ZAGAT®

New York City
Shopping
2007

EDITORS
Catherine Bigwood, Randi Gollin and Troy Segal

Published and distributed by
Zagat Survey, LLC
4 Columbus Circle
New York, NY 10019
T: 212.977.6000
E: nycshopping@zagat.com
www.zagat.com

ACKNOWLEDGMENTS

We thank Nancy Bilyeau, Michael Cohen, Jacques Dehornois, Angela Gaimari, Dana Gordon, Ki Hackney, Paul Himmelein, Faran Alexis Krentcil, Laura Mitchell, Nancy Peretsman, Steven Shukow, Will Snyder, Neeraja Viswanathan and Mary Zubritsky, as well as the following members of our staff: Victoria Elmacioglu (assistant editor), Rachel McConlogue (editorial assistant), Sean Beachell, Maryanne Bertollo, Sandy Cheng, Reni Chin, Larry Cohn, Carol Diuguid, Jeff Freier, Michelle Golden, Caroline Hatchett, Karen Hudes, Roy Jacob, Natalie Lebert, Mike Liao, Dave Makulec, Andre Pilette, Josh Rogers, Becky Ruthenberg, Thomas Sheehan, Kilolo Strobert, Donna Marino Wilkins, Sharon Yates and Kyle Zolner.

Contents

About This Survey

This **2007 New York City Shopping Survey** is an update reflecting significant developments since our last *Survey* was published.

WHAT IT COVERS: 2,324 of the city's best stores, including 167 important additions – a treasure trove of sources for everything from fashion to furniture, eyeglasses to undies, jeans to jewelry. We've also indicated new addresses, phone numbers and other major changes.

HELPFUL LISTS: Whether shopping for yourself or for the perfect gift, our top lists should help you find exactly the right store. See Most Popular (page 10), Top Ratings (pages 11–21) and Good Values (page 22). We've also provided 68 handy indexes.

WHO PARTICIPATED: Over 7,500 avid shoppers' input forms the basis for the ratings and reviews in this guide (their comments are shown in quotation marks within the reviews). Their collective experience adds up to over one million shopping trips a year. We sincerely thank each participant – this book is really "theirs."

OUR EDITORS: We're also grateful to our contributing editors, Donna Bulseco, a fashion editor who's been on staff at *WWD* and *W*; Erin Clack, a children's editor and shoe editor who has worked at *Children's Business* and *Footwear News*; and Kelly McMasters, who writes about home design for *CITY* and *Elle Decor,* among other publications.

ABOUT ZAGAT: This marks our 28th year reporting on the shared experiences of consumers like you. What started in 1979 as a hobby involving 200 people rating NYC restaurants has come a long way. Today we have over 250,000 surveyors and now cover dining, entertaining, golf, hotels, movies, music, nightlife, resorts, shopping, spas, theater and tourist attractions worldwide.

AVAILABILITY: Zagat guides are available in all major bookstores, by subscription at **zagat.com**, and for use on BlackBerry, Palm, Windows Mobile devices and mobile phones.

MAKE YOUR OPINION COUNT: We invite you to join any of our upcoming surveys – just register at **zagat.com**, where you can rate and review establishments year-round. Each participant will receive a free copy of the resulting guide when published.

FEEDBACK: There is always room for improvement. Therefore, we appreciate your comments and suggestions about any aspect of our performance. Just contact us at nycshopping@zagat.com.

New York, NY
March 7, 2007

Nina and Tim

Nina and Tim Zagat

What's New

NYC continued to grow in shopping stature this year, with locals and tourists alike discovering new finds among the 2,324 stores in this guide. True, 52% of Zagat surveyors feel prices have risen since last year. But factor in Mayor Bloomberg's proposal to eliminate the 4.25% city sales tax for all clothing and footwear, and shopping around town is likely to become even more enticing.

SOHO STRIKES BACK: After a post-9/11 slump, the area has bounced back, becoming an even bigger retail draw than ever – not to mention being voted our surveyors' favorite shopping neighborhood. This past year alone, they've been drawn by hot newcomers like Kiki De Montparnasse, M Missoni, Tarina Tarantino, Tibi, True Religion and UGG Australia, whose apparel, accessories and footwear have lent more spice to the SoHo streets.

EURO-ASIAN INVASION: Much of SoHo's renaissance has been fueled by foreign retailers. Japanese companies big and small established a toehold, led by Nave, Onward Kashiyama's collaborative designer concept; Trico Field, a hip childrenswear find; and Uniqlo, the super-sized kingpin of affordable wear (Tokyo also landed Uptown by way of Samantha Thavasa, the brand that traffics in brightly colored celeb-designed handbags). And if the Italians have *their* way, SoHo might be renamed the new Little Italy, since a trio of that country's home-oriented establishments – contemporary accessories arbiter Alessi, tile-leviathan Sicis and the Murano-based glass company Salviati – opened U.S. outposts there. The Brits have exported emissaries like mod clothier Ben Sherman, the arm-candy avatar Mulberry, with its in-demand 'it' bags, and the fine-furniture design firm Ochre. Not to be outdone, Northern Europe offers easy-fit fashions via Germany's Oska and Swedish skateboarder- and snowboard-inspired attire at WeSC.

DOWNTOWN IS UP: In fact, all of Manhattan south of 14th Street is hot – particularly Bleecker, which has blossomed with the arrival of Brunello Cucinelli, Juicy Couture (the largest of three new NYC stores) and SEE Eyewear. The Meatpacking District blitz continues: Diane von Furstenberg relocated to a new showroom/performance complex, Esthete upped the aesthetic ante and Theory debuted a gigantic flagship near boldface designers Tracy Reese and Trina Turk. In TriBeCa, class-act Nili Lotan and hipster jeans haunt Rogan surfaced, while Leontine, a lone-wolf boutique among a cluster of chains, dropped anchor in the South Street Seaport – a stone's throw away from Wall Street, where tony uptown types like Tiffany and Hermès will open offshoots this year.

GUYS ON THE RISE: Traditionally, womenswear dominates the fashion news, but this year has seen an especially strong showing of new men's stores, from the British-style bespoke suits at Lord Willy's in NoLita to the big-bucks jeans of SoHo's Blue in Green to the witty basics offered at Oliver Spencer in the West Village to the alternative-chic styles at Williamsburg's Yoko Devereaux. In addition, popular East Villager Odin spawned an offshoot in NoLita, and shrunken-suit master Thom Browne moved to larger TriBeCa digs.

GADGETS & GIZMOS: Accompanying the rise in men's retailers was the arrival of stores specializing in boy toys (though girls play with them too). A huge translucent cube marked the entrance of the new Apple store under the General Motors Plaza. Porsche Design drove into Midtown with high-tech accessories for the sports car driver's lifestyle, while neighbor Nokia debuted with three dramatically lit floors of cell phones and other electronics.

FLASHY FLAGSHIPS: What most influences consumers to check out a store? Quite simply, the way it looks, 61% of our surveyors say. Small wonder, then, that retailers are constructing huge showplaces, second or third branches that often outdo the original. Along with the aforementioned Apple, there's Anthropologie – whose two-story Rockefeller Center branch boasts an art gallery – and Puma, whose new Union Square site features a futuristic look distinctly different from its siblings. Designer threads and toiletries for him, her and baby are available under one roof at the new Scoop, which – in a departure from its multi-, mini-boutique approach – is opening a lower Broadway megastore.

STOP 'N' SHOP: Many surveyors characterize shopping as a leisure activity – something more than one-third of them (36%) estimate they do every weekend. To encourage such behavior, many new stores are pitching themselves as places to socialize *and* shop. Some do it with services: a customer can sip tea while she tries on shoes at SoHo's té casan, take knitting classes at the Williamsburg womenswear boutique Treehouse or get a bikini waxing after sampling the hip threads at Valley on the LES; her male counterpart can get an old-fashioned shave as he contemplates the suits at Freemans Sporting Club nearby. Other retailers figure a mix of merchandise will make shoppers linger: you can buy both crystal for your table and creams for your body at the enlarged Arcadia in Chelsea, browse old LPs at the LES maverick men's store Bblessing and peruse a roomful of art and fashion books at designer Paul Smith's new Greene Street emporium.

COMING SOON: The rest of 2007 promises plenty of other international arrivals – including the clothier Cotélac of France; Evisu, a Japanese jeans maker; mobile manufacturer Helio (a joint venture of Earthlink and Korea's SK Telecom); the U.K.'s womenswear chain Karen Millen; and the Spanish fast-fashion goliath Mango. They're all waiting in the wings in – where else? - SoHo.

New York, NY
March 7, 2007

Catherine Bigwood
Randi Gollin
Troy Segal

Ratings & Symbols

Zagat Top Spot	Name	Symbols			Zagat Ratings		
			QUALITY	DISPLAY	SERVICE	COST	

Area,
Address,
Subway
Stop,
Contact

Ⓩ Tim & Nina's ◐

▽ 23 | 9 | 13 | I

W 50s | 4 Columbus Circle (8th Ave.) | 1/A/B/C/D to 59th St./Columbus Circle | 212-977-6000 | www.zagat.com

Review,
surveyor
comments
in quotes

Paradoxically packed with both "prime pet products" and iPods (Nina's the pooch-lover, Tim handles the hardware), this "cutting-edge" Columbus Circle canine/computer boutique attracts "bargain-hounds", who trot over for color-coordinated chew toys and chargers – plus bootlegged versions of 'How Much Is That Doggie in the Window?' to download; but even tail-waggers growl the "snappish staff" "should be sent to the doghouse."

Ratings
Quality, Display and **Service** are rated on a scale of 0 to 30. Newcomers or write-ins are listed without ratings.

0	–	9	poor to fair
10	–	15	fair to good
16	–	19	good to very good
20	–	25	very good to excellent
26	–	30	extraordinary to perfection

▽ low response | less reliable

Cost reflects our surveyors' estimate of each store's price range.

I Inexpensive
M Moderate
E Expensive
VE Very Expensive

Symbols
Ⓩ Zagat Top Spot (highest ratings, popularity and importance)
◐ usually open after 7 PM
Ⓢ closed on Sunday
Ⓜ closed on Monday
⊄ no credit cards accepted

Locations
For chains with over 10 locations in NYC, only the flagship address is listed.

Maps
Maps in indexes show the locations of stores with the highest overall ratings, popularity and importance.

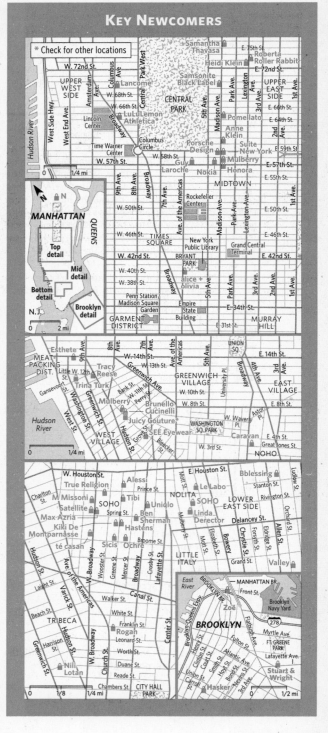

KEY NEWCOMERS

* Check for other locations

UPPER WEST SIDE
W. 72nd St.
Lancome
W. 68th St.
LuLuLemon Athletica
Lincoln Center
Time Warner Center
Columbus Circle
W. 57th St.

CENTRAL PARK

Samantha Thavasa
Heidi Klein
Samsonite Black Label
Roberta Roller Rabbit
E. 75th St.
E. 72nd St.
UPPER EAST SIDE
E. 66th St.
E. 64th St.
Pomellato
Anne Klein
Porsche Design
Suite New York
Guy Laroche
Mulberry
Nokia
Honora
E. 59th St.
E. 57th St.

MIDTOWN
Rockefeller Center
W. 50th St.
W. 46th St.
TIMES SQUARE
New York Public Library
W. 42nd St.
BRYANT PARK
Grand Central Terminal
W. 40th St.
W. 38th St.
alice + olivia
Penn Station/ Madison Square Garden
Empire State Building
E. 34th St.
E. 31st St.
MURRAY HILL
GARMENT DISTRICT

MANHATTAN
N
QUEENS
Top detail
Mid detail
Bottom detail
Brooklyn detail
N.J.
0   1/4 mi
0   2 mi

MEAT-PACKING DIST.
Esthete
Tracy Reese
Trina Turk
Mulberry
Juicy Couture
SEE Eyewear
WEST VILLAGE
Brunello Cucinelli
GREENWICH VILLAGE
W. 14th St.
W. 13th St.
W. 10th St.
W. 8th St.
WASHINGTON SQ. PARK
Caravan
EAST VILLAGE
E. 8th St.
E. 4th St.
Great Jones St.
NOHO
UNION SQ.
E. 14th St.
Hudson River

TRIBECA
True Religion
Missoni
Satellite
Max Azria
Kiki De Montparnasse
té casan
Sicis
Ochre
Rogan
Nili Lotan
SOHO
Alessi
Tibi
Ben Sherman
Hastens
NOLITA
Uniqlo
Le Labo
LOWER EAST SIDE
Linda Derector
Bblessing
Valley
LITTLE ITALY
W. Houston St.
E. Houston St.
Canal St.
CITY HALL PARK

BROOKLYN
MANHATTAN BR.
BROOKLYN BR.
Zoë
Brooklyn Navy Yard
FT. GREENE PARK
Stuart & Wright
Hasker
East River

0   1/8   1/4 mi
0   1/2 mi

Key Newcomers

'If I can make it here, I can make it anywhere' – so goes one version of the song 'New York, New York,' and so seemingly goes the attitude of the newest retailers in town. Here's our take on the past year's most notable arrivals. (For a full list of additions to this book, see page 410.)

Alessi	Nili Lotan
alice + olivia	Nokia
Anne Klein	Ochre
Bblessing	Pomellato
Ben Sherman	Porsche Design
Brunello Cucinelli	Roberta Roller Rabbit
Caravan	Rogan
Esthete	Samantha Thavasa
Guy Laroche	Samsonite Black Label
Hasker	Satellite
Hastens	SEE Eyewear
Heidi Klein	Sicis
Honora	SOHO
Juicy Couture	Stuart & Wright
Kiki De Montparnasse	Suite New York
Lancôme	té casan
Le Labo	Tibi
Linda Derector	Tracy Reese
LuLuLemon Athletica	Trina Turk
Max Azria	True Religion
M Missoni	Uniqlo
Mulberry	Valley
N	Zoë

The year to come shows plenty of potential with a number of high-profile projects in the works: an over-the-top **Christian Lacroix** outpost in the former Oxxford Clothes 57th Street site; Roberto Cavalli's younger, but still eye-opening line **Just Cavalli** in A. Testoni's old 665 Fifth Avenue digs; in the East 60s, decorating diva **Charlotte Moss**' haute home-furnishings shop, Paris-based **Louis Féraud** in Stephane Kelian's now-shuttered Madison Avenue space, stiletto-heel innovator **Roger Vivier**'s highly anticipated shoe and bag boutique, and a few blocks up, former Gucci/YSL powerhouse **Tom Ford**'s first freestanding menswear mecca; Downtown, there's bridal behemoth **Vera Wang**'s ready-to-wear store on Mercer Street; **Rachel Roy**'s glamorous showcase on Hudson Street; and **Yohji Yamamoto**'s second haven of haute couture, this time in the Meatpacking District.

Most Popular Stores

Each surveyor has been asked to name his or her five favorite places. This list reflects their choices. They are also plotted on the map at the back of the book.

CHAINS

1. Bed Bath & Beyond
2. Banana Republic
3. H&M
4. Sephora
5. Met. Museum of Art
6. Williams-Sonoma
7. Tiffany & Co.
8. Anthropologie
9. Crate & Barrel
10. Ann Taylor
11. Ann Taylor Loft
12. Gap
13. Home Depot
14. Kiehl's
15. Pearl Paint
16. Brooks Brothers
17. buybuy Baby
18. Virgin Megastore
19. Coach
20. Talbots
21. Chico's
22. J.Crew

DEPARTMENT STORES

1. Bloomingdale's
2. Saks Fifth Ave.
3. Macy's
4. Bergdorf Goodman
5. Barneys New York
6. Lord & Taylor
7. Target
8. Henri Bendel

DISCOUNTERS

1. Century 21
2. B&H Photo-Video
3. Costco Wholesale
4. J&R Music/Computer
5. Loehmann's
6. Daffy's
7. T.J. Maxx
8. Best Buy
9. DSW
10. Filene's Basement
11. Marshalls
12. Syms

INDEPENDENTS

1. Zabar's
2. Kate's Paperie
3. ABC Carpet & Home
4. Gracious Home
5. MoMA Store
6. Paragon
7. Takashimaya
8. Apple Store
9. Bergdorf Men's
10. Broadway Panhandler

While the above lists contain obvious big names, it's interesting that many of the stores, such as ABC Carpet & Home, B&H Photo-Video, Bergdorf Goodman, Broadway Panhandler, Gracious Home, Henri Bendel, Kate's Paperie and Zabar's, are of the "born in NY" variety, proof that New Yorkers love – and support – individuality in their shopping choices. What's more, if you turn to page 22 you'll see that shopping here can also be a world-class bargain.

Top Ratings

Department stores receive separate scores for different categories. Top lists exclude places with low votes, unless marked ▽.

TOP QUALITY: FASHION/BEAUTY

29 Harry Winston
Van Cleef & Arpels
John Lobb
Chopard
Hermès
Fred Leighton
Mikimoto*
Balenciaga
A La Vieille Russie
Cesare Paciotti
Wempe
Loro Piana
Bergdorf Goodman
Cartier
Chanel
Tod's
Bottega Veneta
Davide Cenci
Giorgio Armani
Akris

28 Turnbull & Asser
Salvatore Ferragamo
Belgian Shoes
Dior New York
Peter Fox Shoes*

Ermenegildo Zegna
Bergdorf Men's
Celine
Piaget*
Christian Louboutin
Oxxford Clothes
Manolo Blahnik
St. John
Brioni
Graff
Spring Flowers
J. Mendel*
Santa Maria Novella
Allen Edmonds
Judith Leiber
Carolina Herrera
Giuseppe Zanotti*
La Perla*
Robert Clergerie*
H. Stern
Barbour/Peter Elliot
Valentino*
Bonpoint
Oscar de la Renta
Fogal/Switzerland

BY CATEGORY

ACCESSORIES
28 Judith Leiber
Marc Jacobs Access.
27 Dunhill
26 Porsche Design
Coach

ACTIVEWEAR
27 Patagonia
25 Orvis
24 North Face
JackRabbit Sports
Capezio

BRIDAL
28 Saks Fifth Ave.
27 Mark Ingram Bridal
Vera Wang Bridal

Amsale
25 Kleinfeld

CLOTHING: CHAINS (MEN'S)
26 Rochester Big/Tall
24 Brooks Brothers
21 Banana Republic Men
20 Express Men
19 Casual Male XL

CLOTHING: CHAINS (MEN'S & WOMEN'S)
22 Talbots
20 Kuhlman
Sisley
J.Crew
French Connection

* Indicates a tie with store above

CLOTHING: CHAINS (WOMEN'S)

24 Adrienne Vittadini
Eileen Fisher
23 Sigrid Olsen
21 Ann Taylor
20 Chico's

CLOTHING: CHILDREN'S

28 Spring Flowers
Bonpoint
27 Petit Bateau
Jacadi
Magic Windows

CLOTHING: DESIGNER (MEN'S)

28 Ermenegildo Zegna
Brioni
26 John Varvatos
BOSS Hugo Boss
Paul Smith

CLOTHING: DESIGNER (MEN'S & WOMEN'S)

29 Hermès
Giorgio Armani
28 Valentino
Etro
27 Louis Vuitton

CLOTHING: DESIGNER (WOMEN'S)

29 Balenciaga
Chanel
Akris
28 Dior New York
Celine

CLOTHING: DISCOUNT

24 Find Outlet
22 Century 21
20 Loehmann's
Gabay's Outlet
18 Syms

CLOTHING: MEN'S (CLASSIC)

29 Davide Cenci
Bergdorf Men's
28 Oxxford Clothes
27 Paul Stuart
Hickey Freeman

CLOTHING: MEN'S (CONTEMPORARY)

29 Jeffrey
27 Barneys New York

24 Camouflage
23 Scoop Men's
Rothman's

CLOTHING: TWEEN/ TEEN

24 Lester's
22 Infinity
21 Berkley Girl
18 Paul Frank
16 Yellow Rat Bastard

CLOTHING: WOMEN'S (BOUTIQUES)

27 Kirna Zabête
24 Searle
Sude
Intermix
CK Bradley

CONSIGNMENT/ VINTAGE

26 Fisch for the Hip
25 Michael's/Consignment
Ina
24 Designer Resale
22 Tokyo Joe

COSMETICS/TOILETRIES (DEPT. STORES)

29 Bergdorf Goodman
28 Takashimaya
Barneys New York
Saks Fifth Ave.
27 Henri Bendel

COSMETICS/TOILETRIES (SPECIALISTS)

28 Santa Maria Novella
Bond No. 9
27 Molton Brown
Penhaligon's
Bathroom

DEPARTMENT STORES

29 Bergdorf Goodman
27 Barneys New York
Saks Fifth Ave.
26 Henri Bendel
23 Bloomingdale's

EYEWEAR

28 Morgenthal Frederics
Alain Mikli
27 Oliver Peoples
H.L. Purdy
Robert Marc

HANDBAGS (DESIGNER)

- 29 Hermès
- Chanel
- Bottega Veneta
- 27 Louis Vuitton
- Gucci

HOSIERY/LINGERIE

- 28 La Perla
- Fogal/Switzerland
- Wolford
- Eres
- 27 Agent Provocateur

JEANS

- 28 Barneys CO-OP
- 26 AG Adriano Goldschmied
- 25 Rogan
- Atrium
- 24 Diesel Denim Gallery

JEWELRY: COSTUME/ SEMIPRECIOUS

- 26 Michal Negrin
- 25 Swarovski
- Alexis Bittar
- Fragments
- 20 Agatha Paris
- Boucher*
- Erwin Pearl*

JEWELRY: FINE

- 29 Harry Winston
- Van Cleef & Arpels
- Mikimoto
- Cartier
- 28 Graff

JEWELRY: VINTAGE

- 29 Fred Leighton
- A La Vieille Russie
- James Robinson∇
- 26 Aaron Faber
- 25 Doyle and Doyle∇

MATERNITY

- 26 Veronique
- 23 Liz Lange Maternity
- 22 Destination Maternity
- 19 Maternity Works
- Mimi Maternity

NEWCOMERS/RATED

- 26 Guy Laroche
- Lancôme
- Porshe Design
- 25 Rogan
- Tracy Reese

SHIRTS/TIES

- 28 Turnbull & Asser
- Robert Talbott
- 26 Charles Tyrwhitt
- Thomas Pink
- 25 Ascot Chang

SHOES: CHILDREN'S

- 26 Tip Top Kids
- 25 Little Eric
- 24 Lester's
- 23 Ibiza Kidz
- 22 Great Feet

SHOES: MEN'S

- 29 John Lobb
- 28 Allen Edmonds
- 27 Barneys New York
- A. Testoni
- 26 J.M. Weston

SHOES: MEN'S & WOMEN'S

- 29 Cesare Paciotti
- Tod's
- 28 Salvatore Ferragamo
- Belgian Shoes
- Walter Steiger
- Warren Edwards*

SHOES: WOMEN'S

- 29 Jeffrey
- 28 Peter Fox Shoes
- Christian Louboutin
- Manolo Blahnik
- Robert Clergerie

SNEAKERS

- 27 New Balance
- 26 Super Runners Shop
- 24 Niketown NY
- Alife
- New York Running

SWIMWEAR

- 27 Vilebrequin
- 26 Malia Mills Swimwear
- Canyon Beachwear
- 21 Quiksilver
- Billabong

WATCHES

- 29 Chopard
- Wempe
- 28 Piaget
- 27 Tourneau
- Cellini

TOP QUALITY: HOME/GARDEN

29 Buccellati
Bernardaud
Steuben*
Frette
Baccarat
Pratesi
Bergdorf Goodman
Cartier
Lalique
Scully & Scully
Georg Jensen

28 Moss
Bridge Kitchenware
Tiffany & Co.
Asprey
Waterworks
Takashimaya
Stickley, Audi & Co.
Ligne Roset
Yves Delorme*

27 Schweitzer Linen
Barneys New York
Christofle
Simon Pearce
B&B Italia

Ann Sacks
Roche Bobois
Broadway Panhandler

26 Zabar's
Simon's Hardware
Michael C. Fina
Avventura
Country Floors
Dean & Deluca
Williams-Sonoma
Harris Levy
Charles P. Rogers
Aero
Carlyle Convertibles*
Maurice Villency
Krup's Kitchen/Bath
Artistic Tile
Pierre Deux
Sur La Table

25 Pompanoosuc Mills
Urban Archaeology
MacKenzie-Childs
S.Feldman Houseware*
Signoria*
ABC Carpets/Rugs

BY CATEGORY

ACCESSORIES

29 Scully & Scully
28 Moss
26 Pierre Deux
25 ABC Carpet & Home
Armani Casa

BATHROOM FIXTURES

28 Waterworks
27 Ann Sacks
26 Country Floors
Artistic Tile
23 Davis & Warshow

COOKWARE

28 Bridge Kitchenware
27 Broadway Panhandler
26 Zabar's
Dean & Deluca
Williams-Sonoma

DEPARTMENT STORES

29 Bergdorf Goodman
27 Barneys New York
Saks Fifth Ave.
23 Bloomingdale's
19 Macy's

FINE CHINA/CRYSTAL

29 Bernardaud
Steuben*
Baccarat
Lalique
27 Simon Pearce

FURNITURE

28 Stickley, Audi & Co.
Ligne Roset
27 B&B Italia
Roche Bobois
26 Aero
Carlyle Convertibles*

GARDEN

29 Takashimaya
25 Gracious Home
24 Smith & Hawken
21 Lowe's
19 Home Depot

HARDWARE STORES

26 Simon's Hardware
24 Dykes Lumber
23 Vercesi Hardware

subscribe to zagat.com

| 22 | Janovic Plaza |
| | Beacon Paint/Hardware |

LIGHTING

25	Oriental Lamp Shade
24	Gracious Home
	Just Bulbs
	Lighting By Gregory
23	Lee's Studio

LINENS

29	Frette
	Pratesi
28	Yves Delorme
27	Schweitzer Linen
26	Harris Levy

MAJOR APPLIANCES

26	Krup's Kitchen/Bath
25	Gringer & Sons
24	Drimmers
23	Bloom & Krup
	Quintessentials

NEWCOMERS/RATED

25	Alessi
	Signoria
24	Kate's At Home
	Madura

SILVER

29	Buccellati
	Cartier
	Georg Jensen
28	Tiffany & Co.
27	Christofle

TILES

28	Waterworks
27	Ann Sacks
26	Country Floors
	Artistic Tile
25	Urban Archaeology

TOP QUALITY: LIFESTYLE

29	Ghurka
28	City Quilter
	Tender Buttons
	Lyric Hi-Fi
	Mrs. John L. Strong*
	Smythson of Bond St.
	Purl
	T. Anthony
	TUMI
	Il Papiro
	Montblanc
	Bang & Olufsen
	Seaport Yarn*
	Downtown Yarns
	Fountain Pen
	Harvey Electronics
27	Louis Vuitton
	B&H Photo-Video
	Bose
	String
	Crane & Co.
	Apple Store
	Dempsey & Carroll
	Babeland
	Kate's Paperie

	Arthur Brown & Bro.
	Other Music
	Trixie and Peanut
	Geppetto's Toy Box
	Sound by Singer*
	Whiskers*
26	Stereo Exchange
	Canine Styles
	Neue Galerie NY
	International Photo
	Leather Man
	Museum Arts/Design
	Mary Arnold Toys
	Joon
	Kidding Around
	Tekserve*
	Toga Bikes*
	Sony Style
	Rita's Needlepoint
	B&J Fabrics
	Pet Stop
	Stitches East
	Adorama Camera
	Greenwich Letterpress
	Yarn Co.*

BY CATEGORY

ART SUPPLIES

- 26 Pearl Paint
- 25 Lee's Art Shop
- New York Central Art
- Blick Art Materials
- 24 A.I. Friedman

AUDIO

- 28 Lyric Hi-Fi
- Bang & Olufsen
- Harvey Electronics
- 27 Bose
- Sound by Singer

CAMERAS/VIDEO

- 27 B&H Photo-Video
- 26 Adorama Camera
- 23 Alkit
- 22 Camera Land
- 21 42nd St. Photo

CDS/VINYL

- 27 Other Music
- 25 Generation Records
- 24 Academy Records
- Colony Music
- 23 Virgin Megastore

COMPUTERS

- 27 Apple Store
- 26 Tekserve
- Sony Style
- 24 J&R Music/Computer
- 21 DataVision

FABRICS/NOTIONS

- 28 City Quilter
- Tender Buttons
- 26 B&J Fabrics
- 25 M&J Trimming
- 23 Zarin Fabrics

GIFTS/NOVELTIES

- 24 Met. Opera Shop
- Delphinium
- 22 Dylan's Candy Bar
- 19 Alphabets
- 18 La Brea

KNITTING/NEEDLEPOINT

- 28 Purl
- Seaport Yarn
- Downtown Yarns
- 27 String
- 26 Rita's Needlepoint

LUGGAGE/LEATHER GOODS

- 29 Ghurka
- 28 T. Anthony
- TUMI
- 27 Louis Vuitton
- 26 Crouch & Fitzgerald

MUSEUM SHOPS

- 26 Neue Galerie NY
- International Photo
- Museum Arts/Design
- Rubin Museum
- 25 MoMA Store

NEWCOMERS/RATED

- 26 Greenwich Letterpress
- 25 Morgan Library
- 24 Samsonite Black Label
- 23 Toy Space
- 22 Nokia

PET SUPPLIES

- 27 Trixie and Peanut
- Whiskers
- 26 Canine Styles
- Pet Stop
- 25 Barking Zoo

SEX SHOPS

- 27 Babeland
- 26 Leather Man
- 24 Eve's Garden
- 22 Pleasure Chest
- 19 Pink Pussycat

SPORTING GOODS

- 26 Toga Bikes
- EMS
- 25 Gerry Cosby
- Tent and Trails
- Burton Store

STATIONERY

- 28 Mrs. John L. Strong
- Smythson of Bond St.
- Il Papiro
- Montblanc
- Fountain Pen

TOYS

- 27 Geppetto's Toy Box
- 26 Mary Arnold Toys
- Kidding Around
- 25 FAO Schwarz
- 24 West Side Kids

subscribe to zagat.com

VIDEOS/DVDS

[24] J&R Music/Computer
Kim's Mediapolis

[23] Virgin Megastore
[20] Best Buy
Disc-O-Rama

TOP QUALITY: BY LOCATION

CHELSEA

[29] Balenciaga
[28] City Quilter
[26] Williams-Sonoma
Comme des Garçons
Carlyle Convertibles
Fisch for the Hip*
Tekserve*

EAST 40S

[28] Allen Edmonds
Bridge Kitchenware
TUMI
[27] Paul Stuart
Robert Marc

EAST 50S

[29] Buccellati
Harry Winston
Van Cleef & Arpels
Bernardaud
Baccarat

EAST 60S

[29] Steuben
Frette
John Lobb
Chopard
Hermès

EAST 70S

[28] Christian Louboutin
Spring Flowers
Carolina Herrera
Il Papiro
Morgenthal Frederics

EAST 80S

[28] Lyric Hi-Fi
Barbour/Peter Elliot
[27] Petit Bateau
H.L. Purdy
Schweitzer Linen*

EAST 90S

[28] Bonpoint
[27] Robert Marc
Jacadi
[26] Veronique
[25] Annie Needlepoint
S. Feldman Housewares*

EAST VILLAGE

[28] Downtown Yarns
[27] Kiehl's
Whiskers
Selima Optique
[25] Arche

FINANCIAL DISTRICT

[27] Hickey Freeman
[26] DeNatale Jewelers
[25] Kenjo
Tent and Trails
[24] J&R Music/Computer

FLATIRON DISTRICT

[28] Bang & Olufsen
Waterworks
Stickley, Audi & Co.
Ligne Roset
[27] Ann Sacks

GARMENT DISTRICT

[27] B&H Photo-Video
Tourneau
[26] B&J Fabrics
[25] M&J Trimming
School Products*

GRAMERCY PARK

[26] Simon's Hardware
Pearl Paint
[24] Sude
Park Ave. Audio
[23] Vercesi Hardware

GREENWICH VILLAGE

[27] Aedes De Venustas
Kate's Paperie
Broadway Panhandler
Geppetto's Toy Box
[26] C.O. Bigelow

LOWER EAST SIDE

[27] Babeland
[26] Harris Levy
[24] Alife
Altman Luggage
Lighting By Gregory

MEATPACKING DISTRICT

- 28 La Perla
- Alexander McQueen
- Jeffrey
- 26 Stella McCartney
- 25 Tracy Reese

MURRAY HILL

- 27 Roche Bobois
- 25 Morgan Library
- 23 Ethan Allen
- Shoe Box
- 22 Yarn Connection

NOHO

- 28 Bond No. 9
- 27 Other Music
- 26 Stereo Exchange
- 25 Atrium
- Blick Art Materials

NOLITA

- 28 Santa Maria Novella
- 26 Malia Mills Swimwear
- Fresh
- 25 Lilith
- Seize sur Vingt

SOHO

- 29 Chanel
- Georg Jensen
- 28 Peter Fox Shoes
- Moss
- La Perla

SOUTH STREET SEAPORT

- 28 Seaport Yarn
- 25 Met. Museum of Art
- 22 Talbots
- 21 Guess
- Brookstone

TRIBECA

- 28 Fountain Pen
- 26 Bu and the Duck
- 25 Issey Miyake
- Pompanoosuc Mills
- Rogan*

UNION SQUARE

- 27 Sound by Singer
- 26 Country Floors
- 25 Paragon
- 24 JackRabbit Sports
- 23 Virgin Megastore

WEST 40S

- 28 TUMI
- Harvey Electronics
- 27 Crane & Co.
- Arthur Brown & Bro.
- New Balance

WEST 50S

- 28 Manolo Blahnik
- Smythson of Bond St.
- TUMI
- Morgenthal Frederics
- 27 Bose

WEST 60S

- 27 Kiehl's
- Robert Marc
- Jacadi
- 26 Lancôme
- Toga Bikes

WEST 70S

- 28 Bang & Olufsen
- 26 Malia Mills Swimwear
- Super Runners Shop
- Tip Top Kids
- Clarins

WEST 80S

- 27 Schweitzer Linen
- Patagonia
- 26 Zabar's
- Avventura
- Greenstones

WEST 90S

- 25 Albee Baby Carriage
- 24 Sude
- 20 Metro Bicycles
- 19 Petco
- 18 La Brea

WEST 100S/HARLEM

- 26 M.A.C. Cosmetics
- 24 Kim's Mediapolis
- Carol's Daughter
- 23 New York Public Library
- Davis & Warshow

WEST VILLAGE

- 28 Christian Louboutin
- Bonpoint
- Marc Jacobs Access.
- Bond No. 9
- 27 Bathroom

OUTER BOROUGHS

BRONX

24	Dykes Lumber
23	Davis & Warshow
21	ABC Carpet/Whse. Outlet
20	Athlete's Foot
	Loehmann's

BROOKLYN: BAY RIDGE/DYKER HEIGHTS

26	Michael C. Fina
22	Century 21
20	United Colors/Benetton
19	Casual Male XL
16	KB Toys

BROOKLYN: BOERUM HILL/DOWNTOWN

24	Flight 001
	Carol's Daughter
23	Something Else
21	DSW
20	Brooklyn Industries

BROOKLYN: HEIGHTS/DUMBO

26	M.A.C. Cosmetics
24	Design Within Reach
20	New York Transit Mus.
	Housing Works Thrift
17	BoConcept

BROOKLYN: PARK SLOPE

26	Clay Pot
25	Baby Bird
24	Lion in the Sun
	Dykes Lumber
	JackRabbit Sports*

BROOKLYN: WILLIAMSBURG

24	Academy Records
21	Triple Five Soul
20	Brooklyn Industries
19	Beacon's Closet
18	S&W

BROOKLYN: OTHER

27	Jacadi
24	Drimmers
	Lester's
	Carol's Daughter
23	Something Else

QUEENS: ASTORIA/L.I.C.

24	Dykes Lumber
22	Costco Wholesale
	Metropolitan Lumber
21	Mimi's Closet
20	United Colors/Benetton

QUEENS: OTHER

25	Bare Escentuals
23	Clarks England
	Geox
	Ethan Allen
	Davis & Warshow

STATEN ISLAND

27	Apple Store
25	Swarovski
23	Ethan Allen
	Crabtree & Evelyn
22	Build-A-Bear

TOP DISPLAY

29 Moss
Bernardaud
Ghurka
J. Mendel

28 Oscar de la Renta
Cartier
Van Cleef & Arpels
Graff
Takashimaya
Harry Winston
Waterworks
Christian Louboutin
Manolo Blahnik
Apple Store
Trixie and Peanut
Bathroom
Steuben
John Lobb
Nicole Farhi
Dior New York
Versace
Chopard
Piaget

27 Hermès
Valentino

Chanel
Giorgio Armani
Chanel Jewelry
Baccarat
St. John
A La Vieille Russie
Alexander McQueen
Judith Leiber
Louis Vuitton
Agent Provocateur
Tiffany & Co.
Comme des Garçons
Frette
Jo Malone
Bulgari
Room & Board*
Smythson of Bond St.*
Ralph Lauren Layette
Bottega Veneta
Fred Leighton*
Michal Negrin*
Scully & Scully*
Yohji Yamamoto*
Gucci
Aedes De Venustas

ARCHITECTURAL INTEREST

Alexander McQueen
Apple Store
Baker Tribeca
Balenciaga
Calvin Klein
Carlos Miele
Cartier
Comme des Garçons
Conran Shop
ddc domus design
Donna Karan
Fendi
Henri Bendel
Hugo Boss
Issey Miyake

Jacob & Co.
Jil Sander
Louis Vuitton
Maurice Villency
Neue Galerie NY
Nicole Farhi
Paul Smith
Phi
Prada
Ralph Lauren
Rubin Chapelle
Stella McCartney
Versace
Vitra
Yves Saint Laurent

HOLIDAY DECORATION

ABC Carpet & Home
American Girl Place
Barneys New York
Bergdorf Goodman
Bloomingdale's
Cartier
FAO Schwarz
Henri Bendel

Lord & Taylor
Macy's
Paul Smith
Ralph Lauren
Saks Fifth Ave.
Sony Style
Takashimaya
Tiffany & Co.

TOP SERVICE

28 Babeland
Oscar de la Renta
Van Cleef & Arpels
Harry Winston

27 Oxxford Clothes
John Lobb
J. Mendel
Graff
Buccellati
Fred Leighton*
Piaget*

26 Baccarat
City Quilter
Sude
Gianfranco Ferré
Cartier
Wempe
Warren Edwards
Ghurka
J.M. Weston
Frette
Mark Ingram Bridal
Chopard
Giorgio Armani
DeBeers
Dunhill

Bulgari

25 Town Shop
Mikimoto
Steuben
Aedes De Venustas
H.L. Purdy
Vercesi Hardware
Asprey
Calling All Pets
Leonard Opticians
Robert Marc
Chanel Jewelry
Turnbull & Asser
H. Stern
A La Vieille Russie
Bond No. 9*
Paul Stuart
Kiehl's
Carolina Herrera
Fountain Pen*
John Varvatos*
Lalique*
Super Runners Shop*
Walter Steiger*
Brioni
Valentino

IN-STORE DINING

ABC Carpet & Home
Alessi
American Girl Place
AsiaStore/Asia Society
Barneys New York
Bergdorf Goodman
Bergdorf Men's
Bloomingdale's
Bodum
Bond No. 9
Build-A-Bear
Dean & Deluca
DKNY
Kiehl's
Lord & Taylor

Lounge
Macy's
Met. Museum of Art
MoMA Store
Morgan Library
Neue Galerie NY
Nicole Farhi
Rubin Museum
Saks Fifth Ave.
Sol Moscot
Takashimaya
té casan
202
Virgin Megastore
Whitney Museum

Aerosoles
Agatha Paris
Aldo
Altman Luggage
Am. Eagle Outfitters
American Apparel
Anbar
Ann Taylor Loft
Babies "R" Us
B&H Photo-Video
Beacon's Closet
Best Buy
Bis Designer Resale
Blick Art Materials
Bodum
Body Shop
Bolton's
Broadway Panhandler
Brooklyn Industries
Burlington Coat
Carol's Daughter
Casual Male XL
Century 21
Chambers Outlet
Children's Place
Container Store
Costco Wholesale
Crate & Barrel
Crumpler Bags
Daffy's
Dave's Army Navy
David's Bridal
Drimmers
Dr. Jay's
DSW
Edith and Daha
Filene's Basement
Find Outlet
Fishs Eddy
For Eyes
Fossil
Gabay's Home
Gabay's Outlet
GapBody
Gentlemen's Resale
Goldy + Mac
H&M
Home Depot
Housing Works Thrift
Jam Paper
J&R Music/Computer

K&G Fashion
Kartell
Kiehl's
Kmart
Kuhlman
LeSportsac
Limited Too
Loehmann's
Lowe's
M&J Trimming
Marshalls
Maternity Works
Mavi
Mish Mish
Missha
My Glass Slipper
Natan Borlam's
Nat'l Wholesale Liquid
Necessary Clothing
Nemo Tile
Nine West
Old Navy
Orchard Corset
Origins
Oska
Payless Shoe
Pearl Paint
Pearl River Mart
Petco
Petland Discounts
Pippin
Pookie & Sebastian
Pottery Barn
Prato Fine Men's Wear
Ray Beauty Supply
RK Bridal
Roberta Freymann
S&W
SEE Eyewear
Skechers
Sol Moscot
Swatch
Syms
Target
Tiny Living
T.J. Maxx
Training Camp
Uniqlo
V.I.M.
William-Wayne
Zara

ALPHABETICAL
DIRECTORY

Aaron Basha ⊠

25 | 22 | 20 | VE

E 60s | 680 Madison Ave. (bet. 61st & 62nd Sts.) | 4/5/6/F/N/R/W to 59th St./Lexington Ave. | 212-935-1960 | www.aaronbasha.com
The "cute baby-shoe charms" are the most emblematic item at this Madison Avenue standby and "still the best gift for the newborn's mom" or granny, but others admire the array of "enameled" and "jewel-encrusted" pieces "with a sense of humor", including "bedazzled frogs", flowers and lucky ladybugs that turn up on necklaces and bracelets; however, detractors are disenchanted by "too much of the same thing" and not-so-cute price tags.

Aaron Faber Gallery ⊠

26 | 24 | 24 | VE

W 50s | 666 Fifth Ave. (53rd St.) | E/V to 5th Ave./53rd St. | 212-586-8411 | www.aaronfaber.com
"Fresh and inspiring", this glass-and-chrome gallery on West 53rd Street makes for "a great stop on the way to MoMA"; its large vitrines display "the best art jewelry in New York" – an "unusual mix of hand-made and custom-made" studio pieces by the "newest artists" – along with "interesting estate" gems, "covetable" vintage watches and a classic to contemporary collection of bridal bijoux.

☑ ABC Carpet & Home ●

25 | 24 | 17 | VE

Flatiron | 888 Broadway (19th St.) | 4/5/6/L/N/Q/R/W to 14th St./ Union Sq. | 212-473-3000 | www.abchome.com
This Flatiron "fantasyland for fancy furnishings" is a "quintessential New York shopping experience" for "fashionable" home goods "whether you love the Renaissance or Wright"; an "eclectic mix of old and new" that includes carpets, chandeliers, organic linens, "rich fabrics" and "unique furniture" from all over the world (like carved Chinese marriage beds and chairs upholstered in vintage Suzani tapestries) is displayed over seven "sprawling" floors of "sensory overload"; count on "beautiful creations", "boggling costs" and a "fairly invisible staff."

☑ ABC Carpet & Home (Carpets/Rugs) ●

25 | 22 | 18 | E

Flatiron | 881 Broadway (bet. 18th & 19th Sts.) | 4/5/6/L/N/Q/R/W to 14th St./Union Sq. | 212-473-3000 | www.abccarpet.com
There's an "overwhelmingly huge inventory" of flat-weave, sisal, needlepoint and wall-to-wall carpeting at this "funky", three-floor Flatiron "bazaar" that's filled with a "never-disappointing" collection ("more than you can possibly look at in a day") of rugs; while some dissatisfied surveyors snipe "you'll have more luck finding a pork chop in a kosher deli than getting help" here, most say the "prices" are "fair", especially the "deals to be had" on closeouts and "great remnants" in the "bargain basement."

ABC Carpet & Home Warehouse Outlet

21 | 14 | 15 | E

Bronx | 1055 Bronx River Ave. (Bruckner Expwy.) | 6 to Whitlock Ave. | 718-842-8772 | www.abchome.com
"If you can find your way here through the potholes" to the Bronx, supporters say it's "worth it if you are looking for big-ticket items like leather sofas", rugs, bedding or other home furnishings featured at the two original Flatiron icons; but you may have to "dig deep" and "sort the treasures from the junk" "to find bargains" in the "overwhelming", "hit-or-miss" two-story space.

	QUALITY	DISPLAY	SERVICE	COST

Abercrombie & Fitch ◑

E 50s | 720 Fifth Ave. (56th St.) | N/R/W to 5th Ave./59th St. |
212-306-0936
Seaport | South Street Seaport | 199 Water St. (Fulton St.) | 2/3/4/5/
A/C/J/M/Z to Fulton St./B'way/Nassau | 212-809-9000
888-856-4480 | www.abercrombie.com

| 18 | 19 | 13 | M |

Bet "if Paris Hilton opened a store", it might be something like this
"staple brand" for "the young and the svelte" with a Fifth Avenue flagship and a South Street Seaport branch where "all-American"
"preppy" tees, jeans and minis serve as "good backbones for wardrobes"; grinches gripe you have to have the "figure of a Popsicle stick",
and snipe about the "thunderous" music and a "modelesque" staff
that's more focused on "looking good" than offering assistance, but
the "under-21" clientele barely notices.

ABH Design ⑤

E 70s | 401 E. 76th St. (bet. 1st & York Aves.) | 6 to 77th St. | 212-249-2276 |
www.abh-design.com

| - | - | - | E |

French style "sans attitude" is found at costume designer
Aude Bronson-Howard's "wonderful" Uptown boutique that's "*waaay*
East, not in Muffy/Buffy land"; the owner's "unique" eye is evident
in women's clothing and accessories such as scarves, silk robes,
lingerie and handbags as well as items for the home like linen
napkins, table runners, pillows and bath towels, making it a "lovely"
"place for gifts."

NEW Abitare Ⓜ

Brooklyn Hts | 309 Henry St. (bet. Atlantic Ave. & State St.) | Brooklyn |
1/2/4/5/M/N/R to Court St./Borough Hall | 718-797-3555 |
www.abitareshop.com

| - | - | - | E |

Named after the Italian verb for 'to live', this modern all-white home-
accessories newcomer located on the ground floor of a Brooklyn
Heights brownstone features a well-edited collection of "lovely items"
(mostly handmade and from small companies) ranging from ceramics, glassware, vases, bowls, blankets and rugs to an exclusive line
of Italian linens.

Abracadabra ⑤ Ⓜ

Flatiron | 19 W. 21st St. (bet. 5th & 6th Aves.) | N/R/W to 23rd St. |
212-627-5194 | www.abracadabrasuperstore.com

| 21 | 22 | 18 | M |

"Not for the faint of heart", this "top-of-the-line" Flatiron District
spook shop is haunted by "Halloween" revelers and thespians alike,
looking to scare up wigs, masks, "costumes and props galore" – not to
mention more than a few "gross effects" too ("like the occasional
severed head"); magician's supplies, clown paraphernalia, swords
and gags round out the "extensive collection" of "fun stuff" that's
"dangling everywhere" you look.

A Brooklyn Table

Cobble Hill | 140 Atlantic Ave. (bet. Clinton & Henry Sts.) | Brooklyn |
F/G to Bergen St. | 718-422-7650 | www.abrooklyntable.com

| - | - | - | E |

Everything you need for a handsome table can be found at this elegant
Cobble Hill shop that sets a stylish example with its vignette displays
consisting of fine china, crystal and linen that combine rich, traditional
lines and colors with sleek, contemporary accents.

	QUALITY	DISPLAY	SERVICE	COST

Academy Records ●

24 | 13 | 15 | I

E Vill | 77 E. 10th St. (bet. 3rd & 4th Aves.) | 6 to Astor Pl. | 212-780-9166
Flatiron | 12 W. 18th St. (bet. 5th & 6th Aves.) | 1 to 18th St. |
212-242-3000 | www.academy-records.com
Williamsburg | 96 N. Sixth St. (bet. Berry St. & Wythe Ave.) | Brooklyn |
L to Bedford Ave. | 718-218-8200 | www.academyannex.com

A "world of music for a pocketful of change" awaits classical connoisseurs at this "excellent" Flatiron "treasure trove" of used and new CDs and LPs as well as its rock, jazz and soul campuses in the East Village and Williamsburg (each a "vinyl paradise"); sure, service is sometimes "snooty", and it may "take digging" to unearth "potluck" "treasures" in the "cramped quarters", but its rapt pupils proclaim it a "sanctuary."

a. cheng ●

▽ 19 | 20 | 20 | E

E Vill | 443 E. Ninth St. (bet. Ave. A & 1st Ave.) | L to 1st Ave. |
212-979-7324 | www.achengshop.com

Expect "exquisite pieces worth trekking" Downtown for at this "easy-going yet elegant" East Villager watched over by "lovely" owner-designer Alice Cheng; her tasteful eye for antique fabrics renders such standards as silk print blouses and versatile shirtdresses "unique" and "classy enough to wear to work", justifying their "pricey" tabs.

Acorn

– | – | – | E

Downtown | 323 Atlantic Ave. (bet. Hoyt & Smith Sts.) | Brooklyn | 2/3 to
Hoyt St. | 718-522-3760 | www.acorntoyshop.com

Take a "trip down memory lane" at this "refreshing" Atlantic Avenue toy shop where, instead of "plastic" playthings, you'll discover a "nice" selection of classic, handcrafted wooden and tin toys reminiscent of your own childhood; admirers also go nuts for the small collection of clothing from local designers, all charmingly displayed in a woodsy setting, and laud the helpful owners' "insightful advice."

Active Wearhouse ●

▽ 18 | 15 | 16 | M

SoHo | 514 Broadway (bet. Broome & Spring Sts.) | 6 to Spring St. |
212-965-2284

"Grab trendy sneakers" and "traditional activewear" (i.e. gym shorts) at this SoHo spot that also boasts a "large, chic selection" of casual wardrobe essentials for men and women from "today's urban designers"; "it's just like Transit" muse comparative shoppers – perhaps "because it's run by the same company."

Add Accessories ●

▽ 20 | 18 | 23 | M

SoHo | 461 W. Broadway (bet. Houston & Prince Sts.) | B/D/F/V to
B'way/Lafayette St. | 212-539-1439

"Add stands for addiction" quip acolytes who can't pass this "adorable" SoHo accessories shop without stopping in – what with the "lollipop-colored bags" and "sweet" staff, you feel like a kid in a "candy store"; the "cute scarves", gloves, jewelry and hats from international designers also "never disappoint", amounting to "great" wardrobe additions.

Addy & Ferro Ⓜ

– | – | – | E

Ft Greene | 672 Fulton St. (bet. S. Elliott Pl. & S. Portland Ave.) | Brooklyn |
C to Lafayette Ave. | 718-246-2900 | www.addyandferro.com

Named after owner Erica Hutchinson's parents, this Fort Greene boutique mixes funky local designers with name brands like Earnest Sewn and Tracy Reese, along with men's items; it's worth the subway ride, especially when the courtyard is open.

Adidas Originals | 23 | 23 | 19 | M |

SoHo | 136 Wooster St. (bet. Houston & Prince Sts.) | N/R/W to Prince St. | 212-673-0398 | 800-289-2724

Adidas Sports Performance ◑

NoHo | 610 Broadway (Houston St.) | B/D/F/V to B'way/Lafayette St. | 212-529-0081
www.adidas.com

"Beautifully designed", the "garage-themed" "Wooster location is the mother ship for all of us Adidas freaks" addicted to the "impressively complete", "old-school" Originals collection of clothing and "sneakers with flair", plus the "so-fly-it-hurts hip-hop" music makes it "feel like a party"; the "name speaks for itself" at the sleek Sports Performance headquarters on Broadway offering "wonderful quality" trainers and "straightforward" athletic apparel along with service that's "attentive, not pushy."

ⓩ Adorama Camera | 26 | 14 | 18 | M |

Flatiron | 42 W. 18th St. (bet. 5th & 6th Aves.) | 4/5/6/L/N/Q/R/W to 14th St./Union Sq. | 212-741-0052 | 800-223-2500 |
www.adorama.com

"If you want it, it's probably here" at this veritable "camera cornucopia", a "legendary" Flatiron "gem" that "has everything" new or used "for beginners and professionals" alike; the "knowledgeable staffers" "know what they're talking about" and offer "some of the best deals in the city"; those who say "oy vey" about the "disheveled environment" and "cluttered", "crowded aisles" may be happy to hear a major expansion is scheduled for early 2007.

Adrien Linford | 22 | 24 | 21 | E |

E 70s | 927 Madison Ave. (74th St.) | 6 to 77th St. | 212-628-4500
E 90s | 1339 Madison Ave. (bet. 93rd & 94th Sts.) | 6 to 96th St. | 212-426-1500

These Upper East Side sister spots showcase "elegantly presented" collections of contemporary decorative arts and home accessories, such as chests, occasional tables and lamps, as well as jewelry; inspired mainly by Asian designs, the items make "unusual" "engagement and housewarming gifts."

Adriennes ⓢⓜ | ▽ 24 | 22 | 21 | M |

LES | 156 Orchard St. (bet. Rivington & Stanton Sts.) | F/V to Lower East Side/2nd Ave. | 212-228-9618

Adriennes Bridesmaid ⓢⓜ

LES | 155 Orchard St. (bet. Rivington & Stanton Sts.) | F/V to Lower East Side/2nd Ave. | 212-475-4206
www.adriennesny.com

"Sort of like shopping for a gown in your friend's apartment, this cozy store on the LES" and its companion shop for bridesmaids offer a "welcoming environment" for brides who "don't want the typical" "experience"; the "chatty owner" and her staff are "professional and excellent at what they do" while aisle-wear from the house-label and designers like Saison Blanche, Alvina Valenta, Jim Hjelm and Lazaro "makes your special day really special."

	QUALITY	DISPLAY	SERVICE	COST

NEW Adrienne Vittadini ⬧

24 | 23 | 21 | E

W 40s | 1180 Sixth Ave. (46th St.) | B/D/F/V to 47-50th Sts./
Rockefeller Ctr. | 212-869-7810 | www.adriennevittadini.com
How suitable that this beloved designer's new flagship is right near
Midtown's Diamond District, as her "stunning classics" are "always a
treasure"; customers are "greeted with a warm smile" as they browse an
"immaculately" arranged assortment of "well-made" knits, "working
woman" suits, sling backs, scarves and "trendy" totes that'll take you
"from South Beach to LA to the Riviera"; most term the tabs "reasonable", but even the "pricey" items are "good deals", given they'll deliver "years of wear."

⬧ Aedes De Venustas ●

27 | 27 | 25 | VE

G Vill | 9 Christopher St. (bet. 6th & 7th Aves.) | 1 to Christopher St./
Sheridan Sq. | 212-206-8674 | 888-233-3715 | www.aedes.com
Celebrities and fashionistas frequent this hip haunt, a "charming"
"little fragrance lover's sanctuary" in Greenwich Village known for its
"well-edited selection of perfumes, soaps", skincare products and
candles from statusy, hard-to-come-by European brands such as
Serge Lutens and Costes; the "knowledgeable staff" is "generous with
samples", and if you are buying a present, you should spring for the
additional charge and "have them gift wrap it" in their "beautiful"
black-and-gold boxes topped with fresh flowers, which adds to
the "divine" experience.

⬧ Aero ⬧

26 | 24 | 20 | VE

SoHo | 419 Broome St. (bet. Crosby & Lafayette Sts.) | 6 to Spring St. |
212-966-1500 | www.aerostudios.com
"Thomas O'Brien rules!" declare devotees of this midcentury modern
studio in SoHo that exudes "great taste"; a stylish mix of "beautiful"
accessories and furnishings like lamps, chairs and sofas, as well as
"one-of-a-kind" pieces and "reproductions" "at top-market prices",
makes this high-design destination "a reason to make novenas to
the lottery deity."

Aerosoles ●

18 | 17 | 17 | M

Garment Dist | 36 W. 34th St. (bet. 5th & 6th Aves.) | B/D/F/N/Q/R/V/W to
34th St./Herald Sq. | 212-563-0610 | 800-798-9478 | www.aerosoles.com
Additional locations throughout the NY area
Perfect "for the girl on the go" seeking "well-fitting" footwear at a
"medium price", this "king of comfy shoes" hits the mark, offering a
"wide range" of styles that "feel like butter"; sure, they're "not
Manolo's", and a handful harrumph they're still "too grandma for me",
but most applaud the chain's "360-degree turnaround" toward
more "fashionable" looks.

AG Adriano Goldschmied

26 | 23 | 21 | E

SoHo | 111 Greene St. (bet. Prince & Spring Sts.) | C/E to Spring St. |
212-680-0581 | www.agjeans.com
Guy and gal hipsters who covet this California-based brand can scoop
up colorful cords and form-fitting jeans from an "amazing selection" of
merchandise at its first East Coast store, a sprawling, skylit SoHo
yearling with "extremely helpful" employees who "aren't afraid to tell
you if that pair makes your butt look too big"; should your new five-

pockets need altering, head to the espresso bar while the in-house tailor nips and tucks your purchase; N.B. the lower level is reserved for VIP fittings.

Agatha Paris

20	20	20	M

E 50s | 611 Madison Ave. (58th St.) | N/R/W to 5th Ave./59th St. | 212-758-4301
W 60s | 159A Columbus Ave. (67th St.) | 1 to 66th St./Lincoln Ctr. | 212-362-0959 ◑
800-242-8427 | www.agatha.fr

For "copies of classic-style jewelry" and "stylish, up-to-the-minute" faux and semiprecious bijoux, boosters head to this Paris-based twosome in the East 50s and West 60s; the "sweet, inexpensive trinkets" are "displayed by category – silver, gold, with stones, without stones" – in neat glass cases and simple wall arrangements, which makes it easy for you to select a "piece that will make you smile" or a "good, safe gift."

Agatha Ruiz de la Prada ⊠

24	23	21	E

SoHo | 135 Wooster St. (Prince St.) | N/R/W to Prince St. | 212-598-4078

"Fabulous colorful designs" for bright young things and women too fill this Spanish designer's slim white SoHo expanse, the perfect showcase in which to peruse her fanciful, heart- and flower-strewn baby and children's clothing, "great kids' shoes" and accessories, plus nightdresses and footwear for mom in vivacious hues; but others admit that while they enjoy eyeballing the vivid palette, they "just wouldn't wear" anything quite so startling.

Agent Provocateur

27	27	23	VE

SoHo | 133 Mercer St. (bet. Prince & Spring Sts.) | N/R/W to Prince St. | 212-965-0229 | www.agentprovocateur.com

"Make your man blush" at this "delightfully decadent", "vampy" British import in SoHo, where the "come-hither lingerie" – ranging from "kinky" briefs with suspenders to "ooh-la-la" bras – transforms you into the "seductive" "star of your own blue movie"; sure, you may feel a "bit naughty" scooping up the "sexy wares", but the "awesome" scanties have a "humorous touch" and no matter which "erotic" unmentionable you dare to buy, the "provocatively" dressed salespeople "don't bat an eye."

Agnès B.

23	22	17	E

E 80s | 1063 Madison Ave. (bet. 80th & 81st Sts.) | 6 to 77th St. | 212-570-9333
SoHo | 103 Greene St. (bet. Prince & Spring Sts.) | N/R/W to Prince St. | 212-925-4649
Union Sq | 13 E. 16th St. (bet. 5th Ave. & Union Sq. W.) | 4/5/6/L/N/Q/R/W to 14th St./Union Sq. | 212-741-2585
888-246-3722 | www.agnesb.net

Left Bank lovers feel right at home perusing the "beautiful French duds" displaying "gorgeous fit" and "timeless styling with attention to details" in crisp shirts, striped tees and smartly cut suits at this trio; but *sceptiques* sigh this "once-so-edgy" brand is now just "boring stuff for lots of bucks", served by an often "uptight" staff; P.S. the "landmark SoHo" locale also sells men's clothes.

A.I. Friedman

24 | 22 | 18 | M

Flatiron | 44 W. 18th St. (bet. 5th & 6th Aves.) | 1 to 18th St. |
212-243-9000 | 800-736-5676 | www.aifriedman.com

Set in a landmark Flatiron building, this "polished" art supply store offers a "fabulous selection" of "high-quality paper", "good portfolios" and "cool gifts" along with "great frames"; some quibble it's "more for the hobbyist than the practicing artist", but even they admit the stock is "well organized", the service "courteous" and prices "competitive."

Airline Stationery Ⓢ

21 | 13 | 19 | M

E 40s | 284 Madison Ave. (40th St.) | 4/5/6/7/S to 42nd St./Grand Central |
212-532-6525 | 800-218-5815 | www.airlineinc.com

"One of the few oldies to survive the Staples challenge", this family-run, "unbelievably well-stocked workhorse" near Grand Central offers "nothing fancy", just a solid selection of paper supplies that meet "obscure office needs" along with popular brands like Filofax; aesthetes who assert the owners of the "cramped" store "don't even know that the concept of display exists" may be pleased to learn that a renovation is scheduled for later this year.

Ⓩ Akris Ⓢ

29 | 25 | 21 | VE

E 60s | 835 Madison Ave. (bet. 69th & 70th Sts.) | 6 to 68th St. |
212-717-1170 | www.akris.ch

You're sure "to find one special piece that's the highlight of the season" at this luxuriously spare East 60s emporium housing Zurich designer Albert Kriemler's "stunning" women's line of slim separates, "business suits that travel well" and trim trench coats in plush double-face wool; while indulgences such as these are "expensive even on sale", they're meant "to be worn forever"; N.B. the savvy take a look-see at Akris Punto, the won't-drain-the-Swiss-bank-account sportswear line as well.

Alain Mikli

28 | 25 | 23 | VE

E 50s | 575 Madison Ave. (bet. 56th & 57th Sts.) | E/V to 5th Ave./
53rd St. | 212-751-6085
E 70s | 986 Madison Ave. (bet. 76th & 77th Sts.) | 6 to 77th St. |
212-472-6085
www.mikli.com

"The French do know from fashionable faces" attest trendsetters who descend on this East 70s–East 50s duo with a "great atmosphere" for "distinctive", "cutting-edge" specs with a Gallic "flair" sold by a staff that's "extremely helpful, not snooty"; the "beautiful modern frames" are both "funky" and "très chic" – *mais oui,* it's the "only eyewear to be seen in" – ensuring you'll "always get compliments."

Ⓩ À La Vieille Russie Ⓢ

29 | 27 | 25 | VE

E 50s | 781 Fifth Ave. (59th St.) | N/R/W to 5th Ave./59th St. |
212-752-1727 | www.alvr.com

"For the czarina in all of us", this fifth-generation family emporium on Fifth Avenue "is the only place to go" for "Russian imperial treasures" "that are some of the most beautiful and rare things on earth"; whether it's "authentic Fabergé", vintage jewelry, silver or porcelain, they are "all one-of-a-kind" pieces presented by "a very informed staff", "but bring a couple of suitcases of cash" if you plan on purchasing.

	QUALITY	DISPLAY	SERVICE	COST

Albee Baby Carriage Co. 🗷

25 | 9 | 19 | M

W 90s | 715 Amsterdam Ave. (95th St.) | 1/2/3 to 96th St. | 212-662-5740 | 877-692-5233 | www.albeebaby.com

"If you can handle the cluttered", "cramped" and "chaotic" conditions, this "dependable" West 90s baby gear outfit, in business since 1933, is "the place to go for full service" infant shopping; while it "can't compete with the scale and offerings of the superstores", you'll find "all the essentials" here, from "brand-name" clothing and cribs to strollers and toys, and "what they don't have", the "knowledgeable" staff "will order for you."

Albertine ❶

- | - | - | E

G Vill | 13 Christopher St. (bet. Greenwich Ave. & Waverly Pl.) | 1 to Christopher St./Sheridan Sq. | 212-924-8515

Shoppers sing the praises of this Greenwich Villager, which "may be small", but has a super-feminine stash of silky dresses, inventive knits and lacy extras that add up to "more than you'd find at stores 10 times the size" due to the unerring eye of owner Kyung Lee, who curates wares from new and local designers like Christina Hatler and Sir; N.B. check out Claudine, a sweet slip of a sister store at 19 Christopher, and its new South Street Seaport sibling, Leontine.

Alcone 🗷

▽ 23 | 13 | 19 | M

W 40s | 322 W. 49th St. (bet. 8th & 9th Aves.) | C/E to 50th St. | 212-757-3734 | 800-466-7446 | www.alconeco.com

"Forget fancy displays and fawning salespeople", this "professional makeup artist's paradise" in Hell's Kitchen is the "real deal" for a "great selection" of stage greasepaint like Mehron and Ben Nye, plus European brands such as Visiora that suit "civilians" as well; it's "small and cluttered", but it's stocked with a moderately priced "secret stash" that "no one else in New York has."

Aldo ❶

16 | 17 | 15 | M

Garment Dist | 15 W. 34th St. (bet. 5th & 6th Aves.) | B/D/F/N/Q/R/V/W to 34th St./Herald Sq. | 212-594-6255 | 888-818-2536 | www.aldoshoes.com
Additional locations throughout the NY area

"Good stuff disappears fast" at this "shoe lover's dream" where "fashion-conscious" guys and gals flock for "trendy, sexy" styles that "don't bust the bank"; "party girls" go "crazy for clubbing" looks while nine-to-fivers latch onto "sassy heels for work" or "loafers with edge" – you "can always count on something different" at this chain; still, protestors pout they're "not the most comfy" and rarely "last more then a season."

Alessandro Dell'Acqua 🗷

▽ 26 | 23 | 21 | VE

E 60s | 818 Madison Ave. (bet. 68th & 69th Sts.) | 6 to 68th St. | 212-253-6861 | www.alessandrodellacqua.com

The couture cognoscenti get the cinematic riffs behind the modernist interior of this Madison Avenue boutique where the Naples-born designer Alessandro Dell'Acqua celebrates the earthy sophistication of movie icons like Sophia Loren and Gina Lollobrigida with filmy chiffon blouses, curvaceous pantsuits and diva dresses for those "wanting something different from their friends"; bring along your Marcello – they sell menswear too, as well as accessories.

	QUALITY	DISPLAY	SERVICE	COST

NEW Alessi
25 25 19 E

SoHo | 130 Greene St. (bet. Houston & Prince Sts.) | B/D/F/V to B'way/Lafayette St. | 212-941-7300 | www.alessi.com

For "all Alessi, all the time", head to the Italian company's new Hani Rashid–designed SoHo space that's as "modern" and "sleek" as its stock of over 3,000 "high-quality designer stainless-steel products for the home"; "pick up all the Graves and Starck you can afford" or find "fun" "housewarming gifts" and gadgets ranging from "the whimsical to the utilitarian", whether it be coffeemakers, wine openers, tea kettles, cookware, tableware or flatware; P.S. you can take a break from all the "cool" stuff by hitting the Joe coffee bar in the front of the store.

☑ Alexander McQueen
28 27 23 VE

Meatpacking | 417 W. 14th St. (bet. 9th & 10th Aves.) | A/C/E/L to 14th St./8th Ave. | 212-645-1797 | www.alexandermcqueen.com

The designer who made dresses with leather harnesses hip delivers a "fashion-forward" Meatpacking District flagship for jet-set types bent on emulating a "super-vixenish Joan of Arc or modern-day Lucrezia Borgia" via skinny pants, zippered jackets or body-conscious gowns; naturally, you need a "serious trust fund" to afford such "couture cutting"-edge creations, but if you lack one, you "can always browse and pretend."

Alexandros ☑
– – – E

Chelsea | 345 Seventh Ave., 4th fl. (bet. 29th & 30th Sts.) | 1 to 28th St. | 212-868-1044
E 50s | 5 E. 59th St., 2nd fl. (5th Ave.) | 4/5/6/F/N/R/W to 59th St./Lexington Ave. | 212-702-0744
www.luxuryouterwear.com

While not as high-profile as some, this "wonderful furrier offers all of the latest styles" profess fans – though critics counter the looks are "a bit long in the tooth"; still, there's no debate that you can get the goods, plus shearlings and home accessories, "at downtown prices", whether you visit the Chelsea showroom (where pelts are produced) or Midtown.

Alexis Bittar
25 24 23 E

SoHo | 465 Broome St. (bet. Greene & Mercer Sts.) | N/R/W to Prince St. | 212-625-8340 | www.alexisbittar.com

"A gem of a store", this "fantastic SoHo space" showcases the eponymous jewelry designer and his original, "vibrant" Lucite creations, along with "very wearable", "wonderfully creative" semiprecious and costume pieces that appeal to celebs like Cameron Diaz, Madonna and Mischa Barton; a "helpful" and "accommodating" staff adds to the "colorful" experience.

NEW alice + olivia ☑
22 23 19 E

W 40s | 80 W. 40th St. (6th Ave.) | 7/B/D/F/V to 42nd St./Bryant Park | 212-840-0887 | www.aliceandolivia.com

"Finally there's a place to find all of this adorable" line – a spacious black-and-white tiled boutique opposite Bryant Park; converts keep chanting "cute, cute, cute" about the capris, pants that make "your butt look amazing" and "skimpy tank tops" that comprise designer Stacey Bendet's "body-conscious" brand; the styles, while "pricey", "are worth the money" – however, they're also seemingly "sized for teens", so stay clear of the Dylan's Candy Bar goodies in the corner.

	QUALITY	DISPLAY	SERVICE	COST

Alife
| | 24 | 24 | 17 | E |

LES | 158A Rivington St. (bet. Clinton & Suffolk Sts.) | F/J/M/Z to Delancey/Essex Sts. | 212-375-8116 | www.alifenyc.com

Alife Rivington Club
LES | 158 Rivington St. (bet. Clinton & Suffolk Sts.) | F/J/M/Z to Delancey/Essex Sts. | 212-375-8128 | www.rivingtonclub.com

"If you haven't been, just go" to this LES double whammy "hidden behind a tinted door, with a doorbell as the only identifying characteristic" – if, of course, you're a dude seeking one of the "best selections of kicks" (especially at the Club), house-label clothing, accessories or a few T-shirts for the ladies; you may not feel "cool enough to shop" at this "original concept", which is "ironic because it is completely unpretentious."

Alixandre Furs 🗷
| ▽ | 24 | 16 | 22 | E |

Garment Dist | 150 W. 30th St., 13th fl. (bet. 6th & 7th Aves.) | 1 to 28th St. | 212-736-5550 | www.alixandrefurs.com

Since the early days of the 20th century, this family-owned furrier has been luring ladies to its large Garment District showroom to try on a plethora of pelts in "au courant styles" (they're the licensees for several designers, including Oscar de la Renta and Isaac Mizrahi), at "well below uptown prices"; the "excellent" staff may also steer you toward their fur-trimmed coats and shearlings for men.

Alkit Pro Camera 🗷
| | 23 | 17 | 18 | E |

Flatiron | 222 Park Ave. S. (18th St.) | 4/5/6/L/N/Q/R/W to 14th St./Union Sq. | 212-674-1515 | 800-285-1698 | www.alkit.com

"When you need camera advice and you're willing to pay for it", go "elbow to reel with" the experts at this "easy-to-shop" family-owned superstore offering "personalized service" and a "manageable" selection; shutterbugs snap up and rent "professional" equipment, while other photogs focus on the outfit's "great quality film developing."

Allan & Suzi
| | 20 | 16 | 15 | E |

W 80s | 416 Amsterdam Ave. (80th St.) | 1 to 79th St. | 212-724-7445 | www.allanandsuzi.net

It's "like your eccentric-but-glamorous aunt's attic" at this Upper West Side vintage/consignment store that's "crowded" with "cool", "crazy fun stuff" "in every style from mostly the '50s on" ("they can't use your normal clothes"); while "expensive", "it's worth a visit for the vibe as well as the products" – just hope the owner is "in a good mood."

◪ Allen Edmonds
| | 28 | 23 | 25 | E |

E 40s | 24 E. 44th St. (bet. 5th & Madison Aves.) | 4/5/6/7/S to 42nd St./Grand Central | 212-682-3144
E 50s | 551 Madison Ave. (55th St.) | E/V to 5th Ave./53rd St. | 212-308-8305
877-817-7615 | www.allenedmonds.com

"You get what you pay for" agree "well-heeled" "conservative" types keen on the "comfortable", "classically styled handmade" men's shoes sold at these Midtown chain offshoots by an "accommodating" staff that "takes fitting" footwear "seriously"; "good old American quality still wins out" – in fact your purchase may "outlast most Manhattan relationships if treated properly" since their "recrafting service is second-to-none."

	QUALITY	DISPLAY	SERVICE	COST

Alpana Bawa ⓜ   – | – | – | E

E Vill | 70 E. First St. (bet. 1st & 2nd Aves.) | F/V to Lower East Side/
2nd Ave. | 212-254-1249 | www.alpanabawa.com

Lush, "lovely colors" and embroidery galore characterize the namesake designer's India-inspired merchandise in her East Village shop,
be it the "nicely" designed shifts and tunics for women, easy-fitting
shirts in vibrant, painterly patterns for men or line of hot-hued pillows
and other furnishings for the home.

Alphabets ⓞ   19 | 18 | 16 | M

E Vill | 115 Ave. A (bet. 7th St. & St. Marks Pl.) | 6 to Astor Pl. | 212-475-7250
G Vill | 47 Greenwich Ave. (bet. Charles & Perry Sts.) | 1/2/3 to 14th St. |
212-229-2966
800-419-3989 | www.alphabetsnyc.com

"Fun, fun, fun" giggle gift-givers – "last-minute" and otherwise – of
this duo offering "clever cards", "novelty tees", "funky" yet functional
housewares and classic toys that are a "trip down memory lane"; the
"witty" merch mix makes these shops a "great source for gifts both
gag and gracious" and a must-"stop before a party."

Altman Luggage   24 | 13 | 20 | M

LES | 135 Orchard St. (bet. Delancey & Rivington Sts.) | F/J/M/Z to
Delancey/Essex Sts. | 212-254-7275 | 800-372-3377 |
www.altmanluggage.com

Whether you're hunting "for that last minute bag" or just a "fair price
on good luggage", this "crowded, out-of-the-way" "legend" "beats all
others' selection", making it "worth the trip to the Lower East Side";
"forget how it looks" and just turn to the "product savvy" staff for "advice" about suitcases, "pens and Filofax" organizers, and remember
there's "lots of room for negotiation."

Amarcord Vintage Fashion ⓞ   – | – | – | E

E Vill | 84 E. Seventh St. (bet. 1st & 2nd Aves.) | 6 to Astor Pl. |
212-614-7133 ⓜ
NEW **SoHo** | 252 Lafayette St. (bet. Prince & Spring Sts.) | B/D/F/V
to B'way/Lafayette St. | 212-431-4161
Williamsburg | 223 Bedford Ave. (bet. N. 4th & 5th Sts.) | Brooklyn | L to
Bedford Ave. | 718-963-4001
www.amarcordvintagefashion.com

Surveyors are in accord about this trio of vintage clothiers – each one
is a "fashionista's dream", specializing in "well-selected" women's
and men's duds, shoes and accessories bearing European designer labels (think Fendi, Fiorucci, Gucci) from the '50s to the '80s; some say
the "prices are high for used clothes", but, with the help of the "wonderful" staff, "you'll definitely find at least a few things you'll love";
N.B. with the opening of the new SoHo location, the Seventh Street
branch has become more of an outlet.

American Apparel ⓞ   19 | 20 | 17 | I

NoHo | 712 Broadway (Washington Pl.) | N/R/W to 8th St. |
646-383-2257 | www.americanapparelstore.com
Additional locations throughout the NY area

"Stock up on reasonably priced", "super-comfy" T-shirts and knits in
"every color under the sun" at this ever-expanding chain appreciated
for its "simple" displays and "plain" but "slightly sexy" styling; "left-

leaning" sorts "love the idea" of shopping "relatively guilt-free" – the goods are "made in the USA" with "no sweatshop labor" – though a number wonder "what's with all the porn-style photos" on the walls?

American Eagle Outfitters ● | 17 | 18 | 17 | M |

Garment Dist | 40 W. 34th St. (bet. B'way & 5th Ave.) | B/D/F/N/Q/R/V/W to 34th St./Herald Sq. | 212-947-1677

SoHo | 575 Broadway (bet. Houston & Prince Sts.) | N/R/W to Prince St. | 212-941-9785

Union Sq | 17-19 Union Sq. W. (15th St. & Union Sq. W.) | 4/5/6/L/N/Q/R/W to 14th St./Union Sq. | 212-645-2086

Kings Plaza | Kings Plaza Shopping Ctr. | 5249 Kings Plaza (Flatbush Ave. & Ave. U) | Brooklyn | 718-377-0342

NEW **Bayside** | 212-55 26th Ave. (Bell Blvd.) | Queens | 7 to Main St. | 718-279-0651

Elmhurst | Queens Ctr. | 90-15 Queens Blvd. (bet. 57th & 59th Aves.) | Queens | G/R/V to Woodhaven Blvd. | 718-699-2874

Staten Island | Staten Island Mall | 2655 Richmond Ave. (bet. Platinum Ave. & Richmond Hill Rd.) | 718-494-2885

888-232-4535 | www.ae.com

It's "*Dawson's Creek* with a dash of *The OC*" at this "frat-boy" (and -girl) chain offering "comfortable", "all-American preppy" clothing for "the teen set"; the "laid-back attire" suitable for everything from "safaris to the movies to Starbucks" leaves "pocketbooks happy", especially items from the "deal"-packed "sale racks" that keep 'em coming back despite quality that's "sometimes wanting."

American Folk Art Museum | 23 | 20 | 20 | M |

W 50s | 45 W. 53rd St. (bet. 5th & 6th Aves.) | E/V to 5th Ave./53rd St. | 212-265-1040

W 60s | 2 Lincoln Sq., Columbus Ave. (bet. 65th & 66th Sts.) | 1 to 66th St./Lincoln Ctr. | 212-595-9533 ● Ⓜ

www.folkartmuseum.org

Folks who favor "one-of-a-kind" "treasures" with a "touch of whimsy" laud this "little" "hidden gem" in Midtown and its larger gallery near Lincoln Center; the "interesting books" and "special" handcrafted contemporary items and reproductions ring in at a "range of prices", and the "lovely ornaments" make it "great" for holiday shopping.

American Girl Place | 24 | 27 | 22 | E |

E 40s | 609 Fifth Ave. (49th St.) | B/D/F/V to 47-50th Sts./Rockefeller Ctr. | 212-371-2220 | 877-247-5223 | www.americangirl.com

Truly a "little girl's fantasy come true", this "over-the-top" Midtown "experience", based on the Chicago original, offers "entertainment" for "hordes of 10-and-unders" who "have a ball" shopping for dolls with "enough of an educational bent to keep parents happy"; take your tyke and her toy to the hair salon for a new 'do, then "treat" them to a "lovely lunch" and a "delightful show" in the theater; if cynics snarl those dollies should "do my laundry" for such "big bucks", enthusiasts rejoin it's "worth it" to "see such smiles."

American Kennels | 17 | 13 | 16 | E |

E 60s | 798 Lexington Ave. (bet. 61st & 62nd Sts.) | 4/5/6/F/N/R/W to 59th St./Lexington Ave. | 212-838-8460 | www.americankennels.com

"A peep show" for puppy and pussycat voyeurs, this UES pet shop attracts "crowds" with window displays of "adorable" animals; the "supplies are excellent" and "the name means a lot" to pedigree proponents, but a few stray opposers posit the four-legged offerings are "priced way over market value."

American Museum of Natural History   22 | 21 | 18 | M

W 70s | Central Park West & 79th St. | B/C to 81st St. | 212-769-5100 | www.amnh.org

From "reasonably priced" "doodads" ranging from "candy-coated bugs" to "beautiful jewelry" and "handcrafted African and Asian textiles", this "bustling" Upper West Side museum store has "something for everyone"; naturally, it's strong on "inspirational" "scientific toys" and books for "smart kids", and even if some lament the "less-than-helpful staff", the "amazing selection" "warrants a look."

Amsale 🖼 Ⓜ   27 | 24 | 21 | VE

E 50s | 625 Madison Ave. (bet. 58th & 59th Sts.) | N/R/W to 5th Ave./ 59th St. | 212-583-1700 | www.amsale.com

Expect "quite a presentation" of "gorgeous" bridal "gowns fit for a princess" at this "sleek", by-appointment-only Madison Avenue "loft space" that's "small enough to be intimate, but with enough choice" "so you don't feel limited"; Amsale Aberra "fulfills every woman's inner Cinderella" with her "heavenly dresses" and "fantastic bridesmaids' ensembles that are comfy and classy"; while admirers applaud the staff, a few huff "for the price, they could be more accommodating."

Anbar 🖼   21 | 11 | 11 | M

TriBeCa | 60 Reade St. (bet. B'way & Church St.) | 1/2/3 to Chambers St. | 212-227-0253

"It's every woman for herself" at TriBeCa's two-floor "warehouse-esque" discount den, a "secret treat filled with designer" footwear and "organized by color, making it easy to navigate"; "don't let the look of the place turn you off" – ambiance and "service are not why you schlep Downtown" – it's the "surprise brands" at a "great price", like Biviel, Delman, Donald J Pliner and even Gucci and Prada "finds", "lurking next to the mall-variety" kicks that keep "shoeaholics" on their toes.

Andy's Chee-Pees ◑   15 | 10 | 11 | M

E Vill | 37 St. Marks Pl. (2nd Ave.) | 6 to Astor Pl. | 212-253-8404
NoHo | 691 Broadway (bet. 3rd & 4th Sts.) | 6 to Bleecker St. | 212-420-5980

"Andy ain't so cheap" anymore virtually every surveyor says about this "cramped", "punk" pair of used-clothing purveyors in NoHo and the East Village – and, argue the antagonistic, "nothing to shout about as far as selection" goes either ("old T-shirts passing as vintage"); still, "if you can stand fishing through the crowded racks", "you can find unique crinoline skirts, army jackets" and "authentic bell-bottoms from 1975."

Angela's Vintage Boutique ◑   – | – | – | M

E Vill | 330 E. 11th St. (bet. 1st & 2nd Aves.) | L to 1st Ave. | 212-475-1571

In a neighborhood (the East Village) chockablock with boutiques selling vintage clothing, this small shop stands out for its oft-changing inventory; though it's famed for flapper dresses, there's also plenty of '50-'70s formalwear, along with shoes, jewelry and other accessories to provide the perfect period look for ladies.

Angel Street Thrift Shop
17 | 16 | 16 | I

Chelsea | 118 W. 17th St. (bet. 6th & 7th Aves.) | 1 to 18th St. | 212-229-0546
"Search well and you shall find" "some decent things" amid the "new clothes", "cool accessories", bric-a-brac and furniture – all "organized with eye appeal" or in "inventive window displays" at this Chelsea thrift; patrons praise the plain but "pristine environs" and "considerate" staff, though skeptics shrug off its new "more upmarket" efforts ("place thinks it's Barneys but it's more like Goodwill").

Anik ◐
21 | 18 | 14 | E

E 70s | 1355 Third Ave. (bet. 77th & 78th Sts.) | 6 to 77th St. | 212-861-9840
E 80s | 1122 Madison Ave. (bet. 83rd & 84th Sts.) | 4/5/6 to 86th St. | 212-249-2417
Upper East Siders "walk in and want everything" in this "cut-above" duo jam-packed with "trendy casual wear", "stylish" suits, "core pieces" like cashmere sweaters and Juicy Couture separates; insiders promote the sale annex in back "full of good surprises" at the Third Avenue location – it's a "gem for great bargains"; still, a handful huff that the mood is "sometimes chaotic" and the service sort of "snotty."

Anna ◐
– | – | – | E

E Vill | 150 E. Third St. (bet. Aves. A & B) | F/V to Lower East Side/2nd Ave. | 212-358-0195 | www.annanyc.com
Owner Kathy Kemp may have studied anthropology, but what she really digs is designing the body-conscious togs that fill the racks and banquette of this East Villager; street-smart Downtowners say her funky silhouettes "get better all the time" as they scoop up her versatile 7-way top in 4-ply silk, a shapely lace skirt or striped rayon dress.

Anna Sui

23 | 23 | 20 | E

SoHo | 113 Greene St. (bet. Prince & Spring Sts.) | N/R/W to Prince St. | 212-941-8406 | www.annasui.com
"Boho chic" reigns at this designer's "little, dark and glam" SoHo boutique with an "always jolly" "vibe that feels like the '60s", what with the lavender-red-black color scheme, "the scent of patchouli" and the "kaleidoscope of psychedelia" emanating from the "inventive", hippie-ish garb and "drag-queen makeup at the front" – "what every NYU girl wants to wear when dressed up"; N.B. scores may not reflect a post-*Survey* expansion in size and into menswear.

Ann Crabtree ▨
23 | 19 | 21 | E

E 90s | 1260 Madison Ave. (90th St.) | 4/5/6 to 86th St. | 212-996-6499
Devotees of this "neighborhood jewel" include Carnegie Hill moms, who proclaim it's "very hard to pass by" the "elegant", "well-chosen selection of tasteful", "good quality" women's dresses, separates and "great accessories"; "it's not your usual boutique" – the vibe is oh-so-"low-key" and the mix "interesting" – and chances are you'll walk away with a "one-of-a-kind" find.

Anne Fontaine
27 | 25 | 24 | E

E 50s | 610 Fifth Ave. (bet. 49th & 50th Sts.) | B/D/F/V to 47-50th Sts./Rockefeller Ctr. | 212-489-1554
E 60s | 687 Madison Ave. (bet. 61st & 62nd Sts.) | 4/5/6/F/N/R/W to 59th St./Lexington Ave. | 212-688-4362

(continued)

(continued)

Anne Fontaine

SoHo | 93 Greene St. (bet. Prince & Spring Sts.) | C/E to Spring St. | 212-343-3154
www.annefontaine.com

"If God were a woman", he'd go to this "blouse heaven" trio to "indulge in the chic simplicity of a classic white shirt" (plus some black and cream versions), whose "steep price tags" are "worth every penny"; loyalists laud the "lovely saleswomen" and how the shops, suffused with proprietary perfume, "even smell luxurious", so while some snap "the selections seem limited", most attest *"j'adore Anne."*

NEW Anne Klein ◐

– | – | – | E

E 60s | 655 Madison Ave. (bet. 60th & 61st Sts.) | 4/5/6/F/N/R/W to 59th St./Lexington Ave. | 212-317-2731

As part of a push to rejuvenate this once-beloved brand, Jones Apparel is rolling out a series of sleek stores and higher-quality goods; the new modern Madison Avenue representative, all chocolate-accented white floors and light woods (actually, wallpaper), emphasizes smart leather accessories – shoes, belts, gloves and bags – in, blissfully, medium as well as the huge trendy sizes; there's also an increasing amount of womenswear – mostly neutral-toned basics now, but designer Isabel Toledo is slated to take over the reins with the fall '07 collection.

Annelore Ⓜ

– | – | – | E

W Vill | 636 Hudson St. (Horatio St.) | A/C/E/L to 14th St./8th Ave. | 212-255-5574

West Village waifs wander into this wee white-washed wonderland for designer-owner Juliana Cho's "creative, edgy" femme fashions made from distinctive fabrics, including menswear textiles like twill and tuxedo cloth, and finished with TLC details like handmade buttons; it's a "delightful haven for the blouse maven" – not to mention seekers of superbly tailored women's jackets and coats, hand-knit pullovers and dresses, tunics and shirts in flirty prints.

Annie & Company Needlepoint Ⓢ

25 | 24 | 24 | E

E 90s | 1325 Madison Ave., 2nd fl. (bet. 93rd & 94th Sts.) | 6 to 96th St. | 212-360-7266 | 888-806-7200 | www.annieandco.com

Stocking a "vast selection of hand-painted canvases" "for every skill level" plus "all the yarns and supplies you could ever need", this Upper East Sider ranks as "one of NYC's best needlepoint stores"; free instruction at two central tables and "great" natural light from the front picture window make it a "wonderful" place to ply your plies, especially since the "super-friendly" staff delivers "expert" advice and "top-quality finishing"; N.B. custom designs available.

☑ Ann Sacks Ⓢ

27 | 26 | 18 | VE

E 50s | 204 E. 58th St. (bet. 2nd & 3rd Aves.) | 4/5/6/F/N/R/W to 59th St./Lexington Ave. | 212-588-1920
Flatiron | 37 E. 18th St. (bet. B'way & Park Ave.) | 4/5/6/L/N/Q/R/W to 14th St./Union Sq. | 212-529-2800
800-278-8453 | www.annsacks.com

"Search no further" – the "best place" for "luxurious, unusual" stone, mosaic and leather tiles in "phenomenal colors and patterns" as well as "magnificent sinks and other fixtures" is this duo in the Flatiron

District and the East 50s; cynics say the "snooty help is no help" and the "staggering prices" mean "you'll have to sell your first born", but the smitten simply sigh "it doesn't get more beautiful than this."

☒ Ann Taylor ●
21 | 21 | 19 | M

E 60s | 645 Madison Ave. (60th St.) | 4/5/6/F/N/R/W to 59th St./ Lexington Ave. | 212-832-9114 | 800-342-5266 | www.anntaylor.com
Additional locations throughout the NY area

"Like your best friend", this "conservative" chain is "always there if you need it", peddling "perfect attire for all things corporate" – i.e. "not for fashionistas, but for their lawyers" – in sizes to "fit average" women, "not just stick figures" (including "great options for petites"); the "willing", "helpful" service alone makes it "worth shopping here", even if trendsters yawn "still boring after all these years."

☒ Ann Taylor Loft ●
20 | 20 | 19 | M

E 40s | 150 E. 42nd St. (Lexington Ave.) | 4/5/6/7/S to 42nd St./Grand Central | 212-883-8766 | 800-342-5266 | www.anntaylorloft.com
Additional locations throughout the NY area

"A less-expensive alternative to Ann Taylor", this "ubiquitous" women's chain draws "office"-oriented types with its "business-casual" suits, dresses and separates (including a "particularly satisfying" petites selection) that perhaps are "not very exciting" but can be had "without breaking the bank"; though to stylesetters it's "double-dull", "conservative" types swear by it, especially at sale time (they "really know how to mark down a garment").

☒ Anthropologie ●
20 | 24 | 17 | E

Flatiron | 85 Fifth Ave. (16th St.) | 4/5/6/L/N/Q/R/W to 14th St./ Union Sq. | 212-627-5885
SoHo | 375 W. Broadway (bet. Broome & Spring Sts.) | C/E to Spring St. | 212-343-7070
NEW **W 50s** | Rockefeller Ctr. | 50 Rockefeller Ctr. (50th St.) | E/V to 5th Ave./53rd St. | 212-246-0386
www.anthropologie.com

Bringing a "French flea market-y" look to "the masses", these "boho chic" chain links brimming with "folkloric", "flirty, frilly" women's clothing, "vintage-inspired" jewelry, home accents and "wonderful trinkets" are the next best thing to "your funky aunt's attic"; the "kitschy" "creative" mix is a "dream" "for the fabulous girl" who's "tired of basics", and while it's "pricey", the "amazing" (if "chaotic") sale section provides "salvation" for those "on a shoestring budget"; N.B. the new, two-floor Rockefeller Center branch features an art gallery.

Anya Hindmarch
25 | 21 | 20 | E

E 60s | 29 E. 60th St. (bet. Madison & Park Aves.) | N/R/W to 5th Ave./59th St. | 212-750-3974 ☒
SoHo | 115 Greene St. (bet. Prince & Spring Sts.) | N/R/W to Prince St. | 212-343-8147
www.anyahindmarch.com

For "lovely handbags with a witty twist", turn to this British designer, the "Kate Spade of the U.K.", whose shops in the East 60s and SoHo boast "cute signature bow purses" along with "elegant leather goods" and shoes; "check out" the be-a-bag service that allows for "fun personalization" – you can "be your own celebrity" and have "your own picture" or even your pooch's put on your tote or clutch "so long as you have celebrity money to afford it."

Apartment 48 Ⓜ
`21` `24` `20` `M`

Flatiron | 48 W. 17th St. (bet. 5th & 6th Aves.) | F/L/V to 14th St./6th Ave. | 212-807-1391 | www.apartment48.com

"Brilliantly laid-out", with seven small rooms "arranged like an actual" apartment, this Flatiron store has "practical" and "beautiful" home and personal accessories aimed at men, women and baby in the bed, bath, kitchen and dining departments; the "interesting" collection includes linens, decanters, decoupage platters, pasta bowls and pitchers.

A.P.C.
`21` `22` `17` `E`

SoHo | 131 Mercer St. (bet. Prince & Spring Sts.) | N/R/W to Prince St. | 212-966-9685 | www.apc.fr

Amis agree this "light, airy" SoHo store with wood plank floors is "very Left Bank", with designer Jean Touitou's "classic" men's and women's trousers, tees and "killer" denim jackets imbued with a "dose of French attitude" - which also applies, alas, to the "too-cool-for school" clerks; it may be "more expensive than you'd expect" for "modern" "everyday-wear", but most say *oui* to the tasteful "basics" "because they fit so well"; N.B. jeans are stowed in the back room addition.

Ⓩ Apple Store ◗
`27` `28` `21` `E`

NEW **E 50s** | 767 Fifth Ave. (bet. 58th & 59th Sts.) | N/R/W to 5th Ave./ 59th St. | 212-336-1440 Ⓢ Ⓜ

SoHo | 103 Prince St. (Greene St.) | N/R/W to Prince St. | 212-226-3126

Staten Island | Staten Island Mall | 2655 Richmond Ave. (bet. Platinum Ave. & Richmond Hill Rd.) | 718-477-4180

800-692-7753 | www.apple.com

"The promised land" "for Mac fans", this "seductive" spot in a former SoHo post office sports "sleek, quality merchandise", including "beautifully laid-out", "cool" computers that "you're allowed to touch", not to mention a "knowledgeable" staff, "great free classes" and a "hipster vibe"; in short, this Apple's got "polish" - even if the "iPod craze has made" it "as crowded as Times Square"; N.B. the Staten Island branch and the GM building's underground store with a huge, translucent cube marking the entrance opened post-*Survey*.

Arcadia ◗
`▽` `25` `26` `24` `M`

Chelsea | 228 Eighth Ave. (bet. 21st & 22nd Sts.) | C/E to 23rd St. | 212-243-5358 | www.arcadianyc.com

"Glory hallelujah - a fun, affordable place to shop" in Chelsea praise proponents of this "well-presented" gift/lifestyle and cosmetics boutique that successfully combines "old-world service with New Age products"; home accessories like candles, crystal and vases mingle with costume jewelry, aromatherapy treatments and "all types of salves and lotions for beautiful men and women" in a two-story space.

Archangel Antiques Ⓜ
`-` `-` `-` `M`

E Vill | 334 E. Ninth St. (bet. 1st & 2nd Aves.) | L to 1st Ave. | 212-260-9313

Divided into two sections, this dark, narrow East Villager carries a magpie's nest of vintage merchandise - from clothing to housewares to costume jewelry; but definitely ask to delve into the drawers of the various chests and cabinets, which house a huge collection of old buttons and cuff links.

Arche
25 | 20 | 20 | E

E 60s | 1045 Third Ave. (bet. 61st & 62nd Sts.) | 4/5/6/F/N/R/W to 59th St./Lexington Ave. | 212-838-1933
E 70s | 995 Madison Ave. (77th St.) | 6 to 77th St. | 212-439-0700
E Vill | 10 Astor Pl. (bet. B'way & Lafayette St.) | 6 to Astor Pl. | 212-529-4808 ●
W 50s | 128 W. 57th St. (bet. 6th & 7th Aves.) | N/Q/R/W to 57th St. | 212-262-5488
www.arche-shoes.com

"Perfect city shoes from Paris" insist boosters who make a beeline to this "candy-store" quartet for "funky, European" footwear in "fabulous colors" and "soft leathers" with "supremely comfortable" natural Latex soles; they're so "inventive" "I could take every pair home in a heartbeat" – they should call it the "Arche de Triomphe!"; but those who skip to another beat archly retort it's a "one-note concept" and too "expensive."

Arden B. ●
17 | 19 | 17 | M

E 60s | 1130 Third Ave. (66th St.) | 6 to 68th St. | 212-628-2003
Flatiron | 104 Fifth Ave. (bet. 15th & 16th Sts.) | 4/5/6/L/N/Q/R/W to 14th St./Union Sq. | 646-638-0361
SoHo | 532 Broadway (bet. Prince & Spring Sts.) | 6 to Spring St. | 212-941-5697
877-274-6722 | www.ardenb.com

"On top of the fashions" and "unafraid to be a little glitzy", this "sweetly sexy" chain appeals to "younger women who haven't yet graduated to real boutiques" but seek "great going-out clothes" and "just-right accessories" to keep them "in vogue but not broke"; though it can be "a bit pricey for the quality", savvy regulars join the "shopper's reward program" so they can afford to "buy it, wear it and throw it away" after "a season or two."

Area
- | - | - | M

Carroll Gdns | 196 Court St. (Wyckoff St.) | Brooklyn | F/G to Bergen St. | 718-222-0869
Carroll Gdns | 233 Smith St. (bet. Butler & Douglass Sts.) | Brooklyn | F/G to Carroll St. | 718-522-6455
Carroll Gdns | 252 Smith St. (bet. Degraw & Douglass Sts.) | Brooklyn | F/G to Carroll St. | 718-246-9453
Carroll Gdns | 331 Smith St. (Carroll St.) | Brooklyn | F/G to Carroll St. | 718-624-2411
Park Slope | 103 Seventh Ave. (bet. President & Union Sts.) | Brooklyn | M/R to Union St. | 718-636-7235
Park Slope | 45 Fifth Ave. (Bergen St.) | Brooklyn | 2/3 to Bergen St. | 718-230-7495
www.areabrooklyn.com

Yoginis, health nuts and earthy mamas congregate at these children's emporiums sprinkled throughout Carroll Gardens and Park Slope – part of the Area spa, yoga studio and retail family – to check out the eclectic offerings; rifle through the racks of organic kids' apparel at some branches, then head to other links to peruse the imported toys, including wooden guitars and ant farms, or test drive the Bugaboos.

	QUALITY	DISPLAY	SERVICE	COST

Armani Casa Ⓜ
| | 25 | 25 | 17 | VE |

SoHo | 97 Greene St. (bet. Prince & Spring Sts.) | N/R/W to Prince St. |
212-334-1271 | www.armanicasa.com

"What doesn't Armani do well?" ask admirers of the Italian icon's take
on home furnishings as displayed at this "sleek", skylit SoHo space;
his "gorgeous minimalist" tableware, furniture and accessories include hand-blown Murano glass vases and side tables covered in crocodile; the "rarefied" atmosphere makes for "an art gallery of a store,
with prices to match."

Artbag Ⓢ
| | 24 | 17 | 23 | E |

E 80s | 1130 Madison Ave. (84th St.) | 4/5/6 to 86th St. | 212-744-2720 |
www.artbag.com

"Unique" handbags and accessories in "rich" Italian "leathers and exotic
skins" at "all sorts of prices" line the maple cabinets of this East 80s
brownstone; "even better" is the repair service declare loyalists who
crown this 75-year-old family-run outfit "great merchants" thanks to a
staff, including European-trained craftsmen, that's "not above" "giving that damaged bag new life" "rather than pushing a sale."

Artemide Ⓢ
| | ▽ 27 | 23 | 23 | E |

SoHo | 46 Greene St. (bet. Broome & Grand Sts.) | A/C/E to Canal St. |
212-925-1588 | www.artemide.us

"If you like modern lighting, this is the place" swear supporters of this
SoHo showroom for the "high-end" namesake Milanese company;
many of its products, like the Boalum table lamp that's shaped like a
snake, are in museum collections, so while it's expensive, even wallet-
watchers window shop here "for design ideas."

Ⓩ Arthur Brown & Brother Ⓢ
| | 27 | 22 | 24 | E |

W 40s | 2 W. 46th St. (bet. 5th & 6th Aves.) | B/D/F/V to 47-50th Sts./
Rockefeller Ctr. | 212-575-5555 | 800-772-7367 | www.artbrown.com
Since 1924, this "class act" stationer near Rockefeller Center has offered an "amazing selection of inks", "paper ephemera", art supplies
and "a great framing department"; still, some say the staff "can vary
from the service-oriented to the sales-oriented."

Arthur's Invitations and Prints ◗
| | ▽ 21 | 19 | 23 | M |

G Vill | 13 E. 13th St. (bet. 5th Ave. & University Pl.) | 4/5/6/L/N/Q/R/W to
14th St./Union Sq. | 212-807-6502 | www.arthursinvitations.com
Party animals promise you'll find "everything but the caterer and flo-
rist" at this soaring Greenwich Village stationery shop offering custom
invitations and printing, thank you notes and table placecards, plus
Larsen-Juhl designer framing; the staff is "helpful but not intrusive",
serving everyone from the graphically oriented Parsons crowd to
locals like Susan Sarandon.

Ⓩ Artistic Tile Ⓢ
| | 26 | 23 | 18 | E |

E 50s | 150 E. 58th St. (bet. Lexington & 3rd Aves.) | 4/5/6/F/N/R/W to
59th St./Lexington Ave. | 212-838-3222
Flatiron | 79 Fifth Ave. (bet. 15th & 16th Sts.) | 4/5/6/L/N/Q/R/W to
14th St./Union Sq. | 212-727-9331
800-260-8646 | www.artistictile.com
"Artistic" vignette-style displays of glass, metal and porcelain tiles
"provide excellent design inspiration" and show off the "enormous

range" of "quality products" in these East 50s and Flatiron stores; still, some say it's best to "know what you are looking for" because the "snooty" staff is "not accommodating."

Artsee
`- | - | - | VE`

Meatpacking | 863 Washington St. (bet. 13th & 14th Sts.) | A/C/E/L to 14th St./8th Ave. | 212-414-0900

"I could find fab frames for every day of the week" vow visionaries who anoint this "service-oriented" Meatpacking District spectacle shop one of "the greatest in the city" – and "one of the few that's not part of a dreaded chain"; "not only can you shop for eyewear", choosing from an "amazing selection" of vintage, designer and custom-made styles, "you can also see great artwork" since it doubles as a gallery.

Ascot Chang 🛇
`25 | 22 | 24 | VE`

W 50s | 7 W. 57th St. (bet. 5th & 6th Aves.) | N/R/W to 5th Ave./ 59th St. | 212-759-3333 | 800-486-9966 | www.ascotchang.com

"You surely pay a premium" at this "premier shirt shop", but most Midtown men say "the money's worth it" to get a garment "as you like it", custom-made Shanghainese-style from the "finest fabrics" and with "superior craftsmanship"; there's also a "conservative collection" of ready-made button-downs and accessories including, yes, ascots; a move to 110 Central Park South is scheduled for summer 2007.

AsiaStore at Asia Society and Museum
`24 | 22 | 20 | E`

E 70s | Asia Society and Museum | 725 Park Ave. (70th St.) | 6 to 68th St. | 212-327-9217 | www.asiastore.org

This recently renovated Park Avenue museum offers a "fantastic selection" of "upscale" "Pan-Asian goods" including "beautiful ceramics", "wonderful jewelry" and "lovely textiles" for the "discerning eye" along with "impressive books"; even though some whisper the wares are "overpriced", most agree it's a "unique" resource for "unusual gifts."

⚂ Asprey 🛇
`28 | - | 25 | VE`

E 70s | 853 Madison Ave. (bet. 70th & 71st Sts.) | 6 to 68th St. | 212-688-1811 | 800-883-2777 | www.asprey.com

"Oh, to be in England" – but if you're not, this "very British" 225-year-old retailer, whose NY flagship is scheduled to relocate to this Madison Avenue address in spring, makes a most "stylish" substitute; it's "a delight to stroll through", perusing "everything from flawless diamonds" ("copies of the Queen's baubles") to the "mother lode of silver accessories", "scarves that last for decades", "well-designed" mens- and womenswear, "exquisite" leather goods and rare books; though a bit "pretentious", the "service matches the quality" of the merch – just be sure to "go loaded"; N.B. as we go to press, its temporary quarters are at 50 East 57th Street.

Atelier New York
`- | - | - | VE`

SoHo | 125 Crosby St. (bet. Houston & Prince Sts.) | N/R/W to Prince St. | 212-941-8435 | www.ateliernewyork.com

"Rare finds for men" make this dark shop, adorned in black (leather) and white (marble) a favorite of the fashion-forward set with a penchant for European apparel à la Ann Demeulemeester or Raf Simons; its "great buyers" stock up on "pieces that can't be found elsewhere", even among the swarms of other SoHo specialty boutiques.

	QUALITY	DISPLAY	SERVICE	COST

A. Testoni
	27	–	23	VE

E 50s | Sherry-Netherland Hotel | 781 Fifth Ave. (bet. 59th & 60th Sts.) | N/R/W to 5th Ave./59th St. | 212-223-0909 | www.testoni.com

"Give your feet the shoes they deserve" urge devotees of this family-owned Italian leather-goods luxury purveyor, newly relocated to the Sherry-Netherland, that radiates a certain "panache"; the "incredibly beautiful high-quality" footwear for men and women with "somewhat conservative taste" comes at such "incredibly high prices" even admirers may find themselves gasping for air, but they're "so comfortable" you almost "don't mind" shelling out the big bucks.

Athlete's Foot, The
	20	16	15	M

Bronx | 2467 Grand Concourse (E. 188th St.) | B/D to 182nd/183rd Sts. | 718-733-1427 ◐

Bronx | 2918 Third Ave. (Westchester Ave.) | 2/5 to 3rd Ave./149th St. | 718-292-3390 ◐

Bronx | 300 E. Fordham Rd. (E. Kingsbridge Rd.) | 4 to Fordham Rd. | 718-367-2502 ◐

East NY | 1053-1055 Liberty Ave. (bet. Crescent & Hemlock Sts.) | Brooklyn | A to Grant Ave. | 718-235-3401

Flushing | 136-92 Roosevelt Ave. (Main St.) | Queens | 7 to Main St. | 718-762-6684 ◐

Jamaica | 163-11 Jamaica Ave. (163rd St.) | Queens | E/J/Z to Jamaica Ctr. Parsons/Archer | 718-883-9300 ◐

888-801-9157 | www.theathletesfoot.com

"The dizzying variety" of "all the latest sneakers" at these chain links "is almost too much" assert sports buffs, "until you speak to a salesperson, who can narrow down the selection, based on your feet's shape, and your personal needs"; but critics caution that the "personnel is not fully knowledgeable" and snipe that the stores are "unattractive", making it a low-on-the-rung "choice for New Yorkers."

Atrium ◐
	25	20	15	E

NoHo | 644 Broadway (Bleecker St.) | 6 to Bleecker St. | 212-473-9200 | www.atriumnyc.com

"Definitely one of the premier" "destinations" for "jeans fanatics", this "clubby", "quintessential" his-and-hers NoHo "hot spot" staffed with "attractive" help offers an "unrivaled selection" of "premium denim" from the "most hyped brands" to the "more underground" labels; while a few huff it's "organized by some mysterious system" and "madly expensive" to boot, most find the "amazing" assortment elevating – "if I could pick one" stop "for my entire wardrobe, this would be it!"

A Uno
	▽ 24	22	24	E

TriBeCa | 123 W. Broadway (Duane St.) | 1/2/3 to Chambers St. | 212-227-6233

A Uno Walk
NEW **TriBeCa** | 119 W. Broadway (bet. Duane & Reade Sts.) | 1/2/3 to Chambers St. | 212-343-2040

Svelte, "trim women" and those with "full figures" saunter down to this "wonderful" TriBeCa duo to peruse the "terrific" well-"curated collection" of "avant-garde" puffy coats, unconstructed jackets, cropped pants and sleek knitwear from labels like Annette Gortz, Marithe + Francois Girbaud, Pierantonio Gaspari and ReSet; the "competent salespeople" help novices navigate the "edgier brands" so customers always take home "pieces to keep forever"; N.B. A Uno Walk is stocked with shoes from hard-to-find labels like Trippen.

auto ◐

| | – | – | – | M |

Meatpacking | 805 Washington St. (bet. Gansevoort & Horatio Sts.) | A/C/E/L to 14th St./8th Ave. | 212-229-2292 | 866-568-2886 | www.thisisauto.com

Husband-and-wife owners Renata Bokalo and Roman Luba apply an artful eye to this minimalist Meatpacking District space stocked with home furnishings ranging from boldly colored bedding to bath towels and pillows from Etro and Missoni, as well as children's accessories like booties and hats; N.B. they've also expanded into the space next door to house their women's and men's jewelry and accessories.

Aveda Environmental Lifestyle Store

| | 26 | 24 | 24 | M |

E 40s | Grand Central, Park Ave. tunnel | 42nd St. (Vanderbilt Ave.) | 4/5/6/7/S to 42nd St./Grand Central | 212-682-5397 ◐
E 50s | 509 Madison Ave. (bet. 52nd & 53rd Sts.) | E/V to 5th Ave./53rd St. | 212-832-2416
E 60s | 1122 Third Ave. (bet. 65th & 66th Sts.) | 6 to 68th St. | 212-744-3113 ◐
Flatiron | 140 Fifth Ave. (19th St.) | 4/5/6/L/N/Q/R/W to 14th St./Union Sq. | 212-645-4797 ◐
SoHo | 233 Spring St. (bet. 6th Ave. & Varick St.) | C/E to Spring St. | 212-807-1492 ◐
SoHo | 456 W. Broadway (bet. Houston & Prince Sts.) | N/R/W to Prince St. | 212-473-0280 ◐
W 50s | The Shops at Columbus Circle, Time Warner Ctr. | 10 Columbus Circle, 3rd fl. (bet. 58th & 60th Sts.) | 1/A/B/C/D to 59th St./Columbus Circle | 212-823-9714 ◐
800-644-4831 | www.aveda.com

"Come for the products, stay for the tea" at this "eco-friendly", "moderately priced" beauty chain famed for "quality" products made from organic plants and flowers, "particularly the best shampoos and conditioners around" like the Sap Moss line "for taming frizzy locks" that's a Hollywood cult favorite; a "well-informed" staff presides over "soothing" settings that are "an instant escape from the stress" outside.

◪ Avventura

| | 26 | 20 | 18 | E |

W 80s | 463 Amsterdam Ave. (bet. 82nd & 83rd Sts.) | B/C to 81st St. | 212-769-2510 | 888-640-9177 | www.forthatspecialgift.com

It's clear that this Upper West Side purveyor of "unusual and distinctive" art glass and ceramics with an emphasis on "well-selected" Italian pieces from Murano and Deruta is a "perfect place" to find a "beautiful wedding gift"; the staff is "knowledgeable and nice", and while some say this "little gem" is "expensive", others reflect that "prices are high, but so is the quality"; N.B. closed Saturdays.

A.W. Kaufman

| | ▽ 26 | 9 | 21 | M |

LES | 73 Orchard St. (bet. Broome & Grand Sts.) | F/J/M/Z to Delancey/Essex Sts. | 212-226-1629 | www.awkaufman.com

"First impressions shouldn't scare you away from" this "too crowded", third-generation–run Lower East Sider that "may look like a rat's nest" but carries a "wide selection" of "top-of-the-line" European lingerie, undergarments, hosiery and "soft like buttah nightgowns" from "great names" like Chantelle, Hanro and La Perla "at discount prices"; the "schlep" Downtown is "worth the effort" – but only if you "don't mind changing without a formal dressing room."

A/X Armani Exchange ⊘

19 | 19 | 16 | E

E 50s | 645 Fifth Ave. (51st St.) | E/V to 5th Ave./53rd St. | 212-980-3037
Flatiron | 129 Fifth Ave. (bet. 19th & 20th Sts.) | N/R/W to 23rd St. | 212-254-7230
SoHo | 568 Broadway (Prince St.) | N/R/W to Prince St. | 212-431-6000
W 50s | The Shops at Columbus Circle, Time Warner Ctr. | 10 Columbus Circle, 3rd fl. (bet. 58th & 60th Sts.) | 1/A/B/C/D to 59th St./Columbus Circle | 212-823-9321
NEW Elmhurst | Queens Ctr. | 90-15 Queens Blvd. (bet. 57th & 59th Aves.) | Queens | G/R/V to Grand Ave./Newtown | 718-271-4879
www.armaniexchange.com

For "a fun taste of the great Giorgio", hit "Armani's cheaper little cousin" carrying an "urban-hip" men's and women's apparel line that's an "edgier", "more wearable" version of Emporio designed for those with "expensive tastes but not-so-big wallets"; perennial sales keep the "budget-conscious" coming back for "cool, casual" shirts, skirts, tees and such, but snobs suggest "X this out of your Rolodex" because "what used to be a fabulous alternative" has "gone down-market."

Azaleas ⊘ Ⓜ

– | – | – | M

E Vill | 223 E. 10th St. (bet. 1st & 2nd Aves.) | 6 to Astor Pl. | 212-253-5484 | www.azaleasnyc.com

"Cute, sassy" unmentionables share space with lingerie-inspired separates, loungewear, swimsuits and shoes at this "great" East Village "neighborhood joint" featuring lots of "darling" designs like Deborah Marquit's glow-in-the-dark undies, Wendy Glez's lace camis and hipster bikinis from Vix; add in plenty of fun accessories and it's easy to see why brevity-boosters yell "yes!" to this one.

B8 ⊘

– | – | – | E

Meatpacking | 27 Little W. 12th St. (bet. 9th Ave. & Washington St.) | A/C/E/L to 14th St./8th Ave. | 212-924-8700

Dark, purple-trimmed walls and sparkling chandeliers enchant customers at this "undiscovered treasure" with a "cool downtown vibe" in the Meatpacking District, where banker-turned–boutique owner Karine Bellil – who comes from a family of eight (hence the name) – amasses menswear that ranges from custom-made shirts and suits to jeans and organic cotton tees; she stocks only one item per size, so it's unlikely you'll see yourself coming and going.

Z Babeland ⊘

27 | 26 | 28 | M

LES | 94 Rivington St. (bet. Ludlow & Orchard Sts.) | F/J/M/Z to Delancey/Essex Sts. | 212-375-1701
SoHo | 43 Mercer St. (bet. Broome & Grand Sts.) | 6/J/M/N/Q/R/W/Z to Canal St. | 212-966-2120
800-658-9119 | www.babeland.com

"All questions and perversions are welcome" at New York's "best" sex stores, a "delicious yet informative" woman-owned duo in SoHo and on the Lower East Side, where "witty" signage, "beautiful displays", "regular classes" and an "up-front" but "non-intimidating" staff (actually voted No. 1 for Service in this *Survey*) make browsing a "wide variety" of "quality" "erotica" a "stylish", "classy" experience; forget the "dirty-old-man-in-a-raincoat" shtick – you'll "never feel sketchy" in these shops that "take the smut out of intimate personal care."

Babies "R" Us ⦿

| | 19 | 18 | 15 | M |

NEW **Union Sq** | 24-30 Union Sq. E. (15th St.) | 4/5/6/L/N/Q/R/W to 14th St./Union Sq. | 212-798-9905
NEW **Bensonhurst** | 8973-95 Bay Pkwy. (W. 10th St.) | Brooklyn | D/M to Bay Pkwy. | 718-714-6400
Starrett City | Gateway Ctr. | 395 Gateway Dr. (bet. Erskine St. & Vandalia Ave.) | Brooklyn | A/C to Euclid Ave. | 718-277-3400
College Pt | 139-19 20th Ave. (Whitestone Expwy.) | Queens | 718-321-8166
888-222-9787 | www.babiesrus.com

This "all-under-one-roof" superstore chain is bursting with "everything for baby", including clothing for tots, furniture, toys, gear, diapers and other supplies at "moderate prices"; given its "warehouselike" proportions and "hard-to-find salespeople", though, it "can be a bit overwhelming for first-time parents" and registry customers, so the uninitiated should "shop with someone who knows what to look for."

Baby Bird

| | 25 | 24 | 23 | E |

Park Slope | 428 Seventh Ave. (bet. 14th & 15th Sts.) | Brooklyn | F to 7th Ave. | 718-788-4506 | www.shopbird.com

Moms and "baby shower" attendees scouting for tweet tyke-wear that's "not your run-of-the-mill" variety flock to this "excellent" pint-sized Park Sloper, within wingspan of its mother store, Bird; expect "lovely personal service" and "gorgeous" playwear bound to make your little chickadee "look devastatingly" "adorable"; still, it takes more than birdfeed to attain "something different and very cute", prompting aspirants to chirp "if only I could win the lottery."

BabyGap ⦿

| | 22 | 20 | 17 | M |

Garment Dist | 60 W. 34th St. (B'way) | B/D/F/N/Q/R/V/W to 34th St./Herald Sq. | 212-760-1268 | 800-427-7895 | www.gap.com
Additional locations throughout the NY area

"You can't go wrong" at this "shower or birthday gift" "mecca" for "adorable" "baby basics" that "wear well" and "don't break the bank"; "easy-to-browse" store setups mean it's a snap "to find something for each age" group, and bargain-hunters note there are "especially good deals" to be found on its ever-present "clearance racks", so never mind if service is "spotty" in some locations.

Babylicious

| | – | – | – | E |

TriBeCa | 51 Hudson St. (bet. Duane & Jay Sts.) | 1/2/3 to Chambers St. | 212-406-7440 | www.babyliciousnyc.com

This "cute, little place" in TriBeCa carries just about everything a modern parent needs for bringing up baby in style from birth to size six, including a hefty helping of tees and onesies; gift-givers also appreciate the extensive selection of unique toys, books, bibs, blankets and other tiny trinkets.

⦿ Baccarat ⊠

| | 29 | 27 | 26 | VE |

E 50s | 625 Madison Ave. (59th St.) | N/R/W to 5th Ave./59th St. | 212-826-4100 | 866-886-8003 | www.baccarat.com

For "the crystal of kings", connoisseurs head to this "elegant" East Side French "classic" whose "exquisite" and "exceptional" stemware, decanters, vases, candlesticks, chandeliers and jewelry set "the gold standard"; their pieces are "perfect for a wedding gift or corporate memento", but since prices are shattering you'll "need a large inheritance to buy anything."

Bag House, The
23 17 18 M

G Vill | 797 Broadway (bet. 10th & 11th Sts.) | N/R/W to 8th St. | 212-260-0940 | www.thebaghouse.com

Get your fill of "every bag you can think of and more" at the Village's "king of canvas" (and leather too) that's staffed with "cool, friendly" salespeople; choose from a "wide selection" of "utilitarian" backpacks, duffels, messenger bags and luggage from "well-known brand names" like Kipling, LeSportsac and Manhattan Portage; still, a smattering say the selection holds more appeal if you're "not too into fashion."

Baker Tribeca
▽ 28 29 25 VE

TriBeCa | 129-133 Hudson St. (Beach St.) | 1 to Franklin St. | 212-343-2956 | 800-592-2537 | www.bakerfurniture.com

"A lovely store with gorgeous furniture", this 12,000-sq.-ft. TriBeCa duplex houses the more-than-100-year-old namesake Midwest manufacturer's collections, which range from traditional to the highly touted contemporary designs of Bill Sofield and Barbara Barry; many of the "quality" chairs, chests, sofas, tables and beds shine with old-world details such as hand-colored wood and gold-leaf, which are not tarnished by the high prices.

☒ Balenciaga
29 26 21 VE

Chelsea | 542 W. 22nd St. (bet. 10th & 11th Aves.) | C/E to 23rd St. | 212-206-0872 | www.balenciaga.com

It's a "cool" if slightly "strange garagelike" space in Chelsea that showcases the creations of Nicolas Ghesquière and reflects the tough-chic aesthetic he's applied to this venerable French fashion house; enthusiasts call the clothes "innovative and intellectual", but the real draw are the accessories – "ever heard of the motorcycle bag" sported by stars such as Uma Thurman and the Olsen twins? – that cause converts to "take the plunge for an incomparably designed" item that's "expensive but timeless (we hope!)."

Bally
28 - 24 E

E 50s | 628 Madison Ave. (59th St.) | N/R/W to 5th Ave./59th St. | 212-751-9082 | www.bally.com

"Low-key consumers of high-end goods" fall for the "discreetly stylish and comfortable luxury footwear", what may be some of the "world's finest crocodile and alligator accessories", "beautiful, classy" bags and even clothing at this his-and-hers "Swiss-made classic", now newly relocated back in their revamped orignal 59th Street digs; its "very conservative" image is bally-anced out with "some mod urban pieces intermixed" and an on-the-ball staff that's "efficient but not pushy."

Bambini
27 18 20 VE

E 80s | 1088 Madison Ave. (82nd St.) | 4/5/6 to 86th St. | 212-717-6742

The "classic", "beautiful" children's finery at this Madison Avenue establishment "sure beats what my parents dressed me in" agree admirers; the tony togs from Italian labels like Magil and pappa & ciccia reveal such "attention to detail" and are so darn "cute" they may even "make your baby say *ciao bella*"; still, the lire-lacking lament that the "out-of-this-world prices" are for "tiny billionaires only."

☑ Banana Republic ●

20	21	18	M

E 50s | 626 Fifth Ave. (50th St.) | E/V to 5th Ave./53rd St. | 212-974-2350 | 888-277-8953 | www.bananarepublic.com
Additional locations throughout the NY area

Touted as "top Banana" by legions who consider it a "sure thing" for "basic business" staples with "easy classic styling", plus "cute accessories", this "ubiquitous" chain provides "lots of bang for the buck"; "easy-to-find-everything" store layouts and "usually helpful" service also contribute to its "standby" status, though even admirers concede "you'll see everyone else wearing" "the same clothes as you."

Banana Republic Men's ●

21	21	18	M

Flatiron | 114 Fifth Ave. (17th St.) | 4/5/6/L/N/Q/R/W to 14th St./ Union Sq. | 212-366-4691
SoHo | 528 Broadway (Spring St.) | 6 to Spring St. | 212-334-3034
888-277-8953 | www.bananarepublic.com

A "safe place for men to buy clothing", these Flatiron-SoHo chain links allow guys to "stock up on work clothes" in styles ranging from "preppy staples" to "cookie-cutter metrosexual" office wear; trendsetters may yawn "boring", but for "clean-cut" types, the "well-made", "well-priced" "moderately cool" apparel and shoes are "a solid buy", especially during the "frequent sales", when staffers "keep the discount racks stuffed."

☑ B&B Italia 🅂

27	27	20	VE

E 50s | 150 E. 58th St. (bet. Lexington & 3rd Aves.) | 4/5/6/F/N/R/W to 59th St./Lexington Ave. | 212-758-4046
NEW **SoHo** | 137 Greene St. (bet Houston & Prince Sts.) | N/R/W to Prince St. | 212-966-3514 🅜
800-872-1697 | www.bebitalia.it

"High-style Italian furniture" is the focus of this "very expensive", "classic modern" East 50s showroom (and its new SoHo offshoot), which both feature "fabulous" designs, like the Charles sofa, in "great colors and forms", plus beds, armchairs and tables; but those who dwell in diminutive digs warn that most pieces are "scaled for an airport lobby."

☑ B&H Photo-Video-Pro Audio

27	20	21	M

Garment Dist | 420 Ninth Ave. (bet. 33rd & 34th Sts.) | 1/2/3/A/C/E to 34th St./Penn Station | 212-444-6600 | 800-947-9950 | www.bhphotovideo.com
The "Disneyland of cameras", this "block-long" Garment District "oasis" boasts an "enormous", "fairly priced" selection managed with an inventive "tracking system" of "overhead bins" and overseen by an "educated sales force" that "turns the retail experience into an assembly line" (in a "great" way); still, some say the "staff is not always the friendliest", while others claim the "busy-as-Grand-Central-at-rush-hour" setting makes them "feel like rats in a maze"; N.B. a scheduled 2007 expansion may help cure the claustrophobia.

☑ B&J Fabrics 🅂

26	18	21	M

Garment Dist | 525 Seventh Ave., 2nd fl. (38th St.) | 1/2/3/7/N/Q/ R/S/W to 42nd St./Times Sq. | 212-354-8150 | 866-354-8150 | www.bandjfabrics.com
"Well-organized" (with samples "on hangers so you can easily go through the racks") and "perfectly lit", this huge Garment District

"mother of all fabric shops" offers a "stunning collection" of "upscale dress and theatrical" material ("interesting chiffons and sheers", "Liberty-print cottons"); the "helpful" "army of staffers" "really knows the trade", so it's "one of the best" options "for choice and service."

☒ Bang & Olufsen
28 | 27 | 23 | VE

E 70s | 952 Madison Ave. (75th St.) | 6 to 77th St. | 212-879-6161
Flatiron | 927 Broadway (bet. 21st & 22nd Sts.) | N/R/W to 23rd St. | 212-388-9792
W 70s | 330 Columbus Ave. (bet. 75th & 76th Sts.) | 1 to 79th St. | 212-501-0926
www.bang-olufsen.com

Strictly "for the serious audio aficionado" who dreams of "stylishly sleek" "fantasy electronic toys" that are beyond "cutting-edge", this over-80-year-old "Danish firm has some of the most sophisticated" and "sinfully beautiful" audio-visual components around (the "clean look of the equipment" makes it "as fascinating 'off'" as when it's on); yes, the "prices are sky-high", but "wealthy" sorts insist the "personalized service" and "amazing" quality make it "worth every penny."

Barami ●
16 | 16 | 16 | M

E 40s | 375 Lexington Ave. (41st St.) | 4/5/6/7/S to 42nd St./Grand Central | 212-682-2550
E 40s | 535 Fifth Ave. (45th St.) | 4/5/6/7/S to 42nd St./Grand Central | 212-949-1000
E 50s | 136 E. 57th St. (Lexington Ave.) | 4/5/6/F/N/R/W to 59th St./Lexington Ave. | 212-980-9333
Garment Dist | 485 Seventh Ave. (36th St.) | 1/2/3/A/C/E to 34th St./Penn Station | 212-967-2990
www.barami.com

"Working babes" believe this brand is "worth checking out" because it "understands" that women want "sexy, but tasteful" clothes that "fit well and last", especially for petites; the "nice selection" includes "business-meeting" – "appropriate, but sassy" suits and "affordable dressy clothes"; P.S. if the staff gets "pushy", just "tell them to back off."

Barbara Bui
27 | 26 | 21 | VE

SoHo | 115-117 Wooster St. (bet. Prince & Spring Sts.) | N/R/W to Prince St. | 212-625-1938 | www.barbarabui.fr

"Creative", "clever and a tad different" describes the style of this French-Vietnamese designer, whose gallerylike SoHo shop is as Zen-elegant as the "tall and sleek" followers who flock here for precisely cut pants, soigné suits, hip-high boots and heavenly handbags; "prices are a little high", *bien sûr*, but strapped-yet-smitten shoppers can always take home a bit of Bui in a perfume bottle.

Barbara Feinman Millinery ●
23 | 21 | 23 | E

E Vill | 66 E. Seventh St. (bet. 1st & 2nd Aves.) | 6 to Astor Pl. | 212-358-7092 | www.feinmanhats.com

Go for "stylish, edgy hats", "come out with jewelry" and "one-of-a-kind handbags" – "you never know what you'll find at this lovely little" East Villager done up with a chandelier and a "fun" retro flair; Fein-fans confide that the toppers are sometimes "eccentric but still very wearable", and what's more, they can be customized with "personal fittings", which exemplifies just one aspect of the "great service."

| | QUALITY | DISPLAY | SERVICE | COST |

Barbara Shaum ⧈Ⓜ

| | – | – | – | E |

E Vill | 60 E. Fourth St. (bet. Bowery & 2nd Ave.) | 6 to Astor Pl. |
212-254-4250

If you're finicky about your sandals, don't sidestep this East Villager,
as it would be a shame to eschew Shaum's handcrafted numbers,
many of which are custom-made to fit your tootsies to a tee; adding a
personal touch to the experience, this cool, modern-day Geppetto
cobbles her funky footwear in an on-site workshop, so take a peek, and
while you're at it, pick up belts, bags and buckles too.

⧈ Barbour by Peter Elliot

| | 28 | 24 | 23 | E |

E 80s | 1047 Madison Ave. (80th St.) | 6 to 77th St. | 212-570-2600 |
www.barbour.com

Decked out like a hunting lodge – "all that's missing is the bird dog and
the shotgun" – this "veddy" "preppy" upper Madison Avenue shop caters to "country gentlemen" and women who want to "nurse their na-
scent Anglophilia" with this impeccably made (since 1894) Brit brand of
quilted jackets, tattersall scarves and the trademark waxed duffle coats;
"there's nothing like" the "expensive but durable" microfiber macs
concur acolytes – they're "all you can dream of" for "a drizzly weekend."

Bardith ⧈⇄

| | – | – | – | VE |

E 70s | 31 E. 72nd St. (Madison Ave.) | 6 to 68th St. | 212-737-8660
E 70s | 901 Madison Ave. (bet. 72nd & 73rd Sts.) | 6 to 68th St. |
212-737-3775
www.bardith.com

For over 30 years the "knowledgeable staff" at this pricey Madison
Avenue duo has been providing "fine pieces" of antique 18th-century
and early-19th-century English and European porcelain and pottery,
along with papier-mâché trays and period glassware, causing window-
shoppers to proclaim "when I win the lottery, this will be one of my
first buying stops."

Bare Escentuals ●

| | 25 | 23 | 22 | M |

E 60s | 1140 Third Ave. (bet. 66th & 67th Sts.) | 6 to 68th St. |
646-537-0070
NEW **Elmhurst** | Queens Ctr. | 90-15 Queens Blvd. (bet. 57th & 59th Aves.) |
Queens | G/R/V to Grand Ave./Newtown | 718-371-3724
800-227-3990 | www.bareescentuals.com

Its "like silk on my face" say supporters of the "excellent" makeup
found at these East 60s and Elmhurst offshoots of the long-standing
San Francisco–based chain; the focus is on their bareMinerals line featuring "natural-looking", preservative-free powder-based founda-
tions, shadows and shimmers; "decent prices" and a "helpful staff"
add to its appeal.

Barking Zoo ●

| | 25 | 19 | 25 | M |

Chelsea | 172 Ninth Ave. (bet. 20th & 21st Sts.) | C/E to 23rd St. |
212-255-0658 | www.thebarkingzoo.com

With the "best service" from a staff "as nice as your dog", it's no wonder this "warm and cuddly" pet store is a "Chelsea institution" where
even your pooch is "ensured a fun shopping experience"; a "great selection" of specialty foods catering to "individual needs", unusual
"duds" for fashion-forward canines and "quality" supplies make it
"worth every penny."

	QUALITY	DISPLAY	SERVICE	COST

Barneys CO-OP
24 21 17 E

Chelsea | 236 W. 18th St. (bet. 7th & 8th Aves.) | 1 to 18th St. |
212-716-8816 ❂
SoHo | 116 Wooster St. (bet. Prince & Spring Sts.) | N/R/W to Prince St. |
212-965-9964
W 70s | 2151 Broadway (75th St.) | 1/2/3 to 72nd St. | 646-335-0978 ❂
www.barneys.com

"Funky, fresh and for flat-bellied guys and gals" sums up the scene at
this trio, "the less intimidating" "side of Barneys", which offers relatively
"more affordable options" "for stylishly edgy fashion hawks" including
"by far the best denim selection in NYC", "hard-to-find" casual lines,
"the latest in accessories" and a "metrosexual paradise" of skincare;
those "over 30 with hips" opine it's "overpriced", and many slam a
"staff that's too hip to help the likes of you", but still, it's a treasure trove
for "trust-fund babies" "who want to look like downtown" types; N.B. the
Madison Avenue mother ship also boasts several CO-OP floors.

☒ Barneys New York ❂
27 26 20 VE

E 60s | 660 Madison Ave. (61st St.) | N/R/W to 5th Ave./59th St. |
212-826-8900 | 888-822-7639 | www.barneys.com

Walking into this elite East 60s emporium is like "entering a cocktail
party – full of excitement and the possibility of naughty encounters"
amid the "desirable goods and beautiful displays"; fashionistas confirm
it's like a "microcosm of the NY dream lifestyle", with "the edgiest looks
from the best-known designers", "new" "pampering" cosmetics and
"luxurious" accessories galore; some genuflect at the "slice of heaven"
shoe floor, others kneel for the home furnishings department, and once
"you convince the help that you're worthy, service can be quite good";
P.S. thanks to Simon Doonan, "the windows are beyond wonderful."

Bath & Body Works ❂
19 21 20 I

Staten Island | Staten Island Mall | 2655 Richmond Ave. (bet. Platinum Ave. &
Richmond Hill Rd.) | 718-982-8546 | www.bathandbodyworks.com
Additional locations throughout the NY area

Fans of this "bright", "fruity and fun" toiletries chain that's known for
"a big variety of scents and body washes" that's "inexpensive" and
"makes you feel like a kid again" are also pleased at the company's image upgrade, which includes a treatment line from Manhattan celeb
dermatologist Dr. Patricia Wexler and the "brilliant addition of
Bigelow and Bendel products"; still, cynics sniff the stores' "sickly
sweet smell" "overwhelms your olfactory senses"' and their cookie-
cutter shelves make them "feel like a mall."

Bathing Ape, A
(aka Bape NY)
▽ 21 22 15 E

SoHo | 91 Greene St. (bet. Prince & Spring Sts.) | N/R/W to Prince St. |
212-925-0222 | www.bape.com

This bright bi-level store in SoHo is as "cool as promised" profess both
first-timers and bona fide sneakerheads; Japanese musician/
designer/retailer Nigo's "limited-edition" T-shirts, streetwear, accessories and shiny conveyor belt of "hip, hip, hip" kicks attract men,
women and kids who find the Wonderwall-designed interior, colorful
merchandise and sometimes "silent staff" "intimidating and hilarious
at the same time."

| | QUALITY | DISPLAY | SERVICE | COST |

☒ Bathroom, The ◐
27 28 22 E

W Vill | 94 Charles St. (bet. Bleecker & W. 4th Sts.) | 1 to Christopher St./
Sheridan Sq. | 212-929-1449 | 800-856-9223 | www.inthebathroom.com

"Eye-catching" and "original" West Village bath-and-body boutique
that's swimming in a sea of "the best brands" of "hard-to-find" "old-
school and new-world" "upscale" beauty products; "everything is
chicly presented" – from Lollia perfume, Olivina Napa Valley scrub
and Gianna Rose seashell soaps to a cache of candles ranging from
Rigaud to Seda France – and "the owner is a charmer."

NEW Bblessing ◐⇥
▽ 21 18 18 E

LES | 181 Orchard St. (Stanton St.) | F/V to Lower East Side/2nd Ave. |
212-378-8005 | www.bblessing.com

"Young, hip men" say it's "surely a blessing to find" this Lower East
Side boutique, with "cutting-edge fashion, art" and tunes from former
music store occupant Breakbeat Science housed within its oxblood
walls; fans applaud the tightly edited, "good-value-for-what-you get"
collection of Preen cashmere, denim from Surface to Air, Giacometti
and Iliad and soft, cool tees, and dig the tongue-in-cheek sensibility –
the upside-down objects suspended from the ceiling, the Parisian bar
and a "secret back door" leading to a DJ-worthy stash of vintage vinyl.

BCBG Max Azria
22 21 19 E

E 60s | 770 Madison Ave. (66th St.) | 6 to 68th St. | 212-717-4225
NEW Flatiron | 168 Fifth Ave. (22nd St.) | N/R/W to 23rd St. |
212-989-7307 ◐
SoHo | 120 Wooster St. (bet. Prince & Spring Sts.) | N/R/W to Prince St. |
212-625-2723
NEW W 60s | 2003-2005 Broadway (bet. 68th & 69th Sts.) | 1 to
66th St./Lincoln Ctr. | 212-496-1853 ◐
NEW Staten Island | Staten Island Mall | 2655 Richmond Ave. (bet.
Platinum Ave. & Richmond Hill Rd.) | 718-983-5938 ◐
www.bcbg.com

BCBG may be French slang for preppy, but the "conservative-with-an-
edge" womenswear strikes a more seductive pose at this expanding
chain where the staff usually "helps you buy the right thing"; while a
"favorite" with "young-adult daughters", "most bodies are flattered"
by the "colorful selection" of "party wear and office attire" ("although
some suits are pretty risqué") and "ageless accessories" displayed in
"high-energy presentations."

BDDW ▨
- - - VE

SoHo | 5 Crosby St. (bet. Grand & Howard Sts.) | 6/J/M/N/Q/R/W/Z to
Canal St. | 212-625-1230 | www.bddw.com

Under the arches of a high cathedral ceiling, this SoHo furniture showroom exhibits heirloom-quality beds, tables, chairs and floor lamps
handcrafted out of American hardwood that proponents pine for;
while the line is "not for the faint of wallet", enthusiasts assure that
"what you can afford you will treasure."

Beacon Paint & Hardware
22 15 23 M

W 70s | 371 Amsterdam Ave. (bet. 77th & 78th Sts.) | 1 to 79th St. |
212-787-1090 | www.beaconpaint.com

The Stark family has helped Upper West Siders cover their walls for
over a quarter-century, offering a full line of Benjamin Moore paints

that can be custom color-matched from other brands, plus "reliable advice" to get novice DIYers started; it's a "cramped" beacon of convenience for "one-stop-shoppers" who stock up on everything from air conditioners to plumbing supplies, especially for early birds, who land at 7:30 AM for the weekday openings.

Beacon's Closet ●   19 | 15 | 13 | I

Park Slope | 220 Fifth Ave. (bet. President & Union Sts.) | Brooklyn | M/R to Union St. | 718-230-1630
Williamsburg | 88 N. 11th St. (bet. Berry St. & Wythe Ave.) | Brooklyn | L to Bedford Ave. | 718-486-0816
www.beaconscloset.com

"Bringing the best of the Midwest vibe to Williamsburg (the much larger of the two) and Park Slope ("more mainstream"), these "hipster havens" offer "thrift shoppers" everything from "wacky party dresses to serious business suits"; while purists cavil the pieces "aren't actually vintage, just secondhand", most enjoy "fishing" through "rack upon rack" of "eye-poppers" for "dirt-cheap prices"; P.S. they buy used threads too, so you can "make and save a buck" at the same time.

Beads of Paradise ●   22 | 19 | 21 | M

Flatiron | 16 E. 17th St. (bet. B'way & 5th Ave.) | 4/5/6/L/N/Q/R/W to 14th St./Union Sq. | 212-620-0642

"When you need a bead", heed the "awesome back room" of this "eclectic" Flatiron District "find" that beckons with "an overwhelming selection" that includes the largest collection of semiprecious stones in the city, as well as African and Asian artifacts hanging overhead; custom-made jewelry, plus re-stringing and repair services, are also part of the mix.

Beasty Feast ●   24 | 20 | 25 | M

W Vill | 630 Hudson St. (bet. Horatio & Jane Sts.) | A/C/E/L to 14th St./8th Ave. | 212-620-7099
W Vill | 680 Washington St. (bet. Charles & W. 10th Sts.) | A/B/C/D/E/F/V to W. 4th St. | 212-620-4055
www.beastyfeast.com

The "knowledgeable", "animal-loving" staff "never looks bored when proud 'pet parents' stop by to chat" at these two longtime West Village "favorites"; along with the "greatest selection" of chow and "all types of supplies", they offer grooming services and are affiliated with an adoption organization, Renaissance Project.

Beau Brummel   22 | 22 | 19 | VE

SoHo | 347 W. Broadway (bet. Broome & Grand Sts.) | C/E to Spring St. | 212-219-2666
W 70s | 287 Columbus Ave. (bet. 73rd & 74th Sts.) | 1/2/3 to 72nd St. | 212-877-3689 ●

Named after the Regency dandy who popularized trousers over knee breeches in the early 1800s, these SoHo and Upper West Side men's stores offer "cutting-edge", "stylish European clothing", from ties to separates to suits with an "anti–Brooks Brothers" appeal; however, some find both prices and staff "a little too uppity."

Bebe ●   17 | 19 | 16 | M

E 50s | 805 Third Ave. (50th St.) | E/V to 5th Ave./53rd St. | 212-588-9060
E 60s | 1127 Third Ave. (66th St.) | 6 to 68th St. | 212-935-2444

(continued)

Bebe

Flatiron | 100 Fifth Ave. (15th St.) | 4/5/6/L/N/Q/R/W to 14th St./Union Sq. | 212-675-2323

NEW **W 50s** | The Shops at Columbus Circle, Time Warner Ctr. | 10 Columbus Circle, ground fl. (bet. 58th & 60th Sts.) | 1/A/B/C/D to 59th St./Columbus Circle | 212-262-2690

NEW **Elmhurst** | Queens Ctr. | 90-15 Queens Blvd. (bet. 57th & 59th Aves.) | Queens | G/R/V to Grand Ave./Newtown | 718-271-2323

Staten Island | Staten Island Mall | 2655 Richmond Ave. (bet. Platinum Ave. & Richmond Hill Rd.) | 718-697-0070

877-232-3777 | www.bebe.com

"If you want the 'in' look", this "young, fun" women's clothing chain "is the place" according to the "skinny minis" and "Pamela Anderson types" who sport its "dressed-up essentials" and racy "club wear"; down-to-earth detractors call the cut-"waaay-too-tight" threads "impractical" and complain that service "can be snooty", but even they concede when you want to "feel like a babe", this outfit's "bling and bedazzle" is hard to beat.

Beckenstein Fabrics & Interiors

`- | - | - | M`

Flatiron | 4 W. 20th St. (bet. 5th & 6th Aves.) | F/V to 23rd St. | 212-366-5142 | 800-348-1327 | www.beckensteinfabrics.com

Founded in 1918, this Flatiron dry-goods dealer specializes in custom draperies and reupholstered furniture (especially headboards), much of it constructed from scratch; the "selection is fab" and there's "a lot to look at" (remnants downstairs, special-ordered designer textiles upstairs), plus the staff is "willing and able to help you with questions and sample cuttings."

Z Bed Bath & Beyond ●

`20 | 19 | 16 | M`

E 60s | 410 E. 61st St. (1st Ave.) | 4/5/6/F/N/R/W to 59th St./Lexington Ave. | 646-215-4702

Flatiron | 620 Sixth Ave. (bet. 18th & 19th Sts.) | 1 to 18th St. | 212-255-3550

W 60s | 1932 Broadway (65th St.) | 1 to 66th St./Lincoln Ctr. | 917-441-9391

Starrett City | Gateway Ctr. | 459 Gateway Dr. (bet. Erskine St. & Vandalia Ave.) | Brooklyn | A/C to Euclid Ave. | 718-235-2049

Elmhurst | 72-15 25th Ave. (72nd St.) | Queens | E/F/G/R/V to Roosevelt Ave. | 718-429-9438

Rego Pk | 96-05 Queens Blvd. (Junction Blvd.) | Queens | G/R/V to 63rd Dr./Rego Park | 718-459-0868

NEW **Staten Island** | 2700 Veterans Rd. W. (Englewood Ave.) | 718-984-2894

Staten Island | 2795 Richmond Ave. (Platinum Ave.) | 718-982-0071

800-462-3966 | www.bedbathandbeyond.com

"Household gadgets galore", all the "major brands" of bedding, a "newlyweds' dream" of cookware and "anything and everything else for the home" – "from Fido's food bowl to Hanukkah candles" – is "stacked to the ceiling" at this "warehouse-style" chain that's "like a 5-and-10 on steroids"; it's "forever popular" for its "forgiving return policy" and "long hours", and while "there are no bargains", "you won't take a bath" on prices either; still, some find the "cavernous" quarters "frightfully chaotic" – and sophisticates sneer the styles are "dorm-room chic" ("bed, bath and boring").

☑ Belgian Shoes ⑤ | 28 | 22 | 25 | E |

E 50s | 110 E. 55th St. (bet. Lexington & Park Aves.) | E/V to Lexington Ave./
53rd St. | 212-755-7372 | www.belgianshoes.com

Like "slippers disguised as shoes", the "comfortable" his-and-hers
"classics" at this East 50s "staple" (founded by Henri Bendel in 1956) are
as "great for work as for around the city"; sure, "one hopes to own" many
handmade loafers with tassels or bows "in any number of color combinations", but "if you can only splurge on one pair, you might want them
to be Belgian"; P.S. they "keep banker's hours", closing at 4:30 PM.

NEW Belle & Maxie Ⓜ | – | – | – | E |

Ditmas Pk | 1209 Cortelyou Rd. (Westminster Rd.) | Brooklyn | Q to
Cortelyou Rd. | 718-484-3302 | www.belleandmaxie.blogspot.com

From its retro tin ceiling to its neighborhood discussion nights, this
Ditmas Park kids' outfitter strives to recapture the charm of an old-
fashioned mom-and-pop shop; the merchandise is anything but old-
school though, thanks to a generous serving of stylish picks, including
snazzy shoes by See Kai Run and teeny-tiny graphic tees and patterned button-down shirts from labels like Fooey and Wonderboy.

Bellini | 23 | 23 | 17 | E |

E 60s | 1305 Second Ave. (bet. 68th & 69th Sts.) | 6 to 68th St. |
212-517-9233 | www.bellini.com

"If money is no object" when it comes to your little cherub, cruise over
to this East 60s satellite of a well-known furniture chain that peddles
"amazing", Italian-crafted nursery and bedroom pieces made to "last
long after kids need them"; still, the more price-sensitive scoff it's "not
worth the investment."

Belly Dance Maternity | – | – | – | E |

W Vill | 548 Hudson St. (bet. Charles & Perry Sts.) | 1 to Christopher St./
Sheridan Sq. | 212-645-3640 | 888-802-1133 |
www.bellydancematernity.com

This Chicago-based chain with a branch in the West Village brings a
boutique approach to pregnancy style, stocking an eclectic selection
of figure-flattering maternity fashions from both established labels
like Chaiken to up-and-coming brands like Juliet Dream; expectant
moms can also scoop up skincare treats and diaper bags so fashionable they almost don't look like the real thing.

Beneath ●Ⓜ | ▽ 22 | 19 | 21 | M |

E 70s | 265 E. 78th St. (2nd Ave.) | 6 to 77th St. | 212-288-3800 |
www.allthingsbeneath.com

Whether you like your lingerie super-saucy or delicately demure,
chances are you'll hit the jackpot at this "no intimidation" East 70s
storefront, the brick-and-mortar companion to Karyn Riale's Web site;
accent your assets with boldface designers including Anna Sui and
Roberto Cavelli and mainstays like Eberjey and Hanky Panky, then top
it all off with casual clothing and jewelry finds.

NEW Ben Sherman ● | 23 | 21 | 19 | E |

SoHo | 96 Spring St. (Mercer St.) | 6 to Spring St. | 212-680-0160 |
www.benshermanusa.com

"London is still calling" for "wannabe mods" enamored of the
"Swingin' '60s" (even if they were born in the '90s) who flock to this

SoHo flagship of the "snappy" British brand; fans find it a "fab shoppe" full of "graphic patterns and slim cut" clothes ("better for blokes than gals", admittedly); the Mick (as in Jagger) mansion look of the place, with its crystal chandelier, blood-red walls, faux antiques and endless English pop soundtrack, creates a "perfect" backdrop for "some fabulous eye candy, both shopping and working."

☑ Bergdorf Goodman ◗

29 | 27 | 24 | VE

E 50s | 754 Fifth Ave. (bet. 57th & 58th Sts.) | N/R/W to 5th Ave./59th St. | 212-753-7300 | 800-558-1855 | www.bergdorfgoodman.com

"There are department stores and then there's Bergdorf's", the "extravagant" emporium opposite The Plaza that's "every woman's" shopping "dream"; "the aura" "may seem intimidating", but "there's always someone to assist you" and a "wealth of riches" await, including "old-world and au courant" top designers "arranged in boutique-y sections", an "awe-inspiring shoe salon" for those "who can't live without the latest Louboutins" and jewelry that's "elegance under glass"; "heaven must buy its linens" in the revamped home department, whose wares now range from Leontine sheets to Deyrolle stuffed birds, while the cosmetics "basement is a must-do, if you want to be beautiful."

☑ Bergdorf Goodman Men's ◗

28 | 27 | 24 | VE

E 50s | 745 Fifth Ave. (58th St.) | N/R/W to 5th Ave./59th St. | 212-753-7300 | 800-558-1855 | www.bergdorfgoodman.com

When "you want to be treated like a king, make BG Men's your court" proclaim peacocks "who have arrived or want to look like they have" about this "silky smooth" "Fifth Avenue experience" whose "elegant" confines offer "designer suitings (Zegna, Brioni, etc.)", "traditional and just-trendy-enough" separates, a "grand cuff link collection", "incredible ties" and "an unusually broad shoe selection"; "you can leave looking like royalty, a rock star or anything in between", and while prices "run high" – "is that someone's zip code or the price of a suit?" – perhaps "if all men shopped here, the city would be a better place."

Berkley Girl

21 | 21 | 18 | E

E 70s | 1418 Second Ave. (74th St.) | 6 to 77th St. | 212-744-9507
W 70s | 410 Columbus Ave. (bet. 79th & 80th Sts.) | B/C to 81st St. | 212-877-4770
www.berkleygirl.com

"From the viewpoint of a tween", this "cute, well-done" West 70s boutique with an East 70s sidekick is "divine", in fact, you "need go no further for trendy wear"; the owner holds frequent focus groups with neighborhood kids to make sure she's stocking the "right" stuff, from Seven jeans and Lemon T-shirts to Sister Sam skirts and Monkey Wear party dresses, to piles of jewelry and accessories – so "if you're 10–13 years old", "you automatically love everything."

Berluti ⊠

- | - | - | VE

E 70s | 971 Madison Ave. (76th St.) | 6 to 77th St. | 212-439-6400 | www.berluti.com

"Truly a work of art" agree aesthetes who fall for these "beautiful" bespoke men's "shoes with a story" from the Berluti family whose company, now under the LVMH umbrella, dates back to 1895; sole seekers with euros to spare make tracks to its Madison Avenue corner shop, a blue-walled gem offering a "gorgeous presentation" of the costly creations made from Venetia leather and meticulously rubbed with essential oils to attain the right patina.

☑ Bernardaud ☒
29	29	24	VE

E 50s | 499 Park Ave. (59th St.) | 4/5/6/F/N/R/W to 59th St./Lexington Ave. | 212-371-4300 | 800-884-7775 | www.bernardaud.fr
Since 1863, this French "classic" has made "beautiful", "expensive" porcelain "almost too pretty to touch" that "dinner guests always compliment"; its well-appointed Park Avenue boutique also carries Baccarat and Hermès crystal and Christofle and Puiforcat sterling silver flatware, making the moneyed maintain "it's hard not to want everything" here.

☑ Best Buy ●
20	17	14	M

E 80s | 1280 Lexington Ave. (86th St.) | 4/5/6 to 86th St. | 917-492-8870
Flatiron | 60 W. 23rd St. (6th Ave.) | F/V to 23rd St. | 212-366-1373
NoHo | 622 Broadway (bet. Bleecker & Houston Sts.) | 6 to Bleecker St. | 212-673-4067
NEW **W 40s** | 529 Fifth Ave. (44th St.) | 7/B/D/F/V to 42nd St./Bryant Park | 212-808-0309
Bensonhurst | Caesar's Bay Shopping Ctr. | 8923 Bay Pkwy. (Shore Pkwy.) | Brooklyn | D/M to Bay Pkwy. | 718-265-6950
Elmhurst | Queens Pl. | 88-01 Queens Blvd. (bet. 55th & 56th Aves.) | Queens | G/R/V to Grand Ave./Newtown | 718-393-2690
LIC | 50-01 Northern Blvd. (bet. 50th St. & Newtown Rd.) | Queens | G/R/V to 46th St. | 718-626-7585
Staten Island | Staten Island Mall | 2795 Richmond Ave. (bet. Platinum Ave. & Richmond Hill Rd.) | 718-698-7546
888-237-8289 | www.bestbuy.com
Browsers love that "you can play" with the "large inventory" at these "mass-market" "electronics supermarkets", "one-stop shops" for "any device that plugs into a wall socket – from refrigerators to computers" and "all kinds of gadgets" in between; still, critics complain the "name is a misnomer" ("wait for a sale") and say "good luck finding help" since the "hit-or-miss staff" is often "nowhere to be found."

Betsey Bunky Nini ☒
23	22	20	E

E 70s | 980 Lexington Ave. (bet. 71st & 72nd Sts.) | 6 to 68th St. | 212-744-6716
Visitors to the "happy environment" of this East 70s women's boutique warm to the "well-edited collection" of "high fashion" lines such as Alberta Ferretti, Ter et Bantine, Piazza Sempione and Paul Smith; "everything looks so good", but a nattering of naysayers squawk it's a bit "on the expensive side."

Betsey Johnson
21	22	20	E

E 60s | 251 E. 60th St. (bet. 2nd & 3rd Aves.) | 4/5/6/F/N/R/W to 59th St./Lexington Ave. | 212-319-7699
E 80s | 1060 Madison Ave. (bet. 80th & 81st Sts.) | 6 to 77th St. | 212-734-1257
SoHo | 138 Wooster St. (bet. Houston & Prince Sts.) | N/R/W to Prince St. | 212-995-5048
W 70s | 248 Columbus Ave. (bet. 71st & 72nd Sts.) | 1/2/3/B/C to 72nd St. | 212-362-3364
www.betseyjohnson.com
Every day is "party dress-up day" at this "wacky" "boudoirlike" quartet where the forever "young-at-heart" designer (the "pink punker of

fashion") is "always a hit" with her "funky, feminine and sexy" dresses; the mature maintain that "only models and teens" "have the flair to pull off" the "trashy" "items that look cheaper than they are"; still, the "impossibly hip" staff is "attentive" and "honest – what a blessing."

Beverly Feldman
| | 20 | 23 | 20 | E |

W 50s | 7 W. 56th St. (bet. 5th & 6th Aves.) | E/V to 5th Ave./53rd St. | 212-484-0000 | 877-776-5477 | www.beverlyfeldmanshoes.com
"When your kooky mood strikes" bop over to this "kitschy" pink, gold and black West 50s shoe shop for an "over-the-top" "pick-me-up" to match your "glitz and bling" style; designer Beverly Feldman's "incredible pizzazz" translates into "fabulous" footwear for fashion heat seekers who abide by the mantra "when more is not enuff"; still, subdued sorts chide "are you kidding?" – only if you're part of the "gold lamé crowd."

Bicycle Habitat
| ▽ | 23 | 13 | 18 | M |

SoHo | 244 Lafayette St. (bet. Prince & Spring Sts.) | 6 to Spring St. | 212-431-3315 | www.bicyclehabitat.com
"For quality, go" to this SoHo "source for custom and fixed-gear" bicycles, a "classic" "greasy, messy, sweaty" shop that "professional riders" and park cruisers alike laud as just "what a bike shop should be", with "reasonably priced" merchandise and repairs "done quickly"; still, while most find the "avid cyclists" on staff to be "knowledgeable", a handful feel that "service is in decline"; N.B. a recent major expansion may not be reflected in the above Display score.

Bicycle Renaissance
| ▽ | 21 | 16 | 12 | E |

W 80s | 430 Columbus Ave. (bet. 80th & 81st Sts.) | 1 to 79th St. | 212-724-2350 | www.bicyclerenaissance.com
Pedalers purport that this "urban bike shop" on the UWS is a "great place to trick out an ordinary" set of wheels and praise the "competent repair" department for "emergency" fix-ups; still, detractors switch to a different gear, griping that the "surly staff" is "not very helpful" and the offerings are "overpriced", advising head "elsewhere for a good deal."

Big Drop ●
| | 21 | 20 | 16 | E |

E 70s | 1321 Third Ave. (bet. 75th & 76th Sts.) | 6 to 77th St. | 212-988-3344
E 70s | 1325 Third Ave. (76th St.) | 6 to 77th St. | 212-472-3200
SoHo | 174 Spring St. (bet. Thompson St. & W. B'way) | C/E to Spring St. | 212-966-4299
SoHo | 425 W. Broadway (bet. Prince & Spring Sts.) | C/E to Spring St. | 212-226-9292
www.bigdropnyc.com
"Go on a skinny day" and "drop big bucks" on "hip" threads from the "latest indie" and boldface designers like Gwen Stefani's L.A.M.B. line, Ya-Ya and Rebecca Taylor at this "well-curated" "trendsetter" that carries everything from a "going-out outfit" to "top-of-the-line" jeans; but while supporters insist the staff "isn't aloof", cynics snap they're "snobby"; N.B. the 1325 Third Avenue branch features menswear.

Bike Works NYC ⊠
| | – | – | – | I |

LES | 106 Ridge St. (Rivington St.) | F/J/M/Z to Delancey/Essex Sts. | 212-388-1077 | www.bikecult.com
Vintage models are an occasional draw at this Lower East Side bike bodega, which carries fixed-gear and single-speed cycles for hipsters

and "messenger wannabes" looking to partake in the old-school scene; service is anything but retro, though, with a staff of enthusiasts who are "hard-core loisida."

Z Billabong ◐   21 | 21 | 19 | M

W 40s | 1515 Broadway (bet. 44th & 45th Sts.) | 1/2/3/7/N/Q/R/S/W to 42nd St./Times Sq. | 212-840-0550 | www.billabong.com

Wave-riders "love the Aussie style" of this "great quality brand" that now has a home for its "surfer stuff", from board shorts to sunglasses; the huge space also features the Element line of skateboard parts, giving "outdoor types" more reasons to coast over to Times Square.

Billy Martin's Western Wear   27 | 25 | 24 | E

E 60s | 220 E. 60th St. (bet. 2nd & 3rd Aves.) | 4/5/6/F/N/R/W to 59th St./Lexington Ave. | 212-861-3100 | www.billymartin.com

"If you're saddling up to go out West", this East 60th Street stockade, gussied up with "memorabilia", a vintage bar and a Coca-Cola machine, is "the place to go" gush guys and gals in search of "fabulous" cowboy boots, "great belt buckles" and rodeo-ready attire "with pizzazz", favored by celebrities like Sheryl Crow and Billy Bob Thornton; the "workmanship is superior" – as are "Texas oil-men" prices.

Bird ◐   ▽ 25 | 25 | 25 | E

NEW **Cobble Hill** | 220 Smith St. (Butler St.) | Brooklyn | F/G to Bergen St. | 718-797-3774
Park Slope | 430 Seventh Ave. (bet. 14th & 15th Sts.) | Brooklyn | F to 7th Ave. | 718-768-4940
www.shopbird.com

Soar into this Park Slope boutique with its "homey, feel-good vibe" and you'll "want to come back again and again" chirp "cutting-edge" chicks; former Barneys New York buyer Jennifer Mankins has "a great eye for patterns and colors", mixing "pieces from unique" labels with "quality designers" and "established" lines like A.P.C., and to go-with, "such cool" accessories, jewelry and shoes; "trendy" doesn't come cheap – it's hard to "leave without spending a paycheck"; N.B. the new Smith Street branch carries a slightly different mix.

Birnbaum & Bullock Z M   – | – | – | E

Chelsea | 151 W. 25th St. (bet. 6th & 7th Aves.) | N/R/W to 23rd St. | 212-242-2914 | www.birnbaumandbullock.com

At this by-appointment-only Flatiron District salon, the "extremely pleasant" namesake designers "custom fit dresses according to the bride's wishes", "making the experience extra special"; hit the sleek blue-and-silver showroom and slip into something sophisticated, like a silk chiffon number – whatever you choose, you can rely on the B&B team to offer "great recommendations for the entire ensemble."

Bisazza Z M   – | – | – | VE

SoHo | 43 Greene St. (bet. Broome & Grand Sts.) | A/C/E to Canal St. | 212-334-7130 | www.bisazzausa.com

The tony Italian tile company's first U.S. showroom is this sparkling, gallerylike SoHo stunner displaying "gorgeous" glass mosaic designs; they'll make a big splash in your bath, kitchen or pool, but the prices may get you in hot water; N.B. as we go to press, they are renovating this space and may be relocating to a temporary showroom, so call ahead.

Bis Designer Resale

`-` `-` `-` `E`

E 80s | 1134 Madison Ave., 2nd fl. (bet. 84th & 85th Sts.) | 4/5/6 to 86th St. | 212-396-2760 | www.bisbiz.com

At this "wonderful consignment shop", which sells a "superb selection of high-end vintage" clothing and accessories (e.g. "Blahniks for a couple hundred" bucks) to ladies and, to some extent, gentlemen, the "inventory always looks immaculate"; labels like Chanel, Ferragamo and Vuitton suggest that it's "targeting an older crowd", but it *is* on the UES, after all – and a "must-visit if you're on a shopping venture."

Blacker & Kooby

`25` `17` `19` `M`

E 80s | 1204 Madison Ave. (88th St.) | 4/5/6 to 86th St. | 212-369-8308

Locals like this long-standing Upper East Side family-owned stationery store primarily because of its "great customer service and selection" of cards, invitations, pens, photo albums and picture frames, along with other "unique items."

Blackman ⊠

▽ `26` `18` `16` `E`

Flatiron | 85 Fifth Ave., 2nd fl. (16th St.) | 4/5/6/L/N/Q/R/W to 14th St./ Union Sq. | 212-337-1000

Flushing | 134-07 Northern Blvd. (bet. College Point Blvd. & Main St.) | Queens | 7 to Main St. | 718-939-7200

Queens Vill | 217-68 Hempstead Ave. (bet. Springfield Blvd. & 217th St.) | Queens | E/J/Z to Jamaica Ctr. Parsons/Archer | 718-479-5533

800-843-2695 | www.blackman.com

The gigantic, "gorgeous" flagship in Union Square displays "excellent lines" of kitchen and bath booty, including faucets, tubs, showers, sinks, hardware and every kind of designer plumbing imaginable "across a wide range of prices", but don't discount the Queens locations, where the establishment has been a fixture since 1921.

Blades Board and Skate ◗

▽ `23` `18` `18` `M`

Garment Dist | Manhattan Mall | 901 Sixth Ave. (bet. 32nd & 33rd Sts.) | B/D/F/N/Q/R/V/W to 34th St./Herald Sq. | 646-733-2738

NoHo | 659 Broadway (bet. Bleecker & 3rd Sts.) | 6 to Bleecker St. | 212-477-7350

W 70s | 156 W. 72nd St. (bet. B'way & Columbus Ave.) | B/C to 72nd St. | 212-787-3911

888-552-5233 | www.blades.com

If shooting the slopes, catching a breaker or riding the halfpipe is your idea of R&R, hit this sports triplet for all things extreme; the stock seems to be more "boards than blades lately", but this outfit still "keeps it real" with a "good selection" of powder-shredding gear sold by a "young, fully pierced" staff that lives the lifestyle and "knows the product", adding to the "home-grown feel."

Blair Delmonico ◗

`-` `-` `-` `E`

W 50s | The Shops at Columbus Circle, Time Warner Ctr. | 10 Columbus Circle, ground fl. (bet. 58th & 60th Sts.) | 1/A/B/C/D to 59th St./Columbus Circle | 212-246-6580 | www.blairdelmonico.com

Founded in 1987, this international mini-chain makes its Big Apple headquarters in the Time Warner Center, where an easy-to-shop layout has the company's classically stylish apparel displayed side by side with its costume and semiprecious jewelry, including Swarovski crystal-coated pearls for the bride.

	QUALITY	DISPLAY	SERVICE	COST

Blanc de Chine ⑤
24 | 24 | 24 | VE

E 50s | 673 Fifth Ave. (53rd St.) | E/V to 5th Ave./53rd St. |
212-308-8688 | www.blancdechine.com

A "luxury" Chinese clothier makes its U.S. debut with this East 50s
emporium, whose cool Zen-like digs – white walls, dark-wood floors and
furnishings – are dominated by a spiral staircase; using sumptuous
materials (velvets, cashmere, silk treated to look like leather), the mens-
and womenswear offers an "elegant" East-meets-West fusion, i.e.
mandarin-collar T-shirts, tweedy wool cheongsams and pants suits in
Asian prints; bed linens, pillows and scarves round out the collection.

Bleecker Bob's Golden Oldies Record Shop ●
20 | 12 | 18 | M

G Vill | 118 W. Third St. (bet. MacDougal St. & 6th Ave.) | A/B/C/D/
E/F/V to W. 4th St. | 212-475-9677 | www.bleeckerbobs.com

"Get lost in the smell of old, dusty album covers" at this "legendary"
Greenwich Village "relic", a "fun" store filled with "oddities", choice
oldies, collectibles and even CDs; it's the "place to go for hard-to-find
music", and though the "arrogant" staffers sometimes "act like the recording execs they never became", they're some of the "best record
geeks in the world."

Bleecker Street Records ◗
23 | 13 | 17 | M

G Vill | 239 Bleecker St. (bet. Carmine & Leroy Sts.) | A/B/C/D/E/F/V to
W. 4th St. | 212-255-7899

"Hearkening back to the good old Village days", this "treat for music
lovers" provides not only a "breath of nostalgia for the commercially
wary" but an "eclectic and diverse collection" "including DVDs", "live
CDs" and "hard-to-find old discs for your turntable"; despite the "self-
serve atmosphere" and "somewhat crowded" presentation, it's "a
classic spot" for late-night browsers.

NEW Blibetroy ●Ⓜ
– | – | – | E

LES | 100 Stanton St. (bet. Ludlow & Orchard Sts.) | F/V to Lower East Side/
2nd Ave. | 212-979-5250 | www.blibetroy.com

Arm-candy connoisseurs seeking bold-colored handbags hit the
mother lode at this new LES purse pantheon; though small in stature,
it makes a big style statement with plyboo (plywood that looks like
bamboo) walls and a cool console table, a modern dais for displaying ar-
chitecturally inspired reversible leather shoulder bags, foldable
clutches, male messenger bags and weekend totes.

Ⓩ Blick Art Materials ◗
25 | 24 | 21 | M

NoHo | 1-5 Bond St. (bet. B'way & Lafayette St.) | 6 to Bleecker St. |
212-533-2444 | www.dickblick.com

This "excellent", "well-organized" NoHo chain link offers a "wealth of
supplies", "amazing papers" and "studio furniture" in a "bright, lofty"
bi-level, pillar-accented space; "reasonable prices" and a "knowledgeable" staff composed of "helpful hipsters" add the final flourishes.

Bloch
– | – | – | M

W 70s | 304 Columbus Ave. (bet. 74th & 75th Sts.) | B/C to 72nd St. |
212-579-1960 | www.blochworld.com

"One of the few places to find" this Aussie dancewear-maker's clothes
is this West 70s flagship outfitting professionals and dilettantes alike;

scoop up leotards and leggings, then slip into pointe, tap or cutting-edge jazz or hip-hop shoes before ponying up to the barre for a pre-view on the plasma TV; even gym rats reveal "if you want to get looks, wear their work-out pants – they mold your butt beautifully."

Blockbuster Video ☻

16	15	11	I

W 50s | 829 Eighth Ave. (51st St.) | C/E to 50th St. | 212-765-2021 | www.blockbuster.com
Additional locations throughout the NY area
It's "movies for the masses" at this "reliable" chain whose "wide", if "predictable", selection of "big-budget Hollywood" flicks is well-suited to "family viewing"; still, cinéastes slam it as a "commercial" giant that can't "compete" when it comes to "older movies or obscure" titles, adding that its "clerks know utterly nothing about film."

Bloom ▣

24	24	20	M

E 40s | 361 Madison Ave. (bet. 45th & 46th Sts.) | 4/5/6/7/S to 42nd St./ Grand Central | 212-370-0068 | www.bloom21llc.citysearch.com
Not to be confused with the Lexington Avenue flower shop, this Madison Avenue offshoot of a Japanese jewelry company sells "crisp", "clean-lined" fine steel, titanium and white gold chokers, chains, rings and bangles in a "sleek" white minimalist setting; if you're "looking for a gift but can't afford Cartier, this is the place."

Bloom & Krup

23	-	16	M

Garment Dist | 347 W. 36th St. (bet. 8th & 9th Aves.) | 1/2/3/A/C/E to 34th St./Penn Station | 212-673-2760 | www.bloomandkrup.net
Newly relocated from its long-standing East Village spot to the Garment District, this "one-stop shop" for kitchen, bath and plumbing supplies has offered "good prices on expensive products" like Bosch dishwashers and Viking and Gaggenau cooking equipment; foes who find the staff "missing in action" wonder if they're "locked in one of the freezers", but fans say the service is "knowledgeable."

⧉ Bloomingdale's ☻

23	20	17	E

E 50s | 1000 Third Ave. (bet. 59th & 60th Sts.) | 4/5/6/F/N/R/W to 59th St./Lexington Ave. | 212-705-2000 | 800-232-1854

⧉ Bloomingdale's SoHo ☻

SoHo | 504 Broadway (bet. Broome & Spring Sts.) | 6 to Spring St. | 212-729-5900
www.bloomingdales.com
"What can you say about a Manhattan institution?" – "from moderately priced merchandise to chic couture", "you can find everything you need" (except "knowledgeable sales help") at this East 50s "mother ship" and its "boutique"-like SoHo satellite; the "venerable" original is stocked with clothing, "baubles, bangles and beads" and "good-quality furniture", plus it's a "bridal shower mecca" for housewares; true, it teems with tourists and "overcrowded" aisles, but despite its sometimes "discombobulated state", it's voted NYC's Most Popular department store; N.B. star chef David Burke has an eatery in the flagship.

Blue

-	-	-	E

E Vill | 137 Ave. A (bet. 9th St. & St. Marks Pl.) | 6 to Astor Pl. | 212-228-7744
"There's a method" to owner-designer Christina Kara's "madness" de-clare devotees, who praise this East Village shop and its madcap pro-

prietor for coming up with "the answer for curves" in her "dress-of-your-dreams" wedding gowns, "creative bridesmaid dresses", cocktail dresses and suits that fit "a real woman's body"; "even if you've got a smallish bridal gown budget", you won't leave singing the blues.

Blue Bag

- | - | - | E

NoLita | 266 Elizabeth St. (bet. Houston & Prince Sts.) | 6 to Spring St. | 212-966-8566

"Feel your troubles melt away" as you step inside this palm-studded, brick-walled, "St. Barts–inspired" boutique and peruse the "exquisite selection" of handbags displayed amid vintage furnishings; the "ever-changing" array of "very modern, chic" evening and day essentials includes "hard-to-find labels" and "independent designers", and it's all sold by a staff that "cares what you like" – no wonder it's a "favorite" of individualists who love being asked "where did you get that bag?"

Blue Bench Ⓜ

- | - | - | VE

TriBeCa | 159 Duane St. (bet. Hudson St. & W. B'way) | 1/2/3 to Chambers St. | 212-267-1500 | www.bluebenchnyc.com

This TriBeCa treasure specializes in "the best in children's furniture" – everything from handmade, hand-painted cribs to bookshelves and beds, plus decorative trimmings like rugs, bedding, lamps, toy chests and picture frames; all this charm is costly, though, leaving the sticker-shocked wondering "who in their right mind would pay these prices?"

Blueberi ◐Ⓜ

- | - | - | E

Dumbo | 143 Front St. (bet. Jay & Pearl Sts.) | Brooklyn | A/C/F to Jay St./Borough Hall | 718-422-7724

For womenswear that has a "cool, 'mark of the hand' designer look", fashionistas duck into this Dumbo den of style, a larger, luxer sibling to owner Carlene Brown's Prospect Heights boutique, Redberi; the grottolike space boasts urban-chic finds from Jill Stuart, LaRok and Mason's, plus a "treasure trove" of handbags and jewelry to complete the "sophisticated, sometimes funky" ensemble.

NEW Blue in Green ◐

▽ 21 | 21 | 20 | E

SoHo | 8 Greene St. (bet. Canal & Grand Sts.) | 6/J/M/N/Q/R/W/Z to Canal St. | 212-680-0555 | www.blueingreensoho.com

Break away from the Canal Street crowds and cruise into this "cool" SoHo spot where dudes who are into duds recognize the exclusive brands of British and Japanese casualwear; while there are a lot of "high-priced items" – especially the denim from labels like Johnbull, Pure Blue and Sugar Cane – guys don't feel blue shelling out the green, cuz it's tough to find this limited-edition stuff stateside.

Blue Tree Ⓢ

24 | 22 | 20 | VE

E 90s | 1283 Madison Ave. (bet. 91st & 92nd Sts.) | 4/5/6 to 86th St. | 212-369-2583 | www.bluetreeny.com

It's the "kind of cute, quirky shopkeeper's boutique that doesn't exist in New York anymore" muse admirers who deem actress Phoebe Cates Kline's double-decker haunt in the East 90s a "unique" "place to browse"; choose from a "highly edited selection of toys, clothes, jewelry" and trinkets for kids, then shake the adult trees for diamonds, antiques, perfume, vintage LPs, chocolates and candles; still, a miffed few wail "everything looks great – until you look at the price tags."

blush ●

21 | 17 | 17 | E

W Vill | 333 Bleecker St. (Christopher St.) | 1 to Christopher St./ Sheridan Sq. | 212-352-0111

"Sexy and sometimes unusual" womenswear tempts at this West Village shop where the lovely wares include filmy tops, flirty knits and body-conscious suits "you must have a 24-inch waist" to wear; the only nays are for the "waaaay too pushy" staff, who may make you blush with their "overly complimentary" comments.

Böc ●

▽ 19 | 22 | 18 | E

W 80s | 491 Columbus Ave. (bet. 83rd & 84th Sts.) | B/C to 81st St. | 212-362-5405 | www.bocnyc.com

"Just what was needed on the Upper West Side" applaud admirers, who say bravo to the "downtown selection of modern, beautiful cloth-ing" from labels like the owner's line, Lemon, along with finds from Vivienne Westwood and Rebecca Taylor and jeans from Citizens of Humanity; the "lofty, spacious" store offers "plenty of space to walk around" or park a stroller when searching for an "adorable" "last-minute Saturday night outfit."

Bochic ▣

- | - | - | VE

E 50s | The Crown Bldg. | 730 Fifth Ave. (bet. 56th & 57th Sts.) | N/R/W to 5th Ave./59th St. | 212-873-0707 | www.bochic.com

Ranging from classic creamy white, gray, black and golden pearls strung into necklaces and bracelets to intricate mogul-inlayed enamel rings and colorful cobblestone-path bracelets of polished gemstones, this jewelry showroom in The Crown Building lives up to its bohemian-chic name; N.B. call ahead for an appointment.

BoConcept .

17 | 22 | 18 | M

Chelsea | 144 W. 18th St. (6th Ave.) | 1 to 18th St. | 646-336-8188
Murray Hill | 105 Madison Ave. (30th St.) | 6 to 33rd St. | 212-686-8188
NEW SoHo | 69 Greene St. (bet. Broome & Spring Sts.) | N/R/W to Prince St. | 212-966-8188
NEW Dumbo | 79 Front St. (bet. Main & Washington Sts.) | Brooklyn | F to York St. | 718-246-8188
www.boconcept.us

"Modular" "Scandinavian furniture at a moderate price" is the point at this "well-laid-out" outfit where "stylish" "modern" pieces come in flexible designs – for example, one sofa style can be ordered in hun-dreds of variations in size, shape and color; still, skeptics question the quality of items that appear to have "more style than substance."

Bodum

25 | 25 | 19 | M

Meatpacking | 413-415 W. 14th St. (bet. 9th & 10th Aves.) | A/C/E/L to 14th St./8th Ave. | 212-367-9125 | 800-232-6386 | www.bodumusa.com

There's "more than just French-press coffeemakers" at this "hip" Scandinavian housewares mecca in the Meatpacking District that's "a must for a new home or apartment", inspiring "huge wish lists" for "bargain-priced", "Euro-modern"-designed products like teapots, gadgets and insulated glasses; the "sleek" space is "customer-friendly" and boasts a "cute cafe", as well as a "great sales area in back."

	QUALITY	DISPLAY	SERVICE	COST

Body Shop, The ◑ `20` `19` `19` `M`
E Vill | 747 Broadway (bet. Astor Pl. & 8th St.) | N/R/W to 8th St. |
212-979-2944 | 800-263-9746 | www.thebodyshop.com
Additional locations throughout the NY area
"The smell of mangos and coconut lures you" into "the original conscious cosmetics company" selling "reasonably priced", environmentally friendly "safe products" like the body butters that "are not tested on animals"; but cynics criticize the "overzealous staff", "hemp and hippie-ish" vibe ("bring your mood ring") and suggest "a face-lift" is in order.

Boffi SoHo 🅂 Ⓜ `-` `-` `-` `VE`
SoHo | 31½ Greene St. (Grand St.) | C/E to Spring St. | 212-431-8282 |
www.boffi-soho.com
Located in a cavernous, multilevel SoHo showroom, this high-end Milan-based kitchen and bath manufacturer is a modernist's dream, with gleaming fixtures, sinks, appliances, custom-made cabinets, bathtubs and showers in materials ranging from steel and glass to wood; just note less costs more when it comes to the price here.

Bolton's ◑ `14` `11` `11` `I`
W 50s | 27 W. 57th St. (bet. 5th & 6th Aves.) | F to 57th St. | 212-935-4431 |
www.boltonsstores.com
Additional locations throughout the NY area
Though this "dingy" discounter definitely "has seen better days", you can still "score" "bargains if you search", rummaging through the racks of "color-coordinated clothing" – "a nice idea", especially since the staff is "not really interested in helping you"; there are "good, cheap accessories too", especially at the "well-located" West 57th Street flagship.

Bombay Company, The ◑ `15` `18` `17` `M`
E 80s | 1542 Third Ave. (87th St.) | 4/5/6 to 86th St. | 212-987-3990
Flatiron | 900 Broadway (20th St.) | N/R/W to 23rd St. | 212-420-1315
Bayside | Bay Terrace Shopping Ctr. | 23-88 Bell Blvd. (24th Ave.) |
Queens | 7 to Main St. | 718-224-2998
NEW Glendale | The Shoppes at Atlas Park | 8000 Cooper Ave. (80th St.) |
Queens | 718-326-0651
Staten Island | Staten Island Mall | 2655 Richmond Ave. (bet. Platinum Ave. &
Richmond Hill Rd.) | 718-494-0426
800-829-7789 | www.bombaycompany.com
"Fill in the nooks and crannies" with budget "bric-a-brac" like mirrors and "traditional reproduction" "dark-wood" furniture, at this chain with "cheerful service"; but aesthetes warn with "poor quality" and "fake English" accessories like "tacky hunting prints", "you need a lot of style to pull a look together" without making your place "look like a Hilton."

Bond No. 9 `28` `26` `25` `E`
E 60s | 680 Madison Ave. (61st St.) | N/R/W to 5th Ave./59th St. |
212-838-2780
E 70s | 897 Madison Ave. (72nd St.) | 6 to 68th St. | 212-794-4480
NoHo | 9 Bond St. (bet. B'way & Lafayette St.) | 6 to Bleecker St. |
212-228-1732 ◑
W Vill | 399 Bleecker St. (11th St.) | A/C/E/L to 14th St./8th Ave. |
212-633-1641 ◑
877-273-3369 | www.bondno9.com
Those who've bonded with this "cool" "perfume line named for different NYC neighborhoods" like Nuits de Noho and Chelsea Flowers say it

sells 26 "unique, sexy smells that you won't find on every other woman"(or guy), along with custom-blend options; N.B. the Bond Street flagship boasts a tearoom and library.

Bond 07 by Selima
_ _ _ E

NoHo | 7 Bond St. (bet. B'way & Lafayette St.) | 6 to Bleecker St. | 212-677-8487 | www.selimaoptique.com

Some fancy her a Bond girl, but Selima Salaun, the creative designer, optician and optometrist behind star-magnet Selima Optique, offers up more than a Goldfinger's worth of glamour at this NoHo boutique, which boasts "gorgeous eyewear", an "eclectic" selection of new and vintage hats, handbags, dresses and jewelry, plus lingerie from Le Corset, her now-shuttered SoHo shop.

Bonne Nuit
▽ 24 | 17 | 18 | E

E 70s | 1193 Lexington Ave. (81st St.) | 6 to 77th St. | 212-472-7300 | www.bonnenuitonline.com

Shoppers are over the moon about the "wonderful selection of imported" ladies' lingerie and childrenswear at this Eastsider where you can snap up "sweet" undies and luxe sleepwear, crib-size quilts, mother-baby pajamas and old-fashioned little-girl dresses from Papo d'Anjo.

☑ Bonpoint
28 | 26 | 19 | VE

E 60s | 810 Madison Ave. (68th St.) | 6 to 68th St. | 212-879-0900 🖹
E 90s | 1269 Madison Ave. (91st St.) | 4/5/6 to 86th St. | 212-722-7720 🖹
NEW **W Vill** | 392 Bleecker St. (Perry St.) | 1 to Christopher St./ Sheridan Sq. | 212-647-1700 ☻
www.bonpoint.com

"Ooh-la-la!" trumpet touters of this trio of *très chic* French children's clothiers, who fawn over the "magnificent", "beautifully made" layette, sportswear and special-occasion creations boasting "sophisticated fabrics and colors" – "mini-couture for the city's elite to drool over and on"; "prices are through the roof" but "it's hard to resist" such "divine" duds – especially when "every piece is a keepsake."

Boomerang Toys
_ _ _ M

NEW **Financial Dist** | 2 World Financial Ctr. (West Side Hwy.) | R/W to Rector St. | 212-786-3011
TriBeCa | 173 W. Broadway (Worth St.) | 1 to Franklin St. | 212-226-7650
www.boomerangtoys.com

You always "walk out with something" after visiting these Financial District and TriBeCa toy boxes, which stock some of the most "unique" playthings around, including European imports like Ravensburger puzzles and Bruder trucks; they're "great to browse in", especially when you're hunting down "hard-to-find" must-haves for kids, and they even keep track of gifts bought for neighborhood parties to avoid duplication.

Borrelli Boutique
_ _ _ VE

E 60s | 16 E. 60th St. (bet. 5th & Madison Aves.) | N/R/W to 5th Ave./ 59th St. | 212-644-9610

On a swanky side street in the East 60s, a stone's throw from Barneys and Tod's, this small shop supplies *signore e signori* with some sunny sartorial style from Napoli, via colorful suits, separates, sweaters and shoes; it's "one of the best for custom shirts – though certainly at tailor-made prices" confide cognoscenti.

ⓩ Bose ◑
27 | 26 | 24 | VE

W 50s | The Shops at Columbus Circle, Time Warner Ctr. | 10 Columbus Circle, 3rd fl. (bet. 58th & 60th Sts.) | 1/A/B/C/D to 59th St./ Columbus Circle | 212-823-9314 | 800-999-2673 | www.bose.com

"Top-notch" home entertainment equipment that'll make you think you're "walking into a fancy concert hall" has earned this sleek Time Warner Center purveyor a reputation for "great quality products" with "fabulous" acoustics (to wit, the Wave radio, which tops many an audiophile's wish list, and the iPod-compatible SoundDock); "excellent service" adds to the "confidence-building experience."

BOSS Hugo Boss ◑
26 | 25 | 22 | VE

W 50s | The Shops at Columbus Circle, Time Warner Ctr. | 10 Columbus Circle, ground fl. (bet. 58th & 60th Sts.) | 1/A/B/C/D to 59th St./ Columbus Circle | 212-485-1900 | 800-484-6267 | www.hugoboss.com

At this sleek multifloor shop in the Time Warner Center, there's plenty of "panache" to please the "manly man" who likes to button up in a "chic", "classy" suit and "great fitting" separates; although this German manufacturer strikes some as "pricey", converts claim "you can never get enough of the Boss" – especially boss ladies, who "wish there were more women's stuff."

ⓩ Bottega Veneta
29 | 27 | 24 | VE

E 50s | 699 Fifth Ave. (bet. 54th & 55th Sts.) | E/V to 5th Ave./53rd St. | 212-371-5511 | www.bottegaveneta.com

Inhale the "smell of great leather" at this luxury label's mammoth Fifth Avenue flagship where the "presentation of goods" from accessories to clothing is "superb" and creative director Tomas Maier's "elegant" touch is evident everywhere; surveyors swoon over "mouthwatering" "soft, buttery" purses that "last forever" and "never go out of style", pronouncing them "worth every dear penny" they'll undoubtedly cost you; still, for most, "nothing beats" the "signature woven bags", which may be "extravagant", but "essential to the well-dressed wardrobe."

Botticelli
25 | 21 | 21 | E

E 40s | 522 Fifth Ave. (bet. 43rd & 44th Sts.) | 7/B/D/F/V to 42nd St./ Bryant Park | 212-768-1430
E 40s | 620 Fifth Ave. (49th St.) | B/D/F/V to 47-50th Sts./Rockefeller Ctr. | 212-582-6313
E 50s | 666 Fifth Ave. (53rd St.) | E/V to 5th Ave./53rd St. | 212-586-7421
www.botticellishoes.com

"Lush leathers with Italian elegance" – what "great stuff for the tootsies" – no wonder this Fifth Avenue "shoe heaven" was "Elaine from *Seinfeld*'s favorite" muse admirers who also tune into the "soundly made" handbags and men's offerings; "excellent quality" and a staff gifted with "unending patience" are its "hallmarks", along with "expensive" prices, so perhaps wait for sale days, when the merchandise "becomes affordable to mere mortals."

Boucher ◑
20 | 20 | 21 | M

Meatpacking | 9 Ninth Ave. (Little W. 12th St.) | A/C/E/L to 14th St./ 8th Ave. | 212-206-3775 | www.boucherjewelry.com

If you love "delicate", colorful and "trendy" baubles in semiprecious and precious gemstones, especially lariats, earrings and briolette bracelets and necklaces, then this "jewel box" in the "super-hot"

Meatpacking District is for you; "good prices" and "friendly service" are other reasons some call the shop their "favorite."

Bowery Kitchen Supplies

22	11	14	I

Chelsea | Chelsea Mkt. | 75 Ninth Ave. (bet. 15th & 16th Sts.) | A/C/E/L to 14th St./8th Ave. | 212-376-4982 | www.bowerykitchens.com

Although no longer on the Bowery, this "bargain-priced", "cheaper-by-the-dozens" Chelsea store still serves up "restaurant-style supplies for the average home" and provides tools and equipment to the Food Network studio upstairs; most say the "cluttered" space is "full" of "everything you need for your kitchen", "except standing room."

Bowery Lighting

21	13	17	M

LES | 132 Bowery (bet. Broome & Grand Sts.) | J/M/Z to Bowery | 212-941-8244 | www.liteelite.com

"It lights up my life!" assert admirers of this Bowery bastion, which offers "a dazzling array" of "mainstream choices" from "over-the-top crystal chandeliers to simple bathroom" fixtures; the endless rows of products leave some "overwhelmed" and with a "stiff neck" from all that looking up, but "fair prices" make it easier to focus.

B. Oyama Homme

–	–	–	E

Harlem | 2330 Seventh Ave. (bet. 136th & 137th Sts.) | 2/3 to 135th St. | 212-234-5128 | www.boyamahomme.com

Bernard Oyama's Parisian sensibility is everywhere in evidence at the Harlem haven for *hommes* near the 135th Street subway stop; there is a detailed elegance to the classy suits, slacks, shirts and knits that all seem to fit neatly into his cozy atelier decorated with old photos of style-setting African-American jazz and pop stars of yesteryear.

Boyd's of Madison Avenue

23	17	17	E

W 70s | 309 Columbus Ave. (bet. 74th & 75th Sts.) | 1/2/3 to 72nd St. | 212-877-3307 | 800-683-2693 | www.boydsonline.com

No longer on Madison, this dowager is now ensconced on Columbus Avenue, where it offers "everything for the face, hair, body" and bath, including cosmetic makeovers, plus jewelry, scarves, lingerie and toys; cynics say one thing that hasn't changed is the "harpy-ish salespeople" who "follow you like hawks."

Bra Smyth

25	16	21	E

E 70s | 905 Madison Ave. (bet. 72nd & 73rd Sts.) | 6 to 68th St. | 212-772-9400

NEW **W 70s** | 2177 Broadway (77th St.) | 1 to 79th St. | 212-721-5111 www.brasmyth.com

With "old-fashioned fitters" who "figure out your perfect size" and make "free alterations on bras", the goods "feel custom-made" at this family-owned duo serving up "sexy lingerie", sleepwear and swimwear that's "not super-luxury, but high-quality"; still, a handful huff that it's too "crowded" and find the staff's attitude a tad "holier than thou."

Bra*Tenders ⊠

–	–	–	M

W 40s | 630 Ninth Ave., 6th fl. (bet. 44th & 45th Sts.) | A/C/E to 42nd St./Port Authority | 212-957-7000 | www.bratenders.com

Overflowing with frilly goods, this lingerie lair tucked away in a Theater District office building specializes in suiting up stage and screen sirens, but regular gals can get star treatment too via one-on-

one bra-sizings; the impeccable fitting undergarments (including shapewear, sports bras and hosiery) don't come cheap, but even with no-pressure service, it's hard not to leave without a bagful of new favorite bras; N.B. appointment required.

Breguet ⑤ | ▽ 29 | 28 | 27 | VE |

E 60s | 779 Madison Ave. (bet. 66th & 67th Sts.) | 6 to 68th St. | 212-288-4014 | 800-331-1577 | www.breguet.com

"Amazing watches with an amazing history" from the Swiss luxury-brand horologist, dating back to 1775 and now part of Swatch, are the focus at this "fabulous" Madison Avenue boutique; whether you choose the timepiece brand worn by Napoléon Bonaparte and Marie Antoinette, select a glittering piece of fine jewelry or pick up a precision pen, the "exceptional staff" makes you "feel you are the most important customer that ever walked in" – "now, all you have to do is win the lottery."

Bric's | ▽ 27 | 26 | 26 | E |

E 50s | 535 Madison Ave. (bet. 54th & 55th Sts.) | E/V to 5th Ave./53rd St. | 212-688-4490 | 866-866-3390 | www.brics.it

If you want "skycaps to compliment your luggage as the nicest they've ever seen", but you also want something "well-made" and "well-priced", zip over to this Midtown shop and peruse the "tasteful selection" of "elegant", "practical" and "brilliantly conceived" Italian-designed travel gear; the "distinctive" pieces come in unconventional shades like lavender and are "very good-looking", and what's more, the staff is "supportive", dispensing "useful information."

Bridal Garden, The ●⑤ | 18 | 10 | 15 | M |

Flatiron | 54 W. 21st St. (bet. 5th & 6th Aves.) | N/R/W to 23rd St. | 212-252-0661 | www.bridalgarden.org

"You have to sift through" the "designer gowns at knockoff prices" and "pray they have your size, but if you're lucky" at this "cramped" Flatiron District shop run by a not-for-profit children's charity, "ahhh . . . what a feeling!"; imagine "professing your love, looking great while you do it and giving back"; some dresses "need TLC before the big day" – but remember, it can be "quite the windfall" too.

NEW Bridal Reflections ⑤Ⓜ | 20 | 18 | 18 | E |

Murray Hill | 286 Fifth Ave., 5th fl. (30th St.) | 6 to 28th St. | 212-764-3040 | www.bridalreflections.com

Family-owned for 35 years, this Long Island wedding-gear retailer is looking to take Manhattan with its new Murray Hill store; but Big Apple brides are being a bit skeptical: while there are "nice selections" among the 20-plus designers represented, ranging from the corseted creations of Justin Alexander to the Thai silks of Alvina Perucci to the bodacious styles of Stephen Yearick, the gowns seem "pricey for the quality", and the "aloof" "help is not so helpful."

Ⓩ Bridge Kitchenware ⑤ | 28 | – | 19 | E |

E 40s | 711 Third Ave., entry on 45th St. (bet. 2nd & 3rd Aves.) | 4/5/6/7/S to 42nd St./Grand Central | 212-688-4220 | 800-274-3435 | www.bridgekitchenware.com

About a year and a half ago, "chef's heaven" officially relocated to East 45th Street assert acolytes who swear that "in addition to the basics", "anything and everything you could ever want for your kitchen is here", including "odd gadgets", "hard-to-find, quality" equipment and other "uncommon things"; they also warn that "if you're not a professional cook, beware" as the staff can be "indifferent to or impatient with the ignorant."

Brief Encounters
- | - | - | E

W 70s | 239 Columbus Ave. (71st St.) | 1/2/3 to 72nd St. | 212-496-5649
Insiders with an intimate knowledge of this black-and-white Columbus Avenue corner lingerie shop say the "goods are high-quality", so whether you're looking for a slinky slip, luxe hosiery or silk pajamas, "wonderful" wares from labels like Elle Macpherson or Ralph Lauren await; the "very knowledgeable staff" is also "exceptional" – "no ill-fitting bras are allowed" to be sold.

☑ Brioni ⑤
28 | 27 | 25 | VE

E 50s | 55 E. 52nd St. (bet. Madison & Park Aves.) | E/V to 5th Ave./ 53rd St. | 212-355-1940
E 50s | 57 E. 57th St. (bet. Madison & Park Aves.) | 4/5/6/F/N/R/W to 59th St./Lexington Ave. | 212-376-5777
888-778-8775 | www.brioni.it
"Conservative, well-heeled gents" are well-served at this elegant East 50s pair that's "simply the best of the best" for "traditional Italian menswear", from the stunning suits to the "beautiful" ties; sure, "you pay top dollar", but the bill includes being made to feel "special" by a staff that can "do anything" – "the hunchback of Notre Dame could walk in and they would fit him."

British American House ⑤
▽ 22 | 19 | 16 | E

E 50s | 488 Madison Ave. (51st St.) | 6 to 51st St. | 212-752-5880
Oddly enough, considering its name, "a good selection of big-name" brands from Italy are the stock-in-trade of this Midtown men's store that's "been around for a long time"; though views vary on the service – some call it "high-pressure", others appreciate the "advice on appropriate looks" – all agree the contemporary-styled goods are "high-quality"; just "keep a stiff upper lip when you pay."

☑ Broadway Panhandler
27 | - | 21 | M

G Vill | 65 E. Eighth St. (bet. B'way & University Pl.) | N/R/W to 8th St. | 212-966-3434 | 866-266-5927 | www.broadwaypanhandler.com
Your "culinary skills automatically increase upon entering" this "one-stop-shopping" "foodies' mecca" that's newly relocated from SoHo to Greenwich Village; supporters say it stocks "the best range of prices for good pots and pans", "top-of-the-line staples", "fun gadgets", bakeware and "more cookie cutters than you can imagine", and they're all sold by a "knowledgeable staff" "that's as sharp as the cutlery."

Brooklyn Collective �androidM
- | - | - | M

Red Hook | 198 Columbia St. (Sackett St.) | Brooklyn | F/G to Carroll St. | 718-596-6231 | www.brooklyncollective.com
Red Hook may be out of the way, but once you hit this boutique/gallery, you won't want to rush back to the Big Apple, as there's hip womenswear aplenty (from Tessa Phillips' camis to Milton Carter's witty tees), art and Brazilian music to hook you into settling down in a gilded chair; as the name implies, much of the "interesting" inventory, which includes photos, jewelry and guitar straps, comes from local talent.

Brooklyn General Store 🛍 Ⓜ — | — | — | E

Carroll Gdns | 128 Union St. (Hicks St.) | Brooklyn | F/G to Carroll St. |
718-237-7753 | www.brooklyngeneral.com

Designed by and for crafty moms (it offers after-hours knitting, crocheting, quilting, sewing and spinning classes every weeknight), this
"cute" and "friendly" West Carroll Gardens nook overflows with "interesting" specialty yarns, vintage fabrics, needlework notions, toys
and clothing for women and kids; as similarly countrified knit competitors spring up all over town, though, the few who've found it feel it's
"not that unique."

Brooklyn Industries ◑ — 20 | 21 | 21 | M

NEW Chelsea | 161 Eighth Ave. (18th St.) | A/C/E/L to 14th St./8th Ave. |
212-206-0477

SoHo | 286 Lafayette St. (bet. Jersey & Prince Sts.) | B/D/F/V to B'way/
Lafayette St. | 212-219-0862

NEW W Vill | 500 Hudson St. (Christopher St.) | 1 to Christopher St./
Sheridan Sq. | 212-206-1488

Boerum Hill | 100 Smith St. (bet. Atlantic Ave. & Pacific St.) | Brooklyn |
F/G to Bergen St. | 718-596-3986

Park Slope | 206 Fifth Ave. (Union St.) | Brooklyn | M/R to Union St. |
718-789-2764

Park Slope | 328 Seventh Ave. (9th St.) | Brooklyn | F to 7th Ave. |
718-788-5250

Williamsburg | 162 Bedford Ave. (bet. N. 8th & 9th Sts.) | Brooklyn | L to
Bedford Ave. | 718-486-6464

Williamsburg | 184 Broadway (Driggs Ave.) | Brooklyn | J/M/Z to
Marcy Ave. | 718-218-9166

800-318-6061 | www.brooklynindustries.com

Now eight shops strong, this "funky" urban brand has the right inventory to keep "any shallow-pocketed hipster happy", with artist-
designed "limited-edition" silk-screened tees, "cool" borough-pride
hoodies "for the Brooklyn lover in you", "sturdy", "unique" messenger
bags, belts, shoes and a line of premium denim that can "handle the
wear and tear of the city"; P.S. the "cute staff" is "always helpful."

Brooklyn Museum Shop Ⓜ — 22 | 19 | 18 | M

Prospect Hts | Brooklyn Museum | 200 Eastern Pkwy. (Washington Ave.) |
Brooklyn | 2/3 to Eastern Pkwy. | 718-501-6259 | www.brooklynmuseum.org

"A shopping spree grows in Brooklyn" brag boosters of this "excellent
museum shop" proffering a "wonderful hodgepodge" of merchandise
including "quality materials thematically linked to the exhibitions",
"wonderful" jewelry and crafts "from around the world" and "creative
toys", all "imaginatively presented"; prices are "reasonable", and its
"original selection" makes it "worth a trip."

☑ Brooks Brothers — 24 | 22 | 22 | E

E 40s | 346 Madison Ave. (44th St.) | 4/5/6/7/S to 42nd St./Grand Central |
212-682-8800

E 50s | 666 Fifth Ave. (bet. 52nd & 53rd Sts.) | E/V to 5th Ave./53rd St. |
212-261-9440 ◑

TriBeCa | 1 Liberty Plaza (B'way) | R/W to Cortlandt St. | 212-267-2400
800-274-1815 | www.brooksbrothers.com

"Classic with a capital 'C'", this "institution" remains the "gold standard in corporate wear" according to "button-down" sorts who seek
out these chain links for "well-made" business suits, dress shirts and

other "board room–appropriate" attire proffered by a "reliably old-school", "courteous" staff; the women's department "feels like an afterthought" to some and draws complaints about "stodgy" styles, but if you're looking to "channel your inner preppy", this "Wasp heaven" is the place to go.

Brookstone
| 21 | 21 | 20 | E |

Garment Dist | Manhattan Mall | 901 Sixth Ave. (bet. 32nd & 33rd Sts.) | B/D/F/N/Q/R/V/W to 34th St./Herald Sq. | 212-947-2144 ●
Seaport | South Street Seaport | 18 Fulton St. (bet. Front & South Sts.) | 2/3/4/5/A/C/J/M/Z to Fulton St./B'way/Nassau | 212-344-8108 ●
W 50s | 16 W. 50th St. (bet. 5th & 6th Aves.) | B/D/F/V to 47-50th Sts./Rockefeller Ctr. | 212-262-3237 ●
W 50s | 20 W. 57th St. (bet. 5th & 6th Aves.) | F to 57th St. | 212-245-1405
NEW Staten Island | Staten Island Mall | 2655 Richmond Ave. (bet. Platinum Ave. & Richmond Hill Rd.) | 718-982-1525 ●
800-846-3000 | www.brookstone.com

Jam-packed with "tantalizing" toys that "dazzle the eye", this "fun novelty store" chain is perfect "for that quirky gift" thanks to scads of "unnecessary but enticing gadgets" and "oddball products" "you didn't even know existed" ("battery-powered nose-hair remover", anyone?); it seems "most people don't go there to buy as much as they do to play" and browse, though, or just to "sit on the massage chair" and unwind.

NEW Brunello Cucinelli ●
| - | - | - | VE |

W Vill | 379 Bleecker St. (bet. Charles & Perry Sts.) | 1 to Christopher St./Sheridan Sq. | 212-627-9202 | www.brunellocucinelli.it

Imagine a rustic house in Umbria complete with white brick walls, wood floors, a twig-filled fireplace and state-of-the-art flat-screen TV, and you'll get a sense of this chic Bleecker Street shop for him and her; cashmere rules the day in plush sweaters, finely tuned skirts, tailored jackets and strictly cut trousers, all with the kind of attention to detail that reflects the quality and warm, gracious service you pay (dearly) for.

Bu and the Duck
| 26 | 25 | 22 | E |

TriBeCa | 106 Franklin St. (bet. Church St. & W. B'way) | 1 to Franklin St. | 212-431-9226 | www.buandtheduck.com

"Unusual finds and splurges" abound at this "cute" TriBeCa mecca for "hip parents with cool kids", where "outrageous" prices and a sometimes "chilly" sales staff fail to deter determined shoppers from snapping up the "truly beautiful and unique", vintage-inspired children's clothes and accessories, handmade rag dolls and European shoes by the armful.

Ⓩ Buccellati Ⓢ
| 29 | - | 27 | VE |

E 50s | 46 E. 57th St. (bet. Madison & Park Aves.) | 4/5/6/F/N/R/W to 59th St./Lexington Ave. | 212-308-2900 | 877-462-8223 | www.buccellati.com

This old-world Milanese manufacturer, which recently moved back to its original East 57th Street location, is renowned for statusy, "substantial" and "strikingly beautiful" sterling silver serving pieces, flatware and tableware that is voted the Tops in this *Survey*'s Home/Garden category, along with "magnificent" jewelry like "great rings"; "the two words that come to mind when you examine the fine work" will be "wow", immediately followed by "ow" when you peek at the "astronomical prices."

	QUALITY	DISPLAY	SERVICE	COST

Buckler
	–	–	–	E

Meatpacking | 13 Gansevoort St. (bet. 8th Ave. & Hudson St.) | A/C/E/L to 14th St./8th Ave. | 212-255-1596 | www.andrewbuckler.com

NYC blokes fulfill their buried rocker tendencies at this garage/band-room of a store in the subterranean surrounds of an old Meatpacking District factory; feel like Franz Ferdinand or Tommy Lee (all fans of the brand) as you hang for a while playing the drums or flipping through the racks of jeans and leather jackets evoking that cooler-than-thou vibe.

☑ Build-A-Bear Workshop ◗
	22	26	23	M

E 40s | 565 Fifth Ave. (46th St.) | B/D/F/V to 47-50th Sts./Rockefeller Ctr. | 212-871-7080
NEW **Staten Island** | Staten Island Mall | 2655 Richmond Ave. (bet. Platinum Ave. & Richmond Hill Rd.) | 718-698-1477
877-789-2327 | www.buildabear.com

"Kids love bringing their bear to life" at the Midtown and Staten Island branches of this "cute concept" chain where they can have a "great-quality" toy animal stuffed, stitched, fluffed and dressed "exactly to their liking" in "novel" outfits like NYPD uniforms; if Grizzly Adams types growl it's "fun to do once – you spend a fortune very quickly" – soft touches shrug "what the heck, seems worth it"; N.B. older girls can create dolls at the adjoining Friends 2B Made shop.

Built by Wendy
	–	–	–	E

Little Italy | 7 Centre Market Pl. (bet. Broome & Grand Sts.) | 6 to Spring St. | 212-925-6538
Williamsburg | 46 N. Sixth St. (bet. Kent & Wythe Aves.) | Brooklyn | L to Bedford Ave. | 718-384-2882
www.builtbywendy.com

You'd expect a convergence of cool at the crossroads of Little Italy, NoLita and SoHo – and in this pale blue gem, you get it, along with the "hipster attitude" of designer-owner Wendy Mullin's edgy women and men's sportswear; bargain-hunters can hit her Williamsburg branch for deals on older collections and clearance items too.

Bulgari
	28	27	26	VE

E 50s | 3 W. 57th St. (bet. 5th & Madison Aves.) | F to 57th St. | 212-315-9000
E 60s | 783 Madison Ave. (bet. 66th & 67th Sts.) | 6 to 68th St. | 212-717-2300 🅂
800-285-4274 | www.bulgari.com

"Showy", "distinctive" gold and gemstone jewelry, "unique" watches, small silver gifts and leather accessories are the luxury wares purveyed by this family-owned Italian firm with two East Side venues; sybarites sigh the only thing that tarnishes the experience is "extraordinary prices"; N.B. as we go to press, the 57th Street store is slated to move back to its original flagship locale at 730 Fifth Avenue.

Burberry
	27	24	22	VE

E 50s | 9 E. 57th St. (bet. 5th & Madison Aves.) | 4/5/6/F/N/R/W to 59th St./Lexington Ave. | 212-371-5010
SoHo | 131 Spring St. (bet. Greene & Wooster Sts.) | 6 to Spring St. | 212-925-9300
www.burberry.com

While they still sell "the best trenches this side of the pond", "they've come a long way from rainwear" at this historic British brand, whose

Midtown and SoHo stores, with their "pitch-perfect layouts" and "lovely" if slightly "snooty" staff, supply men, women and even pets with "awesome" "basics and trendy collection pieces" sporting the familiar black, white and beige pattern (the Prorsum line is "as hip as plaid gets"); cynics cry it's "almost a cliché" – "like wearing a neon bulb for the status-oriented" – but none dispute that the "well-made" merch "measures up" to the "sky-high prices"; N.B. 57th Street also stocks children's clothing.

Burlington Coat Factory ●

15	9	8	I

Chelsea | 707 Sixth Ave. (bet. 22nd & 23rd Sts.) | F/V to 23rd St. | 212-229-2247
Downtown | Atlantic Ctr. | 625 Atlantic Ave. (bet. Ft. Greene Pl. & S. Portland Ave.) | Brooklyn | 2/3/4/5/B/D/M/N/Q/R to Atlantic Ave. | 718-622-4057
Staten Island | 1801 South Ave. (West Shore Expwy.) | 718-982-0300
800-444-2628 | www.coat.com

Calling all "bargain queens", kings and princelings to this discount chain, which carries "not just coats" – though those "really are their forte" – but "decent" adult, baby and kids' apparel, shoes and linens at "cheap prices"; but with its "dreary" decor, "piles of unrelated merchandise" and plethora of "last year's styles", it resembles "an indoor swap meet", and that – plus the "unhelpful assistants" – make naysayers nix it as "not worth the hunt."

Burton Store

25	23	22	E

SoHo | 106 Spring St. (Mercer St.) | C/E to Spring St. | 212-966-8068 | www.burton.com

"If you snowboard or ski", you'll "think you're in Arctic heaven" at this "cool concept store in SoHo", the sports manufacturer's showcase; in a space that mimics the slopes with tilted flooring, they've got "the best gear" for snowboarding, plus "the most innovative, cutting-edge clothes anywhere"; staffers "know your questions before you ask", but don't take their word for it – put the goods to the test in the 20-below-zero fitting room.

Butik Ⓜ

-	-	-	E

W Vill | 605 Hudson St. (bet. Bethune & W. 12th Sts.) | A/C/E/L to 14th St./8th Ave. | 212-367-8014

The name means 'shop' in old Danish, and that's exactly what supermodel Helena Christensen and pal Leif Sigersen have created in this cozy boutique, which brings the Scandinavian spirit to the West Village with an eclectic mix of "bohemian bric-a-brac", including antique furniture, modern and vintage clothing, flowers and organic chocolates that are all "beautifully presented."

Butter

▽ 23	23	17	E

Downtown | 389 Atlantic Ave. (bet. Bond & Hoyt Sts.) | Brooklyn | A/C/G to Hoyt/Schermerhorn Sts. | 718-260-9033

"Everything is breathtaking" at this newly renovated and expanded Atlantic Avenue destination owned by stylemeister-sisters Robin and Eva Weiss agree admirers who melt at the "exquisitely edited selection" of "unique must-haves" from Dries Van Noten, Henry Beguelin, Martin Margiela and Rick Owens, all arranged by color, along with super-"stylish" jewelry and shoes in a "gallerylike" setting; but the price-sensitive pout that the "lovely" looks are too "expensive for words", "especially in Downtown Brooklyn", griping it's the sort of shop that's "best left to SoHo."

Butter and Eggs

▽ 22 | 24 | 23 | E

TriBeCa | 83 W. Broadway (bet. Chambers & Warren Sts.) | 1/2/3 to Chambers St. | 212-676-0235 | www.butterandeggs.com

The "very friendly and organized owner" of this "lovely" TriBeCa boutique fills it with a "well-chosen selection" of "adorable home accessories" like pillows, lamps, candlesticks and "modern furniture" including sofas and tables; the name pays homage to the area's history as a dairy district at the turn of the century.

☒ buybuy BABY ●

23 | 21 | 19 | M

Chelsea | 270 Seventh Ave. (bet. 25th & 26th Sts.) | 1 to 23rd St. | 917-344-1555 | www.buybuybaby.com

"Bed Bath & Beyond meets the baby world" at Chelsea's "one-stop shop" "wonderland" – a "welcome suburban intrusion" that "covers all categories with ease", offering the "broadest assortment" of clothing, furniture, gear, toys and supplies; throw in a well-oiled, "awesome registry" process, a staff that "knows their products (how refreshing)" and prices "for everyone's wallet" and "all you want to do is buy, buy, buy."

By Boe
(fka Annika Inez)

- | - | - | M

E 70s | 243 E. 78th St. (bet. 2nd & 3rd Aves.) | 6 to 77th St. | 212-717-9644 | ☒
NEW **SoHo** | 172 Prince St. (bet. Sullivan & Thompson Sts.) | C/E to Spring St. | 212-226-5200
www.byboe.com

Though the name recently changed, this "cute", understated East 70s shop and its new SoHo offshoot still keep devotees coming back for Swedish designer Annika Salame's clean-lined, simple jewelry – from a sliver of a gold crescent pendant and thin, wire-styled earrings to chunky vintage bead necklaces and colored enamel chains; though quantities are limited, the reasonably priced gems and accessories are always changing, and the service is laid-back.

Caché

18 | 19 | 18 | E

E 40s | 805 Third Ave. (bet. 49th & 50th Sts.) | 6 to 51st St. | 212-588-8719
W 50s | The Shops at Columbus Circle, Time Warner Ctr. | 10 Columbus Circle, ground fl. (bet. 58th & 60th Sts.) | 1/A/B/C/D to 59th St./Columbus Circle | 212-823-9693 ●
Staten Island | Staten Island Mall | 2655 Richmond Ave. (bet. Platinum Ave. & Richmond Hill Rd.) | 718-370-8843 ●
800-788-2224 | www.cache.com

Make a beeline for this "black-tie" bonanza to emulate your favorite *Dynasty* diva via "flashy", spangly, "dressy" eveningwear in "all lengths, all colors and all styles", all "on the pricy side"; though it's a standard chain-stop on the hunt for a "great prom dress", "larger-size women" chide "not everyone is a size 2 or 4."

Cadeau

▽ 25 | 23 | 23 | E

NoLita | 254 Elizabeth St. (bet. Houston & Prince Sts.) | N/R/W to Prince St. | 212-674-5747 | 866-622-3322 | www.cadeaumaternity.com

Expectees who can't part with their pre-pregnancy style head to this "amazing" NoLita maternity shop, a labor of love from Barneys alum

Emilia Fabricant offering some of the "most beautiful, well-made" and on-trend clothing for those all-important nine months; yes, the "chic" Italian garments are "expensive", but moms-to-be believe that "feeling hip" "rather than frumpy" makes the dent in the wallet "worthwhile."

Calling All Pets

24 | 16 | 25 | M

E 70s | 301 E. 76th St. (bet. 1st & 2nd Aves.) | 6 to 77th St. | 212-734-7051
E 80s | 1590 York Ave. (bet. 83rd & 84th Sts.) | 4/5/6 to 86th St. | 212-249-7387

"Loved by all two- and four-legged critters in the neighborhood", this "cozy" UES duo boasts the "nicest", most "informed" staff as well as the "best selection of top pet products" at "good prices"; in addition to their "awesome" delivery service, they can also special-order birthday cakes and cookies to help your creatures celebrate in style.

Calvin Klein

25 | 26 | 22 | VE

E 60s | 654 Madison Ave. (60th St.) | N/R/W to 5th Ave./59th St. | 212-292-9000 | 877-256-7373

The "austere, sanitized rooms are a perfect showcase for the clean lines" of the "subtle", "sexy, American" men- and womenswear offered at this trendsetting designer flagship in the East 60s; "as a New Yorker, you should always dress in black and they have plenty" of it – though Francisco Costa, who took over a few years ago, has added color to the clothes; the Calvin clan also "loves to browse" the "wonderful home section", aided by "salespeople who help when needed."

Calvin Klein Underwear ◗

21 | 19 | 17 | M

SoHo | 104 Prince St. (bet. Greene & Mercer Sts.) | N/R/W to Prince St. | 212-274-1639 | 877-258-7646
W 50s | The Shops at Columbus Circle, Time Warner Ctr. | 10 Columbus Circle, ground fl. (bet. 58th & 60th Sts.) | 1/A/B/C/D to 59th St./Columbus Circle | 212-246-8200
www.cku.com

"If you're comfortable in your 'Calvins'" head to this pair of minimalist shops in SoHo and the Time Warner Center kitted out with captivating photos of scantily clad models and start from the first layer, picking up "sexy" "casual-to-dressy" undies for men and women, plus "nicely styled" sleepwear; the "staff makes you feel welcome" and "prices are reasonable", so acolytes are in-Kleined to "definitely return."

NEW Calvin Tran

– | – | – | E

NoLita | 246 Mulberry St. (bet. Prince & Spring Sts.) | 6 to Spring St. | 212-431-2576 | www.calvintran.com

The Zen-garden aura at this NoLita boutique invites shoppers to contemplate the "chic and refined" threads of this young designer, whose "terrific staff is ready to help but not harass" the female clientele (which has included Iman, Drew Barrymore and Brooke Shields); patrons praise the "pieces that can go just about anywhere", be they "well-priced" slinky gowns, ruffly face-framing jackets, Red Engine denim or "multifunctional" garments, like shirts that turn into skirts.

Calypso

23 | 24 | 18 | E

NEW E 60s | 815 Madison Ave. (68th St.) | 6 to 68th St. | 212-585-0310
E 70s | 935 Madison Ave. (74th St.) | 6 to 77th St. | 212-535-4100
(continued)

(continued)

Calypso

NoLita | 280 Mott St. (bet. Houston & Prince Sts.) | B/D/F/V to B'way/Lafayette St. | 212-965-0990
NEW **SoHo** | 191 Lafayette St. (Broome St.) | B/D/F/V to B'way/Lafayette St. | 212-941-6512
SoHo | 424 Broome St. (bet. Crosby & Lafayette Sts.) | 6 to Spring St. | 212-274-0449
NEW **TriBeCa** | 137 W. Broadway (bet. Duane & Thomas Sts.) | 1/2/3 to Chambers St. | 212-608-2222
W Vill | 654 Hudson St. (bet. Gansevoort & W. 13th Sts.) | A/C/E/L to 14th St./8th Ave. | 646-638-3000
www.calypso-celle.com

No "matter which outpost" of this "dreamy" boutique you visit, you'll uncover "boho chic by the boatload" with the help of a "gorgeous", "caring" staff; owner-designer Christiane Celle creates a "visual feast", "dressing" each shop "like a rainbow" – "you feel the beat of the islands" as you sift through the "breezy", "floaty" tunics and dresses, "au courant" cashmere sweaters and "girlie" fashions from "hard-to-find" labels that walk the line between "urban vintage and tropical exoticism"; even her sexy trademark "perfumes brighten up" your mood; N.B. the 424 Broome Street branch is now a Calypso outlet.

Calypso Bijoux

∇ 25 | 26 | 22 | E

NoLita | 252 Mott St. (bet. Houston & Prince Sts.) | N/R/W to Prince St. | 212-334-9730 | www.calypso-celle.com

This NoLita jewel in the Christiane Celle network of "great, hip stores" for everything from resort wear to home furnishings is "a great place to send your boyfriend for a winning present", whether it's a costume or semiprecious piece; though on the "expensive" side, "there are some great finds" in the high-end selection from around the world, including signature silver or gold ID disc necklaces that can be custom-engraved.

Calypso Enfant & Bebe

26 | 23 | 21 | E

SoHo | 426 Broome St. (bet. Crosby & Lafayette Sts.) | 6 to Spring St. | 212-966-3234

Calypso Kids & Home

NEW **SoHo** | 407 Broome St. (bet. Centre & Lafayette Sts.) | 6 to Spring St. | 212-941-9700
www.calypso-celle.com

The apple doesn't fall far from the tree at these "beautiful" Downtown kids' offshoots of the "trendy" Calypso women's empire; duck into the Enfant & Bebe boutique for "mini-me" versions of the signature beachy duds and "amazing cashmere sweaters", then skip over to the new Kids & Home hub on the NoLita-SoHo border for more high-end childrenswear, plus furniture finds and limited-edition toys.

Calypso Home ●

- | - | - | E

NoLita | 199 Lafayette St. (Broome St.) | 6 to Spring St. | 212-925-6200 | www.calypso-celle.com

If you want to "channel St. Barts' style into your home", hit this "gorgeous" NoLita shop, part of Christiane Celle's wildly popular, ever-expanding Caribbean-inspired consortium; it's a well-edited showcase for handmade wooden furniture and international accessories like gold leather ottomans, Mexican silver bowls, snake quilts from India,

Italian pottery and colorful cashmere throws, plus the "relaxing" space makes fans feel as if they are "in a spa", so they "want to move in."

Camera Land

22	15	23	E

E 50s | 575 Lexington Ave. (bet. 51st & 52nd Sts.) | 6 to 51st St. | 212-753-5128 | 866-967-8427 | www.cameralandny.com

"There are not that many real camera stores" of the "traditional neighborhood" variety left and this "surprisingly price-competitive" East 50s standby is one of "the best NY can offer" attest photo fiends; the "professional, competent" staff provides "great service and advice", while the space boasts "the latest" equipment to purchase or rent, digital printing kiosks and a gallery of "attractive picture frames."

Camilla Dietz Bergeron

–	–	–	E

E 60s | 818 Madison Ave., 4th fl. (bet. 68th & 69th Sts.) | 6 to 68th St. | 212-794-9100 | www.cdbltd.com

This Madison Avenue charmer, tucked away on the fourth floor, is so "personal" it's like "family" to fans who turn to the owners for their "exquisite taste" and "high level of knowledge" when looking for "beautiful" estate and antique jewelry with "pizzazz" from Cartier, Van Cleef & Arpels, Paul Flato, Jean Schlumberger and Mauboussin, as well as the eponymous designer's own pieces; N.B. by appointment only.

Camouflage

24	24	22	E

Chelsea | 139 Eighth Ave. (17th St.) | A/C/E/L to 14th St./8th Ave. | 212-691-1750
Chelsea | 141 Eighth Ave. (17th St.) | A/C/E/L to 14th St./8th Ave. | 212-741-9118

A "neighborhood asset" since the '70s, these Chelsea twins project sophistication with their "nice mix" of men's dress-up-or-down designers like Etro and Marc Jacobs that are always "of the moment" but also "thoughtfully chosen" "with an eye to what a [regular] guy wants to wear"; N.B. the branch on the 'uptown' side of Eighth Avenue carries more familiar labels, while the 'downtown' site's sportswear is edgier.

Camper

23	21	17	E

SoHo | 125 Prince St. (Wooster St.) | N/R/W to Prince St. | 212-358-1841 | www.camper.com

"Love the way" the "buttery leather" "styles are laid out" – they're so "easy to see and touch" at this "nicely designed" SoHo stomping ground showcasing his-and-hers "match-everything shoes" from the "eccentric Spanish label"; "hipsters with deep pockets" "don't come here looking for high heels and pointy toes", but they do come for "unique Euro" looks with "splashes of color and whimsy", sold by a staff that's "cool" but still "helpful."

Canal Hi-Fi

16	10	13	M

Chinatown | 319 Canal St. (bet. Greene & Mercer Sts.) | 6/J/M/N/Q/R/W/Z to Canal St. | 212-925-6575 | www.canalhifi.com

"Typifying Canal Street's bargain-basement reputation" for "cheap electronics", this "mom-and-pop" fixture features "help that can lead you to the right choices" in DJ equipment and home-audio components (and since some "stuff is connected", you might get a demo); still, the cash-conscious caution you'd "better know how much you should be paying before going" so you can "haggle to get the best bargains."

	QUALITY	DISPLAY	SERVICE	COST

Canal Jean Company ●

	17	13	13	M

G Vill | 718 Broadway (bet. Washington & Waverly Pls.) | N/R/W to 8th St. | 212-226-3663

Flatbush | 2236 Nostrand Ave. (bet. Aves. H & I) | Brooklyn | 2/5 to Brooklyn College/Flatbush Ave. | 718-421-7590

"You'll find a funky selection" of "eclectic jeans" and "everything you need for your wardrobe, from lingerie to shoes", to "unique" used clothing at this Village-Flatbush duo; it's "awesome" for "teenagers" on the hunt for "trendy" threads, yielding "great buys if you dig for them"; but the less-entrenched declare that while the Broadway sibling "used to be great" in its former location, it's "lost the panache of the past."

☑ Canine Styles

	26	25	21	VE

E 60s | 830 Lexington Ave. (bet. 63rd & 64th Sts.) | F to Lexington Ave./ 63rd St. | 212-838-2064

E 80s | 1195 Lexington Ave. (bet. 81st & 82nd Sts.) | 6 to 77th St. | 212-472-9440 ⧄

G Vill | 43 Greenwich Ave. (bet. Charles & Perry Sts.) | A/B/C/D/E/F/V to W. 4th St. | 212-352-8591 ●

www.caninestyles.com

The "cute" Downtown pet shop for the "style-conscious" formerly known as Fetch recently joined forces with this East 80s canine couture club – and even spawned a new East 60s offspring, all offering a "beautiful selection" of "unique" goods for beloved bowwows; the vibe is still "Gucci for poochie" so expect to "dish out a fortune" for "fancy beds", "adorable" catwalk-worthy "doggy duds" and "superb" toys and "colorful collars and leashes."

Cantaloup

	22	19	18	E

E 70s | 1036 Lexington Ave. (74th St.) | 6 to 77th St. | 212-249-3566

Cantaloup: Destination Denim ⧄

E 70s | 1359 Second Ave. (72nd St.) | 6 to 77th St. | 212-288-3569

Cantaloup Luxe ●

NEW **E 70s** | 1217 Third Ave. (bet. 70th & 71st Sts.) | 6 to 68th St. | 212-249-1241

www.cantaloupny.com

A "cute stop" for "chic" clothing, this "friendly" East 70s trio appointed with antique tables and chandeliers ap-peels to women with a fine-tuned sense of "their own style"; the Destination Denim shop boasts an LA vibe, stocked with "all the jeans" you could possibly need, including "fun", of-the-moment labels like Earnest Sewn, Rock & Republic and True Religion, while the Lexington Avenue standby and new Luxe shop carry lots of "unique pieces from the trendiest up-and-coming designers."

Canyon Beachwear ●

	26	18	21	E

E 60s | 1136 Third Ave. (66th St.) | 6 to 68th St. | 917-432-0732 | 800-863-6681 | www.canyonbeachwear.com

If you have a "hard time finding swimwear to fit" and "nice cover-up choices", this East 60s "nirvana" "is the place to go" agree the sea-and-sand set who promise "you won't feel intimidated" here; the staff is "attentive" and "knowledgeable", bringing you a "wonderful selection" of the "latest styles" that "flatters even the most bathing-suit averse"; it's "worth every penny", and what's more, you "leave feeling like Elle Macpherson."

	QUALITY	DISPLAY	SERVICE	COST

Capezio

| | 24 | 18 | 19 | M |

E 60s | 136 E. 61st St. (Lexington Ave.) | 4/5/6/F/N/R/W to 59th St./
Lexington Ave. | 212-758-8833
E 90s | 1651 Third Ave., 3rd fl. (bet. 92nd & 93rd Sts.) | 6 to 96th St. |
212-348-7210
W 50s | 1650 Broadway, 2nd fl. (51st St.) | 1 to 50th St. | 212-245-2130 ◑
W 50s | 1776 Broadway, 2nd fl. (57th St.) | 1/A/B/C/D to 59th St./
Columbus Circle | 212-586-5140
877-532-6237 | www.capeziodance.com

"If you dance or want to look like you do", give this "legendary" "life-saver" a twirl; sure it's twinkle-toe "heaven", offering "work-out clothes that dancers crave", with "fine-quality" footwear and leotards in every "color you need for any show", but the "great gear" also "wows" "stylish gym-goers who want to look sexy while sweating."

Capitol Fishing Tackle Co. ⊠

| | – | – | – | M |

Garment Dist | 132 W. 36th St. (bet. B'way & 7th Ave.) | B/D/F/N/Q/R/V/W
to 34th St./Herald Sq. | 212-929-6132 | 800-528-0853 |
www.capitolfishing.com

Reeling in tyros and experts alike for nearly four decades, this vintage Chelsea anglers' paradise recently relocated to the Garment District but brought its refreshingly raffish neon sign along for the ride; according to fin fans who hook "excellent equipment for salt-" and fresh-water fishing – from Penn to Shimano – from its well-stocked shelves and appreciate its staff of *Old Man and the Sea* types who dole out tackle tips, it remains the "best in New York" City.

Cappellini

| | – | – | – | VE |

SoHo | 152 Wooster St. (Houston St.) | N/R/W to Prince St. |
212-620-7953 | www.cappellini.it

Decked out in floor-to-ceiling red, this SoHo space showcases modern chairs, sofas, beds, dressers and lighting accessories, all of which are made by the venerable Italian design house that was founded in the 1930s; "cutting-edge" fashion for your home comes at a "large price", but when you "fall in love" with this furniture as some of our respondents did, cost seems inconsequential.

Capucine ◑

| | – | – | – | E |

TriBeCa | 20 Harrison St. (bet. Greenwich & Hudson Sts.) | 1/2/3 to
Chambers St. | 212-219-4030

Svelte trendseekers as well as expectant women unwilling to see their style vanish along with their waistlines count on Capucine Vacher's TriBeCa shop to keep them in top fashion form; the first camp covets finds from lines like Diane von Furstenberg while pregos scout out "beautiful, original" maternity clothing from labels like Belly Basics, Home Mummy and yes, DvF too; rounding out the mix: kids clothing, furniture, bedding and home furnishings.

NEW Caravan ◑

| | ▽ 20 | 24 | 16 | M |

NoHo | 2 Great Jones St. (B'way) | 6 to Astor Pl. | 212-260-8189 |
www.shopcaravan.com

Embrace the vagabond spirit at this airy NoHo shop (the new, station-ary home of a "moving store" on wheels), where indie designers like Sretsis, Rojas and Lincoln Maynes showcase their "beautiful clothing" for both sexes in a "very original, very chic" high-ceilinged space; you can also catch up with these fashionable gypsies in their original van (weekends-only), or at the by-appointment offshoot at 128 E. 91st St.

Cardeology ◑
19 | 15 | 15 | I

E 80s | 1200 Lexington Ave. (bet. 81st & 82nd Sts.) | 4/5/6 to 86th St. | 212-734-8170
W 70s | 314 Columbus Ave. (bet. 74th & 75th Sts.) | B/C to 72nd St. | 212-579-9310
W 80s | 452 Amsterdam Ave. (bet. 81st & 82nd Sts.) | 1 to 79th St. | 212-873-2491

Thank god there's "no Hallmark here" exhale admirers of this "cute" stationery trio carrying a "creative selection of cards and gifts" ranging from journals and calendars to Crabtree & Evelyn toiletries.

Carlos Miele
– | – | – | E

Meatpacking | 408 W. 14th St. (bet. 9th Ave. & Washington St.) | A/C/E/L to 14th St./8th Ave. | 646-336-6642 | www.carlosmiele.com.br

It's not only the São Paulo sexpots who dig this Brazilian designer's Meatpacking shop with its "amazing" curvy walls and rows of "gorgeous" dresses that "fit like a dream"; NYC fashionistas also flock here for the red-carpet–worthy eveningwear, stylish suits, shoes and clutches.

⊠ Carlyle Custom Convertibles
26 | 19 | 24 | E

Chelsea | 122 W. 18th St. (bet. 6th & 7th Aves.) | 1/2/3 to 14th St. | 212-675-3212
E 60s | 1056 Third Ave. (bet. 62nd & 63rd Sts.) | 4/5/6/F/N/R/W to 59th St./Lexington Ave. | 212-838-1525
www.carlylesofa.com

Sellers of sofa beds since the '60s, this Chelsea and UES duo has a "reputation for being the best of any convertibles" available, with a "great selection", "good upholstery", "excellent mattresses" and "lovely fabrics", as well as an option to work with your own material; the only thing about these sleepers that will keep you awake is the "high price."

⊠ Carolina Herrera
28 | 27 | 25 | VE

E 70s | 954 Madison Ave. (75th St.) | 6 to 77th St. | 212-249-6552 | www.carolinaherrera.com

"Get dressed to go" to the "most elegant house of chic on [upper] Madison Avenue", where you'll encounter "refined, can't-go-wrong" dresses and suits in a "classic style like the designer herself", as well as an expanded floor of wedding gowns for "brides who want the best"; the "ladies who lunch" also love the "luxurious" alterations process and "personal service (they know your name every time)", which help offset the "ouch"-inducing prices.

Carol's Daughter ◑
24 | 22 | 21 | M

Harlem | 24 W. 125th St. (bet. 5th & Lenox Aves.) | 2/3 to 125th St. | 212-828-6757
NEW **Downtown** | Atlantic Terminal Mall | 139 Flatbush Ave. (bet. Atlantic & 4th Aves.) | Brooklyn | 2/3/4/5/B/D/M/N/Q/R to Atlantic Ave. | 718-622-4514
Ft Greene | 1 S. Elliot Pl. (DeKalb Ave.) | Brooklyn | G to Fulton St. | 718-857-0282
877-540-2101 | www.carolsdaughter.com

Owner Lisa Price started out by concocting lotions in her kitchen sink for friends and family, and her "positive-vibe" Fort Greene original shop and Harlem offshoot continue the tradition with homemade "natural products that are great for glowing skin" and making tresses "do what they are supposed to do"; fans like Will Smith and Jay-Z have invested big bucks in the homegrown brand – and yes, Oprah loves it too; N.B. the Flatbush Avenue mall store is new.

Caron Paris

25 | 22 | 20 | E

E 60s | 675 Madison Ave. (bet. 61st & 62nd Sts.) | 4/5/6/F/N/R/W to 59th St./Lexington Ave. | 212-319-4888

"Sensuous" "old-school scents for those who love the classics" are showcased at this *"très elegant"* and "intoxicating" Madison Avenue offshoot of the over one-century-old Paris fragrance house; a chic gray-and-gold chandeliered setting is the backdrop for the brand's 34 "pricey" perfumes as well as Lierac skin- and haircare products.

☑ Cartier

29 | 28 | 26 | VE

E 50s | 653 Fifth Ave. (52nd St.) | E/V to 5th Ave./53rd St. | 212-753-0111
E 60s | 828 Madison Ave. (69th St.) | 6 to 68th St. | 212-472-6400 Ⓢ
800-227-8437 | www.cartier.com

In 1917, Pierre Cartier traded a string of pearls plus $100 for a Fifth Avenue neo-Renaissance mansion, which is still the U.S. headquarters for this jeweler that's joined by a renovated East 60s spin-off; an "extraordinary" staff purveys the "best baubles", bangles and beads, watches, silver *objets* and stationery, all "status symbols" of "classic elegance"; sure, you "shell out big bucks for small things", but "nothing says 'I love you' like that red box."

Cassina USA

- | - | - | VE

E 50s | 155 E. 56th St. (bet. Lexington & 3rd Aves.) | 4/5/6/F/N/R/W to 59th St./Lexington Ave. | 212-245-2121 | 800-770-3568 | www.cassinausa.com

For those who feel that "classic is best", this sexy, high-voltage red-and-white East 50s showroom for the famed Italian furniture manufacturer features The Masters Collection from industry icons like Le Corbusier and Charlotte Perriand, as well as pieces from newer luminaries like Piero Lissoni and Philippe Starck; although prices range "from high to extra high", enthusiasts applaud the "impressive quality" and a buying option that promises 10-day delivery of select beds, chairs, lounges and tables straight from The Boot.

Castor & Pollux ●Ⓜ

- | - | - | E

W Vill | 238 W. 10th St. (bet. Bleecker & Hudson Sts.) | 1 to Christopher St./Sheridan Sq. | 212-645-6572 | www.castorandpolluxstore.com

Owner-designer Kerrilynn Pamer moved her "lovely little" women's boutique from Prospect Heights into a West Village space that's twice the size but no less charming thanks to its glam retro vibe; choose from hip-girl goodies from Filippa K, Mint, 3.1 Phillip Lim and the proprietress' own collection – and don't forget to peruse the display cases filled with jewelry and beauty finds like Poppy King's coveted Lipstick Queen line.

Casual Male XL

19 | 16 | 20 | M

(fka Casual Male Big & Tall)
Gramercy | 291 Third Ave. (bet. 22nd & 23rd Sts.) | 6 to 23rd St. | 212-532-1415

(continued)

(continued)

Casual Male XL

Bronx | Bay Plaza Shopping Ctr. | 2094 Bartow Ave. (CoOp City Blvd.) | 6 to Pelham Bay Park | 718-379-4148 ●
Bronx | 945 White Plains Rd. (bet. Bruckner Blvd. & Story Ave.) | 718-239-0761 ●
Canarsie | 1110 Pennsylvania Ave. (bet. Cozine & Flatlands Aves.) | Brooklyn | L to Canarsie/Rockaway Pkwy. | 718-649-2924
Dyker Hts | 527 86th St. (bet. 5th Ave. & Fort Hamilton Pkwy.) | Brooklyn | R to 86th St. | 718-921-9770
Mill Basin | 2435 Flatbush Ave. (bet. Aves. T & U) | Brooklyn | 2/5 to Brooklyn College/Flatbush Ave. | 718-252-1313 ●
Staten Island | 2295 Richmond Ave. (bet. Nome & Travis Aves.) | 718-370-7767 ●
866-844-6595 | www.casualmale.com
This chain for larger-than-average men carries casual "hard-to-find" items for the big boys including suits, shirts, jeans and tees from brands like Polo, Cutter & Buck and Levi's; the "good selection" and "not-so-fancy" offerings make this store "the Jeep of clothing" dispensing practical, somewhat "mundane" items that "will wear for years."

Caswell-Massey

| 25 | 23 | 22 | M |

E 40s | 518 Lexington Ave. (48th St.) | 6 to 51st St. | 212-755-2254 | 800-326-0500 | www.caswellmassey.com
In 1752, Great Britain still owned America, Ben Franklin was flying his kite and this company was selling its first cologne, called Number Six and favored by George Washington; "America's oldest chemist and perfumer" still purveys soaps, fragrances and lotions that are "classic" like the "wonderful almond-scented" potions, plus shaving gear and children's items at this Lexington Avenue shop.

Catbird ●

| - | - | - | E |

NEW **Williamsburg** | 219 Bedford Ave. (N. 4th St.) | Brooklyn | L to Bedford Ave. | 718-599-3457
Williamsburg | 390 Metropolitan Ave. (Marcy Ave.) | Brooklyn | L to Bedford Ave. | 718-388-7688
www.catbirdnyc.com
Trek out to this tiny robins-egg-blue shop near the BQE and you'll find it chock-full of wearable well-priced finds among the racks of boutique-label clothing, stacks of Wrangler and J Brand jeans, accessories and shoes; their new outpost on Bedford Avenue focuses on jewelry, showcasing delicate charm necklaces and pendants by local artisans like Bing Bang and St. Kilda displayed in whitewashed antique china cabinets.

Catherine Malandrino

| 24 | 24 | 20 | VE |

SoHo | 468 Broome St. (Greene St.) | C/E to Spring St. | 212-925-6765
W Vill | 652 Hudson St. (13th St.) | A/C/E/L to 14th St./8th Ave. | 212-929-8710
www.catherinemalandrino.com
"Paris takes NYC by storm" at this duo in SoHo and on the West Village/Meatpacking border filled with "printed tunics, flowy skirts" and "romantic, flirty frocks" that Demi Moore, Heidi Klum and "young women of style and substance" love since they "make you feel feminine" "in a modern way"; but while most find the French designer's styles "flattering", a few deem them "ill-fitting" – unless you're "six feet tall and rich"; N.B. the Broome Street branch carries home furnishings as well.

Catherine Memmi
- | - | - | VE

SoHo | 45 Greene St. (bet. Broome & Grand Sts.) | N/R/W to Prince St. |
212-226-8200 | www.catherinememmi.com

Laid out like a large, lavish apartment, this SoHo home furnishings and
accessories shop showcases the eponymous Parisian designer's
warm, neo-minimalist collection; tables in precious woods like wenge,
lavish linens in unusual colors like chocolate and room sprays and candles in refreshing scents like white orchid and cucumber make it a
haunt for well-heeled Francophiles.

Cath Kidston
▽ 27 | 27 | 23 | E

NoLita | 201 Mulberry St. (bet. Kenmare & Spring Sts.) | 6 to Spring St. |
212-343-0223 | www.cathkidston.com

"Cute housewares and odds and ends" including "fun", "vintage"
"prints on a wide array" of fabrics, wallpaper, china, towels, totes and
"even pretty tents for camping" (that no straight guy will ever crawl
into) "from the British Martha Stewart" are on offer at this bright, bi-
level NoLita shop; fans who "love" her look feel lucky to have access to
the "wonderful" London-based label, but blame the "conversion rate"
for the "expensive" price tags.

Catimini
26 | 25 | 18 | VE

E 80s | 1125 Madison Ave. (84th St.) | 4/5/6 to 86th St. | 212-987-0688 |
www.catimini.com

City parents who want their offspring "to look different than all the other
Gap toddlers" and kiddies on the playground frequent this Madison
Avenue shop, the sole U.S. branch of the popular French childrenswear
chain whose forte is "unique" "but don't-let-your-child-eat-a-bite-in-
this" clothing; the "stylish" and "adorable tot togs" come in "cute mix-
and-match outfits", making shopping a snap for the time-pressed.

Catriona Mackechnie ●
- | - | - | E

Meatpacking | 400 W. 14th St. (9th Ave.) | A/C/E/L to 14th St./8th Ave. |
212-242-3200 | www.catrionamackechnie.com

For unmentionables your partner won't stop talking about and you may
not see anywhere else, head to this Meatpacking District den of desire
and linger over "very sexy lingerie" from unique Italian, French and
British labels including Damaris, Dolce & Gabbana and Guia La Bruna;
order custom-made knickers, then get in the swim of showing off your
hot bod with brazen bathing suits from handpicked European designers.

CB I Hate Perfume ⊠Ⓜ
- | - | - | VE

Williamsburg | 93 Wythe Ave. (N. 10th St.) | Brooklyn | L to Bedford Ave. |
718-384-6890 | www.cbihateperfume.com

Owner Christopher Brosius (ex Kiehl's and Demeter) considers himself
an artist and, accordingly, his Williamsburg storefront looks more like a
gallery than a *parfumerie*, but what's lining the shelves are bottles of
handmade, non-alcohol-based original scents like Fir Tree, Lavender Tea
and Gathering Apples, and cutting-edge aromas including custom-
blends are in the air.

Cécile et Jeanne
▽ 24 | 24 | 23 | M

E 80s | 1100 Madison Ave. (bet. 82nd & 83rd Sts.) | 4/5/6 to 86th St. |
212-535-5700

(continued)

QUALITY DISPLAY SERVICE COST

(continued)

Cécile et Jeanne

SoHo | 436 W. Broadway (bet. Prince & Spring Sts.) | C/E to Spring St. | 212-625-3535 ◗
www.cecilejeanne.com

"It's great that I can indulge my obsession without having to fly to Paris" assert admirers of this French jeweler with Uptown and Downtown offshoots; "wearable" handcrafted pieces – like the signature doves, "spectacularly colored" resin gems or the newer Renaissance-like Opera styles – are offered by a "friendly" staff at reasonable prices.

☑ Celine ⑤

28 | 24 | 24 | VE

E 60s | 667 Madison Ave. (bet. 60th & 61st Sts.) | N/R/W to 5th Ave./ 59th St. | 212-486-9700 | www.celine.com

"Ladies who lunch do their thing" at this Upper East Side boutique, which houses "high-end", "sophisticated Parisian" goods from the established French luxury label; some suggest it "can't decide if it wants to cater to the young and stylish or the old" "since Michael Kors left" off designing the line; still, it's perfect for "people with expense accounts" who find the "understated, timeless elegance" of the nipped-in suits, lusted-after Inca loafers and Boogie bags "worth the investment."

Cellini ⑤

27 | 23 | 24 | VE

E 40s | Waldorf-Astoria | 301 Park Ave. (49th St.) | 6 to 51st St. | 212-751-9824
E 50s | 509 Madison Ave. (bet. 52nd & 53rd Sts.) | E/V to 5th Ave./ 53rd St. | 212-888-0505

Whether it's the Waldorf-Astoria shop or the pint-sized Madison Avenue branch a few blocks uptown, watch aficionados say "you can't go wrong" with this "great place for the very best" brands like Franck Muller and Richard Mille; the "knowledgeable staff" is "surprisingly friendly" and "treats regulars like family"; N.B. check out the chic pink and yellow diamond jewelry.

Centricity Ⓜ

– | – | – | I

E Vill | 63 E. Fourth St. (bet. Bowery & 2nd Ave.) | 6 to Bleecker St. | 212-979-7601

It helps "to be a garage/tag sale person", but even vintage-savvy East Villagers find this nook "a fun, different place to browse", to the tune of two chirping parakeets; most of the merch seems straight from the malls of the '70s and '80s: polyester jumpsuits, woolly purses and pouf dresses, plus costume jewelry and racks crammed with kitchen items and tchotchkes; prices for the menswear and womenswear are as friendly as the owner.

☑ Century 21 ◗

22 | 10 | 9 | M

Financial Dist | 22 Cortlandt St. (bet. B'way & Church St.) | R/W to Cortlandt St. | 212-227-9092
Bay Ridge | 472 86th St. (bet. 4th & 5th Aves.) | Brooklyn | R to 86th St. | 718-748-3266
www.c21stores.com

This "Downtown discount destination" and its Bay Ridge relative is "a financially strapped fashionista's dream", with "designer duds" "at pauper prices", "plus undies and accessories galore", "orgasmic discoveries" in shoes and "a veritable cornucopia" of cosmetics, housewares and electronics; get ready to "do some hunting" – "shoving when necessary" – and "be in a patient, forgiving mood" with the "infuriatingly disorganized" displays, "tight, open fitting rooms", "busloads of tourists" and near-"useless staff", because "when you find a treasure, you'll be bragging for years."

Ceramica ▽ | 29 | 25 | 22 | E |

SoHo | 59 Thompson St. (bet. Broome & Spring Sts.) | C/E to Spring St. | 212-941-1307 | 800-228-0858 | www.ceramicadirect.com

For "the next best thing to buying ceramics in Tuscany" and Umbria, touters turn to this SoHo shop for "authentic", "high-quality", "handmade" pieces ranging from "dinner services to vases" and platters that are definitely "not the knockoffs you see in some catalogs."

☑ Cesare Paciotti ☒ | 29 | 27 | 22 | VE |

E 60s | 833 Madison Ave. (bet. 69th & 70th Sts.) | 6 to 68th St. | 212-452-1222 | www.cesare-paciotti.com

"Edgy" boots, "sporty" styles and stilettos so "scorchingly hot" you could "wear them to bed" lure trendsetters to this modern Madison Avenue mecca like hornets to honey; sure, loyalists "love" the "must-have" men's shoes and "cool" handbags, jewelry and eyewear, but patrons really pour on the accolades for the "wonderful" feminine designs, maintaining this is "the reason why women's feet exist."

Chambers Outlet Store ◐ | 24 | 16 | 18 | M |

E 70s | 1451 Second Ave. (76th St.) | 6 to 77th St. | 212-396-2463 | www.wshome.com

Perfect for "finicky people who must have 500-count sheets" but must also have "bargain" prices, this Upper East Side outlet offers its own "high-quality" bed linens, towels and bath mats as well as those from Frette and parent company Williams-Sonoma at "steep discounts" of 50%–80% off catalog prices; loyalists also like the inexpensive bath salts and shower gels, but they wish the "not-so-great presentation" was better organized.

Champs ◐ | 17 | 16 | 14 | M |

Harlem | 208 W. 125th St. (bet. 7th & 8th Aves.) | A/B/C/D to 125th St. | 212-280-0296
W 40s | 5 Times Sq. (42nd St. & 7th Ave.) | 1/2/3/7/N/Q/R/S/W to 42nd St./Times Sq. | 212-354-2009
Elmhurst | Queens Ctr. | 90-15 Queens Blvd. (bet. 57th & 59th Aves.) | Queens | G/R/V to Woodhaven Blvd. | 718-760-0095
Staten Island | Staten Island Mall | 2655 Richmond Ave. (bet. Platinum Ave. & Richmond Hill Rd.) | 718-698-1560
www.champssports.com

Bargain fans cheer this chain for its "low prices" on sports equipment, including bats, balls, helmets and shoes as well as a "good selection of team merchandise"; in short, most "would shop here again", even if foes find the "decent products" and "sketchy service" "disappointing."

☑ Chanel | 29 | 27 | 23 | VE |

E 50s | 15 E. 57th St. (bet. 5th & Madison Aves.) | N/R/W to 5th Ave./59th St. | 212-355-5050 | 800-550-0005
E 60s | 737 Madison Ave. (bet. 64th & 65th Sts.) | N/R/W to 5th Ave./59th St. | 212-535-5505 ☒

(continued)

(continued)

☑ Chanel

SoHo | 139 Spring St. (Wooster St.) | N/R/W to Prince St. | 212-334-0055 | 800-550-0005

www.chanel.com

The "doorman almost dares you to enter" these havens of "haute logo couture" to peruse Karl Lagerfeld's "traditional tweeds", quilted bags, signature shoes and eyewear that, whether "fabulous or silly", are the "embodiment of perfection"; some suggest that "unless you're dropping mega-cash" and dressed "in your best", the otherwise-"helpful" staff may not even "acknowledge your presence"; but even if "you have to be 20 to wear it and 70 to afford it", Coco's brand's been the "epitome of taste, trends and snob appeal" "for almost a century"; N.B. 737 Madison Avenue is exclusively bags, shoes and accessories.

Chanel Fine Jewelry ☒

27 | 27 | 25 | VE

E 60s | 733 Madison Ave. (64th St.) | F to Lexington Ave./63rd St. | 212-535-5828 | 800-550-0005 | www.chanel.com

For the "ultimate in classy flash", whether it's very-Mademoiselle-Chanel masses of pearls, the signature quilted Matelesse line or a bijoux from the Eléments Céleste collection, this Madison Avenue outpost offers "grandly proportioned breathtaking pieces"; of course, "jewelry for the stars" comes at "out-of-this-world prices."

Charles Nolan ●

– | – | – | E

Meatpacking | 30 Gansevoort St. (Hudson St.) | A/C/E/L to 14th St./ 8th Ave. | 212-924-4888 | 888-996-6526 | www.charlesnolan.com

In the still-hot Meatpacking District, how refreshing to find an "adorable store" with a "friendly, knowledgeable staff" say the few familiar with this American designer (best-known for rejuvenating the Anne Klein label); the colorful, spacious boutique houses his signature chic tees, silk gowns, tailored wool jackets and pencil skirts, as well as "one-of-a-kind treasures from resin bangles to lace-up gloves", along with furniture, housewares and even books.

☑ Charles P. Rogers ●

26 | 21 | 23 | E

Flatiron | 55 W. 17th St. (bet. 5th & 6th Aves.) | 4/5/6/L/N/Q/R/W to 14th St./Union Sq. | 212-675-4400 | 800-582-6229 | www.charlesprogers.com

"From sleigh beds to day beds", in wood, wrought iron, brass or leather, there's a "great selection of styles" at this Flatiron manufacturer that dates back to 1835; "excellent and attentive" customer service, including "right-on-time delivery", also adds to the relaxed experience.

Charles Tyrwhitt

26 | 24 | 23 | E

E 40s | 377 Madison Ave. (46th St.) | 4/5/6/7/S to 42nd St./Grand Central | 212-286-8988

W 50s | 745 Seventh Ave. (49th St.) | N/R/W to 49th St. | 212-764-4697 ●

www.ctshirts.com

Whether "for work or formal occasions", "comfortable", colorful, "classy shirts in the English tradition" are available at these Midtown shops for men (and women); an ample selection of "gorgeous ties" "and cuff links makes putting an outfit together a snap", and while the "lovely" goods are "a bit on the expensive side", "there are always terrific sales" going on; N.B. the Seventh Avenue store opened post-*Survey*.

	QUALITY	DISPLAY	SERVICE	COST

Charlotte Russe ●

| 10 | 13 | 11 | I |

Garment Dist | Manhattan Mall | 1275 Broadway (bet. 32nd & 33rd Sts.) | B/D/F/N/Q/R/V/W to 34th St./Herald Sq. | 212-465-8425
Staten Island | Staten Island Mall | 2655 Richmond Ave. (bet. Platinum Ave. & Richmond Hill Rd.) | 718-761-0020
www.charlotte-russe.com

"Teens on a limited budget" swamp these "flashy" Manhattan Mall and Staten Island chain links offering "disposable junior-size duds" and "inexpensive accessories" perfect for gals looking to put together a "last-minute outfit" while only "dropping a few bucks"; sure, they "could use more salespeople to assist and clean up" (watch out for the "piles of clothing dumped around"), but given that they're "packed" with "trendy stuff for cheap", most don't mind much.

Cheap Jack's ●

| 14 | 12 | 12 | M |

Garment Dist | 303 Fifth Ave. (31st St.) | B/D/F/N/Q/R/V/W to 34th St./Herald Sq. | 212-777-9564 | www.cheapjacks.com

"Though not as cheap as the name would suggest", this "fairly large" Garment District used-clothing purveyor is a "place to find the quirky and antique" among its vast variety of vintage mens- and womens-wear, from "lazy weekend tees" to "leather '70s-era coats"; but critics carp that while "there's a huge inventory, there's not enough good stuff", and "you need to be in the mood to look at overloaded racks" and deal with "help that isn't terribly helpful."

Chelsea Girl

| - | - | - | E |

SoHo | 63 Thompson St. (bet. Broome & Spring Sts.) | C/E to Spring St. | 212-343-1658

Chelsea Girl Couture

NEW **SoHo** | 186 Spring St. (bet. Sullivan & Thompson Sts.) | C/E to Spring St. | 212-343-7090
www.chelsea-girl.com

"Vintage vixens seeking fabulous" finds "should flock to this adorable" store on a "sleepy" stretch of Thompson Street, whose intimate, "creaky wood" environs are literally covered with century-spanning clothes and accessories; their current emphasis is on American labels from the '40s and early '50s, and there's "a particularly solid collection of handbags" too; N.B. Chelsea Girl Couture nearby features upscale designers like YSL.

Cherry ●

| - | - | - | E |

W Vill | 19 Eighth Ave. (bet. Jane & W. 12th Sts.) | A/C/E/L to 14th St./8th Ave. | 212-924-1410

Cherry Men ●

W Vill | 17 Eighth Ave. (bet. Jane & W. 12th Sts.) | A/C/E/L to 14th St./8th Ave. | 212-924-5188
www.cherryboutique.com

Whether you patronize the original store, now devoted solely to women, or the newer adjacent men's branch, this Village vintage clothing pair is a "great couture and near-couture designerwear resource"; both are crammed with "cool-looking" mannequins and displays (many featuring the wares of custom shoemaker Joseph LaRose), but if you don't have a weakness for flamboyant, rock 'n' roll rags and costume-y creations from the '60s–'70s, the prices may seem "crazy."

	QUALITY	DISPLAY	SERVICE	COST

Chico's ●
| | 20 | 19 | 21 | M |

E 70s | 1310 Third Ave. (75th St.) | 6 to 77th St. | 212-249-9105
Bayside | Bay Terrace Shopping Ctr. | 23-60 Bell Blvd. (24th Ave.) |
Queens | 7 to Main St. | 718-224-1256
888-669-4911 | www.chicos.com

"Made for me!" cry "forgotten over-40s" of these chain links in the East 70s and Bayside catering to "non-model-shaped women" with "reasonably priced", "stylish" yet "forgiving" suits, separates and dresses in "mix-and-match" styles, many of them "machine-washable"; the "nicest saleslADies in the world" ensure "great shopping" despite interiors that are often "too crowded", so never mind if upstarts dismiss its "no-wrinkle" duds as strictly "frumpy."

Children's General Store
| | ▽ 27 | 21 | 21 | E |

E 40s | Grand Central | 42nd St. (Vanderbilt Ave.) | 4/5/6/7/S to 42nd St./Grand Central | 212-682-0004 ●
E 90s | 168 E. 91st St. (bet. Lexington & 3rd Aves.) | 6 to 96th St. | 212-426-4479

A popular "stopover" for Grand Central commuters and now East·90s residents too, this "old-fashioned" toy duo steers clear of "commercial brands" in favor of items that "emphasize learning" like puzzles and science kits, making it "every intelligent parent's dream"; there are "no bargains", but the "cute gift-wrapping" compensates.

Children's Place, The ●
| | 16 | 16 | 15 | M |

Garment Dist | 22 W. 34th St. (bet. 5th & 6th Aves.) | B/D/F/N/Q/R/V/W to 34th St./Herald Sq. | 212-904-1190 | 800-527-5355 |
www.childrensplace.com
Additional locations throughout the NY area

"Considering how fast children grow", it's nice to have a chain where "cheerful" duds for the little ones are "inexpensive enough to stock up on", especially staples like jeans and T-shirts; some report hit-or-miss quality (some things "wear well, others fall apart"), but with "prices this cheap", no one complains too loudly.

Chip & Pepper ●
| | 23 | 22 | 20 | E |

NoLita | 250 Mulberry St. (bet. Prince & Spring Sts.) | 6 to Spring St. | 212-343-4220 | www.chipandpepper.com

Complete with a deer antler chandelier, pine-wood shelving and fishing rods, the vibe at twin brothers Chip and Pepper Foster's NoLita nook is more log cabin than designer boutique, emphasizing the lived-in look of their "flattering" "vintage-inspired" jeans; fans (including Naomi Campbell, who allegedly whacked her maid with a BlackBerry over a lost pair) judge the brand a "winner in the overcrowded high-end denim market" and also collect California-cool T-shirts and hoodies.

Chloé ▣
| | 26 | 25 | 20 | VE |

E 70s | 850 Madison Ave. (70th St.) | 6 to 68th St. | 212-717-8220 |
www.chloe.com

"Everything the twentysomething with a handbag of cash would want" crows the chorus of Chloé converts, who single out the "fantastic fit" and "gamine styling" of this "so-cool" French label for the "younger jet set" housed in a glossy Madison Avenue boutique; the "boho-chic" line is now designed by Paulo Melim Andersson (ex Marni), who replaced creative director Phoebe Philo, which may outdate the above scores.

	QUALITY	DISPLAY	SERVICE	COST

ⓩ Chopard Ⓢ
29 | 28 | 26 | VE

E 60s | 725 Madison Ave. (bet. 63rd & 64th Sts.) | 6 to 68th St. | 212-218-7222 | www.chopard.com

"If you love bling, get buzzed into" this "elegant" East 60s branch of an 1860 firm, whose old-world appointments like mahogany paneling and a marble fireplace create the backdrop for "gorgeous" watches like the signature Happy Diamond timepieces with loose gems floating inside the face and fine jewelry; needless to say, "time is money", so the "beautiful merchandise ranges from very expensive to ridiculously expensive."

ⓩ Christian Louboutin
28 | 28 | 24 | VE

E 70s | 941 Madison Ave. (bet. 74th & 75th Sts.) | 6 to 77th St. | 212-396-1884 Ⓢ

W Vill | 59 Horatio St. (bet. Greenwich & Hudson Sts.) | A/C/E/L to 14th St./8th Ave. | 212-255-1910

"The red soles are the giveaway . . . you spent a fortune!"; *mais oui*, it's "worth every penny" because the French designer's "killer stilettos" and "incredibly sexy", "luxurious footwear" for the "shoe fetishist" showcased at these West Village and East 70s "gems" are "beyond chic"; "can't live without" his "beautifully crafted" "high-fashion" heels vow the wowed – they're among the "most comfortable and the most sublime" "classy styles" around, plus the staff is "low on attitude"; N.B. the Madison Avenue shop is slated to relocate in 2007.

ⓩ Christofle Ⓢ
27 | 26 | 24 | VE

E 60s | 680 Madison Ave. (62nd St.) | N/R/W to 5th Ave./59th St. | 212-308-9390 | www.christofle.com

For "gorgeous everything" in "heavy-weight, beautiful silver", head to the crisp rosewood interior of this Madison Avenue mecca that's particularly known for its "clean-lined" flatware; you can find other "exquisite gifts" in silver plate, crystal and porcelain, but no matter what the material, the prices are consistently "not for the faint of wallet."

Christopher Fischer
▽ 23 | 27 | 23 | VE

SoHo | 80 Wooster St. (bet. Broome & Spring Sts.) | N/R/W to Prince St. | 212-965-9009 | www.christopherfischer.com

This knitwear designer's namesake SoHo shop may be pristine white, but there's nothing muted about the "many gorgeous colors" of cashmere goods that fill the shelves and racks; the ultramodern, "stunning presentation" offsets the "to-die-for sweaters", both "conservative" and cut down to there, kittenish crocheted cardigans, flirty skirts and high-style wraps, plus there's a cache of colorful luxe accessories and soft-touch items for men, kids and the home.

Christopher Totman
– | – | – | E

NoLita | 262 Mott St. (bet. Houston & Prince Sts.) | N/R/W to Prince St. | 212-925-7495

Urbanites ready to go natural applaud this American designer's "genius way of recycling materials [like kimono fabrics] into high fashion" at his NoLita shop; fans "love the atmosphere", which features a fish tank and actual tree-trunk shelves to hold the harvest of nubby knit pullovers, bright gauzy tops and a few smart-looking separates for men; prices seem "decent", given the "extremely high quality" and "great service."

| | QUALITY | DISPLAY | SERVICE | COST |

Chrome Hearts ⊠
▽ 28 | 28 | 24 | VE

E 60s | 159 E. 64th St. (bet. Lexington & 3rd Aves.) | 6 to 68th St. |
212-327-0707 | www.chromehearts.com

A garden with a fish-pond fountain separates the wings of this "mysterious little company" in an unmarked brownstone on East 64th Street "with a loyal, almost cult following" that includes "rock stars"; "alternate" signature sterling silver that is "hot" and Goth ("great crosses") and loads of bling like diamond-studded dog tags dominate, but don't overlook the watches, flexi-lense sunglasses and "exquisite" leather goods in the "too cool for school" handmade mix.

Chuckies ●
25 | 21 | 15 | VE

E 60s | 1073 Third Ave. (bet. 63rd & 64th Sts.) | F to Lexington Ave./
63rd St. | 212-593-9898

E 80s | 1169 Madison Ave. (86th St.) | 4/5/6 to 86th St. | 212-249-2254

It's "like visiting a museum of shoes" agree aesthetes who amble over to this Upper East Side duo to view a "wealth" of the "hottest styles" from "top" names like Marc Jacobs and Jimmy Choo as well as "unique" "stuff" from "lesser-knowns"; but while a handful find "the help delightful", most are put off by the "nose-in-the-air" 'tude, huffing they're "not so friendly unless you're dressed in designer duds."

Church's Shoes
25 | 21 | 21 | E

E 60s | 689 Madison Ave. (62nd St.) | 6 to 68th St. | 212-758-5200

"Fine English shoes for fine English men" and Anglophiles-in-the-making are the backbone of this "top-caliber", "friendly" Madison Avenue shop; "don't look for trendy" stuff here, instead, zero in on the "impeccable", "handcrafted" "super-establishment" footwear that "wears like iron – you'll pass them on to your grandchildren" – and "never goes out of style"; if a few wail "it ain't what it used to be", worshipers retort this "classic" is a keeper.

Circuit City ●
19 | 15 | 12 | M

E 80s | 232 E. 86th St. (bet. 2nd & 3rd Aves.) | 4/5/6 to 86th St. |
212-734-1786

Union Sq | 52 E. 14th St. (bet. 4th & 5th Aves.) | 4/5/6/L/N/Q/R/W
to 14th St./Union Sq. | 212-387-0730

W 80s | 2232 Broadway (80th St.) | 1 to 79th St. | 212-362-9850

Clinton Hill | Atlantic Ctr. | 625 Atlantic Ave. (bet. Ft. Greene Pl. &
S. Portland Ave.) | Brooklyn | 2/3/4/5/B/D/M/N/Q/R to Atlantic Ave. |
718-399-2990

Starrett City | Gateway Ctr. | 369 Gateway Dr. (bet. Fountain &
Vandalia Aves.) | Brooklyn | A/C to Euclid Ave. | 718-277-1611

College Pt | 136-03 20th Ave. (Whitestone Expwy.) | Queens | 7 to
Main St. | 718-961-2090

Rego Pk | 96-05 Queens Blvd. (Junction Blvd.) | Queens | G/R/V to
63rd Dr./Rego Park | 718-275-2077

Staten Island | 2505 Richmond Ave. (Richmond Hill Rd.) | 718-982-1182
800-843-2489 | www.circuitcity.com

"Good values" are the draw for fans of this "mass-market chain" offering "all those electronics that we can no longer live without" – "from computers to microwave ovens" – within a "warehouse atmosphere"; just "do your research first" and "don't expect in-depth answers", for "when it comes to customers", the "know-nothing help" forgot to "plug in their circuit."

City Cricket

	-	-	-	E

W Vill | 215 W. 10th St. (Bleecker St.) | 1 to Christopher St./Sheridan Sq. | 212-242-2258 | www.citycricket.com

"There's always something adorable to buy here" chirp acolytes who fly over to this "perfect little West Village spot", which tucks a surprisingly "great selection" of treasures for tots into such a "tiny" space; it's a haven for "gift-givers", filled with a "unique" array of old-fashioned toys, handmade quilts, silver and pewter keepsakes and even kiddie-sized wing and Adirondack chairs.

City Opera Thrift Shop

	22	20	17	M

Gramercy | 222 E. 23rd St. (bet. 2nd & 3rd Aves.) | 6 to 23rd St. | 212-684-5344

"A theater buff's trash may be your treasure" at this Gramercy thrift shop run by the New York City Opera, whose digs – dominated by a wrought-iron staircase – are rather "serene and elegant" compared to the usual charity outlet; though "the stock is limited, you can always find something" among "the well-organized" items, "especially books, jewelry", "costume castoffs" and "new designer stuff, tags and all"; critics carp that the "highbrow" goods sometimes come with "high-end prices", "but think of it as an investment in your inner diva."

◪ City Quilter, The Ⓜ

	28	24	26	M

Chelsea | 133 W. 25th St. (bet. 6th & 7th Aves.) | 1 to 23rd St. | 212-807-0390 | www.cityquilter.com

"What a store!" proclaim pieceniks who prize this "welcoming" Chelsea specialist where "quilting enthusiasts" can get square deals on a "fantastic selection" of fabrics, notions and other supplies or take the "best classes"; it can be "somewhat expensive" since it's the "only game in town", but the "friendly" staffers "care" enough to "want you to get what you need for perfect results"; P.S. it's a "great place to buy gifts for quilters" too.

City Sports ◕

	20	15	17	M

E 50s | 153 E. 53rd St. (bet. Lexington & 3rd Aves.) | E/V to Lexington Ave./53rd St. | 212-317-0541
NEW **Murray Hill** | 390 Fifth Ave. (36th St.) | 6 to 33rd St. | 212-695-0171 www.citysports.com

"Your plain-Jane, gym-rat stores for when you want practical, not flashy" activewear and gear agree urban athletic types who sprint to these Midtown and East 30s outposts of a Boston-based chain "for the basics"; "show your ID" from select NYC sports clubs "for an on-spot discount" and score a "great sneaker deal" too – "if you buy two pairs"; still, a handful lament the "presentation is nothing to write home about" and find the staff "helpful – if you can locate them."

CK Bradley

	24	23	23	E

E 70s | 146 E. 74th St. (bet. Lexington & 3rd Aves.) | 6 to 77th St. | 212-988-7999 | www.ckbradley.com

Almost as "preppy as a grosgrain headband", this "cheerful", "whimsical" East 70s boutique lures loyalists with its "weekends in Connecticut essentials" including "fabulous totes", "colorful belts", "cute, feminine" "summer cocktail dresses" and "fun patterned skirts", all designed by owner Camilla Bradley; the "Wasp-cubed" clothing is such a "guilty pleasure" – all you "need is a house in" Greenwich "to go with your wardrobe."

Claire's Accessories

8 | 11 | 11 | I

Garment Dist | 1385 Broadway (bet. 37th & 38th Sts.) | B/D/F/N/Q/R/V/W to 34th St./Herald Sq. | 212-302-6616 | www.claires.com
Additional locations throughout the NY area

"Cash-strapped" "teenyboppers" "trying to look flashy" "play all day" among a "mishmash maze" of "cheap jewelry and accessories", from chandelier earrings to fake tattoos, headbands and makeup; "you get what you pay for" so "don't expect their items to last forever."

Clarins

26 | 25 | 24 | E

E 80s | 1061 Madison Ave. (bet. 80th & 81st Sts.) | 6 to 77th St. | 212-734-6100 ●
SoHo | 146 Spring St. (Wooster St.) | C/E to Spring St. | 212-343-0109
W 70s | 247 Columbus Ave. (bet. 71st & 72nd Sts.) | 1/2/3 to 72nd St. | 212-362-0190 ●
www.clarins.com

This "high-end French line" with a trio of outlets around town has a "no-nonsense, botanical approach" to beauty that "really works"; besides their famous self-tanner (known for no streaks and "no carrot"-like color), fans favor items like Le Rouge lipstick and Line Prevention Cream; an "attentive" staff adds to the "terrific top-to-toe experience."

Clarks England

23 | 18 | 19 | M

E 40s | 363 Madison Ave. (45th St.) | 4/5/6/7/S to 42nd St./Grand Central | 212-949-9545
Elmhurst | Queens Ctr. | 90-15 Queens Blvd. (bet. 57th & 58th Aves.) | Queens | G/R/V to Woodhaven Blvd. | 718-271-7505 ●
www.clarksusa.com

If you "gotta walk", slip on a pair of "well-wearing casual shoes" from this "friendly", "fun place to shop" in the East 40s and Queens; "here, as in the U.K.", the "great conservative" men's and women's styles are some of the "most comfortable on the planet, especially if that planet is the desert" and the footwear of choice is the signature "desert boot."

Classic Kicks Ⓢ

▽ 25 | 23 | 21 | E

NoHo | 298 Elizabeth St. (bet. Bleecker & Houston Sts.) | 6 to Bleecker St. | 212-979-9514 | www.classickicks.com

"As the name implies, a classic collection" of "awesome" "old-school sneaks", in imported, limited-edition, collectible and fashion-forward versions, "keeps hipsters coming back" to this NoHo haunt; sneaker buffs scoop up footwear from faves like Adidas, Nike, Lacoste, Puma and Vans "in all-new styles and colors" and to-go-with, way-"trendy threads", all dispensed by "wonderful, warm owners."

Classic Sofa

▽ 23 | 17 | 20 | E

Flatiron | 5 W. 22nd St. (bet. 5th & 6th Aves.) | N/R/W to 23rd St. | 212-620-0485 | www.classicsofa.com

There are "lots of choices" at this "high-quality" sofa store in the Flatiron District, which offers couches constructed out of hardwood and down-fill in modern and traditional styles, and "if you don't see what you want", they'll custom-design it for you; loyalists like the "quick turnaround" time of about two weeks average, although the sticker-shocked wonder "what is this stuff made of, gold?"

	QUALITY	DISPLAY	SERVICE	COST

Claudia Ciuti 🗷
25	24	20	E

E 70s | 955 Madison Ave. (75th St.) | 6 to 77th St. | 212-535-3026 | www.claudiaciuti.com

"*Bella bella bella*" – "have I made my point clear?" – "Ms. Ciuti is a genius!" agree adoring fans of the Florentine footwear designer, who fall head over heels for the "divine, utterly feminine" suede stiletto boots, T-straps, platform pumps and "hot bling sandals" at her "lovely" East 70s shop; add in exotic leathers, alluring color combos and "excellent service" and it's plain to see these luxe kicks are "worth the money."

Clay Pot ●
26	24	23	E

Park Slope | 162 Seventh Ave. (bet. 1st St. & Garfield Pl.) | Brooklyn | B/Q to 7th Ave. | 718-788-6564 | 800-989-3579 | www.clay-pot.com
"Beautiful crafts chosen with a classy eye" are the draw at this "cute", "eclectic" Park Slope stalwart representing 75 different U.S. artists and specializing in handblown glass and "great handmade jewelry", including engagement rings and wedding bands; though it's "a little on the high side", most maintain it's a good "place for a special gift."

Clea Colet 🗷 Ⓜ
▽ 26	21	20	E

E 70s | 960 Madison Ave. (bet. 75th & 76th Sts.) | 6 to 77th St. | 212-396-4608
You'll have a "wonderful time trying on the beautiful" bridalwear at this by-appointment-only Madison Avenue salon where you'll be looked after by an "easygoing staff"; the "well-made" gowns come in a "variety of materials from Duchess satin to silk organza" and work well "for any shape" especially since the namesake designer (who "specializes in simpler styles" – sans-"glitz") will custom-"fit the dress to your body type"; P.S. "such great sample sales" too.

Clio
-	-	-	E

SoHo | 92 Thompson St. (bet. Prince & Spring Sts.) | C/E to Spring St. | 212-966-8991 | www.clio-home.com
This "stylish" SoHo tabletop shop sells "unique" international accessories ranging from teardrop vases from San Francisco and bone china dinnerware from Germany to handblown glass lighting from Brooklyn and palm wood trays from Bali; no wonder supporters say it's a "great resource for wedding and housewarming gifts."

Cloak ◑
-	-	-	VE

SoHo | 10 Greene St. (Canal St.) | C/E to Spring St. | 212-625-2828 | www.cloakdesign.com
A "dark" "moody ambiance" reigns at this librarylike lair in SoHo, the flagship for designer Alexandre Plokhov's label that's also big in Japan; men wishing to shroud themselves in "high-fashion" mystery uncover Gothic coats galore, "sharply tailored" suits, special-order fabrics and somber separates with dashing details; a bookcase that features coffee-table titles from DAP also conceals a dressing room – just a touch of cloak-and-dagger mystique; N.B. since the wholesale end of the business will close this spring, the store's future remains uncertain.

Cloth Ⓜ
-	-	-	E

Ft Greene | 138 Fort Greene Pl. (Hanson Pl. & Lafayette Ave.) | Brooklyn | C to Lafayette Ave. | 718-403-0223 | www.clothclothing.com
For tasteful womenswear, fashion insiders duck into Zoe van de Wiele's hip Fort Greene gem behind the BAM Cultural District; the owner's fash-

ion training has made her a stickler for construction and the result is an unassumingly chic selection including labels like Loomstate and Matta, plus edgy jewelry and beauty wares from Rhode Island's Farmaesthetics.

Club Monaco ❷

18 | 20 | 16 | M

E 60s | 1111 Third Ave. (E. 65th St.) | 6 to 68th St. | 212-355-2949
Flatiron | 160 Fifth Ave. (21st St.) | N/R/W to 23rd St. | 212-352-0936
SoHo | 121 Prince St. (bet. Greene & Wooster Sts.) | N/R/W to Prince St. | 212-533-8930
SoHo | 520 Broadway (bet. Broome & Spring Sts.) | N/R/W to Prince St. | 212-941-1511
W 50s | 6 W. 57th St. (bet. 5th & 6th Aves.) | F to 57th St. | 212-459-9863
W 80s | 2376 Broadway (87th St.) | 1 to 86th St. | 212-579-2587
Elmhurst | Queens Ctr. | 90-15 Queens Blvd. (bet. 57th & 59th Aves.) | Queens | G/R/V to Woodhaven Blvd. | 718-760-9282
www.clubmonaco.com

When you "don't feel like shelling out for the real designer outfit" hit this "cleanly" styled men's and women's clothing chain that draws "young" "trendsetters" and others with its "runway" "knockoffs" and "hip, but not slick" suits, dresses and jeans that amount to "great value" considering the overall "quality"; the service, however, is perhaps best-suited for those "with low expectations."

Clyde's ❷

27 | 23 | 22 | E

E 70s | 926 Madison Ave. (74th St.) | 6 to 77th St. | 212-744-5050 | 800-792-5933

"Classy right down to the shopping bags", this Upper East Sider remains among "the last of the old-world drug and beauty stores" that's "great for hard-to-find and imported items" like Versace makeup, Boucheron fragrance and almost anything else that "keeps the ladies who lunch looking good"; most maintain "the sales people are generally great", so the only issue is the cost, which leads customers to complain the establishment "could double as a comedy club with those prices!"

☑ Coach ❷

26 | 24 | 22 | E

E 50s | Fuller Bldg. | 595 Madison Ave. (57th St.) | N/R/W to 5th Ave./59th St. | 212-754-0041 | 888-262-6224 | www.coach.com
Additional locations throughout the NY area

"Durable" "bags that age better than some people do" in "timeless" styles you'll "will to your daughters" and "trendy" designs "irresistible" to "fashionable" folk are "displayed in an appealing way" at this "marvelous" chain where the staff "meets and greets" "addicts" of all ages; customers concur the "craftsmanship is apparent" collection-wide – "nothing beats the leather line" of accessories and jackets, plus their "warranty is one of the best in the business"; but critics coach "ease up" on the "logo-ed" merchandise, adding it's become too "ubiquitous."

C.O. Bigelow Chemists ❷

26 | 21 | 21 | M

G Vill | 414 Sixth Ave. (bet. 8th & 9th Sts.) | A/B/C/D/E/F/V to W. 4th St. | 212-533-2700 | 800-793-5433 | www.bigelowchemists.com

Founded in 1838 as an apothecary, this Greenwich Village institution "is a gold mine for toiletry divas" with common brands crammed alongside Greek body scrubs from Propoline, jasmine and ginger toothpaste from Marvis and their own in-house line of face and body products in vintage packaging along with oodles of hair accessories and "products you never knew existed"; though it's "stuffed to the gills", it has a "cool, old-school feel" leading loyalists to exclaim "if I could, I would live upstairs."

Coclico ●   - | - | - | E

NoLita | 275 Mott St. (bet. Houston & Prince Sts.) | B/D/F/V to B'way/Lafayette St. | 212-965-5462

Europe rules at this cute, colorful NoLita shop where fashionistas flock for "fabulous" east-of-the-pond labels; choose from lesser-known names, including the house brand and finds from Costume National and Fornarina, then try on accessories to complete the head-to-toe look.

CoCo & Delilah ●   - | - | - | E

E Vill | 115 St. Marks Pl. (bet. Ave. A & 1st Ave.) | 6 to Astor Pl. | 212-254-8741 | www.coco-nyc.com

Smack dab in the "funky" East Village sits this pretty shop, complete with a crystal chandelier and coveted womenswear (Da-Nang, Nanette Lepore, Petro Zillia), super-cool denim (Blue Cult, Hudson and James Jeans) and tees (Trunk Ltd, Three Dots); followers of owner Collette LoVullo's Web site feel "thrilled" to have a go-to spot for her inspired choices that "run the gamut" of getups for "work and weekends."

Cog & Pearl ● M   21 | 21 | 15 | M

Park Slope | 190 Fifth Ave. (Sackett St.) | Brooklyn | M/R to Union St. | 718-623-8200 | www.cogandpearl.com

Crafty Slopers make a beeline to this "lovely venue" on Fifth Avenue to peruse the gallerylike "showcase" of "unique items" from "local talent and amazing artisans" including "one-of-a-kind" handmade jewelry, "very cute" handbags, accessories, journals, T-shirts and "original" ceramics and home knickknacks, like John Derian decoupage; while many of the "edgy products" are made from recycled materials, "happily" they don't have that "crunchy, re-used-burlap feel."

Cohen's Fashion Optical ●   19 | 16 | 16 | M

E 60s | 767 Lexington Ave. (60th St.) | 4/5/6/F/N/R/W to 59th St./Lexington Ave. | 212-751-6652 | 800-393-7440 | www.cohensfashionoptical.com
Additional locations throughout the NY area

"The same wherever you go", this "Woolworth's of eyewear" ("glasses for the masses") can "come through with the goods" and some "decent" "deals"; but "wary" customers caution that the "final price" rarely "lives up to the ads" and find the service "lame", concluding "this isn't your store if you wanna resemble Paris Hilton."

Cole Haan   25 | 23 | 22 | E

E 50s | 620 Fifth Ave. (50th St.) | B/D/F/V to 47-50th Sts./Rockefeller Ctr. | 212-765-9747
E 60s | 667 Madison Ave. (61st St.) | 4/5/6/F/N/R/W to 59th St./Lexington Ave. | 212-421-8440
W 50s | The Shops at Columbus Circle, Time Warner Ctr. | 10 Columbus Circle, ground fl. (bet. 58th & 60th Sts.) | 1/A/B/C/D to 59th St./Columbus Circle | 212-823-9420
800-488-2000 | www.colehaan.com

"Talk about a reinvention!" this "high-quality" outfit boasting "solidly crafted" footwear, bags and outerwear "isn't your mama's store anymore!"; the staff is "patient" and what's more, "you'll be hooked" on the "hip and trendy (but in a good way)" shoes and the "amazingly comfortable, sexy" styles from the "funky" "G-series, designed with Nike"; if a few pout it's become "more generic", most retort just "treat your feet" – "you can wear them next season too."

Colony Music ●

| 24 | 15 | 19 | E |

W 40s | 1619 Broadway (49th St.) | 1 to 50th St. | 212-265-2050 | www.colonymusic.com

Broadway babies boast this "fantastic" Theater District "original" in the Brill Building has "stuff no one else has" in the way of "obscure sheet music", "vintage vinyl", "fun memorabilia" and karaoke machines; sure, the "know-it-all staff" and "laughably high prices" can strike a sour note, but the "remarkable selection" and late hours make it just the ticket for most; N.B. a refurb may outdate the Display score.

Comme des Garçons

| 26 | 27 | 24 | VE |

Chelsea | 520 W. 22nd St. (bet. 10th & 11th Aves.) | C/E to 23rd St. | 212-604-9200

"Even veteran shoppers are surprised" by this Chelsea boutique with its tunnel leading to a "womblike space" filled with Japanese designer Rei Kawakubo's "fantastic", if "way, way out", his-and-hers garments; critics cry "the clothes are more a curiosity than something to be worn in public", "but if you feel daring and have money to burn", these "avant-garde" "art pieces" could become "an addictive acquired taste" – or else, "display them as textile sculptures."

Compact Impact ●⊠

| – | – | – | E |

Financial Dist | 71 Broadway (Trinity Pl.) | R/W to Rector St. | 212-677-0500 | www.compactimpact.com

This innovative, by-appointment-only electronic-gadget gallery in the Financial District offers the latest in trendy Tokyo technology and urban lifestyle design, from Japanimation-inspired gizmos and solar-powered backpacks that'll juice up your cell phone to conceptual contraptions like an iDog whose byte is all digital, but whose bark is all music.

CompUSA ●

| 19 | 15 | 10 | M |

Garment Dist | 420 Fifth Ave. (37th St.) | B/D/F/N/Q/R/V/W to 34th St./Herald Sq. | 212-764-6224
W 50s | 1775 Broadway (57th St.) | 1/A/B/C/D to 59th St./Columbus Circle | 212-262-9711
Rego Pk | 97-77 Queens Blvd. (64th Dr.) | Queens | G/R/V to 63rd Dr./Rego Park | 718-793-8663
800-266-7872 | www.compusa.com

"Nerds" and "techno-illiterates" alike can obtain "anything related to computers" and "everything for audio and video" at this chain of "grocery stores" for "true high-tech stuff"; expect to "find it yourself", though, as the salespeople are so "few and far between" that "you could die from old age waiting" – or locate one only to discover that "not all geeks are knowledgeable."

Conran Shop, The ●

| 23 | 25 | 18 | E |

E 50s | Bridgemarket | 407 E. 59th St. (1st Ave.) | 4/5/6/F/N/R/W to 59th St./Lexington Ave. | 212-755-9079 | www.conran.com

English style icon Sir Terence Conran's "cool, slick store" is "like a museum of design" where there are "stunning displays" of "beautiful modern" furniture and housewares ranging from "dishes to divans, from towels to telephones"; it's "waaaay out of the way", tucked beside the 59th Street Bridge, but enthusiasts insist it's worth the schlep.

NEW Consignment
— | — | — | E

Downtown | 371 Atlantic Ave. (bet. Bond & Hoyt Sts.) | Brooklyn | A/C/G to Hoyt/Schermerhorn Sts. | 718-522-3522

Butter fans are sure to whip themselves into a frenzy over the consignment clothing culled from seasons past at its new offspring on Atlantic Avenue; like its stylish big sister, the setting here is understated yet chic, with never-been-worn, gently used and still-pricey finds from labels like Gucci, Isabel Marant, Mayle and Rick Owens carefully merchandised beside a select few pieces of Danish Modern furniture, jewelry, shoes and bags.

Container Store, The
22 | 22 | 21 | M

Chelsea | 629 Sixth Ave. (bet. 18th & 19th Sts.) | 1 to 18th St. | 212-366-4200 ◐
NEW **E 50s** | 725 Lexington Ave. (58th St.) | 4/5/6/F/N/R/W to 59th St./Lexington Ave. | 212-366-4200 ⊠ Ⓜ
800-733-3532 | www.containerstore.com

"First-timers walk around dazed", but pros know how to navigate this Chelsea "nirvana" for nesters "with small apartments" that's an "organizational dreamland" "containing everything you need to contain anything" – including "a great closet line" – and all sold by staffers that are "so friendly you think they're part of a cult"; it's an "addictive" "place that was made for Manhattan" and, with any luck, the crushing "crowds" of fellow "obsessive-compulsives" will be minimized now that there's a second city store in the East 50s.

Cooper-Hewitt National Design Museum Shop Ⓜ
24 | 21 | 17 | M

E 90s | Cooper-Hewitt | 2 E. 91st St. (5th Ave.) | 4/5/6 to 86th St. | 212-849-8355 | www.cooperhewitt.org

Devotees of both "classic and innovative design" delight in this Upper East Side "find" offering a "great selection" of "modern housewares" and "decorative accessories" from "top" names as well as "fantastic books" at "varied prices"; the space is "nicely laid out", and though a few gripe the goods are "sometimes uninspired" and "disappointing", more maintain it's "one of the best of the museum shops."

Cosmophonic Sound
— | — | — | E

E 80s | 1622 First Ave. (84th St.) | 4/5/6 to 86th St. | 212-734-0459 | www.cosmophonic.com

Whether you need "same-day service for a complicated television hookup" or "to repair your old Betamax", head to this East 80s home-theater specialty shop, a family-run biz with a staff that forgoes the "high-pressure sale pitch"; audiophiles also turn to the "wonderful" help to customize a multiroom automated system to specifications or to purchase a plasma TV, confiding, "they know their products intimately."

∅ Costco Wholesale ◐
22 | 12 | 12 | I

Sunset Pk | 976 Third Ave. (39th St.) | Brooklyn | D/M/N/R to 36th St. | 718-965-7603

(continued)

(continued)

☒ Costco Wholesale

LIC | 32-50 Vernon Blvd. (B'way) | Queens | N/W to Broadway |
718-267-3680
Staten Island | 2975 Richmond Ave. (Staten Island Expwy.) |
718-982-9525
www.costco.com

Ah, "the joys of buying in bulk" for all your household and personal needs; "from batteries to steaks", this "essential" "big-box" chain "has everything you need" attest addicts who also adore the "excellent optical and pharmacy departments" and the "great brand names" from Cartier to Canon; it all makes the $50 annual "membership fee pay for itself" – that is, if you have "storage space in your home" ("everything's large, except the prices"); don't expect anything in the way of amenities, unless you count the "endless samples" of snacks.

Costume National

SoHo | 108 Wooster St. (bet. Prince & Spring Sts.) | N/R/W to Prince St. |
212-431-1530 | www.costumenational.com

Embrace the dark side in the ebonized interior of this sophisticated SoHo boutique with its "great shoes" and "funky, cool, chic pieces" for men and women designed by Ennio Capasa in "shiny monochromatic fabrics, most of them black" and tailored so cleverly that they would even make Darth Vader "the paradigm of sexiness."

Council Thrift Shop

E 80s | 246 E. 84th St. (bet. 2nd & 3rd Aves.) | 4/5/6 to 86th St. |
212-439-8373 | www.ncjwny.org

If you feel "Upper East Side thrift stores are the place to be", then this veteran, established by the National Council of Jewish Women in 1952, is definitely one "to check out", thanks to its "frequently changing", "very good selection" of "brand-name" clothes, furniture, housewares and china; some say the staff's "on the snobbish side", "but it's worth it" to "find that discarded pair of $600 shoes selling for $50."

☒ Country Floors ☒

Union Sq | 15 E. 16th St. (bet. 5th Ave. & Union Sq. W.) | 4/5/6/L/N/Q/R/W to 14th St./Union Sq. | 212-627-8300 | www.countryfloors.com

Proof that "you don't have to go to Italy to find wonderful tiles", this "dream store" in Union Square has provided connoisseurs with a "fabulous place to troll for ideas" for over 40 years; terra-cotta, natural stone and glass with unusual textures and finishes mix with mosaic designs from the 17th century and "magnificent hand-painted" pieces, making this a "favorite place for over-the-top" purchases "if you have the budget for them."

NEW C.P.W. ●

W 80s | 495 Amsterdam Ave. (84th St.) | 1 to 86th St. | 212-579-3737

After stocking up on must-have items like J Brand jeans for yourself, pick up shrunken versions of all the latest adult styles for the youngest members of your fashion clan at this West 80s boutique for women and kids; tiny trendseekers also find it hard to resist super-soft C&C California tees, denim duds from Joe's Jeans and Lacoste polo shirts in a rainbow of colors.

	QUALITY	DISPLAY	SERVICE	COST

Crabtree & Evelyn
23 | 22 | 21 | M

E 40s | Rockefeller Ctr. | 620 Fifth Ave. (bet. 49th & 50th Sts.) | B/D/F/V to 47-50th Sts./Rockefeller Ctr. | 212-581-5022
E 50s | 520 Madison Ave. (bet. 53rd & 54th Sts.) | E/V to 5th Ave./ 53rd St. | 212-758-6419 🔊
W 50s | The Shops at Columbus Circle, Time Warner Ctr. | 10 Columbus Circle, ground fl. (bet. 58th & 60th Sts.) | 1/A/B/C/D to 59th St./Columbus Circle | 212-823-9584 ●
Staten Island | Staten Island Mall | 2655 Richmond Ave. (bet. Platinum Ave. & Richmond Hill Rd.) | 718-982-8252 ●
800-272-2873 | www.crabtreeandevelyn.com

An "oasis" "for the woman who's outgrown candy-scented products", this English chainlet and "blast from the past" founded in 1800 offers soaps, scents, potpourri and room sprays that rely on "classic" ingredients like lavender and "don't smell syrupy sweet"; prices are moderate and there are "excellent sales", but cutting-edge it ain't.

☑ Crane & Co., Paper Makers
27 | 23 | 21 | E

W 40s | Rockefeller Ctr. | 59 W. 49th St. (bet. 5th & 6th Aves.) | B/D/ F/V to 47-50th Sts./Rockefeller Ctr. | 212-582-6829 | www.crane.com
For "beautiful, traditional paper" that's "pricey but worth it" and the "finest quality engraved stationery" that will "make an impression", "you can't go wrong" at this small Rockefeller Center branch of an "American classic" dating back to 1801; fashionistas claim they can't find "trendy" designs, but admirers insist "no one's ever turned down any of the invitations" they've bought here.

☑ Crate & Barrel ●
21 | 24 | 20 | M

E 50s | 650 Madison Ave. (59th St.) | N/R/W to 5th Ave./59th St. | 212-308-0011
NoHo | Cable Bldg. | 611 Broadway (Houston St.) | B/D/F/V to B'way/ Lafayette St. | 212-780-0004
800-967-6696 | www.crateandbarrel.com

"Lock, stock and barrel", these NoHo and Midtown "you-want-it-they-got-it" "from furniture to flower pots" housewares mega-stores are "popular for a reason" – a "wide range" of "nicely laid-out", "high-quality" "chic designs" and "terrific value" make them "great for a first apartment or home" and "bring good taste to the masses."

Crembebè ●
– | – | – | E

E Vill | 68 Second Ave. (bet. 3rd & 4th Sts.) | F/V to Lower East Side/ 2nd Ave. | 212-979-6848 | www.crembebe.com
Trendsetters are sweet on this Second Avenue confection, well-stocked with all of the ingredients needed to "dress your baby in East Village funk from head-to-toe" like cute finds from Appaman, Pure Pensée and other new designers high on the most-wanted list; P.S. for a bona fide sugar high, indulge in "cool" accessories, toys and other gift-worthy goodies.

🆕 Crew Cuts ●
– | – | – | M

SoHo | J.Crew | 99 Prince St. (Greene St.) | N/R/W to Prince St. | 212-966-2739 | www.jcrew.com
J.Crew courts the milk-and-cookies crowd with this splurge-inducing new kids' shop, tucked inside its SoHo adults' store, which serves up tiny takes on its signature collegiate styles; tomorrow's prepsters

score everything from classic candy-colored cableknit sweaters and corduroy pants to rugby shirts and tartan kilts, plus shoes, slippers and rainboots to match; the icing on the cake: prim party dresses and spiffy gold-buttoned blazers and bow ties for dress-up occasions.

C. Ronson
▽ | 16 | 18 | 20 | E

NoLita | 239 Mulberry St. (bet. Prince & Spring Sts.) | B/D/F/V to B'way/Lafayette St. | 212-625-9074 | www.cronson.com

Always good for a girlie-girl fix, designer Charlotte Ronson's tiny NoLita boutique reveals her groovy-gal-about-town sensibility with "cute" "but not cheap" finds like "casualwear with hearts and cherries", undies and iPod-pocketed hoodies; while you're there, check out the "fun" clothing and accessories with a decidedly downtown vibe from other "emerging" lines.

Crouch & Fitzgerald
26 | 21 | 22 | E

E 40s | 400 Madison Ave. (bet. 47th & 48th Sts.) | B/D/F/V to 47-50th Sts./Rockefeller Ctr. | 212-755-5888 | 800-627-6824 |
www.crouchandfitzgerald.com

A "NYC tradition among the moneyed crowd", this "dependable" Madison Avenue luggage leviathan is the "real thing", "one of those rare places that make shopping a fulfilling treat"; loyalists insist that the "outstanding range" of "classy leather items", including "chic" suitcases, handbags and accessories "at top prices", "age better than" themselves; still, a few Crouch-grouchers wonder "what has happened to the venerable" store, the "one my mother" patronized?

Crumpler Bags ●
24 | 19 | 20 | M

NoLita | 45 Spring St. (bet. Mott & Mulberry Sts.) | 6 to Spring St. | 212-334-9391
W Vill | 49 Eighth Ave. (bet. Horatio & W. 4th Sts.) | A/C/E/L to 14th St./8th Ave. | 212-242-2535
www.crumplerbags.com

"Proof" that "superb functional utility" accessories "don't have to be in black", or cross the "over-designed" line, the totable "wonders from Down Under" at this Downtown duo come in "odd color pairings that work", including custom creations at the newer West Village shop; choose from "sturdy" camera bags, laptop cases and "backpacks galore" "full of useful" details, like the third leg strap, an "invention bicycle messengers have been waiting for."

Crunch ●
15 | 16 | 14 | M

E Vill | 404 Lafayette St. (bet. Astor Pl. & 4th St.) | 6 to Astor Pl. | 212-614-0120 | 888-227-8624 | www.crunch.com
Additional locations throughout the NY area

"Hip" hoodies, sweats, leggings and T-shirts so "playful and unique" you may "live in" them draw muscle-meisters to the "crowded retail areas" of this urban-gym chain; if a few sniff this outfit "should stick to exercise and leave" the activewear to "experts", for most it's crunchy "fun."

Custo Barcelona
21 | 23 | 20 | E

SoHo | 474 Broome St. (bet. Greene & Wooster Sts.) | C/E to Spring St. | 212-274-9700 | www.custo-barcelona.com

The brothers Dalmau originally made a name for themselves with their "exuberantly creative" "paper-thin T-shirts" for "funky" gals and guys, and they've evolved and extended their line at this sleek SoHo boutique, whose decor changes with the seasons; the "hip" apparel "with Euro flair" delivers "bold prints", "color and pattern" galore in suits and separates "that always exude sexiness and garner compliments."

Cynthia Rowley ◐

23 | 22 | 22 | E

W Vill | 376 Bleecker St. (bet. Charles & Perry Sts.) | 1 to Christopher St./Sheridan Sq. | 212-242-3803 | www.cynthiarowley.com

Slip into this silvery little West Village gem to pick up "girlie-girl-to-the-max" garb from the *Swell* book series co-creator whose "vibrant" styles, from sweet coats to party dresses, "look so cute" and make "material girls" "feel pretty as a princess"; unfortunately, the "price tags can be pretty pricey too" – though several "middle-income" mademoiselles maintain they're "decent" enough.

☒ Daffy's ◐

17 | 10 | 9 | M

Garment Dist | 1311 Broadway (34th St.) | B/D/F/N/Q/R/V/W to 34th St./Herald Sq. | 212-736-4477 | 877-933-2339 | www.daffys.com
Additional locations throughout the NY area

"For those with a strong hunter's gene", it's "possible to find outstanding labels at bargain prices" at this "crowded discount" chain carrying "wacky Euro styles" for men and women, "Italian clothing for infants", accessories and home decor items; but even "if you're willing to dig", "you can never find salespeople", and the merch "seems to be in a constant state of disarray", leading foes to fume you're "daft" to shop here.

Damiani ☒

- | - | - | VE

E 60s | 796 Madison Ave. (67th St.) | 4/5/6/F/N/R/W to 59th St./Lexington Ave. | 212-375-6474 | www.damiani.com

"Italians know about good jewelry" according to admirers of this third-generation, family-owned, Milan-based business dating back to 1924; its Madison Avenue outpost offers the sleek, D-Side collection co-designed with Brad Pitt and more opulent diamond- and gemstone-encrusted pieces with plenty of eye appeal.

Dana Buchman

25 | 23 | 23 | E

E 50s | 65 E. 57th St. (bet. Madison & Park Aves.) | N/R/W to 5th Ave./59th St. | 212-319-3257 | 800-522-3262 | www.danabuchman.com

A master at careerwear for the nine-to-five crowd, this American maker's "designs are changing" from "very conservative" to "well-made, not ultra-expensive" wide-leg trousers, colorful suede jackets and tile-print tunics at her East 50s boutique; skeptics still say it's "stuffy", but devotees "love the fit" and all applaud the employees who, while "not obsequious", are "eager to find you what you want."

D & G ◐

24 | 24 | 21 | VE

SoHo | 434 W. Broadway (bet. Prince & Spring Sts.) | C/E to Spring St. | 212-965-8000 | www.dolcegabbana.it

Housed in a "sparse" concrete jungle of a boutique in SoHo, what some call "the slutty younger sister of Dolce & Gabbana" holds sway with both sexes, and "if you're looking to add something tight in a leopard print to your closet, this is the place"; while the body-baring tops and plastered-on jeans may be a bit "bizarre for those past 30", the "Italian-with-an-attitude" apparel keeps the "young and hip" happy; N.B. divas-in-training can shop for D & G Junior childrenswear here too.

Dane 115
— | — | — | E

SoHo | 115 Crosby St. (bet. Houston & Prince Sts.) | 6 to Spring St. | 212-431-1295
Treasure-seekers are bound to discover lots of luxe finds at this minuscule SoHo shop that feels like a Parisian attic; owner Robin Fonseca and her daughter, Dana, fill their elegant nook with a mélange of rare wares including Loyd Maish handbags from Florence, unique footwear from London's Emma Hope and former Givenchy designer Laurence Dacade along with clothing from coveted labels like Borne; N.B. don't deign to depart Dane without poring over the high-end vintage and estate jewelry.

Danskin ●
23 | 18 | 19 | M

W 60s | 159 Columbus Ave. (bet. 67th & 68th Sts.) | 1 to 66th St./Lincoln Ctr. | 212-724-2992 | 800-288-6749 | www.danskin.com
Find "just the right tutu at just the right price" at this "tried-and-true" women's and children's "standby" set "close to Lincoln Center for performers'" convenience; sure, it's "been known for its ballet" apparel since 1882, but gym buffs are "happy" to find "comfortable" activewear here too; if a few bemoan the "boring" displays, most applaud the "great selection of clothing that looks great in or out of the studio."

Darling ●
— | — | — | E

W Vill | 1 Horatio St. (8th Ave.) | A/C/E/L to 14th St./8th Ave. | 646-336-6966 | www.darlingnyc.com
Devotees whisper that former Broadway costume designer Ann French Emont's "charming boutique" is "possibly the best-kept shopping secret in the West Village"; the "extremely friendly" owner sets the stage for "flirtation" with "dreamy", "vintage and vintage-inspired" "girlie-girl" party dresses and sexy separates that "flatter all figures, not just underfed models'", from designers like Nieves Lavi, Shoshanna and Zola; P.S. on warm Thursday nights, treat yourself, darling, to "champagne in the back" garden.

Daryl K
▽ 23 | 19 | 23 | E

NoHo | 21 Bond St. (bet. Bowery & Lafayette St.) | B/D/F/V to B'way/Lafayette St. | 212-529-8790 | www.darylk.com
"Downtown dressing for city girls" describes the duds of Daryl Kerrigan, a designer idolized as "still an innovator" – or perhaps a contemporary-minded nostalgist, since cheeky minis, sexy short shorts and naughty-girl baby-dolls never go out of style in her ice-cool world; so channel your inner Edie Sedgwick at her stripped-to-the-necessities NoHo shop, which also features vintage boots and bags.

DataVision ●
21 | 14 | 12 | M

Murray Hill | 445 Fifth Ave. (39th St.) | 4/5/6/7/S to 42nd St./Grand Central | 212-689-1111 | www.datavis.com
"They have everything you could want in electronics", including a "wide selection of computer items", at this "great place" near the 42nd Street Library; critics contend that management "could clean up" the "cluttered, claustrophobic" layout and complain that the "variable" staff is "either all over you or totally absent", but "if you know your stuff", "you can bargain a bit here and get a good deal."

	QUALITY	DISPLAY	SERVICE	COST

Daum Ⓢ
▽ 27 | 25 | 25 | VE

E 60s | 694 Madison Ave. (bet. 62nd & 63rd Sts.) | N/R/W to 5th Ave./
59th St. | 212-355-2060 | www.daum.fr

For some of "the most unique crystal around", this "small" Upper East
Side shop offers "one-of-a-kind" French glassware including *pâte de
verre* vases, perfume bottles, bowls, lamps and jewelry with signature
frosted floral, animal and insect-inspired motifs.

Dave's Army Navy
21 | 12 | 18 | I

Chelsea | 581 Sixth Ave. (bet. 16th & 17th Sts.) | F/L/V to 14th St./6th Ave. |
212-989-6444 | 800-543-8558

"Rock 'n' roll and join the army – they got all the authentic stuff" you
need at this "longtime Chelsea favorite"; surveyors hail it for having
"hands down, the best selection of work-clothes brands like Carhartt
and Levi's" "at great prices"; sure, the digs are "basic", but just think
of it as a store that serves "steak without the sizzle."

Dave's Quality Meat
– | – | – | E

E Vill | 7 E. Third St. (bet. Bowery & 2nd Ave.) | F/V to Lower East Side/
2nd Ave. | 212-505-7551 | www.davesqualitymeat.com

It may look like a retro butcher shop, but the prime pickings hanging
from the metal meat racks at this "very cool" East Village spot owned
by three skateboarders happen to be limited-edition sneakers, not
steaks, from "boss" labels like Adidas, Converse, Nike and Vans; adding gravy to the mix: house-brand T-shirts, shrink-wrapped and displayed in a refrigerator case, plus clothing from other grade-A labels.

☑ Davide Cenci Ⓢ
29 | 22 | 24 | VE

E 60s | 801 Madison Ave. (bet. 67th & 68th Sts.) | 6 to 68th St. |
212-628-5910 | www.davidecenci.com

Men who appreciate a full-service shop will find a most "enjoyable experience" at this multilevel townhouse whose "fine merchandise" includes "classic Italian threads", ready-made and made-to-measure
shirts, coats, ties and "Tod's shoes to boot", along with a smaller
selection of womenswear that also gets "high marks"; the sterling
"service can be a little stuffy, but hey, this *is* Madison Avenue."

David Lee Holland Ⓜ
– | – | – | E

SoHo | 69 Sullivan St. (bet. Broome & Spring Sts.) | C/E to Spring St. |
212-925-1944 | www.davidleeholland.com

The eponymous owner-designer of this serene SoHo jewelry "oasis"
says he is inspired by nature and proves it with "unique" pieces like 18-
karat gold oncidium orchid earrings, a laurel leaf necklace and a beech
burr pendant appointed with a black Tahitian pearl; for the younger
set, there's a collection of silver pieces mixed with oversized, brightly
colored gem stones; "excellent one-on-one service" adds to its appeal.

David's Bridal ●
13 | 12 | 14 | I

LIC | 35-00 48th St. (Northern Blvd.) | Queens | G/R/V to 46th St. |
718-784-8200 | 888-480-2743 | www.davidsbridal.com

Penny-pinchers proclaim "it's hard to pass up" the mostly inexpensive
wedding regalia found at this LIC chain link that feels like a "department
store for the bride"; if "you have the patience and don't need to be ca-
tered to" it's "great for quicky shopping", but most blast the "run-of-
the-mill" dresses and would "rather pay more to go somewhere else."

David Webb 🛃

E 60s | 789 Madison Ave. (bet. 66th & 67th Sts.) | 6 to 68th St. | 212-421-3030 | www.davidwebb.com

"Quintessentially New York", this Upper East Side gem dating back to 1948 is still home to sparkling signature tiger-, zebra- and armadillo-inspired jewelry in enamel, gold or gemstones, plus other "overscaled, overpriced and unique" designs that are the "Palm Beach–chic" "alternative to Kenny Lane" "for the truly affluent."

David Yurman 🛃

25 | 24 | 23 | VE

E 60s | 729 Madison Ave. (64th St.) | 6 to 68th St. | 212-752-4255 | 877-226-1400 | www.davidyurman.com

Loyalists "love" this "right-on-the-money" Madison Avenue jeweler, including his signature "silver and gold look", plus pearls with sterling or gem-set bijoux that are "not for the faint of heart"; but detractors dub the designs "overly expensive", "stylish suburban soccer-mom" stuff, and give the staff "mixed reviews."

David Z. ●

19 | 14 | 15 | M

Flatiron | 655 Sixth Ave. (21st St.) | F/V to 23rd St. | 212-807-8595
G Vill | 821 Broadway (12th St.) | 4/5/6/L/N/Q/R/W to 14th St./Union Sq. | 212-253-5511
Murray Hill | 384 Fifth Ave. (bet. 35th & 36th Sts.) | 6 to 33rd St. | 917-351-1484
NoHo | 620 Broadway (Houston St.) | B/D/F/V to B'way/Lafayette St. | 212-477-3826
SoHo | 487 Broadway (Broome St.) | 6 to Spring St. | 212-625-9391
SoHo | 556 Broadway (bet. Prince & Spring Sts.) | 6 to Spring St. | 212-431-5450
Union Sq | 12 E. 14th St. (bet. 5th Ave. & University Pl.) | 4/5/6/L/N/Q/R/W to 14th St./Union Sq. | 212-229-4790
Union Sq | 862 Broadway (17th St.) | 4/5/6/L/N/Q/R/W to 14th St./Union Sq. | 212-420-8627
www.davidz.com

It's a "good resource for sneakers" and the "latest in urban", "trendy" footwear with "lots of choices" and "deals to be found" attest throngs of shoppers who swarm to this "hectic" chain around town; "it's a zoo, but someone will eventually help you", though "you better take a seat" and you may have to put up with attitude that's either "nonchalant" or as "aloof as a bad nightclub crowd."

DaVinci Artist Supplies

23 | 19 | 20 | E

Chelsea | 132 W. 21st St. (bet. 6th & 7th Aves.) | 1 to 23rd St. | 212-871-0220 | www.davinciartistsupply.com

"With a name like that it has to be good" concur creative sorts who feel like "Alice in an artists' wonderland" at this "lovely" Chelsea art supply shop offering brushes, paints, pads, paper and canvas by the yard and a custom framing department too; "selection, quality and experienced help – a great combination" – and "DaVinci's got it!"; but it's different strokes for less-impressed folks who sigh "nothing special here."

Davis & Warshow, Inc. 🛃

23 | 18 | 19 | E

E 50s | A&D Bldg. | 150 E. 58th St., 4th fl. (bet. Lexington & 3rd Aves.) | 4/5/6/F/N/R/W to 59th St./Lexington Ave. | 212-980-0966
Harlem | 207 E. 119th St. (bet. 2nd & 3rd Aves.) | 6 to 116th St. | 212-369-2000

| | QUALITY | DISPLAY | SERVICE | COST |

(continued)

Davis & Warshow, Inc.

Harlem | 251 W. 154th St. (bet. 8th Ave. & Macombs Pl.) | B/D to
155th St. | 212-234-5100
Bronx | 3150 Jerome Ave. (bet. Bedford Park Blvd. & Mosholu Pwky.) |
4 to Bedford Park Blvd. | 718-584-1351
Maspeth | 57-22 49th St. (bet. 56th Rd. & Maspeth Ave.) | Queens |
718-937-9500
www.daviswarshow.com
A favorite of the wholesale set, this well-stocked "one-stop-shopping"
quintet of showrooms is "the jumping-off point" for 150 products for
the kitchen and bath – from bronze basins and Japanese tubs to saunas
and bar sinks from the likes of Kohler and Kallista.

NEW DC Shoes ◑   22 | 21 | 19 | M

SoHo | 109 Spring St. (bet. Greene & Mercer Sts.) | 6 to Spring St. |
212-334-4500 | www.dcshoes.com
Skate rats, snowboarders, surfers and rally racers all roll into this slick
SoHo newcomer to scope out the sweet selection of "cool" sneakers,
boots, hoodies, parkas and caps with an arty spin at "reasonable"
prices; the gnarly goods are displayed amid a futuristic "teen"-perfect
atmosphere featuring free-floating chrome fixtures and 16 plasma
screens beaming the brand's edgy film projects and team tour footage.

ddc domus design collections ⊠   ▽ 27 | 28 | 24 | VE

Murray Hill | 181 Madison Ave. (34th St.) | 6 to 33rd St. |
212-685-0800 | www.ddcnyc.com
If it's sleek and chic, it can probably be found at this three-story
Murray Hill showroom featuring contemporary furniture, lighting and
accessories that's housed in a landmark building designed by Grand
Central Station architects Warren & Wetmore.

DDC Lab   - | - | - | E

Meatpacking | 427 W. 14th St. (bet. 9th & 10th Aves.) | A/C/E/L to
14th St./8th Ave. | 212-414-5801 | www.ddclab.com
Technology pays off in "superbly designed" trendy wear at this sleek
Meatpacking District hot spot where the "innovative urban styles" of
owners Roberto Crivello and Savania Davies-Keiller draw those in
search of premium Japanese jeans, washable suede or leather separates and climate-control hoodies that regulate the body temperature
of the guy and gal hotties who shop here.

☑ Dean & Deluca ◑   26 | 24 | 18 | E

SoHo | 560 Broadway (Prince St.) | N/R/W to Prince St. | 212-226-6800 |
800-781-4050 | www.deandeluca.com
Truly a "SoHo pioneer", this "high-end" "specialty gourmet store"
where "beautiful" "produce is arranged like a still life" and "brownies
are the size of a small child" also sells "posh cookware", cutlery,
housewares and serving pieces; the practical point out that "prices are
beyond belief", so you better "have Bloomberg's wallet."

Dear Fieldbinder ◑   - | - | - | E

Cobble Hill | 198 Smith St. (bet. Baltic & Warren Sts.) | Brooklyn | F/G
to Bergen St. | 718-852-3620 | www.dearfieldbinder.com
It's "a pleasure to shop here and find what you want" amid the "well-
edited selection of hipster clothes" croon fashionistas about this

Cobble Hill emporium, a retro-modern mecca filled with "feminine" looks from both style stalwarts (Cynthia Rowley, Ted Baker) and lesser-known labels; Lara Fieldbinder, "the owner, is always at your service", which mitigates the fact that her wares "demand my whole paycheck."

Debbie Fisher Ⓜ
- | - | - | M

Carroll Gdns | 461 Court St. (bet. 4th Pl. & Luquer St.) | Brooklyn | F/G to Carroll St. | 718-625-6005 | www.debbiefisher.com
Inspired by museum collections of ancient and ethnic art, this Carroll Gardens jewelry shop mainly features the "beautiful" work of its eponymous owner-designer whose "unique, understated and feminine" pieces are crafted from precious and semiprecious stones, Thai, Indian and African beads or 18- or 22-karat gold and silver.

DeBeers Ⓢ
27 | 23 | 26 | VE

E 50s | 703 Fifth Ave. (55th St.) | E/V to 5th Ave./53rd St. | 212-906-0001 | 800-929-0889 | www.debeers.com
A joint venture between the eponymous South African firm and prestigious Louis Vuitton, this jewelry store brings "amazing diamonds from the source" to Fifth Avenue; of course, there are "sell-your-house-before-going-shopping-here" pieces like enormous engagement rings, but for those intimidated by the price of all that ice, the "beautiful presentation" also includes a clearly marked under-$1,000 section.

de Grisogono Ⓢ
- | - | - | VE

E 60s | 824 Madison Ave. (69th St.) | 6 to 68th St. | 212-439-4220 | www.degrisogono.com
This wildly expensive Geneva-based fine jewelry company is housed in a dramatic black and lime-green Madison Avenue space (complete with spiral staircase) – an apt backdrop for their bold designs; glittering gemstones in colorful, often arresting contrasting combinations (emerald with amethyst for example) turn up in witty pieces like eggplant or apple earrings, floral rings and spiraling snake neckaces.

delfino ●
22 | 20 | 18 | M

E 70s | 1351A Third Ave. (bet. 77th & 78th Sts.) | 6 to 77th St. | 212-517-5391
W 50s | Rockefeller Ctr. | 56 W. 50th St. (bet. 5th & 6th Aves.) | B/D/F/V to 47-50th Sts./Rockefeller Ctr. | 212-956-0868
www.delfinoshop.com
Loyalists "love to wander" this pair of "stylish" spots in the East 70s and West 50s searching for "unique" "of-the-moment" handbags and accessories "not everyone has", including the house line and "delicious" brands from Europe (Longchamp, Hervé Chapelier, etc.) that take you "from day to play"; it's just too bad the "bored sales staff" doesn't help you navigate the "excellent array."

Delphinium Cards & Gifts ●
24 | 20 | 22 | M

W 40s | 358 W. 47th St. (bet. 8th & 9th Aves.) | C/E to 50th St. | 212-333-7732

Delphinium Home ●
W 40s | 653 Ninth Ave. (bet. 45th & 46th Sts.) | A/C/E to 42nd St./Port Authority | 212-333-3213
These "cute" "hole-in-the-wall" Hells Kitchen shops with "helpful service" are "full of cool stuff for your home and kitchen" (or someone else's for a "last-minute gift") that isn't "found on every other corner",

like umbrellas with imprints of blue skies on their underbellies and matte silver leaf Zen photo albums; "it can get cramped but it's worth getting shoved for" their "delightful", moderately priced "small things."

DeMask
▽ 22 | – | 18 | E

LES | 144 Orchard St. (bet. Rivington & Stanton Sts.) | F/J/M/Z to Delancey/Essex Sts. | 212-466-0814 | www.demask.com

Rubber lovers reveal you'll be "hot, hot, hot", literally and figuratively, squeezed into a "top-quality latex" ensemble from this European import, which recently relocated from Chelsea to the Lower East Side, where it still peddles "the world's finest fetishwear"; the "awesome", fashion-forward selection is only for females, but guys can perch on a red leather couch and let their "imaginations run wild" while their lady friends model duds that are "divine for the dominatrix."

Demolition Depot/
Irreplaceable Artifacts 🏠⇄
– | – | – | E

Harlem | 216 E. 125th St. (bet. 2nd & 3rd Aves.) | 4/5/6 to 125th St. | 212-777-2900 | www.demolitiondepot.com

For "great finds from back in time", hit this Harlem outlet for all things old whose inventory of unique architectural works and ornaments changes daily, as pieces are switched in and out of the numerous New England warehouses operated by this salvage sultan; antique elevator and entrance doors are popular, as are the plentiful plumbing fixtures, but there are smaller pieces like deco door knockers too.

☑ Dempsey & Carroll 🏠
27 | 22 | 24 | VE

E 50s | 136 E. 57th St., 4th fl. (bet. Lexington & 3rd Aves.) | 4/5/6/F/N/R/W to 59th St./Lexington Ave. | 212-750-6055 | www.dempseyandcarroll.com

"Mingle with the socialites" at this "old-world" East 57th Street shop (which was relaunched under new ownership in 2004) where "Edith Wharton would feel at home"; a "dignified staff" purveys "classy", "traditional engraved stationery", wedding invitations and address books in a "postage-stamp-size" space; of course, "you pay for what you get" – "premium products" that "others aren't likely to be using."

DeNatale Jewelers, Inc. 🏠
26 | 25 | 24 | E

E 40s | 400 Madison Ave. (bet. 47th & 48th Sts.) | 4/5/6/7/S to 42nd St./Grand Central | 212-317-2955
Financial Dist | 170 Broadway (Maiden Ln.) | 2/3/4/5/A/C/J/M/Z to Fulton St./B'way/Nassau | 212-349-2355
www.denatale.com

Whether you're searching for a gold-link bracelet or a radiant-cut canary diamond engagement ring, supporters say you "can always find what you are looking for" at this family-owned-and-operated Wall Street and Midtown jewelry duo dating back to 1908; "quality" "in all price ranges" and "friendly", "old-world service" help guarantee you'll have "a good shopping experience"; N.B. they also do custom designs and repairs and offer a full selection of china, crystal and other giftware.

Denimaxx
– | – | – | VE

E 40s | 444 Madison Ave. (bet. 49th & 50th Sts.) | 6 to 51st St. | 212-207-4900 | www.denimaxx.com

Truly for those who walk on the wild side when it comes to fur, this Madison Avenue store delivers its me-Tarzan-you-Jane look in luxurious and sexy men's and women's coats, jackets and dresses, plus eccentric and handsome belts, gloves and wallets; sure, the prices are sky-high, but at least it beats flying to their shops in Aspen or Coral Gables to pick up a fox-collared shearling or two.

Dennis Basso
▽ 24 | 26 | 22 | VE

E 60s | 765 Madison Ave. (bet. 65th & 66th Sts.) | 6 to 68th St. | 212-794-4500 | www.dennisbasso.com

"You'll be a showstopper" in one of the "warm, extravagant" shearlings and furs, including "the ne plus ultra of sables", produced by this black-and-gold-accented, elegant East 60s salon whose "beautifully hand-embroidered" "styles are exquisite" without "nodding to what is supposedly 'in'"; not surprisingly, they're also "super-duper expensive – don't expect to pay any less than a year of college tuition" (but do "the kids really need to learn", anyway?).

Dernier Cri ⦿
- | - | - | E

Meatpacking | 869 Washington St. (bet. 13th & 14th Sts.) | A/C/E/L to 14th St./8th Ave. | 212-242-6061

The store's name translates to the 'latest fashion' or 'newest discovery', which is just what you'd expect to find at this Meatpacking District spot owned by MTV alum Stacia Valle who knows how to keep it real – and "worth a look", kitting the space out with celery-green walls, industrial "metal racks" and a rebellious mix of renegade silhouettes and rocker tees for righteous babes from lines including Daryl K, Preen, Maharishi and Vivienne Westwood.

Designer Resale
24 | 20 | 18 | E

E 80s | 311 E. 81st St. (bet. 1st & 2nd Aves.) | 6 to 77th St. | 212-734-2836
E 80s | 324 E. 81st St. (bet. 1st & 2nd Aves.) | 6 to 77th St. | 212-734-3639
www.resaleclothing.net

Set in two facing townhouses on 81st Street, this "grande dame of thrift shops" offers a "well-presented", "impressive selection of upscale designer threads" and accessories of a "definitely Upper East Side" nature ("nothing too trendy or too cool"); however, the "haughty sales clerks" "are not so helpful", and some find the consigned goods "overpriced" – although the "twice-annual sales can be phenomenal" ("Coach and Kate Spade at knockoff prices!").

Design Within Reach
24 | 22 | 20 | E

E 60s | 27 E. 62nd St. (bet. Madison & Park Aves.) | 4/5/6/F/N/R/W to 59th St./Lexington Ave. | 212-888-4539
NEW Flatiron | 903 Broadway (20th St.) | 6 to 23rd St. | 212-477-1155
Meatpacking | 408 W. 14th St. (bet. 9th & 10th Aves.) | A/C/E/L to 14th St./8th Ave. | 212-242-9449
SoHo | 142 Wooster St. (bet. Houston & Prince Sts.) | N/R/W to Prince St. | 212-475-0001
TriBeCa | 124 Hudson St. (bet. Beach & N. Moore Sts.) | 1 to Franklin St. | 212-219-2217
W 70s | 341 Columbus Ave. (76th St.) | 1/2/3 to 72nd St. | 212-799-5900
Brooklyn Hts | 76 Montague St. (Hicks St.) | Brooklyn | 1/2/4/5/M/N/R to Court St./Borough Hall | 718-643-1015
800-944-2233 | www.dwr.com

Within the space of three years, this San Francisco–based furniture firm has exploded across the city, opening seven locations, and democratizing the "midcentury" modern mystique by offering "haute design for the masses"; a "helpful", "well-informed staff" can talk you through classics like Charles and Ray Eames and Isamu Noguchi or newer pieces from Karim Rashid and Philippe Starck; still, surveyors are split on the cost, with proponents praising "almost reasonable prices", while critics who call the store's name a "misnomer" declare that tabs are only "within reach of the well-heeled"; N.B. they've also introduced a children's line.

Desiron

▽ 22	26	24	VE

SoHo | 151 Wooster St. (bet. Houston & Prince Sts.) | N/R/W to Prince St. | 212-353-2600 | www.desiron.com

"Wonderful lines", "custom-made quality" and "beautiful finishes and detail" make aesthetes aspire to the "absolute minimalism" of this "high-fashion" furniture shop in SoHo that spans 6,000 sq. ft. and showcases the Carfaro brothers' collection of tables, seating, beds, bureaus and storage pieces; everything here is stylishly spare except the prices.

Destination ●

▽ 23	25	22	E

Meatpacking | 32-36 Little W. 12th St. (bet. 9th Ave. & Washington St.) | A/C/E/L to 14th St./8th Ave. | 212-727-2031 | www.destinationny.net

The plaster pig on the sidewalk outside signals that this Meatpacking District destination is no ordinary fashionista stomping ground; clotheshorses and art-lovers alike wander the large, contemporary shop that doubles as an art gallery, perusing the "well-curated selection" of apparel, shoes and accessories from an international coterie of under-the-radar designers – this is definitely "not run-of-the-mill stuff."

Destination Maternity

22	20	22	M

E 50s | 575 Madison Ave. (57th St.) | E/V to 5th Ave./53rd St. | 212-588-0220 | 800-291-7800 | www.destinationmaternity.com

It's the "mother ship for expectant mothers, literally" proclaim pregnant patrons who find an Edamame spa, Pea in the Pod, Mimi Maternity and Motherhood Maternity clothing and accessories "all at your fingertips" at this three-level Madison Avenue mecca; you "feel like a fashion plate" whether you "pick up a cheap top or glam it up" – there's something for "everyone in every price range"; still, a few grumble it's "somewhat understaffed, which can make a cranky prego impatient."

Diana Kane ●

-	-	-	E

Park Slope | 229B Fifth Ave. (bet. Carroll & President Sts.) | Brooklyn | M/R to Union St. | 718-638-6520

NEW **Park Slope** | 78A Seventh Ave. (bet. Berkeley & Union Sts.) | Brooklyn | M/N/R to Union St. | 718-638-5674
www.dianakane.com

"Diana's got the best taste" – and now fashionistas can reap the benefits of the namesake owner's clean, elegant style at two Park Slope locations; the Fifth Avenue original can be "torture" for those who "want it all", including "great lingerie" (Cosabella, Hanky Panky) and womenswear (Erica Tanov, Velvet), Repetto ballet flats, Vix swimsuits and Kane's own "gorgeous handmade jewelry", but can "afford little"; the all-white Seventh Avenue newcomer traffics in similar temptations, plus choice pieces from Lewis Cho and Saltwater.

Diane T ●Ⓜ

-	-	-	E

Cobble Hill | 174 Court St. (bet. Amity & Congress Sts.) | Brooklyn | F/G to Bergen St. | 718-923-5777

"Displaced Manhattan fashionistas" can forgo the F train and make tracks to this gleaming white, "stylish outpost" in Cobble Hill, where owner Diane Tkacz stocks plenty of desirables from Rebecca Taylor and Marc by Marc Jacobs along with the latest jeans from Juicy Couture and 7 for All Mankind; it's also "an excellent resource" for smart stuff from Milly, Paul & Joe, Vanessa Bruno and emerging designers, and, to go-with, "pricey" handbags and shoes.

Diane von Furstenberg

(aka DVF the Shop)

24	-	22	E

Meatpacking | 874 Washington St. (14th St.) | A/C/E/L to 14th St./ 8th Ave. | 646-486-4800 | www.dvf.com

When craving "eye candy for your wardrobe" from Ms. Furstenberg, the "Manhattan maven of comfortable, chic, body-conscious" design, head west to her recently relocated boutique, now on the ground floor of the new DVF Studio, a multifloor Meatpacking District complex; while cultists clamor for her "feminine and flattering" wrap dresses that "can handle many figure shapes", there's lots more on hand, plus you may see "the queen" herself, as she "treats this store as if it's her own closet."

Didi's Children's Boutique

-	-	-	E

E 80s | 1196 Madison Ave. (bet. 87th & 88th Sts.) | 4/5/6 to 86th St. | 212-860-4001 | www.didis.com

A nice alternative to the big-box behemoths, this "friendly, welcoming" East 80s emporium (with an elder sibling in Bedford, NY) aims to please with its imaginative, albeit "pricey", inventory of playthings for tykes, ranging from "adorable wooden European toys", train sets, puppet theaters and picture books to "cute" clothing, accessories and even mother-daughter tote bags.

Diesel

23	21	17	E

E 60s | 770 Lexington Ave. (60th St.) | 4/5/6/F/N/R/W to 59th St./ Lexington Ave. | 212-308-0055 ◗
SoHo | 135 Spring St. (bet. Greene & Wooster Sts.) | C/E to Spring St. | 212-625-1555
Union Sq | 1 Union Sq. W. (14th St.) | 4/5/6/L/N/Q/R/W to 14th St./ Union Sq. | 646-336-8552 ◗
www.diesel.com

It's the "king" of "everything denim" declare denizens who worship the "always hip" label that helped "start it all" at these huge Lex, SoHo and Union Square outposts; if you're "lucky enough to have a Diesel body", these "high-priced", "cutting-edge" styles "deliver" and "keep you coming back"; but a miffed minority fumes about the staff of "absolute prima donnas", grumbling "just remember you're not allowed to touch" the "carefully stacked inventory."

Diesel Denim Gallery

24	23	18	E

SoHo | 68 Greene St. (bet. Broome & Spring Sts.) | C/E to Spring St. | 212-966-5593 | www.diesel.com

"If you want sharp, unique, imported limited-edition jeans" that make your butt "look super", this "trendy", half-gallery, half-shop is the SoHo "spot for you"; some pairs "seem to fit better than others" and service veers from "helpful" to "terribly hip", but instead of singing the blues, remember that "buying new" denim "isn't supposed to be easy", plus there's a silver lining: "great" options to "suit anyone's body."

Diesel Kids
▽ 25 | 23 | 19 | E

SoHo | 414-416 W. Broadway (bet. Prince & Spring Sts.) | C/E to Spring St. | 212-343-3863 | www.dieselkids.com

Budding fashionistas get their fill of the Italian fashion phenomenon at this spacious SoHo shop done up with stainless-steel fixtures and chocolate-colored wood floors; the "very friendly staff" helps steer you through the selection of seasonal streetwear and footwear and, of course, the giant jeans wall, stuffed to the seams with its highly covetable premium denim for babies through teens.

Dinosaur Designs
– | – | – | E

NoLita | 250 Mott St. (bet. Houston & Prince Sts.) | B/D/F/V to B'way/ Lafayette St. | 212-680-3523 | www.dinosaurdesigns.com

The three Aussies behind this Sydney-based business with an offshoot in NoLita began with organic-inspired, brightly colored and "quirky" resin jewelry like rings, bangles and necklaces and have branched out using the same modern material to shape housewares, vases and bowls in equally vibrant shades.

Dinosaur Hill
▽ 24 | 24 | 24 | M

E Vill | 306 E. Ninth St. (2nd Ave.) | 6 to Astor Pl. | 212-473-5850 | www.dinosaurhill.com

"Expect the unexpected" at this "simply marvelous" East Village "wonderland", where every "nook and cranny" is filled with "magical" toys, making it "fun to wander through with a child"; it has "all the basics", but it's also jammed with the "sort of stuff you would've gone nuts for when you were" a kid like kaleidoscopes, marionettes from around the world, stained-glass fairies, wooden dollhouses, steel drums and figurines.

Dior Homme
▽ 26 | 26 | 21 | VE

E 50s | 17 E. 57th St. (bet. 5th & Madison Aves.) | N/R/W to 5th Ave./ 59th St. | 212-421-6009 | www.dior.com

Hip *hommes* "highly recommend" house designer Hedi Slimane's slim suits, narrow ties and jewelry at this sleek, polished sliver of a store next to Dior's main 57th Street boutique; the black slate floors and white laminated shelving show off the merch, which is "good value, given the quality"; nevertheless, some caution that given the costs and the cuts, these clothes are "only for the rich and skinny."

⚠ Dior New York
28 | 28 | 23 | VE

E 50s | 21 E. 57th St. (bet. 5th & Madison Aves.) | N/R/W to 5th Ave./ 59th St. | 212-931-2950 | www.dior.com

"If you're on an expense account", "start shopping here" at this luxury-laden, multifloor haven for logo-loco ladies with "displays that are some of the best in NY" and an "unpretentious staff"; not many designers alive today can "match designer John Galliano's wit, visual flair and pure madness" of design – be it in bustier bikinis or corseted gowns – all of which enable "your days to be a continuous Sarah-Jessica-Parker-in-*Sex-and-the-City* moment."

Disc-O-Rama Music World

	QUALITY	DISPLAY	SERVICE	COST
	20	9	14	I

G Vill | 186 W. Fourth St. (bet. 6th & 7th Aves.) | A/B/C/D/E/F/V to W. 4th St. | 212-206-8417 ●
G Vill | 44 W. Eighth St. (bet. MacDougal St. & 6th Ave.) | A/B/C/D/E/F/V to W. 4th St. | 212-477-9410 ●
Union Sq | 40 Union Sq. E. (bet. 16th & 17th Sts.) | 4/5/6/L/N/Q/R/W to 14th St./Union Sq. | 212-260-8616
866-606-2614 | www.discorama.com

"New releases" of "top CDs" plus "current videos and games" can be found at this "no-frills" trio; the "crowded", "small spaces" are "difficult to browse" and some of the "knowledgeable" staffers are "nasty", but with such "low prices" you'll think the merchandise "must have fallen off the truck" – strike quickly, though, as "popular product goes fast."

Disrespectacles

	QUALITY	DISPLAY	SERVICE	COST
	▽ 27	27	27	E

TriBeCa | 117 W. Broadway (bet. Duane & Reade Sts.) | 1/2/3 to Chambers St. | 212-608-8892
W Vill | 82 Christopher St. (bet. Bleecker St. & 7th Ave. S.) | 1 to Christopher St./Sheridan Sq. | 212-741-9550
www.disrespectacles.com

At this "cool" TriBeCa–West Village duo, a "learned", "extremely accommodating" staff proffers "the most unique eyewear in the city" ranging from "understated to outlandish" with "hard-to-find vintage" and "funky" eyeglasses in between; you'll have "hours of fun trying on" the "excellent quality" specs that "get more compliments than your jewelry" and make "New Yorkers the envy of mall-bound" vision-questers.

Diva

	QUALITY	DISPLAY	SERVICE	COST
	-	-	-	E

Midwood | 1409 Ave. M (bet. 14th & 15th Sts.) | Brooklyn | Q to Ave. M | 718-645-9797

Little fashion plates make regular pilgrimages to this pink-and-chocolate-colored Midwood boutique, which aims to bring out the inner diva in every girl, particularly tweens, with its racks of runway-worthy sportswear and special-occasion finery from hip European labels like Miss Blumarine, Parrot and Simonetta, and its stockpile of stylin' shoes from designers D & G Junior and Moschino.

DKNY ●

	QUALITY	DISPLAY	SERVICE	COST
	21	22	18	E

E 60s | 655 Madison Ave. (60th St.) | N/R/W to 5th Ave./59th St. | 212-223-3569
SoHo | 420 W. Broadway (bet. Prince & Spring Sts.) | C/E to Spring St. | 646-613-1100
www.dkny.com

Whether they're sipping a smoothie at the Madison Avenue shop's organic cafe or sampling the fruity Be Delicious fragrance at the SoHo site, disciples declare Donna Karan's "got it down" with her lower-priced line, aka "staple urbanwear" for men and women seeking "stylish" items for work or play; but views vary on the clothes' price-value ratio ("excellent" vs. "not always affordable") and whether the staff comes with or "without any attitude."

D/L Cerney ●

	QUALITY	DISPLAY	SERVICE	COST
	-	-	-	M

E Vill | 13 E. Seventh St. (bet. 2nd & 3rd Aves.) | 6 to Astor Pl. | 212-673-7033
Retro works best when it's well made – and a bit cheeky – which is why this East Village fixture attracts guys and gals with a weakness for the

house label's "unusual, top-quality", vintage-inspired rayon gabardine shirts and silk wrap skirts, ratcheted up a style notch with "details like special antique buttons", '40s-esque prints and topstitching; you'll look right in step to stop by McSorley's Old Ale House (dating back to 1854) for a post-purchase pint.

Doggystyle

-	-	-	E

SoHo | 100 Thompson St. (bet. Prince & Spring Sts.) | C/E to Spring St. | 212-431-9200 | www.doggystylenyc.com

"Pampered pooches" make tracks for this "amazing" SoHo shop showcasing an "excellent selection of hip apparel" and "unique" accessories; "special" services like pet portraiture are other reasons some say it's the "best" boutique for "spoiled puppies."

Dö Kham ◑

▽ 22	21	22	M

NoLita | 51 Prince St. (bet. Lafayette & Mulberry Sts.) | N/R/W to Prince St. | 212-966-2404

This NoLita shop features the "best of Tibet in Manhattan" with its "amazing array of boho-chic" fashion ranging from "unique chandelier earrings" and vibrant tunics to tiered skirts "embellished with sequins"; devotees can also decorate their digs with "perennially fashionable" Silk Road must-haves, including colorful bedspreads and pillows.

Dolce & Gabbana

27	26	22	VE

E 60s | 825 Madison Ave. (bet. 68th & 69th Sts.) | 6 to 68th St. | 212-249-4100 | www.dolcegabbana.it

The dynamic duo of Domenico Dolce and Stefano Gabbana never disappoints those types – "tall, skinny and a bit loud in their taste" – who visit this well-appointed East 60s showcase for the label synonymous with "pure sex appeal"; an "amazing staff" offers help with the "original", corsetry-inspired collections for her and "edgy suits" for him, inspiring those who live to "imagine their inner rock star" to declare "when money is no object, this is the place to shop – even when it *is* an object, this is the place to shop."

Dolce Vita ⧄

23	19	18	E

LES | 122 Orchard St. (bet. Delancy & Livington Sts.) | F/J/M/Z to Delancey/Essex Sts. | 212-533-2231 | www.shopdolcevita.com

No "sticker shock" here – just "trendy shoes" for a heck of a lot less money than similar styles at "neighboring stores" marvel admirers of this Lower East Sider; check out the extensive collection of house-brand women's footwear, then move on to the "great selection" of hip womenswear from under-the-radar labels like Alex Gaines, H. Fredriksson, United Bamboo and Vivienne Westwood – there's lots of sweet "stuff" here.

Domain

20	20	18	E

E 60s | Trump Palace | 1179 Third Ave. (69th St.) | 6 to 68th St. | 212-639-1101

Flatiron | 938 Broadway (22nd St.) | N/R/W to 23rd St. | 212-228-7450

W 60s | 101 West End Ave. (65th St.) | 1 to 66th St./Lincoln Ctr. | 917-441-2397

800-888-1388 | www.domain-home.com

Trio of home stores that is the domain of European-inspired, "oversized" "traditional furniture" such as armoires, couches, chaises, bookcases and beds with "ornate" decorative elements like wrought-iron flourishes, fluted pilasters, hand-painted details and other frills as well as "antiquey accessories"; modernists maintain the styles can be a "little foofie", but bargain-hunters boast that "good deals can be had at sale time."

Domenico Vacca
-│-│-│VE

E 50s | 781 Fifth Ave. (bet. 59th & 60th Sts.) | 4/5/6/F/N/R/W to 59th St./Lexington Ave. | 212-759-6333
E 60s | 702 Madison Ave. (bet. 62nd & 63rd Sts.) | 6 to 68th St. | 212-421-8902
SoHo | 367 W. Broadway (Broome St.) | C/E to Spring St. | 212-925-0010 ◑
www.domenicovacca.com

Sartorial sybarites feel right at home at this threesome of high-end haberdasheries where well-dressed CEOs go for alligator shoes hand-crafted in Naples, overcoats lined in cashmere and colorful, custom-made suits and eveningwear that reflect their prestigious bank accounts; intelligent salespeople and plush surroundings – wool-paneled walls and soft leather couches – add to the allure.

Donna Karan
25│25│23│VE

E 60s | 819 Madison Ave. (bet. 68th & 69th Sts.) | 6 to 68th St. | 212-861-1001 | www.donnakaran.com

Art imitates life at this "clever" multilevel Madison Avenue store, "which mixes clothing and objects in a magical manner", placing this admired American designer's his-and-hers collections in "silks and natural fibers that titillate the senses" against the backdrop of a bamboo and Japanese sculpture garden; a few feel the line's "lost some of its glamour" of late, but most "monotone-dressing NYers" maintain these "consistently excellent pieces become never-dated classics", and applaud the "amazing service."

Donzella ⊠
-│-│-│VE

TriBeCa | 17 White St. (bet. 6th Ave. & W. B'way) | 1 to Franklin St. | 212-965-8919 | www.donzella.com

You'll find "high-end furnishings with all the trimmings" (including "very expensive" price tags) at this TriBeCa store; "a helpful staff" guides you through the museum-worthy collection of vintage or period furniture and accessories from Europe and America, ranging from ebonized mahogany seating from Edward Wormley and cork-top side tables circa 1950 from Paul Frankl to Murano glassware from Italy.

Dooney & Bourke
25│23│22│E

E 60s | 20 E. 60th St. (bet. Madison & Park Aves.) | 4/5/6/F/N/R/W to 59th St./Lexington Ave. | 212-223-7444 | 800-347-5000 | www.dooney.com

"Even if D.B. aren't your initials", the "lovely" leather backpacks, "preppy" "colorful" drawstring purses and other luxe accessories at this "great" East 60s store will have you "obsessed"; the "cheerful", "helpful" staff may be another reason why loyalists "own almost every handbag they've made."

Door Store
17│16│17│M

Chelsea | 123 W. 17th St. (bet. 6th & 7th Aves.) | 1 to 18th St. | 212-627-1515
E 50s | 969 Third Ave. (bet. 58th & 59th Sts.) | 4/5/6/F/N/R/W to 59th St./Lexington Ave. | 212-421-5273

(continued)

Door Store

Gramercy | 1 Park Ave. (33rd St.) | 6 to 33rd St. | 212-679-9700
W 80s | 601 Amsterdam Ave. (89th St.) | 1 to 86th St. | 212-501-8699
🆕 **Downtown** | 475 Atlantic Ave. (bet. Nevins St. & 3rd Ave.) |
Brooklyn | 2/3/4/5/B/D/M/N/Q/R to Atlantic Ave. | 718-237-6888 ◗
www.doorstorefurniture.com

"Decent-quality furniture" "at great prices" is "the reason this chain's been around for 52 years"; it's "not known for the coolest" presentation, and "there's not a door in sight", but "practical" pieces like "casual so-fas", bedroom sets, tables and entertainment units that are "attractive" and appropriate for a "first apartment" keep customers coming back.

Dosa
▽ 24 | 23 | 23 | E

SoHo | 107 Thompson St. (bet. Prince & Spring Sts.) | C/E to Spring St. |
212-431-1733 | www.dosainc.com

"Pretty, bohemian, arty" are adjectives that all apply to the womenswear in this nearly "unnoticeable" SoHo shop, whose eco-friendly owner-designer, Christina Kim, specializes in "better-quality" cotton and silk pieces (pajamas are particularly popular), accessories and home furnishings; she employs hand-loomed fabrics, organically grown wool, natural pigments and metallic threads – so "be prepared for high prices."

Douglas Cosmetics ◗
22 | 18 | 18 | M

E 40s | Grand Central | 42nd St. (Vanderbilt Ave.) | 4/5/6/7/S to 42nd St./
Grand Central | 212-599-1776 | 800-770-0081 | www.douglascosmetics.com

"When you forget that last-minute hostess gift or your makeup bag on your way to a weekend rendezvous", this cosmetics purveyor in Grand Central gets an "A for commuter convenience"; at other times, "limited space" and "service that's offhand at best" aren't nearly as impressive.

ⓩ Downtown Yarns
28 | 25 | 25 | E

E Vill | 45 Ave. A (bet. 3rd & 4th Sts.) | F/V to Lower East Side/2nd Ave. |
212-995-5991 | www.downtownyarns.com

"The screen door is a clue" to the "laid-back" vibe of this "inviting" "Vermont country store on Avenue A", a neighborhood knitters' "retreat" where the "kind" staff is "willing to help you on all fronts" and the "beautiful" wools and tools "spur [one's] creativity"; though a few frown on the "tiny", "dim" confines ("not good for color matching"), there's one big plus: "you'll pay less here than at some more upscale joints."

Doyle and Doyle ⓜ
▽ 25 | 27 | 28 | E

LES | 189 Orchard St. (bet. Houston & Stanton Sts.) | F/V to Lower East Side/
2nd Ave. | 212-677-9991 | www.doyledoyle.com

"Charming" and "helpful" sister-owners Pamela and Elizabeth Doyle have a "great eye" and it shows at this "small", "laid-back" Lower East Side shop with "fantasyland" displays of "gorgeous" and "eclectic" vintage and estate jewelry; styles range from Georgian to art deco, and prices from "affordable to extravagant."

Drimmers
24 | 12 | 20 | M

Midwood | 1608 Coney Island Ave. (bet. L & M Aves.) | Brooklyn | Q to
Ave. M | 718-773-8483 | 877-338-3500 | www.drimmers.com

"When you are ready for the ultimate kitchen", this 30-year-old, family-owned Coney Island Avenue appliance store offers "some of the best prices" on high-end domestic and European refrigerators, dishwashers, washer/dryers and ovens, as well as "great service"; it may be a "trek" getting out there, but once you do and order your goods, there's no charge for their delivery within the five boroughs.

Dr. Jay's ●

	18	14	12	M

Garment Dist | 33 W. 34th St. (bet. 5th & 6th Aves.) | B/D/F/N/Q/R/V/W to 34th St./Herald Sq. | 212-695-3354 | www.drjays.com
Additional locations throughout the NY area

This "Midtown mega-shop for all things streetwear" does a good job at serving up "basic urban thugwear" from popular brands like Ecko and Triple Five Soul for "hip-hoppers" of all ages and sexes; while the "lines are usually long" and the service "lax", your "cred will be impeccable" in these "ultracool" threads that won't "break your bank account."

Ⓩ DSW ●

	21	16	11	M

Financial Dist | 102 N. End Ave. (Vesey St.) | A/C to Chambers St. | 212-945-7419
Union Sq | 40 E. 14th St., 3rd fl. (bet. B'way & University Pl.) | 4/5/6/L/N/Q/R/W to 14th St./Union Sq. | 212-674-2146
Downtown | Atlantic Terminal | 139 Flatbush Ave. (bet. Atlantic & 4th Aves.) | Brooklyn | 2/3/4/5/B/D/M/N/Q/R to Atlantic Ave. | 718-789-6973
Elmhurst | Queens Pl. | 88-01 Queens Blvd. (bet. 55th & 56th Sts.) | Queens | G/R/V to Grand Ave./Newtown | 718-595-1361
800-477-8595 | www.dswshoe.com

"If you don't mind last year's styles" from labels like "Coach and Carlos Santana", you can let "your inner Imelda run wild" at this chain, which carries "row after row" of "everything from stilettos to sneakers" – "oh, and they have men's too"; though it's all discounted, "check the clearance rack first" for the "really good deals"; P.S. it's especially rewarding "if you're a fan of self-serve: there's no waiting for someone to fetch your shoes because they're all out on the floor."

Dudley's Paw Ⓢ

	–	–	–	E

TriBeCa | 327 Greenwich St. (bet. Duane & Jay Sts.) | 1/2/3 to Chambers St. | 212-966-5167

A "teeny-weeny shop with a big heart", this TriBeCa longtimer "barks and meows NYC" "neighborhood store"; the staff "couldn't be nicer", and even if the "small space" means the "selection is minimal", it offers "all the essentials" and the pet food's "good quality."

NEW Dulcinée ●

	–	–	–	M

LES | 127 Stanton St. (bet. Essex & Norfolk Sts.) | F/V to Lower East Side/2nd Ave. | 212-253-2534 | www.dulcineenyc.com

At this LES vintage clothier, the selection is small but chic: women's couture labels like YSL, Alaïa and Ungaro, mostly from the '60s–'80s (though you never know when there'll be an older "great find, like a mint Claire McCardle with tags, from – what, 50 years ago?"), plus a large array of leather goods; only drawback to the streamlined white space is the dressing room – actually, a corner with a ringed curtain around it.

Duncan Quinn ●Ⓜ

	–	–	–	E

NoLita | 8 Spring St. (bet. Bowery & Elizabeth St.) | J/M/Z to Bowery | 212-226-7030 | www.duncanquinn.com

Make an appointment at this "candy-box" of a shop for "the dandy in your life", who'll relish this cheeky namesake Brit who's made his rep applying Savile Row refinement to rather racy clothes (the "boldest pinks and purples"); though it's about the size of a walk-in closet, the NoLita digs offer ready-made and bespoke suits and shirts, luggage and all sorts of accessories, from suspenders to sterling silver collar stays, plus custom-tailored haberdashery for her.

Dunderdon Workshop
-	-	-	E

SoHo | 272 Lafayette St. (Prince St.) | B/D/F/V to B'way/Lafayette St. | 212-226-4040 | www.dunderdon.com

It may be super-small in size, but this "wonderful" SoHo Swedish import is big on style, supplying trendsetting guys with functional yet fashion-forward finds; the detail-happy don't have to dig deep to uncover "the best" sturdy, multipocketed canvas and denim pants, plus padded and pile-lined casual jackets, and to go-with, cool hoodies, T-shirts and accessories; N.B. womenswear is slated to arrive in spring '07.

Dune 🗷
-	-	-	E

TriBeCa | 88 Franklin St. (bet. B'way & Church St.) | 1 to Franklin St. | 212-925-6171 | www.dune-ny.com

Housed in a soaring former painting studio in TriBeCa is this "minimalist" showroom for made-to-order, cutting-edge American contemporary furniture like funky ottomans and sectional sofas; if you don't see what you need, "just ask for what you want – they'll make it."

Dunhill
27	27	26	VE

E 50s | 711 Fifth Ave. (bet. 55th & 56th Sts.) | E/V to 5th Ave./53rd St. | 212-753-9292 | 800-776-4053 | www.dunhill.com

"Bringing the refined style of the English elite" to Midtown, this "bastion of civilized living" offers men of means an "absolutely marvelous shopping experience", from the "impeccable service" to the "totally unnecessary but totally desirable objects"; "check out" the "high-quality" bespoke clothing, shoes and "genuine gentlemen's accessories" including leather goods, watches and "lighters that'll last a lifetime" (a flashback to its cigar-specialist past); it's the "best – if you can afford it."

Dusica Dusica ●
-	-	-	E

SoHo | 67 Prince St. (Crosby St.) | N/R/W to Prince St. | 212-966-9099 | www.dusicadusica.com

Cultists who consider footwear art get their culture fix at designer Dusica Sacks' playfully minimalist SoHo boutique set in, what else, a former gallery, with the "unique" shoes, boots and handbags displayed against a dramatic white backdrop enhanced by 20-ft.-high curtains; you "won't see yourself coming and going" in these colorful heels and flats decked out with straps, buckles, fur and other "inventive" details.

Dykes Lumber 🗷
24	13	22	M

W 40s | 348 W. 44th St. (bet. 8th & 9th Aves.) | 1/2/3/7/N/Q/R/S/W to 42nd St./Times Sq. | 212-246-6480

Bronx | 1777 W. Farms Rd. (174th St.) | 2/5 to W. Farms Sq. | 718-784-3920

Park Slope | 167 Sixth St. (bet. 2nd & 3rd Aves.) | Brooklyn | F/M/R to 4th Ave./9th St. | 718-624-3350

LIC | 26-16 Jackson Ave. (bet. 44th & Purves Sts.) | Queens | E/V to 23rd St./Ely Ave. | 718-784-3920

www.dykeslumber.com

"When you need wood" "delivered fast" for that home project or "molding for your pre-war apartment", head to this borough-wide "mom-and-pop lumberyard" outfit staffed with "friendly" folk "who know their stuff" and put first-time DIYers "at ease"; constructionists confide that you can also nail down windows from specialists like Andersen or Marvin, and even order custom millwork or "doors and the like" here – "who'd a thunk it?"

Dylan's Candy Bar

22 | 26 | 16 | M

E 60s | 1011 Third Ave. (60th St.) | 4/5/6/F/N/R/W to 59th St./Lexington Ave. | 646-735-0078 | www.dylanscandybar.com

Devotees drool over this East 60s "sugary wonderland" whose colorful, "chaotic" premises promise the sweet-toothed and "chocoholics every conceivable fix", from "your favorite childhood bar" to "the latest craze", from "hard-to-find flavors" to "ordinary" brands in bulk; some get a toothache from the prices (it "costs how much"?), but most agree "this is what's at the end of the rainbow"; N.B. check out the candy-hued clothing and accessories too.

Earnest Cut & Sew, An

▽ 25 | 19 | 19 | VE

Meatpacking | 821 Washington St. (bet. Gansevoort & Little W. 12th Sts.) | A/C/E/L to 14th St./8th Ave. | 212-242-3414 | www.earnestsewn.com

The Earnest Sewn "jeans everybody wants", you know, the ones "people always ask about" with "just the right amount of distress and whimsy", can be found at this Meatpacking District concept shop duded down with salvaged wood plank floors; these "top-quality", label-less light-weight must-haves from the co-founder of Paper Denim & Cloth are "pricey", particularly the "custom-fit-for-your-bum" styles, made for you within hours, but there's lots to "love", including the general store decor, which reveals a rustic sort of "taste and philosophy."

E.A.T. Gifts

23 | 21 | 17 | E

E 80s | 1062 Madison Ave. (bet. 80th & 81st Sts.) | 6 to 77th St. | 212-861-2544

Eli Zabar's "crowded" Madison Avenue kids' mecca is the "perfect" place to "get stuck on a rainy afternoon", especially if you relish "rummaging through the bins" for "obsession-worthy knickknacks and toys"; you'll find "whimsical, fun" "finds in every nook and cranny", from "Tin-Tin to Olivia to creative gifts for adults" to "last-minute" "party favors"; sure, some "prices are insane, but they do have some cute" "tchotchkes."

E. Braun & Co. 🔣

– | – | – | E

E 60s | 717 Madison Ave. (bet. 63rd & 64th Sts.) | F to Lexington Ave./63rd St. | 212-838-0650 | www.ebraunandco.com

Since 1943, this Madison Avenue "classic" has been providing "beautifully detailed linens" imported from Europe for the bed, dining table and bath; if the luxury of embroideries, appliqués and scalloped edges on Egyptian cotton, silk and linen is not enough to lure you in, there's also a myriad of customization options – monogramming, patterning, quilting and coloring – offered.

Edge nyNoHo 🅼

24 | 20 | 21 | M

NoHo | 65 Bleecker St. (bet. B'way & Lafayette St.) | B/D/F/V to B'way/Lafayette St. | 212-358-0255 | www.edgeny.com

"An impressive gathering of independent designers" – "all eager to spill every detail about how their goods were made" – collects in mini-boutiques at this large, bright bazaar created by Market NYC founder

Nicholas Petrou in NoHo's historic Louis Sullivan building; it's "the best place to pick up something unique" and "not too expensive", whether your needs run to "one-of-a-kind" jewelry or "something new" in men's and women's apparel and accessories.

NEW Ed Hardy ◐

Meatpacking | 425 W. 13th St. (bet. 9th Ave. & Washington St.) | A/C/E/L to 14th St./8th Ave. | 212-488-3131 | www.donedhardy.com

From its doorman ropes to its hip-hop vibe to its "eclectic clientele of rock stars and star stalkers", this warehouse-turned–"Meatpacking District hideaway" feels more like a nightclub than store – but that's to be expected from designer Christian Audigier, who tapped the tattooing talent of inker Don Ed Hardy to create illustration-adorned "flashy and cashy" clothes ("tattoo chic for the needle phobic"); "if you're looking for skull design" merch, this is the place, so "grab a T-shirt", rhinestone cap, sneakers or energy drink, while it's "still the fad of the moment."

Edith and Daha ◐

LES | 104 Rivington St. (bet. Essex & Ludlow Sts.) | F/J/M/Z to Delancey/Essex Sts. | 212-979-9992

"You actually get great vintage for vintage prices" gush groupies of this Lower East Side basement-level boutique, whose namesake owners "are the best at selecting" clothing of a feminine, flirty nature – plus period purses and shoes to match; they also sell their own line of "cool, original pieces" with a retro look.

Eidolon ◐ M

Park Slope | 233 Fifth Ave. (bet. Carroll & President Sts.) | Brooklyn | M/R to Union St. | 718-638-8194 | www.eidolonbklyn.com

Shoppers desiring the "image of perfection" (that's what Eidolon means) don't mind the "microscopic size" of this Park Slope cooperative, which sells "trendy, but nice" womenswear from local designers, including co-owners Andrea Fisher's "beautifully sewn", "1940s-inspired" dresses, Amara Felice's harmoniously hued separates, Yukie Ohta's one-of-a-kind handbags and totes, plus colorful, retro-inspired shoes from Lisa Nading/Gentle Souls.

Eileen Fisher

E 50s | 521 Madison Ave. (bet. 53rd & 54th Sts.) | E/V to 5th Ave./53rd St. | 212-759-9888

E 70s | 1039 Madison Ave. (bet. 79th & 80th Sts.) | 6 to 77th St. | 212-879-7799

E Vill | 314 E. Ninth St. (bet. 1st & 2nd Aves.) | 6 to Astor Pl. | 212-529-5715 ◐

Flatiron | 166 Fifth Ave. (bet. 21st & 22nd Sts.) | N/R/W to 23rd St. | 212-924-4777

SoHo | 395 W. Broadway (bet. Broome & Spring Sts.) | C/E to Spring St. | 212-431-4567

W 50s | The Shops at Columbus Circle, Time Warner Ctr. | 10 Columbus Circle, 2nd fl. (bet. 58th & 60th Sts.) | 1/A/B/C/D to 59th St./Columbus Circle | 212-823-9575 ◐

W 70s | 341 Columbus Ave. (bet. 76th & 77th Sts.) | 1 to 79th St. | 212-362-3000

800-345-3362 | www.eileenfisher.com

This "comfy" chain "offers new things without straying from its core concept" – "beautiful clothing that never dates" – pleasing "women of a certain age" who appreciate the "forgiving", "unstructured" fit of its basics made to "flatter figures that are less than (or perhaps more than) perfect" as well as "fabulous salespeople"; never mind if a few dis its "upscale frump"-wear as "formless"; N.B. the original East Ninth Street branch carries samples and discounted merchandise.

Einstein-Moomjy
24 | 20 | 21 | E

E 50s | 141 E. 56th St. (bet. Lexington & 3rd Aves.) | 4/5/6/F/N/R/W to 59th St./Lexington Ave. | 212-758-0900 | 800-864-3633 | www.einsteinmoomjy.com

"What a range of rugs" – from Aubusson, Arts & Crafts, tribal and traditional hand-knotted ones to broadloom Berbers and a kids' collection – can be found at this East 50s emporium that also offers furniture like leather ottomans and sofas.

Eisenberg & Eisenberg
▽ 22 | 16 | 20 | M

Flatiron | 16 W. 17th St. (bet. 5th & 6th Aves.) | F/L/V to 14th St./6th Ave. | 212-627-1290 | www.eisenbergandeisenberg.com

"Been buying clothes here for 50 years" say surveyors about this family-owned Flatiron fixture for men's formalwear that's famed for "very good values" in purchases and rentals, whether one favors forward styles from Andrew Fezza or traditional looks from the likes of Lord West; amid a simple warehouse setting, all the appropriate accessories are available too, from patent-leather shoes to cummerbunds.

Elgot Ⓢ
▽ 25 | 19 | 16 | VE

E 60s | 937 Lexington Ave. (bet. 68th & 69th Sts.) | 6 to 68th St. | 212-879-1200 | www.elgotkitchens.com

For half a century, this "reliable" Upper East Side kitchen and bath showroom has featured some of "the best" quality manufacturers like Gaggenau, Wolf and Sub-Zero, as well as custom and semi-custom cabinetry and countertops.

Elie Tahari ●
24 | 22 | 21 | E

SoHo | 417 W. Broadway (bet. Prince & Spring Sts.) | C/E to Spring St. | 212-334-4441 | www.elietahari.com

A sparkling ballroom-sized chandelier welcomes women to waltz right into this sweeping SoHo store where Elie Tahari's "well-tailored" "classics with a kick" please "ladies with curves" who collect the "well-made" silk-lined coats, brocade jackets and "sassy, sexy" separates; "expensive embellishments" like filigree buttons, plus "attentive service", make purchases "worth the extra dollars."

Elizabeth Charles ●Ⓜ
- | - | - | E

Meatpacking | 639½ Hudson St. (bet. Gansevoort & Horatio Sts.) | A/C/E/L to 14th St./8th Ave. | 212-243-3201 | www.elizabeth-charles.com

The "decor and layout are the best" assert insiders, who, much like celeb customers Gemma Ward and Hilary Swank, covet everything about Melbourne-born tastemaker Elizabeth Charles' Meatpacking District shop bordering the West Village; antiques and midcentury-modern furniture create a madcap living-room–like feel while the Down Under designs from Karen Walker, Lover and Maticevski, rarely found outside of Oz, inspire unbridled lust; try on the goodies in the huge boudoir to the rear while reflecting on the splendor of the garden.

	QUALITY	DISPLAY	SERVICE	COST

Elizabeth Locke ⑤   ▽ 29 | 29 | 26 | VE

E 70s | 968 Madison Ave. (bet. 75th & 76th Sts.) | 6 to 77th St. | 212-744-7878

"Gorgeous" "handmade" earrings, brooches, chokers and charm bracelets are adorned with miniature "mosaics, Venetian glass intaglios", Roman coins and precious or semiprecious stones and set in signature hammered 19-karat gold; the palazzolike interior of the East 70s shop is an appropriate backdrop for the designer's "supreme artistry."

Ellen Christine Ⓜ   – | – | – | E

Chelsea | 255 W. 18th St. (bet. 7th & 8th Aves.) | 1 to 18th St. | 212-242-2457 | www.ellenchristine.com

"Booming personality Ellen Christine has created a little" Chelsea "nook filled with crannies" that boast "amazing vintage creations" and "contemporary" finds, from pre-1920s toppers and chic modern-day cloches to Victorian-inspired capelets and jewelry that "complete a look"; this milliner/costumer/stylist custom-makes "fun, wacky" hats too and the *chapeaux*-crazed confide "she knows what works on people."

El Museo Del Barrio Ⓜ   ▽ 20 | 18 | 20 | M

E 100s | 1230 Fifth Ave. (104th St.) | 6 to 103rd St. | 212-831-7272 | www.elmuseo.org

From "superb jewelry" to "lovely ceramics" to "interesting" crafts such as *santos* and masks, "hidden treasures" abound at this "small shop" in an Upper East Side museum focused on Latin American and Caribbean art and history; the "great products" also include books, posters and CDs, and its amigos report some "incredible deals."

Emanuel Ungaro ⑤   28 | 26 | 23 | VE

E 60s | 792 Madison Ave. (67th St.) | 6 to 68th St. | 212-249-4090 | www.emanuelungaro.fr

Some things never change – like the "beautiful creations" at this "so-chic" Madison Avenue fixture – and that's a good thing for Gallic-crazy gals who "love, love, love this line" with its bustiers, poufy skirts and sensuous gowns in a mélange of sun-drenched florals or geometric prints; the "out-of-this-world prices" mean "if your last name is Trump, you'll be a regular"; otherwise, you best Ungar-go elsewhere.

NEW EMc2 ●   23 | 24 | 21 | E

NoLita | 240 Elizabeth St. (Houston St.) | N/R/W to Prince St. | 212-431-4134 | www.emmettmccarthy.com

A "haven for those who need their *Project Runway* fix", this "cute new NoLita shop" carries "gorgeous" womenswear from a "mix and match of [the show's] winners and losers", including designers Chloe Dau, Kara Janx and the store's owner, Emmett McCarthy; "never knowing when you might run into Tim Gunn" (McCarthy designed his bobblehead doll) "makes it even more fun", even if some would wave *auf Wiedersehen* to a scene they call "tragically hip (more tragic than hip)."

Emmelle   ▽ 21 | 22 | 18 | E

E 70s | 1042 Madison Ave. (bet. 79th & 80th Sts.) | 6 to 77th St. | 212-570-6559

E 80s | 123 E. 89th St. (bet. Lexington & Park Aves.) | 4/5/6 to 86th St. | 212-289-5253

"Park Avenue" types head to this Upper East Side twosome to peruse the rows and rows of "lovely" "classic designs" including "great special-occasion dresses", and "truly timeless" suits that fit well, even "if you're not stick thin" – and chances are you won't "see someone else wearing the same thing"; still, "service varies" – "you take the good with the bad and the rude."

Emporio Armani

23 | 23 | 20 | E

E 50s | 601 Madison Ave. (bet. 57th & 58th Sts.) | N/R/W to 5th Ave./59th St. | 212-317-0800

SoHo | 410 W. Broadway (Spring St.) | C/E to Spring St. | 646-613-8099
www.emporioarmani.com

"Beginner Armani"-ites of both sexes can savor the great Giorgio's "sophisticated, yet simple" secondary line, sold in stand-alone stores in SoHo and the East 50s; but while the "impeccably tailored" slouchy jackets and crêpe separates sell "for a fraction of his black label", many moan the "prices keep getting steeper", and sometimes the "distinct, flamboyant" styles "can turn heads both toward and away from you."

EMS (Eastern Mountain Sports) ●

26 | 21 | 21 | M

SoHo | 591 Broadway (bet. Houston & Prince Sts.) | N/R/W to Prince St. | 212-966-8730 | 888-463-6367 | www.ems.com

"You can almost smell the fresh pine" at this SoHo shop that caters to both experienced nature "sporting enthusiasts" and "aspiring outdoorsy" types "looking to gear up" with a "phenomenal selection" of "camping, whitewater", "hiking and climbing stuff" (as well as "work-out clothes" for dedicated urbanites); plus, the "friendly, knowledgeable staffers" are so "helpful" they'll even "put up a tent in the middle of the store if you ask."

Encore

20 | 14 | 13 | M

E 80s | 1132 Madison Ave. (bet. 84th & 85th Sts.) | 4/5/6 to 86th St. | 212-879-2850 | www.encoreresale.com

"If you like upscale designer merchandise", "great resale finds are possible at this second-floor Upper East Side institution", which for over 50 years has been supplying women and men with "conservative" consignment clothing, costume jewelry and "more shoes than my girlfriend should be looking at"; on the downside, the sales help can seem "hostile" and "the surroundings are not very pleasant", particularly the "curtainless communal dressing room."

Eneslow

▽ 28 | 23 | 24 | E

Murray Hill | 470 Park Ave. S. (bet. 31st & 32nd Sts.) | 6 to 33rd St. | 212-477-2300

Little Neck | Little Neck Shopping Ctr. | 254-61 Horace Harding Expwy. (Little Neck Pkwy.) | Queens | 718-357-5800
www.eneslow.com

There's nary a flimsily constructed stiletto to be found at this "source for comfort and superb fit" on Park Avenue South and the Little Neck Shopping Center, home of solid-to-the-ground footwear from the house label, plus names like Birkenstock, MBT and New Balance; "if you have foot problems", "walk no further", as the "knowledgeable staff" tends to "special needs."

environment337

- | - | - | E

NEW **G Vill** | 56 University Pl. (10th St.) | 4/5/6/L/N/R/Q/W to Union Square 14th St. | 212-254-3400 Ⓢ

(continued)

environment337

Carroll Gdns | 337 Smith St. (Carroll St.) | Brooklyn | F/G to Carroll St. | 718-522-1767 Ⓜ
www.environment337.com

Way "before there were a million housewares stores on Smith Street", there was this "pleasant" lifestyle emporium whose edited "with a great eye" collection includes pillows, lighting and furniture, ensuring that "one-of-a-kind gifts" can always be found here; N.B. Manhattanites' environment is now enlivened by a new Greenwich Village branch.

Enzo Angiolini ❶   20 | 18 | 18 | M

E 50s | 551 Madison Ave. (55th St.) | E/V to 5th Ave./53rd St. | 212-339-8921
Garment Dist | Manhattan Mall | 901 Sixth Ave. (bet. 32nd & 33rd Sts.) | B/D/F/N/Q/R/V/W to 34th St./Herald Sq. | 212-695-8903
www.ninewest.com

"On-trend", "office-worthy" shoes for the "sexy corporate woman" rule at these Midtown chain links that footwear fans find a "significant step up" from its "Nine West brethren"; it's "always dependable for affordable prices" that "won't break the bank", "decent comfort and current fashions" that "aren't too out there", but "if you're looking for something more fun and flashy, it's not the place to go."

Equinox Energy Wear ❶   22 | 19 | 17 | E

E 60s | 140 E. 63rd St. (Lexington Ave.) | 4/5/6/F/N/R/W to 59th St./Lexington Ave. | 212-752-5360 | www.equinoxfitness.com
Additional locations throughout the NY area

"Hip activewear that you'd expect from an equally hip club" is what proponents posit who are pumped over this gym chain's "trendy" selection that's as "stylish and comfy for running errands as it is for working out"; if it's "a little overpriced", check out the "discount bin."

Eres   28 | 25 | 22 | VE

E 50s | 621 Madison Ave. (bet. 58th & 59th Sts.) | 4/5/6/F/N/R/W to 59th St./Lexington Ave. | 212-223-3550 🛇
SoHo | 98 Wooster St. (bet. Prince & Spring Sts.) | C/E to Spring St. | 212-431-7300
800-340-6004 | www.eresparis.com

"The thing to wear" when you want to "feel like a sophisticated Paris jet-setter" – and spend like one too – jest Francophiles who gladly "break the bank" at the "fabulous" French lingerie chain's sleek Madison Avenue and SoHo branches; the bras, panties and "wonderful swimsuits" are "elegant and sexy" (and guys, just right for your "wife or significant other"), and while the designs are "subtle, they're never boring" – *oui*, they make any "woman look great."

Eric   24 | 19 | 22 | E

E 70s | 1333 Third Ave. (bet. 76th & 77th Sts.) | 6 to 77th St. | 212-288-8250
E 80s | 1222 Madison Ave. (bet. 88th & 89th Sts.) | 4/5/6 to 86th St. | 212-289-5762

It's "dangerous to live" within strolling distance of this Upper East Side duo declare shoehounds who exult in the "good variety" of "classy" footwear; choose from the "best flats!" imbued "with a great sense of style", designer "looks" from the retro-inspired line Bettye Muller and house-label "knockoffs of very expensive brands"; while it "can be pricey" you can always score at the "frequent sales."

Erica Tanov

QUALITY	DISPLAY	SERVICE	COST
–	–	–	E

NoLita | 204 Elizabeth St. (bet. Prince & Spring Sts.) | 6 to Spring St. | 212-334-8020 | www.ericatanov.com

This huge white shop with quirky lighting "makes you feel a lot cooler than usual" confide insiders, who "soak in the NoLita-ness of it", perusing the namesake designer's dreamy collection for women, which includes fluttery dresses and "beautiful" jackets, pants and skirts imbued "with a sense of earnestness, in spite of the very New York prices"; splurge on compatible lines like John Smedley knitwear along with "especially lovely linens, children's clothing", jewelry and delicate lingerie.

Z Ermenegildo Zegna

QUALITY	DISPLAY	SERVICE	COST
28	26	24	VE

E 50s | 663 Fifth Ave. (bet. 52nd & 53rd Sts.) | E/V to 5th Ave./53rd St. | 212-421-4488 | www.zegna.com

"Who needs A to Z when Z is all you need" ask the well-appointed of this "understatedly elegant" Fifth Avenue store with a "knowledgeable staff" selling "dress-to-impress" menswear (plus a little for ladies) in "beautiful fabrics" "with a subtle hint of Euro-style"; "sure, it's expensive", but "if clothes make the man, Zegna makes them immortal" – so, if you can't "buy your entire wardrobe here, at least get a tie", or try the lower-priced Z Zegna and Zegna Sport lines.

Erwin Pearl

QUALITY	DISPLAY	SERVICE	COST
20	22	20	M

E 40s | Grand Central, Lexington Ave. passage | 42nd St. (Vanderbilt Ave.) | 4/5/6/7/S to 42nd St./Grand Central | 212-922-1106 ◗
E 60s | 697 Madison Ave. (bet. 62nd & 63rd Sts.) | 4/5/6/F/N/R/W to 59th St./Lexington Ave. | 212-753-3155
NEW **Financial Dist** | Winter Garden | 3 World Financial Ctr. (West St.) | R/W to Rector St. | 212-227-3400
W 50s | Rockefeller Ctr. | 70 W. 50th St. (bet. 5th & 6th Aves.) | B/D/F/V to 47-50th Sts./Rockefeller Ctr. | 212-977-9088
800-379-4673 | www.erwinpearl.com

Costume-jewelry quartet specializing in "fantastic fakes", from "the best faux pearls" to "cubic-zirconium studs in every size and color" starting at under $100 "so there are no tears if you lose one"; a few question the "disappointing quality", but most praise their "good-looking" "classic pieces at modest prices."

Escada

QUALITY	DISPLAY	SERVICE	COST
27	26	24	VE

E 50s | 715 Fifth Ave. (56th St.) | N/R/W to 5th Ave./59th St. | 212-755-2200 | www.escada.com

"For the woman with a little Ivana in her", this Midtown boutique stands ready to supply "sexy socialite" garb (structured suits, fur- and leather-trimmed sportswear) and accessories (crystal-encrusted cell phones); some call the look a bit "aggressive", like the help (though they do "find exactly what looks best on you"), but most marvel the "clothing is runway-worthy, you just need the body for it" – not to mention the bucks.

Eskandar ⑤

QUALITY	DISPLAY	SERVICE	COST
–	–	–	VE

G Vill | 33 E. 10th St. (bet. B'way & University Pl.) | N/R/W to 8th St. | 212-533-4200 | www.eskandar.com

"Understated, quiet and refined" describes this British designer's collection showcased at his light-filled, loftlike Greenwich Village shop;

guys and girls alike fall for his "forever pieces" including cowlneck tops, drawstring trousers and tunics that achieve an "almost monklike perfection" in "gorgeous" wool, cashmere and silk "fabrics and knits" that help "justify" the prices; penny-pinchers who "pray for the euro/dollar ratio to make it viable" can content themselves with a vase or a bottle of ginger-blossom body wash.

Esprit ⊘   17 | 19 | 17 | M

SoHo | 583 Broadway (bet. Houston & Prince Sts.) | N/R/W to 8th St. | 646-823-0183
Union Sq | 110 Fifth Ave. (16th St.) | 4/5/6/L/N/Q/R/W to 14th St./Union Sq. | 212-651-2121
W 50s | The Shops at Columbus Circle, Time Warner Ctr. | 10 Columbus Circle, 2nd fl. (bet. 58th & 60th Sts.) | 1/A/B/C/D to 59th St./Columbus Circle | 212-823-9922
Staten Island | Staten Island Mall | 2655 Richmond Ave. (bet. Platinum Ave. & Richmond Hill Rd.) | 347-745-3020
www.esprit.com

Fans who feel like they've "grown up alongside" this San Francisco label "are glad to see it back", hailing the "relatively inexpensive" items in "great colors and fabrics" with a "classic flair" that "manage to keep pace with trends without going overboard"; but critics kvetch that the "narrow selection", "weird sizing" and only "nice-ish" clothes are "not as cutting-edge as in days of yore."

Essentials ⊘   20 | 16 | 16 | M

E 70s | 1392 Third Ave. (79th St.) | 6 to 77th St. | 212-517-4447
NEW **Flatiron** | 123 19th St. (5th Ave.) | 4/5/6/L/N/Q/R/W to 14th St./Union Sq. | 212-228-8141
W 80s | 2259 Broadway (81st St.) | 1 to 79th St. | 212-721-2818

Customers "could die happy (and well moisturized)" at this "really essential" trio of "resources for beauty supplies", from cosmetics to haircare products and appliances; plus you're guaranteed to "find what they tried to sell you at your fancy salon at a fraction of the price", so "what more could you ask for?"

Estella   ∇ 25 | 25 | 22 | E

G Vill | 493 Sixth Ave. (bet. 12th & 13th Sts.) | F/L/V to 14th St./6th Ave. | 212-255-3553 | www.estella-nyc.com

Fetching "window displays" draw passersby into this easygoing Greenwich Village children's shop where a thoughtfully assembled selection of "adorable" European clothing from Belgium, England and Italy – along with a smattering of Bugaboo strollers and "unique" furniture – awaits, displayed on an antique table or minimalist racks; but party-poopers put off by the "shockingly expensive" sticker prices decree "gimme a break" and "wait for the sales."

NEW Esthete Ⓜ   - | - | - | VE

Meatpacking | 416 W. 14th St. (bet. 9th & 10th Aves.) | A/C/E/L to 14th St./8th Ave. | 212-620-3120

Beauty is in the eye of the beholder and there's plenty of it to be eyed at this Meatpacking District brick-lined bell jar where esthetes of both sexes savor "sophisticated designer clothing with an urban point of view" (think thigh-high boots for her, skull motif scarves for him); a Goth aura permeates the place, with weathered wall vitrines displaying silver rings and chunky pendants like the works of art they resemble; if you "don't mind having clothes cooler than you are", the haughty clerks won't bother you either.

Etcetera ●
- | - | - | M

E 70s | 1465 Second Ave. (bet. 76th & 77th Sts.) | 6 to 77th St. | 212-794-2704
Murray Hill | 481 Third Ave. (bet. 33rd & 34th Sts.) | 6 to 33rd St. | 212-481-6527
www.etceteragiftsny.com

Cute children's outfits share space with sparkly purses, costume jewelry jostles pretty painted pottery and overall a cornucopia of "great finds" draws gift-givers into this Upper East Side and Murray Hill pair; the dizzying displays can "overwhelm the eyes", but not the budget – though the classy "wrapping alone will make friends and family think you spent a fortune."

Ethan Allen
23 | 23 | 22 | E

E 60s | 1107 Third Ave. (65th St.) | 4/5/6/F/N/R/W to 59th St./ Lexington Ave. | 212-308-7703
Murray Hill | 192 Lexington Ave. (32nd St.) | 6 to 33rd St. | 212-213-0600
W 60s | 103 West End Ave. (bet. 64th & 65th Sts.) | 1 to 66th St./ Lincoln Ctr. | 212-201-9840
Forest Hills | 112-33 Queens Blvd. (76th Rd.) | Queens | F to 75th St. | 718-575-3822
Staten Island | Heartland Shopping Ctr. | 2275 Richmond Ave. (Nome Ave.) | 718-983-0100
888-324-3571 | www.ethanallen.com

"Well-made furniture" that is "not one-of-a-kind but still lovely" sums up this long-standing chain offering "pricey" but "lasts forever" sofas, tables, beds, bureaus, lighting and other home accessories; still, sophisticates sniff the pieces "shout suburbia" and "won't fit into the average NYC apartment", and add they "hate the assigned salesperson" policy that means a staff member "follows you around" everywhere.

Etherea ●
- | - | - | M

E Vill | 66 Ave. A (bet. 4th & 5th Sts.) | F/V to Lower East Side/2nd Ave. | 212-358-1126 | www.etherea.net

Specializing in "obscure titles", this East Village music "mecca" satisfies "your electronic music needs", and when it comes to indie rock they "have all the new releases", including the often-overlooked emerging artist; though sometimes "snobby", the "knowledgeable" staff will allow you to preview any CD in stock, even "if you aren't wearing the right clothes."

Etro
28 | 27 | 23 | VE

E 60s | 720 Madison Ave. (bet. 63rd & 64th Sts.) | F to Lexington Ave./ 63rd St. | 212-317-9096 | www.etro.it

"For the cognoscenti of color, paisley and pattern-mixing", this East 60s boutique holds "so much under one roof", from "beautiful quality" his-and-hers clothing to "awesome printed" scarves, leather goods and home furnishings "with flair"; "it takes a special sort of fashionista to pull off" this "high-Renaissance" look – "only the Italians understand" "the art of how it all fits together" – but happily the "discreet" staff helps offset the "drama" of the designs.

Eve's Garden ⊠

24	19	24	M

W 50s | 119 W. 57th St. (bet. 6th & 7th Aves.) | N/Q/R/W to 57th St. | 212-757-8651 | 800-848-3837 | www.evesgarden.com

"You can go in to buy a dildo, and people will think you are just visiting an office" when you hit this "discreet and comfortable" "femme-friendly" "paradise" of "pleasure" devices on the 12th floor of a West 57th high-rise; the "no-storefront entry" also makes for a "non-pervy environment" in which to browse merchandise meant for "all levels of knowledge and sexuality."

Express ◗

16	17	15	M

Garment Dist | 7 W. 34th St. (bet. 5th & 6th Aves.) | B/D/F/N/Q/R/V/W to 34th St./Herald Sq. | 212-629-6838 | www.expressfashion.com
Additional locations throughout the NY area

"Good staples for work and play" are the province of this "fun" chain whose "moderately priced" pieces run the gamut from "conservative" suits and separates to "throwaway trend" wear; though the "quality of some pieces is decent enough for the office", most agree the goods are "not built to last", leading a few to complain it's "expensive for what you get" – but then again, "items don't stay full price very long", so just "wait for the sales."

Express Men ◗

20	18	19	M

Seaport | South Street Seaport | 89 South St., Pier 17 (Fulton St.) | 2/3/4/5/A/C/J/M/Z to Fulton St./B'way/Nassau | 212-766-5709
Kings Plaza | Kings Plaza Shopping Ctr. | 5350 Kings Plaza (Flatbush Ave. & Ave. U) | Brooklyn | 718-377-6334
www.expressfashion.com

Polished basics ("go for the jeans") plus some "edgier" items "to make a man look good" occupy the racks at this male counterpart to Express; critics fail to find "much flair" in the styling and pout that the "items are a bit pricey" for the quality, but even they suggest you should "run, not walk" when the "slash-and-burn monthly sale" is going on.

Eye Candy ◗

▽ 24	24	20	M

NoHo | 329 Lafayette St. (bet. Bleecker & Houston Sts.) | 6 to Bleecker St. | 212-343-4275 | www.eyecandystore.com

"Their name says it best" profess fans who feast on the "sparkly, sparkly" "faux jewels, bags", hats and "tremendous selection of shoes" at this moderately priced NoHo specialist in antique accessories; while generally known as a place for "the downtown set" "to get its fix" on "funky, edgy vintage items", "they also carry stunning [things] by new designers."

Eye Man, The

▽ 25	21	26	E

W 80s | 2264 Broadway (bet. 81st & 82nd Sts.) | 1 to 79th St. | 212-873-4114 | www.eyeman.com

"An institution on the West Side", this "warm and cozy" "neighborhood store" maintains a faithful following for its "dozens of colorful frames coming out of neat rows of drawers", including "prescription and non-prescription glasses from top designers" and lots of children's options; perhaps even better is the "helpful" staff of opticians that takes such "excellent care" of customers – "once you shop here you'll never go elsewhere."

	QUALITY	DISPLAY	SERVICE	COST

Fabulous Fanny's ❷

| | - | - | - | M |

E Vill | 335 E. Ninth St. (bet. 1st & 2nd Aves.) | 6 to Astor Pl. | 212-533-0637 | www.fabulousfannys.com

Stocking the "absolute best in vintage frames", this "true" eyewear "find" in the East Village offers a "fabulous", "fairly priced" selection from the 1700s to the present, and also does custom rhinestone work on glasses; "the owners are great guys" who're "pretty excited to show you the coolest stuff", some of which is snapped up for Broadway productions (*Spamalot*) and movies (*Little Miss Sunshine*).

FACE Stockholm

| | 22 | 24 | 22 | M |

SoHo | 110 Prince St. (Greene St.) | N/R/W to Prince St. | 212-966-9110

W 50s | The Shops at Columbus Circle, Time Warner Ctr. | 10 Columbus Circle, ground fl. (bet. 58th & 60th Sts.) | 1/A/B/C/D to 59th St./Columbus Circle | 212-823-9415 ❷

W 70s | 226 Columbus Ave. (bet. 70th & 71st Sts.) | 1/2/3/B/C to 72nd St. | 212-769-1420

888-334-3223 | www.facestockholm.com

Mother-and-daughter-owned Swedish cosmetics chain that's famed for its "vast selection" of colors and moderately priced, "no-frills" products like Pearl Eyeshadow and Aura Blush, but the brand's big secret weapon is undoubtedly the "super-durable nail polish that's a must for manicure mavens."

Facial Index

| | - | - | - | VE |

SoHo | 104 Grand St. (bet. Greene & Mercer Sts.) | 6/J/M/N/Q/R/W/Z to Canal St. | 646-613-1055

Hipsters on the hunt for "something different" to frame their peepers hit the jackpot at this "immaculate" eyewear emporium where the handmade specs and sunglasses come in a variety of fashion-forward hues, shapes and materials; "let the expert staff pick a frame" to suit your face, and turn a blind eye to the fact that its consumer price index is commensurate with the "sleek" SoHo digs.

Façonnable ❷

| | 27 | 25 | 24 | E |

E 50s | 636 Fifth Ave. (51st St.) | E/V to 5th Ave./53rd St. | 212-319-0111 | www.faconnable.com

Though now "owned by Nordstrom", a "discreet French flair" still pervades this Gallic label that specializes in "Euro-hip meets preppy" looks for men and women; whether you're seeking "jet-set-casual" separates, "super-proper" accessories or "timeless" tailored garments, the two-floor beaux arts flagship in Rockefeller Center "has it all", including a "smile and a helping hand" from the staff; sure, it's "expensive", but the "sophisticated" clientele gladly shells out for "Côte d'Azur chic with American comfort."

Family Jewels, The

| | - | - | - | E |

Chelsea | 130 W. 23rd St. (bet. 6th & 7th Aves.) | F/V to 23rd St. | 212-633-6020 | www.familyjewelsnyc.com

With stock that ranges from Victorian petticoats to '50s beaded sweaters to '70s ties, "they have an undeniably great selection" of women and menswear "in good condition" at this "crowded" "Chelsea vintage shop"; however, if the vibe's "hipper-than-thou", the staff's "unfriendlier than most", and malcontents mutter its popularity among fashion and show-biz stylists means "unforgivable prices" for "mediocre finery."

FAO Schwarz
25 | 26 | 20 | E

E 50s | 767 Fifth Ave. (58th St.) | N/R/W to 5th Ave./59th St. | 212-644-9400 | www.fao.com

Still the "ultimate playground" for "tourists and New Yorkers alike" following a face-lift, this "rare" Fifth Avenue "treat" "brings out the little kid in everyone" with its "magical", "overwhelming" assortment; "live out your *Big* fantasy" with spectacles like the 22-ft. floor piano and the "pricey ice cream parlor that must be tried", then "be prepared to knock over Fort Knox to pay for" "out-of-this-world" "specialty toys" from the newborn doll nursery and Hot Wheels custom car factory; still, the price-sensitive snipe "nice place to visit, wouldn't want to buy here."

Fat Beats ◐
– | – | – | M

G Vill | 406 Sixth Ave., 2nd fl. (bet. 8th & 9th Sts.) | A/B/C/D/E/F/V to W. 4th St. | 212-673-3883 | www.fatbeats.com

Scratch the competition cuz the "best place" for rap and hip-hop "vinyl junkies" may well be this Greenwich Village vanguard with outposts in Amsterdam and Los Angeles; collectors sing the praises of a "better-quality" queue of CDs and records and "excellent selection of DJ mixes" and beat a path for the "great" in-store events.

Federico de Vera
– | – | – | E

SoHo | 1 Crosby St. (Howard St.) | 6/J/M/N/Q/R/W/Z to Canal St. | 212-625-0838 | www.deveraobjects.com

"You didn't know you wanted or needed it until you saw it" at this "beyond comparison" SoHo gallery where antique *objets* share space with jewelry, much of which is made in-house; one-of-a-kind pieces include intricate Japanese lacquer boxes, Buddhas, Indian dagger hilts and cameos carved from lava rock.

Femmegems Nolita
▽ 17 | 19 | 19 | M

NoLita | 280 Mulberry St. (bet. Houston & Prince Sts.) | 6 to Bleecker St. | 212-625-1611 | www.femmegems.com

NoLita *bijouterie* that draws DIYers, fashionistas and celebrities alike who applaud the "fun" idea of "creating their own jewelry", choosing from a bountiful inventory of colorful beads, gemstones and findings to create unique necklaces, bracelets and earrings; for the craft-impaired, founder Lindsay Cain keeps a supply of ready-made styles on hand.

Fendi
27 | – | 23 | VE

E 50s | 677 Fifth Ave. (bet. 53rd & 54th Sts.) | E/V to 5th Ave./53rd St. | 212-759-4646 | 800-336-3469 | www.fendi.com

This venerable Italian label opened its Fifth Avenue store post-*Survey* – a cool, high-tech showcase, complete with a digital 'waterfall' over the staircase and movies playing on the walls – and now, more than ever, it's a "must-stop" in Midtown for femme-fatale fans who favor Karl Lagerfeld's "fun styles" in furs, frilly dresses or a statusy, "well-made" purse; granted, the goods are geared to "those who don't have to ask 'how much'" – but those who do needn't Fendi for themselves, since the staff makes anyone feel "like a queen."

| | QUALITY | DISPLAY | SERVICE | COST |

Fila ●

E 40s | 340 Madison Ave. (bet. 43rd & 44th Sts.) | 4/5/6/7/S to 42nd St./
Grand Central | 646-502-2100 | 866-758-3452 | www.fila.com

| | 23 | 20 | 19 | E |

"Bright and airy", this modern East 40s shop designed by Palermo-born visionary architect Giorgio Borruso "makes you look" at this "solid" Italian activewear label "with new eyes"; "love" the "preppy but fun" finds like the "hip tennis line" ("retro is back in fashion") as well as the "unique, practical" golf and running apparel, accessories and custom-configured sneakers – "looks like" this "old favorite" has "come back to life."

☑ Filene's Basement ●

Flatiron | 620 Sixth Ave. (18th St.) | 1 to 18th St. | 212-620-3100
Union Sq | 4 Union Sq. S. (14th St.) | 4/5/6/L/N/Q/R/W to 14th St./
Union Sq. | 212-358-0169
W 70s | 2222 Broadway (79th St.) | 1 to 79th St. | 212-873-8000
Flushing | 18704 Horace Harding Expwy. (188th St.) | Queens | 718-479-7711
888-843-8474 | www.filenesbasement.com

| | 18 | 10 | 9 | I |

So maybe "it's better in Boston" where it began, but NYers still file in to this "mother of discount department stores" – especially the Union Square behemoth, whose "real quality" items have earned admirers; "the others leave a little to be desired", with their "cramped quarters" and often "hard-to-find employees"; still, if you're "prepared to dig", "you can grab great deals here on everything from socks to jewelry" to bath items, with special praise going to "the Vault area for designer brands that mere mortals don't often see in real life."

Find Outlet

Chelsea | 361 W. 17th St. (bet. 8th & 9th Aves.) | A/C/E/L to 14th St./
8th Ave. | 212-243-3177 Ⓜ
NoLita | 229 Mott St. (bet. Prince & Spring Sts.) | 6 to Spring St. |
212-226-5167
www.findoutlet.com

| | 24 | 15 | 17 | M |

While these Chelsea and NoLita "stores are barely the size of a closet", their stock of "unlikely-to-see-elsewhere" "designers at a discount" (Paul & Joe, Lauren Moffatt) is "a must for stylish PYTs looking for fantastic bargains"; true, it's "slim pickings unless you wear 2 to 6", but if you're "the right size in the right place at the right time", you'll revel in the "finds"; N.B. the 17th Street location is open Thursday–Sunday.

Finyl Vinyl Ⓜ

E Vill | 208 E. Sixth St. (Cooper Sq.) | 6 to Astor Pl. | 212-533-8007

| | – | – | – | M |

Dedicated solely to "rare vinyl" spanning the 1940s to the late '70s, this East Village disc depot is a "great spot" to search for that obscure punk band or elusive Delta-blues 45; it's "not cheap", but it's a "must" "for the true music hound" – including "any proper DJ."

Fisch for the Hip

Chelsea | 153 W. 18th St. (bet. 6th & 7th Aves.) | 1 to 18th St. | 212-633-9053

| | 26 | 21 | 19 | E |

"Heads above the other consignment" places is this "classy" Chelsea clothier chock-full of "the current season's latest and greatest" from "the best" labels for both genders, plus shoes and "more Hermès bags than Hermès itself"; some "prices are high", particularly the purses' ("the rationale is, you avoid designer waiting lists"), but that doesn't deter devotees who declare "I could've bought the whole store."

	QUALITY	DISPLAY	SERVICE	COST

Fishs Eddy ⬤
| 18 | 18 | 17 | I |

Flatiron | 889 Broadway (19th St.) | N/R/W to 23rd St. | 212-420-9020 | 877-347-4733 | www.fishseddy.com

"Unusual dinnerware" dotted with "odd monograms or names of schools and clubs" as well as "funky" cutlery and glasses from restaurants and diners are some of the options for "avoiding traditional" table settings at this "non-snob's paradise of possibilities" for cute, inexpensive kitchen "kitsch" in the Flatiron District; although some say the store has "lost some of its unique flavor" and gone a bit "mainstream", you can still "buy a set of martini glasses for less money than the liquor you fill them with."

Flight 001 ⬤
| 24 | 24 | 20 | E |

W Vill | 96 Greenwich Ave. (bet. Jane & W. 12th Sts.) | A/C/E/L to 14th St./8th Ave. | 212-989-0001
NEW **Boerum Hill** | 132 Smith St. (bet. Bergen & Dean Sts.) | Brooklyn | F/G to Carroll St. | 718-243-0001
www.flight001.com

"There's something here for every jet-lagged soul – even those who just traversed the NYC" subway quip "hipster" voyagers who get carried away at this "lovely", retro-inspired Village "must-go" stop for "design-conscious, streamlined travel goods" and its new Boerum Hill offshoot; "these guys get it, with style", packing a punch with "funky luggage", "unique passport holders", "practical miniature kits of things you'll forget" and even "going-away presents" with "creative gift-wrapping."

flora and henri
| ▽ 23 | - | 20 | E |

E 70s | 1023 Lexington Ave. (bet. 73rd & 74th Sts.) | 6 to 77th St. | 212-249-1695 | www.florahenri.com

Parents with a penchant for "classics with a hip, modern twist" "love buying" wardrobe essentials for their little ones like "ribbed tees and leggings" and "pleated" skirts at this standby, which recently moved from Madison to Lexington Avenue; European fabrics, soft colors and traditional details give the collection a vintage charm that's sweet, but not too twee, and while it's sure "expensive", there's no denying that the craftsmanship and "quality are excellent."

Floris of London ▣
| 27 | 24 | 20 | E |

E 60s | 703 Madison Ave. (bet. 62nd & 63rd Sts.) | 4/5/6/F/N/R/W to 59th St./Lexington Ave. | 212-935-9100 | 800-535-6747 | www.florislondon.com

For Anglophiles, this "adorable" import dating back to 1730 offers "classic scents that don't assault the senses", including the very feminine Edwardian Bouquet; there's also a men's grooming line and "cute gifts for the home" like lavender linen freshener.

Florsheim Shoe Shops
| 20 | 18 | 18 | M |

E 50s | 444 Madison Ave. (50th St.) | 6 to 51st St. | 212-752-8017
Garment Dist | 101 W. 35th St. (6th Ave.) | B/D/F/N/Q/R/V/W to 34th St./Herald Sq. | 212-594-8830 ⬤
www.florsheim.com

After clocking 115 years, this "service-oriented" chainster with links in Midtown deserves its "classic" crown, and indeed some men still swear by its "solid, dependable", "well-made" footwear that stands up to "years of wear"; but the less-impressed note that while it's a "great first-paycheck place" for young bucks "starting" out, these shoes are "not made to impress", adding it's "gliding on its faded laurels."

Flou
`–` `–` `–` `VE`

SoHo | 42 Greene St. (bet. Broome & Grand Sts.) | C/E to Spring St. | 212-941-9101 | www.flou.com

The slickest of clever, contemporary Italian beds (more than 40 models including ones with stylish storage space options) are showcased at this SoHo specialist housed in an old converted factory with brick walls and tin ceilings; a collection of other bedroom-oriented items, including linens, lighting, mattresses and even pajamas, makes it a one-stop shop for sleep.

Flying A
`17` `18` `14` `E`

SoHo | 169 Spring St. (bet. Thompson St. & W. B'way) | C/E to Spring St. | 212-965-9090 | www.flyinganyc.com

There are "volumes of vintage for the hipster set" (especially "original" tees) at this SoHo shop that also carries a "very cool mix" of "retro to brand-new" men's and women's "finds" from A Design (their signature line), "unique" indie names and "great stuff" from Fred Perry and Paul Frank; whether you scoop up "cute" Birkenstocks or Spitfire sunglasses, remember, "getting the free vinyl totebag is worth almost any purchase!"

Flying Squirrel, The
`–` `–` `–` `M`

Williamsburg | 96 N. Sixth St. (bet. Berry St. & Wythe Ave.) | Brooklyn | L to Bedford Ave. | 718-218-7775 | www.flyingsquirrelbaby.com

If you want your kid to look like a million bucks without spending a lot of greens, scurry over to this wallet-friendly Williamsburg boutique, which peddles new and nearly new children's clothes, shoes, toys, books and baby gear; since fresh stock is always arriving, buddy up with the "helpful" sales people and "they'll call you when new items come in."

F.M. Allen ⑤
`–` `–` `–` `M`

E 70s | 962 Madison Ave. (bet. 75th & 76th Sts.) | 6 to 77th St. | 212-737-4374 | www.fmallen.com

Named after a safari outfitter from the '40s, this intriguing UES shop for all things African Colonial is replete with antique campaign furniture, Victorian-era whips, pith helmets and brass compasses, as well as new canvas and leather luggage and clothing; "everything is so Indiana Jones" that "you'll want to take a trip just to be able to sport the gear."

② Fogal of Switzerland ⑤
`28` `24` `25` `VE`

E 50s | 515 Madison Ave. (53rd St.) | E/V to 5th Ave./53rd St. | 212-355-3254 | www.fogal.com

You'll find "Swiss quality all the way around" at this small Madison Avenue outpost of the European lingerie outfit, from the "cool" sales staff to the "neatly arranged" "sexy" stockings and legwear that run the "rainbow gamut"; "wow, I didn't know pantyhose could cost this much" whisper wallet-watchers, to which savvy sorts retort yes, but these "last for years."

Foley + Corinna ●
`21` `22` `20` `E`

LES | 114 Stanton St. (bet. Essex & Ludlow Sts.) | F/V to Lower East Side/2nd Ave. | 212-529-2338 | www.foleyandcorinna.com

It's a Lower East Side "shopping gem" declare devotees of owners Anna Corinna and Dana Foley's "really pretty" flea-markety space; the "great mix of vintage finds" and "new stuff" boasting an "eclectic, feminine" feel (e.g. "gorgeous Grecian-inspired tops", "satiny, classy creations in "fantastic colors") elicit "endless compliments", making it a "hipster-chick" "favorite."

Foot Locker ●

21	18	15	M

Garment Dist | 120 W. 34th St. (bet. 6th & 7th Aves.) | 1/2/3/A/C/E to 34th St./Penn Station | 212-629-4419 | 800-991-6815 | www.footlocker.com
Additional locations throughout the NY area

The "place to go for all sports footwear" say supporters who "stand by" this "classic" chain "found all over NYC"; "if you want to run, walk or just look stylish the variety is there to choose from", including the "current must-have sneaker"; but an unhinged handful huffs it's a "cookie-cutter" outfit with "lackadaisical service."

Forever 21

10	13	9	I

Garment Dist | 50 W. 34th St. (B'way) | B/D/F/N/Q/R/V/W to 34th St./ Herald Sq. | 212-564-2346 ●
G Vill | 49 E. 14th St. (bet. B'way & University Pl.) | 4/5/6/L/N/Q/R/W to 14th St./Union Sq. | 212-228-0598 ●
Downtown | 1 DeKalb Ave. (bet. Bond & Fulton Sts.) | Brooklyn | A/C/G to Hoyt/Schermerhorn Sts. | 718-797-9634
Kings Plaza | Kings Plaza Shopping Ctr. | 5250 Kings Plaza (Flatbush Ave. & Ave. U) | Brooklyn | 718-434-9368 ●
Elmhurst | Queens Ctr. | 90-15 Queens Blvd. (bet. 57th & 59th Aves.) | Queens | G/R/V to Woodhaven Blvd. | 718-699-5630 ●
Staten Island | Staten Island Mall | 2655 Richmond Ave. (bet. Platinum Ave. & Richmond Hill Rd.) | 718-477-2121 ●
800-966-1355 | www.forever21.com

"No trend is below the style radar" at this "cheap, cheerful" and "sometimes trashy" chain where the "dizzying array" of "snazzy" apparel and accessories for "young lads and lasses" "changes from one day to the next"; sure, the "long lines at the fitting rooms and registers" can make you "feel like you'll be there forever", but for "party-girl" garb and other "disposable" duds, it's hard to beat.

For Eyes 🔲

▽ 23	21	21	M

E 40s | Graybar Bldg. | 420 Lexington Ave. (bet. 43rd & 44th Sts.) | 4/5/6/7/S to 42nd St./Grand Central | 212-697-8888 | www.foreyes.com

Right "next to Grand Central" – a "great location for commuters" – this Midtown eyewear chain outpost offers a "two-for-$99 deal" (you "can't beat it") that's ideal for those seeking "an extra pair or two of glasses for a different look"; maybe the frames "won't be top-of-the-line", but they're "nice enough" considering the "great price."

Forréal

19	14	14	M

E 70s | 1335 Third Ave. (bet. 76th & 77th Sts.) | 6 to 77th St. | 212-734-2105
E 70s | 1375 Third Ave. (bet. 78th & 79th Sts.) | 6 to 77th St. | 212-396-9535
www.forrealnyc.com

"Trendy" Upper East Side high-schoolers and the "young at heart" latch onto this "teenybopper paradise" where "you can find everything you need" from babe-a-licious basics and "your favorite jeans" from the label-likes of Big Star and Diesel at the 1375 address to dressier threads (BCBG, Nicole Miller) "to go clubbing" at the 1335 locale; even "moms shop here", as this pair is "fair with their price points" – and that's for real.

	QUALITY	DISPLAY	SERVICE	COST

Fort Street Studio 🗷📵   - | - | - | VE

SoHo | 578 Broadway (bet. Houston & Prince Sts.) | N/R/W to Prince St. |
212-925-5383 | www.fortstreetstudio.com

The fine, hand-knotted wild-silk carpets found at this fifth-floor SoHo
showroom are based on ethereal abstract watercolor designs created
by husband-and-wife owners Brad Davis and Janis Provisor; of course,
the wildly expensive prices will leave some spinning; N.B. closed
Saturdays and Sundays.

Fortunoff   24 | 21 | 21 | M

E 50s | 681 Fifth Ave. (54th St.) | E/V to 5th Ave./53rd St. | 212-758-6660 |
800-367-8866 | www.fortunoff.com

"No one gets taken" at this "trustworthy" Fifth Avenue source for
"excellent quality and prices" on diamond, pearl and gold jewelry as
well as china, crystal and flatware that make wedding attendees
"come here like lemmings" for "classy gifts"; "informed" and "polite
service" also means "it's a more pleasant place to shop" than others
of its ilk.

45rpm 🗷   ▽ 23 | 23 | 20 | E

E 70s | 17 E. 71st St. (bet. 5th & Madison Aves.) | 6 to 68th St. |
212-737-5545
R by 45rpm
SoHo | 169 Mercer St. (W. Houston St.) | N/R/W to Prince St. |
917-237-0045
www.rby45rpm.com

Über-premium jeans with a "Japanese aesthetic" made from "environmentally" friendly fabrics (and woven on antique looms) lure acolytes
to these spare Shinto shrines to denim on the Upper East Side and in
SoHo; though the "beautiful line" and "amazing environments" may be
"like nothing you've ever seen before", the stratospheric prices
prompt a few to label the brand "R for ripoff."

42nd Street Photo   21 | 14 | 14 | M

Garment Dist | 378 Fifth Ave. (bet. 35th & 36th Sts.) | B/D/F/N/Q/R/V/W to
34th St./Herald Sq. | 212-594-6565 | www.42photo.com

"Been a-shopping here since I was a kid" and it's still "a pleasure to
stop in" to this "gigantic" Garment District "mail-order icon" that fulfills "all of your electronic needs", from cameras, cell phones and
iPods to "the latest gadgets"; "educate yourself and check prices online beforehand or you may find them as inflated as a hot-air
balloon" – but bear in mind that there's wiggle room since the
"brusque", "hard-sell" staff is oftentimes "willing to bargain."

Fossil ◗   19 | 19 | 18 | M

E 40s | 530 Fifth Ave. (bet. 44th & 45th Sts.) | 4/5/6/7/S to 42nd St./
Grand Central | 212-997-3978
Elmhurst | Queens Ctr. | 90-15 Queens Blvd. (bet. 57th & 59th Aves.) |
Queens | G/R/V to Woodhaven Blvd. | 718-592-2528
800-449-3056 | www.fossil.com

This Dallas-based chainlet with links in Midtown and Queens Center
features lots of "cute", "inexpensive novelty watches" "for every time
and place at startlingly good prices" so "you can wear a different one
every day of the week"; strap one on, then check out the "cool handbags", sunglasses and other accessories.

	QUALITY	DISPLAY	SERVICE	COST

☑ Fountain Pen Hospital ☒ | 28 | 21 | 25 | E |

TriBeCa | 10 Warren St. (bet. B'way & Church St.) | R/W to City Hall |
212-964-0580 | www.fountainpenhospital.com

Proponents proclaim it's "Pen central" at this "high-quality", "old New
York" TriBeCa shop with a "mind-boggling selection" that ranges
"from the everyday" to "rarefied" vintage models to calligraphy pens
with 14-karat-gold nibs, as well as an "excellent repair" service ("if it
writes or used to they can fix it"); the "incredibly knowledgeable" staff
also leaves an indelible impression.

4PlayBK | - | - | - | M |

Park Slope | 360 Seventh Ave. (bet. 10th & 11th Sts.) | Brooklyn | F to
7th Ave. | 718-369-4086

Tweens, teens and twentysomethings congregate at this "cute,
kitschy", "strictly-for-the-under-30-set" South Slope hangout; gab
and gobble up the "cool, eclectic mix of trend-right" hoodies, jeans,
jackets and accessories at wallet-friendly prices from faves like Le
Tigre and Paul Frank, then share your borough pride and pick up "T-shirts
for all your Brooklyn-crazed friends."

Fragments | 25 | 24 | 20 | E |

E 70s | 997 Madison Ave. (77th St.) | 6 to 77th St. | 212-537-5000
SoHo | 116 Prince St. (bet. Greene & Wooster Sts.) | N/R/W to Prince St. |
212-334-9588
888-637-2463 | www.fragments.com

"It's almost impossible to walk away empty handed from these stores"
in SoHo and on Madison Avenue – just ask J. Lo, Britney, Debra
Messing or anyone else who's looking for "stellar designs" "by everyone who's who in jewelry" (both costume and fine) that is "hard to find
elsewhere"; loyalists like the warm "compliments" they get when
wearing their goods, but service with "attitude" leaves critics cold.

Frank Stella Ltd. | 22 | 19 | 19 | E |

E 70s | 1326 Third Ave. (bet. 75th & 76th Sts.) | 6 to 77th St. |
212-744-5662 ☻
W 50s | NY Athletic Club | 921 Seventh Ave. (58th St.) | N/Q/R/W to
57th St. | 212-957-1600
W 80s | 440 Columbus Ave. (81st St.) | B/C to 81st St. | 212-877-5566 ☻
www.frankstellanyc.com

When "looking for a little style, the business-casual set" finds this trio
"a great place to splurge" on suits and sportswear from the likes of
Robert Graham and Nat Nast as well as Mason and Ben Sherman; "in
a city of ever-larger department stores, it's one of the few small men's
shops left" – like "the haberdasher your mother told you to have" – and
those who buy gifts here find they've "never had one item returned."

Fratelli Rossetti | 27 | 24 | 23 | E |

E 50s | 625 Madison Ave. (58th St.) | 4/5/6/F/N/R/W to 59th St./
Lexington Ave. | 212-888-5107 | www.rossetti.it

While you may not actually see "Italian cobbling masters at work",
you do have the opportunity to slip into the "pricey", "good-fitting" results of such craftsmanship at this Madison Avenue standby backed
by "excellent service"; the luxe men's and women's "shoes wear on
and on", plus the Flexa comfort line is "like walking on air", and to top
it off, the handbags and "leather coat selection have fabulous style."

☑ Fred Leighton ☒

29 | 27 | 27 | VE

E 60s | 773 Madison Ave. (66th St.) | 6 to 68th St. | 212-288-1872 | www.fredleighton.com

"Glitz and glamour" abound at this Madison Avenue über-jeweler where the "drool" factor is sky-high; a 1920s-style salon is the backdrop for "wonderful gems from old India", "beautiful" "$10,000 baubles at the bracelet counter", old-mine and cushion-cut diamond estate and antique engagement rings and opulent art deco designs that all go for "buckets of bucks"; P.S. "there really is a Fred, and he's a charmer."

NEW Freemans Sporting Club ●Ⓜ

- | - | - | E

LES | 8 Rivington St. (bet. Bowery & Christie St.) | F/V to Lower East Side/ 2nd Ave. | 212-673-3209

Sartorial studs with a PC bent appreciate the union-made, hand-tailored menswear at this new LES address; it's part barbershop (haircuts and straight razor shaves available in vintage chairs), part haberdasher (made-to-measure and ready-to-wear suits, handmade Le Chameau boots and Quoddy moccasins), part apothecary (grooming goods from Geo F. Trumper and D.R. Harris) and yes, part social club for the owners of the nearby hipster hangout Freemans restaurant right down the alley.

French Connection ●

20 | 19 | 17 | M

NoHo | 700 Broadway (4th St.) | N/R/W to 8th St. | 212-473-4486
SoHo | 435 W. Broadway (Prince St.) | N/R/W to Prince St. | 212-219-1197
W 50s | 1270 Sixth Ave. (bet. 50th & 51st Sts.) | B/D/F/V to 47-50th Sts./ Rockefeller Ctr. | 212-262-6623
888-741-3285 | www.frenchconnection.com

"Find a staple" or an "of-the-moment add-on" for your wardrobe at this Brit chain that's "worth a pass-through"; but detractors who "don't get the hype" declare the clothing "far too expensive for what it's worth" and exhort "don't bother if you're above a size 10" – and even admirers aver it's time to "drop the FCUK" logo ("the shock value is gone").

French Sole

▽ 24 | 13 | 15 | M

E 70s | 985 Lexington Ave. (bet. 71st & 72nd Sts.) | 6 to 68th St. | 212-737-2859 | www.frenchsoleshoes.com

"You feel like you've gone to ballet-flat heaven" at this East 70s "shoebox" that may be a "little crammed-in, but makes you feel like you've discovered something" truly "adorable"; nothing compares to "walking the city streets" in any of the 300 variations, from "beautiful" Italian calfskin to hand-beaded "one-of-a-kind" numbers, so swan on over.

Fresh

26 | 25 | 22 | E

E 70s | 1367 Third Ave. (78th St.) | 6 to 77th St. | 212-585-3400 ●
E 70s | 922 Madison Ave. (bet. 73rd & 74th Sts.) | 6 to 77th St. | 212-396-4545
Flatiron | 872 Broadway (18th St.) | 4/5/6/L/N/Q/R/W to 14th St./ Union Sq. | 212-477-1100 ●
NoLita | 57 Spring St. (bet. Lafayette & Mulberry Sts.) | 6 to Spring St. | 212-925-0099 ●
W Vill | 388 Bleecker St. (bet. Perry & W. 11th Sts.) | 1 to Christopher St./ Sheridan Sq. | 917-408-1850 ●
800-373-7420 | www.fresh.com

"The cleanest store you've ever seen" is this "chic" chain known for skincare, haircare and fragrances based on "ingredients like sugar and lychee fruit that smell so good, you want to eat them"; a "knowledgeable staff" sells "beautifully packaged", "ahead-of-the-pack" products that are "Fresh and original without being overpowering."

NEW Fresh Kills Ⓜ

-	-	-	M

Williamsburg | 50 N. Sixth St. (bet. Kent & Wythe Aves.) | Brooklyn | L to Bedford Ave. | 718-388-8081 | www.freshkillsforthepeople.com

Two former set decorators set the quirky tone at this sprawling new home-furnishings purveyor in a split-level converted warehouse/garage in Williamsburg's burgeoning design district; midcentury modern sofas, lighting, mirrors, consoles and chairs share space with a cache of Milo Baughman tables and frames and fresh pieces from Brooklyn-based designers.

Z Frette Ⓢ

29	27	26	VE

E 60s | 799 Madison Ave. (bet. 67th & 68th Sts.) | 6 to 68th St. | 212-988-5221 | www.frette.com

Posh patrons demanding the "ultimate" in "luxurious" Italian sheets that make you feel like you're "sleeping on a cloud" head for this Upper East Side shop that also sells table linens, robes, home fragrances and candles; while fans of the "crisp cotton bedding" include the Vatican and "royalty and their consorts", most who "Frette over" "the ridiculously expensive cost" can only sigh "ah to have money!"

Frick Collection Ⓜ

22	18	18	M

E 70s | 1 E. 70th St. (5th Ave.) | 6 to 68th St. | 212-288-0700 | www.frick.org

Housed in an "intimate museum" with a "high masterpiece-per-square-footage quotient", this "small" shop at the UES Frick Collection offers a "precise", "classy", "moderate-sized" selection of "art objects" and "reference volumes"; though a few rue it's "unremarkable" and even a bit "boring", more generous sorts insist it's "great" for "unique gifts."

Frock Ⓢ Ⓜ

-	-	-	M

LES | 148 Orchard St. (bet. Rivington & Stanton Sts.) | F/J/M/Z to Delancey/Essex Sts. | 212-594-5380 | www.frocknyc.com

The '70s and '80s live on – sartorially, at least – within the clean, white confines of this LES women's boutique; explore the vintage styles of Stephen Burrows, Ossie Clark, Norma Kamali, Calvin Klein (when Calvin still designed it) and Stephen Sprouse, all neatly arrayed on the walls, with Maud Frizon and SusanBennisWarrenEdwards pumps down the middle of the floor; returns are limited, but the owners are happy to consult about a garment's fit (yes, children, pants once sat at the waist, not the hip).

Furla

25	23	21	E

E 50s | 598 Madison Ave. (57th St.) | N/R/W to 5th Ave./59th St. | 212-980-3208
E 60s | 727 Madison Ave. (64th St.) | 6 to 68th St. | 212-755-8986
www.furla.com

A trip to either the newly renovated East 60s link or its East 50s sibling will "transport you" to Europe laud leather-fiends who claim that a "well-deserved splurge" on this Bologna-based Italian outfit's "timeless bags and gorgeous shoes" "last forever"; better yet, the "no-pressure" service "with a smile" makes it all "worth the price."

	QUALITY	DISPLAY	SERVICE	COST

Furry Paws ◑
21 | 15 | 19 | M

E 50s | 1036 First Ave. (bet. 56th & 57th Sts.) | 4/5/6/F/N/R/W to 59th St./Lexington Ave. | 212-486-8661
E 90s | 1705 Third Ave. (bet. 95th & 96th Sts.) | 6 to 96th St. | 212-828-5308
Gramercy | 310 E. 23rd St. (bet. 1st & 2nd Aves.) | 6 to 23rd St. | 212-979-0920
G Vill | 9 E. Eighth St. (bet. 5th Ave. & University Pl.) | 6 to Astor Pl. | 212-979-0685
Murray Hill | 120 E. 34th St. (bet. Lexington & Park Aves.) | 6 to 33rd St. | 212-725-1970
W 60s | 141 Amsterdam Ave. (66th St.) | 1 to 66th St./Lincoln Ctr. | 212-724-9321

Proponents of this paws-itively ubiquitous Manhattan mini-chain maintain it's a "great source" for "natural pet foods and products" and hail the "helpful staff" and "reasonable prices"; sure, some snarl the stock is "hit-or-miss" and the service "impersonal", but diehards demur "the free delivery makes it worthwhile."

Future Perfect, The
- | - | - | E

Williamsburg | 115 N. Sixth St. (Berry St.) | Brooklyn | L to Bedford Ave. | 718-599-6278 | www.thefutureperfect.com

"Cutting-edge" Williamsburg home-furnishings shop that's a show-case for the industry's emerging talents; items like antler chandeliers, sheaths of intensely graphic wallpaper and recycled wood furniture will woo loft-lovers, although those with less avant-garde taste point out that, while interesting, these things are "not necessarily practical."

f.y.e. ◑
18 | 16 | 13 | M

W 50s | 1290 Sixth Ave. (51st St.) | N/R/W to 49th St. | 212-581-1669 | www.fye.com

This Midtown link of a "chain that sometimes gets it right" offers "cur-rent CDs and DVDs"; still, critics cavil that "full-price" offerings mean there's "no incentive to shop" at this "cookie-cutter" outfit, while "eso-teric" sorts seeking "obscure" titles blast the "dull", "Top 40" choices.

NEW Gabay's Home
15 | 10 | 14 | M

E Vill | 227 First Ave. (bet. 13th & 14th Sts.) | L to 1st Ave. | 212-529-4036 | www.gabaysoutlet.com

The likes of Calvin Klein linens, Waterford tableware, Cuisinart appli-ances, cappuccino machines and furniture at "closeout" prices are haphazardly displayed in an industrial setting at this new East Village home-furnishings outlet next door to its discount designer "clothing sister"; while bargain-hunters gloat there are "great values" to be had, naysayers note that after all that "rummaging" around it's a total "crapshoot" whether you'll find something special.

Gabay's Outlet
20 | 7 | 14 | M

E Vill | 225 First Ave. (bet. 13th & 14th Sts.) | L to 1st Ave. | 212-254-3180 | www.gabaysoutlet.com

With its "amazing bargains, particularly on top brands of shoes and handbags" (think Gucci, Fendi, Marc Jacobs), this East Village dis-counter is "a treasure trove for label-astute fashionistas" who've vowed "never to pay retail again"; "the store's not much to look at and it can be hit-or-miss", but "they seem to get new merchandise regularly", so "keep stopping in."

	QUALITY	DISPLAY	SERVICE	COST

Gallery of Wearable Art ⊠Ⓜ

−	−	−	E

E 60s | 34 E. 67th St. (bet. Madison & Park Aves.) | 6 to 68th St. |
212-570-2252 | www.galleryofwearableart.com

Brides and event-going ladies who march to their own drummer beat
a path to this East 60s atelier decorated with a pinch of Parisian flair;
the one-of-a-kind collectible creations, including extravagant gowns,
film-noirish suits and lavish coats recall eras past via silhouettes,
detailing and antique and vintage textiles.

Galo

22	20	21	E

E 60s | 825 Lexington Ave. (bet. 63rd & 64th Sts.) | 6 to 68th St. |
212-832-3922
E 70s | 1296 Third Ave. (bet. 74th & 75th Sts.) | 6 to 77th St. |
212-288-3448
E 70s | 895 Madison Ave. (72nd St.) | 6 to 68th St. | 212-744-7936
www.galoshoes.com

"I gallivant everywhere in my Galo shoes" gloat gals about town who
"treat their feet" – and their kids' too – to "something special" at this
Upper East Side trio; the "fashionable but not way-out" "variety" of
boots, pumps and sandals is "perfect for someone who likes" their
shoes "stylish yet classic", but you'll also find "pricey", "glamorous
surprises" peeking out from among the more "practical" purchases.

Gant

22	20	20	E

E 50s | 645 Fifth Ave. (bet. 51st & 52nd Sts.) | B/D/F/V to 47-50th Sts./
Rockefeller Ctr. | 212-813-9170 | www.gant.com

From its tailored tops to its V-necked sweaters, this American label
(now foreign-owned) has, for half a century, epitomized "good taste"
for men and women too; so what if the rugby shirts "lack genuine
ruggedness" – "you get what you pay for" at its Rockefeller Center
shop: "stylish clothes" and "nice" service.

ⓩ Gap ◑

18	17	16	M

Garment Dist | 60 W. 34th St (B'way) | B/D/F/N/Q/R/V/W to 34th St./
Herald Sq. | 212-760-1268 | www.gap.com
Additional locations throughout the NY area

"After all these years", this "inexpensive" wonder-chain remains a "reliable" resource for "classic", "good-quality" and "easygoing" men's
and women's "wardrobe staples" from jeans to sweaters to T-shirts;
the faithful maintain it's "always worth a look-see" because even
those with a "Gap in their wallets" can "afford these prices"; if more
daring sorts declare the seasonal lines a little "vanilla ice cream", even
they may reevaluate now that this standby is collaborating with designers like Roland Mouret on capsule collections.

GapBody ◑

19	18	16	I

E Vill | 1 Astor Pl. (B'way) | 6 to Astor Pl. | 212-253-0452 |
www.gap.com

"When your wallet can't handle a hit from Cosabella", head to this
Gap spin-off offering "affordable" lingerie including signature seam-
less bras, "quality cotton undies", "cozy bathrobes" and "around the
house clothes" (as well as yoga togs and swimwear); though a few
lace into "weak" service and pout it's "limited" sizewise, it compensates with "fabulous sales", making it a great place to "stock up"
on "the basics."

	QUALITY	DISPLAY	SERVICE	COST

GapKids ●

	21	19	17	M

Garment Dist | 60 W. 34th St. (B'way) | B/D/F/N/Q/R/V/W to 34th St./ Herald Sq. | 212-760-1268 | www.gap.com
Additional locations throughout the NY area

"Dress your little darling" in "well-made, good-looking" "basics" from this chain outfitting kids, tweens and teens in "versions of adult clothes" that they'll "actually wear"; the "fair prices" become even more so during its "fantastic sales", so "what would we do without them?".

Garrard 🖎

	–	–	–	VE

SoHo | 133 Spring St., 3rd fl. (bet. Greene & Wooster Sts.) | C/E to Spring St. | 212-688-2209 | www.garrard.com

Designated the Crown jeweler by Queen Victoria, this 270-year-old British dowager has been given a face-lift by creative director Jade Jagger, whose gold, platinum, enamel or gem-studded pieces that range from charms to tiaras exude a hip, modern vibe, and are sold at this homey salon in the heart of SoHo.

G.C. William

	▽ 20	14	16	E

E 80s | 1137 Madison Ave. (bet. 84th & 85th Sts.) | 4/5/6 to 86th St. | 212-396-3400
W 70s | 111 W. 72nd St. (bet. Amsterdam & Columbus Aves.) | 1/2/3 to 72nd St. | 212-873-2314
www.gcwilliam.com

Once a magnet for trendsetting tweens, these bookend boutiques on the Upper East and West Sides are gearing their merchandise more toward teenagers and twenty- and thirtysomethings, dishing up funky fare from the likes of Hudson and True Religion; still, some profess to a "love-hate thing" for the place, since they're intrigued by the inventory but put off by the "expensive" prices and "unfriendly staff."

Geminola 🅜

	–	–	–	E

W Vill | 41 Perry St. (bet. 7th Ave. S. & W. 4th St.) | A/B/C/D/E/F/V to W. 4th St. | 212-675-1994

Just down the block from hot eatery Sant Ambroeus sits this "quirky" shop that "exemplifies West Village cool" with its tulle skirts, candy-colored satins, repurposed tweed jackets and reworked Moulin Rouge-style slip gowns hand-dyed to enchanting effect by owner Lorraine Kirke and favored by stars like Nicole Kidman and Sarah Jessica Parker; fashionistas also indulge in finds like La Voleuse flats and Rogan jeans.

Generation Records ●

	25	19	19	M

G Vill | 210 Thompson St. (bet. Bleecker & W. 3rd Sts.) | A/B/C/D/E/F/V to W. 4th St. | 212-254-1100 | www.generationrecords.com

"Hardcore" and "indie" rock fans "who like their music with an edge" swear this Greenwich Village haunt has "the city's best selection" of "affordable" LPs and CDs (DVDs too), including "rare recordings" and other "fabulous finds" you "couldn't buy on the Internet"; just "don't expect courteous service" from the "too-cool-for-school" staff.

Gentlemen's Resale

	▽ 24	22	19	M

E 80s | 322 E. 81st St. (bet. 1st & 2nd Aves.) | 4/5/6 to 86th St. | 212-734-2739 | www.resaleclothing.net

"Fashionable suits, dress shirts and ties" from A(rmani) to Z(egna) are "nicely presented" in this Upper East Side townhouse, one of the few consignment stores devoted to guys (they're a male relation of Designer Resale down the block); "other than the occasional wrinkle" or "minor flaw", "the wares are as you'd find them at Saks – just a lot less costly."

George Smith Ⓢ

			VE
-	-	-	VE

SoHo | 315 Hudson St. (Spring St.) | 1 to Canal St. | 212-226-4747 | www.georgesmith.com

"Great goods" and more than 70 silhouettes of the "most fabulous" bespoke furniture, including "lovely overstuffed" sofas, chaises and chairs, are available at this London transplant's sprawling showroom, which recently moved from Spring to Hudson Street; much of the handmade-to-order selection is based on original 19th-century designs with beech or birch wood framing and the finest natural fabrics, and while the "first-class quality" doesn't come cheap, respondents remind "you get what you pay for."

☒ Georg Jensen

29	27	24	VE

E 60s | 685 Madison Ave. (bet. 61st & 62nd Sts.) | 4/5/6/F/N/R/W to 59th St./Lexington Ave. | 212-759-6457 Ⓢ
SoHo | 125 Wooster St. (Prince St.) | C/E to Spring St. | 212-343-9000
800-546-5253 | www.georgjensen.com

Supporters swear "the gold standard for silver" is to be found at these Upper East Side and SoHo stores purveying cutlery, hollowware and jewelry crafted with "Scandinavian simplicity and elegance", whether in "classic old-style or cutting-edge contemporary" designs; they're "expensive", but enthusiasts also extol their "excellent value."

Geox

23	20	19	M

E 50s | 575 Madison Ave. (57th St.) | E/V to 5th Ave./53rd St. | 212-319-3310
E 50s | 731 Lexington Ave. (bet. 58th & 59th Sts.) | 4/5/6/F/N/R/W to 59th St./Lexington Ave. | 212-319-3321 ☽
Elmhurst | Queens Ctr. | 90-15 Queens Blvd. (bet. 57th & 59th Aves.) | Queens | G/R/V to Woodhaven Blvd. | 718-760-1002 ☽
800-992-4369 | www.geox.com

Like "walking on marshmallows" sigh comfort-seeking families who step lightly to this Italian innovator's "sleek" Midtown and Queens Center branches for "stylish" patented "breathable" footwear that's "air-cooled from the sole" – you "can't beat the technology" – what a "great commuting" find; if a few wail "waited for ages" for "unfriendly" help, insiders retort go to the Madison Avenue flagship – the "staff is knowledgeable", the space-shuttlelike presentation is really "inviting" and they stock the "full selection."

☒ Geppetto's Toy Box

27	24	23	E

G Vill | 10 Christopher St. (bet. Gay St. & Greenwich Ave.) | A/B/C/D/E/F/V to W. 4th St. | 212-620-7511 | 800-326-4566 | www.nyctoys.com

"Both kids and kids-at-heart" are charmed by this "quintessential neighborhood toy store" in Greenwich Village, which purveys an "unparalleled" selection of playtime favorites including Colorforms, Corolle dolls, Wild Planet spy gadgets, Steif plush animals and Groovy Girls fashion dolls; the "friendly" staff offers cart-"loads of useful and creative suggestions" even for gift-givers without offspring of their own – no lie, it's everything a children's "store should be."

Gerry Cosby & Co. ◐

	QUALITY	DISPLAY	SERVICE	COST
	25	14	18	E

Garment Dist | Madison Square Garden | 3 Penn Plaza (7th Ave. & 32nd St.) | 1/2/3/A/C/E to 34th St./Penn Station | 212-563-6464 | www.cosbysports.com

"A hockey oasis in the concrete jungle", this Madison Square Garden "landmark" is a "mecca" for puck proponents looking to find "any jersey or [piece of] equipment"; true, the "cramped" space is "a zoo" when it's crowded, making a visit feel like spending time in the penalty box, but it's worth the roughing up to be "properly fitted by professionals"; N.B. baseball, basketball and football gear is also offered.

Gerry's ◐

	QUALITY	DISPLAY	SERVICE	COST
	24	19	21	E

Chelsea | 110 Eighth Ave. (bet. 15th & 16th Sts.) | A/C/E/L to 14th St./ 8th Ave. | 212-243-9141
Chelsea | 112 Eighth Ave. (bet. 15th & 16th Sts.) | A/C/E/L to 14th St./ 8th Ave. | 212-691-2188
W Vill | 353 Bleecker St. (bet. Charles & W. 10th Sts.) | 1 to Christopher St./ Sheridan Sq. | 212-691-0636

Though they're "not exactly a destination", admirers say this Downtown trio is "excellent" for "neighborhood shopping": at the West Village branch, the "good selection" includes the best of business-casual, including Ben Sherman and Ted Baker among others, while the Chelsea branches – one for him, the other for her – stock an assortment of "practical yet cool" brands (True Religion, Seven For All Mankind and Gwen Stefani's L.A.M.B. line, plus Puma and Adidas sneakers).

Ghost

	QUALITY	DISPLAY	SERVICE	COST
	–	–	–	E

NoHo | 28 Bond St. (bet. Bowery & Lafayette St.) | 6 to Bleecker St. | 646-602-2891 | www.ghost.co.uk

Flesh out your feminine side at this Parisian flea market–inspired shop in NoHo, with "clothing you can float in" from founder-designer Tanya Sarne; made of delicate-toned satin, vintage crêpe and velvet, her sensuous, fluid "basics with a flair" are such that surveyors and stars like Jennifer Aniston, Julia Roberts and Catherine Zeta-Jones "can't get enough of them."

Z Ghurka

	QUALITY	DISPLAY	SERVICE	COST
	29	29	26	VE

E 60s | 683 Madison Ave. (bet. 61st & 62nd Sts.) | N/R/W to 5th Ave./ 59th St. | 212-826-8300 | 800-587-1584 | www.ghurka.com

What "great stuff" fawn fans – you'll "want every piece" of the "well-crafted" luggage from this "high-end" Madison Avenue shop, voted No. 1 in this guide's Lifestyle category; the "excellent goods", ranging from leather carry-ons to duffels and travel bags, have moved further away from "classic styling" into more exotic terrain, thanks to the use of über-expensive skins like alligator, a beefed-up selection of luxury handbags and the expansive vision of creative director John Bartlett, who joined the company post-*Survey*.

Gianfranco Ferré Ø

	QUALITY	DISPLAY	SERVICE	COST
	27	26	26	VE

E 70s | 870 Madison Ave. (bet. 70th & 71st Sts.) | 6 to 68th St. | 212-717-5430 | www.gianfrancoferre.com

This Italian-born designer refines his "sexy" men's and women's collections with "amazing fabrics" and "sophisticated" construction that reveal his roots as an architect; likewise, his aesthetically pleasing Upper East Side boutique is "the place to have your fashion dreams come true" with its inventory of strictly tailored skirts, classic white shirts and serene eveningwear that suit even "if you're not a stick-girl" or boy.

Giggle
25 | 26 | 23 | E

E 70s | 1033 Lexington Ave. (74th St.) | 6 to 77th St. | 212-249-4249
SoHo | 120 Wooster St. (bet. Prince & Spring Sts.) | N/R/W to 8th St. | 212-334-5817
800-495-8377 | www.egiggle.com

Owner Allison Wing brings her infants' lifestyle concept from "San Fran to the Big Apple", specifically SoHo and the East 70s, wowing "trendy NYC parents" with "well-edited merch that makes choosing stylish baby items a breeze"; leave your stroller by the 'parking meters', then wander through the "modern" digs filled with "colorful" organic clothing, crib bedding, furniture and all-natural skincare products – "it's the perfect place to dream about how cute your kids can be."

☑ Giorgio Armani ☒
29 | 27 | 26 | VE

E 60s | 760 Madison Ave. (65th St.) | 6 to 68th St. | 212-988-9191 | www.giorgioarmani.com

Now in his 70s, this "top-of-the-list" designer still has his finger on the pulse of what celebs like Cate Blanchett, Heidi Klum and Julia Roberts love "for those red-carpet moments"; the "four floors of absolute perfection" of his East 60s store boasts his-and-hers "drool, drool, pant, pant" suits and separates that are "tailored and timeless", plus "elegant" accessories and "runway clothing at runway prices"; and even if you feel like you should dress up before entering the premises, once in, the "service is impeccable."

NEW Giorgio Fedon 19 ☻
- | - | - | E

W 40s | Rockefeller Ctr. | 30 Rockefeller Ctr. (49th St.) | B/D/F/V to 47-50th Sts./Rockefeller Ctr. | 212-582-3232 | www.giorgiofedon1919.it

Add a splash of Euro style to your work space or wardrobe with orange, black, brown or red accessories from this dramatic-looking Rock Center newcomer, the Italian stalwart's first U.S. shop; while craftsmanship is key, the small leather (and leatherlike) luxury goods, including men's and women's totes, briefcases and wallets, along with desk accoutrements, still convey an urbane 21st-century elegance.

Giraudon ☻
▽ 22 | 20 | 19 | E

Chelsea | 152 Eighth Ave. (bet. 17th & 18th Sts.) | 1 to 18th St. | 212-633-0999 | 800-278-1552 | www.giraudonnewyork.com

"Nice and airy", Chelsea's "go-to place for cool (but not too cool) shoes" lures fashion-conscious men and women with its pointy-toed ankle boots, Victorian-inspired side-button styles and more casual, sportier numbers with cushy soles; diehards declare that this "good-quality" footwear, all made by the French company that's been a style staple since 1977, is among the "best and most fabulous" around.

Girl Props
11 | 14 | 13 | I

G Vill | 33 E. Eighth St. (University Pl.) | N/R/W to 8th St. | 212-505-7615
SoHo | 153 Prince St. (bet. Thompson St. & W. B'way) | C/E to Spring St. | 212-505-7615 ☻
www.girlprops.com

"Take your bored tween or teen daughter" to these "funky" Greenwich Village and SoHo stores for "sweatshop baubles" like "zillions of sparkly" necklaces and earrings, beaded barrettes, feather boas, bags and belts; these spots aren't long on quality or service, but they do provide "cheap thrills."

Girlshop

19 | 19 | 18 | M

Meatpacking | 819 Washington St. (bet. Gansevoort & Little W. 12th Sts.) | A/C/E/L to 14th St./8th Ave. | 212-255-4985 | www.girlshop.com

"If you're a fan of indie designers, you'll love" this copper-walled Meatpacking District "treasure" that "brings the well-known Web site to life", giving "little-known names" like Louis Verdad and Nieves Lavi "an opportunity to show what they've got"; the "emphasis is on girlie" looks, including "fun and funky accessories", all so "affordable" "you may go a little nuts!"; P.S. "there's something for everyone", including your guy who can cop a snooze on the couch outside the dressing-room lounge.

Girly NYC ●

21 | 22 | 21 | M

E Vill | 441 E. Ninth St. (bet. Ave. A & 1st Ave.) | L to 1st Ave. | 212-353-5366

Femme-finds are the name of the game at this "fun and flirty" lingerie boutique full of "East Village flair" and done up with a Pucci-esque patterned floor and art for sale on the walls; channel sirens of yore with noirish nighties or play the gamine with cute-as-heck camis, then pick up "trendy" accessories and clothing essentials that also work the feminine angle.

☑ Giuseppe Zanotti Design

28 | 26 | 22 | VE

E 60s | 806 Madison Ave. (bet. 67th & 68th Sts.) | 6 to 68th St. | 212-650-0455 | www.giuseppe-zanotti-design.com

Not just for "high-style" trophy wives and "*Sex and the City*" disciples coo cultists who go cuckoo for the "unusual, gorgeous" footwear at this "fab" Madison Avenue stomping ground; "if you want shoes that are a piece of art" – think "hot" boots "with lots of gems", specifically Swarovski crystals, jewel-encrusted sandals and "over-the-top" stilettos in eye-popping colors – and don't want to see "yourself coming and going", this "beautiful" shop is a "real find"; N.B. the store will be revamped in spring 2007.

Givenchy

▽ 27 | 29 | 26 | VE

E 60s | 710 Madison Ave. (63rd St.) | 4/5/6/F/N/R/W to 59th St./ Lexington Ave. | 212-688-4338 | www.givenchy.com

"Oooh, *magnifique*" maintain moneyed mavens of this legendary French label, known for the relaxed chic of its womenswear immortalized by Audrey Hepburn; in this expansive East 60s space, a new generation of luxurious trench coats, trousers and – of course – form-fitting little black dresses designed by Italian Riccardo Tisci attract a couture-conscious clientele; N.B. equally expensive, well-tailored menswear is housed upstairs.

Global Table

- | - | - | M

SoHo | 107-109 Sullivan St. (bet. Prince & Spring Sts.) | C/E to Spring St. | 212-431-5839 | www.globaltable.com

To immediately "improve" your home's "style", hit this Asian-influenced Sullivan Street spot for an "unusual selection" of "cute" tabletop things like bamboo bowls, blue-and-white pineapple vases from Thailand and black ceramic tea sets from Japan; it's "the perfect place to find a gift", especially since the prices are "moderate" "by SoHo standards."

Goldy + Mac ◗

	QUALITY	DISPLAY	SERVICE	COST
	▽ 22	23	22	M

Park Slope | 219 Fifth Ave. (bet. President & Union Sts.) | Brooklyn | M/R to Union St. | 718-230-5603 | www.goldyandmac.com
Pals, partners and jewelry designers Ashley Gold and Susan McInerney lure local fashionistas to their brick-walled and gilt-mirrored Park Slope yearling offering "boutique-style clothing without the SoHo prices"; thanks to "trendy" threads from "won't-break-the-bank" labels like BCBG's To The Max, Free People, Gold Hawk and Rebecca Beeson and "wonderful", "friendly" service, it's a "great treat" to shop at this "neighborhood" nook.

NEW Golfsmith

23	21	19	E

E 50s | 641 Lexington Ave. (bet. 54th & 55th Sts.) | 4/5/6/F/N/R/W to 59th St./Lexington Ave. | 212-317-9720 | www.golfsmith.com
"Everything you need is in one place" at this new East 50s sports "supermarket" specializing in "golf stuff galore" and "impressive tennis offerings" too; prices for the "newest gear" and "top-notch equipment" are "competitive", if "not cheap"; and while the "service is uneven, ranging from old pros" to those who "think there are 14 holes on a course", the "fun indoor driving range" ("try before you buy!") hits "a hole in one" with most.

Good, the Bad & the Ugly, The ◗

-	-	-	M

NoLita | 85 Kenmare St. (Mulberry St.) | 6 to Spring St. | 212-473-3769 | www.goodbaduglynyc.com
Loyalists "love the name" of this psychedelic boutique, newly relocated from the East Village to NoLita, because it encapsulates all that owner-designer Judi Rosen has to offer, like eccentric high-waisted blue jeans, slouchy, sexy knit tops and on-the-mark accessories from her Miss Dater line, including gauntlet-style gloves and thigh- and knee-highs, plus trendy totes and sexy 1950s-inspired mules.

Goodwill Industries ◗

12	9	11	I

Downtown | 258 Livingston St. (Bond St.) | Brooklyn | A/C/G to Hoyt/Schermerhorn Sts. | 718-923-9037 | www.goodwill.org
Additional locations throughout the NY area
In between the often "messy" displays and sometimes "seriously unsavory items" ("the clothes scare me"), this century-old chain of "pretty cheap" charity stores may represent the "lowest common denominator of thrift shopping", "but still, God bless 'em" say those willing "to really rummage" "through a lot of junk" "to find the occasional treasure"; P.S. "truly dedicated bargain"-hunters hail the East 23rd Street branch as "having more to offer, better presented."

Gotham Bikes

▽ 24	18	22	E

TriBeCa | 112 W. Broadway (bet. Duane & Reade Sts.) | 1/2/3 to Chambers St. | 212-732-2453 | www.gothambikes.com
The staff "sure knows" and "loves their bikes" at this TriBeCa boutique, "Toga's twin", that's especially "great for mountain and hybrid" models; the combination of a "no-bull atmosphere" and a "no-hard-sell" approach adds up to "terrific service", making it a good place for your inner Lance to find the right wheels with "all the accoutrements."

Gothic Cabinet Craft

15 | 9 | 13 | M

W 40s | 730 11th Ave. (51st St.) | C/E to 50th St. | 212-246-9525 | www.gothiccabinetcraft.com
Additional locations throughout the NY area

"They will build it if you come" to these finished and unfinished "starter" furniture stores featuring bookcases, beds and dressers for "a fraction" of what their painted and primped brethren cost; but critics counter "don't expect master craftsmanship", and add the "aggravation of the terrible customer service is not worth the bang for your buck."

Gotta Knit

21 | 15 | 12 | E

G Vill | 498 Sixth Ave., 2nd fl. (bet. 12th & 13th Sts.) | F/L/V to 14th St./6th Ave. | 212-989-3030 | 800-898-6748 | www.gottaknit.net

Trendy NYU and New School students who've gotta knit swarm this "convenient", sunny second-floor shop in the Village, where the cubbyholed yarns are "high-end" and "fabulous" but "the prices are intimidating" ("what if you look awful in it?"); despite "great classes", many maintain this place "disappoints" due to "disorganization" and "attitude" ("the staff needs smiling lessons").

⧉ Gracious Home

25 | 18 | 20 | E

E 70s | 1201 Third Ave. (bet. 69th & 70th Sts.) | 6 to 68th St. | 212-517-6300 | 800-338-7809
E 70s | 1217 & 1220 Third Ave. (70th St.) | 6 to 68th St. | 212-517-6300 | 800-338-7909
W 60s | 1992 Broadway (67th St.) | 1 to 66th St./Lincoln Ctr. | 212-231-7800 | 800-338-7809 ◗
www.gracioushome.com

It's "crowded and claustrophobic" and you often have "to wait while others get the gracious service", but "everything the well-maintained home" requires resides at these "premier hardware/houseware stores", "from a $10 screw to a $1,000 vacuum"; the array "makes for tempting shopping", "and they deliver with a smile" "for free" (in Manhattan); granted, much of the merch "may be cheaper" elsewhere, but "if you need it, they have it" and "if you can't find it here – you really don't need it"; N.B. the 1201 Third Avenue branch focuses on lamps, lighting and bathroom fixtures.

⧉ Graff ⧉

28 | 28 | 27 | VE

E 60s | 721 Madison Ave. (bet. 63rd & 64th Sts.) | 6 to 68th St. | 212-355-9292 | www.graffdiamonds.com

Devotees "can't walk past the window without stopping to drool over the dazzlers" at this London-based jeweler lighting up Madison Avenue with rainbows of enormous, "beautifully displayed and designed" diamonds – think one to 100+ karats, in colors ranging from deep-yellow to icy white; the "nice staff is helpful", but ordinary ooglers assert that "overwhelming" applies both to the size of the stones and their "money-is-no-object" price.

Grand Central Racquet

– | – | – | E

E 40s | 341 Madison Ave. (44th St.) | 4/5/6/7/S to 42nd St./Grand Central | 212-292-8851 ⧉
E 40s | Grand Central, 45th St. passageway | 42nd St. (Vanderbilt Ave.) | 4/5/6/7/S to 42nd St./Grand Central | 212-856-9647 ⧉

(continued)

Grand Central Racquet

NEW **Flushing** | USTA National Tennis Ctr., Flushing Meadows Park | 11101 Corona Ave. (Saultell Ave.) | Queens | 7 to Main St. | 718-760-6227 ◑ www.grandcentralracquet.com

Rail-riding racquet-eers report that the "excellent stringing service" at this East 40s outfit is the "best" for commuters thanks to "knowledge-able staffers", same-day service and convenient locations – a "cramped" kiosk "in a hallway between train tracks" on Grand Central Terminal's main floor and a Madison Avenue big brother boasting shoes, clothing, equipment and a "great pro-shop atmosphere"; N.B. Flushing folk can now net the goods at their NTC Pro shop inside the USTA National Tennis Center.

Granny-Made

24	20	23	E

W 70s | 381 Amsterdam Ave. (bet. 78th & 79th Sts.) | 1 to 79th St. | 212-496-1222 | 877-472-6691 | www.granny-made.com

Purl-seekers pop by this 20-year-old West 70s standby to scoop up "wonderful" hand-knit children's sweaters and hats just like "your granny made but you don't have the time to", along with "whimsical" Polar fleece scarves, "unusual" blankets, slippers, toys and even "nice knitware" for adults; still, Granny's not everyone's bag: a handful jab that it's a "bit pricey" – "unless daddy's a Trump."

GRDN Bklyn

▽ 23	25	21	M

Boerum Hill | 103 Hoyt St. (bet. Atlantic & Pacific Sts.) | Brooklyn | 2/3/4/5/B/D/M/N/Q/R to Atlantic Ave. | 718-797-3628 | www.grdnbklyn.com

Exuding "country charm in the city", this "delightful" Boerum Hill stripling stocks "healthy plants", plus seeds, topiaries, trees, tools and containers; it's run by a "lovely staff" who are experts on organic farm-ing, but "even those without a garden" will find plenty of "beautiful, itching-to-be-bought items" like French soaps, scents, chimes, cards and carafes, along with Francis Palmer Pearl tableware and vases.

Great Feet

22	19	17	M

E 80s | 1241 Lexington Ave. (84th St.) | 4/5/6 to 86th St. | 212-249-0551 | www.striderite.com

Parents who want their wee ones well-heeled swear by this "great all-around" East 80s standby, which stocks a "diverse selection" of footwear for newborns to age 12, from "sneakers to rain boots and everything in between" from brands like Stride Rite, Merrell and Primigi; the "knowledgeable" staff "knows how to fit your child" – "just make sure you have plenty of time" if you stop in "before school starts in September."

Green Onion, The ⧄Ⓜ

▽ 24	20	10	E

Cobble Hill | 274 Smith St. (bet. Degraw & Sackett Sts.) | Brooklyn | F/G to Carroll St. | 718-246-2804

You're "always sure to find something new and interesting" at this "sweet" Cobble Hill kiddie shop avow admirers aflutter over its hand-picked, "unique assortment of clothes, toys and books" at a variety of price points, all housed inside antique armoires and other unique dis-play pieces; however, a few "neighborhood moms" who gripe about the "unfriendly", "off-putting" sales help "dub it The Mean Onion."

	QUALITY	DISPLAY	SERVICE	COST

Greenstones
26 | 18 | 21 | E

NEW **E 70s** | 1410 Second Ave. (bet. 73rd & 74th Sts.) | 6 to 77th St. | 212-794-0530

E 80s | 1184 Madison Ave. (bet. 86th & 87th Sts.) | 4/5/6 to 86th St. | 212-427-1665

W 80s | 442 Columbus Ave. (bet. 81st & 82nd Sts.) | B/C to 81st St. | 212-580-4322

For "lovely high-end and European children's" togs "with a modern twist" or the "perfect baby gift", trek to these "excellent" crosstown cousins, including the latest Second Avenue addition, that also boast one of the "best assortments of play clothes"; if a few fret that the racks are "not well organized", the green team points out that the "staff helps you make selections", which "makes shopping here a delight."

NEW Greenwich Letterpress
26 | 23 | 23 | M

W Vill | 39 Christopher St. (bet. 6th & 7th Aves.) | 1 to Christopher St./ Sheridan Sq. | 212-989-7464 | www.greenwichletterpress.com

"Oh-so-civilized, so lovely" and yes, oh-so-"great for cards" and "whimsical gifts" too, this "highly recommended" bright pink-and-brown wallpapered West Village stationer with a "wonderful, knowledgeable staff" oozes "vintage-style charm"; the "cute, handmade stock and special papers at an affordable price" "make you wish it weren't so easy to e-mail" concur correspondents who also practice their penmanship with "unique", custom-made invitations that elicit "compliments from guests."

Gringer & Sons ⊠
25 | 11 | 18 | M

E Vill | 29 First Ave. (2nd St.) | F/V to Lower East Side/2nd Ave. | 212-475-0600 | www.gringerandsons.com

Since 1918, this East Village "expert on making the most of cramped city spaces" has been offering a "huge selection" of "fairly priced" appliances spanning low-end to "midrange to luxe" manufacturers, i.e. from Frigidaire to Viking; "it's not a pretty" place and you "don't always get helped right away", but eventually a "know-their-stuff staff" can show you "everything you would ever want for your dream kitchen" or bath.

Groupe
– | – | – | E

(aka Groupe 16sur20)

NoLita | 267 Elizabeth St. (bet. Houston & Prince Sts.) | B/D/F/V to B'way/Lafayette St. | 212-343-0007 | www.groupe1620.com

If James Bond were the least bit nerdy, he'd feel right at home in this spacious garagelike NoLita storefront (a casual menswear cousin of nearby Seize sur Vingt) where edgy classics – think wide-wale cord jackets, bespoke cotton shirting, two-tone shoes – from house brands like Troglodyte Humongous and 16sur20 hang next to a bright yellow Ferrari parked at the front; take time to ponder the changing photo exhibits on the wall, while deciding which cut of trouser makes your behind look oh-so-sexy.

Gruen Optika
25 | 21 | 23 | E

E 50s | 599 Lexington Ave. (52nd St.) | 6 to 51st St. | 212-688-3580 ⊠

E 60s | 1076 Third Ave. (64th St.) | 6 to 68th St. | 212-751-6177

E 60s | 740 Madison Ave. (bet. 64th & 65th Sts.) | 6 to 68th St. | 212-988-5832 ⊠

E 80s | 1225 Lexington Ave. (83rd St.) | 4/5/6 to 86th St. | 212-628-2493

(continued)

Gruen Optika

W 60s | 2009 Broadway (bet. 68th & 69th Sts.) | 1 to 66th St./Lincoln Ctr. | 212-874-8749
W 80s | 2382 Broadway (87th St.) | 1 to 86th St. | 212-724-0850
www.grueneyes.com

This "upscale" eyewear chain stands out with its "well-edited", "beautiful collection of designer frames" and sunglasses from Chanel to Kate Spade to Oakley that "varies from store to store"; some feel "you're paying for" the "overpriced" "aura of German optical excellence", but even though it's "not the mom-and-pop optician it started out as", the "always-helpful" salespeople add value because they "know what you want even if you don't."

G-Star Raw ❂   ▽ 23 | 20 | 19 | E

SoHo | 270 Lafayette St. (Prince St.) | B/D/F/V to B'way/Lafayette St. | 212-219-2744 | www.g-star.com

"Rock-star clothes", particularly "gorgeous" raw-denim jeans with distinctive details "sure to look good on anyone", form the backbone of this Netherlands-based company's two-floor SoHo showcase awash in cement, steel and raw wood; if a handful harrumph they're a "li'l too trendy" and "slightly overpriced", true-blue "believers" "spend the money", "tight budget" be damned, "because they're worth it!"

Gucci   27 | 27 | 23 | VE

E 50s | 685 Fifth Ave. (54th St.) | E/V to 5th Ave./53rd St. | 212-826-2600
E 60s | 840 Madison Ave. (bet. 69th & 70th Sts.) | 6 to 68th St. | 212-717-2619
www.gucci.com

"You definitely feel like you're shopping on Fifth Avenue" (Madison too) at this "beautifully appointed" modernistic duo where all "runs like clockwork" from the "impressive entrance" to the sales associates, now "much friendlier than in the past" as they "please" the patrons forever perusing the "revealing cuts" in clothing, "snobbissimo" leather goods and "everything from shoes to ice trays" stamped with the ubiquitous logo or horse-bit; if a few quibble it's "not as hip" "post-Tom Ford", supporters retort that with creative director Frida Giannini holding the reins it's still "happening."

Guess ❂   21 | 20 | 19 | M

SoHo | 537 Broadway (bet. Prince & Spring Sts.) | N/R/W to Prince St. | 212-226-9545
Seaport | South Street Seaport | 23-25 Fulton St. (Water St.) | 2/3/4/5/A/C/J/M/Z to Fulton St./B'way/Nassau | 212-385-0533
Kings Plaza | Kings Plaza Shopping Ctr. | 5351 Kings Plaza (Flatbush Ave. & Ave. U) | Brooklyn | 718-421-5075
Staten Island | Staten Island Mall | 2655 Richmond Ave. (bet. Platinum Ave. & Richmond Hill Rd.) | 718-370-1594
800-394-8377 | www.guess.com

The "true test" of how "flattering" this chain's "cool" jeans are is "walking down the street and watching the heads turn" as you strut by in your "moderately priced" low-riders; while there's no question that the "nice selection" has "teen set" –appeal, and even some adults find it has a "bit of edge", snobs simply pass, pointing to "cheap-looking ads" – "hello, Paris Hilton."

| | QUALITY | DISPLAY | SERVICE | COST |

Guggenheim Museum Store
22 | 19 | 17 | M

E 80s | Guggenheim Museum | 1071 Fifth Ave. (89th St.) | 4/5/6 to
86th St. | 212-423-3615 | 800-329-6109 | www.guggenheimstore.org
Echoing this Museum Mile's gem of a building, the Guggenheim store's
offerings are "well rounded", featuring "arty scarves, books and jewelry"
as well as "great gadgets and mobiles" along with "decorative accessories"; some frankly fret over the "too-tight" space with "limited"
merch, but more report the "esoteric" selection has the Wright stuff.

NEW Guy Laroche
26 | 23 | 23 | VE

W 50s | 47 W. 57th St. (bet. 5th & 6th Aves.) | F to 57th St. | 212-935-4747 |
www.guylaroche.com
You may not immediately realize you're in the lap of couture luxury at
this West 50s boutique, but once you start fingering the plush, sculptural cashmere women's suits, "well-displayed menswear" or Hilary
Swank-y gowns (she wore one to the Oscars), the message is clear:
don't visit this French designer's new American flagship "unless
you've won the lottery – then go with a truck."

Gymboree
22 | 20 | 20 | M

E 60s | 1049 Third Ave. (62nd St.) | 4/5/6/F/N/R/W to 59th St./
Lexington Ave. | 212-688-4044
E 70s | 1332 Third Ave. (bet. 76th & 77th Sts.) | 6 to 77th St. | 212-517-5548
E 80s | 1120 Madison Ave. (bet. 83rd & 84th Sts.) | 4/5/6 to 86th St. |
212-717-6702
W 60s | 2015 Broadway (69th St.) | 1 to 66th St./Lincoln Ctr. |
212-595-7662 ●
W 80s | 2271 Broadway (81st St.) | 1 to 79th St. | 212-595-9071 ●
NEW Glendale | The Shoppes at Atlas Park | 80-28 Cooper Ave.
(bet. 80th & 83rd Sts.) | Queens | 718-386-6139 ●
Staten Island | Staten Island Mall | 2655 Richmond Ave. (bet. Platinum Ave. &
Richmond Hill Rd.) | 718-370-8679 ●
877-449-6932 | www.gymboree.com
"Mommies and mommies-to-be go wild" for the "durable", "ever-
adorable" kids' duds, accessories and toys at these "reasonably
priced" stores that are always "stocked to the rafters"; "casual", "colorful" clothing with "very cute themes (especially for girls)" mean for
many it's the "first stop for shower and birthday presents" sure to
make a tot "look like a million bucks."

Gym Source ⧄
▽ 26 | 23 | 26 | VE

E 50s | 40 E. 52nd St. (bet. Madison & Park Aves.) | 6 to 51st St. |
212-688-4222 | 888-496-7687 | www.gymsource.com
Fans turn back flips for this "excellent resource" in Midtown for "top-
quality gym equipment" – "both residential and commercial" varieties –
including Cybex, Nautilus and Stairmaster brands; athletes ranging
from bodybuilders to runners appreciate the "knowledgeable" salespeople and "great delivery service", even if they come at "high prices."

Hable Construction Ⓜ
- | - | - | E

W Vill | 117 Perry St. (bet. Hudson & Greenwich Sts.) | A/C/E/L to
14th St./8th Ave. | 212-989-2375 | www.hableconstruction.com
Now that sister-owners Susan and Katharine Hable have shuttered
their NoLita nugget, habitués head to their West Village yearling to
peruse the screen-printed canvas and linen handbags, baskets, pil-

lows, oven mitts and sun hats in "original, artistic fabrics"; choose from "wonderful" light-hearted prints like Charcoal Checker and Scarlet Branch, plus colorful alpaca throws and a line of embroidered cotton voile quilts.

Habu Textiles

| - | - | - | E |

Chelsea | 135 W. 29th St. (bet. 6th & 7th Aves.) | 1 to 28th St. | 212-239-3546 | www.habutextiles.com

For an "amazing selection" of "wonderful" Japanese "yarns and fabrics you will find nowhere else" (made from such substances as pineapple, bamboo and a stainless-steel-and-silk combo), artists and fashionistas wend their way to this Chelsea textile specialist near FIT, which also houses a weaving studio and gallery; the "minimalist" space displays one-of-a-kind hand-dyed pieces for garments or home furnishings that are also fabu as artworks in their own right.

NEW Hairy Mary's

| - | - | - | I |

LES | 149 Orchard St. (bet. Rivington & Stanton Sts.) | F/V to Lower East Side/2nd Ave. | 212-228-8989 | www.hairymarysvintage.com

Its blue, pink and fuchsia walls enlivened by the proprietor's own vibrant paintings, this "way cool", pint-size boutique presents a pretty picture to LES passersby; roughly one side consists of vintage womenswear – mostly everyday garb from the '70s and '80s and slightly older coats and fur stoles; the other carries reconstructed items – "really, some lovely things" – while rows of timeless shoes and boots line the floor.

halcyon the shop

| - | - | - | M |

Dumbo | 57 Pearl St. (Water St.) | Brooklyn | F to York St. | 718-260-9299 | www.halcyonline.com

One-stop shopping for hipsters, this high-concept Dumbo music store/boutique/gallery offers the latest in electronica, house, techno, soul, funk, avant-garde, Afrobeat and bossa lounge, plus a slew of vintage and used records; the groovy, eco-themed interior, complete with bark-accented walls and sod-and-stone flooring, also showcases local art, cool threads and pro DJ accessories as well as in-store happenings.

Half Pint

| - | - | - | M |

Dumbo | 55 Washington St. (bet. Front & Water Sts.) | Brooklyn | F to York St. | 718-875-4007 | 877-543-7186 | www.babybazaar.com

The brick-and-mortar offshoot of Babybazaar.com, this spacious Dumbo shop, blocks from the Brooklyn Bridge, stocks an A to Z assortment of loot for little people, from furniture, bedding and strollers to toys, diaper bags and gifts; it's also home to an impressive selection of clothing from both old favorites like Levi's and Zutano and of-the-moment labels like Appaman, Tea Collection and Small Paul.

Hammacher Schlemmer & Co. ⑤

| 25 | 25 | 22 | E |

E 50s | 147 E. 57th St. (bet. Lexington & 3rd Aves.) | 4/5/6/F/N/R/W to 59th St./Lexington Ave. | 212-421-9000 | 800-421-9002 | www.hammacher.com

An "oasis of the unlikely and improbable", this "high-tech gift" store in the East 50s "keeps up with the latest outlandish items", many of which are destined for the "Gadget Hall Of Fame"; penny-wise perusers protest that the "cool" "toys for big boys" can be as "expensive" as a "vacation to Paris" ("$4,000 for a massage chair?"), but it's never-theless "a fun place to browse", "try out new items" and "dream."

⨀ H&M ●
12 | 14 | 9 | I

E 50s | 640 Fifth Ave. (51st St.) | E/V to 5th Ave./53rd St. | 212-489-0390 | www.hm.com
Additional locations throughout the NY area

How to handle this "cheap, cheap, cheap" Swedish chain: "shop before noon" (when the "mob" descends and the "messiness begins"), buy without trying on to avoid "ridiculous fitting-room lines" and "bring armloads of patience" to endure staff attitude that's "demanding at best"; "annoyances" aside, though, most "cannot resist" its "of-the-moment" fashions "for the whole family" – including one-off lines from top designers (most recently, Victor & Rolf) – packing "huge bang for the buck"; N.B. a new Midtown branch is slated to open in 2007.

⨀ Harris Levy
26 | 13 | 19 | M

LES | 98 Forsyth St. (bet. Broome & Grand Sts.) | B/D to Grand St. | 212-226-3102 | 800-221-7750 | www.harrislevy.com

"My mother brought me here when I was getting married and I brought my kids here when they started college" is a typical statement from supporters who frequent this fourth-generation, family-owned Lower East Side purveyor of "very good quality" "discount bedding" (especially Italian 600-thread-count sheets) as well as towels, shower curtains and comforters; there's a "good selection", but "know what you want beforehand", as the space "isn't great for browsing."

Harry's Shoes
24 | 16 | 18 | M

W 80s | 2299 Broadway (83rd St.) | 1 to 86th St. | 212-874-2035 | 866-442-7797 | www.harrys-shoes.com

Staffed with "efficient" folks "who measure your feet", this "crowded", "chaotic" "old-school" West 80s "standard" offers a "staggering inventory" of "trendy and traditional" footwear for men and women – and now that the kids have their own store nearby, the ladies' selection is even more extensive; forget Jimmy Choos – instead, think "sturdy sport shoes" from Timberland, Merrill and Teva offset by "excellent" offerings from Camper, Frye and Puma.

NEW Harry's Shoes for Kids
– | – | – | M

W 80s | 2315 Broadway (83rd St.) | 1 to 86th St. | 212-874-2034 | www.harrys-shoes.com

Now settled into its own spacious digs just a skip and a hop from its parent store, this old-guard West 80s children's shoe shop sticks to its winning formula: customer service, expert fitting and an A-to-Z assortment of American and European brands, including Geox, Ecco, Keen, Merrell and Puma; while the lines can stretch long, especially on Saturdays, the staff knows how to treat kids' feet, making it well worth the wait.

⨀ Harry Winston ⨂
29 | 28 | 28 | VE

E 50s | 718 Fifth Ave. (56th St.) | N/R/W to 5th Ave./59th St. | 212-245-2000 | 800-988-4110 | www.harrywinston.com

"Who isn't wild about Harry?" ask acolytes of this "exceptional", "elegant, expensive" and "imposing" Fifth Avenue icon voted this *Survey*'s No. 1 for Fashion/Beauty that's known for "amazing diamonds" that are "the best there is"; since 1920 they've had a "rich, famous" and "red-carpet" following, including stars like Gwyneth Paltrow and Halle Berry, and "once they open the gates for you, you'll feel like royalty too."

⚡ Harvey Electronics

	QUALITY	DISPLAY	SERVICE	COST
	28	24	20	VE

W 40s | 2 W. 45th St. (bet. 5th & 6th Aves.) | B/D/F/V to 47-50th Sts./ Rockefeller Ctr. | 212-575-5000 | 800-254-7836 | www.harveyonline.com

"Audiophiles are at home" at this "gold-standard" electronics outlet in the West 40s with "nice sound rooms" for novices looking to "learn" and a staff of "audio specialists" that is "a pleasure to deal with"; in fact, the main gripe about this "high-end", "high-quality" hi-fi haven is its "high prices", though sound zealots insist you "suck up the expense" – "you won't be disappointed."

NEW Hasker Ⓜ

	QUALITY	DISPLAY	SERVICE	COST
	-	-	-	E

Carroll Gdns | 333 Smith St. (bet. Carroll & President Sts.) | Brooklyn | F/G to Carroll St. | 718-222-5756 | www.haskerhome.com

This "spectacular" shop in Carroll Gardens is the newest neighbor on "Smith Street's home furnishings row"; the modern, clean space's exposed-brick walls, dim lighting and eclectic music is a soothing backdrop for unique and fairly priced handcrafted goods that range from furniture, fine china, ceramics, linens and lamps to jewelry – all from a mix of Brooklyn and Scandinavian designers.

NEW Hastens

	QUALITY	DISPLAY	SERVICE	COST
	-	-	-	VE

SoHo | 80 Greene St. (bet. Broome & Spring Sts.) | C/E to Spring St. | 212-219-8022 | www.hbeds.com

If you don't loose sleep at the thought of investing five figures in a mere mattress then a purchase at this new SoHo offshoot of a 150-year-old Swedish firm should be a dream come true; only natural materials such as cotton, flax, wool and purified hand-flailed horsehair from Argentina are used on the handmade beds, which are bound in signature blue-and-white gingham; but some just keep on counting sheep when it comes to the price tag, which can climb to $49,500.

Hastings Tile & Il Bagno Collection Ⓢ

	QUALITY	DISPLAY	SERVICE	COST
	▽ 26	-	19	VE

E 50s | A&D Bldg. | 150 E. 58th St., 10th fl. (bet. Lexington & 3rd Aves.) | 4/5/ 6/F/N/R/W to 59th St./Lexington Ave. | 212-674-9700 | 800-351-0038 | www.hastingstilebath.com

It's "a museum for tiles, plus kitchen and bath" accessories including faucets and basins praise proponents of this top-notch showroom that moved post-*Survey* to the A&D Building in the East 50s; it's got "great stuff" particularly for those looking for trendsetting designs (think chic crocodile-patterned squares), but "you'll pay dearly for them."

Hat Shop, The

	QUALITY	DISPLAY	SERVICE	COST
	24	24	24	E

SoHo | 120 Thompson St. (bet. Prince & Spring Sts.) | C/E to Spring St. | 212-219-1445 | www.thehatshopnyc.com

"*J'adore* – there's nothing else like it in NYC" declare devotees who descend on this SoHo "favorite" for "fabulous", "top-notch" quality toppers from over 30 local milliners; chances are you'll find "just the right hat with just the right fit" but don't forget to ask the "lively, informative", "hands-on owner" about custom designs – "there's nothing like having a great" chapeau "made just for you."

Hazel's House of Shoes
18 | 9 | 17 | I

Bayside | 35-16 Bell Blvd. (35th Ave.) | Queens | 7 to Main St. | 718-423-8666

"Now that everyone knows" about this converted Bayside house, a "hole-in-the-wall" offering a "huge selection of work, casual", "dressy" and "bridal shoes" "especially dyeables" and "great bags" at a "fabulous" discount, you "need to go early to get the good pickings"; subways here are nonexistent (take the LIRR), but the "good deals" keep your budget on track.

NEW Heidi Klein 🅢
- | - | - | E

E 70s | 1018 Lexington Ave. (bet. 72nd & 73rd Sts.) | 6 to 77th St. | 212-327-1700 | www.heidiklein.com

It's a "vacation just to shop" at this "charming UES" newcomer, a breezy British import filled with everything you need to jump-start your warm-weather holiday – no matter when you're jetting to the tropics; the resort-bound flip for "beautiful" bikinis, sarongs, swim trunks, sunglasses and totes, plus "cute sundresses and cover-ups" sure to "wow the East Hampton crowd", from labels like Apsara, Emamo, Eres, Maji, Melissa Odabash and Vilebrequin.

Heights Kids
- | - | - | E

Brooklyn Hts | 85 Pineapple Walk (bet. Cadman Plaza & Henry St.) | Brooklyn | 2/3 to Clark St. | 718-222-4271 | www.heightskids.com

For nearly two decades, this "excellent" Brooklyn Heights emporium has remained a "reliable" source for all things *enfant*; admirers not only applaud the "wonderful selection" of educational toys, French and Italian clothing and all-natural bath products that scale the heights of expectations, they also head here for a snazzy, new set of wheels for baby from "high-end" stroller brands like Bugaboo and Silver Cross.

Helen Ficalora
- | - | - | E

NoLita | 21 Cleveland Pl. (bet. Kenmare & Spring Sts.) | 6 to Spring St. | 212-219-3700 | 877-754-2676 | www.helenficalora.com

This fine jewelry designer is known for her alphabet charm necklaces and a celeb clientele that includes Sarah Jessica Parker and Katie Holmes; her first shop, on the NoLita/SoHo border, is a pink-and-gold bandbox and an apt backdrop for such "sweet" pieces as delicate diamond and gemstone bands inspired by blooms like daffodils and dogwood that are "a wonderful way to mark a special occasion for a woman."

Helen Wang
- | - | - | E

SoHo | 69 Mercer St. (Broome St.) | N/R/W to Prince St. | 212-997-4180 | www.helenwangny.com

Browsers of Barneys and Bergdorf who know the Shanghai-born Wang's wares now also alight at this designer's own shop, an airy SoHo loft brimming with her characteristic cute, colorful dresses, classic coats and cashmere cardigans that channel an updated Doris Day; there's also kids' wear named after her daughter, Mina, and a smattering of pillows, candles and fragrant soaps.

☑ Henri Bendel ◗
26 | 25 | 21 | VE

E 50s | 712 Fifth Ave. (bet. 55th & 56th Sts.) | N/R/W to 5th Ave./59th St. | 212-247-1100 | 800-423-6335

"Feeling more like a boutique than a department store", this Fifth Avenue *femmes* favorite is "always up on the latest styles", nestling "unique items among the name brands"; though known for "expensive" creations from "hard-to-find indie designers", it also carries its own line of "cashmere sweaters at reasonable prices", plus "cutting-edge skincare", "absolutely amazing" accessories and "cute" costume jewelry; "service is friendly", if *un peu* pushy, and while the lachrymose lament the "lost edge" of elegance to "teenybopper-time" threads, at least navigating the "confusing multilevel maze" lets you "look at the beautiful Lalique windows."

Henry Beguelin

	-	-	-	E

Meatpacking | Gansevoort Hotel | 18 Ninth Ave. (13th St.) | A/C/E/L to 14th St./8th Ave. | 212-647-8415 | www.henrybeguelin.it

"Boho-luxe leatherwear for those most in-the-know" is on show at this tiny shop adjacent to the Gansevoort Hotel, where nearly everything – from the floor to the furnishings to the "arty" his-and-hers clothing and signature Spazzatura and Tribu belts – is made of handcrafted cowhide; and while some ask "what's up with the prices?", the "understated, anti-Louis (Vuitton)" crowd confides this is "the ultimate in paying a lot to look like you've paid very little."

Henry Lehr

▽ 24	21	22	E

NoLita | 11 Prince St. (bet. Bowery & Elizabeth St.) | J/M/Z to Bowery | 212-274-9921
NoLita | 9 Prince St. (bet. Bowery & Elizabeth St.) | J/M/Z to Bowery | 212-274-9921

It may be "well-edited", but the "manageable" denim and cord selection at this NoLita nook is one of the "best in town" according to fit-minded guys and girls; the "part-guru/part-genius" staff "will put you in the hottest jeans" from J Brand to Rogan – they "know what looks best on you the minute you walk in the door", so go ahead, "trust them" – then duck through the doorway to 11 Prince Street for T-shirts to match.

Here Comes the Bridesmaid ⑤ Ⓜ

17	9	14	M

Chelsea | 238 W. 14th St. (bet. 7th & 8th Aves.) | A/C/E/L to 14th St./8th Ave. | 212-647-9686 | www.bridesmaids.com

If you're looking for a "moderately priced gown that your bridesmaids won't hate you for picking out" and flower girl outfits too, "roll up your sleeves" and sift through "tons of dresses shoved onto racks" at this by-appointment Chelsea nook; while some wedding party frocks are "beautiful", the "worn-out" "samples require imagination", plus "service is as good as it could be in such a closet" that's in need of "sprucing up."

⊿ Hermès ⑤

29	27	23	VE

E 60s | 691 Madison Ave. (62nd St.) | N/R/W to 5th Ave./59th St. | 212-751-3181 | 800-441-4488 | www.hermes.com

"Be prepared to drop your inheritance on your first visit" to this "exceptional" Parisian "status store" and "tourist magnet" on Madison Avenue that lovers of "unparalleled" luxury "worship" as a "temple of high-quality" apparel and the "holy grail of accessories"; "go, gawk and gasp" at the wait-listed Birkin and Kelly bags, "gorgeous" "investment scarves", leather goods "that will outlast our lives", "crème de la crème" ties and even "doggy chew toys"; however, while many find the service "*fantastique*", some shoppers say "Oprah wasn't entirely wrong" about the "haughty" help.

H. Herzfeld 🗷

▽ 26 | 20 | 22 | VE

E 50s | 118 E. 57th St. (bet. Lexington & Park Aves.) | 4/5/6/F/N/R/W to 59th St./Lexington Ave. | 212-753-6756 | www.herzfeldonline.com

Even a newish East 50s locale can't take away that "bygone age" feel of this venerable haberdasher, with its "quiet" air, "custom clothes", "nice selection" of accessories, from umbrellas to underwear, and "salesmen of an antediluvian tradition"; "discriminating men" head here for "classic goods" (Sea Island cottons, Scottish cashmeres), but "don't go if you have to ask about the prices", which reflect the "rarity" of the tailoring tradition.

Hickey Freeman

27 | 24 | 24 | VE

E 50s | 666 Fifth Ave. (bet. 52nd & 53rd Sts.) | E/V to 5th Ave./53rd St. | 212-586-6481

Financial Dist | 111 Broadway (Thames St.) | 4/5 to Wall St. | 212-233-2363 🗷

888-603-8968 | www.hickeyfreeman.com

Ok, so the style's "a little old-school" ("makes a 30-year-old look like a 50-year-old" jesters jibe), but "if you want an American-made" suit, "hand-tailored" from "the finest" fabric (whether off-the-rack or made-to-measure), this Midtown–Financial District duo is "what a quality men's haberdasher should be"; "great" staffers also guide you through the "very good selection of accessories" and sportswear, and while prices are "not for the faint of wallet", the "business-crowd" clientele amortizes the cost, knowing their purchase "will last forever."

Highway

– | – | – | E

NoLita | 238 Mott St. (bet. Prince & Spring Sts.) | 6 to Spring St. | 212-966-4388 | www.highwaybuzz.com

"The street-chic factor hasn't" changed since its Hiponica days – reason enough for cutting-edgers to continue cruising this Highway in NoLita for "colorful", "quirky" handbags, "cool" laptop totes and other accessories done up in "fun" materials like felt, flannel, nylon and velvet; it's the wheel deal declare diehards who wear the gear "for years", so expect to be "complimented by everyone from Japanese tourists to New Zealand shopgirls."

H.L. Purdy 🗷

27 | 25 | 25 | VE

E 50s | 501 Madison Ave. (bet. 52nd & 53rd Sts.) | E/V to 5th Ave./53rd St. | 212-688-8050

E 80s | 1171 Madison Ave. (86th St.) | 4/5/6 to 86th St. | 212-249-3997

E 80s | 1195 Lexington Ave. (81st St.) | 6 to 77th St. | 212-737-0122

www.hlpurdy.com

"Beautiful", "elegant" specs presented by a "superb" and "profoundly knowledgeable" staff have eye-ficionados tagging this Uptown troika the "Harry Winston" of eyewear; "skillful" on-site opticians can finesse even the "trickiest lenses" and cater to fashion-forward kiddies (Lexington location), and even if it's admittedly "expensive", the selection and service are "worth the extra cost."

Hogan

26 | 26 | 21 | VE

SoHo | 134 Spring St. (bet. Greene & Wooster Sts.) | C/E to Spring St. | 212-343-7905 | 888-604-6426 | www.hogancatalog.com

Pick up a "dream bag" with "great classic style and lines" at this funky, "friendly" SoHo sibling to Tod's that "makes shopping a real pleasure";

the "beautifully presented" goods by designer Diego Della Valle include "high-quality" footwear too but budget-watchers warn the "tried-and-true" finds can "cost a great deal."

NEW Hollander & Lexer Ⓜ | - | - | - | E |

Boerum Hill | 358 Atlantic Ave. (bet. Bond & Hoyt Sts.) | Brooklyn | 2/3/4/5/B/D/M/N/Q/R to Atlantic Ave. | 718-797-9190

Boerum Hill locals feel right at home sifting through the menswear in this black-as-night boutique that, with its curio-shop vitrines and stuffed roosters, feels like a cross between Atlantic Avenue's antique shops and a London haberdashery; but a closer look at its wares reveals a hipness factor in the shape of Rag & Bone tweed jackets, Steven Alan cardigans and Santa Maria Novello toiletries cool enough to satisfy the snobbiest of metrosexuals.

Hollywould Ⓢ | 24 | 23 | 21 | VE |

NoLita | 198 Elizabeth St. (bet. Prince & Spring Sts.) | 6 to Spring St. | 212-219-1905 | www.ilovehollywould.com

"Where's Holly [Dunlap] been all our lives?" wonder admirers who "can't get enough" of the owner-designer's "funky" pumps, "hot, hot, hot!" stilettos for that "go-out outfit", "classic flats-made-sexy – an 'it' girl staple" – and "Palm Beach" –perfect sandals, all showcased at her "convenient"; cabana-striped NoLita shop; but there's more: she also offers a "clothing line with style" and "fun bags" too; if a handful huff "too expensive", others wait for the "insane sales."

Hom Boms | - | - | - | M |

E 70s | 1500 First Ave. (78th St.) | 6 to 77th St. | 212-717-5300

"Great doesn't say enough" about this East 70s "stalwart", one of the "best toy stores in NYC" offering a really "nice selection" including Lego sets, dolls, arts-and-crafts kits and puzzles; if a few humbugs grumble that "everything is crowded and smushed together", happy campers rationalize that the "knowledgeable staff makes up for the really cramped space", adding "leave the stroller and kids at home."

Ⓩ Home Depot ◗ | 19 | 16 | 14 | M |

Flatiron | 40 W. 23rd St. (bet. 5th & 6th Aves.) | F/V to 23rd St. | 212-929-9571 | 800-430-3376 | www.homedepot.com
Additional locations throughout the NY area

"Forget the suburbs, we've got doormen" at the chain's Flatiron flagship, anyway, quip "home-handy" "hardware-starved New Yorkers" who "feed" their DIY "fantasies" at this "big-box" "superstore"; "whether you need screws, toilet seats" or "how-to classes" or want to "finish" renovating "your apartment without leaving Manhattan" it's a "godsend" with a "surprisingly deep inventory"; but detractors suggest "packing survival supplies" before hitting the "interminable check-out lines" and deem the staff a "bunch of amateurs", adding, "for expert advice shop late when the contractors go."

Homer Ⓢ | - | - | - | E |

E 70s | 939 Madison Ave. (bet. 74th & 75th Sts.) | 6 to 77th St. | 212-744-7705 | www.homerdesign.com

Named after American artist Winslow Homer, this modern space just a few doors down from the Whitney showcases contemporary tables, desks, seating, lighting and accessories from American and European designers alongside owner-architect Richard Mishaan's signature collection of elegant offerings including limed-oak bookcases.

NEW Honora — | — | — | E

E 50s | 30 E. 57th St. (Madison Ave.) | N/R/W to 5th Ave./59th St. | 212-308-8707 | www.honora.com

If you have a passion for pearls you won't feel stranded at this new East 50s jewelry store that's a first in New York City for the 50-year-old company; Chinese freshwater cultured pearls as well as ones from the South Seas may be combined with silver, gold or leather and turn up in everything from bracelets, belts, necklaces, earrings and watches, in prices ranging from $50–$50,000.

Hooti Couture ◐ ▽ 21 | 21 | 23 | M

Prospect Hts | 321 Flatbush Ave. (7th Ave.) | Brooklyn | B/Q to 7th Ave. | 718-857-1977 | www.hooticouture.com

"Pretty cool place" purr Prospect Heights patrons of this "funky shop" whose owner not only "has a great eye" for "good vintage bags", clothing (mostly midcentury) and furs, but is "so entertaining to watch" as she zips around the small Victorian storefront, offering "attentive service" and even price adjustments; N.B. you'll hoot with laughter at the phrases scrawled on the tags (e.g. 'new mom's first night out').

Hot Toddie Ⓜ — | — | — | E

Ft Greene | 741 Fulton St. (bet. S. Elliott Pl. & S. Portland Ave.) | Brooklyn | C to Lafayette Ave. | 718-858-7292 | www.hottoddieonline.com

Bridget Williams' buzzworthy Fort Greene children's boutique beckons with an arsenal of the hottest sportswear brands du jour, including Armani Junior, Lipstik and Nolita Pocket, along with vintage-distressed Diesel and Levi's denim and a sprinkling of shoes and accessories; everything is artfully displayed within a cozy, chandelier-lit space, peppered with antique prams, doll carriages and tricycles.

House of Oldies Ⓢ Ⓜ — | — | — | E

G Vill | 35 Carmine St. (bet. Bedford & Bleecker Sts.) | A/B/C/D/E/F/V to W. 4th St. | 212-243-0500 | www.houseofoldies.com

"What an amazing selection" sing "pop-music fans" who're "happy to pay" the prices at this "expensive" record store, a Greenwich Village fixture since 1968 specializing in rare mint-condition vinyl from the '50s on up (no CDs or cassettes); true, most folks' "closet is bigger" than the minuscule digs, but speak up if you can't find that "obscure 45" because they may have it in their off-limits block-long basement or Long Island storage annex.

Housing Works Thrift Shop 20 | 17 | 16 | I

Chelsea | 143 W. 17th St. (bet. 6th & 7th Aves.) | 1 to 18th St. | 212-366-0820

E 70s | 202 E. 77th St. (bet. 2nd & 3rd Aves.) | 6 to 77th St. | 212-772-8461

NEW E 80s | 1730 Second Ave. (90th St.) | 4/5/6 to 86th St. | 212-722-8306 Ⓢ Ⓜ

Gramercy | 157 E. 23rd St. (bet. Lexington & 3rd Aves.) | 6 to 23rd St. | 212-529-5955

W 70s | 306 Columbus Ave. (bet. 74th & 75th Sts.) | 1/2/3/B/C to 72nd St. | 212-579-7566

(continued)

Housing Works Thrift Shop

NEW **W Vill** | 245 W. 10th St. (bet. Bleecker & Hudson Sts.) | 1 to Christopher St./Sheridan Sq. | 212-352-1618

NEW **Brooklyn Hts** | 122 Montague St. (Henry St.) | Brooklyn | A/C/F to Jay St./Borough Hall | 718-237-0521

www.housingworks.org

Known for "witty windows" "you want to move into", this "benchmark of thrifts" around NYC draws crowds for its "interesting mix" of "high-quality" "clothes, furniture, books and bric-a-brac" "previously owned by folks with good taste"; "prices are ok, not cheap", "some stores have friendly staffers and some don't", and impulse-buyers are irritated that "the most coveted pieces are always on auction", but isn't it nice to know "the money you spend on a Burberry coat goes directly toward helping others"?

☑ H. Stern 🗷   28 | 26 | 25 | VE

E 50s | 645 Fifth Ave. (51st St.) | E/V to 5th Ave./53rd St. | 212-688-0300 | 800-747-8376 | www.hstern.net

Brazilian-based jeweler, with over 150 international branches, that mines and designs its own precious and semiprecious pieces and is particularly known for "beautiful colored stones" like aquamarine, tourmaline and citrine and "modern" shapes that "make a statement", although they are starting to add some "daintier" things; the Fifth Avenue store is "accessible", "nicely organized" and run by an "attentive", "gracious" staff.

H2O Plus ●   23 | 22 | 21 | M

E 50s | 511 Madison Ave. (52nd St.) | E/V to 5th Ave./53rd St. | 212-750-8119 | 800-242-2284 | www.h2oplus.com

This water-oriented chain with a Madison Avenue link relies on "natural ingredients without naturally high prices", and specializes in hydration as "fresh products" with names like Ebb Tide Shower Gel and Natural Spring Cream attest; the aqueous theme continues with white-and-blue settings that are as "soothing" as the sea.

Hugo Boss   25 | 25 | 23 | VE

E 50s | 717 Fifth Ave. (56th St.) | N/R/W to 5th Ave./59th St. | 212-485-1800
SoHo | 132 Greene St. (bet. Houston & Prince Sts.) | N/R/W to Prince St. | 212-965-1300
www.hugoboss.com

Executive wizards who want to "land a spot on *The Apprentice*" stop at this Fifth Avenue flagship, which boasts "beautifully cut" business-wear for those desiring to "strut in the latest power suits", supplied by "salespeople who know their stuff"; there's also "crisp and stylish" womenswear on the main floor and sportswear in the basement; the SoHo branch sticks to trendier threads from the red label line, but whichever you prefer, take a "wad of money" "if you want to look great."

Hunting World   - | - | - | E

SoHo | 118 Greene St. (bet. Prince & Spring Sts.) | N/R/W to Prince St. | 212-431-0086 | www.huntingworld.com

Urban adventurers and jungle trekkers alike head to this SoHo shop for luggage, carryalls and handbags made of sturdy canvas or lightweight, durable Battue nylon, and to go-with safari-inspired attire; the functional, fashionable pieces are based on the vision of the company's founder who created the first line of resilient travel gear following an African expedition over 40 years ago.

Hyde Park Stationers ⧉
∇ 23 | 16 | 15 | M

E 80s | 1070 Madison Ave. (81st St.) | 6 to 77th St. | 212-861-5710

Hyde-seekers head to this quiet Madison Avenue shop for a "sweet selection of cards", invitations, office supplies, personalized stationery and scrapbooks, along with bath items and fragrances – almost "all the things a tony neighborhood needs."

Hyman Hendler & Sons ⧉
∇ 28 | 11 | 19 | M

Garment Dist | 67 W. 38th St. (bet. 5th & 6th Aves.) | B/D/F/N/Q/R/V/W to 34th St./Herald Sq. | 212-840-8393 | www.hymanhendler.com

"Good enough even for Martha Stewart", this multigenerational ribbon specialist in the Garment District peddles an "exquisite selection" of "absolutely gorgeous" grosgrains, laces, straps, strings, tassels and novelty trims (including "fantastic antique" versions) that "stir the imagination"; sure, the "clerks" can be "disinterested" and the surroundings are so-so, nevertheless, this "NYC classic" remains a "favorite retreat" of dressmakers, florists, milliners and crafters.

Ibiza Kidz ●
23 | 23 | 21 | E

G Vill | 42 University Pl. (bet. 9th & 10th Sts.) | N/R/W to 8th St. | 212-505-9907

G Vill | 61 Fourth Ave. (9th & 10th Sts.) | 6 to Astor Pl. | 212-228-7990

www.ibizakidz.com

"Crammed with fun stuff", these "relaxed", "friendly" Greenwich Village tot shops help "you turn your babies, toddlers and children into the New York City style mavens they ought to be"; the relocated University Place branch specializes in "high-quality" European clothing "just funky enough that your kids will love them", while its Fourth Avenue sidekick zeroes in on toys and "colorful shoes"; but shoppers "not only love what's inside – the windows are always so inviting" too.

Ibiza NY ●
21 | 23 | 18 | E

G Vill | 46 University Pl. (bet. 9th & 10th Sts.) | N/R/W to 8th St. | 212-533-4614

It's "one of my favorite neighborhood stores" vow Villagers who covet this boutique's "wonderful hippiesque" women's apparel imbued with a "one-of-a-kind" vibe; drink in the "fabulous funk" of sun-drenched tanks, flirty tiered skirts and gypsy-gorgeous jewelry, some of which seems "more Marrakech- than Ibiza"-inspired, and pat yourself on the back for looking "creative and cool at the same time!"

NEW IC Zinco
- | - | - | E

SoHo | 85 Mercer St. (bet. Broome & Spring Sts.) | 6 to Spring St. | 212-680-1414 | www.zincozone.com

The beefier the cardigan, the higher the price at this new Italian import in SoHo, a 'bottega'-type concept shop that charges by the weight of the Mongolian cashmere (and come summer, the Sea Island cotton); choose men's and women's styles from wooden baskets affixed to the walls of the modern, loftlike space, then hit the digital scales, paying by the ounce for solid and novelty patterned sweaters, hats and scarves; N.B. wool items are sold at set prices.

	QUALITY	DISPLAY	SERVICE	COST

Ideal Tile ⊠
▽ 20 | 16 | 19 | M

E 50s | 405 E. 51st St. (1st Ave.) | 6 to 51st St. | 212-759-2339 |
www.idealtileimporting.com

"Go to the high-end places to get your ideas" suggest some, then head
to this "enlarged" East 50s franchise outpost that stocks floor and wall
tiles made of granite, marble and porcelain, as well as bathroom faucets and sinks; while some feel the selection is a bit "limited", chances
are "if they have what you are looking for, the price is good."

IF
- | - | - | VE

SoHo | 94 Grand St. (bet. Greene & Mercer Sts.) | 6/J/M/N/Q/R/W/Z to
Canal St. | 212-334-4964

Look in the fashion dictionary under "avant-garde at its best", and
you'll find this SoHo pioneer, which established its "cutting-edge"
roots over 30 years ago and continues to lure stylesetters today in an
unassuming, tin-ceilinged space lined with one-of-a-kind pieces and
rarefied wear for him and her from a roll call of the finest, including
Comme des Garçons, Dries Van Noten, Ivan Grundahl, Junya
Watanabe, Martin Margiela, Paul Harden and Veronique Branquinho.

I Heart ●
- | - | - | E

NoLita | 262 Mott St. (bet. Houston & Prince Sts.) | B/D/F/V to B'way/
Lafayette St. | 212-219-9265 | www.iheartnyc.com

Descend "several feet below ground level" to this NoLita cavern, a
"best-kept secret" boasting a smartly edited, "interesting collection of
hip foreign labels" including an ever-changing stash of "indie designers" (Emma Cook, Hengst) and names that are "well-known", at least
in certain fashion circles (Isabel Marant, Lover, United Bamboo); don't
miss the art on the walls, the Phaidon books or the repurposed china
by Sarah Cihat.

Il Bisonte
▽ 27 | 22 | 24 | E

SoHo | 120 Sullivan St. (bet. Prince & Spring Sts.) | C/E to Spring St. |
212-966-8773 | 877-452-4766 | www.ilbisonte.com

Invest in "classic" bags made of "subtle, sublime hides" that "look better as they age" say bullish boosters of the "beautiful" vacchetta
leather offerings at the SoHo branch of this Florence-based brand; the
briefcases, totes, luggage, small goods and a new line of tapestries are
presented in an airy space decorated with antique bison figures.

Il Makiage
▽ 23 | - | 18 | E

E 50s | 830 Third Ave. (bet. 50th & 51st Sts.) | E/V to Lexington Ave./
53rd St. | 212-371-0551 | www.il-makiage.com

Founded by makeup guru Ilana Harkavi in 1972, this cosmetics maven,
which recently relocated from the East 60s to the East 50s, is "still one
of the best" in the city, with "great stuff for the artist or Joe Schmo off
the street"; although professionals receive discounts on products like
non-smearing lip pencils and brow-lash brushes, "good prices" are a
draw for everyone; N.B. closed Saturdays.

⊠ Il Papiro ⊠
28 | 25 | 23 | E

E 70s | 1021 Lexington Ave. (bet. 73rd & 74th Sts.) | 6 to 77th St. |
212-288-9330

"Cheaper than a trip to Florence", this 23-year-old Upper East Side
staple is the source for "beautiful", "elegant" marbleized papers *fatto*

a mano in Italy, as well as desk accessories, photo albums and picture frames that are "great for gifts" – for yourself or others.

Ina

25	19	13	E

E 70s | 208 E. 73rd St. (bet. 2nd & 3rd Aves.) | 6 to 68th St. | 212-249-0014
NoLita | 21 Prince St. (bet. Elizabeth & Mott Sts.) | B/D/F/V to B'way/Lafayette St. | 212-334-9048
NoLita | 262 Mott St. (bet. Houston & Prince Sts.) | 6 to Spring St. | 212-334-2210
SoHo | 101 Thompson St. (bet. Prince & Spring Sts.) | C/E to Spring St. | 212-941-4757
www.inanyc.com

"Top-notch" "trendy labels find a home" at this string of consignment shops for her and, at Mott Street, just him; "although priced higher than you'd expect for 'used'", the "precisely selected" clothes "from recent seasons" are "in great shape" – "many worn only once in fashion shoots" – and "attractively presented"; true, the "staff couldn't be more haughty", but most "deal with it" 'cuz "where else can you get a Dries Van Noten cardigan to go with your patent leather Helmut Lang shoes?"

Infinity 🖻

22	10	14	E

E 80s | 1116 Madison Ave. (83rd St.) | 4/5/6 to 86th St. | 212-517-4232 | www.infinitynyc.com

This "terrific" East 80s shop is overrun by "trendy NY teens" and tweens armed with "daddy's credit card", combing through the "hottest" "of-the-minute fashions" from Juicy Couture and Miss Sixty and ordering custom tees, sweats and jeans affixed with their name; if a few sulk that "you must be a regular" to receive attention from the "attitudinal help", others counter "have patience" – "if I was that age I'd shop here too."

Ingo Maurer Making Light 🅼

-	-	-	VE

SoHo | 89 Grand St. (Greene St.) | A/C/E to Canal St. | 212-965-8817 | www.ingo-maurer.com

"I see the light!" exclaim electrical enthusiasts when they look at some of the "best creative" modern pieces – like the flotation hanging lamp with a three-tiered paper shade – from this eponymous German designer; his "witty" works are sold in this soaring SoHo landmark building and are on display at MoMA as well as other museums around the world.

In Living Stereo ◗

-	-	-	E

NoHo | 13 E. Fourth St. (bet. B'way & Lafayette St.) | 6 to Astor Pl. | 212-979-1273 | www.inlivingstereo.com

The exclusive NYC retailer for many top lines, this elite electronics showroom in NoHo has an experienced staff that'll demo the different "options available, even for beginning audiophiles"; the patient pros give the same attention to patrons purchasing an all-out home entertainment center as those choosing connecting cables.

Innovation Luggage

20	14	16	M

E 40s | 300 E. 42nd St. (2nd Ave.) | 4/5/6/7/S to 42nd St./Grand Central | 212-599-2998 ◗
E 60s | 1186 Third Ave. (69th St.) | 6 to 68th St. | 212-717-2740 ◗
Flatiron | 134 Fifth Ave. (bet. 18th & 19th Sts.) | 4/5/6/L/N/Q/R/W to 14th St./Union Sq. | 212-924-0141 ◗
NEW **W 50s** | 1392 Sixth Ave. (bet. 56th & 57th Sts.) | B/D/F/V to 47-50th Sts./Rockefeller Ctr. | 212-586-8210

(continued)

Innovation Luggage

W 50s | 1755 Broadway (bet. 56th & 57th Sts.) | 1/A/B/C/D to 59th St./
Columbus Circle | 212-582-2044 ◗
W 60s | 2001 Broadway (68th St.) | 1 to 66th St./Lincoln Ctr. |
212-721-3164 ◗
800-903-8728 | www.innovationluggage.com

"They always seem to have everything in stock" at this "reliable", "not
fancy" outfit carrying "important luggage names" like Samsonite, Tumi
and Victorinox, but critics counter there are "no great deals here."

Innovative Audio ◗   ▽ 29 | 26 | 24 | VE

E 50s | 150 E. 58th St. (bet. Lexington & 3rd Aves.) | 4/5/6/F/N/R/W to
59th St./Lexington Ave. | 212-634-4444 | www.innovativeaudiovideo.com

A sound experience "you won't forget" can be found at this East 50s
"high-end stereo store" that's been a "favorite" "for the audiophile"
since its Brooklyn-basement beginnings; aficionados are addicted to
its "truly fine" home-entertainment systems and "great service" from
a "nice" staff that "takes time to work with customers" and "will let
you linger with the equipment" in a listening room "until you decide."

Institut NYC ◗   19 | 18 | 17 | E

SoHo | 97 Spring St. (bet. B'way & Mercer St.) | 6 to Spring St. |
212-431-5521

"The windows draw you in" to "shop by color" at this Spring Street
standby jammed with "overwhelmingly crowded racks" of "eclectic
Euro-boutique-y" womenswear and accessories (bedazzled jeans,
mohair vests, studded bags) from "next season's wave of indie designers"; "you can score great deals at their sales", but don't be daunted
by a staff that "seems to have no interest in selling the clothes."

Intermix   24 | 21 | 15 | E

E 70s | 1003 Madison Ave. (bet. 77th & 78th Sts.) | 6 to 77th St. |
212-249-7858
Flatiron | 901 Broadway (20th St.) | N/R/W to 23rd St. | 212-533-9720 ◗
SoHo | 98 Prince St. (bet. Greene & Mercer Sts.) | N/R/W to Prince St. |
212-966-5303 ◗
W 60s | 210 Columbus Ave. (bet. 69th & 70th Sts.) | B/C to 72nd St. |
212-769-9116 ◗
W Vill | 365 Bleecker St. (Charles St.) | 1 to Christopher St./Sheridan Sq. |
212-929-7180 ◗
www.intermixonline.com

"My go-to place" for that "sexy night out" outfit or "that one pair of
jeans" vow "fashionistas" who count on these "hipster destinations"
for "hot, of-the-moment pieces" sure to invite the "envy of girlfriends"; there's "lots of bling", making it the "best place to go broke" –
hey, dressed in Geren Ford, Matthew Williamson and Robert
Rodriguez, "at least you'll look good in bankruptcy court"; still, service
can be "frosty", which is "just plain mixed up"; N.B. plans are underway
to expand the Madison Avenue branch.

☑ International Center of Photography   26 | 19 | 20 | M

W 40s | 1133 Sixth Ave. (43rd St.) | 7/B/D/F/V to 42nd St./Bryant Park |
212-857-9725 | www.icp.org

"Photojournalism enthusiasts" celebrate this Midtown museum's
"first-rate" selection of "wonderful" and otherwise "hard-to-find"

"coffee-table" books as well as "fun, inexpensive" novelty cameras and other "good photography-related items" such as frames and albums; "helpful service" makes it a snap to sort through the "great variety" of "gems."

Intimacy
▽ 28 | 21 | 27 | E

E 90s | 1252 Madison Ave. (90th St.) | 4/5/6 to 86th St. | 212-860-8366 | www.myintimacy.com

With the "nicest pj's and robes", "tons" of underthings and a "discreet" staff that "won't sell you a bra without a proper fitting", this "intimate" peach-colored Madison Avenue shop is a "great resource" for "basic to tarty" lingerie; fans who "keep coming back" say you may have to "wait your turn" for the "excellent" service.

Irma
- | - | - | E

W Vill | 378 Bleecker St. (bet. Charles & Perry Sts.) | A/B/C/D/E/F/V to W. 4th St. | 212-206-7475

At this stripped-down West Village womenswear boutique, the seductive threads seem sewn for arty individualists who embrace the moody, anarchistic beauty of designers like Vivienne Westwood, Hannoh, Inhabit and Castle Starr, as well as va-va-vroom motorcycle and aviator gear from Belstaff; if you don't see your size, do ask – the just-friendly-enough staff will gladly fetch a frock from the back if you need it.

IS: Industries Stationery
- | - | - | M

SoHo | 91 Crosby St. (bet. Prince & Spring Sts.) | N/R/W to Prince St. | 212-334-4447 | www.industriesstationery.com

If you care as much about the look of your journals as what goes into them, this SoHo store is "the best" for sleek, chic styles, along with stationery, memo pads and note cards with colorful, modern graphics that change with the seasons; also in stock here are über-stylish Lexon desk accessories.

Issey Miyake
25 | 25 | 23 | VE

E 60s | 802 Madison Ave. (bet. 67th & 68th Sts.) | 6 to 68th St. | 212-439-7822 | www.isseymiyake.com
TriBeCa | 119 Hudson St. (bet. Franklin & N. Moore Sts.) | 1 to Franklin St. | 212-226-0100 | www.tribecaisseymiyake.com

Followers of this "cool-as-it-gets" Japanese "genius" plan a pilgrimage to the Frank Gehry–designed TriBeCa flagship or the Uptown destination, newly relocated to the East 60s, to revel in the "unusual but beautifully made" male and female garb, designed by Naoki Takizawa; admittedly, one woman's "wearable art" is another's "weird clothes", but those "looking for something edgy" enjoy it, and certainly the "wow" fragrances "never go out of style."

Itsasickness ●Ⓜ
- | - | - | M

LES | 132A Ludlow St. (Rivington St.) | F/V to Lower East Side/2nd Ave. | 212-995-9171

Imagine a "concept" store that feeds off of customers' addictive habits and you get the drift behind this "fun" LES novelty nook; obsessive sorts can't help but indulge their inner shopaholic with leather tote bags, quirky T-shirts that riff on weaknesses like smoking and gambling, chocolates, activewear and assorted gizmos – after all, it's a sickness.

Jacadi

E 60s | 787 Madison Ave. (bet. 66th & 67th Sts.) | 6 to 68th St. | 212-535-3200
E 70s | 1260 Third Ave. (bet. 72nd & 73rd Sts.) | 6 to 68th St. | 212-717-9292
E 90s | 1296 Madison Ave. (92nd St.) | 6 to 96th St. | 212-369-1616
W 60s | 1841 Broadway (60th St.) | 1/A/B/C/D to 59th St./
Columbus Circle | 212-246-2753
Borough Pk | 5005 16th Ave. (bet. 50th & 51st Sts.) | Brooklyn | D/M to
50th St. | 718-871-9402
www.jacadiusa.com

"Darling clothes from France for baby" and kids that "really hold up" are the focus of these "lovely" chain links with a Parisian pedigree, where you can find everything from "chic", "one-of-a-kind" dresses and coats to "beautiful" bedding for the nursery; still, a miffed few mutter that service can be "apathetic" and are put off by "laugh-out-loud prices", suggesting "catch them at seasonal sales" instead.

Jack Gomme

NoLita | 252 Elizabeth St. (bet. Houston & Prince Sts.) | F/V to Lower East Side/2nd Ave. | 212-925-6414 | www.jackgomme.com

Housed in a former butcher shop with its old tile floor still intact, this NoLita boutique turns out "incredibly beautiful" "city smart" handbags created by the namesake French designer and his wife; fans who find "innovative" totes in calf leather, nylon and printed canvas, along with umbrellas, sun hats in season, men's laptop bags and weekenders swear by their "lasting quality."

Jackie Rogers ⊠

E 70s | 1034½ Lexington Ave. (bet. 73rd & 74th Sts.) | 6 to 77th St. | 212-535-0140 | www.jackierogers.com

After a stint in the Meatpacking District, the peripatetic couturier returns to her roots with this East 70s atelier catering to pampered party gals (who also patronize her Palm Beach and East Hampton shops); with her "elegant" eveningwear, she dishes out a "definite look" that devotees describe as "high drama in organza and satin."

JackRabbit Sports ●

NEW **Union Sq** | 42 W. 14th St. (bet. 5th & 6th Aves.) | 4/5/6/L/N/Q/R/W to 14th St./Union Sq. | 212-727-2980
Park Slope | 151 Seventh Ave. (bet. Carroll St. & Garfield Pl.) | Brooklyn | B/Q to 7th Ave. | 718-636-9000
www.jackrabbitsports.com

"Thank goodness they made it over to Manhattan!" rejoice runners and triatheletes who hop over to the "great" Union Square flagship (as well as the smaller Park Slope sibling) for "expert advice and high-quality" activewear; vaunters vow you'll "never buy running shoes anywhere else" after staffers who "actually look like they exercise" "pop you on a treadmill for a test drive", complete with a video analysis that lets you compare kicks.

Jack Spade

SoHo | 56 Greene St. (bet. Broome & Spring Sts.) | C/E to Spring St. | 212-625-1820 | www.jackspade.com

"Kate's hubby (Andy) follows her recipe", "dishing out" "classic style with a mod attitude" "in Spades" at this SoHo haunt with a "cool, at-home atmosphere"; "practical and affordable", the "snazzy" yet "subtle designs" appeal to "guys who want to look hip without pushing it"; the "trump" card: these "beautiful leather", canvas or nylon messenger styles and briefcases can take "abuse and still look fantastic."

Jacob & Co. ▣

▽ 24 | 26 | 23 | VE

E 50s | 48 E. 57th St. (bet. Madison & Park Aves.) | 4/5/6/F/N/R/W to 59th St./Lexington Ave. | 212-398-1224 | www.jacobandco.com

"Calling all ballers and shot callers" to this four-story building on East 57th Street that's home to Jacob Arabo, who was discovered by Faith Evans and her late husband, Notorious B.I.G., and dubbed "Jacob the Jeweler" by Sean "Diddy" Combs; huge diamond crosses and signature Multi Time Zone watches are just two of the oversized, "bling is blinging" styles favored by the rock, rap and sports sets.

Jaded

▽ 25 | 25 | 22 | E

E 80s | 1048 Madison Ave. (80th St.) | 6 to 77th St. | 212-288-6631 | www.jadedjewels.com

"Consistently interesting" styles, "good quality" and a "nice selection" are the hallmarks of this veteran Upper East Side jeweler with a celeb and social register clientele; its owner-designers still make 22-karat-gold-plated pieces by the "lost wax" process and use heaps of lustrous pearls and colorful semiprecious stones like quartz, carnelian and peridot to produce items that often look like antiques.

Jaime Mascaró

▽ 21 | 21 | 18 | E

NEW **E 70s** | 976 Lexington Ave. (bet. 70th & 71st Sts.) | 6 to 68th St. | 212-472-9200 ▣

SoHo | 430 W. Broadway (bet. Prince & Spring Sts.) | C/E to Spring St. | 212-965-8910 ◗

www.jaimemascaro.com

"What's Spanish for 'I spent my whole paycheck on shoes'?" quip customers who stake out "highly styled" artfully showcased kicks and handbags from this SoHo mainstay and new Lexington Avenue sidekick; the family-owned European outfit may be the "best-kept secret in the city" confide acolytes enchanted by colorful pumps festooned with bows, floral-trimmed ballet flats and leopard-print numbers.

James Perse ◗

24 | 22 | 21 | M

NEW **W Vill** | 361 Bleecker St. (bet. Charles & Perry Sts.) | 1 to Christopher St./Sheridan Sq. | 212-255-5801

W Vill | 411 Bleecker St. (W. 11th St.) | 1 to Christopher St./Sheridan Sq. | 212-620-9991

www.jamesperse.com

Lovers of the "coolest T-shirts on the planet" applaud this West Village yearling, which lays out its "super-soft", "easy-to-wear" women's basics in a "fresh", "minimalist" nature-inspired setting; the "more-than-willing-to-help" staff and the "mix-and-match color palette" of the hip wares "make life simple" for the "fashion-impaired"; in short, "cotton never looked and felt so good"; N.B. the new offshoot nearby at 361 Bleecker stocks guys' apparel only.

James Robinson ▣

▽ 29 | 26 | 28 | VE

E 50s | 480 Park Ave. (58th St.) | 4/5/6/F/N/R/W to 59th St./ Lexington Ave. | 212-752-6166 | www.jrobinson.com

"Very pricey" Park Avenue aristocrat that's "the epitome of classical good taste", from the "outstanding selection of vintage jewelry", particularly 19th-century gems, 20th-century art deco pieces, signature cuff links and engagement rings, to the "best sterling silver flatware" ("made the old-fashioned way – by hand in England"), prestigious European porcelain dinner services and antique table glass; the atmosphere is "super-swanky", but the "staff is friendly."

Jamin Puech
	–	–	–	E

NoLita | 247 Elizabeth St. (bet. Houston & Prince Sts.) | 6 to Bleecker St. | 212-431-5200 | www.jamin-puech.com

What a "little jewel" sigh tastemakers smitten by the French designer's "quirky" handbag "treasures" with a decidedly boho flair showcased at this "warm, inviting", intimate NoLita nook; peruse the big old-fashioned cabinets filled with "tiny evening" purses, rock-chick satchels and tony totes bearing "super-luxurious embellishments" like beads, feathers and embroidery in a riot of color and leather combos, and be prepared to get carried away.

Jammyland ●
	–	–	–	I

E Vill | 60 E. Third St. (bet. 1st & 2nd Aves.) | F/V to Lower East Side/ 2nd Ave. | 212-614-0185 | www.jammyland.com

"One of those shops that makes you proud to live in this city", this East Village music store slakes the thirst of both "hard-core enthusiasts and newbies" faster than a Red Stripe with "excellent" reggae, ska, rock steady and dub as well as African and Carib grooves; rude boys also give big ups to the "niche"-like digs jammed with vintage LP covers and posters.

Jam Paper & Envelope
	18	10	11	I

Gramercy | 135 Third Ave. (bet. 14th & 15th Sts.) | 4/5/6/L/N/Q/R/W to 14th St./Union Sq. | 212-473-6666 | www.jampaper.com

Crafters, students and arty types of all stripes swear by the "deep but not large" selection of funky colored "paper, paper everywhere" (including stationery, folders, portfolios, gift-wrapping, boxes and "odd-sized envelopes") at this "cluttered" "warehouse" east of Irving Place; sure, it's "cheap", but some "frustrated" fans fume the "self-serve" attitude means "they just Jam it in and don't help you pull it out"; N.B. the Sixth Avenue site closed.

⊠ J&R Music & Computer World ●
	24	17	17	M

Financial Dist | 1-34 Park Row (bet. Ann & Beekman Sts.) | R/W to City Hall | 212-238-9000 | 800-221-8180 | www.jr.com

"You name it" – you can probably find it at this "Park Row legend" whose "great selection of electronics, appliances, music, movies", "etc." seems to include "every techie gadget under the moon", all peddled by a "brusque" but "efficient" staff; the "bustling", "Byzantine" complex "spread out in multiple buildings" "can be overwhelming", so insiders advise "go early" or "use the online store and avoid the lines" altogether.

Jane ⊠
	–	–	–	E

E 70s | 1025 Lexington Ave. (bet. 73rd & 74th Sts.) | 6 to 77th St. | 212-772-7710 | www.janeboutique.com

Rest assured there's no plain-Jane garb at this elegant boutique that feels like a dream closet where the color-coded womenswear from European and American labels, including Blumarine and John Smedley, play off an artistic pale pink backdrop; while the look is classically stylish, there's a smart edginess to the silhouettes – and attentive customer service – to keep fans returning to this Upper East Sider.

Jane Wilson-Marquis 🗷Ⓜ | - | - | - | E |

E 70s | 42 E. 76th St. (bet. Madison & Park Aves.) | 6 to 77th St. | 212-452-5335 | www.bridalgowns.net

Brides and social butterflies who want custom-made choices that aren't "just what Vera Wang is showing this season", plus affordable ready-to-wear gowns, make an appointment at this namesake designer's atelier, now located in the East 70s; the "romantic", "vintage-looking" couture creations seem straight out of a fairy tale, while the lower-priced off-the-rack line appeals to women with more modern – and retro-modern – sensibilities; N.B. guys can also dress the part with big-day essentials from the JWM collection.

Janovic Plaza ❶ | 22 | 17 | 17 | M |

E 60s | 1150 Third Ave. (67th St.) | 6 to 68th St. | 212-772-1400 | 800-772-4381 | www.janovic.com
Additional locations throughout the NY area

If you "need to refresh your home or apartment", this is "the place to go for paint, wallpaper and window treatments" assert "city dwellers" who find this outfit "convenient", "well stocked" and "easy" to "comb through"; however, servicewise, it's different strokes for different folks, with fans hailing the salespeople as "helpful" and others sniping that they're "knowledgeable but not forthcoming" – "it would be great if they'd be more willing to share it."

Jay Kos 🗷 | - | - | - | VE |

E 50s | 475 Park Ave. (bet. 57th & 58th Sts.) | 4/5/6/F/N/R/W to 59th St./Lexington Ave. | 212-319-2770
E 70s | 986 Lexington Ave. (bet. 71st & 72nd Sts.) | 6 to 68th St. | 212-327-2382

These "pricey but excellent" shops in the East 50s and 70s have earned a devoted following over the past decade for their superior selection of classic, old-world men's business attire enlivened by "lots of color" for a kind of "edgy conservative" feel; besides brand-name and bespoke suits, "interesting" ties, hats, cuff links and cigars abound at both boutiques where the "friendly owner" often offers style advice; N.B. the Lexington Avenue store boasts a full boys' section, a rare find.

Jazz Record Center 🗷 | - | - | - | M |

Chelsea | 236 W. 26th St., 8th fl. (bet. 7th & 8th Aves.) | 1 to 28th St. | 212-675-4480 | www.jazzrecordcenter.com

There's nothing "run-of-the-mill" about the world-class selection at this eighth-floor Chelsea hideaway with "drawers of great CDs" and "lots of vinyl"; whether "you want jazz", Latin, gospel, blues or fusion, fans insist "there's no better place" to score that coveted recording, and an extensive assortment of T-shirts, books and ephemera such as magazines, posters and "great photos" completes the experience.

J.Crew | 20 | 21 | 18 | M |

E 40s | 347 Madison Ave. (45th St.) | 4/5/6/7/S to 42nd St./Grand Central | 212-949-0570
Flatiron | 91 Fifth Ave. (bet. 16th & 17th Sts.) | 4/5/6/L/N/Q/R/W to 14th St./Union Sq. | 212-255-4848 ❶

(continued)

J.Crew

SoHo | 99 Prince St. (bet. Greene & Mercer Sts.) | N/R/W to Prince St. | 212-966-2739 ◗

Seaport | South Street Seaport | 203 Front St. (bet. Beekman & Fulton Sts.) | 2/3/4/5/A/C/J/M/Z to Fulton St./B'way/Nassau | 212-385-3500 ◗

W 50s | The Shops at Columbus Circle, Time Warner Ctr. | 10 Columbus Circle, 2nd fl. (bet. 58th & 60th Sts.) | 1/A/B/C/D to 59th St./Columbus Circle | 212-823-9302 ◗

W 50s | Rockefeller Ctr. | 30 Rockefeller Ctr. (bet. 5th & 6th Aves.) | B/D/F/V to 47-50th Sts./Rockefeller Ctr. | 212-765-4227 ◗

800-562-0258 | www.jcrew.com

Complete your "prepster look" at this "traditional" chain that's "never been better" with its "quality cashmere sweaters in fun colors", "flirty dresses with a vintage bent", bathing suits and other "classics that are easily funkied up"; plus, who can resist its "classy-looking" stores sporting "reasonable" prices, a "great return policy" and "helpful staff"?

Jean Shop

— — — VE

Meatpacking | 435 W. 14th St. (9th Ave.) | A/C/E/L to 14th St./8th Ave. | 212-366-5326 | www.jean-shop.com

"If you could put a price on cool", then this "grand" Meatpacking District destination is "pretty darn cool" – so "be prepared to shell out a pretty penny for some of the finest" his-and-hers Japanese denim around confide hipsters; "don't bother looking for Diesel or Earl jeans here" because the spare, sprawling confines contain their own label goods with a few styles distressed to your specifications.

Jeffrey New York ◗

28 23 22 VE

Meatpacking | 449 W. 14th St. (bet. 9th & 10th Aves.) | A/C/E/L to 14th St./8th Ave. | 212-206-1272

"La crème de la crème" of his-and-hers "high fashion, with an accent on the high" is hosted by this "shopping heaven" in the Meatpacking District with "too-chic-to-be-chic atmosphere" and an "eager", slightly "intrusive" staff; it "shines in shoes", with "unique models" from all the names, but the wares also include "edgy" threads (bound to "raise eyebrows at even the most open-minded" offices) and "seductive" jewelry; malcontents moan "prices are exorbitant" but "if you're sufficiently thin and adventurous", it's worth it for what converts call "the best-curated clothing collection in the city."

Jennifer Convertibles ◗

13 12 13 M

Flatiron | 902 Broadway (20th St.) | N/R/W to 23rd St. | 212-677-6862 | www.jenniferfurniture.com

Additional locations throughout the NY area

Wallet-watchers maintain that this chain offers "decent" sofa beds, love seats and cocktail tables "for a starter home" at "insanely cheap prices", but the unconverted tersely assert that "poor workmanship" makes for "disposable furniture."

Jennifer Miller Jewelry ⊠

— — — M

E 70s | 972 Lexington Ave. (bet. 70th & 71st Sts.) | 6 to 68th St. | 212-734-8199 | www.jewelsbyjen.com

Whether you're a fan of the faux or the fine, you'll find it at this tiny, all-white, crystal-chandeliered jewelry boutique on the Upper East

Side; the store's namesake designer offers a "lovely selection" of contemporary and classic looks in precious stones as well as a popular collection of replicas in man-made diamonds; N.B. there's also a small sampling of handbags, clothing and tabletop accessories.

Jensen-Lewis
19 | 18 | 16 | M

Chelsea | 89 Seventh Ave. (15th St.) | 1/2/3 to 14th St. | 212-929-4880 | www.jensen-lewis.com

For almost 40 years this Chelsea showroom has sold "functional" "contemporary furniture" "at a decent price"; choices range from canvas to metal, wood and leather so "you are sure to find something" here, except perhaps for consistent service.

Jeri Cohen Fine Jewelry 🖪
▽ 27 | 27 | 25 | VE

E 60s | Trump Plaza | 1036 Third Ave. (bet. 61st & 62nd Sts.) | 4/5/6/F/N/R/W to 59th St./Lexington Ave. | 212-750-3172 | www.jericohenjewelry.com

Trained in the arts, jeweler Jeri Cohen loves what she does, and while she might be playing with her pugs when you step into her bright shop in the East 60s, her passion for "beautiful" "quality" diamonds is certainly on display – especially understated ones for daytime – from stacks of glittering, slightly oval bangles to signature flower studs and pendants that she also produces in miniature for the younger set; all tagged as "fairly" as possible in this pricey medium.

Jewish Museum Stores, The
25 | 22 | 20 | M

E 90s | The Jewish Museum | 1109 Fifth Ave. (92nd St.) | 6 to 96th St. | 212-423-3211

W 70s | Jewish Community Ctr. | 334 Amsterdam Ave. (76th St.) | 1 to 79th St. | 646-505-5730

www.thejewishmuseum.org

"Browse to the tunes of *Fiddler on the Roof*" at the two "lovely" shops within the Jewish Museum, one that specializes in "high-end" Judaica and ceremonial objects and another filled with "gorgeous" jewelry, "wonderful books" and art exhibit–related items "with a Jewish bent" – or find the whole "interesting" *megillah* at the Upper West Side offshoot; though a few kvetch over sometimes "expensive" tabs, with such "quality" and a "helpful" staff to boot, "what's not to like?"

Jill Platner
– | – | – | E

SoHo | 113 Crosby St. (bet. Houston & Prince Sts.) | N/R/W to Prince St. | 212-324-1298 | www.jillplatner.com

A "stark" SoHo space is an apt backdrop for the designer's "bold", "organic", hammered silver and gold jewelry that's a sculptural "modern" take on nature – from a 19-karat forget-me-not pendant on a string to wild-bean earrings; though "a bit pricey", the pieces are "striking", and "when you wear them, you can't stop touching them."

Jill Stuart
▽ 22 | 19 | 17 | E

SoHo | 100 Greene St. (bet. Prince & Spring Sts.) | N/R/W to Prince St. | 212-343-2300 | www.jillstuart.com

It's an Edwardian-inspired combination of innocence and sensuality that's the calling card of this American designer, whose "uncluttered" SoHo stomping ground trips the light fantastic with its baby-doll dresses, high-collared blouses and "fun, girlie" separates lined in lace, tulle, crochet and chiffon; insiders collect her "extraordinary shoes" or descend downstairs to shop collections past, and soon men will find their own line here too; N.B. the Display score may not reflect a recent redo.

Jil Sander ⑤ | 25 | 23 | 22 | VE

E 50s | 11 E. 57th St. (bet. 5th & Madison Aves.) | E/V to 5th Ave./
53rd St. | 212-838-6100 | 800-704-7317 | www.jilsander.com
"How can one resist" when "you feel just wonderful" in the plush fabrics and "elegant", subtle stylings of this visionary mens- and womenswear, housed in a limestone-floored boutique on East 57th Street; still, some miss the "true eye" of the namesake designer, saying the line is "not as well-designed as it used to be" since she left.

Jimmy Choo | 28 | 27 | 23 | VE

E 50s | 645 Fifth Ave. (51st St.) | E/V to 5th Ave./53rd St. |
212-593-0800
E 60s | 716 Madison Ave. (bet. 63rd & 64th Sts.) | 4/5/6/F/N/R/W to
59th St./Lexington Ave. | 212-759-7078
www.jimmychoo.com
"If I don't make it to heaven, I'll opt for" my "favorite place on the planet" fawn "fashion-lovers" who feed their "addictive habit" with designers Tamara Mellon and Sandra Choi's "sexy", "ultra-expensive eye candy" at this East Side duo; "comfortable stilettos? somehow JC makes it happen" – "you'll want every pair" (it's "worth the extra cashola") – and if a few scoff "who can walk in stilts?", groupies gush "gimme Jimmy!"

J.J. Hat Center ⑤ | ▽ 27 | 23 | 25 | E

Garment Dist | 310 Fifth Ave. (bet. 31st & 32nd Sts.) | B/D/F/N/Q/R/V/W to
34th St./Herald Sq. | 212-239-4368 | 800-622-1911 | www.jjhatcenter.com
Perhaps the "only place in NYC for a man to buy a real hat", this topper titan, established in 1911, housed in the fresco-filled former IBM building and staffed with some of the "most knowledgeable" help "in town", makes you feel like "you've stepped into the past"; slip on a Borsalino fedora or a porkpie number and embrace your inner nostalgist; N.B. there are some women's styles too.

NEW J.J. Marco ⑤ | ▽ 24 | 23 | 24 | VE

E 80s | 1070 Madison Ave. (81st St.) | 4/5/6 to 86th St. | 212-744-3202 |
www.jjmarco.com
"Nothing says I'm sorry like a designer piece of 18-karat gold" and "if you really mean it, throw in some diamonds" too, just like those found on the "classic", "colorful and beautiful" earrings and necklaces at this elegant little Upper East Side shop fitted out with cherry cabinets filled with their own brand of eye candy.

J. Lindeberg Stockholm ❶ | 26 | 23 | 20 | E

SoHo | 126 Spring St. (Greene St.) | N/R/W to Prince St. | 212-625-9403 |
www.jlindeberg.com
Hard to believe it's been 10 years since Johan Lindeberg left Diesel to launch his vision of contemporary sports- and activewear that continues to earn "cool points with those in-the-know"; the "stylish duds" – kind of a "Swedish take on the preppy look" – for men (with a few for women) are served up amid the "hip" retro-'70s environment of his SoHo store, one of only two in the U.S.

	QUALITY	DISPLAY	SERVICE	COST

J. McLaughlin
| 22 | 21 | 21 | E |

NEW **E 70s** | 1008 Lexington Ave. (72nd St.) | 6 to 68th St. | 212-879-9565
E 90s | 1311 Madison Ave. (bet. 92nd & 93rd Sts.) | 6 to 96th St. |
212-369-4830
www.jmclaughlin.com

Ivy Leaguers unsure of what to wear to the dean's house for dinner head to this Carnegie Hill townhouse – and now a new East 70s off-shoot too – where the "nice, classic" sportswear, "proper" skirts, "country-club" pants and rich cashmere cable knits "in every color of the rainbow" are "just conservative enough" to satisfy; but edgier sorts sneer the styling is exclusively for "frumpy preps or preppy frumps" and rather "pricey for what it is."

Z J. Mendel Ⓢ
| 28 | 29 | 27 | VE |

E 60s | 723 Madison Ave. (bet. 63rd & 64th Sts.) | 4/5/6/F/N/R/W to 59th St./Lexington Ave. | 212-832-5830 | www.jmendel.com

The "furs are without peer" at this East 60s "branch of a Parisian classic", whose "novel, whimsical creations (sheared mink in colors is a specialty)" represent the "ultimate in self-indulgence" – as does the "smart" clothing; "salespeople who know what they're talking about" and a salon decorated with a dramatic, curved staircase create a "luxurious" shopping experience; of course, you better "bring your bank account with you" to cover the "incredible prices" – but "who can argue when you're getting the Rolls-Royce of designer" skins?

J.M. Weston Ⓢ
| 26 | 23 | 26 | VE |

E 60s | 812 Madison Ave. (68th St.) | 6 to 68th St. | 212-535-2100 | 877-493-7866 | www.jmweston.com

"If you can afford it you should have at least one pair" of "wonderful quality" hand-sewn shoes from this 120-year-old famed French company opine men "in-the-know" who shop at this East 60s emporium for footwear made the old-world way; what "excellent craftsmanship and great service" exclaim big spenders who tout the "tony", "very expensive" collection, opting for "classic" loafers and wingtips or more contemporary offerings like Chelsea boots and trainers designed by Michel Perry, all made from naturally tanned leathers.

Joan Michlin Gallery
| ▽ 27 | 26 | 24 | E |

SoHo | 449 W. Broadway (bet. Houston & Prince Sts.) | N/R/W to Prince St. | 212-475-6603 | 800-331-1335 | www.joanmichlin.com

"You won't see yourself coming and going" if you're wearing a piece of this pioneering SoHo designer's "unique", "well-crafted jewelry" in gold or gold with gemstones; still, some wish her "aggressive" sales staff weren't like "piranhas in a feeding frenzy" when it comes to pursuing customers.

Joël Name Optique de Paris Ⓢ
| - | - | - | E |

SoHo | 448 W. Broadway (Prince St.) | N/R/W to Prince St. | 212-777-5888

This longtime SoHo specialty retailer excels at "eyewear with flair", including frames and sunglasses from boldface brands like Chanel, Judith Leiber and Silhouette; although there's "no same-day service", they do "quality work" according to regulars – and what's more, you "can always find a pair" of specs that "will earn compliments."

Joe's Fabrics and Trimmings

- - - M

LES | 102-110 Orchard St. (Delancey St.) | F/J/M/Z to Delancey/ Essex Sts. | 212-674-7089

Located at the corner of Orchard and Delancey, this Lower East Side draper displays a "fantastic selection" of "upholstery fabrics, lace and diaphanous sheers", plus trims and tassels; owing to "aisles and aisles of fabric" this place is "not easy" to browse, but worthwhile if you're "going for one particular thing" – especially since you can consult the "human encyclopedias" who staff the store.

John Derian

- - - E

E Vill | 6 E. Second St. (bet. Bowery & 2nd Ave.) | F/V to Lower East Side/ 2nd Ave. | 212-677-3917

John Derian Dry Goods Ⓜ

E Vill | 10 E. Second St. (bet. Bowery & 2nd Ave.) | F/V to Lower East Side/ 2nd Ave. | 212-677-8408

www.johnderian.com

The eponymous owner of this "artistic" East Village shop offers his own "expensive" and "unique" decoupage designs – fanciful flowers, birds, bats and insects – on tableware, lamps, coasters and paper-weights, along with exotic items like giant clam shells and sea sponges; an offshoot, just two doors down, showcases softer goods such as bedding and pillows, along with vintage Pakistani quilts and refurbished sofas, all "perfect for the person with everything."

John Fluevog Shoes

23 21 20 E

NoLita | 250 Mulberry St. (Prince St.) | N/R/W to Prince St. | 212-431-4484 | 800-381-3338 | www.fluevog.com

If you want "funky, baby", as in "super-sturdy", "kickin' shoes" with a "cool edge" that "can take anything that the mean streets of New York throws at them", follow the "downtown crowd" to this Canadian outfit's way-"different" NoLita nook; it's "easy" for dudes and dolls alike "to become addicted to Fluev's friendly attitude" and "consistently creative" "leather-lined and well-designed" "trendy styles" ranging from "clunky to diva"-esque to flat-out "unique" numbers.

Ⓩ John Lobb Ⓢ

29 28 27 VE

E 60s | 680 Madison Ave. (bet. 61st & 62nd Sts.) | 4/5/6/F/N/R/W to 59th St./Lexington Ave. | 212-888-9797 | www.johnlobb.com

"Simply the best, if you can afford them" agree well-shod aesthetes who fall head over heels over the "amazing craftsmanship" of the "beautiful" ready-to-wear collection of men's shoes, handmade in England by this Hermès Group outfit and sold by an "extremely knowl-edgeable" sales staff at this Madison Avenue mecca; while that line, ranging from classic oxfords and loafers to contemporary ankle boots, is undoubtedly "excellent", the made-to-measure styles, crafted in Paris, each pair involving 300 steps, reach unparalleled "perfection."

Johnston & Murphy

25 22 22 E

E 40s | 345 Madison Ave. (44th St.) | 4/5/6/7/S to 42nd St./Grand Central | 212-697-9375

E 50s | 520 Madison Ave. (54th St.) | E/V to 5th Ave./53rd St. | 212-527-2342 888-324-6189 | www.johnstonmurphy.com

"For the businessman in" you, turn to this Madison Avenue twosome offering "real classic", "well-made", "excellent men's shoes that last" and are "worth every penny"; if a few quip that a "Greenwich zip code is a must in order to purchase" a pair, for most, these "straight-laced" "styles can't be matched", and ditto for the apparel and leather goods.

John Varvatos | 26 | – | 25 | VE |

SoHo | 122 Spring St. (bet. Greene & Mercer Sts.) | N/R/W to Prince St. | 212-965-0700 | 800-689-0151 | www.johnvarvatos.com

"How 21st-century man is intended to dress" declare the "designer-shy" of the "understated" collection – a "well-edited balance of color and cut with no gimmicks" – developed by this alum of Calvin Klein and Ralph Lauren; in late 2005, the store relocated to a more spacious SoHo location, taking its "easygoing sportswear and business attire" and "the best staff anywhere" along.

Jo Malone | 27 | 27 | 24 | E |

E 70s | 946 Madison Ave. (bet. 74th & 75th Sts.) | 6 to 77th St. | 212-472-0074
Flatiron | Flatiron Bldg. | 949 Broadway (23rd St.) | N/R/W to 23rd St. | 212-673-2220 ◑
866-566-2566 | www.jomalone.com

"Perfection in a bottle" is found at these "pricey but exquisite" scent shops in the Flatiron District and Upper East Side with 18 naturally inspired fragrances like Lime Basil and Mandarin that can be "mixed and matched", along with a line of "good facial products" and candles; "elegant packaging" adds visual impact to the "olfactory adventure."

Jonathan Adler | ▽ 26 | 24 | 20 | E |

E 80s | 1097 Madison Ave. (83rd St.) | 4/5/6 to 86th St. | 212-772-2410
SoHo | 47 Greene St. (bet. Broome & Grand Sts.) | C/E to Spring St. | 212-941-8950
877-287-1910 | www.jonathanadler.com

Whether at his original SoHo shop or younger Madison Avenue locale, "cult" pottery pop star Jonathan Adler's "awesome" line of lacquered furniture is "as appealing" as his "pricey" "trademark" ceramics, textiles and pillows; both branches boast a "lively" "carnival of kitsch and color" for the "young at heart."

▣ Joon | 26 | 21 | 23 | E |

E 40s | Grand Central | 42nd St. (Vanderbilt Ave.) | 4/5/6/7/S to 42nd St./Grand Central | 212-949-1700 ◑
E 50s | Trump Tower | 725 Fifth Ave. (bet. 56th & 57th Sts.) | 4/5/6/F/N/R/W to 59th St./Lexington Ave. | 212-317-8466
E 60s | 795 Lexington Ave. (bet. 61st & 62nd Sts.) | 4/5/6/F/N/R/W to 59th St./Lexington Ave. | 212-935-1007 ▣
800-782-5666 | www.joon.com

Serious scribes jones for Joon – "a palace" for an "astonishing selection" of "quality" pens, from a simple Sheaffer to a mighty Montblanc, and "hard-to-find refills" presented by a "patient" staff; the recent expansion of the Lexington Avenue flagship may outdate the above Display score.

Jos. A. Bank ◑ | 18 | 19 | 20 | M |

E 40s | 366 Madison Ave. (46th St.) | 4/5/6/7/S to 42nd St./Grand Central | 212-370-0600 | 800-285-2265 | www.josabank.com

Part of a nationwide chain, this bi-level building in the East 40s offers "inexpensive" but "decent" "work dress clothes" that are "perfectly ok "if you wanna look like every other businessman" some sophisticates sneer; still, the average Jos. can bank on a "knowledgeable staff" presenting plenty of suits, separates, golfwear and accessories for all sizes that are seemingly "always on sale."

Joseph
23 | 20 | 21 | E

E 60s | 816 Madison Ave. (bet. 68th & 69th Sts.) | 6 to 68th St. | 212-570-0077

SoHo | 106 Greene St. (bet. Prince & Spring Sts.) | N/R/W to Prince St. | 212-343-7071 ●

Shoppers of both sexes, start your search for "beautifully cut pants" and "great knits" at this earthy, wood-and-leather SoHo shop (but it's ladies' apparel only at the Madison Avenue branch); though a few fear "my American bottom will never fit" this British line's low-rise rockers, supporters say the other "practical", "professional" styles are quite "flattering."

Joseph Edwards
▽ 22 | 18 | 18 | E

E 40s | 500 Fifth Ave. (42nd St.) | 4/5/6/7/S to 42nd St./Grand Central | 212-730-0612

Since 1978, this Midtowner has been a staple for an "outstanding" array of "middle-tier watches", but what really charges fans' batteries is "more reasonable pricing than their competitors"; Swarovski crystals add sparkle to their fine jewelry collection; N.B. plans are underway to relocate to 452 Fifth Avenue in 2007.

Joyce Leslie
8 | 9 | 7 | I

G Vill | 20 University Pl. (8th St.) | N/R/W to 8th St. | 212-505-5419 ●

Bay Ridge | 2147 86th St. (bet. Bay Pkwy. & 21st Ave.) | Brooklyn | D/M to Bay Pkwy. | 718-266-0100 ●

Kings Plaza | Kings Plaza Shopping Ctr. | 5225 Kings Plaza (Flatbush Ave. & Ave. U) | Brooklyn | 718-252-6488 ●

Mill Basin | Georgetown Shopping Ctr. | 2109 Ralph Ave. (Ave. K) | Brooklyn | 2/5 to Brooklyn College/Flatbush Ave. | 718-251-3219 ●

Flushing | 37-28 Main St. (38th Ave.) | Queens | 7 to Main St. | 718-353-8419 ●

Ridgewood | 56-48 Myrtle Ave. (bet. Catalpa & Hancock Sts.) | Queens | L/M to Myrtle/Wycoff Aves. | 718-381-3031

Staten Island | Staten Island Mall | 2655 Richmond Ave. (bet. Platinum Ave. & Richmond Hill Rd.) | 718-370-1705 ●

www.joyceleslie.com

"A paradise for noncommittal fashionistas on a budget", this "teen hot spot" chain peddles "cheap" "party clothes" and accessories that may be "poor quality", but then they'll "only be trendy for a few weeks" anyway; young things willing to "plow through the mess" and endure "rude salespeople" are rewarded with "astoundingly low prices" and the occasional "interesting" "impulse item."

J. Press ☒
23 | 21 | 22 | E

E 40s | 7 E. 44th St. (bet. 5th & Madison Aves.) | 4/5/6/7/S to 42nd St./Grand Central | 212-687-7642 | 800-765-7737 | www.jpressonline.com

"Old school is the only school" at this East 40s "bastion" of "classic ivy league style" and formalwear; double-majoring in "beautiful blazers" and "first-year ties" for undergrads as well as plentiful knits and "preppy accessories" for the "post-college set", it offers a look that's "stylish but not hip"; "marvelous salespeople" also earn honors.

	QUALITY	DISPLAY	SERVICE	COST

Jubilee

▽ 16 | 17 | 21 | M

E 50s | 649 Lexington Ave. (bet. 54th & 55th Sts.) | E/V to Lexington Ave./ 53rd St. | 212-308-5505
E 70s | 1331 Third Ave. (76th St.) | 6 to 77th St. | 212-327-4555 ●
G Vill | 57 W. Eighth St. (bet. 5th & 6th Aves.) | A/B/C/D/E/F/V to W. 4th St. | 212-598-1050
W 70s | 2169 Broadway (bet. 76th & 77th Sts.) | 1 to 79th St. | 212-875-0095 ●
NEW **Forest Hills** | 71-54 Austin St. (bet. Continental & 71st Aves.) | Queens | E/F/G/R/V to Forest Hills/71st Ave. | 718-575-0650 ●
When beset with the blues, buying new shoes can be like a shot of St. John's Wort, and the aptly named Jubilee, now flying its flag around town, provides a cheerful "fashion fix" with its "cute young" offerings; latch onto "lots of flats", wedges and boots – "so many different" kicks and none "budget busters" – from the house label, Durango and Seychelles; N.B. the East Side shops stock women's styles only.

✓ Judith Leiber ⊠

28 | 27 | 23 | VE

E 60s | 680 Madison Ave. (61st St.) | 4/5/6/F/N/R/W to 59th St./ Lexington Ave. | 212-223-2999 | 866-542-7167 | www.judithleiber.com
"You feel like a million" carrying one of this designer's "tiny treasures" – animal-shaped, "expensive minaudières" "encrusted with Austrian crystals" that are basically "handbag bling for ladies who lunch" and the "favored clutches at most black-tie events"; these "works of art", all on display at the "gorgeous" Madison Avenue shop, add "dazzle" to "any outfit", but take note, she's also "got the skinny" on "exotic skins" and some of the "best shoes to boot."

Judith Ripka

25 | 24 | 22 | VE

E 60s | 673 Madison Ave. (61st St.) | 4/5/6/F/N/R/W to 59th St./ Lexington Ave. | 212-355-8300
E 60s | 777 Madison Ave. (bet. 66th & 67th Sts.) | 6 to 68th St. | 212-517-8200 ⊠
800-575-3935 | www.judithripka.com
Once inside either the tiny 673 Madison Avenue boutique or the grander jewelry salon slightly further uptown, "even the most self-controlled shopper will have difficulty leaving empty-handed, despite the prices"; whether it's a trademark loop-and-toggle bracelet, a glittering gold-and-colored crystal Lola ring or something from the less expensive JR2 collection, pros praise her "gorgeous", "wearable pieces" that emit "enough sparkle to elevate your outfit to *Vogue* standards."

NEW Juicy Couture

20 | 21 | 17 | E

E 70s | 860 Madison Ave. (bet. 70th & 71st Sts.) | 6 to 68th St. | 212-327-2398
Flatiron | 103 Fifth Ave. (bet. 17th & 18th Sts.) | 4/5/6/L/N/Q/R/W to 14th St./Union Sq. | 212-727-8029 ●
W Vill | 368 Bleecker St. (Charles St.) | 1 to Christopher St./Sheridan Sq. | 646-336-8151 ●
www.juicycouture.com
"What took them so long?" cry converts of this California brand that recently hit NYC with "a juicy explosion" of "brightly colored" Uptown and Downtown shops; you'll have "no arguments with your teens and pre-teens" – or "mothers who dress like teens" – as they wiggle into the signature "cute" velour sweatsuits and "sweet jeans"; but while

the smitten swear "you're never too old or fat" for a fix, opponents of the "overpriced" garb opine "isn't their 15 minutes up yet?"; N.B. the Bleecker Street mother ship offers goodies for the whole family.

Julian & Sara

-	-	-	E

SoHo | 103 Mercer St. (bet. Prince & Spring Sts.) | N/R/W to Prince St. | 212-226-1989 | www.julianandsara.com

This "great little neighborhood" nook, located in an old SoHo carriage house, is chock-full of "charm and character" – "unlike those huge chain stores"; shop here for your tot or teen, picking from a parade of "pretty" things from some of Europe's most exclusive labels, among them Kenzo, Miniman and Monnalisa.

NEW Jumelle ●

-	-	-	E

Williamsburg | 148 Bedford Ave. (N. 9th St.) | Brooklyn | L to Bedford Ave. | 718-388-9525 | www.shopjumelle.com

A bevy of Williamsburg boho babes parade under the black chandelier of this open, airy boutique boasting chic and feminine frocks, knits and trousers from labels as eclectic as Lauren Moffatt, Grey Ant, Sonia by Sonia Rykiel and Lyell; a mix of exposed brick and vintage wallpaper, the year-old store's decor is as diverse as the inventory, which also includes delicate jewelry from Camille Hempel and bags from Alek Wek.

Just Bulbs

24	16	20	M

Flatiron | 5 E. 16th St. (bet. 5th Ave. & Union Sq. W.) | 4/5/6/L/N/Q/R/W to 14th St./Union Sq. | 212-228-7820

"From Christmas lights to fridge bulbs", this 1,500-sq.-ft. Flatiron space stocks 26,000 specimens, making for a "great selection", including "odd things like fluorescent kitchen rings" or "wacky" items like party strings decorated with Sponge Bob, palm trees or flamingos; their next-door sibling, Superior Light & Fan, offers more bright ideas.

Just Shades 🗵 Ⓜ

▽ 24	16	22	M

NoLita | 21 Spring St. (Elizabeth St.) | 6 to Spring St. | 212-966-2757 | www.justshadesny.com

Since 1966, this NoLita "specialty store" has provided ready-made and custom shades for those New Yorkers tired of bare-bulbing it; decorative finials and bespoke options allow you to fashion a one-off creation, which is a good option opine opponents, who find the selection "limited."

Jutta Neumann ●🗵 Ⓜ

-	-	-	E

LES | 158 Allen St. (bet. Rivington & Stanton Sts.) | F/V to Lower East Side/2nd Ave. | 212-982-7048 | www.juttaneumann-newyork.com

If you fancy your leather sandals, handbags, belts, wallets and wristbands "handmade" and "earthy", in an "overwhelming" variety of vivid and natural colors, look no further than this Lower East Side boutique; trained by an old-school craftsman, the German-born namesake designer has her "own vibe going on", which translates to understated pieces that stand out in their simplicity.

J.W. Cooper ●

-	-	-	VE

W 50s | The Shops at Columbus Circle, Time Warner Ctr. | 10 Columbus Circle, ground fl. (bet. 58th & 60th Sts.) | 1/A/B/C/D to 59th St./Columbus Circle | 212-823-9380 | www.jwcooper.com

Whether you want to "be a cowboy, New York–style" or just stand out in the crowd, dig deep into your trust fund then head to this "lovely" Time

Warner Center shop specializing in luxury accessories; well-heeled habitués "find plenty of gifts" including exotic leather belts, sterling silver, 14-karat and 18-karat buckles, some inlaid with jade or turquoise, alligator wallets and some of the "best Western boots" around.

Kaas GlassWorks Ⓜ
`- | - | - | E`

W Vill | 117 Perry St. (bet. Greenwich & Hudson Sts.) | 1 to Christopher St./ Sheridan Sq. | 212-366-0322 | www.kaasglassworks.com

Husband-and-wife-team Chris and Carol Kaas combine the art of decoupage with their love of vintage prints and the result is a distinctive handmade collection brimming with glass trays, coasters, plates and paperweights decorated with playful parrots, ferns, flowers and the like and displayed in a sweet, shoebox-sized West Village shop whose antique fixtures and tin ceilings reflect the old-fashioned aesthetic.

NEW Kaight ●
`- | - | - | E`

LES | 83 Orchard St. (bet. Broome & Grand Sts.) | B/D to Grand St. | 212-680-5630

Take a page from Kermit – it's easy bein' green nowadays, or rather, finding cool green garb – just hightail it to owner Kate McGregor's airy, eco-conscious LES womenswear boutique; everything in the spanking new space is made from recycled and/or organic materials, from the dark brown bamboo floors to the stylish (no-crunch) clothing from Stewart + Brown and J'aime by Jaime Pressley, to the Lulu Frost jewelry and Beyond Skin footwear.

NEW K & G Fashion Superstore ●
`15 | 13 | 12 | I`

E 40s | 122 E. 42nd St. (Lexington Ave.) | 4/5/6/7/S to 42nd St./ Grand Central | 212-682-9895 | www.kgstore.com

"Bargain-hunters who don't want to hunt too hard" have a field day at this multifloor Midtown discounter where a "vast assortment" of "neatly displayed", "moderately priced work and casual clothes" ("from items that look like Kmart to low-end designer collections") for guys and gals awaits; but the "not very helpful" clerks dissuade detractors, who also find the merchandise and atmosphere "unappealing" ("bring a sense of fashion – you won't find it here").

Kangol Columbus Ave. ●
`23 | 21 | 19 | M`

W 60s | 196 Columbus Ave. (bet. 68th & 69th Sts.) | 1 to 66th St./ Lincoln Ctr. | 212-724-1172

"Friendly and helpful", the staff "never makes you feel creepy for trying on 73 different hats" at this "fad-fabulous" West 60s accessories haunt; sure, you'll find the "ubiquitous cap", but this "candy store" also stocks a "wide range" of the British label's toppers from the "sporty" to the "trendy" in "every color and size", plus a clutch of "cute purses" too.

Karim Rashid Shop Ⓜ
`- | - | - | M`

Chelsea | 137 W. 19th St. (bet. 6th & 7th Aves.) | 1 to 18th St. | 212-337-8078 | www.karimrashidshop.com

Colorful Chelsea lifestyle shop showcasing the omnipresent Cairo-born, Canadian-bred designer's take on everyday objects for the home from garbage cans to tabletop and dinnerware pieces, as well as funky fashion statements like silver leather sneakers; still, the less-impressed assert "innovation for the sake of innovation doesn't do a thing for me."

QUALITY	DISPLAY	SERVICE	COST

Kartell | - | - | - | E |

SoHo | 39 Greene St. (bet. Broome & Grand Sts.) | C/E to Spring St. | 212-966-6665 | 866-854-8823 | www.kartell.it

SoHo home-furnishings showroom featuring "great plastic" pieces that are relatively "cheap but stylish"; floor-to-ceiling displays include Philippe Starck's best-selling Bubble Club and Louis Ghost chairs, along with tables, stools, storage units and shelving.

NEW **Kate's At Home** | 24 | 25 | 20 | E |

SoHo | 72 Spring St. (bet. Crosby & Lafayette Sts.) | 6 to Spring St. | 212-334-1010 | www.katespaperie.com

Kate's Paperie has expanded into home furnishings with this "striking" new SoHo space that formerly housed Portico; "brightly colored" pillows and bedding, a "large collection of floral rugs", upholstered furniture, leather dining chairs, lamps and, natch, a plethora of cheerful paper goods like napkins and plates lead proponents to proclaim "it's so happy in here."

Kate Spade | 24 | 25 | 20 | E |

SoHo | 454 Broome St. (Mercer St.) | N/R/W to Prince St. | 212-274-1991 | www.katespade.com

"My love affair started with the bags, and now I love" the recently renovated, super-"spacious" SoHo shop too, with its "polite" staff and "perfect presentation" of "whimsical" "adorable" accessories and home furnishings; "you ache to wake up in her world where coiffed girls adorned with satchels sit on tuffets and drink tea out of polka-dot china" – "it seems impossible to be hip, country-club-ish, quirky and classic at the same time, but Kate does it"; P.S. if you're a fan, "you won't mind the mind-boggling prices."

Z **Kate's Paperie** | 27 | 26 | 20 | E |

E 70s | 1282 Third Ave. (bet. 73rd & 74th Sts.) | 6 to 77th St. | 212-396-3670
G Vill | 8 W. 13th St. (bet. 5th & 6th Aves.) | F/L/V to 14th St./6th Ave. | 212-633-0570 ◐
SoHo | 561 Broadway (bet. Prince & Spring Sts.) | N/R/W to Prince St. | 212-941-9816 ◐
W 50s | 140 W. 57th St. (bet. 6th & 7th Aves.) | N/Q/R/W to 57th St. | 212-459-0700 ◐
888-941-9169 | www.katespaperie.com

These "arty" "must-stops" for the "serious writer and inviter" feature the "most beautiful selection of paper goods" from stationery, "thoughtful cards", scrapbooks and "buttery leather journals" to hundreds of "lush" handmade decorative papers, "exquisite ribbons" and a custom gift-wrapping service; it's "pricey", but proponents proclaim "the quality and quantity" of "unique merchandise" are "worth it."

Katz in the Cradle | - | - | - | M |

Midwood | 2920 Ave. L (bet. Nostrand Ave. & 29th St.) | Brooklyn | 2/5 to Brooklyn College/Flatbush Ave. | 718-258-1990

Its "small" size and "sloppy" demeanor can't tarnish the appeal of this Midwood mainstay where you can furnish your child's bedroom under the guiding hand of the store's "extremely knowledgeable and polite sales staff"; for those on the prowl for an "excellent deal" on brand-name wooden cribs, beds, dressers, armoires, mattresses and more, this place is the 'Katz' meow.

Kavanagh's 🗷Ⓜ   - | - | - | VE

E 40s | 146 E. 49th St. (bet. Lexington & 3rd Aves.) | 6 to 51st St. | 212-702-0152

The "highest-quality designer stuff" – think Chanel suits and Valentino dresses – from seasons past is carried by this elegant East 40s consignment shop, decorated with antiques and artwork (and that's not counting the Hermès bags lining the walls); those used to thrift-shop tags note "this is not for bargains, but you know what you're getting" – and it's still well below the retail prices at, say, Bergdorf Goodman, where owner Mary Kavanagh worked as director of personal shopping.

KB Toys ●   16 | 10 | 9 | I

Garment Dist | Manhattan Mall | 901 Sixth Ave. (bet. 32nd & 33rd Sts.) | B/D/F/N/Q/R/V/W to 34th St./Herald Sq. | 212-629-5386

Bay Ridge | 424 86th St. (bet. 4th & 5th Aves.) | Brooklyn | R to 86th St. | 718-745-7994

Flushing | 136-45 Roosevelt Ave. (bet. Main & Union Sts.) | Queens | 7 to Main St. | 718-460-6092

Jackson Hts | 37-48 82nd St. (bet. Roosevelt & 37th Aves.) | Queens | 7 to 82nd St./Jackson Hts. | 718-803-3702

Ridgewood | 56-29 Myrtle Ave. (Cypress Ave.) | Queens | L/M to Myrtle/Wycoff Aves. | 718-418-9388

Staten Island | Staten Island Mall | 2655 Richmond Ave. (bet. Platinum Ave. & Richmond Hill Rd.) | 718-698-8686

877-552-8697 | www.kbtoys.com

They're real "madhouses" but shoppers with the stamina to "sift through the mess" and deal with "cramped" conditions at these "budget" chain links score "terrific deals" on the "fad toys" "every kid wants" and a few "classics" too; "if you want ambiance, go to FAO Schwarz" but "if all you need is a cheap" game "for a birthday present, this is where to find it."

KD Dance & Sport ●   - | - | - | M

NoHo | 339 Lafayette St. (Bleecker St.) | 6 to Bleecker St. | 212-533-1037 | www.kddance.com

Performers and would-bes striving for a limelight-worthy look head to this tranquil NoHo corner nook for ballet slippers plus high-style, body-conscious dance and sports clothing in a cache of colors just right for stage- or streetwear; the New York–made line is designed for movement, so slip into the big green dressing room, wiggle into sexy knit wrap tops and shrugs or stretchy leotards and strike a pose.

Kenjo 🗷   25 | 22 | 21 | E

Financial Dist | 40 Wall St. (William St.) | 2/3 to Wall St. | 212-402-7000

W 50s | 40 W. 57th St. (bet. 5th & 6th Aves.) | N/Q/R/W to 57th St. | 212-333-7220

"One of the most helpful and engaging watch stores in the city", this 57th Street staple stocks "hard-to-find" items like a "full line of Fortis" styles, as well as popular tickers like Omega and Breitling; its "post-purchase care is excellent", as the "knowledgeable" staff includes a watchmaker; N.B. the Wall Street offshoot is younger and smaller.

Kenneth Cole New York ●   21 | 21 | 20 | M

E 40s | Grand Central | 42nd St. (Vanderbilt Ave.) | 4/5/6/7/S to 42nd St./Grand Central | 212-949-8079

E 40s | Rockefeller Ctr. | 610 Fifth Ave. (49th St.) | B/D/F/V to 47-50th Sts./Rockefeller Ctr. | 212-373-5800

(continued)

Kenneth Cole New York

E 50s | 130 E. 57th St. (Lexington Ave.) | 4/5/6/F/N/R/W to 59th St./
Lexington Ave. | 212-688-1670
Flatiron | 95 Fifth Ave. (17th St.) | 4/5/6/L/N/Q/R/W to 14th St./
Union Sq. | 212-675-2550
SoHo | 597 Broadway (Houston St.) | N/R/W to Prince St. | 212-965-0283
W 70s | 353 Columbus Ave. (77th St.) | B/C to 81st St. | 212-873-2061
800-536-2653 | www.kennethcole.com

"Feel like a New Yorker" from head to toe at this "easy-to navigate"
"lifestyle" chain specializing in "great hip men's and women's basics
with a flair", "handbags that last an eternity" and, of course, "unbelievably feet-friendly" footwear for "young, sophisticated professionals", all from the designer who's as recognized for his "infamous"
"social-conscience" ads; if quibblers snap "he still makes much better
shoes than he does clothing", there's no controversy when it comes to
the "courteous", "good-looking" staff.

Key ●   – | – | – | E

SoHo | 41 Grand St. (bet. Thompson St. & W. B'way) | C/E to Spring St. |
212-334-5707 | www.shopkeynyc.com

Head off SoHo's main drag and hit this spacious skylit shop, a former
artists' studio that's now trend-central for "J Brand jeans, vintage bags
and slouchy cashmere sweaters"; there are also pieces from under-
the-radar womenswear designers like Corey Lynn Calter, Yumi Kim
and Manoush; the "personnel are personable", and your guy can rest
comfortably on the "cute" canvas couches or out on the back patio
while you lock down key garments in the quirkily cool fitting rooms.

☑ Kidding Around   26 | 24 | 22 | M

Flatiron | 60 W. 15th St. (bet. 5th & 6th Aves.) | F/L/V to 14th St./6th Ave. |
212-645-6337 | www.kiddingaround.us

For arguably "the best selection of traditional" playthings "this side of
the North Pole", look no further than this Flatiron favorite, which proffers an "unusual mix of merchandise you don't see elsewhere", with an
emphasis on "smart" toys like chemistry sets and educational games
and a "great dress-up section"; the "friendly" staff can even assemble
party favor bags, pulling from their stash of "adorable" trinkets.

kid o.   22 | 23 | 18 | E

G Vill | 123 W. 10th St. (Greenwich Ave.) | F/L/V to 14th St./6th Ave. |
212-366-5436 | www.kidonyc.com

Design diehards descend on this "wonderful", "friendly" Greenwich
Village children's shop to drool over the über-contemporary eye
candy, including kid-size Eames and Bertoia chairs, Oeuf cribs, arty
mobiles and wall hangings, Montessori "high-quality educational"
toys and other "creative", "one-of-a-kind" gifts that "will wow moms
and please kids"; no kidding – the "stylish selection" is "enough to
keep you returning" again and again.

Kid Robot   – | – | – | E

SoHo | 126 Prince St. (bet. Greene & Wooster Sts.) | N/R/W to Prince St. |
212-966-6688 | 877-762-6543 | www.kidrobot.com

More like a museum than a toy store, this "cool, little" SoHo shop "for
the Japanese toy enthusiast" draws crowds with its cache of limited-

edition collectibles; carefully displayed in glass cases are two-inch-tall treasures like urban vinyl figurines, art miniatures and action figures of all the covetable Asian characters of the moment, along with old-school classics like Gumby and G.I. Joe; N.B. the store recently renovated, and now sells apparel too.

Kids Rx
`- | - | - | M`

W Vill | 523 Hudson St. (W. 10th St.) | 1 to Christopher St./Sheridan Sq. | 212-741-7111 | www.cherryspharmacy.com

If your kid seems to be coming down with something, bundle him up and trundle him into this West Village pharmacy catering to children with such healthcare, bath and body products as California Baby calming massage oil; while you're consulting with the druggist, your little one is being distracted by a toy train that chugs around the store and a Thomas the Tank table; N.B. there's a sister shop called Cherry's Pharmacy at 207 East 66th Street.

Kidville Boutique
`22 | 19 | 18 | E`

E 80s | 163 E. 84th St. (bet. Lexington & 3rd Aves.) | 4/5/6 to 86th St. | 212-772-8435

NEW **W 80s** | 466 Columbus Ave. (82nd St.) | B/C to 81st St. | 212-362-7792

www.kidvilleny.com

What a "nice addition to the kiddie parade" muse parents who "can't stop shopping for adorable clothes" at these East 80s–West 80s siblings, also home to a giant gym and and tot-friendly courses like 'Bach to Rock'; if a few find the offerings "limited" and "overpriced like the classes", most retort there are "gems within the mix", including "wonderful" togs from "trendy" labels like Shoshanna, Kule, Splendid and Tea Collection.

ⓩ Kiehl's
`27 | 23 | 25 | M`

E Vill | 109 Third Ave. (13th St.) | 4/5/6/L/N/Q/R/W to 14th St./ Union Sq. | 212-677-3171

W 60s | 154 Columbus Ave. (bet. 66th & 67th Sts.) | 1 to 66th St./ Lincoln Ctr. | 212-799-3438 ●

800-543-4571 | www.kiehls.com

"As NY as cheesecake", this "classic" toiletries duo Downtown and Uptown is a "favorite" of "moms, models and more"; it's "a terrific place" that "makes you feel as if you're in an old-fashioned drug store" with a "beyond helpful" staff that talks you through "no-frills" "quality products that work" like Protein Chamomile Shampoo and "the best lip balm this side of the Nile"; prices are "affordable" and there's a "liberal sample policy", leading loyalists to lament "I would Kiehl myself without Kiehl's!"

Kieselstein-Cord
`▽ 28 | - | 23 | VE`

E 80s | 1058 Madison Ave. (80th St.) | 6 to 77th St. | 212-744-1041 | 888-252-7009 | www.kieselstein-cord.com

Anyone who can attract a clientele as diverse as Oprah and Armani must be offering "some of the most original jewelry and accessories" around; this designer's "gorgeous works of art" (all signed, dated and copyrighted) include silver belt buckles, ornate animal jewelry like signature alligators in matte-finish green-gold, as well as trophy handbags and shades; "absolutely stunning" applies to the products and the prices; N.B. the store recently moved from SoHo to swanky Upper East Side digs.

	QUALITY	DISPLAY	SERVICE	COST

NEW Kiki De Montparnasse · 25 | 26 | 22 | VE

SoHo | 79 Greene St. (bet. Broome & Spring Sts.) | N/R/W to Prince St. | 212-965-8150 | 888-965-5454 | www.kikidm.com

"Get your kink on" at this "naughty" but "tasteful" new SoHo salon named after Man Ray's mistress where black-and-white erotic photographs line the walls and "gorgeous" "high-end European lingerie" dominates the display racks; "saucy" shoppers seek out the "classy", "very expensive" (ahem) "adult" products displayed like museum pieces in glass cases, while shyer sorts peruse the selection of luxurious house brand body products, candles and chocolates.

Kim's Mediapolis ● · 24 | 16 | 14 | M

W 100s | 2906 Broadway (bet. 113th & 114th Sts.) | 1 to 110th St. | 212-864-5321

Kim's Video ●

W Vill | 89 Christopher St. (Bleecker St.) | 1 to Christopher St./ Sheridan Sq. | 212-242-4363

Mondo Kim's ●

E Vill | 6 St. Marks Pl. (3rd Ave.) | 6 to Astor Pl. | 212-505-0311 www.kimsvideo.com

The "video stores to end all video stores", this triumvirate features a film collection that seemingly spans "every hard-to-find", "rare or foreign" title; though the West Village branch solely supplies DVDs, the East Village and Uptown outposts also offer videocassettes, books and a "fabulous CD selection" that'll "please a wide variety of musical palates", all at "college-student" prices – if only the "snotty", "pretentious" staffers weren't "so damn mean."

NEW Kipepeo · – | – | – | M

NoLita | 250 Elizabeth St. (bet. Houston & Prince Sts.) | N/R/W to Prince St. | 212-219-7555

More is more at this pink-and-cream NoLita accessories haven bursting with Lucite bangles, earrings and vintage-y lockets (like the one worn by celeb Lindsay Lohan); once you have jewelry in the bag, hunt down affordable arm candy like the standout Nairobi tote.

Kirna Zabête · 27 | 26 | 15 | VE

SoHo | 96 Greene St. (bet. Prince & Spring Sts.) | N/R/W to Prince St. | 212-941-9656 | www.kirnazabete.com

Stylesetters hungering for "lovely, trendy" clothing "priced in the outer limits" need look no further than SoHo's candy-colored, Nick Dine-designed double-decker destination that "pioneered the boutique as interior-design-mecca" concept; with-it owners Beth Buccini and Sarah Easley "sway" tastemakers with an "amazing", "well-edited selection" of "high-end" European and American designers including Chloé, Proenza Schouler and Rick Owens, leading sybarites to sigh "wish my closet looked like this"; if a few quibble that the staff doesn't "go out of its way" to help, others applaud the "no-pressure" service.

Kiton ⑤ · – | – | – | VE

E 50s | 4 E. 54th St. (bet. 5th & Madison Aves.) | E/V to 5th Ave./53rd St. | 212-813-0272 | www.kiton.it

This East 50s brownstone houses Neapolitan made-to-measure menswear, finely tailored women's clothes and handmade shoes; the superb cuts and meticulous details of these "greatest-ever" garments, plus a staff that's "better" than any department store's, underscore the couture sensibility and pricing, but some wonder "who can afford this?"

Kleinfeld ⓜ | 25 | 19 | 20 | E |
Chelsea | 110 W. 20th St. (bet. 6th & 7th Aves.) | C/E to 23rd St. | 212-352-2180 | www.kleinfeldbridal.com

"The cadillac of bridal salons" is "finally in Manhattan!" – "thanks for crossing the river" gush the gleeful agog over the Brooklyn "icon's" "awesome new" by-appointment-only Chelsea digs; "grandmothers, mothers, daughters – what a tradition" – "there's a reason they've been in business" since 1941: the selection of "sensational" gowns is "huge", and the "patient staff" "takes care of every need" – "I thought it would be too posh but it was everything you could ask for and more"; still, the put-off pout that the salespeople "push too hard."

Kmart ☯ | 12 | 10 | 7 | I |
Garment Dist | 250 W. 34th St. (bet. 7th & 8th Aves.) | 1/2/3/A/C/E to 34th St./Penn Station | 212-760-1188
G Vill | 770 Broadway (Astor Pl.) | 6 to Astor Pl. | 212-673-1540
Bronx | 1998 Bruckner Blvd. (bet. Pugsley Ave. & White Plains Rd.) | 6 to Parkchester | 718-430-9439
Bronx | 300 Baychester Ave. (bet. Bartow Ave. & Hutchinson River Pkwy.) | 6 to Pelham Bay Park | 718-671-5377
Middle Vill | 66-26 Metropolitan Ave. (bet. Audley St. & Grosvenor Rd.) | Queens | M to Middle Vill./Metropolitan Ave. | 718-821-2412
Staten Island | 2660 Hylan Blvd. (Ebbitts St.) | 718-351-8500
Staten Island | 2875 Richmond Ave. (Yukon Ave.) | 718-698-0900
866-562-7844 | www.kmart.com

"If you can find it – a big if – you can get good value at this chain of barnlike" megastores that carry "all the basic things" – "and Martha Stewart, of course" – for the home and person; supporters single out the "wide selection" of "going-off-to-college" cookware, "cheap bed and bath needs" and "simple" watches; even so, given the "glacial-in-speed service", "junky" looks and the fact they're often "out of what you came for", most say they're pretty "sad to shop in."

Knit-A-Way of Brooklyn | – | – | – | M |
Boerum Hill | 398 Atlantic Ave. (bet. Bond & Hoyt Sts.) | Brooklyn | A/C/G to Hoyt/Schermerhorn Sts. | 718-797-3305 | www.knitaway.com

This bi-level Boerum Hill boutique (successor to Knitting Hands) affords "hours of yarn browsing" thanks to wares that range from budget brands (Brown Sheep) to loftier labels (Karabella, Tahki); frequent classes, held in the basement, cover basic technique as well as specialized skills, while regular on-site knitting and crocheting circles give learners the chance to click with a likeminded clique.

Knit New York ☯ | 25 | 23 | 20 | E |
E Vill | 307 E. 14th St. (2nd Ave.) | L to 1st Ave. | 212-387-0707 | www.knitnewyork.com

At this "super-hip" yet "comfortable" 14th Street "wonderland for knitters", the "unusual" range of "gorgeous yarns" and "excellent pattern collection" are supplemented by a "wonderful cafe" where stitchers can "have a coffee while browsing the books" or "chatting about future projects"; the "good product" and lessons can be "expensive", however, and service seems somewhat "inconsistent" – fans find staffers "easygoing" and "knowledgeable" but foes fret "prepare to be ignored."

Knits Incredible ▽ 20 | 16 | 17 | M

E 70s | 971 Lexington Ave., 2nd fl. (bet. 70th & 71st Sts.) | 6 to 68th St. | 212-717-0477

With its "great selection of beautiful skeins" (including many novelties and hand-dyed lines) plus funky buttons and needlework notions, this second-floor shop near Hunter College attracts Upper East Side stitchers who often commission custom-designed patterns from owner and knitting-world maven Ann Regis; a few yarnheads yearn for a bit more order on the premises ("boxes everywhere").

Knitting 321 🗟 Ⓜ — | — | — | E

E 70s | 321 E. 75th St. (bet. 1st & 2nd Aves.) | 6 to 77th St. | 212-772-2020 | www.knitting321.com

Knit-wits head to this "small" basement-level shop in the East 70s for trendy natural-fiber yarns from around the world, some of which come prepackaged as projects along with instructions and trimmings; the few who've found this nook say service is "good", but prices can be "crazy."

Knoll 🗟 — | — | — | VE

Chelsea | 76 Ninth Ave., 11th fl. (bet. 15th & 16th Sts.) | A/C/E/L to 14th St./8th Ave. | 212-343-4000 | www.knoll.com

"Modern equals Knoll" assert aesthetes about this furniture pioneer that holds the license for midcentury masters such as Mies; its Chelsea showroom, formerly open to the trade only, displays iconic residential and office seating and tables that are the "real deal"; N.B. appointments preferred.

Koh's Kids — | — | — | E

TriBeCa | 311 Greenwich St. (bet. Chambers & Reade Sts.) | 1/2/3 to Chambers St. | 212-791-6915

Despite its shoebox size, this TriBeCa treasure manages to stuff a surprisingly vast selection of children's clothing and accessories within its walls – you'll love sampling all of the European fashion eye candy here; for something truly one-of-a-kind, check out the store's own original collection of colorful, handknit sweaters, dresses and hats.

Kraft Hardware 🗟 ▽ 26 | 23 | 23 | E

E 60s | 315 E. 62nd St. (bet. 1st & 2nd Aves.) | 4/5/6/F/N/R/W to 59th St./Lexington Ave. | 212-838-2214 | www.kraft-hardware.com

For 70 years, this "wonderful" two-story Upper East Sider has been known for a "great selection" of hardware, plumbing fixtures, faucets, sinks, vanities, toilets and cast-iron tubs ranging in price "from moderate to expensive"; enthusiasts also appreciate the "great" attentive staff; N.B. closed Saturday and Sunday.

Kreiss Collection 🗟 ▽ 26 | 26 | 21 | VE

E 50s | 215 E. 58th St. (bet. 2nd & 3rd Aves.) | 4/5/6/F/N/R/W to 59th St./Lexington Ave. | 212-593-2005 | www.kreiss.com

Custom-made "California modern" sectional couches, chairs and tables in neutral tones and all-natural fibers are showcased in the company's East 50s store alongside accessories like bed linens and lamps; the big, "beautiful" pieces are "perfect for your place in the Hamptons", and "worth the large price tags."

| | QUALITY | DISPLAY | SERVICE | COST |

Kremer Pigments 🛒

▽ 29 | – | 24 | E

Chelsea | 247 W. 29th St. (bet. 7th & 8th Aves.) | 1 to 28th St. | 212-219-2394 | 800-995-5501 | www.kremer-pigmente.com

"The finest selection of ground pigments, resins and varnishes available" can be found at this painters' outpost, which still evokes a "medieval apothecary" in its new Chelsea digs with shelves showcasing jars of "superb" raw materials for "real artists" and restorers; a "patient" staff helps you find any hue "imaginable" at this sole American satellite of a Germany-based company, though take note: "it's not for novices."

Krizia 🛒

– | – | – | E

E 60s | 769 Madison Ave. (66th St.) | 6 to 68th St. | 212-879-1211 | www.krizia.it

Follow your animal instincts to Mariuccia Mandelli's Madison Avenue boutique where her label's iconic tiger adorns "young, sexy designs" such as fluttery chiffon dresses, trendy-with-a-twist suits and signature, you'll-have-'em-"forever" knits; your Tarzan can get into the swing of things too, as the airy limestone premises also houses cashmere coats, silk ties and a sensual scent for him.

⚡ Krup's Kitchen & Bath, Ltd. 🛒

26 | 14 | 19 | E

Flatiron | 11 W. 18th St. (bet. 5th & 6th Aves.) | 1 to 18th St. | 212-243-5787

This long-standing, family-owned Flatiron store features "quality" kitchen appliances from the likes of Bosch and Sub-Zero and custom-made cabinets and countertops as well as bathroom and plumbing fixtures; the space is "overcrowded" and "in need of renovation", but "very good prices" and a "helpful" and "knowledgeable" staff help straighten things out.

Kuhlman Company

20 | 18 | 20 | M

G Vill | 484 Sixth Ave. (bet. 12th & 13th Sts.) | F/L/V to 14th St./6th Ave. | 212-414-4678 🌑

SoHo | 96 Grand St. (bet. Greene & Mercer Sts.) | 1 to Canal St. | 212-226-7208

W 50s | Rockefeller Ctr. | 30 Rockefeller Ctr. (bet. 49th & 50th Sts.) | B/D/F/V to 47-50th Sts./Rockefeller Ctr. | 212-581-5631 🛒 www.kuhlmancompany.com

Many a Manhattanite is "impressed" by this Minneapolis-based chain carving rapidly into the Big Apple, as it offers suits and separates that are "colorful and flashy, but still office-wearable" for "guys and girls alike"; maybe the merchandise is "not of the best quality, but you can't beat" their "won't-break-the-bank" prices.

La Boutique Resale

▽ 23 | 18 | 20 | M

E 60s | 803 Lexington Ave., 2nd fl. (62nd St.) | 4/5/6/F/N/R/W to 59th St./Lexington Ave. | 212-588-8858

E 70s | 1045 Madison Ave., 2nd fl. (bet. 79th & 80th Sts.) | 6 to 77th St. | 212-517-8099

W 70s | 160 W. 72nd St., 2nd fl. (bet. B'way & Columbus Ave.) | 1/2/3 to 72nd St. | 212-787-3098 www.laboutiqueresale.com

"If you hit it right" you'll "find hidden treasures" at this trio – perhaps a piece of Prada, or a St. John suit, or a chemise among the Chanels; prices are "reasonable", given the "high-quality goods", but what really makes it "one of the best of its kind" is its "friendly staff";

P.S. there's "interesting vintage" stock at the Madison Avenue mother ship, and the Upper West Side branch now carries menswear.

La Brea ●   18 | 18 | 13 | M

E 40s | 500 Lexington Ave. (47th St.) | 6 to 51st St. | 212-371-1482
E 60s | 1321 Second Ave. (bet. 69th & 70th Sts.) | 6 to 68th St. | 212-879-4065
E 80s | 1575 Second Ave. (bet. 81st & 82nd Sts.) | 6 to 77th St. | 212-772-2640
W 70s | Beacon Hotel | 2130 Broadway (bet. 74th & 75th Sts.) | 1/2/3 to 72nd St. | 212-873-7850
W 90s | 2440 Broadway (90th St.) | 1 to 86th St. | 212-724-2777
www.labrea.com

These "essential resources" for "witty, funny cards" (think "upscale Hallmark") also house "an eclectic assortment" of gifts and gag items from T-shirts to Freud bobbleheads; the "wonderful variety" of products makes browsing "always interesting"; however, some shrug off the "cute stuff" as "too cute for me."

La Cafetière ●   – | – | – | M

Chelsea | 160 Ninth Ave. (bet. 19th & 20th Sts.) | C/E to 23rd St. | 646-486-0667 | 866-486-0667 | www.la-cafetiere.com

"Charming" Chelsea shop that sells "beautiful housewares and linens" in a "setting that makes you feel like you've traveled abroad" to the South of France; "unusual items" include peg-and-groove constructed furniture in over 30 patinas, hand-blown glassware, colorful quilts and mohair throws that will make you and your *maison* smile.

NEW Laces ⊠ Ⓜ   – | – | – | E

NoLita | 252 Mott St. (bet. Houston & Prince Sts.) | 6 to Spring St. | 212-334-5457 | www.laces-nyc.com

Ladies luck out with this women's-only sneaker boutique in NoLita, the brainchild of Louis Colon III, creator of sneaker collector magazine *Kicksclusive*; glammed out with gold walls, chandeliers and velvet chairs, the shop is stocked solid with limited-editions, reissues and other exclusive styles from brands like Nike, Reebok and Cr8tive Recreation, as well as loads of laces and coordinating accessories.

Lacoste   24 | 22 | 19 | E

E 40s | 608 Fifth Ave. (49th St.) | E/V to 5th Ave./53rd St. | 212-459-2300
E 50s | 575 Madison Ave. (bet. 56th & 57th Sts.) | 4/5/6/F/N/R/W to 59th St./Lexington Ave. | 212-750-8115
SoHo | 134 Prince St. (bet. W. B'way & Wooster St.) | N/R/W to Prince St. | 212-226-5019
800-452-2678 | www.lacoste.com

"Anyone can pull off a simple polo", but it helps if it has a "cute little crocodile" as a logo and "fits great", like this "classic" brand's versions, which come "in every color and permutation"; though the "shirts are still its staple", the "styles are updated" and accessorized with leather bags, sporty watches and sneakers; but you might need a serve like supporter/tennis champ Andy Roddick's to "get help" in the often "overcrowded stores."

LaCrasia Gloves ⊠   25 | 17 | 18 | M

Chelsea | 15 W. 28th St. (bet. B'way & 5th Ave.) | N/R/W to 23rd St. | 212-803-1600 | www.weloveyou.com

"Your fingers can find fashionable coverage all year round" at this "great focused resource" in Chelsea offering every "glove you can imagine" from "arm-length" numbers "for that black-tie outfit" to "racy fine leather driving" styles; hand mavens vow "this place is a trip", even if your digits don't need protection; N.B. the Grand Central shop of the same name carries their merchandise but is separately owned.

LaDuca Shoes

-	-	-	E

Garment Dist | 534 Ninth Ave. (bet. 39th & 40th Sts.) | A/C/E to 42nd St./Port Authority | 212-268-6751 | www.laducashoes.com

Broadway hoofers and studio savants consider choreographer Phil LaDuca's "beautiful", flexible Italian-made character shoes displayed in his vintagey-looking Garment District stomping ground the "most coveted dance" numbers "in the city"; nothing "makes you look like a star" and "tells people you are serious" about your floor moves like these custom-crafted or off-the-shelf designs made for jazz, tap or can-can classes and performances.

Lady Foot Locker ●

22	19	17	M

Garment Dist | 120 W. 34th St. (B'way) | B/D/F/N/Q/R/V/W to 34th St./Herald Sq. | 212-629-4626
NEW SoHo | 523 Broadway (Spring St.) | 6 to Spring St. | 212-965-0493
Kings Plaza | Kings Plaza Shopping Ctr. | 5364 Kings Plaza (Flatbush Ave. & Ave. U) | Brooklyn | 718-253-9631
Sunset Pk | 5314 Fifth Ave. (bet. 53rd & 54th Sts.) | Brooklyn | R to 53rd St. | 718-439-4669
Elmhurst | Queens Ctr. | 90-15 Queens Blvd. (bet. 57th & 59th Aves.) | Queens | G/R/V to Woodhaven Blvd. | 718-760-3271
Staten Island | Staten Island Mall | 2655 Richmond Ave. (bet. Platinum Ave. & Richmond Hill Rd.) | 718-370-0505
800-991-6815 | www.ladyfootlocker.com

There's "always something new on the shelves" assert sneaker fans who also find this chain is "getting better with activewear"; the "good selection and prices make for a pleasant shopping experience", and the "salespeople are willing and able to get you the right size"; still, it doesn't rock everyone's locker – a handful wail it "seems to fall short, from its lack of style diversity to its bland presentations."

Laila Rowe ●

14	18	17	I

E 40s | 8 E. 42nd St. (5th Ave.) | 7/B/D/F/V to 42nd St./Bryant Park | 212-949-2276 | www.lailarowe.com
Additional locations throughout the NY area

If you've "outgrown plastic jewelry" but don't want to "blow a month's rent", head to this "well-laid-out" "cheap thrill" of a local chain for "bling-bling without the ka-ching"; be it "colorful baubles" or "bohemian trinkets", "you'll find just the thing for pennies and look like you've spent lots more"; the "rapidly changing stock" gives you reasons to visit anew and "makes it hard to leave empty-handed."

Laina Jane

-	-	-	E

G Vill | 45 Christopher St. (bet. 7th Ave. & Waverly Pl.) | 1 to Christopher St./Sheridan Sq. | 212-807-8077 ●
W 80s | 416 Amsterdam Ave. (80th St.) | 1 to 79th St. | 212-875-9168
www.lainajane.com

"I always find something" at these "small" "attitude-free" shops in the Village and on the Upper West Side – "it's my favorite place to buy" "fine lingerie" laud loyalists who take a shine to the stash of "sweet nothings" fashioned from silk and lace or delicate cotton; "from engagement and bridal shower gifts" to unmentionables "for myself" from brands such as Chantelle, and Cosabella to "hard-to-find" labels, "everything they carry is sophisticated and pretty."

Lalaounis Ⓢ ▽ 29 | 24 | 23 | VE

E 60s | 739 Madison Ave. (bet. 64th & 65th Sts.) | 6 to 68th St. | 212-439-9400 | www.iliaslalaounis.com

Ancient civilizations are the inspiration for this fourth-generation Greek jeweler in a cozy, burgundy-and-beige bijouterie in the East 60s; "magnificent", "very original" and very expensive designs of hand-hammered 18- and 22-karat gold incorporate classical techniques such as granulation, filigree and repoussé.

Ⓩ Lalique Ⓢ 29 | 26 | 25 | VE

E 60s | 712 Madison Ave. (bet. 63rd & 64th Sts.) | 6 to 68th St. | 212-355-6550 | 800-214-2738 | www.lalique.com

"Madison Avenue is the right place" to house this "elegant" "museum" of "beautiful", "incomparable quality" opalescent French "crystal that will stand the test of time" and "should be handed down from generation to generation", whether it's vases, bar ware, perfume bottles or jewelry; while "nothing here is cheap", respondents remind "you're buying art."

Lana Marks Ⓢ ▽ 28 | 29 | 21 | VE

E 60s | 645 Madison Ave. (bet. 59th & 60th Sts.) | N/R/W to 5th Ave./59th St. | 212-355-6135 | www.lanamarks.com

"Where else can you buy a handbag to match your dog's eyes" and find over 150 styles in ostrich, alligator, crocodile and lizard ask aficionados who pledge their loyalty to the Palm Beach–based designer (aka the "queen of leather goods") and her Madison Avenue shrine; the "simplicity of design", "fabulous quality" and "craftsmanship speak for themselves" – just ask celeb customers like Oprah Winfrey and Julianne Moore – but your wallet may be rendered speechless.

NEW Lancôme ● 26 | 24 | 22 | E

W 60s | 201 Columbus Ave. (69th St.) | B/C to 72nd St. | 212-362-4858 | www.lancome.com

The first NYC outpost of the French firm and "a pleasant addition to the Upper West Side's" beauty row is this "bright and airy" "place to indulge one's self" with "pick-me-up" cosmetics, fragrances and "classic" skincare "products that serve a wide range of ages"; a "supportive" staff that can "help you find your look" also adds to its appeal.

LaoLao Handmade ●Ⓜ – | – | – | M

E Vill | 149 Ave. C (bet. 9th & 10th Sts.) | L to 1st Ave. | 212-979-1855 | www.laolaohandmade.com

Adding Southeast Asian spice to Avenue C, this bright boutique full of "gorgeous" handmade silk textiles and accessories for women, men and the home is named after the traditional moonshine of Laos; the luxurious loot also includes a proprietary line of ceramic dishes and Burmese teak furniture from the '30s.

Ⓩ La Perla 28 | 25 | 23 | VE

E 60s | 803 Madison Ave. (bet. 67th & 68th Sts.) | 6 to 68th St. | 212-570-0050
Meatpacking | 425 W. 14th St. (bet. 9th Ave. & Washington St.) | A/C/E/L to 14th St./8th Ave. | 212-242-6662

(continued)

(continued)

⊡ La Perla

SoHo | 93 Greene St. (bet. Prince & Spring Sts.) | C/E to Spring St. |
212-219-0999
866-527-3752 | www.laperla.com

"If God wears underwear, she shops here" proclaim parishioners who
worship at this "amazingly indulgent" trio that traffics in "classy",
"high-end lacy" thongs, bustiers, garter belts and other "beautiful"
unmentionables that act like "Kryptonite for men"; while you're
indulging "all the senses", pour yourself into "sexy" swimwear and hosiery that will "make him want to touch" your "perfect body" – but remember that in order to drive this "incredible" "Mercedes of lingerie",
you may need to "rob a bank."

La Petite Coquette   26 | 23 | 23 | E

G Vill | 51 University Pl. (bet. 9th & 10th Sts.) | 6 to Astor Pl. |
212-473-2478 | 800-240-0308 | www.thelittleflirt.com

From the "littlest creation to full-body lace coverings", Rebecca
Apsan's "delightfully naughty" "lingerie candy store" for "women of
exquisite taste and deep pockets" is "a great place to watch celebrities"
(Sarah Jessica Parker, Winona Ryder) buying "barely there" unmentionables from designers like Chantelle, Lise Charmel and Myla; with
a "friendly" "gossipy" staff on hand, you'll always "find the perfect
thing" at this Village boudoir – or "spend your last dollar" trying to.

Lara Hélène   – | – | – | VE

E 60s | 13 E. 69th St. (bet. 5th & Madison Aves.) | 6 to 68th St. |
212-452-3273 | www.larahelene.com

"Definitely worth a stop by all brides", this by-appointment-only
atelier on the UES offers a customized collection of its own creations
(the work of a sisterly duo), along with exclusive European and Latin
American lines; samples of the sophisticated gowns hang from the
ceiling in the airy, elegant space, shimmering against the dark wood
floor and furniture; there's also a garden and large fitting room,
providing ample room for clients to play with the garments, unique
veils and crystal bouquets.

Larry & Jeff's Bicycle Plus   – | – | – | M

E 70s | 1400 Third Ave. (bet. 79th & 80th Sts.) | 6 to 77th St. | 212-794-2929
E 80s | 1690 Second Ave. (bet. 87th & 88th Sts.) | 4/5/6 to 86th St. |
212-722-2201
www.bicyclesnyc.com

This pair of pedal peddlers on the Upper East Side offers a "good selection" of wheels, including "specialized road" rigs; whether you're
looking for big bikes from names such as Cannondale and Giant or
Kettler tricycles for toddlers graduating from strollers, the "helpful",
"courteous" staff will match the perfect ride to your specs.

L'Artisan Parfumeur   26 | 25 | 23 | E

NEW **E 80s** | 1100 Madison Ave. (bet. 82nd & 83rd Sts.) | 6 to 77th St. |
212-794-3600
SoHo | 68 Thompson St. (Spring St.) | C/E to Spring St. | 212-334-1500 ◐
www.artisanparfumeur.com

The first U.S. offshoot of this premier French fragrance house is an
"intimate" pink-and-purple SoHo boutique showcasing pretty gold-

capped bottles filled with "unique" scents based on natural ingredients like almond milk, figs and orange blossoms, along with candles and body creams concocted from fruit and flower extracts; the products are pricey but "you'll never smell like the person next to you"; N.B. the Madison Avenue branch opened post-*Survey*.

L' Avenue des Reves 🛇 | - | - | - | E |

E 70s | 1028 Lexington Ave. (bet. 73rd & 74th Sts.) | 6 to 77th St. | 212-396-9500

To preserve their pre-pregnancy style, expectant moms head straight to Michelle Ronty's dreamy Upper East Side maternity boutique where all of the beautiful pieces are made-to-order from store samples, sketches, photos and customers' own favorite pieces; you can also shop here for unique, imported home accessories and even pillows for your canine companion.

Layla Ⓜ | - | - | - | E |

Boerum Hill | 86 Hoyt St. (bet. Atlantic Ave. & State St.) | Brooklyn | A/C/G to Hoyt/Schermerhorn Sts. | 718-222-1933

At this "great" Brooklyn homage to all things Indian tucked away from Atlantic Avenue, shoppers discover brightly colored bed linens, cushions and quilted silk coverlets, most of them handmade and detailed; bangle bracelets and an eponymous clothing line using all natural materials add to the earthy ethnic emphasis.

Laytner's Linen & Home ◐ | 20 | 18 | 16 | M |

E 80s | 237 E. 86th St. (bet. 2nd & 3rd Aves.) | 4/5/6 to 86th St. | 212-996-4439

W 80s | 2270 Broadway (82nd St.) | 1 to 79th St. | 212-724-0180 800-690-7200 | www.laytners.com

Many locals laud these long-standing Upper East and West Side home-furnishings emporiums for being "convenient", "decently priced" "saviors" "when you need something in a pinch", including sheets, towels, candles, place mats, folding chairs and Shaker-style furniture; "the selection isn't huge" and "nothing is out of this world or unique", but "frequent sales help makes up for shortcomings in the coolness factor."

☒ Leather Man, The ◐ | 26 | 22 | 24 | E |

W Vill | 111 Christopher St. (bet. Bleecker & Hudson Sts.) | 1 to Christopher St./Sheridan Sq. | 212-243-5339 | 800-243-5330 | www.theleatherman.com

"Even experts periodically have to ask 'what the hell is that for?'" when they peruse the "wicked stuff" at this duplex "leather S/M" shop in the "gay central" section of the West Village; "the store is overflowing with goods" "packed in every nook and cranny" – speaking of which, "young guys" in particular "should prepare for manhandling" by the staff, whose "touchy-feely"approach is "helpful" to "fetishists" being fitted for custom-made apparel.

Le Chien Pet Salon | ▽ 23 | 23 | 17 | VE |

E 60s | Trump Plaza | 1044 Third Ave. (bet. 61st & 62nd Sts.) | 4/5/6/F/N/R/W to 59th St./Lexington Ave. | 212-861-8100 | 800-532-4436 | www.lechiennyc.com

Fashionistas who "can afford to schlep Fifi" in Chanel-like carriers frequent this "luxurious" Trump Plaza fixture boasting digs reminiscent of a "museum"; it offers "beautiful" puppies and "top-quality" accessories, but down-to-earth doggies and kitties declare "you have to own a very well-off human" to handle the "high price" tags.

Lederer de Paris 🖾

	QUALITY	DISPLAY	SERVICE	COST
	25	19	20	E

E 50s | 457 Madison Ave. (51st St.) | 6 to 51st St. | 212-355-5515 | 888-537-6921 | www.ledererdeparis.com

It's a mixed bag for this "classic" Madison Avenue leather goods shop that's been a staple since the 1940s: proponents predict "when all else fails, you'll find something" amid its "always dependable" purses, briefcases, luggage and business accessories, but faultfinders fume there's "attitude for no reason" since the prices make "you feel like you're just paying their rent."

Lee Anderson

	QUALITY	DISPLAY	SERVICE	COST
	-	-	-	VE

E 60s | 23 E. 67th St. (Madison Ave.) | 6 to 68th St. | 212-772-2463

Each season, discriminating women make an appointment at this namesake designer's intimate East 60s boutique to order custom-made everyday essentials and special-occasion wear ranging from corduroy coats that look like fur to sophisticated mother-of-the-bride dresses; customers peruse the chic samples, choose from an "abundant" array of special high-end fabrications (brocade, silk faille, chiffon) and walk away six weeks later with one-of-a-kind creations.

Lee's Art Shop ●

	QUALITY	DISPLAY	SERVICE	COST
	25	23	19	E

W 50s | 220 W. 57th St. (bet. B'way & 7th Ave.) | N/Q/R/W to 57th St. | 212-247-0110 | www.leesartshop.com

"Hours of browsing" await at this multilevel West 50s "wonderland", which "got even better as it got bigger"; "you can't beat" the "staggering selection" of "fantastic art supplies", "terrific writing instruments" and other "fun finds", plus there's also a "great framing department"; "solicitous service" completes the picture, though bashers brush off the "uptown" prices (hence the "term 'starving artist'").

Lee's Studio ●

	QUALITY	DISPLAY	SERVICE	COST
	23	19	17	E

W 50s | 220 W. 57th St., 2nd fl. (bet. B'way & 7th Ave.) | N/Q/R/W to 57th St. | 212-581-4400 | 877-544-4869 | www.leesstudio.com

Located above Lee's Art Shop in Midtown, this 6,000-sq.-ft. space features furniture and fans, but the main focus is on lighting from the likes of Leucos, Flos and Artemide; however, "expensive" prices and "indifferent" salespeople "with attitude" leave many customers in the dark.

Le Fanion 🖾

	QUALITY	DISPLAY	SERVICE	COST
	-	-	-	E

W Vill | 299 W. Fourth St. (Bank St.) | 1 to Christopher St./Sheridan Sq. | 212-463-8760 | 800-258-8760 | www.lefanion.com

Small West Village home-furnishings shop that evokes the French countryside with pretty pieces ranging from antique armoires and zinc weathervanes to rustic pitchers, platters and delicate bronze chandeliers dripping with crystal fruits.

NEW Le Labo

	QUALITY	DISPLAY	SERVICE	COST
	-	-	-	VE

NoLita | 233 Elizabeth St. (bet. Houston & Prince Sts.) | 6 to Spring St. | 212-219-2230 | www.lelabofragrances.com

At this atmospheric, interactive, new NoLita perfume lab, clients sniff from giant glass apothecary jars containing 10 fragrances based on essences from Grasse, France's olfactory capital, and choose a scent that a "helpful" staff member will blend and pour into plain-Jane packaging with your hand-lettered name and an expiration date; it's a "cool concept", but of course all this personalization comes at a price.

Leonard Opticians 🗷

E 70s | 1264 Third Ave. (bet. 72nd & 73rd Sts.) | 6 to 68th St. | 212-535-1222
W 50s | 40 W. 55th St. (bet. 5th & 6th Aves.) | F to 57th St. | 212-246-4452
www.leonardopticians.com

"You're guaranteed the best quality" at this longtime UES and Midtown pair of spectacle shops stocking the "latest styles" from leading designers alongside "tried-and-true classics"; the "terrific" staff "won't sell it to you if it doesn't flatter", and "prices are fair" for the chic selection.

NEW Leontine ●

Seaport | 226 Front St. (bet. Beekman St. & Peck Slip) | 2/3/4/5/A/C/J/M/Z to Fulton St./B'way/Nassau | 212-766-1066

With her latest undertaking, a warmly lit, fragrant gem on the South Street Seaport waterfront, Kyung Lee (owner of Albertine) goes where few specialty shopkeepers have gone to date; the signless store boasts handpicked finds ranging from Kathy Kemp dresses and jewelry from Delphine to delicate toile linens and antique furnishings, making visitors feel like they've wandered into a charming brownstone rather than a boutique – except that everything's for sale.

Léron 🗷

E 60s | 804 Madison Ave. (bet. 67th & 68th Sts.) | 6 to 68th St. | 212-753-6700 | 800-954-6369 | www.leron.com

Since 1910, this Upper East Side doyenne has been purveying "beautiful and classic" bath, bed, baby and table linens; they can also "custom-make anything" in the aforementioned categories, plus lingerie; while wallet-watchers warn "don't even enter this store unless you just robbed a bank", the only thing enthusiasts advise is "love what you purchase because it will be around for a long, long time."

Le Sabon and Baby Too ●

| 23 | 23 | 18 | E |

E 60s | 834 Lexington Ave. (63rd St.) | F to Lexington Ave./63rd St. | 212-319-4225 | www.lesabon.com

When you "can't hold back on your little one" or need a "nattily packaged" baby shower gift, head to this "tiny" East 60s newcomer and scoop up "cute" stuff like leather bibs and onesies, plus "fragrant creams", soy candles and Dead Sea bath products from the "eye-catching displays"; if a handful get in a lather about "hard to come by" help, most retort it's a "great stop after shopping Bloomie's."

Les Petits Chapelais

∇ 25 | 23 | 20 | E |

SoHo | 86 Thompson St. (Spring St.) | C/E to Spring St. | 212-625-1023 | www.lespetitschapelais.com

"Reminds me of shopping in French baby stores" reminisce browsers who tip their hats to this SoHo tot shop named for designer Nathalie Simonneaux's generations-old family farm in Brittany; the whimsical wearables "for kids go beyond the Gap" with "beautiful fabrics", bright colors and a flair for creative combinations taking center stage – just what you'd expect from the visionary who once dreamed up costumes for Le Cirque du Soleil.

| | QUALITY | DISPLAY | SERVICE | COST |

LeSportsac
`20` `19` `17` `M`

E 80s | 1065 Madison Ave. (bet. 80th & 81st Sts.) | 6 to 77th St. | 212-988-6200

SoHo | 176 Spring St. (bet. Thompson St. & W. B'way) | C/E to Spring St. | 212-625-2626

877-397-6597 | www.lesportsac.com

For "funky", "inexpensive" "knockaround" ripstop parachute-nylon satchels that "wear forever", stop by these SoHo and Upper East Side branches where you'll find "the most up-to-date" selections that are "perfect when your shoulder hurts from 50-lb. designer bags"; there's an "unbelievably helpful staff", but snooty sorts snark "if it weren't for Gwen Stefani's L.A.M.B." collection (and playful Japanese anime prints from tokidoki) "they'd be relegated to the closet."

Lester's
`24` `19` `19` `E`

E 80s | 1534 Second Ave. (80th St.) | 6 to 77th St. | 212-734-9292

Gravesend | 2411 Coney Island Ave. (Ave. U) | Brooklyn | Q to Ave. U | 718-645-4501

www.lestersnyc.com

"Why aren't there more stores like this?" ponder parents bewitched by this "been-around-forever" "one-stop shopping" destination in the East 80s and Gravesend boasting "cute kids' clothing" "from dress-up to camp-trunk" essentials; the "trendy" juniors section is "teenybopper heaven", and "you can't beat the selection" in the stellar shoe department; still, it gets "zoo-y" – "your child may grow a size while waiting."

Levi's Store, The ●
`23` `18` `18` `M`

E 50s | 750 Lexington Ave. (59th St.) | 4/5/6/F/N/R/W to 59th St./Lexington Ave. | 212-826-5957

SoHo | 536 Broadway (bet. Prince & Spring Sts.) | N/R/W to Prince St. | 646-613-1847

NEW **Union Sq** | 25 W. 14th St. (bet. 5th Ave. & Union Sq. E.) | F/L/V to 14th St./6th Ave. | 212-242-2128

800-872-5384 | www.levi.com

"Keep your designer jeans – this is the real deal" pledge the true-blue who pick up their "perennial favorite" brand at this "attitude-free" denim trio; whether "you've got a rumpshaker like J.Lo's" or just want an "all-American" "classic" cut, the "personable staff" is "willing to pull and pull" from the "very organized", "right-on-trend" selection until you find your "extremely well-fitting" pair.

Lexington Gardens ⊠
`-` `-` `-` `E`

E 70s | 1011 Lexington Ave. (bet. 72nd & 73rd Sts.) | 6 to 68th St. | 212-861-4390

Long-standing Upper East Sider providing "super-fine", "top-of-the-line custom-made dried flower arrangements" for local patricians and visiting princes and heads of state; interspersed among the bespoke bouquets are "unique" antiques, which add to the atmospheric setting.

Lexington Luggage
`21` `10` `21` `M`

E 60s | 793 Lexington Ave. (bet. 61st & 62nd Sts.) | 4/5/6/F/N/R/W to 59th St./Lexington Ave. | 212-223-0698 | 800-822-0404 | www.lexingtonluggage.com

If prices seem high "at first blush", just rely on your "old-fashioned haggling" skills advise insiders who consider this Lex luggage haunt a "find"; rely on the "patient" staff that's "willing to go the extra mile to help find the perfect gear" and you'll wheel away "incredible deals."

LF Stores

| | | | |
|17|14|17|E|

Flatiron | 150 Fifth Ave. (bet. 19th & 20th Sts.) | 4/5/6/L/N/Q/R/W to 14th St./Union Sq. | 212-645-1334 ●
SoHo | 149 Spring St. (bet. W. B'way & Wooster St.) | C/E to Spring St. | 212-966-5889 ●
Cobble Hill | 227 Court St. (bet. Baltic & Warren Sts.) | Brooklyn | F/G to Bergen St. | 718-797-3626
www.lfstores.com

This trifecta of trendiness is housed in "cool digs" – and dig you must, through a "cluttered closet" –like inventory of "fun, young clothes to mix, match and layer", à la the Olsen twins; still, some sigh that these "items that look like what you'd make yourself if you were a crafty girl", cost "three times what they should."

Liberty House

| | | | |
|▽ 25|20|21|E|

W 90s | 2466 Broadway (bet. 91st & 92nd Sts.) | 1/2/3 to 96th St. | 212-799-7640
W 100s | 2878A Broadway (112th St.) | 1 to 116th St. | 212-932-1950
www.libertyhousenyc.com

Opened during the civil rights era as a nonprofit retailer peddling wares made by craft cooperatives, this separately owned "socially conscious" duo on the Upper West Side now features "funky", "politically correct" clothing and gift items for women (and at the more Uptown branch, kids too), plus "globally" sourced "tchotchkes" and "charming" jewelry made by artisans; just note that "one-of-a-kind pieces" come at a price.

Lightforms

| | | | |
|▽ 23|–|23|E|

Chelsea | 142 W. 26th St. (bet. 6th & 7th Aves.) | 1 to 28th St. | 212-255-4664
W 80s | 509 Amsterdam Ave. (bet. 84th & 85th Sts.) | 1 to 86th St. | 212-875-0407
www.lightformsinc.com

The enlightened head to this duo for a swell selection of "funky to sedate" lighting from over 200 companies such as Halo, Kovacs, Flos, Juno, Lightolier and Leucos, plus bulbs, shades and dimmers; the Amsterdam Avenue store is more traditional, but "good service and prices" keep respondents returning to both places; N.B. the Chelsea branch recently moved to the larger location listed above.

Lighting By Gregory

| | | | |
|24|16|19|M|

LES | 158 Bowery (bet. Broome & Delancey Sts.) | J/M/Z to Bowery | 212-226-1276 | 888-811-3267 | www.lightingbygregory.com

Supporters say it's "worth the trek" to the Bowery for this "fairly priced" lighting store's "great selection" of over 155 different lines ranging "from contemporary to traditional", plus ceiling fans; but while some are satisfied with the "knowledgeable" service, detractors take a dimmer view and dub the staff "surly."

☑ Ligne Roset

| | | | |
|28|25|21|VE|

Flatiron | 250 Park Ave. S. (bet. 19th & 20th Sts.) | 6 to 23rd St. | 212-375-1036
SoHo | 155 Wooster St. (Houston St.) | N/R/W to Prince St. | 212-253-5629
800-297-6738 | www.ligne-roset-usa.com

"Sleek" and "sexy" French home-furnishings stores in the Flatiron District and SoHo selling "beautiful" beds, tables, seating, accessories and other "first-rate quality designs" with "clean modern lines" but "without an icy cold attitude"; Antoine Roset founded the business in 1860, and today his grandsons oversee the production of "almost flawless" pieces at "very expensive" prices.

Lilith
                                                                    25 | 23 | 24 | E

NoLita | 227 Mulberry St. (bet. Prince & Spring Sts.) | 6 to Spring St. | 212-925-0080 | www.lilith.fr

Housed in a warm red NoLita boutique, this "French designer brand" by Lily Bareth includes "beautiful", "drapey", "cosmopolitan clothes", complete with "unusual cuts", "original" colors and "luxe fabrics"; the "attentive staff provides a high level of service" "for hip women of a certain age", "a certain style" and definitely "with deep pockets."

Lilliput
                                                                    - | - | - | E

NoLita | 265 Lafayette St. (bet. Prince & Spring Sts.) | 6 to Spring St. | 212-965-9567

SoHo | 240 Lafayette St. (bet. Prince & Spring Sts.) | 6 to Spring St. | 212-965-9201

www.lilliputsoho.com

Named for that land of little people in *Gulliver's Travels,* these sibling stores – situated a stone's throw across Lafayette – are filled to the gills with "cute" children's clothing, shoes and toys from all of the top brands; but neat freaks snap it's so cluttered that it "would be a miracle to find anything"; N.B. the 265 branch offers more newborn–toddler sizes.

Limited Too ❂
                                                                    16 | 16 | 14 | M

Kings Plaza | Kings Plaza Shopping Ctr. | 5301 Kings Plaza (Flatbush Ave. & Ave. U) | Brooklyn | 4 to Utica Ave. | 718-951-7830

Elmhurst | Queens Ctr. | 90-15 Queens Blvd. (bet. 57th & 59th Aves.) | Queens | G/R/V to Woodhaven Blvd. | 718-592-2857

Staten Island | Staten Island Mall | 2655 Richmond Ave. (bet. Platinum Ave. & Richmond Hill Rd.) | 718-698-6207

www.limitedtoo.com

A little slice of "tween heaven", these "always reliable" chain links are stuffed with "trendy", "well-priced" "cute disposables" including clothes, shoes, accessories and other "plastic delights" for the "budding fashionista" who changes or "outgrows her wardrobe every two weeks"; while a few grouches gripe of "crowded" conditions and "sloppy displays", most young girls love the "shrunken teen togs."

NEW Linda Derector M
                                                                    - | - | - | E

NoLita | 211 Mott St. (bet. Prince & Spring Sts.) | 6 to Spring St. | 212-680-3023

Even fashion visionaries may be blindsided by stylehound Linda Derector's sleek red NoLita nook featuring an expertly curated collection of vintage eyeglass frames and sunglasses from boldface and under-the-radar names dating back to the '60s along with covetable costume jewelry; channel your favorite silver-screen icon or rock star with purr-fect cat eye specs, Italian aviators and enormous '70s styles.

Linda Dresner ⬚
                                                            ∇ 25 | 21 | 23 | VE

E 50s | 484 Park Ave. (bet. 58th & 59th Sts.) | 4/5/6/F/N/R/W to 59th St./Lexington Ave. | 212-308-3177 | www.lindadresner.com

This pristine Park Avenue space provides the clarity for "NYC matrons" "who can afford" to contemplate and meditate on which Tuleh

dress, Viktor + Rolf blouse or Dsquared suit they might buy; the refined interior and tasteful selection of "classy choices" reveal the
sharp eye of owner Linda Dresner, who keeps her clientele "delighted
with everything about the experience and the purchase."

Lingerie on Lex   ▽ 24 | 20 | 22 | E

E 60s | 831 Lexington Ave. (bet. 63rd & 64th Sts.) | 6 to 68th St. |
212-755-3312

With a "wide selection" of mostly European lingerie, sleepwear and
hosiery from "popular" labels like Lise Charmel and La Perla, plus a
"sweet" staff, this Lexington lair is a favorite for the wedding-bound bent
on "big-ticket items" as well as those looking for "moderately priced"
"basics"; it's "small", but with "lots of storage", they'll "find your size."

Links of London   24 | 22 | 22 | E

E 40s | MetLife Bldg. | 200 Park Ave. (45th St.) | 4/5/6/7/S to 42nd St./
Grand Central | 212-867-0258 🗷
E 50s | 535 Madison Ave. (bet. 54th & 55th Sts.) | E/V to Lexington Ave./
53rd St. | 212-588-1177 🗷
SoHo | 402 W. Broadway (bet. Broome & Spring Sts.) | C/E to Spring St. |
212-343-8024
800-210-0079 | www.linksoflondon.com

It's the men's cuff links that inspired the name of this trio, but they also
offer gold and silver everyday jewelry for women and a wide array of
charms; supporters say its "reliable" quality makes it "good for gifts."

Lion in the Sun   24 | 20 | 21 | M

Park Slope | 232 Seventh Ave. (4th St.) | Brooklyn | F to 7th Ave. |
718-369-4006 | www.lioninthesunps.com

"Even better since their recent move to a more visible location" agree
paperie tigers who "love to impulse-buy their way through" this
"neighborly, friendly", family-owned Park Slope "treasure"; scribes
scope out the "lovely cards", "beautiful stationery" and gift items like
photo albums and scrapbooks while party-throwers and the nuptials-
bound order "creative" custom-printed invitations to the rear, attended
by a staff that's "helpful, but not too in-your-face."

NEW Lisa Levine Jewelry ●Ⓜ   - | - | - | E

Williamsburg | 536 Metropolitan Ave. (bet. Lorimer St. & Union Ave.) |
Brooklyn | G/L to Metropolitan Ave./Lorimer St. | 718-349-2824 |
www.lisalevinejewelry.com

The namesake designer's new store-cum-workroom in Williamsburg
displays her delicate silver, oxidized silver and gold jewelry; the clean,
organic shapes range from long hoop earrings to multirow necklaces,
some incorporating intricate miniaturized chains that may be
threaded with feathers or capped with a colored stone or coins.

Little Eric   25 | 21 | 24 | E

E 80s | 1118 Madison Ave. (bet. 83rd & 84th Sts.) | 4/5/6 to 86th St. |
212-717-1513

Put your kid's best foot forward at this East 80s stomping ground,
which boasts a "really nice assortment you may not see elsewhere"
from Italy including "first-time walkers", boots, loafers, sneakers,
Mary Janes and party shoes, in styles that span the spectrum from
"classic" to "avant-garde"; still, budget-minded shoppers turn up their
heels, quipping "they're only shoes, not Fabergé eggs."

	QUALITY	DISPLAY	SERVICE	COST

NEW **Little Stinkers Shoe Company** Ⓜ | – | – | – | M |

E Vill | 280 E. 10th St. (bet. Ave. A & 1st Ave.) | L to 1st Ave. | 212-253-0282

An alternative to pricey tot shops, this East Village newcomer takes the sticker shock out of shopping for kids' shoes by stocking wallet-friendly finds, ranging from Birkenstock sandals and Minnetonka moccasins to Kidorable rain boots and Bobux baby booties; while parents peruse the American kicks, their little stinkers – er, kids – keep busy digging through old-fashioned metal buckets filled with wooden airplanes, whoopee cushions and other toys and trinkets.

Living on Fifth ◐ | – | – | – | M |

Park Slope | 327 Fifth Ave. (bet. 3rd & 4th Sts.) | Brooklyn | F to 7th Ave. | 718-499-0098

Living on Seventh

Park Slope | 219 Seventh Ave. (bet. 3rd & 4th Sts.) | Brooklyn | F to 7th Ave. | 718-788-1651

Living on Smith Ⓜ

Carroll Gdns | 289 Smith St. (bet. Sackett & Union Sts.) | Brooklyn | F/G to Carroll St. | 718-222-8546

Nearly everything you need for nesting with flair can be found at this hip Park Slope–Carroll Gardens lifestyle trio chock-full of home furnishings and women's casualwear; accent your pad with handcrafted vases and ceramics, mod lamps, decorative pillows and custom-made rugs, then treat yourself to Calypso sweaters, Claus Porto candles and soaps and Cosabella undies; N.B. the Smith Street original and the Fifth Avenue offshoot concentrate more on clothing.

Livi's Lingerie | ▽ 20 | 7 | 24 | M |

E 80s | 1456 Third Ave. (bet. 82nd & 83rd Sts.) | 4/5/6 to 86th St. | 212-879-2050

Owner "Livi is a legend" declare devotees of this "old-fashioned corsetiere" who can "tell you're a 34B from one block away" – or from the "tight quarters" of her East 80s shop where her staff will also "take time" with you; designer and specialty lingerie, including bodyshapers, are at your fingertips, but you'll have to "ask for the racey stuff."

Liz Lange Maternity | 23 | 24 | 23 | VE |

E 70s | 958 Madison Ave. (bet. 75th & 76th Sts.) | 6 to 77th St. | 212-879-2191 | 888-616-5777 | www.lizlange.com

One trip to the namesake designer's Madison Avenue boutique and "you'll keep your style during nine tough months" proclaim pregnant patrons who pay "high prices" for "fabulous-looking" jeans, tailored trousers, blouses and suits that are "great for working moms"; most praise the "intelligent" staff that "understands what you're going through", but a "disappointed" few find "nothing special."

L'Occitane ◐ | 25 | 24 | 22 | E |

SoHo | 92 Prince St. (Mercer St.) | N/R/W to Prince St. | 212-219-3310 | www.loccitane.com

Additional locations throughout the NY area

Provençal phenomenon with a "European-meadow vibe" purveying "high-qualtiy soaps, creams and candles", whose supporters single out "the excellent shea butter products"; still, snobs sniff "it was better when it didn't seem to be in every mall in the country."

| | QUALITY | DISPLAY | SERVICE | COST |

Lockes Diamonds
- | - | - | VE

E 60s | 683A Madison Ave. (bet. 61st & 62nd Sts.) | 4/5/6/F/N/R/W to 59th St./Lexington Ave. | 212-756-9912 | www.lockesdiamonds.com

This family-owned diamond retail store with a flagship on Madison Avenue starts at the beginning, educating customers about the stones, then offers a range of classic to contemporary designs to choose from or lets you create your own custom piece.

☑ Loehmann's ●
20 | 11 | 9 | M

Chelsea | 101 Seventh Ave. (bet. 16th & 17th Sts.) | 1 to 18th St. | 212-352-0856
Bronx | 5740 Broadway (236th St.) | 1 to 238th St. | 718-543-6420
Coney Is | 2807 E. 21st St. (Emmons Ave.) | Brooklyn | Q to Sheepshead Bay | 718-368-1256
www.loehmanns.com

"Don't put that sweater down, even for an instant" lest you lose it amid the "garage-sale atmosphere" of this chainster where insiders beat a path to the Back Room for the "bonanza of bargains" on designers "from Jean-Paul Gaultier to Anne Klein"; the communal dressing rooms are "like boarding school, with lots of sharing", and if the "lack of service" leaves fans lamenting it's "not like the old days", most maintain it still delivers "damn good" deals; N.B. a West 70s link is slated to open in spring 2007.

Longchamp
26 | 23 | 21 | E

E 60s | 713 Madison Ave. (bet. 63rd & 64th Sts.) | 6 to 68th St. | 212-223-1500 🗷
NEW • SoHo | 132 Spring St. (bet. Greene & Wooster Sts.) | 6 to Spring St. | 212-343-7444
866-566-4242 | www.longchamp.com

Addicts of this Paris-based line's Le Pliage bag "buy a new color every year" even though the "always-in-style" lightweight nylon totes "great for traveling" hold up so "fabulously" you can wear one "from now to eternity"; this Madison Avenue "favorite" offers "fashionable" accessories, a "can't-be-beat repair policy" and a staff of champs "willing to go that "extra mile" – and the recently opened SoHo flagship offers even more of the same – plus a new collection of womenswear.

Loom ●
▽ 23 | 19 | 21 | M

Park Slope | 109A Seventh Ave. (bet. Carroll & President Sts.) | Brooklyn | B/Q to 7th Ave.
Park Slope | 115 Seventh Ave. (bet. Carroll & President Sts.) | Brooklyn | B/Q to 7th Ave.
718-789-0061

"You're sure to find that little gift you need" for everyone from "babies to grandmothers" at this "friendly", modern Park Slope stop that fills its birch-wood shelves with "reliably funky" wares, from "fun handbags" in unique colors, to unusual jewelry, soaps, candles, home accessories, toys and "great cards"; N.B. the tiny offshoot at 109A Seventh Avenue sells women's clothing from labels like Ella Moss and Velvet.

NEW Loopy Mango ●Ⓜ
- | - | - | E

Dumbo | 117 Front St. (bet. Adams & Washington Sts.) | Brooklyn | F to York St. | 718-858-5930

(continued)

(continued)

NEW Loopy Mango

Dumbo | 68 Jay St. (bet. Front & Water Sts.) | Brooklyn | F to York St. | 718-222-0595
www.loopymango.com

There's nothing loopy about the "one-of-a-kind garments" at this Dumbo duo, which savvy owners have made into a fashion maven's must-go; the Jay Street branch offers the "most amazing" new and vintage womenswear, while "their newer store on Front Street", with its "really cool" decor of gold-framed mirrors and antique furniture (also for sale), specializes in über-feminine, fresh party dresses and eclectic workwear; all's "well worth the prices", because you'll "get tons of compliments on anything you buy."

☑ Lord & Taylor ❶   22 | 20 | 19 | M

Murray Hill | 424 Fifth Ave. (bet. 38th & 39th Sts.) | 4/5/6/7/S to 42nd St./Grand Central | 212-391-3344 | 800-223-7440 | www.lordandtaylor.com

"One of the last of the old-guard NY department stores", "focusing on American-made products", this "quiet" Murray Hill "mainstay" "contains level after level of clothing and accessories for men, women and children"; while it's trying "to accommodate younger looks", "people perceive it as fuddy-duddy" – perhaps because many styles reflect "not high fashion, but good middle-of-the-road taste"; still, if you need "professional" garb, "classic" shoes or ("pardon the oxymoron") "the biggest petite section", this "grande dame" "is a great place to find something that fits and is probably marked-down"; P.S. "don't miss the Christmas windows."

Lord of the Fleas ❶   15 | 14 | 15 | I

W 70s | 2142 Broadway (75th St.) | 1/2/3/B/C to 72nd St. | 212-875-8815

"A blast of a store" confide Flea fanatics of this West 70s teen magnet, who concur that "with a little digging" you'll find that "exact thing" you don't need, but "fall in love with" because it's so "unexpectedly cool" and "doesn't cost a fortune"; the inventory turns over constantly so it's "just plain fun" to browse often, but remember, it can also be "hit-or-miss."

NEW Lord Willy's Ⓜ   – | – | – | E

NoLita | 223 Mott St. (bet. Prince & Spring Sts.) | B/D to Grand St. | 212-680-8888 | www.lordwillys.com

Owners Alex and Betty Wilcox and their two Jack Russell terriers hold court in this NoLita matchbook-size wonder, which produces bespoke, English-tailored suits and coats in vintage wools; signature three-button-cuff or French cuff men's shirts in "bold designs" and hues line the tasteful interior, with a few inches devoted to candy-colored ties (matching boxers available); hot lads hail it as all "good, if pretentious" – though "if you're not a *GQ*-er, skip it."

☑ Loro Piana Ⓢ   29 | 25 | 23 | VE

E 60s | 821 Madison Ave. (bet. 68th & 69th Sts.) | 6 to 68th St. | 212-980-7961 | www.loropiana.com

Catering to the "oh-so-affluent" with a variety of "luxurious fibers", this Upper East Side brick-front shop carries "cashmere that will ruin you for anyone else's", be it in the shape of "gorgeous" his-and-hers sweaters, "a bit staid" "but eminently wearable sportswear", home furnishings and even game boards; admittedly, the staff can seem "disinterested" at times, and "prices are steep – but better [to buy] one fabulous piece than 10 mediocre ones."

Louis Vuitton

QUALITY	DISPLAY	SERVICE	COST
27	27	22	VE

E 50s | 1 E. 57th St. (5th Ave.) | N/R/W to 5th Ave./59th St. | 212-758-8877
SoHo | 116 Greene St. (bet. Prince & Spring Sts.) | N/R/W to Prince St. | 212-274-9090
866-884-8866 | www.vuitton.com

Vuitton vixens "swear by" the world's biggest, "never-to-be-topped" luxury brand designed by Marc Jacobs, which "has grown with the times" by ensuring its "simply stunning" flagship on 57th Street and SoHo sister are "dream-come-true" draws for stars like Uma Thurman and Salma Hayek; you "feel like royalty" ogling the "to-die-for" rich-girl garb, "impeccable" menswear, collectible purses "costing more than a car" and leather goods that "last a lifetime (and maybe even your daughter's too)"; while some voters lament the "logo overload" and slam the "snooty-to-anyone-not-a-celebrity" salespeople, the consensus is "everyone should own a piece" of Louis.

Lounge ●

QUALITY	DISPLAY	SERVICE	COST
19	21	15	E

SoHo | 593 Broadway (bet. Houston & Prince Sts.) | N/R/W to Prince St. | 212-226-7585 | www.loungesoho.com

"Come for the music, the fun and the cool setup" say the "wealthy tee-nyboppers" who frequent SoHo's "large multifloor" lifestyle store offering an "eclectic mix of labels" from Sacred Blue and Junk Food to True Religion and Antik Denim; troll through the fringe-y CD bar and "listen to music", "get a drink" in the Casablanca tearoom, a trim in the hair salon or shop till you drop during the sales – otherwise, the "trendy-to-the-max" merchandise will max out your credit line.

NEW Love Brigade ● ⊠ Ⓜ

QUALITY	DISPLAY	SERVICE	COST
–	–	–	E

Williamsburg | 103 Havemeyer St. (bet. Grand & Hope Sts.) | Brooklyn | L to Bedford Ave. | 718-715-0430 | www.lovebrigade.com

Just off Williamsburg's main drag sits the fledgling flagship of this U.K. label, which makes slightly "ghoulish", but still "pretty clothes with an edgy twist", like heart-pocketed skinny jeans and fur vests for rock 'n' roll babes, and arty tees with 'soul-dier' or aorta appliqués for their tattooed bandmates; while the staff is "friendly and helpful", some find the shop hours erratic, so call before trooping over.

Loveday31 Ⓜ

QUALITY	DISPLAY	SERVICE	COST
–	–	–	M

Astoria | 33-06 31st. Ave. (bet. 33rd & 34th Sts.) | Queens | N/W to 30th Ave. | 718-728-4057

"Manhattanites are just discovering" this "small" boutique in Astoria, a vintage-challenged neighborhood – until now; the owner, a "former Screaming Mimi's buyer, knows her stuff", picking the perfect dresses, coats, tops and accessories for guys and dolls", including a floor-to-ceiling tower of belts.

Love Saves The Day ●

QUALITY	DISPLAY	SERVICE	COST
17	18	15	M

E Vill | 119 Second Ave. (7th St.) | 6 to Astor Pl. | 212-228-3802

"Still kooky after all these years" (41, to be exact), this "cluttered" East Village venue for "vintage toys, dolls", games, "cool" collectibles and clothing (plus gag gifts) remains "the perfect store for a rainy day"; even if "funky" isn't your forte, "it's worth going in and just looking around" the "narrow, tight aisles and display cases of memorabilia" guaranteed to "make you kick yourself for not saving the metal lunch box you had when growing up."

Lowell/Edwards 🗷   `-` `-` `-` `E`

E 50s | D&D Bldg. | 979 Third Ave., 5th fl. (bet. 58th & 59th Sts.) | 4/5/6/F/N/R/W to 59th St./Lexington Ave. | 212-980-2862 | 800-778-7249 | www.lowelledwards.com

Audio-visual design meets interior design at this sleek showroom cocooned on the fifth floor of the Upper East Side's D&D Building that attracts celebs and Fortune 500 types; it specializes in classy custom cabinetry that exposes exotic electronics with the click of a button, as well as "top-end" home theaters replete with nine-ft. screens and room-shaking speakers.

Lower East Side Tenement Museum   `21` `19` `21` `M`
(Home Economics)

LES | 90 Orchard St. (Broome St.) | B/D to Grand St. | 212-387-0341 | www.tenement.org

"Access your inner immigrant" at this "charming store" "across the street from the Lower East Side Tenement Museum" offering "an eclectic presentation" of "nostalgic household items"("terrific Depression glass", "neat old china"), plus new novelties (candles, cards, etc.); the staff gives "the impression they're not there to make money, but to remind you of a long-forgotten time"; P.S. the museum Visitor Center a few doors up also sells a "thoughtful collection of historically themed gifts, books and toys."

Lowe's ●   `21` `19` `17` `M`

Gowanus | 118 Second Ave. (Hamilton Pl.) | Brooklyn | F/G to Smith/9th Sts. | 718-249-1151
Staten Island | 2171 Forest Ave. (bet. Grandview Ave. & Samuel Pl.) | 718-682-9027
800-445-6937 | www.lowes.com

"Blows Home Depot away with a helpful staff" "you don't have to search for", "easy-to-navigate" aisles and "variety" vow "DIY sorts" wowed by this "more civilized" "welcome alternative" chain with links in Gowanus and Staten Island; decorate or "build your house and find all the supplies" you need, from hammers and hasps to "small appliances, home furnishings and organizing products"; still, a handful wish there was "more lumber and real construction hardware" in stock and insist "service depends on which employee you ask."

Luca Luca   `25` `24` `25` `VE`

E 60s | 690 Madison Ave. (62nd St.) | 4/5/6/F/N/R/W to 59th St./Lexington Ave. | 212-753-2444
E 70s | 1011 Madison Ave. (78th St.) | 6 to 77th St. | 212-288-9285
www.lucaluca.com

"Sexy, yet appropriate; fun, but timeless", this Italian "favorite" designed by Luca Orlandi – whose front-row fans include Mary J. Blige and the Williams twins – specializes in dresses for "big galas" in brocade, taffeta and chiffon, as well as "feminine, comfortable" suits that Luca "great for work"; some say the wares are "pricey, even for Madison Avenue", but an "extremely friendly" staff helps offset sticker shock.

Lucien Pellat-Finet

-	-	-	VE

G Vill | 14 Christopher St. (Gay St.) | 1 to Christopher St./Sheridan Sq. |
212-255-8560 | www.lucienpellat-finet.com

Sporting "cutting-edge" intarsias with hemp-leaf, dollar-sign and skull-and-crossbones designs, the "best-quality sweaters around" abound at this art-filled Greenwich Village shop, which also offers luxe bed covers, belts and silk umbrellas, all in luscious candy colors or Gothic hues; they don't call this designer 'the king of cashmere' for nothing, but the "unbelievable prices" mean you better cash in the crown jewels before you arrive.

Lucky Brand Jeans ⬤

23	21	22	E

E 60s | 1151 Third Ave. (67th St.) | 6 to 68th St. | 646-422-1192
Flatiron | 172 Fifth Ave. (22nd St.) | N/R/W to 23rd St. |
917-606-1418
SoHo | 38 Greene St. (Grand St.) | A/C/E to Canal St. | 212-625-0707
NEW **SoHo** | 535 Broadway (Spring St.) | 6 to Spring St. | 212-680-0130
W 70s | 216 Columbus Ave. (70th St.) | 1/2/3 to 72nd St. | 212-579-1760
800-964-5777 | www.luckybrandjeans.com

For "great-looking", "well-fitting" "made in the USA" jeans that suit "everyone from the bird-legged bean pole" guy to the "luscious, curvy" hottie aiming for a "rock-chick-meets-new-country" look, "steer" over to this national chain; let the "easygoing" "urban cow"-hands round you up a pair, plus other items designed with "good taste", and you'll agree it's "worth the extra cost for how great your butt looks."

NEW Lucky Kid ⬤

-	-	-	E

SoHo | 127 Prince St. (Wooster St.) | N/R/W to Prince St. |
212-466-0849 | 800-964-5777 | www.luckybrandjeans.com

SoHo browsers who have the good fortune to stumble upon Lucky Brand Jeans' new sibling for pint-sized trendsetters are rewarded with a cool-looking shop decorated with green-and-white leaf frond-patterned wallpaper and whimsical window displays; lucky kids, from babies to toddlers to children up to size 10, hit pay dirt with funky, laid-back looks including rocker tees, hoodies, leggings, denim jackets and jeans.

Lucky Wang

▽ 25	22	19	E

Chelsea | 82 Seventh Ave. (bet. 15th & 16th Sts.) | 1/2/3 to 14th St. |
212-229-2900
G Vill | 799 Broadway (bet. 10th & 11th Sts.) | 4/5/6/L/N/Q/R/W to
14th St./Union Sq. | 212-353-2850
866-353-2850 | www.luckywang.com

"At last!" sigh the fortunate few who've happened upon this Greenwich Village–Chelsea twosome where the "adorable" Asian-inspired kiddie creations on tap, from miniature kimonos packaged sushi-style to printed tees and tinsel coin purses, come in "wonderful colors"; with such "funky-chic" finds, the only hitch is that there "isn't enough" of the stuff in the smaller Broadway original.

Lucy Barnes

-	-	-	E

Meatpacking | 320 W. 14th St. (bet. 8th & 9th Aves.) | A/C/E/L to
14th St./8th Ave. | 212-255-9148 | www.lucybarnes.biz

"We love Lucy" avow the arty aficionados who applaud this Scottish designer's "feminine, yet edgy clothes for all body types"; at her sparkling shop in the Meatpacking District, period '70s chandeliers shine down on handcrafted corsets, silk party skirts, accessories and embroidered jeans whose vintage fabrics or detailing make them "amazing buys for the money."

Ludivine ● | - | - | - | E |

G Vill | 172 W. Fourth St. (Jones St.) | A/B/C/D/E/F/V to W. 4th St. | 646-336-6576 | www.boutiqueludivine.com

Parisienne to the core, this Greenwich Village find has light pink walls that serve as a feminine backdrop for insouciant styles that are somewhat reminiscent of what actress Julie Delpy wore in *Before Sunset* while marathon-chatting with Ethan Hawke; along with Les Prairies de Paris' strictly tailored coats, Tsumori Chisato's boldly printed dresses and Vanessa Bruno's floaty camis, you'll find shoes and totes to round out the *c'est magnifique* chic of owner Ludivine Gregoire's divine taste.

Luilei ● | - | - | - | E |

Park Slope | 682 Union St., 2nd fl. (5th Ave.) | Brooklyn | M/R to Union St. | 718-399-7799 | www.luileiny.com

For grooming groupies and beauty buffs long bewildered by Park Slope's paucity of potions, this neighborhoody apothecary – an airy expanse perched above Union Street – feels like a mini-Manhattan dream come true; treat yourself to niche brands including cosmetics from Hourglass, home fragrances from Anthousa, perfume from Aftelier, Child, i Profumi di Firenze and Yosh and skincare from Ren, and if you're curious about an unfamiliar indie, ask for a pre-purchase sample.

NEW Lulu Castagnette | - | - | - | M |

NoLita | 244 Mulberry St. (Prince St.) | 6 to Spring St. | 212-226-7044 | www.lulucastagnette.com

Amélie-wannabes, both young and old, feel right at home *chez* Lulu, a confection of a shop in the heart of NoLita; bubble-gum pink reigns in sweet tees, pleated kilts and lacy starter bras for *jeune filles* ("love the clothes for my nieces"), alongside *très* chic knit tunics, fitted denim and trendy print blouses for 21st-century Catherine Deneuves; be prepared for your *petite coquette* to beg for a Lulu teddy bear too.

Lulu Guinness | 24 | 25 | 19 | E |

W Vill | 394 Bleecker St. (bet. Perry & W. 11th Sts.) | 1 to Christopher St./ Sheridan Sq. | 212-367-2120 | www.luluguinness.com

"What a hoot" – "how can you not love" this "British eccentric's" "fabulously" "quirky" handbags, shoes, makeup cases and umbrellas, all showcased at her "funky", "friendly" West Village shop boasting "great window displays"; the "whimsical contents" are the "perfect" "pick-me-up" – like "a breath of fresh air on a hot summer day" – but the willpower-less should beware a lulu of a bill as they may "spend lots of money for lots of fun."

NEW LuLuLemon Athletica | - | - | - | E |

TriBeCa | 145 Chambers St. (W. B'way) | 1/2/3 to Chambers St. | 212-732-0511
W 60s | 1928 Broadway (64th St.) | 1 to 66th St./Lincoln Ctr. | 212-712-1767 ●
www.lululemon.com

Guy and gal yoginis with a yen for Zen essentials zone in on ultra-fashionable down-dog-wear and cycling and running garb too at this

Canadian company's West 60s flagship and TriBeCa offshoot inside Naga Yoga studio; the colorful, dry wick cropped pants, leggings, sweats, fitted hoodies, tights, tanks, even tunics flatter the bod with the extra boost of organic and natural fabrics.

L'Uomo ❿

▽ 24 | 21 | 20 | VE

W Vill | 383 Bleecker St. (Perry St.) | 1 to Christopher St./Sheridan Sq. | 212-206-1844

As one might deduce from the name, which translates from Italian as 'the man', most of the slightly "avant-garde" offerings at this West Village boutique come with a distinctly Euro bent; choose from a selection of Hugo Boss, CP and Stone Island or, if indecision strikes, the "owner knows what looks good on everyone."

Lush ❿

23 | 23 | 22 | M

Garment Dist | 1293 Broadway (bet. 33rd & 34th Sts.) | B/D/F/N/Q/R/V/W to 34th St./Herald Sq. | 212-564-9120

W 70s | 2165 Broadway (bet. 76th & 77th Sts.) | 1 to 79th St. | 212-787-5874

NEW **Elmhurst** | Queens Ctr. | 90-15 Queens Blvd. (bet. 57th & 59th Aves.) | Queens | G/R/V to Grand Ave./Newtown | 718-699-8969
www.lush.com

"The best British import since the Beatles" cheer fans of these "funky, playful" chain links where "quirky" "handmade toiletries" like Guinness shampoo, Vegan Karma soap and famous Bath Bombs in "flavors you'd never think of" like Bollywood (coconut, orange and ginger) are stacked in colorful "deli-style displays"; but delicate types decry "gimmicky" products and "smelly", "overpowering" premises that "assault the senses."

Lyell

– | – | – | E

NoLita | 173 Elizabeth St. (bet. Kenmare & Spring Sts.) | J/M/Z to Bowery | 212-966-8484 | www.lyellnyc.com

Emma Fletcher pleases ladylike stylesetters who like a hint of nostalgia in their sexy and sheer black dresses, a dash of retro-daring in a flutter-sleeved blouse and a touch of silver-screen class in a cinched-waist jacket; with its delicate 1940s-era wallpaper and tiled floor, her pearl of a shop on the SoHo-NoLita border picks up the hip, yet old-fashioned vibe of her femme-fabulous designs.

⊠ Lyric Hi-Fi, Inc. ⊠

28 | 25 | 23 | VE

E 80s | 1221 Lexington Ave. (bet. 82nd & 83rd Sts.) | 4/5/6 to 86th St. | 212-439-1900 | www.lyricusa.com

Enter "the inner sanctuary for high-end sound and video" at this "conservative" yet state-of-the-art store on the UES; some say the audio "high priests" on staff "can be forbidding", but beyond that "stuffy" facade awaits "expert" advice and "outstanding recommendations" on "top-tier" equipment, the likes of which has even seduced Bill Clinton.

M.A.C. Cosmetics

26 | 24 | 20 | M

Flatiron | Flatiron Bldg. | 1 E. 22nd St. (B'way) | N/R/W to 23rd St. | 212-677-6611 ❿

Harlem | 202 W. 125th St. (bet. Adam Clayton Powell & Frederick Douglass Blvds.) | A/B/C/D to 125th St. | 212-665-0676 ❿

SoHo | 113 Spring St. (bet. Greene & Mercer Sts.) | 6 to Spring St. | 212-334-4641

(continued)

(continued)

M.A.C. Cosmetics

W 60s | 148 Columbus Ave. (bet. 66th & 67th Sts.) | 1 to 66th St./ Lincoln Ctr. | 212-769-0725 ●

Brooklyn Hts | 152 Montague St. (bet. Clinton & Henry Sts.) | Brooklyn | A/C/F to Jay St./Borough Hall | 718-596-1994 ●

800-387-6707 | www.maccosmetics.com

"Once you go M.A.C. you don't go back" maintain mavens of this makeup chain "mecca" that attracts actors, artists and drag queens alike with "a vast array" of products in a "rainbow of colors" that "last long and wear well" at "prices that will not break your budget"; however, service is "highly variable" as some of the staffers seem "too self-obsessed to actually serve customers", while others apply "clown"-quality cosmetic jobs.

Z MacKenzie-Childs   25 | 27 | 22 | E

E 50s | 14 W. 57th St. (bet. 5th & 6th Aves.) | N/R/W to 5th Ave./59th St. | 212-570-6050 | 888-665-1999 | www.mackenzie-childs.com

It's a "visual frenzy" at this Midtown purveyor of clashingly colored and patterned ceramics, painted furniture and other "feminine and frilly" products for the home like ramekins that resemble cupcakes, black-and-white check fondue sets and "quirky" chairs decorated with fish; the "very expensive" "eye candy" here has its admirers, but cynics sniff "wasn't this a fad whose time has passed?"

Z Macy's ●   19 | 15 | 12 | M

Garment Dist | 151 W. 34th St. (bet. B'way & 7th Ave.) | 1/2/3/A/C/E to 34th St./Penn Station | 212-695-4400 | 800-343-0121 | www.macys.com
Additional locations throughout the NY area

You can do "all your shopping under one roof" at this block-long "Herald Square landmark", "riding the old wooden escalators" to peruse the "affordable accessories", "a corridor of cool" cookware, "a nice variety" of cosmetics and clothing and "good bets in beds and mattresses"; "if you can't find it here, you're not looking hard enough" – but look hard you will, given "too many tourists", "mostly non-helpful help" and "chaotic" aisles; cynics sigh "if only Macy's ran its store like it runs the Thanksgiving Day parade" – still, even though it's "often maddening", NYC "couldn't live without it."

NEW Madura   24 | 25 | 21 | E

E 80s | 1162 Madison Ave. (bet. 85th & 86th Sts.) | 4/5/6 to 86th St. | 212-327-2681 | www.madurahome.com

This family-owned French firm makes an "excellent addition to home stores on the Upper East Side" by offering "well-presented" and "colorful" ready-made curtains with "coordinated household items" like blinds, bedspreads, pillows and tablecloths that are not your "typical" "Bed Bath & Beyond" look; the "helpful" and "efficient" staff enables you to navigate the somewhat "complicated" concept.

Magic Windows   27 | 20 | 19 | E

E 80s | 1186 Madison Ave. (87th St.) | 4/5/6 to 86th St. | 212-289-0028 | www.magic-windows.com

"If you want to drop a bundle on your little bundle", this "Upper East Side institution" has "got it all"; no high-fashion hocus-pocus here, just "ducky duds" that range from "high-quality" layette pieces to "adorable" "special-occasion" outfits for girls and "very European boys stuff" to dreamy prom dresses for your teen; still, a handful huff that the "sales staff could lower their noses a notch."

Maison Martin Margiela
- | - | - | VE

W Vill | 803 Greenwich St. (bet. Jane & W. 12th Sts.) | A/C/E/L to 14th St./8th Ave. | 212-989-7612 | www.maisonmartinmargiela.com
"The quintessential *enfant terrible* of fashion finally gets an outpost to showcase his exquisitely constructed pieces of art" – deceptively simple designs boasting unexpected details like snipped banding, raw edges and asymmetrical closures; the presentation in the sign-free Village building is "reflective of the Margiela image" (bright lights, all-white and off-kilter), and while some giggle at the "wacked-out" womenswear, it's "well worth the bankruptcy" to those who believe in "inspirational, not aspirational" clothing.

Make Up For Ever Ⓜ
▽ 28 | - | 20 | M

G Vill | 8 E. 12th St. (bet. 5th Ave. & University Pl.) | 4/5/6/L/N/Q/R/W to 14th St./Union Sq. | 212-941-9337 | 877-757-5175
Geared to "the professional makeup artist as well as the everyday girl or boy", the cosmetics at this "user-friendly" store (which recently moved from SoHo to Greenwich Village) boast "high amounts of pigment and lots of staying power" – maybe not enough to last forever but supporters swear sufficient "to last all night long without turning funny or runny."

Maleeka
- | - | - | M

Downtown | 327 Atlantic Ave. (bet. Hoyt & Smith Sts.) | Brooklyn | F/G to Bergen St. | 718-596-0991 | www.maleeka.com
With its entrancing windows and cabinets filled with glittering jewelry, ornamented slippers and sumptuous coverlets, this bright spot on Atlantic Avenue may evoke the vibrancy of a Bollywood flick – but there's more to the picture; insiders focus on the fashionable pedigree of lines like Aoyama Itchome, along with brocade coats from Julie Haus, Spy Exchange's deconstructed jackets and Rangoon's fringed capelets.

Malia Mills Swimwear
26 | 21 | 23 | E

E 70s | 1031 Lexington Ave. (bet. 73rd & 74th Sts.) | 6 to 77th St. | 212-517-7485 🏁
NoLita | 199 Mulberry St. (bet. Kenmare & Spring Sts.) | 6 to Spring St. | 212-625-2311
W 70s | 220 Columbus Ave. (70th St.) | 1/2/3 to 72nd St. | 212-874-7200
800-685-3479 | www.maliamills.com
"Bathing suit shopping has been redesigned" at this eponymous designer's trio where the "dreaded experience of trying on bikinis" becomes an opportunity "to make any woman feel good" about her "unique" shape; the "mix-and-match" selection "flatters" "different" bodies, even "lumpy" ones, plus the "warm staff" further "justifies" the "expensive" prices, helping you "find just the right top and bottom" in "lovely colors" and "fabrics that hold up nicely."

Malin + Goetz ●
▽ 22 | 24 | 23 | E

Chelsea | 177 Seventh Ave. (bet. 20th & 21st Sts.) | 1 to 23rd St. | 212-727-3777 | www.malinandgoetz.com
Matthew Malin (ex Kiehl's) and Andrew Goetz's "real up-and-coming-brand" of "high-quality" unisex face, body and haircare products has

"such nice packaging" that "you almost hate to break the seal", but once you do the "goods are incomparable" – especially the eucalyptus scrub seen in many an upscale Manhattan bathroom; the futuristic, all-white Chelsea space also features a lab on the premises, which adds to its modern apothecary aura.

M&J Trimming ⊠

25	19	20	M

Garment Dist | 1000-1010 Sixth Ave. (bet. 37th & 38th Sts.) | B/D/F/N/Q/R/V/W to 34th St./Herald Sq. | 212-204-9595 | 800-965-8746 | www.mjtrim.com

Do-it-yourselfers "drool over the choices" at this 71-year-old Garment District "candy store for trimmings" that "looks like it was designed by Willy Wonka", with "zillions" of "colorful, enticing" ribbons, crystals, "beads, buttons and notions" stacked all the way up to the 30-ft. ceiling; ok, it's "not inexpensive but it's certainly consumer-friendly", since "everything's easy to find" and the "knowledgeable", "non-harassing staff" "allows you to wander while you envision your creations."

Manhattan Center for Kitchen & Bath

-	-	-	E

Flatiron | 29 E. 19th St. (bet. B'way & Park Ave.) | N/R/W to 23rd St. | 212-995-0500 | www.mckb.com

This "beautiful" 10,000-sq.-ft., two-story showroom in the Flatiron District features products from over 84 manufacturers, including the highly coveted Euro brands Aga and Liebherr, in categories ranging from high-end appliances and custom cabinetry to tile and stone, plumbing fixtures and home theater equipment; the megalith is a joint venture between Brooklyn's Drimmers and Kitchen Expressions.

Manhattan Saddlery ⊠

-	-	-	E

Gramercy | 117 E. 24th St. (bet. Lexington & Park Aves.) | 6 to 23rd St. | 212-673-1400 | www.manhattansaddlery.com

Saddle up and run for the roses at this Gramercy haunt, a standby since 1912 where equestrian enthusiasts pony up greenbacks aplenty for stylish barnyard fashions from jodhpurs, bridles and tack to outfits for the track; there's no need to be a horse whisperer, though, since helpful "salespeople" will take you by the reins and "spend" plenty of time guiding you to the best for fox hunts, steeplechases and polo matches.

⊿ Manolo Blahnik ⊠

28	28	24	VE

W 50s | 31 W. 54th St. (bet. 5th & 6th Aves.) | E/V to 5th Ave./53rd St. | 212-582-3007

"Carrie Bradshaw made us all dream" about investing in "foot candy" with "fabulously high heels" from the Midtown "house of the famous and expensive" designer shoes, but "even if you're not sexy and single", "true shoe addicts" insist "you'll glide on air when you slip into" the "ultimate" "must-have" stilettos; "depleting my Swiss bank account never felt so good" – "every woman should experience the royal treatment of shopping" at this "pinnacle" of "luxury" – does there "live a dame who wouldn't if she could"?

Marc and Max ◐

-	-	-	E

W Vill | 342 Bleecker St. (bet. Christopher & W. 10th Sts.) | 1 to Christopher St./Sheridan Sq. | 212-647-1688

This petite and unpretentious West Village shop is well-stocked with lingerie and loungewear from the likes of Cosabella, Huit, Princess

Tam Tam and Wolford, including racks of camisoles so stylish you may not want to hide them under your clothing; a small selection of fine jewelry, candles and glamorously old-fashioned high-heeled slippers make it a perfect girlie stop when shopping on the Bleecker Street strip.

Marc by Marc Jacobs ◐

	25	24	20	E

W Vill | 403-5 Bleecker St. (W. 11th St.) | 1 to Christopher St./
Sheridan Sq. | 212-924-0026 | www.marcjacobs.com

Those jonesin' for some Jacobs start off at these "trendy-to-the-max" adjoining men's and women's stores on Bleecker Street to get a taste of the "cute clothes, cute bags, cute everything" from this beloved designer's "colorful and fresh" diffusion line; the staff "is such fun" that the "serious prices come as a bit of a shock", but guys and "girls with a sense of humor" are "hooked" on these "quirky" re-Marc-able pieces.

Marc by Marc Jacobs Accessories ◑

	28	26	21	E

W Vill | 385 Bleecker St. (Perry St.) | 1 to Christopher St./Sheridan Sq. | 212-924-6126 | www.marcjacobs.com

"Love is all I can say!" avow acolytes who anoint this boldface designer the "god of accessories" and covet his "cherished" bags, truly the "holy grail for fashionistas"; you'll "want everything" at Bleecker Street's "funky yet chic" "hipster heaven" (oftentimes boasting "terrific windows" that make political points) because the shoes, gloves, leather goods and perfumes are also the "most lovely of lovelies" and "worth every penny"; N.B. it now exclusively carries the Marc by Marc Jacobs line, which may outdate the scores.

Marc Jacobs

	27	25	20	VE

SoHo | 163 Mercer St. (bet. Houston & Prince Sts.) | N/R/W to Prince St. | 212-343-1490 | www.marcjacobs.com

On your Marc, get set, go to this "cool, casual mecca" in SoHo "for all things achingly hip and modern with a vintage twist" from the designer whose "amazing" American sportswear is defined as "the epitome of NYC chic" by "tall, skinny supermodels" and "very, very rich skater dudes"; housing both mens- and womenswear, the loftlike space is "a great place to blow your rent", although some say you may "need a raise and cosmetic surgery to be comfortable shopping here" ("unless you're a movie star, don't expect any service").

Marie-Chantal 🖼

	25	24	17	VE

E 80s | 1192 Madison Ave. (bet. 87th & 88th Sts.) | 4/5/6 to 86th St. | 212-828-7300 | www.mariechantal.com

"Cute setup, cute clothing" characterizes this quaint East 80s boutique, home to the Greek Princess and über-socialite/shopper Marie-Chantal's children's collection; her designs slow down the hands of time with "*très* chic", age-appropriate fashions that actually let kids be kids; so even if the staff exhibits some "attitude from hell" and the "exquisite" garb costs a king's ransom, your offspring will feel like royalty.

Mariko 🖼

	–	–	–	E

E 70s | 998 Madison Ave. (bet. 77th & 78th Sts.) | 6 to 77th St. | 212-472-1176 | www.marikopalmbeach.com

Several generations of Upper East Side blue bloods and social climbers alike have relied on this costume-jewelry shop for its stash of pedigreed and pricey "knockoffs", from fake pearl ropes and beaded chokers to very Schlumberger-like enamel bangles and Verdura-inspired cross-decorated cuff bracelets; some say one thing that's genuine though is the staff's "attitude."

Marimekko
24 | 23 | 21 | E

E 70s | 1262 Third Ave. (bet. 72nd & 73rd Sts.) | 6 to 68th St. | 212-628-8400 | 800-527-0624 | www.kiitosmarimekko.com

"Bright", "bold", "eye-catching prints" characterize this East 70s haven for fans of the Finnish brand, whose "forever '60s" aesthetic "inspires" nostalgia for "fun stuff for the home", "adorable accessories and clothing" and "fabrics by the yard"; "it's hard not to smile when you see" the "rainbow" of colors; still, "for the price of a couple" of "supercool" women's "frocks" you could "be on your way to Helsinki."

Market NYC
▽ 20 | 18 | 20 | M

NoLita | 268 Mulberry St. (bet. Houston & Prince Sts.) | B/D/F/V to B'way/Lafayette St. | 212-580-8995 | www.themarketnyc.com

Hip-hunters dedicated to scouting out "unique items" that "distinguish them from the pack" make this "awesome" NoLita bazaar their "first stop"; held only on Saturday and Sunday in a school gym, this "best-kept secret" fashion collective presents "funky, original" "jewelry, bags and tees" by young designers who are "excited to tell you about their product" and may even "give you a better price" than what's at retail.

Mark Ingram Bridal Atelier ☒
27 | - | 26 | E

E 50s | 110 E. 55th St. (bet. Lexington & Park Aves.) | 4/5/6/F/N/R/W to 59th St./Lexington Ave. | 212-319-6778 | www.bridalatelier.com

Owner "Mark Ingram knows his stuff", in fact, he and his "very mellow", "outstanding staff" at this "low-key, upscale", by-appointment-only bridal atelier (now in new East 50s quarters) "treat you like the special lady you are", "offering input" to "ensure you won't look like a big bonbon" on your wedding day; it's an "excellent place" to view a "beautifully edited selection" of "high-quality gowns" that includes "designers not a lot of others carry", like Angel Sanchez, Karl Lagerfeld and Monique Lhuillier.

Marmalade ◐
- | - | - | M

LES | 172 Ludlow St. (bet. Houston & Stanton Sts.) | F/V to Lower East Side/ 2nd Ave. | 212-473-8070 | www.marmaladevintage.com

Set in a spacious, sunny storefront on the Lower East Side, this vintage clothing store serves up a sweet collection of casual clothes that convey a curiously contemporary quality, even though they date from the '50s to the '80s; there are also lots of midprice accessories and shoes (remember Pappagallo?) – mostly for her, though there's a small assortment for him and the kiddies too.

Marni
▽ 24 | 25 | 21 | VE

SoHo | 161 Mercer St. (bet. Houston & Prince Sts.) | N/R/W to Prince St. | 212-343-3912 | www.marni.com

Boasting milky-glass floors and silvery tree-limb fixtures, this "slick environment showcases lovingly dreamed-up womenswear" – plus "inventive" clothing for men and kids – from Milanese designer Consuelo Castiglioni; her loosely fitted dresses and duster coats are "definitely a distinctive look", but a big hit with the "bohemian-chic crowd" that urges "purchase early, as this SoHo location sells out of the hot items fast."

Marsha D.D.
∇ 20 | 16 | 14 | E

E 80s | 1574 Third Ave. (bet. 88th & 89th Sts.) | 4/5/6 to 86th St. | 212-831-2422

A "one-stop shop" for all things tween and teen, this East 80s hot spot with a red rubber floor and zebra-carpeted dressing rooms hooks 'em with a stash of stuff "kids crave" like Paul Frank PJs, Puma bags, Mavi jeans and Trunk rock tees; the shop also stocks Adidas activewear, Billabong board shorts and The North Face jackets, making it a "good place for boys" too.

☑ Marshalls ●
16 | 9 | 8 | I

W 100s | 105 W. 125th St. (Lenox Ave.) | 1 to 125th St. | 212-866-3963
Bronx | Bay Plaza Shopping Ctr. | 2100 Bartow Ave. (Co-Op City Blvd.) | 6 to Pelham Bay Park | 718-320-7211
Bronx | 50 W. 225th St. (bet. B'way & Kingsbridge Ave.) | 1 to 225th St. | 718-933-9062
Bensonhurst | 1832 86th St. (bet. 18th & 19th Aves.) | Brooklyn | N to 86th St. | 718-621-0784
Downtown | Atlantic Ctr. | 625 Atlantic Ave. (bet. Ft. Greene Pl. & S. Portland Ave.) | Brooklyn | 2/3/4/5/B/D/M/N/Q/R to Atlantic Ave. | 718-398-5254
Starrett City | Gateway Ctr. | 351 Gateway Dr. (bet. Fountain & Vandalia Aves.) | Brooklyn | A/C to Euclid Ave. | 718-235-8142
LIC | 48-18 Northern Blvd. (48th St.) | Queens | G/R/V to Northern Blvd. | 718-626-4700
Rego Pk | 96-05 Queens Blvd. (Junction Blvd.) | Queens | G/R/V to 63rd Dr./Rego Park | 718-275-7797
Staten Island | 2485 Richmond Ave. (Richmond Hill Rd.) | 718-370-3313
888-627-7425 | www.marshallsonline.com

If you go to this discount chain with no specific needs, you "can really score a hit" among "an amazing variety of clothes and housewares", with "some of the items looking like they should cost more" (perfect for "furnishing your overpriced studio"); however, it "depends on the location" as "stores vary tremendously" – though scores suggest the "nasty treatment from employees" and the "messy" digs ("worse than the kids' room") are universal.

Marston & Langinger ☒
- | - | - | E

SoHo | 117 Mercer St. (bet. Prince & Spring Sts.) | N/R/W to Prince St. | 212-965-0434 | www.marston-and-langinger.com

It seems fitting that this veddy upscale British import that's best known for custom-made timber-and-glass conservatories opened its first stateside shop in SoHo in a 19th-century warehouse; the cavernous, yet calm, space is home to outdoor-inspired items like garden tools, textiles, tiny Christian Tortu dried rose arrangements, wire tables and planters, pastel pressed-glass plates, classic willow or contemporary furniture, stone fountains and aged teak benches.

Mary Adams The Dress Ⓜ
- | - | - | E

LES | 138 Ludlow St. (bet. Rivington & Stanton Sts.) | F/V to Lower East Side/2nd Ave. | 212-473-0237 | www.maryadamsthedress.com

Nonconformist brides and left-of-center party girls jonesing for one-of-a-kind, fanciful eveningwear head to this by-appointment shop on

| | QUALITY | DISPLAY | SERVICE | COST |

the Lower East Side where designer Mary Adams whips up flirty off-the-rack and custom-made confections; the gowns, minis and separates are infused with a sense of wit, fun and, at times, a bit of retro flair, playing into every woman's dress-up fantasy.

🅩 Mary Arnold Toys 🆂

| | 26 | 19 | 20 | E |

E 70s | 1010 Lexington Ave. (bet. 72nd & 73rd Sts.) | 6 to 68th St. | 212-744-8510

"Save yourself the hassle" of the "big" chains and skip over to this "wonderfully old-fashioned", "friendly" East 70s toy-meister that's "been around forever"; you'll find "all of the usual suspects" crammed into the "close" quarters, from the "hottest, most cutting-edge" playthings to the "thinking child's" "goodies", including early developmental games, books, art kits and dress-up duds; the added edge: "they always have" stuff "in stock", plus "they deliver!"

Mason's Tennis Mart

| | ▽ 26 | 19 | 23 | E |

E 50s | 56 E. 53rd St. (bet. Madison & Park Aves.) | E/V to 5th Ave./53rd St. | 212-755-5805 | www.masonstennis.com

Perhaps "the only shop a serious tennis player needs" is how swinging supporters sum up this Midtown racquet retailer, a "regular" stop thanks to its "great selection" of "unique clothes", "top-of-the-line" equipment, "solid stringing" and "affable", "helpful staffers"; if a few fault it as "too pricey", insiders advise that its January "annual sale is the best" way to score that "perfect" something at a serious markdown.

Mastic Spa ◐

| | - | - | - | E |

SoHo | 438 W. Broadway (Prince St.) | N/R/W to Prince St. | 212-219-3251 | www.masticspa.com

The Mastic tree only grows on the Greek island of Chios, and the gummy resin it exudes is believed to have healing properties; here at this family-owned SoHo spa the exotic ingredient turns up in tony treatment products like moisturizers, soaps, salts and shampoos for both sexes.

Maternity Works

| | 19 | 12 | 15 | I |

W 50s | 16 W. 57th St., 3rd fl. (bet. 5th & 6th Aves.) | F to 57th St. | 212-399-9840 | www.maternitymall.com

If you're "willing to spend the time picking through" the racks, this Midtown maternity outpost (owned by the same parent company as A Pea in the Pod and Mimi Maternity) will reward the "average cost-conscious buyer" with "fabulous bargains" on a "wide variety of styles"; the staff is "friendly and helpful", but the "too-small space" feels over-"packed" to "tomorrow's mamas."

Matta

| | - | - | - | E |

NoLita | 241 Lafayette St. (bet. Prince & Spring Sts.) | 6 to Spring St. | 212-343-9399 | www.mattany.com

This spare, airy, high-ceilinged shop on Lafayette makes a big impact with its "fabulous bohemian" women's and children's clothing, delicate jewelry and home furnishings; Italian designer/co-owner Christina Gitti travels the world to find inspiration for her lightweight cotton sarongs, kurtas, tees and button-downs in lush colors and patterns and covetable quilts and pillows; compatible lines like Antipast, Lucky Fish, Velvet and Orla Kiely reflect her flair for mild-mannered chic.

| | QUALITY | DISPLAY | SERVICE | COST |

Matter — | – | – | E

Park Slope | 227 Fifth Ave. (bet. Carroll & President Sts.) | Brooklyn |
M/R to Union St. | 718-230-1150 | www.mattermatters.com
To patrons of this Park Slope purveyor, every "well-designed" thing
does Matter; whether it's housewares like ceramics, vases, glasses,
rugs and lighting or personal accessories such as jewelry and handbags, most maintain they "always want to buy everything" here.

☑ Maurice Villency 26 | – | 21 | VE

E 50s | 949 Third Ave. (57th St.) | 4/5/6/F/N/R/W to 59th St./
Lexington Ave. | 212-725-4840 | 877-845-5362 | www.villency.com
Since 1932, this luxury furniture company has offered "quality" "modern" "European design" and pieces that "last many years in top condition", "especially sofas and sectionals" in "fabulous leather" and at
"high prices"; the Midtown flagship, now in new East 50s digs, still
stretches a city block, boasts an in-house coffee shop and is full of
salespeople that are "helpful without being pushy."

Mavi ● 22 | 21 | 20 | M

E Vill | 832 Broadway (bet. 12th & 13th Sts.) | 4/5/6/L/N/Q/R/W to
14th St./Union Sq. | 917-289-0520 | 866-628-4575 | www.mavi.com
Mavens of the Mavi-lous Turkish brand maintain that this Broadway
flagship, a modern steel-and-wood showroom with a rotating gallery,
is a mecca for "inexpensive yet trendy jeans"; rely on a "helpful staff"
to help you nail down booty-enhancing denim as well as a "good selection" of his-and-hers jackets, hoodies and casual wear.

NEW Max Azria – | – | – | VE

SoHo | 409 W. Broadway (Spring St.) | C/E to Spring St. | 212-991-4740 |
www.maxazria.com
Women who are mad for Max and have much moolah should motor to
this new SoHo boutique, devoted to the designer's year-old, upscale
collection; taking nature as its inspiration, the small shop has an organic
ambiance – it's centered around an actual tree trunk, and images of
leaves and shrubbery abound amid the racks of clothes; the garments
have the same flowy, loose feel as Azria's BCBG label, but are edgier
and more luxurious, with higher-quality fabrics and attention to detail.

Maxilla & Mandible ▽ 25 | 22 | 20 | E

W 80s | 451 Columbus Ave. (bet. 81st & 82nd Sts.) | B/C to 81st St. |
212-724-6173 | www.maxillaandmandible.com
For an "only in NYC" experience, cut a path to this "tiny, but treasure-
laden" osteological shop (strategically located a stone's throw from
the American Museum of Natural History) where kids, collectors, "aspiring taxidermists and bone collectors" alike "love" to dig through the
"weird" array of skeletons, fossils, insects and quarry curios "you can't
see anywhere else"; "it's worth a visit, even just to look in the window."

MaxMara 25 | 24 | 22 | VE

E 60s | 813 Madison Ave. (68th St.) | 6 to 68th St. | 212-879-6100 |
SoHo | 450 W. Broadway (bet. Houston & Prince Sts.) | C/E to Spring St. |
212-674-1817
"Sleek and classy", this Italian womenswear powerhouse takes a prag-
matic approach in its "treasure trove" of "well-made classics" at
"costly" but – given the quality – "correct prices", including "wool

coats to die for", "nice-fitting" suits and other "tailored clothing" just "fashionable" enough that "you don't see yourself coming and going"; amid the "minimalist decor" of the East 60s or SoHo shops, the "clothes could sell themselves – thankfully, since the salespeople", though "attentive", do have some "attitude."

Max Studio

| 20 | 21 | 18 | E |

SoHo | 426 W. Broadway (bet. Prince & Spring Sts.) | C/E to Spring St. | 212-431-8995 | www.maxstudio.com
No need to max out your MasterCard at this SoHo boutique, which has "an edge over its" competition with its ever-changing stock of skirts and shirts in "flowy fabrics", "fun work clothes", lean outerwear and hip sandals and boots; however, malcontents moan over the "mixed quality."

Mayle

| - | - | - | E |

NoLita | 242 Elizabeth St. (bet. Houston & Prince Sts.) | B/D/F/V to B'way/Lafayette St. | 212-625-0406
One of NoLita's first, this little shop is now a fixture for sweet-but-not-sugary stylemakers, who adore owner/ex-model Jayne Mayle's "original offbeat takes on classic styles"; the designer reveals her "different eye" with chic, unique, vintagey ladylike looks that also have a definite downtown edge and, *mais oui,* a "French feeling."

McGuire ⊠

| - | - | - | VE |

Murray Hill | 200 Lexington Ave. (32nd St.) | 6 to 33rd St. | 212-689-1565 | www.mcguirefurniture.com
Based in San Francisco, this fine furniture company was founded in 1948 and opened its first New York store in Murray Hill last year; designers like Barbara Barry and Adam Tihany are on board and bring an urban eye to traditionally outdoor materials like rattan and teak to produce "beautiful" high-end pieces that are at home in upscale interiors.

Me & Ro

| 23 | 24 | 21 | E |

NoLita | 241 Elizabeth St. (bet. Houston & Prince Sts.) | B/D/F/V to B'way/Lafayette St. | 917-237-9215 | 877-632-6376 | www.meandrojewelry.com
Against a backdrop of silk ceiling lamps and a floating flower pond, this small NoLita shop showcases "hip" Indian, Chinese and Tibetan jewelry "with a mystical edge" (think symbols and lotus petal motifs) in silver and gold; the rich boho look "makes you feel like a Hollywood or fashion insider", but cynics question "how something so tiny can cost so much?"

Mecox Gardens

| - | - | - | VE |

E 70s | 962 Lexington Ave. (bet. 70th & 71st Sts.) | 6 to 68th St. | 212-249-5301 | www.mecoxgardens.com
An "expensive" urban outpost of an upscale Hamptons flagship designed for those with second (and third) homes, this Upper East Side garden-inspired furnishings shop showcases a blend of antique, reproduction and custom pieces and tony tabletop accessories, like pewter-rimmed hurricane lamps; devotees declare if you're looking for the likes of a limestone frieze, this is the place.

Medici ◗

| 20 | 17 | 17 | M |

W 80s | 420 Columbus Ave. (bet. 80th & 81st Sts.) | B/C to 81st St. | 212-712-9342
It's "one of my regular stops" assert admirers who hit this Columbus Avenue standby for "stylish" footwear that's "a bit different"; the

| | QUALITY | DISPLAY | SERVICE | COST |

"breadth and depth can satisfy any shoe aficionado who wants a break from the mass-marketers", plus the "great prices" and "leather quality" make it a "good bet" – though you'll look like "you spent a fortune."

NEW Meg Cohen Design Shop
| | – | – | – | E |

SoHo | 59 Thompson St. (bet. Broome & Spring Sts.) | C/E to Spring St. | 917-805-0189 | www.megcohendesign.com

With its painted white brick walls and airy feel, this accessories designer's new modern nook feels like an oasis of calm in SoHo; soft-touch seekers score plush cashmere finds, from feminine hoods, fingerless gloves and arm socks for her to ski caps and long skinny scarves for him, all in luscious solids or stripes; nesters zero in on bull's-eye pillows and trays with collapsible stands to create instant coffee tables.

Memorial Sloan-Kettering Cancer Center Thrift Shop 🛇
| | 22 | 17 | 15 | M |

E 80s | 1440 Third Ave. (bet. 81st & 82nd Sts.) | 4/5/6 to 86th St. | 212-535-1250 | www.memorialthriftshop.org

There's "always something to buy" "and it's all for a good cause" (cancer research and patient care) at this veteran, "airy" Upper East Side thrift store where shopping is "like picking through your rich aunt's closet" – not to mention her living room, kitchen and library – for "high-end" items; down 'n' dirty bargain-hunters find it a "little too coolly genteel", but "sometimes you get a great bargain for a quality item."

Men's Wearhouse ☻
| | 17 | 16 | 19 | M |

E 40s | 380 Madison Ave. (46th St.) | 4/5/6/7/S to 42nd St./Grand Central | 212-856-9008 | 800-851-6744 | www.menswearhouse.com
Additional locations throughout the NY area

When in need of business attire or a "rented tux", fellas head for this menswear chain that even carries sizes to fit "nontraditional shapes"; "nice displays" of its "ordinary" but "not high-priced" clothing (suits, dress shirts, slacks, shoes, ties, outerwear) and salesmen who greet you upon arrival add up to a "pleasant shopping" experience for most, though more sensitive sorts find the floor crew "overly pushy."

Metro Bicycles
| | 20 | 15 | 20 | M |

E 80s | 1311 Lexington Ave. (88th St.) | 4/5/6 to 86th St. | 212-427-4450
E Vill | 332 E. 14th St. (bet. 1st & 2nd Aves.) | 4/5/6/L/N/Q/R/W to 14th St./Union Sq. | 212-228-4344
Flatiron | 546 Sixth Ave. (15th St.) | A/C/E/L to 14th St./8th Ave. | 212-255-5100
TriBeCa | 417 Canal St. (6th Ave.) | 1 to Canal St. | 212-334-8000
W 40s | 360 W. 47th St. (9th Ave.) | A/C/E to 42nd St./Port Authority | 212-581-4500
W 90s | 231 W. 96th St. (B'way) | 1/2/3 to 96th St. | 212-663-7531
www.metrobicycles.com

Not only will you find "good prices" at this chainlet, but you'll also "get what you pay for" – namely, "quality" cycles including "medium range" models such as Raleigh, LeMond and Trek; the "helpful", "no-attitude" staffers are "patient", which one especially "needs when buying kids' bikes", and the numerous locations throughout Manhattan make it "convenient for parts" too.

| | QUALITY | DISPLAY | SERVICE | COST |

Metropolitan Lumber & Hardware
22 | 12 | 17 | M

SoHo | 175 Spring St. (bet. Thompson St. & W. B'way) | C/E to Spring St. | 212-966-3466
W 40s | 617 11th Ave. (bet. 45th & 46th Sts.) | A/C/E to 42nd St./ Port Authority | 212-246-9090
Astoria | 34-35 Steinway St. (bet. 34th & 35th Aves.) | Queens | G/R/V to Steinway St. | 718-392-4441
Corona | 108-56 Roosevelt Ave. (108th St.) | Queens | 7 to 111th St. | 718-898-2100
Jamaica | 108-20 Merrick Blvd. (109th Ave.) | Queens | E/J/Z to Jamaica Ctr. Parsons/Archer | 718-657-0100
www.themetlumber.com

Go "where the local builders buy" suggest plaksters who get on board at these "convenient full-service lumberyards in Manhattan" and Queens offering a "great selection" at "fair prices"; service is "nice and old-fashioned", which means "they'll go out of their way for you" – "if you get the right person, you're set for life"; they can also help you choose tools and electrical and plumbing equipment.

⚡ Metropolitan Museum of Art Store, The
25 | 23 | 20 | M

E 80s | 1000 Fifth Ave. (81st St.) | 6 to 77th St. | 212-570-3894 Ⓜ
Seaport | South Street Seaport Museum | 14 Fulton St. (bet. Front & South Sts.) | 2/3/4/5/A/C/J/M/Z to Fulton St./B'way/Nassau | 212-248-0954
Washington Hts. | The Cloisters, Fort Tryon Park | 799 Fort Washington Ave. (190th St.) | A to 190th St. | 212-650-2277 Ⓜ
W 40s | Rockefeller Ctr. | 15 W. 49th St. (5th Ave.) | B/D/F/V to 47-50th Sts./ Rockefeller Ctr. | 212-332-1360
800-468-7386 | www.metmuseum.org

"Dazzle your friends while supporting the arts" when you "prospect" for gifts at Fifth Avenue's "gold standard for all museum shops" and its three branches; the "eye-popping" selection features "fantastic books", "high-quality reproductions", "amazing" accessories and "inspired" toys as well as "creative holiday items"; service is "knowledgeable", "prices vary" from "expensive" to "modest" and insiders suggest checking out the clearance tables for "dirt-cheap" tchotchkes.

Metropolitan Opera Shop
24 | 22 | 20 | E

W 60s | Lincoln Ctr., Metropolitan Opera Hse., north lobby | Columbus Ave. (bet. 62nd & 65th Sts.) | 1 to 66th St./Lincoln Ctr. | 212-580-4090 | www.metoperashop.org

The Met's lobby shop hums, especially on show nights when the culture crowd peruses an "expansive" array of CDs, DVDs, posters, accessories, jewelry and other "*bibelots*" – all "keyed to the lover of music" (e.g. pseudo-Egyptian earrings to suggest *Aida*, kimonolike bathrobes à la *Madame Butterfly*); at the very least, it's a "pleasant intermission diversion", although "helpful salespeople" and "bargains" actually make it a fine stop for a "last-minute" gift.

Mexx ●
19 | 19 | 18 | M

E 50s | 650 Fifth Ave. (52nd St.) | E/V to 5th Ave./53rd St. | 212-956-6505
SoHo | 500 Broadway (bet. Broome & Spring Sts.) | N/R/W to Canal St. | 212-343-7954
866-444-1344 | www.mexx.com

Considered a "wardrobe essential" by fans but a "roll of the dice" for the less-enchanted, this Dutch import with chain links in SoHo and

Midtown allows shoppers to travel through easily navigable spaces in search of "Euro city-style" men's and women's clothing for when they "want to be trendy" but "still have money left to go out."

Michael Anchin Glass Company

— | — | — | M

Williamsburg | 51 S. First St. (bet. Kent & Wythe Aves.) | Brooklyn | L to Bedford Ave. | 212-925-1470 | www.michaelanchin.com

The "incredibly talented" artist-owner of this colorful by-appointment-only glass gallery, which recently moved from NoLita to Williamsburg, hand-blows "lovely" vessels, vases, lamps and bright bowls; moreover, "you can own an original piece for an incredibly reasonable price."

Michael Ashton 🗷

— | — | — | VE

E 70s | 933 Madison Ave. (74th St.) | 6 to 77th St. | 212-517-6655 | www.michaelashtonwatches.com

Passionate and worldly, the owner of this by-appointment corner shop near the Whitney Museum specializes in rare vintage watches from 1900–1990s, especially from Rolex (encompassing limited-edition Jean-Claude Killy or Paul Newman styles), Patek Philippe and Vacherin & Constantine; there's also a collection of estate jewelry, mostly art deco, along with European-cut diamond engagement rings.

🗷 Michael C. Fina

26 | 23 | 20 | E

E 40s | 545 Fifth Ave. (45th St.) | 4/5/6/7/S to 42nd St./Grand Central | 212-557-2500

Bay Ridge | 8211 Fifth Ave. (82nd St.) | Brooklyn | R to 86th St. | 718-491-6238 800-289-3462 | www.michaelcfina.com

Family-owned since 1935, this "wedding registry mecca" in Midtown and now Bay Ridge too offers an "excellent selection" of "lovely", "high-end merchandise", from classic and contemporary fine china (Kate Spade to Spode), crystal, silver, cookware and giftware at "a discount" that is often "below regular department store prices"; however, surveyors are split on service, with pros pronouncing it "knowledgeable" and cons calling it "disorganized and slow."

Michael Kors 🗷

26 | 24 | 23 | VE

E 70s | 974 Madison Ave. (76th St.) | 6 to 77th St. | 212-452-4685 | www.michaelkors.com

What some deem "the best selection of low-key luxe" lives at this *Project Runway* guru's East 70s flagship designed by architect Dan Rowen, whose subdued colors create the perfect backdrop for the boldface designer's "classic chic" silhouettes for him or her done up in "cashmere, fur and leather", plus there are also "fab shoes and bags"; the "excellent tailors" and "eye-candy" staff add to the "great experience."

Michael's, The Consignment Shop for Women 🗷

25 | 19 | 20 | E

E 70s | 1041 Madison Ave. (bet. 79th & 80th Sts.) | 6 to 77th St. | 212-737-7273 | www.michaelsconsignment.com

"Still the Upper East Side's best resource for gently used Chanel, Hermès, etc." confide consignment acolytes about this vet (est. 1954), whose "helpful staff" supplies ladies with "designer merch at a discount" (it's also "one of the few to specialize in wedding dresses"); some bargain-hunters blanch at the cost, but fans find the "quality vs. price ratio superb", plus, it's "the only way I can wear Armani."

	QUALITY	DISPLAY	SERVICE	COST

Michal Negrin
26 | 27 | 24 | E

E 70s | 971 Madison Ave. (bet. 75th & 76th Sts.) | 6 to 77th St. |
212-439-8414 | 800-773-4319 | www.michalnegrinnyc.com
From gilded swag molding, crystal chandeliers and heaps of roses to
the nymphs painted on the check-out counter, this East 70s yearling –
the "olde timey", "feminine" vision of veteran Israeli designer Michal
Negrin and the 39th outpost in her global chain – is a Victoriana lover's
delight; the emphasis is on crystal, metal and bead-encrusted baubles, but the lifestyle collection also includes hand-printed tunics,
tiles and wrought-iron shelving.

Michele Varian
- | - | - | E

SoHo | 35 Crosby St. (bet. Broome & Grand Sts.) | 6 to Spring St. |
212-343-0033 | www.michelevarian.com
For "fabrics rich and luxurious in color", head to this "lovely little store"
in SoHo, "where you can always find something precious", including
handmade pillows, throws and duvet covers in silk, suede and leather,
along with "a good collection of jewelry and tableware"; the eponymous owner-designer runs the shop and is "ever-accommodating."

Michelle New York
- | - | - | M

Boerum Hill | 376 Atlantic Ave. (bet. Bond & Hoyt Sts.) | Brooklyn | A/C/G to
Hoyt/Schermerhorn Sts. | 718-643-1680

Michelle New York Brides 🅼
Boerum Hill | 396 Atlantic Ave. (bet. Bond & Hoyt Sts.) | Brooklyn | A/C/G to
Hoyt/Schermerhorn Sts. | 718-643-1680
www.michellenewyork.com
Designer-owner Michelle Fields dresses women for their everyday
lives as well as for their wedding date at her Boerum Hill duo; the spacious, loftlike womenswear shop boasts her edgy, sexy collection plus
lines from around the world, funky jewelry and accessories, while a
few doors up she caters to brides of all budgets; to-bes can also get
ready on the big day in the on-site salon.

Mick Margo 🅼
- | - | - | E

W Vill | 19 Commerce St. (bet. Bedford St. & 7th Ave. S.) | 1 to
Christopher St./Sheridan Sq. | 212-463-0515 | www.mickmargo.com
With a "cozy" ambiance that artfully mixes English wallpaper with
red-leather upholstery, framed photos of the store's namesake who
happens to be the "attentive" owner's grandfather and a distinctively
downtown merch mix that traffics in off-the-beaten-path lines like Clu
and Vena Cava, this "cute West Village shop" sets fashionistas' hearts
aflutter; leave your significant other on the mohair cushioned bench,
pop into the pinstripe-curtained dressing room and emerge with
exclusive find in hand.

Mika Inatome 🅂
- | - | - | E

TriBeCa | 93 Reade St. (bet. Church St. & W. B'way) | 1/2/3 to
Chambers St. | 212-966-7777 | www.mikainatome.com
"The personalized attention" that "passionate, extremely talented"
designer "Mika Inatome provides is priceless" at her TriBeCa studio
where brides actually look "forward to every fitting" of their custom-
crafted gowns; made from natural fabrics like Japanese or Italian silk and
enhanced by touches like distinctive embroidery, hand-stitched beading

	QUALITY	DISPLAY	SERVICE	COST

and European lace, the luxe creations walk the line between timeless and contemporary, making an "already special event more memorable."

Z Mikimoto ☒ | 29 | 26 | 25 | VE |

E 50s | 730 Fifth Ave. (bet. 56th & 57th Sts.) | N/R/W to 5th Ave./59th St. | 212-457-4600 | 888-701-2323 | www.mikimotoamerica.com

If you "live for" "pretty, perfect pearls", this elegant Fifth Avenue store hasn't lost its luster as the "prime place to go" since its founder invented the cultured version, plus it carries everything from classic Japanese Akoya to bigger South Sea varieties; admirers assert "their reliability is worth the cost", and add after all, dahling, "you are buying an heirloom."

miks ● | – | – | – | M |

LES | 100 Stanton St. (bet. Ludlow & Orchard Sts.) | F/V to Lower East Side/ 2nd Ave. | 212-505-1982

This cheerful Lower East Side jewel box is so tiny you may bump into the creative clerk, who's styling the mannequins in the window, but that's part of the charm of exploring Japanese designer Mitsuyo Toyoda's womenswear – smart separates in a chic array of colors, some adorned with oversized buttons or polka dots; also on display are cashmere hand-knits from Peru, well-priced Topkapi leather purses and gorgeous gloves, scarves and hats.

Mimi Maternity | 19 | 18 | 20 | M |

Borough Pk | 4420 13th Ave. (45th St.) | Brooklyn | D/M to Fort Hamilton Pkwy. | 718-871-9430
Staten Island | Staten Island Mall | 2655 Richmond Ave. (bet. Platinum Ave. & Richmond Hill Rd.) | 718-761-0097 ●
877-646-4666 | www.mimimaternity.com

Moms-to-be love the "bang for the buck" at this mega maternity chain where the "looks aren't too pricey" and there's a "decent selection" of everyday wear like "basic black pants" and jeans good enough "for a few months"; but cutting-edgers who complain "it's not the most trendy" say utilize the "extremely helpful staff" and "shop wisely or you'll look like a pregnant Carol Brady."

NEW Mimi's Closet ●☒Ⓜ | 21 | 22 | 23 | E |

Astoria | 21-10 31st St. (21st Ave.) | Queens | N/W to Ditmars Blvd. | 718-278-4585 | www.mimiscloset.net

"Bring along a decent amount of cash" so that you won't have to "leave a gem behind" at this "quaint" blue-and-green Astoria store where former Issey Miyake assistant Mimi Yamanobe and her "knowledgeable staff" provide "excellent service" to those browsing a "small collection" of "simply sexy", whimsical frocks and tops designed by the owner, plus "NYC-made, one-of-a-kind" – looking purses, accessories and jewelry.

Mini Mini Market ● | – | – | – | M |

Williamsburg | 218 Bedford Ave. (bet. N. 4th & 5th Sts.) | Brooklyn | L to Bedford Ave. | 718-302-9337 | www.miniminimarket.com

Adventurous Gothamites maintain it's "worth crossing the bridge" to get to this "ultracool" red-and-pink-colored "kitschy boutique that embodies the flavor of the 'Burg"; the "big draw": a "great sampling of the most current fashions", from "cute accessories" and jewelry (shoot for "unique" pieces like a "gold-gun necklace") to "hipster-fabulous" shoes, lingerie and dresses from Asian and local independent designers.

	QUALITY	DISPLAY	SERVICE	COST

Min-K ◑

| | − | − | − | M |

E Vill | 334 E. 11th St. (bet. 1st & 2nd Aves.) | L to 1st Ave. | 212-253-8337
NoLita | 219 Mott St. (bet. Prince & Spring Sts.) | N/R/W to Prince St. | 212-219-2834
www.mink-nyc.com

"Every city girl needs a good frock", and shoppers deem this East Village original and its NoLita sidekick "ideal spots for scoring beautiful party dresses" that "you won't see another woman wearing"; owner Mingi Kim also parlays her "genius design" abilities into "reasonably priced" wool jumpsuits, tailored trousers and silk halter dresses – for sizes 2–6 – plus stocks a few jewels and heels, which help seal its status as a "sanctuary for funky boutique lovers."

Miriam Rigler ⊠

| | ∇ 28 | 23 | 26 | VE |

E 60s | 41 E. 60th St. (bet. Madison & Park Aves.) | 4/5/6/F/N/R/W to 59th St./Lexington Ave. | 212-581-5519

This elite purveyor of evening- and weddingwear has "been around 'forever'", but only just moved into the East 60s digs shared with the Jeanmarie Gallery (hence, all the oil paintings decorating the walls); the long, narrow space is crammed with colorful "clothing that's great for women of a certain age" – indeed, dressing the mother of the bride has long been the store's specialty; but it also offers custom-made gowns, plus jewelry and accessories, for all participants in the happy day, so "if you're an old-fashioned bride with traditional class, come here."

Mish ⊠

| | − | − | − | VE |

E 70s | 131 E. 70th St. (bet. Lexington & Park Aves.) | 6 to 68th St. | 212-734-3500 | www.mishnewyork.com

Set in a magnificent East 70s townhouse, with a garden entrance, this tiny shop (with workrooms in back) is the home of the eponymous, bow-tied jeweler to the ladies who lunch; they adore his "very few but very beautiful" and very expensive designs – from deliciously colorful, multistrand gemstone necklaces, coral and bamboo collections, whimsical brooches and a charm bracelet or two to cuff links for men.

NEW Mish Mish

| | − | − | − | M |

E 90s | 1435 Lexington Ave. (bet. 93rd & 94th Sts.) | 6 to 96th St. | 212-996-6474

New to the neighborhood, this Israeli import in the East 90s makes shopping for even the most finicky kids a snap with its well-merchandised collection of colorful cotton separates made for easy mixing and matching; from peasant skirts and embellished T-shirts for girls to military jackets and cargo pants for boys, the fresh fashions here deliver a dose of European style – without the steep European price tags.

Missha ◑

| | − | − | − | I |

E 40s | 516 Fifth Ave. (43rd St.) | 4/5/6/7/S to 42nd St./Grand Central | 212-596-4012
SoHo | 513 Broadway (bet. Broome & Spring Sts.) | N/R/W to Prince St. | 212-334-5630
Woodhaven | Queens Ctr. | 90-15 Queens Blvd. (bet. 57th & 59th Aves.) | Queens | G/R/V to Woodhaven Blvd. | 718-271-6268

This Korean superstore trio in Manhattan and Queens is "the H&M of makeup" with over 500 products like lipsticks and eyeshadows for under $5 a pop, plus bath and body products at "bargain-basement prices"; but sophisticates sniff at settings dominated by blaring pop soundtracks and "teenybopper employees."

Missoni 🔣
26 | 25 | 22 | VE

E 70s | 1009 Madison Ave. (78th St.) | 6 to 77th St. | 212-517-9339 | www.missoni.com

On Madison Avenue, a "modernist interior serves as a glass box displaying the vibrant knit garments" of the Italian label like "rare gems" (appropriate, given the "oh-so-expensive" prices); the "beautiful" signature prints and "fantasy" weaves, now designed by heir to the house Angela Missoni, "still reign" for their "originality" – but given the high-voltage hues, you better "like color."

Miss Sixty
21 | 20 | 16 | E

SoHo | 386 W. Broadway (bet. Broome & Spring Sts.) | C/E to Spring St. | 212-334-9772 | www.misssixty.com

"You can't put a price on sexy", but at this "funky" shop on SoHo's main drag the "fit is amazing" on the "fabulous" Italian jeans, which are "guaranteed to make anyone into a goddess"; although the "casually stylish" "urban-chic" "weekend wear" and "cute" chunky boots rock in a Sienna Miller boho kind of way, mischief-makers hiss that it's "expensive for what it is" and "should be called Miss 18" for the teen "poseurs" it attracts.

Miu Miu
25 | 24 | 20 | E

E 60s | 831 Madison Ave. (bet. 69th & 70th Sts.) | 6 to 68th St. | 212-249-9660 🔣

SoHo | 100 Prince St. (bet. Greene & Mercer Sts.) | N/R/W to Prince St. | 212-334-5156

www.miumiu.com

"Prada's funky cousin" draws in '60s-style *gamines,* indie starlets and cool Condé Nasties at its "very friendly" SoHo flagship and its "beautifully designed" Madison Avenue branch; both boast baby-doll print dresses, "well-cut pants, couture-ish detailed shirts and fun" high-heeled platform shoes – all with an "edgy, earthy" spirit that saves it from being a chic clone of Miuccia Prada's signature line (not to mention "more affordable").

Mixona ●
– | – | – | E

NoLita | 262 Mott St. (bet. Houston & Prince Sts.) | B/D/F/V to B'way/Lafayette St. | 646-613-0100 | www.mixona.com

Stocked with "pretty" lacy dainties as well as sizzling bustiers, garter belts and thongs from hot tickets including Eberjay, Hanky Panky and Siren, this large and airy white-walled "fave lingerie" shop in NoLita makes a seductive prelude to that "special date"; saunter in to scan the easy-to-navigate racks for "great underwear and swimsuits too" and you may be rewarded with a "celeb sighting" at the same time.

NEW M Missoni
– | – | – | E

SoHo | 426 W. Broadway (bet. Prince & Spring Sts.) | A/C/E to Canal St. | 212-431-6500 | www.m-missoni.com

When that craving for Italian zigzag knits with a hip bent hits, make tracks to Angela Missoni's new light, airy, well-lit SoHo boutique and scoop up the creative director's lively luxury line; the inventive coterie of colorful, patterned womenswear is actually a bit more affordable, sexy and youthful than the mother ship collection – little wonder it's caught on with boldface names like Lindsay Lohan and Mischa Barton, not to mention company muse/daughter Margherita Missoni.

Modell's Sporting Goods ●

16	11	10	VE

Garment Dist | 1293 Broadway (34th St.) | B/D/F/N/Q/R/V/W to 34th St./ Herald Sq. | 212-244-4544 | 800-275-6633 | www.modells.com
Additional locations throughout the NY area

"Anything athletic they'll have" at this ubiquitous sporting goods chain, a "true New York original" that fans feel is "the place to go" for "inexpensive supplies"; but detractors deride its "awful presentation" as a "disorganized mess" and claim the "couldn't-care-less staff" "barely knows where the products are, much less how to use them."

Modernica

–	–	–	E

SoHo | 57 Greene St. (bet. Broome & Spring Sts.) | C/E to Spring St. | 212-219-1303 | www.modernica.net

Step off the teeming SoHo sidewalk and into this "nice place to dream about the furniture you would buy if you had a TriBeCa loft"; the focus is on reproductions of midcentury classics like Case Study sofas and Noguchi coffee tables, and prices are surprisingly "ok."

Molton Brown

27	24	24	E

E 50s | 515 Madison Ave. (53rd St.) | E/V to Lexington Ave./53rd St. | 212-755-7194 ⬛
E 60s | 1098 Third Ave. (bet. 64th & 65th Sts.) | 6 to 68th St. | 212-744-6430
NEW **SoHo** | 128 Spring St. (bet. Greene & Wooster Sts.) | N/R/W to Prince St. | 212-965-1740
www.moltonbrown.co.uk

This English import with East Side offshoots and now a new SoHo addition too offers "quietly sophisticated", "beautifully packaged" cosmetics and toiletries like "unbeatable bath oils", "the world's best haircare products" and "shower gels to die for"; its jet-set clientele doesn't seem to object to paying "premium prices" – but you might.

⛝ MoMA Design and Book Store

25	24	18	E

SoHo | 81 Spring St. (Crosby St.) | 6 to Spring St. | 646-613-1367 ●
W 50s | 11 W. 53rd St. (5th Ave.) | E/V to 5th Ave./53rd St. | 212-708-9700
W 50s | 44 W. 53rd St. (bet. 5th & 6th Aves.) | E/V to 5th Ave./53rd St. | 212-708-9669
800-793-3167 | www.momastore.org

"Midcentury modern" mavens and "design-forward" hipsters "feel like kids in a candy store" at MoMA's "breathtaking" flagship, across-the-street annex and the forever-"fresh" SoHo satellite; "sophisticated" shoppers find "fabulous" furniture and housewares, "excellent books" and "whimsical" children's items, and though it can be "hectic" and prices "expensive", it's a "unique" resource for "stylish" gifts.

⛝ Montblanc

28	26	24	VE

E 50s | 598 Madison Ave. (57th St.) | N/R/W to 5th Ave./59th St. | 212-223-8888
SoHo | 120 Greene St. (bet. Prince & Spring Sts.) | N/R/W to Prince St. | 212-680-1300
www.montblanc.com

Those who have a pen-chant for "absolutely exquisite" "classic" writing instruments that "everyone wants" head to these SoHo and Madison

Avenue shops that also sell watches, briefcases, leather goods and "gifts designed for all important celebrations"; proponents praise "superb service", but warn be prepared for prices as "high as your golden parachute."

Montmartre
| | 22 | 20 | 18 | E |

E 80s | 1157 Madison Ave. (85th St.) | 4/5/6 to 86th St. | 212-988-8962
Financial Dist | 22150 World Financial Ctr., 2nd fl. (West Side Hwy.) | R/W to Rector St. | 212-945-7858
W 50s | The Shops at Columbus Circle, Time Warner Ctr. | 10 Columbus Circle, 3rd fl. (bet. 58th & 60th Sts.) | 1/A/B/C/D to 59th St./Columbus Circle | 212-823-9821 ●
W 70s | 2212 Broadway (bet. 78th & 79th Sts.) | 1 to 79th St. | 212-875-8430 ●
www.montmartreny.com

It's "impossible to walk out empty-handed" from this "friendly" quartet "packed" with "funky, stylish" casualwear, "bright happy-hip" "going-out" garb and "sophisticated cocktail attire" "with an extra ladylike oomph"; *mais oui*, it's "expensive", but the "well-edited collection" of "wearable, trendy" "cool designers" like Elie Tahari and Nanette Lepore reveals this outfit's "keen eye" for "what's in fashion now."

Mood Designer Fabrics ⑤
| ▽ | 25 | 13 | 20 | M |

Garment Dist | 225 W. 37th St., 3rd fl. (7th Ave.) | 1/2/3/A/C/E to 34th St./Penn Station | 212-730-5003 | www.moodfabrics.com

"Horizontally stacked bolts" of "eye-candy" fabrics (including closeouts from Calvin Klein, Donna Karan and Marc Jacobs) fill the 25,000 sq. ft. of this Garment District behemoth, giving its clientele of clothing and stage designers "loads to choose from" at "low prices"; still, a few turn moody muttering "sometimes it's hard to see what's there" because "they have so much" – and it can be "hard to track down help."

NEW MoonSoup
| ▽ | 24 | 21 | 22 | M |

E 50s | 1059 Second Ave. (bet. 55th & 56th Sts.) | 4/5/6/F/N/R/W to 59th St./Lexington Ave. | 212-319-3222 | www.moonsoup.net

Midtown moms are astir over this "cute, little" East 50s children's emporium, which combines play and learning classes, a party center and "great shopping for all things kid" under one roof, including clothing, toys and diaper bags you don't see everywhere; the selection may be "tiny", nevertheless it can't be beat for "picking up unique gifts" in a pinch; P.S. "put this store on your gift registry."

Morgane Le Fay
| | 26 | 24 | 21 | VE |

E 60s | 746 Madison Ave. (bet. 64th & 65th Sts.) | N/R/W to 5th Ave./59th St. | 212-879-9700
SoHo | 67 Wooster St. (bet. Broome & Spring Sts.) | C/E to Spring St. | 212-219-7672
www.morganelefay.com

You feel like you're in a BAM New Wave Festival at this SoHo and Madison Avenue twosome where surreal statues model a fantasy array of apparel that's "awesome, elegant and classical, with a downtown twist" (and uptown prices); still, cynics say the gauzy gowns and separates look "just perfect for having tea in the forest with elves and fairies – but, how many times do you have tea in the forest with elves and fairies?"

NEW Morgan Library & Museum Shop Ⓜ | 25 | 23 | 20 | E |

Murray Hill | Morgan Library | 225 Madison Ave. (36th St.) | 6 to 33rd St. |
212-590-0300 | www.themorgan.org

"So glad they're open again" cry connoisseurs of this museum shop "in
the original J.P. Morgan home" in Murray Hill; "much airier than the
previous" incarnation, the "hushed", "rarefied" "atmosphere induces
one to spend" on a "small but exquisite selection" of "interesting" art
books, "special papers and cards" and other "gift shop goodies" "for a
cultured friend"; "service can be a bit leisurely" and some find "prices
are on the high side – but so is the quality"; besides, "someone has to
pay for the renovations" to the "redone" Morgan Library.

Morgenthal Frederics | 28 | 26 | 24 | VE |

E 60s | 699 Madison Ave. (bet. 62nd & 63rd Sts.) | 4/5/6/F/N/R/W
to 59th St./Lexington Ave. | 212-838-3090
E 70s | 944 Madison Ave. (bet. 74th & 75th Sts.) | 6 to 77th St. |
212-744-9444
SoHo | 399 W. Broadway (Spring St.) | C/E to Spring St. | 212-966-0099 ◗
W 50s | The Shops at Columbus Circle, Time Warner Ctr. | 10 Columbus
Circle, ground fl. (bet. 58th & 60th Sts.) | 1/A/B/C/D to 59th St./
Columbus Circle | 212-956-6402
www.morgenthalfrederics.com

"Forget contact lenses" – this "quality" quartet offers the "coolest"
handcrafted frames as well as "top-of-the-line sunglasses" that will
"make your face stand out"; the "soothing" David Rockwell–designed
spaces and "fabulous" service (including "outstanding opticians") ensure a "pleasant experience", and even if you may "never spend more"
on specs, you'll also "never want to buy them anywhere else."

Morris Brothers | 19 | 11 | 14 | M |

W 80s | 2322 Broadway (84th St.) | 1 to 86th St. | 212-724-9000

A go-to source for "all of your kid's camp clothes" for generations, this
West 80s stalwart is also clued into "what the boys" and girls "are
wearing", filling its metal racks with "realistically" priced, "no-
nonsense basics" "in brands teens like", including Hurley, Juicy Couture,
Mavi, Nike and The North Face; however, a few grumble that it's a "bit
sparse for the younger set" and find service a "bit gruff."

Ⓩ Moss | 28 | 29 | 21 | VE |

SoHo | 146 & 150 Greene St. (Houston St.) | N/R/W to Prince St. |
212-204-7100 | 866-888-6677 | www.mossonline.com

"Murray Moss has an exceptional eye" and "is on top of what's hot" in
high-end home furnishings, so much so that "an hour of browsing" the
"museumlike" "glass cases" in this "quirky, clever", ever-mushrooming
and "insanely priced" SoHo "temple of cool" "is like a college course in
classic" "modern design"; voted this *Survey*'s Tops for Display, the
"outstanding selection" includes items for the kitchen, office, living
and bedroom and ranges from "the silly to the fabulous", including a
flock of life-sized sheep stools by Hanns-Peter Krafft and an intricate
Marcel Wanders Crochet table constructed of cotton and epoxy.

NEW Moulin Bleu | - | - | - | E |

TriBeCa | 176 Franklin St. (Hudson St.) | 1 to Franklin St. | 212-334-1130

If you're feeling kind of *bleu*, hit this TriBeCa newcomer for a home furnishings pick-me-up that includes a charming selection of pricey an-

tique furniture, affordable glassware made from vintage molds, perfume bottles capped with rose-shaped stoppers, delicate dishes, scented soaps and a bounty of other gift-ready items reminiscent of the South of France.

Movado | 26 | 26 | 23 | E |

SoHo | 138 Spring St. (Wooster St.) | C/E to Spring St. | 212-431-0249
W 40s | Rockefeller Ctr. | 610 Fifth Ave. (bet. 49th & 50th Sts.) | B/D/F/V to 47-50th Sts./Rockefeller Ctr. | 212-218-7555
www.movado.com

Many have "made the move" to these "simple", "sleek and statusy" watches that are "sold all over the city" but have home stores in SoHo and Rockefeller Center; proponents praise the "not insanely priced" pieces and a "helpful", "patient" staff that "even sends thank-you notes" to its customers.

⧉ Mrs. John L. Strong ⧉ | 28 | 24 | 23 | VE |

E 60s | 699 Madison Ave., 5th fl. (62nd St.) | 4/5/6/F/N/R/W to 59th St./ Lexington Ave. | 212-838-3775 | www.mrsstrong.com

"When only the very best will do", debs and dowagers head to this statusy fifth-floor stationer on Madison Avenue founded in 1929 for "beautiful" hand-engraved invitations, letter paper, holiday cards and custom-leather accessories like albums; but "wildly expensive" prices mean the merchandise is "out of the range of most" mortals.

NEW Mulberry | - | - | - | VE |

E 50s | 605 Madison Ave. (58th St.) | N/R/W to 5th Ave./59th St. | 212-835-4700 ext. 102
W Vill | 387 Bleecker St. (Perry St.) | 1 to Christopher St./Sheridan Sq. | 212-835-4700 ext. 101
www.mulberry.com

Though it's been selling its long-lasting leather goods for 35 years, this British brand became a big deal when Kate Moss began toting its Bayswater bag around; now the label's making a huge splash this side of the pond with its new shops in the East 50s and the West Village; in addition to the rugged-yet-sexy, oak-toned clutches and shoulder bags, the Madison Avenue location – done up with leather and wood accents, like a sophisticated log cabin – stocks ready-to-wear clothing for blokes and birds too.

Munder-Skiles ⧉ | - | - | - | VE |

E 60s | 799 Madison Ave., 3rd fl. (bet. 67th & 68th Sts.) | 6 to 68th St. | 212-717-0150 | www.munder-skiles.com

'Exterior decorator' and owner of this pricey Madison Avenue garden furnishings shop John Danzer showcases tables, chairs, benches and urns – many of which are modeled on historic classics from places like Monticello – designed to make the outside of your property as enticing as the inside.

⧉ Museum of Arts & Design Store | 26 | 24 | 20 | E |

W 50s | 40 W. 53rd St. (bet. 5th & 6th Aves.) | E/V to 5th Ave./53rd St. | 212-956-3535 | www.madmuseum.org

It's "always a pleasure to browse" at this "beautiful" Midtown shop showcasing "one-of-a-kind jewelry and scarves from American crafts-people" along with "stunning glasswork", "extraordinary tableware" and other "conversation pieces"; wallet-watchers warn "there are no bargains", but the wowed say it's "worth it" for "gifts you won't find anywhere else"; N.B. plans are underway to relocate to architect Edward Durell Stone's 'Lollipop' building at 2 Columbus Circle in 2008.

Museum of Sex

19 | 20 | 18 | M

Gramercy | 233 Fifth Ave. (27th St.) | N/R/W to 28th St. | 212-689-6337 | www.museumofsex.com

"Never realized the selling of sex could be so sophisticated" say surveyors seduced by this industrial-looking, red-and-gray Gramercy emporium stocked with underwear, "interesting books" and the "highlight: sex toys almost pretty enough to pass as decorative works of art" (some actually are, like the anatomically correct origami man); all the items are "displayed in good taste" – though critics cavil the "understocked" inventory is "not risqué enough"; even so, "few museum shops sell such functional products" (just "stay away from any floor samples").

Museum of the City of New York 🅼

21 | 18 | 18 | M

E 100s | 1220 Fifth Ave. (103rd St.) | 6 to 103rd St. | 212-534-1672, ext. 3330 | www.mcny.org

"Nostalgic New Yorkers" laud this "little-known" museum shop in the East 100s celebrating "Big Apple quality" with "delightful jewelry and art objects" as well as "books and games for the whole family"; the "small but impressive" inventory, "helpful staff" and "decent prices" make it a must for folks seeking "thoughtful gifts" for "city buffs."

Mxyplyzyk

21 | 23 | 18 | M

W Vill | 125 Greenwich Ave. (bet. Horatio & 13th Sts.) | A/C/E/L to 14th St./8th Ave. | 212-989-4300 | 800-243-9810

If you're the West Village, this is the "perfect" "quick-stop" for a "quirky" "gift on the run" or "stylish tchotchkes" that run the gamut from scented candles and retro train cases to pet products and toys; space is tight and service "can be snooty", but the frugal feel the price is right.

My Glass Slipper

▽ 25 | 22 | 20 | M

Flatiron | 20 W. 22nd St., 6th fl. (bet. 5th & 6th Aves.) | N/R/W to 23rd St. | 212-627-0231 | www.myglassslipper.com

Yes, "it's all wedding shoes, all the time" at this "great concept", Web-based sixth-floor shop in the Flatiron District that's "even better in person"; would-be Cinderellas engage in "discount name-brand" footsie, slipping into "everything from Vera Wang to" "surprisingly inexpensive" lesser-known finds and dance away with purses, jewelry and hosiery too; if a few snarl that this Slipper "doesn't fit all", supporters retort "they can order" whatever you want.

Myla 🆂

– | – | – | E

E 60s | 20 E. 69th St. (bet. 5th & Madison Aves.) | 6 to 68th St. | 212-570-1590 | www.myla.com

You'd never expect so much naughtiness on a quiet Upper East Side block, but this high-end Londoner that hit New York a few years ago with a chic collection of lingerie and a handful of rechargeable adult toys in seductive designs delivers bad-girl paraphernalia aplenty; the mirrored back wall and leather-stooled fitting rooms are perfect for modeling pricey feathered mules, see-thru silk teddies and split-cup bras.

Mylo Dweck Maternity

                                             – | – | – | E

Bensonhurst | 366 Ave. U (bet. E. 1st & West Sts.) | Brooklyn | F to Ave. U | 718-333-0420

Style-minded moms-to-be make tracks to the Brooklyn shop of maternity maven Mylo Dweck, who's got a knack for finding the most sought-after fashions from name-brand lines like Childish, Japanese Weekend and Seven; sure, these designer duds come with designer prices, but sometimes you deserve to be spoiled, if only for nine months.

Myoptics

                                         25 | 21 | 24 | E

Chelsea | 96 Seventh Ave. (bet. 15th & 16th Sts.) | 1/2/3 to 14th St. | 212-633-6014

E Vill | 42 St. Marks Pl. (bet. 1st & 2nd Aves.) | 6 to Astor Pl. | 212-533-1577

SoHo | 123 Prince St. (bet. Greene & Wooster Sts.) | N/R/W to Prince St. | 212-598-9306

TriBeCa | 327 Greenwich St. (bet. Duane & Jay Sts.) | 1/2/3 to Chambers St. | 212-334-3123 🎦

www.myoptics.com

"Urban chic without attitude" is the appeal at this slightly "edgy" eyewear chain that offers a "fantastic" selection of frames with designer names like Oliver Peoples and Paul Smith; a befuddled few find the "presentation a bit confusing", but most report it's "fun to buy here", particularly since there are "no high-pressure sales" tactics in play.

M Z Wallace

                                         – | – | – | E

SoHo | 93 Crosby St. (bet. Prince & Spring Sts.) | 6 to Spring St. | 212-431-8252 | 888-600-5559 | www.mzwallace.com

This large, airy SoHo shop showcases "beautiful", colorful, quilted fabric and canvas bags "for the independent" New Yorker who blazes her own trail, with compartments for cell phones, Metrocards and Palm Pilots, all made by owners-designers Lucy Wallace Eustice and Monica Zwirner; the dynamic duo also offers a line of "nice stuff" for men too, including briefcases, laptop totes and overnighters, each named after a movie star.

NEW N 🌗M

                                         – | – | – | E

Harlem | 114 W. 116th St. (bet. Lenox & 7th Aves.) | 2/3 to 116th St. | 212-961-1036 | www.nharlemnewyork.com

Couture comes to Harlem with this pioneering two-level clothing emporium, a spacious 4,000-sq.-ft. loft space; like a mini-department store, the ground floor offers cosmetics, home furnishings by Jonathan Adler, leather goods and womenswear that ranges from Nicole Miller to Tracy Reese, from Miss Sixty to Marimekko – plus local designers and a proprietary label; downstairs, in the exposed-stone basement, boys can browse among the Hugo Boss, Ike Behar, Diesel and Denim Factor threads.

Nakedeye

                                         – | – | – | E

LES | 192 Orchard St. (bet. Houston & Stanton Sts.) | F/V to Lower East Side/2nd Ave. | 212-253-4935 | www.nakedeyeoptical.com

Naked fans consider this eyewear resource "the best" and proprietor George Lee "just the kind of hip cat you want decking out your specs" so you "walk out of there looking good"; with "the coolest" frames from top-notch names like Christian Roth, and a "great" Asian-style "environment" with an art gallery and "cool furnishings", it's clear to see why it's a Lower East Side must.

	QUALITY	DISPLAY	SERVICE	COST

Nancy & Co.
23 | 20 | 21 | E

E 80s | 1242 Madison Ave. (89th St.) | 4/5/6 to 86th St. | 212-427-0770 |
www.nancycony.com

"Keep up the good work!" say fans of Nan, an "old-time" Madison
Avenue "fave"; you "always find something you can't find elsewhere",
be it "great quality staples", "accessories to complete the outfit" or
some "funky stuff" to add to the "mix" in a "wide size range"; if a few
snipe "service could be less snooty", devotees vow the "knowledgeable staff understands what looks good on you."

Nancy Koltes at Home
▽ 28 | 22 | 23 | VE

NoLita | 29-31 Spring St. (bet. Mott & Mulberry Sts.) | 6 to Spring St. |
212-219-2271 | www.nkah.com

Cognoscenti claim you'll "sleep deeply and dream imaginatively"
tucked into "beautiful", "high-quality" Italian bed linens from this cozy
NoLita store, which recently added a new room next door stuffed with
"great home stuff"; a "very helpful staff" also sells towels, throws,
napkins, place mats and "wonderful down pillows and comforters."

Nanette Lepore
25 | 24 | 23 | E

SoHo | 423 Broome St. (bet. Crosby & Lafayette Sts.) | 6 to Spring St. |
212-219-8265 | www.nanettelepore.com

Free spirits favor this namesake designer's perky pink SoHo birdcage for
"precious but hip" "creative togs" with a "'50s cuteness that works for
today"; "universally flattering", these "demure yet sexy" threads, including "well-tailored suits" and "girlie-chic" "dresses cut really well",
display a "rare attention to detail" with trims, buttons and loads of
"unique" prints that make each outfit look "just totally clever."

NEW Napapijri
- | - | - | E

SoHo | 149 Mercer St. (bet. Houston & Prince Sts.) | B/D/F/V to
B'way/Lafayette St. | 212-431-4490 | www.napapijri.com

Outward-bound men, women and kids as well as city folk who aspire
to the great outdoors–look converge at this Italian company's "beautiful" new SoHo stomping ground stocked with "excellent casualwear
and activewear" like rugged parkas, fashionable fleece and camo-
patterned ski overalls; "if you want to look good" in your board shorts,
"this is the place to be" – just bring lots of lira.

Natalie and Friends ◗
▽ 28 | 25 | 26 | E

E 60s | 205 E. 60th St. (bet. 2nd & 3rd Aves.) | 4/5/6/F/N/R/W to
59th St./Lexington Ave. | 212-759-9077 | www.natalieandfriends.com

For way-"cute" fashions that'll have you wishing you were "small again",
head to this East 60s kids' and tweens' emporium "deliciously close to
Dylan's Candy Bar", where owner Natalie Mayer is "on a first name basis
with customers"; with a host of "hip" labels like Tina Neumann, and even
a "store mascot, Raider" Potader, a Labrador with "a line of clothing"
named after him, the only drawback is that it's "hard to make a decision."

Natan Borlam's
▽ 28 | 11 | 24 | M

Williamsburg | 157 Havemeyer St. (bet. S. 2nd & 3rd Sts.) | Brooklyn |
G/L to Metropolitan Ave./Lorimer St. | 718-782-0108 |
866-782-0108 | www.boysitaliansuits.com

"Don't be scared off by the location" because it's well "worth the trip"
to this sprawling, old-guard children's boutique, a family-owned

Williamsburg fixture for over half a century; brave the "barely present-able" displays and you'll be rewarded with some of the "best buys" around on spiffy Italian suits for boys and "beautiful European" fashions for infants and toddlers from labels like Baby Graziella and Clayeux.

National Wholesale Liquidators ⏺ | 11 | 6 | 6 | I |

NoHo | 632 Broadway (Houston St.) | B/D/F/V to B'way/Lafayette St. | 212-979-2400
Bronx | 691 Co-Op City Blvd. (bet. Carver Loop & Peartree Ave.) | 6 to Pelham Bay Park | 718-320-7771
Bensonhurst | 2201 59th St. (Bay Pkwy.) | Brooklyn | F to Ave. N | 718-621-3993
Borough Pk | 4802-22 New Utrecht Ave. (48th St.) | Brooklyn | D/M to 50th St. | 718-438-2604
Flushing | 71-01 Kissena Blvd. (71st Ave.) | Queens | 7 to Main St. | 718-591-3900
LIC | 35-00 48th St. (bet. Northern Blvd. & 35th Ave.) | Queens | G/R/V to 46th St. | 718-389-3311
Staten Island | 1565 Forest Ave. (Decker Ave.) | 718-815-6533
www.nationalwholesaleliquidators.com

In between "the rudest salespeople" and the "messy aisles", this "circus"-like chain has "all the charms of a bus station", but pricewise you "can't beat it for staples" "for your bedroom, bathroom, living room, dining room" and kitchen; at select locations, the "new gourmet food department is worth checking out", and since 'dirt' is the opera-tive word at this dirt-cheap discounter, "wash anything you buy here before using" it.

Naturino | ▽ 28 | 26 | 23 | VE |

E 70s | 1410 Second Ave. (bet. 73rd & 74th Sts.) | 6 to 77th St. | 212-794-0570
E 80s | 1184 Madison Ave. (bet. 86th & 87th Sts.) | 4/5/6 to 86th St. | 212-427-0679
www.naturino.com

A household name overseas, this Italian children's footwear firm is making strides stateside, bringing a colorful cast of "very pricey", "cool" kicks for kids to its Madison Avenue and East 70s offshoots; "what a selection" cheer cohorts who choose from the namesake label as well as splurge-worthy styles from designer brands like Moschino and Oilily.

Natuzzi | ▽ 27 | 23 | 21 | E |

SoHo | 101 Greene St. (bet. Prince & Spring Sts.) | N/R/W to Prince St. | 212-334-4335 | www.natuzzi.com

"Well-made", "attractive modern" leather furniture like sofas, day-beds and chairs handcrafted in Italy is featured at this airy, Zen-feeling SoHo showroom selling what supporters cite is an "unbeatable com-bination of comfort and reasonable prices" for the quality.

NEW Nave | - | - | - | M |

SoHo | 159 Mercer St. (Houston St.) | B/D/F/V to B'way/Lafayette St. | 212-274-1255 | www.naveny.com

What a "cool concept" from Japanese apparel leader Onward Kashiyama confide style sleuths who find "fresh, fun" women's cloth-ing and handbags created by a collaborative coterie of designers that changes with the season at this SoHo newcomer; "love this store!" proclaim fashionistas who fall for "great pieces" in a "range of styles", from flowing dresses and fitted blazers to handmade knits in "different fabrics", all arranged on accessible circular racks.

NBA Store

| 21 | 23 | 16 | E |

E 50s | 666 Fifth Ave. (52nd St.) | E/V to 5th Ave./53rd St. | 212-515-6221 | 877-622-0206 | www.nba.com/nycstore

Grab your "hyperactive teenage sons" and dribble over to this "kid-friendly" Midtown mecca, an "enduring concept" for all things NBA where "excitement abounds" and you may even catch a "famous" player appearance; jump-start hoop dreams with "high-quality, authentic" jerseys, activewear and footwear, then whoosh down the circular ramp to shoot baskets or "play" video games; still, the "tourist"-fatigued yawn "yeah, if you're from Kansas."

Necessary Clothing ◐

| ▽ 17 | 15 | 15 | I |

NoHo | 676 Broadway (bet. Bond & Great Jones Sts.) | B/D/F/V to B'way/Lafayette St. | 212-473-2208
SoHo | 470 Broadway (bet. Broome & Grand Sts.) | N/R/W to Prince St. | 212-966-9011
www.necessaryclothes.com

When you're "on a budget but still want to look faboo when you go out with your girlfriends", this Downtown duo serves up what's necessary "for work or play" with "cute" knit shrugs, dressy capris, "surprisingly flirty and feminine" halter dresses, a tube top or two, tailored vests and velour tracksuits, all "for a fraction of the price" you pay at other SoHo emporiums nearby.

Nellie M. Boutique ◐

| 22 | 17 | 17 | E |

E 80s | 1309 Lexington Ave. (88th St.) | 4/5/6 to 86th St. | 212-996-4410 | www.nelliem.com

We "like" this "cute neighborhood" standby "better than some of the other small Upper East Side boutiques" reveal loyalists who laud the staff that's "generally friendlier" as well as the "assortment of T-shirts", "competitively priced jeans" and "very trendy" but a bit expensive designer collections; bridal parties get big-time pampering, and if you're lucky, you'll be there for one of their "spur-of-the-moment sales."

Nemo Tile Company ⊠

| 21 | 15 | 17 | M |

Flatiron | 48 E. 21st St. (bet. B'way & Park Ave. S.) | 6 to 23rd St. | 212-505-0009
Jamaica | 177-02 Jamaica Ave. (177th St.) | Queens | F to Hillside | 718-291-5969
800-636-6845 | www.nemotile.com

Since 1921, this "contractors' source" in Queens and the newer two-story showroom in the Flatiron District have offered a "good selection of tiles" for "budget-conscious bathroom renovation", along with a discount area and plumbing and accessories like mirrors, medicine cabinets and shower doors.

Nest

| - | - | - | E |

Park Slope | 396A Seventh Ave. (bet. 12th & 13th Sts.) | Brooklyn | F to 7th Ave. | 718-965-3491 | www.nestbrand.com

In a neighborhood where there's slim pickin's when it comes to home-design stores, this Park Slope boutique offers something "different" for *nouveau* nesters or anyone looking for an apartment revamp; choose from the funky, the fanciful (Tord Boontje lighting) or the just plain practical like bath linens, shelving and Blu Dot furniture, along with toys, trimmings and other "lovely things for a child's room."

☑ Neue Galerie New York
26	23	20	E

E 80s | 1048 Fifth Ave. (86th St.) | 4/5/6 to 86th St. | 212-628-6200 | www.neuegalerie.org

Even the "gift store is a museum" at this "amazing" landmark building on upper Fifth Avenue featuring the "*wunderbar*" fine and decorative arts of Germany and Austria; the "superior silver and crafts" ("replicas of work by designers such as Josef Hoffmann) and "fantastic books" are "as much of a treat" as the exhibitions (and the "first-class" restaurants, Cafe Sabarsky and the Cafe Fledermaus downstairs), but "high prices" have *nein*-sayers sniffing it's "not for the average shopper."

New Balance
27	20	22	M

E 50s | 821 Third Ave. (50th St.) | 6 to 51st St. | 212-421-4444
W 40s | 51 W. 42nd St. (bet. 5th & 6th Aves.) | 7/B/D/F/V to 42nd St./ Bryant Park | 212-997-9112
www.newbalance.com

"If you're an athlete, or work out on a regular basis", sprint over to these Midtown "runner's meccas" for a "wide selection" of "long-lasting", "high-performance shoes for the big race" and styles "light, comfortable and tough enough" for "pavement pounders"; the "excellent staff" "doesn't just try to sell you the latest trend – it helps you figure out what is best for your foot and your sport."

New Museum of
Contemporary Art Store ☒ Ⓜ
-	-	-	M

Chelsea | 556 W. 22nd St. (11th Ave.) | C/E to 23rd St. | 212-343-0460 | www.newmuseum.org

"Edgy, unique gifts for yourself" from artists such as Chrissy Conant, John Waters, Marcel Dzama, Mike Giant, Neckface and Ryan McGinness are displayed at this Chelsea museum shop where T-shirts, housewares and other affordably priced objects are on display; the new Bowery digs will be completed in 2007, but until then, the store will also offer "great" unusual books, lomographic cameras and DVDs of esoteric art-related films.

New York & Company ☒
17	17	16	M

Financial Dist | 83 Nassau St. (bet. Fulton & John Sts.) | 2/3/4/5/A/C/J/M/Z to Fulton St./B'way/Nassau | 212-964-2864 | 800-723-5333 |
www.newyorkandcompany.com
Additional locations throughout the NY area

"Constant sales and discounts" make this the spot to get "trendy, comfortable" women's attire and accessories; still, the "sizing is significantly off-base" with "everything running two sizes too big", which doesn't bother some ladies who don't mind being an 8 rather than a 12 when they visit this affordable chain; also be aware that "it's always tough to get a dressing room."

New York Central Art Supply ☒
25	16	21	M

E Vill | 62 Third Ave. (11th St.) | 4/5/6/L/N/Q/R/W to 14th St./ Union Sq. | 212-473-7705 | 800-950-6111 | www.nycentralart.com

"What an art supply shop is supposed to be" profess patrons of this "small" East Village "indie" veteran vending both the "esoteric and the ordinary" including a "mind-boggling", "top-of-the-line" array of "beautiful papers for book artists" and watercolorists; service can be "hit-or-miss" (some note it's "a cut above", others detect "arti-tude"), but the "good prices" and "interesting inventory" make it "worth a visit."

New York Doll Hospital

▽ 28 | 19 | 25 | E

E 60s | 787 Lexington Ave., 2nd fl. (bet. 61st & 62nd Sts.) | 4/5/6/F/N/R/W to 59th St./Lexington Ave. | 212-838-7527

When "their favorite" dollie, teddy or toy is in need of "repair or reha-bilitation", little kids rush them straight to this East 60s "haven" where, with a little TLC, the "master-craftsman" "owner, Irving Chais – an "institution in-and-of himself" – nurses "modern and antique" cherished ones; this "landmark" has been a "New York tradition" for over a century, and "no one does it better" insist loyalists.

New York Elegant Fabric

– | – | – | E

W 40s | 222 W. 40th St. (bet. 7th & 8th Aves.) | 1/2/3/7/N/Q/R/S/W to 42nd St./Times Sq. | 212-302-4980

Conveniently sited just off Times Square and around the corner from Parsons Fashion Design Center, this basters' bastion may look basic but material witnesses swear it's 20,000 sq. ft. of "lovely fabric" (spe-cialties include European brocades and silks) proffered by "lovely peo-ple"; high-quality weaves for upholstery and draperies draw decorators and DIYers as well.

New York Golf Center

24 | 20 | 20 | E

Chelsea | Golf Club at Chelsea Piers | Pier 59 (18th St. & West Side Hwy.) | A/C/E/L to 14th St./8th Ave. | 212-242-8899
Garment Dist | 131 W. 35th St. (bet. B'way & 7th Ave.) | B/D/F/N/Q/R/V/W to 34th St./Herald Sq. | 212-564-2255
888-465-7890 | www.nygolfcenter.com

With 9,000 sq. ft. of showroom, this Garment District mainstay is "the place to go" for the "best golf selection in the city"; an "excellent staff" can caddy you through "all the major brands" from Titlest to Taylor, and while the merchandise is "on the pricey side, you get what you need"; P.S. "try out a new club" at the Chelsea Piers branch boasting an expansive "indoor driving range."

New York Look, The

20 | 17 | 15 | E

E 40s | 551 Fifth Ave. (45th St.) | 4/5/6/7/S to 42nd St./Grand Central | 212-557-0909
SoHo | 468 W. Broadway (bet. Houston & Prince Sts.) | C/E to Spring St. | 212-598-9988 ◕
W 40s | 570 Seventh Ave. (41st St.) | 1/2/3/7/N/Q/R/S/W to 42nd St./Times Sq. | 212-382-2760 ☒
W 60s | 2030 Broadway (69th St.) | 1/2/3 to 72nd St. | 212-362-8650 ◑
W 60s | 30 Lincoln Plaza (bet. 62nd & 63rd Sts.) | 1/A/B/C/D to 59th St./Columbus Circle | 212-245-6511 ◑

"Check out" this fashionista chain with a name "reminiscent of the '80s" and the "latest" looks for work, "trendy", "up-to-date" party dresses, shoes and "excellent costume jewelry"; while no one denies this outfit's "knack" for "quality and style", shoppers say the staff practically "air-kisses you on arrival" and can be "more aggressive than primitive cavemen" – in fact their *"Glengarry Glen Ross* sales tech-nique is a major detraction."

	QUALITY	DISPLAY	SERVICE	COST

New York Pipe Dreams

	QUALITY	DISPLAY	SERVICE	COST
	-	-	-	E

E 80s | 1623 York Ave. (bet. 85th & 86th Sts.) | 4/5/6 to 86th St. |
866-666-6973 | www.newyorkpipedreams.com

Whether the equipment of choice is surf, skate or snow, board members are big believers in this East 80s sporting goods store, which handles a "large selection" of gear, plus all the garb and accessories that accompany these activities; "prices are good", considering the range of brands, and the store also offers sign-up services for bus trips to mountains, beaches and skate parks.

New York Public Library Shop, The Ⓜ

	QUALITY	DISPLAY	SERVICE	COST
	23	20	18	M

E 40s | 476 Fifth Ave. (42nd St.) | 7 to 5th Ave. | 212-930-0641
Harlem | Schomburg Ctr. | 515 Malcolm X Blvd. (135th St.) | 2/3 to
135th St. | 212-491-2206 Ⓩ
www.thelibraryshop.org

Paging all "book-lovers": the New York Public Library's "interesting" shop (and its Schomburg Center outpost) constitutes "heaven for literary" lions lured by "everything from pencils to huge coffee-table" tomes; like the "NYPL system", it's a "treasure" trove of "gifts galore" including maps, writing instruments, "innovative cards" and apparel that's "not too pricey", and though a few whisper there's "not much there", more maintain it's "worth a visit."

New York Replacement Parts Corp. Ⓩ

	QUALITY	DISPLAY	SERVICE	COST
	22	10	20	M

E 90s | 1456 & 1464 Lexington Ave. (bet. 94th & 95th Sts.) | 6 to 96th St. |
212-534-0818 | 800-228-4718 | www.nyrpcorp.com

"Can't find it? – they can", so for "older fixtures" that need "rare" or "replacement parts", "pros go" to this "essential" plumbing showroom and supply house in the East 90s that "covers a range of prices"; it's always "packed" so "be prepared to wait"; N.B. closed weekends.

New York Running Company ◑

	QUALITY	DISPLAY	SERVICE	COST
	24	24	23	E

W 50s | The Shops at Columbus Circle, Time Warner Ctr. | 10 Columbus
Circle, 2nd fl. (bet. 58th & 60th Sts.) | 1/A/B/C/D to 59th St./
Columbus Circle | 212-823-9626 | www.therunningcompany.net

"If you need shoe guidance" and a "lot of good running gear and sneakers", dash over to this Time Warner Center standby "well situated to Central Park"; the "excellent" staff "evaluates you on the treadmill" and "helps" "even the most serious" athlete "find shoes that match your stride and improve efficiency"; such scrutiny "results in perfect fit, if not the perfect price."

New York Transit Museum

	QUALITY	DISPLAY	SERVICE	COST
	20	18	17	M

E 40s | Grand Central, main concourse | 42nd St. (Vanderbilt Ave.) |
4/5/6/7/S to 42nd St./Grand Central | 212-878-0106 ◑
Brooklyn Hts | Corner of Boerum Pl. (Schermerhorn St.) | Brooklyn |
1/2/4/5/M/N/R to Court St./Borough Hall | 718-694-1600
www.transitmuseumstore.com

"Be true to your train line" at these sister shops in Downtown Brooklyn and Grand Central Station, where the "transit-themed tchotchkes" roam from "vintage token jewelry" to "subway map mugs" to "cute" apparel covered with "MTA insignia"; you'll also find "great" authentic memorabilia from retired fleets (air gauges, signs, straps) and "unique" gifts for kids – "the only thing missing is that underground aroma."

	QUALITY	DISPLAY	SERVICE	COST

Nicholas Perricone 🖂
E 60s | 791 Madison Ave. (67th St.) | 6 to 68th St. | 212-734-2537 | www.nicholasperricone.com

| 22 | 21 | 21 | VE |

This "spacious and serene" Upper East Side store touts the teachings of its dermatologist founder Dr. Nicholas Perricone, who believes great skin comes from diet (salmon, salmon and more salmon), vitamin supplements and his own "patented" 35-piece, anti-aging treatment line that includes the likes of Amine Complex Face Lift; but foes fume that the "overpriced" products are "so costly I thought they would just scare my wrinkles away!"

Nicole Farhi
E 60s | 10 E. 60th St. (bet. 5th & Madison Aves.) | N/R/W to 5th Ave./59th St. | 212-223-8811 | www.nicolefarhi.com

| 25 | 28 | 24 | VE |

"Scrumptious" is a word that sums up this British designer in more ways than one: in her "beautiful" East 60s shop, both he and she "can have lunch" in the lower-level restaurant before or after shopping for "sexy-to-slouchy" suits and belted coats, "gorgeous" graceful dresses and an "extremely well-edited collection" of home accessories, from rabbit fur pillows to Tunisian glassware.

Nicole Miller
E 60s | 780 Madison Ave. (bet. 66th & 67th Sts.) | 6 to 68th St. | 212-288-9779
SoHo | 77 Greene St. (bet. Broome & Spring Sts.) | N/R/W to Prince St. | 212-219-1825
www.nicolemiller.com

| 24 | 22 | 21 | E |

"Relatively affordable for Madison Avenue" and SoHo too (especially with the "faboo sales"), this duo specializes in "event dresses" and "true-to-size" eveningwear "you can actually wear", plus a few "funky pieces to add to your work separates"; despite the "classic cuts", this designer "always" delivers "something original to fit the occasion", thanks to the highly "helpful staff."

Niketown New York ●
E 50s | 6 E. 57th St. (bet. 5th & Madison Aves.) | 4/5/6/F/N/R/W to 59th St./Lexington Ave. | 212-891-6453 | www.niketown.com

| 24 | 25 | 17 | E |

"Like an amusement park for the feet" and the bod too, this Midtown "athlete's dream" is "so big, with so many floors" and so many "stylish, yet functional" sneakers and clothing items you can "make a day event out of just "browsing"; the "cool vibe" puts "motivated" types and "couch potatoes alike" "in the work-out mood" and so may the "very eager staff"; still, the "crowd"-adverse cry it's "impossible to make a quick in/out purchase", warning, "avoid on weekends."

NEW Nili Lotan Ⓜ
TriBeCa | 188 Duane St. (Greenwich St.) | 1/2/3 to Chambers St. | 212-431-7788 | www.nililotan.com

| – | – | – | E |

Imagine rocker Patti Smith dressing for a job interview and you'll get a sense of the crisp shirts, skinny pants and masculine-feminine tailoring offered at this "individual and interesting" Israeli designer's elegantly spare TriBeCa flagship/design studio; while "beautiful people shop here", the vibe is more art gallery than boutique, with a dry cleaner's conveyer belt circulating the "well-designed" womenswear coveted by cool Downtowners prepared to "break the bank."

			QUALITY	DISPLAY	SERVICE	COST

99X ⬤

▽ 18 | 17 | 19 | M

E Vill | 84 E. 10th St. (bet. 3rd & 4th Aves.) | 6 to Astor Pl. | 212-460-8599 | www.99xnyc.com

"Head up the stairs for the best of King's Road" British apparel advise guys who "look and feel like a trendster" shopping at this "East Village punk store" that's been "rocking" for decades; admirers mark it as a spot for one of the "best selections of Fred Perry" and Ben Sherman clothing, plus "essential mod gear" like Tuk creepers, "cool" Doc Martens and Gola trainers, and while the stock's mostly for blokes, there's a bit for birds too.

Nine West

17 | 18 | 16 | M

E 50s | 675 Fifth Ave. (bet. 53rd & 54th Sts.) | E/V to 5th Ave./53rd St. | 212-319-6893 | 800-999-1877 | www.ninewest.com
Additional locations throughout the NY area

"Without" this "solid-bet" chain, "I'd be barefoot" quip shoppers who circle the "constantly changing" racks for "on-trend footwear at prices that allow you to treat yourself to more than one pair"; "for those that can't afford the Manolos and the Choos", the "sexy", "stylish" shoes "for work and play" "make us feel almost Sarah-Jessica-y"; but naysayers not "willing to put up with" "knockoffs" "you'll see all over the city" concur it's "not worth the inexpensive price tag."

Nintendo World ⬤

▽ 25 | 25 | 22 | M

E 40s | Rockefeller Ctr. | 10 Rockefeller Ctr. (bet. 5th & 6th Aves.) | B/D/F/V to 47-50th Sts./Rockefeller Ctr. | 646-459-0800 | www.nintendoworldstore.com

Nirvana for Nintendoheads, this "slick" Rockefeller Center superstore "rocks" thanks to a "fantastic" retailtainment "setup" split between the Game Boy Advance, DS and GameCube systems; kids make a beeline for the sampling bar or the giant gaming wall, then settle into the surround-sound gaming pods and software library; P.S. fans of former inhabitant Pokémon Center need not "miss" Pikachu and pals – they still live here in their own area.

Noisette

– | – | – | E

Williamsburg | 54 N. Sixth St. (Kent Ave.) | Brooklyn | L to Bedford Ave. | 718-388-5188 | www.noisettenyc.com

This once-deserted strip of Williamsburg is fast becoming shopping central due to style-magnets like this seductive store, whose name means 'hazelnut' in French; it's owned by Stéphanie Deleau, whose "beautiful" taste in all things Gallic – Aoyama Itchome ethnic-print dresses, Bash knits, Maje cashmeres, Aridza Bross carryalls – "is worth the cost" for seriously sleek gamines; N.B. don't miss Jerome Lagarrigue's stunning oil painting on the back wall.

NEW Nokia ⬤

22 | 21 | 18 | E

E 50s | 5 E. 57th St. (bet. 5th & Madison Aves.) | N/R/W to 5th Ave./59th St. | 212-758-1980 | www.nokia.com

Fans of the Finnish brand reach "high-tech" "heaven" at this "flashy" new "futuristic" three-floor Midtown flagship showcasing a "well-organized" selection of the "latest" mobile phones, accessories, electronics and other "geek stuff"; "if you have lots of bucks" head upstairs where upwards of $5,000 can buy you a customized Vertu cell, otherwise "go here to look and then go elsewhere to buy."

Nom de Guerre ◗ ▽ | 20 | 20 | 16 | E |

NoHo | 640 Broadway (Bleecker St.) | 6 to Bleecker St. | 212-253-2891 | www.nomdeguerre.net

With a name that means 'pseudonym', it's no wonder that this sign-less "guerrilla"-style boutique is located "underground" in a NoHo building reputed to be a "former Black Panthers' hangout"; the "cool, if limited merchandise" is just as "unexpected", from the house line of men's urbanwear to the "wildly exclusive kicks", including collaborative collections with Converse Jack Purcell and Adidas to the Comme des Garçons scents; still, snipers sling arrows at "snotty service."

Noose, The ◗ ▽ | 24 | 17 | 15 | E |

Chelsea | 261 W. 19th St. (bet. 7th & 8th Aves.) | 1 to 18th St. | 212-807-1789

"I like it like that!" say submissive boys and dominant girls sorting through the "good stuff" "crowded" into this small, "dark" Chelsea nook that fills the bill for fetishists; the "somewhat limited" stock of European sex toys, bondage wear and rarities like the P.E.S. electrical system might be shockingly "overpriced", but it's all "quality" merch, and the "extremely rude staff" might just be trying to treat you right.

Norman's Sound & Vision ◗ | – | – | – | I |

E Vill | 67 Cooper Sq. (3rd. Ave., bet. 7th & 8th Sts.) | 6 to Astor Pl. | 212-473-6599 | www.normanssound.com

"Searching through the cases can be time consuming but it's so worth it" is the sound advice from admirers of this East Village vet that's light on vinyl but heavy on "tough-to-find" jazz CDs; "overlooked deals abound", and owner Norman Isaacs' vision includes plans for a Brooklyn outpost.

North Face, The | 24 | 20 | 18 | E |

NEW **SoHo** | 139 Wooster St. (bet. Houston & Prince Sts.) | N/R/W to Prince St. | 212-260-1000
W 70s | 2101 Broadway (73rd St.) | 1/2/3 to 72nd St. | 212-362-1000 ◗
800-362-4963 | www.thenorthface.com

"Serious hikers" as well as "urban dwellers who want to" dress to "match their SUVs" trek to this shop in the Ansonia – and now its new SoHo sibling too – for "top-of-the-line gear" and clothing that "holds up to wear and tear"; whether you're searching for a "phat puffy" jacket or tents and backpacks, "nobody has a better selection of the brand that defines outdoor adventure"; still, a lost few "wish they were more inventive" and question the "clueless" staff.

Nort/Recon | – | – | – | E |
(fka Nort 235)

NoHo | 359 Lafayette St. (bet. Bond & Great Jones Sts.) | 6 to Bleecker St. | 212-777-6102 | www.reconstore.com

At this NoHo streetwear/sneaker specialist owned by legendary graffiti artists Stash and Futura, cool-hunters stock up on T-shirts, pants, jackets and bags while in-the-know Nike nuts hit the mother lode, tracking down unique kicks from the activewear label's limited-edition, imported and collaborative footwear collections; chances are you won't see yourself coming or going.

No. 6 Ⓜ | - | - | - | E |

Little Italy | 6 Centre Market Pl. (bet. Broome & Grand Sts.) | 6 to Spring St. | 212-226-5759 | www.no6store.com

Down a Little Italy alleyway ("never even knew of this street") lies this vintage clothier, which separates itself from the pack by specializing in everyday, if slightly "expensive", European garb; its light-filled digs, artfully if minimally decorated with white wood floors, leather couches and painted windows, highlight the womenswear, which includes both pure old pieces (primarily from the '40s–'70s) and some reconstituted ones; Jacqueline Schnabel footwear and new accessories round out the Continental collection.

Number (N)ine | - | - | - | E |

TriBeCa | 431 Washington St. (Vestry St.) | 1 to Canal St. | 212-431-8699 | www.numberniners.com

The interior almost outshines the clothes at this tiny TriBeCa boutique, as everything within its shadowy, draped interior seems made of 'found' objects: stereo speakers comprise the back wall and books sandwiched between wood slabs are tables; on the racks (erstwhile iron gate posts) hang casual mens- and womenswear from Japanese designer Takahiro Miyashita, whose stylings are for small-boned folks who enjoy neutral or earth-toned basics with that little extra twist – a tuxedo-frilled shirt here, a tab-fronted military jacket there – thrown in.

NYC Velo ◑ | ▽ 20 | 19 | 19 | E |

E Vill | 64 Second Ave. (bet. 3rd & 4th Sts.) | F/V to Lower East Side/ 2nd Ave. | 212-253-7771 | www.nycvelo.com

This family-owned East Village cycle shop offers more than a set of wheels; enthusiasts can latch onto every aspect of the bicycle lifestyle, from "beautiful" rides by Bianchi, Ridley and Turner to clothing and gear from the likes of Campagnolo, Descente and Giro, and even turn to the "knowledgeable staff" that bikes to work everyday for advice about the right fit; stop by the lounge to mingle with messengers and commuters over a free coffee and bagel.

Oak Ⓜ | - | - | - | E |

Park Slope | 668 President St. (bet. 5th & 6th Aves.) | Brooklyn | M/R to Union St. | 718-857-2080
Williamsburg | 208 N. Eighth St. (bet. Driggs & Roebling Sts.) | Brooklyn | L to Bedford Ave. | 718-782-0521
www.oaknyc.com

While the original Oak (and its women's counterpart, Canary) may be history, a new one grows in Williamsburg, a cool-as-ever sibling to the Park Slope standby that sprouted up a few years ago in a spare white carriage house; willowy hipsters of both sexes fall for boldface and emerging designer names, including Farhi, Hussein Chalayan, Imitation of Christ and Vivienne Westwood, plus jeans from Nudies and Acne and Truefitt + Hill shaving cream.

Oakley ◑ | ▽ 21 | 23 | 21 | E |

SoHo | 113 Prince St. (Greene St.) | N/R/W to Prince St. | 212-673-7700 | www.oakley.com

"Making people look good under the sun" for over 30 years, this SoHo outpost of an international chain offers "stylish shades" (including a line incorporating MP3 technology) preferred by "surfer dudes" and snowboarders as well as "sleek" eyeglasses; the "great" store also offers apparel and gear for those leading a high-performance lifestyle.

Occhiali 🖾 | 24 | 22 | 21 | E |

E 80s | 1188 Lexington Ave. (81st St.) | 6 to 77th St. | 212-639-1188
"Always satisfied" asserts the spec-set that sets its sights on this sleek, modern East 80s eyewear maven, "one of the best-designed stores in NYC", when it's time to see straight; "everything is good quality", from the funky frames to the Zeiss lenses, plus the "staff takes top-notch service to a new level", offering "polite but firm advice if you've gone astray in your choices."

NEW Ochre | - | - | - | VE |

SoHo | 462 Broome St. (bet. Greene & Mercer Sts.) | N/R/W to Prince St. | 212-414-4332 | www.ochre.net
"Amazing style" and high-quality craftsmanship mark this new stateside SoHo flagship of a decade-old British home-furnishings firm known for sexy signature seating, luxe day beds and chairs in plush velvet, suede and leather, along with lighting and bespoke chandeliers; of course, this kind of posh comes at a pretty price.

Oculus 20/20 ● | - | - | - | E |

NEW Carroll Gdns | 267 Smith St. (Degraw St.) | Brooklyn | F/G to Carroll St. | 718-554-6230
Carroll Gdns | 552 Henry St. (Carroll St.) | Brooklyn | F/G to Carroll St. | 718-852-9871
Williamsburg | 189 Bedford Ave. (bet. N. 6th & 7th Sts.) | Brooklyn | L to Bedford Ave. | 718-666-0040
For "beautiful frames not found anywhere else", head over the bridge to these attractive Brooklyn eyewear emporiums, boasting 20/20 fashion vision; the broad selection of high-end specs focuses on spectacular names like Francis Klein, Judith Leiber and Robert Marc, so chances are "you'll pay a lot" for the luxury of looking good.

Odin ● | - | - | - | E |

NEW NoLita | 199 Lafayette St. (bet. Broome & Kenmare Sts.) | 6 to Spring St. | 212-966-0026
Odin on 11th ●
E Vill | 328 E. 11th St. (2nd Ave.) | L to 1st Ave. | 212-475-0666
www.odinnewyork.com
"The vibe is so right" at this sophisticated "little" East Village "outfitter" (and its new NoLita offshoot) for the "modern metro man" featuring timely and fashionable urban wear from labels like Umbro by Kim Jones and Comme des Garçons alongside exclusive jewelry and accessories; "look in the back" for a small but well-edited selection of "perfect" gifts for "picky" guys, such as design books, grooming products and cameras from Lomo and Holga.

Oilily | 23 | 25 | 21 | E |

E 60s | 820 Madison Ave. (bet. 68th & 69th Sts.) | 6 to 68th St. | 212-772-8686
NEW SoHo | 465 W. Broadway (bet. Prince & W. Houston Sts.) | N/R/W to Prince St. | 212-871-0201
800-977-7736 | www.oililyusa.com
Catering to the "nonconformist" "future bohemian" "who marches to a different beat", Madison Avenue's Dutch treat (and its gigantic new

SoHo flagship) with a "sweet staff" stirs the senses with its "quirky" brand of kids' clothing (and adult offerings too) that comes in "happy" "showstopping" colors and patterns sure to "brighten up a gray New York day"; though too "wacky" for some, diehards decree that their "rugrats have never looked so good"; N.B. the Downtown store sells a different merchandise mix.

NEW Olá Baby Ⓜ
▽ 27 | 24 | 21 | E

Carroll Gdns | 315 Court St. (bet. Degraw & Sackett Sts.) | Brooklyn | F/G to Carroll St. | 718-422-1978 | www.olababy.com

Stroller pushers steer straight to this "interesting" "gem of a store" in Carroll Gardens when they want to spoil their little bundle with a "fantastic variety" of ultramodern nursery furniture and bedding, including Stokke Collection items from Sweden, baby clothing, toys, books and other "cool", "unusual design-y stuff"; throw in "fair prices" and a "pleasant, helpful staff" and you've got the perfect "neighborhood place."

O'Lampia Studio
▽ 29 | 26 | 28 | E

LES | 155 Bowery (bet. Broome & Delancey Sts.) | 6 to Spring St. | 212-925-1660 | www.olampia.com

For "unique and carefully crafted" custom lighting ranging from floor and table models to chandeliers, pendants and sconces, loyalists like this Bowery studio known for "sky-high quality without prices to match."

Olatz Ⓢ
– | – | – | VE

W Vill | 43 Clarkson St. (bet. Greenwich & Hudson Sts.) | 1 to Houston St. | 212-255-8627 | www.olatz.com

Two huge sleigh beds and a dramatic black-and-white checkered floor dominate this West Village shop owned by Olatz Schnabel, the wife of the painter Julian Schnabel; "high-quality" hand-embroidered linens, towels and crib sets are offered at equally elevated prices.

Olde Good Things
▽ 18 | 14 | 21 | M

Chelsea | 124 W. 24th St. (bet. 6th & 7th Aves.) | F/V to 23rd St. | 212-989-8401
G Vill | 19 Greenwich Ave. (bet. 6th & 7th Aves.) | A/B/C/D/E/F/V to W. 4th St. | 212-229-0850 ☽
888-551-7333 | www.oldegoodthings.com

The "goods" at these Chelsea and Greenwich Village salvage stores are indeed "old" and range from "outdoor fountains" and fireplace mantels to dressers, doorknobs, drawer pulls, tin mirrors, panels and "perfect period fixtures" and architectural elements for those "renovating turn-of-the-century brownstones"; the "presentation is haphazard at best" and "you are on your own" in terms of service, but there are lots of "unique artifacts" to be unearthed.

Olden Camera & Lens Company, Inc. Ⓢ
20 | 10 | 16 | M

Garment Dist | 1263 Broadway, 4th fl. (bet. 31st & 32nd Sts.) | B/D/F/N/Q/R/V/W to 34th St./Herald Sq. | 212-725-1234

"Worth a stop", this Garment District "oldie but goodie" lives up to its "wonderful reputation" as a "neat place" for analogue "camera nuts" "hunting for bargains" thanks to its "good selection of lenses" and "excellent used equipment" (such as "classic" Leicas and Super 8s) sold by "intelligent salespeople" "at reasonable prices"; still, some digital devotees declare it "outdated."

	QUALITY	DISPLAY	SERVICE	COST

Old Navy ⏱

Garment Dist | 150 W. 34th St. (bet. 6th & 7th Aves.) | B/D/F/N/Q/R/V/W to 34th St./Herald Sq. | 212-594-0115 | 800-653-6289 | www.oldnavy.com
Additional locations throughout the NY area

QUALITY 14 | DISPLAY 14 | SERVICE 13 | COST I

"Thrifty is the word" at this "no-frills" "upbeat" chain, which may provide "the best value out there" for "cheap basics" as well as "trendy pieces" for the entire family crew; you may "have to hunt forever for a size" given that everything's "so stuffed onto the racks" and the stores are often a "mob scene"; nonetheless to most it's always "worth a look."

Olive & Bette's

QUALITY 22 | DISPLAY 19 | SERVICE 19 | COST E

E 80s | 1070 Madison Ave. (bet. 80th & 81st Sts.) | 6 to 77th St. | 212-717-9655

SoHo | 158 Spring St. (bet. W. B'way & Wooster St.) | C/E to Spring St. | 646-613-8772

W 70s | 252 Columbus Ave. (bet. 71st & 72nd Sts.) | 1/2/3 to 72nd St. | 212-579-2178 ⏱

W Vill | 384 Bleecker St. (Perry St.) | 1 to Christopher St./Sheridan Sq. | 212-206-0036 ⏱
www.oliveandbettes.com

"Knock yourself out" at this "quirky" quartet – it's the "go-to place for what's hot for the moment" confirm fashionistas; the "mix of froufrou and basics is ideal for one-stop shopping", particularly if you're jonesing for "cute T-shirts", "in-vogue accessories" and "anything sequined" from "popular" labels; as to the "witty staff", hey, "salespeople who actually deign to help find the perfect pair of jeans make my day."

Oliver Peoples

QUALITY 27 | DISPLAY 25 | SERVICE 23 | COST VE

E 60s | 755 Madison Ave. (bet. 65th & 66th Sts.) | 6 to 68th St. | 212-585-3433
SoHo | 366 W. Broadway (Broome St.) | N/R/W to Prince St. | 212-925-5400
888-568-1655 | www.oliverpeoples.com

"For LA style" at "NYC prices" tastemakers "go no further" than this spec-tacular, "top-notch" Uptown-Downtown duo with "courteous" service; slip on a pair of "chic shades to cruise around SoHo like a native" or check out the "hip eyewear", the "sportier" Mosley Tribes spin-off collection (a "great addition") and Paul Smith numbers; sure, "seeing is believing" when it comes to the "expensive prices", but fans insist they're the "most interesting glasses out there, bar none."

NEW Oliver Spencer

QUALITY – | DISPLAY – | SERVICE – | COST E

W Vill | 750 Greenwich St. (11th St.) | 1/9 to Christopher St. | 212-337-3095 | www.oliverspencer.co.uk

With scuffed-up antique furniture and shirts stuffed into bell jars, this intimate West Villager resembles the study of a slightly daft Victorian gent; but the clothing is all contemporary – quality sportswear from the namesake British designer whose U.K. clientele includes Paul McCartney, Daniel Day Lewis and Pierce Brosnan, plus sweaters, tees and jeans from Trovata, Engineered Garments and Rag & Bone; Sharp toiletries and a few leather goods round out the lot.

OMO Norma Kamali ✗

QUALITY 22 | DISPLAY 26 | SERVICE 24 | COST E

W 50s | 11 W. 56th St. (bet. 5th & 6th Aves.) | N/Q/R/W to 57th St. | 212-957-9797 | 800-852-6254 | www.normakamalicollection.com

"Diversity and quality are always an element in the style" of this truly original designer, whose museumlike Midtown store displays her wares like works of art; converts confide the classic, wrinkle-free polyester jersey separates, pin-up girl maillots and signature "sleeping bag coats last forever" – a good thing, since there is and "will only be one Norma."

Only Hearts

21 | 18 | 17 | E

NoLita | 230 Mott St. (bet. Prince & Spring Sts.) | 6 to Spring St. | 212-431-3694
W 70s | 386 Columbus Ave. (bet. 78th & 79th Sts.) | 1 to 79th St. | 212-724-5608
www.onlyhearts.com

"Everything is soo cute and lacy" sigh the smitten aflutter over the "beautiful lingerie" at this "lovely" NoLita–West 70s twosome; whether you're scouting for "comfy" camis, come-hither thongs, a "fun bridal gift" or even "unique jewelry", the "exceptional finds make any woman happy and mend any" broken "ties with a lover"; still, "go on a day when you don't need to" worry about the cost because some scanties seem priced "too high."

On Stage Dance Shop 🖪

– | – | – | M

Murray Hill | 197 Madison Ave. (bet. 34th & 35th Sts.) | 6 to 33rd St. | 212-725-1174 | www.onstagedancewear.com

"A bit more personal" than the boldface-name competitors with a "staff that's eager to assist", this Murray Hill shop "chock-full of dance attire" for "professional wear" outfits both Broadway performers from shows like *The Lion King* and plain ol' exercise-buffs; the leotards, unitards, skatewear and tutus are assembled on barrellike racks with ballet, salsa, jazz, flamenco and tap shoes to match.

Opening Ceremony ●

– | – | – | E

SoHo | 35 Howard St. (bet. B'way & Crosby St.) | N/R/W to Canal St. | 212-219-2688 | www.openingceremony.us

You're invited to an ever-changing celebration of "the most cutting-edge clothes in town" at this SoHo rite of style passage, where you'll find "often gorgeous, always credit-card-maxing" dresses, suits, sweatshirts and tempting T-shirts for men and women from emerging American and European designers, plus a temporary boutique-within-a-boutique upstairs devoted to Topshop, the British cheap-chic chain; chances are "few others" will be wearing this "one-off" garb "on the number 4 train."

Orange Blossom 🖪 🅼

– | – | – | E

Park Slope | 180 Lincoln Pl. (bet. 7th & 8th Aves.) | Brooklyn | B/Q to 7th Ave. | 347-247-5917 | www.orangeblossomnyc.com

Get your fashion juices flowing at this "sweet" Park Slope shop, run by Texas transplants Tracey and Shane Selberg, who favor "cool", "creative" threads from under-the-radar brands like Mr. Tiny, Tea Collection and Wonderboy; extras such as sterling-silver keepsakes, blankets and hand-knit stuffed animals add to its a-peel, making it a "great place to run to when you need a gift quick."

Orchard Corset Center

– | – | – | M

LES | 157 Orchard St. (bet. Rivington & Stanton Sts.) | F/J/M/Z to Delancey/Essex Sts. | 212-674-0786 | 877-267-2427 | www.orchardcorset.com

It's "worth a trip to the Lower East Side" for the "uplifting" New York experience at this "tiny" veteran that's been selling lingerie since 1968; "everything is in boxes" but that's ok since the owner and his mom "will pick the right size" "just by looking at you" – in other words, "be prepared to throw your inhibitions away."

Oriental Lamp Shade Co. 🖼

25	18	23	E

E 60s | 816 Lexington Ave. (bet. 62nd & 63rd Sts.) | 4/5/6/F/N/R/W to 59th St./Lexington Ave. | 212-832-8190
W 70s | 223 W. 79th St. (bet. Amsterdam Ave. & B'way) | 1 to 79th St. | 212-873-0812
www.orientallampshade.com

You can find classic lamps and the largest selection of ready-made and custom shades in hand-sewn silk, paper, linen, hide and metal at these "been-around-forever", family-run East Side and West Side siblings with an "excellent", "knowledgeable" staff; while prices are "on the expensive side", the glowing result is "worth it."

Original Penguin ●

–	–	–	M

W 40s | 1077 Sixth Ave. (41st St.) | 7/B/D/F/V to 42nd St./Bryant Park | 646-443-3520 | www.originalpenguin.com

The march of the penguins continues across from Bryant Park at this flagship for the venerable golf-clubhouse label (relaunched as a his-and-hers sportswear line in '03); the revisionist-retro palette "freshens up casual" clothing with a "smattering of wit"; with a staff that "makes everyone feel welcome" who wouldn't be down with OP?

Origins ●

24	23	22	M

E 40s | Grand Central | 42nd St. (Vanderbilt Ave.) | 4/5/6/7/S to 42nd St./Grand Central | 212-808-4141
Flatiron | Flatiron Bldg. | 175 Fifth Ave. (22nd St.) | N/R/W to 23rd St. | 212-677-9100
SoHo | 402 W. Broadway (Spring St.) | C/E to Spring St. | 212-219-9764
W 80s | 2327 Broadway (bet. 84th & 85th Sts.) | 1 to 86th St. | 212-769-0970
800-674-4467 | www.origins.com

"It even smells calm" say supporters of this skincare, bath and body chain that "knows how to cater to its clientele" with "not too pricey" "eco-conscious products" made from aromatic natural ingredients like mint and white tea, along with a mushroom-based treatment line from alternative medicine guru Dr. Andy Weil; a "knowledgeable staff" "encourages sampling", and you don't have to be a "crunchy granola type" to appreciate the "soothing, soulful" "spalike" experience here.

Orvis Company, The

25	23	22	E

E 40s | 522 Fifth Ave. (44th St.) | 4/5/6/7/S to 42nd St./Grand Central | 212-827-0698 | 888-235-9763 | www.orvis.com

"Perfect" for the "sophisticated" "sporting set", this Midtown outpost of the 150-year-old, family-owned Vermont chain reels in "adventurous" "blue-blood types" as well as "outdoorsy" aspirants who "just want to look like they're going fly fishing" or hunting; no need to wade unaided through the "high-quality equipment" and "excellent" clothing (including one of the "best Barbour selections") – just turn to the "extremely friendly" staff for "first-class fashion advice" and angling pointers too.

☑ Oscar de la Renta 🖼

28	28	28	VE

E 60s | 772 Madison Ave. (66th St.) | 6 to 68th St. | 212-288-5810 | www.oscardelarenta.com

"When you want a classy, timeless look, it's Oscar" opine the ladies who not only lunch, but party all night long – preferably in a sizzling cocktail dress or red-carpet–ready gown from the consummate designer, who still "keeps up with the moment" after more than 40 years; his "beautiful" Madison Avenue boutique offers exclusive evening collections, as well as "classic" daytime suits and extravagant accessories, all overseen by "an amazing staff."

NEW Oska
`- | - | - | M`

SoHo | 415 W. Broadway (bet. Prince & Spring Sts.) | C/E to Spring St. | 212-625-2772 | www.oska.de

Collect five easy pieces – or six or seven – from the unstructured separates made by this German mens- and womenswear label, which is celebrating its 10th anniversary with a new SoHo store; made in a rainbow of soft colors (shown to advantage in the white, boxy space) and forgiving fabrics (boiled wool, linen, corduroy), the vaguely Asian loose tunics, wide-legged pants, long skirts and shirts seem especially suited to middle-aged torsos – not to mention any soul who's sick of the super-skinny look.

☑ Other Music ◑
`27 | 19 | 20 | M`

NoHo | 15 E. Fourth St. (bet. B'way & Lafayette St.) | 6 to Astor Pl. | 212-477-8150 | www.othermusic.com

"*High Fidelity* with a PhD" proclaim "indie snobs" of NoHo's "aptly named" "hip, happening" "music source" "designed to scare Top 40 types" with its "exceptional" selection of "hard-to-find" alternative and underground CDs and vinyl; if you "pay attention to the knowledgeable staff", you'll "find that next undiscovered gem" (the "more obscure the better"), and even though it's admittedly "expensive", few mind because it may be the "most influential record shop" around.

Otte ◑
`▽ 26 | 25 | 17 | E`

W Vill | 121 Greenwich Ave. (bet. Jane & W. 13th Sts.) | A/C/E/L to 14th St./8th Ave. | 212-229-9424
Williamsburg | 132 N. Fifth St. (bet. Bedford Ave. & Berry St.) | Brooklyn | L to Bedford Ave. | 718-302-3007

Devotees declare "you're guaranteed to love" the young, elegant lines like Rebecca Taylor, 3.1 Phillip Lim, Vanessa Bruno and Eberjay lingerie at the West Village shop, and casually chic, "up-to-the-second" finds from Acne Jeans, Velvet and Wrangler at the Williamsburg branch; all are sanely presented by color, and while the "lock on the door" can be annoying if the "staff isn't paying attention", once you're in, you'll be in fashion.

Otto Tootsi Plohound ◑
`23 | 22 | 17 | E`

Flatiron | 137 Fifth Ave. (bet. 20th & 21st Sts.) | N/R/W to 23rd St. | 212-460-8650
NoLita | 273 Lafayette St. (Prince St.) | N/R/W to Prince St. | 212-431-7299

"Entire outfits can be planned around" the "avant-garde footwear" for both sexes at this "nonconformist" outfit, which recently downsized from a quartet to a Flatiron-NoLita duo; the selection is so "dizzying it'll give anyone a shoe fetish" – "whether you need something sassy, classy" or "funky", you'll find it at this "spacious, mod" "city staple" stocked with "seriously unique" offerings from "as-of-yet-unheard-of" labels and "veteran designer brands" alike; still, a few grumble "the only thing more preposterous than the designs are the prices."

| | QUALITY | DISPLAY | SERVICE | COST |

☑ Oxxford Clothes ☒
E 50s | 717 Fifth Ave. (E. 56th St.) | N/R/W to 5th Ave./59th St. |
212-593-0204 | www.oxxfordclothes.com

28 | – | 27 | VE

Worshipers can now pledge their allegiance to the 91-year-old
American brand at its new "temple" in Midtown, where hand-tailored
menswear is often made-to-order for clients that include President
Bush; the special-order crowd shells out a lot of Benjamins, but it's
"ooh so worth it" for what the sartorial majority declares the "best suits
made in the USA" – not to mention shirts, coats and even walking sticks.

Pan Aqua Diving
W 40s | 460 W. 43rd St. (bet. 9th & 10th Aves.) | A/C/E to 42nd St./
Port Authority | 212-736-3483 | 800-434-0884 | www.panaqua.com

– | – | – | E

One of the "best dive shops in the tri-state area", this Times Square–area
water-world offers the upscale aqua man or woman "top-of-the-line"
snorkeling equipment, fins, regulators, wetsuits and swimwear – nearly
everything except perhaps a pair of gills; the "knowledgeable, enthu-
siastic" staff also lives the life aquatic, which means the instructors
are "genuinely interested in teaching" certification classes.

P&S Fabrics
TriBeCa | 355 Broadway (bet. Franklin & Leonard Sts.) | 1 to Franklin St. |
212-226-1534 | www.psfabrics.com

▽ 22 | 13 | 18 | I

"Just steps from Chinatown", this "general-purpose sewing store"
proffers a plethora of "basic items that can be hard to find in
Manhattan" – and may also be the borough's "one affordable place for
mainstream yarn", with "enormous selections of Lion Brand, Patons
and Bernat blends" plus tools, patterns and notions; "bargain-
hunters" willing to tolerate the bare-bones setting and variable service
can find some "incredible values on upholstery fabrics."

Paparazzi ●
Gramercy | 202 E. 23rd St. (bet. 2nd & 3rd Aves.) | 6 to 23rd St. |
212-689-1968

▽ 21 | 21 | 12 | M

Whether it's "to pick up a gift for someone or a pick-me-up for yourself", supporters "love this eclectic little boutique of trinkets and treasures" near Gramercy Park, whose wares range from "subtle to
outlandish, from good girl to bad" clothes, accessories and jewelry –
along with "good cards" and "last-minute gifts"; however, like the
store's namesake, the staff sometimes "breathes down your neck."

Paper Presentation
Flatiron | 23 W. 18th St. (bet. 5th & 6th Aves.) | 1 to 18th St. |
212-463-7035 | 800-727-3701 | www.paperpresentation.com

25 | 20 | 19 | M

"They have it all" at this block-long Flatiron favorite with its "amazing
stock" of "all things paper", from stationery and scrapbooking supplies
to "do-it-yourself invitations" and business cards; "it's filled with lots
of ideas and things you never knew you needed" at "bargain" prices.

Papyrus ●
NEW W 40s | 11 W. 42nd St. (bet. 5th & 6th Aves.) | 7/B/D/F/V to
42nd St./Bryant Park | 212-302-3053 | www.papyrusonline.com
Additional locations throughout the NY area

23 | 20 | 17 | M

Those who prefer their greeting cards "edgier than Hallmark" prize this
"convenient" and "crammed" chain – with a new Midtown flagship –

for its "tasteful", "original" selection (heavy on company founder Marcel Schurman's brand), along with stationery, wrapping paper and "cute extras" like stickers, frames and "little gifty things"; the "frequent-buyer program" keeps loyalists coming back as do the "great sales."

☒ Paragon Sporting Goods ◐ | 25 | 18 | 18 | M |

Union Sq | 867 Broadway (18th St.) | 4/5/6/L/N/Q/R/W to 14th St./ Union Sq. | 212-255-8036 | 800-961-3030 | www.paragonsports.com
"Serious sports enthusiasts", "obsessive exercisers" and "ordinary" gym rats find "everything they need and then some" at Union Square's "friendly" "king of sports" "supermarket" that sets the "gold standard" with its "dizzying" "A-to-Z" selection of "hiking, biking, tennis, camping and urban living goods"; weekends are so "mobbed" "it can be harrowing" and "tough to navigate", plus a few fume "you practically have to beg" for a salesperson; nevertheless, there are plenty of "intriguing discoveries to be stumbled upon."

NEW Parasuco ◐ | 21 | 20 | 18 | E |

NoLita | 60 Spring St. (Lafayette St.) | 6 to Spring St. | 212-925-8858 | www.parasuco.com
"Canadian street couture" geared toward a "younger" crowd comes to NYC via this new NoLita denim emporium peddling name brand jeans and sportswear in an "opulent" chandeliered ex-bank building with "soaring" ceilings; if the "terrific" space impresses shoppers, the "underrepresented label" still leads some to wonder "why everything needs to have the Parasuco name on it?"

Park Avenue Audio | 24 | 19 | 20 | VE |

Gramercy | 425 Park Ave. S. (29th St.) | 6 to 28th St. | 212-685-8101 | www.parkavenueaudio.com
Owned and operated by three generations of a single family, this Gramercy Park electronics store is brimming with "nice stuff", namely "high-end" entertainment equipment; the "expert" consultants enlighten customers with "honest advice" and can even team up with your interior designer to customize and install a home theater or multiroom music system that will have you curled up on the couch purring.

Parke & Ronen ◐ | – | – | – | M |

Chelsea | 176 Ninth Ave. (21st St.) | C/E to 23rd St. | 212-989-4245 | www.parkeandronen.com
The namesake NY-based design duo doles out seasonal collections that are "nice spins on everyday wear" for men at their one-room boutique in Chelsea; although the "body-conscious" cuts of their svelte shirts, denim and skimpy underwear leave some warning "the waistline-challenged need not shop here", alterations and custom-orders are readily available.

Paron Fabrics ☒ | 20 | 13 | 18 | M |

W 40s | 206 W. 40th St. (bet. 7th & 8th Aves.) | A/C/E to 42nd St./ Port Authority | 212-768-3266 | www.paronfabrics.com
Bring your "upholsterer, tailor or dressmaker" to this Times Square trove for some "wonderful buys" (e.g. "mill ends of designers' bolts"), "especially in the half-price" annex – but you'll "have to be patient to wade through all the stock"; if a handful huff it's "overrated", most insist that perks like the proprietors' "old-world knowledge" make it "well worth the trip."

Patagonia
27 | 22 | 22 | E

SoHo | 101 Wooster St. (bet. Prince & Spring Sts.) | C/E to Spring St. | 212-343-1776

W 80s | 426 Columbus Ave. (81st St.) | B/C to 81st St. | 917-441-0011
800-638-6464 | www.patagonia.com

"Must-have fleece" apparel "for every New Yorker" and "top-notch" "technical" "performance"-wear for any "outdoor adventure" draw "SUV"-owning "urban fantasizers" and "real expeditioners" alike to this activewear duo that "takes you out of SoHo" and the West 80s and "into the wilderness" with its "old-school hiking atmosphere"; made of organic and recycled materials, the "superb quality", "nothing-flashy" "clothing is legendary", if a bit pricey ("aka Patagucci"), while the "employees are knowledgeable" "users and thus great advisors."

Paterson Silks
▽ 18 | 11 | 14 | I

W 70s | 151 W. 72nd St. (bet. Amsterdam & Columbus Aves.) | 1/2/3 to 72nd St. | 212-874-9510

NEW **Floral Pk** | 178 Jericho Tpk. (bet. Tyson & Whitney Aves.) | Queens | 718-776-5225 ⑤
www.patersonmills.com

"Printed cottons", wools and, yes, silks "abound" at this "no-frills" outfit in the West 70s and now Floral Park, Queens, too; the "fair prices" and a "good selection" create a "pleasant" shopping experience for DIY types.

Patina
– | – | – | E

SoHo | 451 Broome St. (bet. B'way & Mercer St.) | 6 to Spring St. | 212-625-3375

Think pink when you enter this high-walled SoHo space – the cheerful hue not only colors the ceiling, but sheds a happy patina over the small-but-select array of '30s–'60s vintage clothing, accessories and tableware; it's frequently patronized by fashion designers seeking that superb sequined clutch, fur-collared sweater or crocodile handbag.

Patricia Field ●
▽ 15 | – | 16 | M
(fka Hotel Venus by Patricia Field)

NoHo | 302 Bowery (bet. Bleecker & Houston Sts.) | F/V to Lower East Side/2nd Ave. | 212-966-4066 | www.patriciafield.com

"If anyone knows hip, it's Pat Field" declare devotees of the "toast-of-the-town" *Sex and the City* costumer whose "wild, colorful" bazaar, a "total throwback to 1980s new wave/punk/industrial clubwear", is now located on the Bowery; "the young and young at heart" stop by for a corset, tube top or provocative T-shirt that can "turn you into a walking fashion statement" from her own collection, plus lines like Cheap Monday, Lip Service and Nu Collective – "cutting-edge" "stuff" for the "next Wigstock."

Paul & Shark
27 | 25 | 22 | E

E 60s | 772 Madison Ave. (66th St.) | 6 to 68th St. | 212-452-9868 | www.paulshark.it

Aging cap'ns and younger able-bodied seamen alike love the classic, boldly colorful "yachty" threads at this East 60s flagship of the Italian chain; customers chant that "you don't need, but have to have" their "incredibly durable and well-made" nautical wear – even if the prices will hoist your credit-card bill "sky-high."

	QUALITY	DISPLAY	SERVICE	COST

Paul Frank Store

	18	22	18	M

NoLita | 195 Mulberry St. (Kenmare St.) | 6 to Spring St. | 212-965-5079 |
www.paulfrank.com

Take your "kitschy friends" to NoLita's "fanciful corner shop" and
make "cute monkey faces" at Julius, the "playful" simian and his "car-
toonish" pals like Bunny Girl and Skurvy the Pirate, which take center
stage on "feel-good" T-shirts, undies and accessories; sure, it's
"crowded", and the "staff exudes a laid-back Southern California" demeanor, but "kids and tweens love" the "quirky items" including
Frank's "irreverent" Andy Warhol "stuff" with bug, banana or cow motifs.

NEW Paulina Quintana

	–	–	–	E

E Vill | 335 E. Ninth St. (bet. 1st & 2nd Aves.) | 6 to Astor Pl. | 212-598-0120 |
www.paulinaquintana.com

Contemporary kids' clothes with a kitschy twist are the province of
this LA-based designer's first Big Apple boutique in the East Village;
burrow through the white display cubes for printed skirts, pants and
party dresses in vibrant hues, an array of solid-colored cotton basics
for mixing and matching, plus diaper bags so chic they can double as
everyday handbags for mom.

Paul Smith

	26	25	20	VE

Flatiron | 108 Fifth Ave. (16th St.) | 4/5/6/L/N/Q/R/W to 14th St./
Union Sq. | 212-627-9770
NEW SoHo | 142 Greene St. (W. Houston St.) | B/D/F/V to B'way/
Lafayette St. | 646-613-3060
www.paulsmith.co.uk

London calling at this "exquisitely hip" Flatiron District menswear
shop, a rosy-hued repository for the "cheeky" British designer's
"dandy" striped shirts, colorful jackets and "quirky" accessories; "total style novices" and "fashion aficionados" alike "drool over" these
"funky" duds, despite "the astronomical prices" ("damn exchange
rate!") and a "staff that's a bit standoffish"; the new SoHo flagship
also carries womenswear, books, home furnishings and accessories
for both sexes in a series of five distinctly styled rooms, some adorned
with vintage furniture.

Paul Stuart

	27	26	25	VE

E 40s | 45th St. & Madison Ave. | 4/5/6/7/S to 42nd St./Grand Central |
212-682-0320 | 800-678-8278 | www.paulstuart.com

Men in need of "traditional looks with a touch of whimsy" buy them
from the stu-ards of style at this multilevel "gold standard" in the East
40s that boasts a "broad selection" of suits, accessories and shoes,
some of them custom-made; while a few fret it's "foppy" and "in need
of younger appeal", most find enough "elegant" goods "across the
board" here, along with "true service", to make anyone "wish for a
larger budget"; P.S. the "lesser-known" women's floor makes "a nice
retreat for the professional lady."

Payless Shoe Source

	11	12	10	I

Garment Dist | 484 Eighth Ave. (bet. 34th & 35th Sts.) | 1/2/3/A/C/E to
34th St./Penn Station | 212-594-5715 | www.payless.com
Additional locations throughout the NY area

The "budget"-minded can "make out like a bandit" on the "bargain"
"faux designer shoes" – and now the real deal too, like footwear from

Abaeté designer Laura Poretzky's capsule collection, and coming up, Lela Rose, all supplied by this chainster; if pessimists are put off by "boxes that litter the floor, and service that's nowhere to be seen", proponents retort if it's "good enough for Star Jones, it's good enough for" me and the kids.

P.C. Richard & Son ●   18 | 12 | 15 | M

Gramercy | 120 E. 14th St. (bet. Irving Pl. & 3rd Ave.) | 4/5/6/L/N/Q/R/W to 14th St./Union Sq. | 212-979-2600 | 800-369-7915 | www.pcrichard.com
Additional locations throughout the NY area

Known for its "surprisingly good" selection of "major appliances" and "fair prices" ("you can definitely negotiate a deal"), this family-run "warehouse" chain is the place to get "that a/c fast"; still, some cite the "jumbled floorful" of "messy" displays and alternately "invisible" or "pushy salespeople" as evidence that "it's not a shopping experience to savor."

Peanutbutter & Jane   ▽ 24 | 12 | 22 | E

W Vill | 617 Hudson St. (bet. Jane & W. 12th Sts.) | A/C/E/L to 14th St./ 8th Ave. | 212-620-7952

Downtown dwellers are stuck on this Village veteran stocked with a "surprisingly large selection" of "goodies" "given its small size"; you can't help but go nuts for the "overwhelming array" of "trendy" clothing from English Roses, Lipstik and Petit Bateau, and fun accessories sandwiched into this cozy space; sure, it's "crowded" and "the presentation can be confusing", but the sales staff "is always friendly."

Pearldaddy ●   – | – | – | M

NoLita | 202A Mott St. (bet. Kenmare & Spring Sts.) | 6 to Spring St. | 212-219-7727 | www.pearldaddy.com

This simple NoLita jewelry store owned by architect-designer Liming "Fish" Yu is all about "reasonably priced" freshwater pearls in various shapes and colors that are mated with coral, vintage carved shell, Austrian crystals, clear quartz and mother of pearl for fun bracelets, necklaces, earrings and other accessories that loyalists "love."

☒ Pearl Paint   26 | 16 | 18 | M

Chinatown | 308 Canal St. (bet. B'way & Church St.) | 6/J/M/N/Q/R/W/Z to Canal St. | 212-431-7932
Gramercy | 207 E. 23rd St. (bet. 2nd & 3rd Aves.) | 6 to 23rd St. | 212-592-2179
www.pearlpaint.com

"Artists, craftsmen and wannabes" agree: this "multifloored" Chinatown "go-to" "institution" (with a "super-small" Gramercy Park satellite) is "heaven on earth" supplying "everything you need" from "poster paint to high-grade papers"; you get a "lotta stuff for notta lotta money", which makes it a "student's dream", and even if the contents are "cluttered", stairs a "drag" and service sometimes "tuned out", most salute this "mother ship of art supplies."

Pearl River Mart ●   16 | 17 | 12 | I

SoHo | 477 Broadway (bet. Broome & Grand Sts.) | 6/J/M/N/Q/R/W/Z to Canal St. | 212-431-4770 | 800-878-2446 | www.pearlriver.com

"Like all of Chinatown condensed into one" "spacious" store, this "inexpensive" SoHo emporium is "jam-packed" with "all things Asian", "from Chinese cleavers", "the biggest chopstick selection this side of Beijing" and a "food section that woks" to "funky silk" kimonos and "cute" flip-flops and doodads ("I was tempted to buy a life-size dragon's head, but common sense prevailed"); still, detractors snarl the "rude staff deters" from the fun and feel "the product displays" are in need of "feng shui"; N.B. plans are underway to add a third floor.

Peggy Pardon ◗

| - | - | - | M |

LES | 153 Ludlow St. (bet. Rivington & Stanton Sts.) | F/V to Lower East Side/2nd Ave. | 212-529-3686 | www.peggypardon.com

Sure, there's not much merch, but what there is, is cherce at this Lower East Side vintage clothing store; within its shoebox-sized confines, the womenswear spans several decades – a Gibson Girl blouse here, a '50s sundress there – and includes a few new retro-style pieces, as well as exotic-skin handbags; everything's in excellent condition, but should you spot a loose hem on your purchase, the personable young owner may well whip out a needle and repair it on the spot.

P.E. Guerin ⌧

| - | - | - | VE |

W Vill | 23 Jane St. (bet. 8th & Greenwich Aves.) | A/C/E/L to 14th St./8th Ave. | 212-243-5270 | www.peguerin.com

Discriminating sorts who sweat the details make a beeline to this by-appointment-only West Village studio showcasing the fine home hardware crafted by the Guerin family since 1857 at their foundries in Valencia, Spain; the extensive catalog is decidedly traditional, featuring over 25,000 samples ranging from furniture pulls, knobs, mounts and doorknockers to plumbing fixtures, but you can request custom reproductions of nearly anything, as long as it can be made in brass.

Penhaligon's

| 27 | 26 | 25 | VE |

E 70s | 870 Madison Ave. (71st St.) | 6 to 68th St. | 212-249-1771 | 877-736-4254 | www.penhaligons.co.uk

Dating back to 1870, this "terribly British" purveyor of "timelessly elegant" fragrances with names like Lavendula and Lily of the Valley is still simmering with "wonderful scents and fragrances" inspired by the English countryside; the "helpful staff" at their small UES offshoot can also show you "great candles", men's toiletries and handmade silver and leather accessories like jewelry boxes that are "perfect for presents."

Penny Whistle

| 23 | 20 | 19 | E |

W 80s | 448 Columbus Ave. (bet. 81st & 82nd Sts.) | B/C to 81st St. | 212-873-9090

"Amazing wonders await" at this "blast from the past" West 80s toy store that tickles nostalgists with its "unique", classic playthings, including pinwheels, pogo sticks, collectible dolls and craft kits; it's "fun to browse", but if you're not into lingering, the staff gets you "in and out with your holiday gifts in record time"; still, a few sing the too-"pricey" blues, grumbling "it should be renamed Dollar Whistle."

Perfumania ◗

| 19 | 14 | 14 | M |

Garment Dist | Empire State Bldg. | 20 W. 34th St. (bet. 5th & 6th Aves.) | B/D/F/N/Q/R/V/W to 34th St./Herald Sq. | 212-736-0414 | 866-557-2368 | www.perfumania.com

There's "definitely no frills" at this "outlet" atmosphere chain that stocks women's and men's designer and drugstore perfumes at "excellent" "discount prices"; but naysayers note "they may not have what you want" and sniff at service that can be less than sweet.

Petco ◗

19 | **17** | **13** | **M**

E 80s | 147 E. 86th St. (bet. Lexington & 3rd Aves.) | 6 to 86th St. | 212-831-8001
Murray Hill | 560 Second Ave. (bet. 31st & 32nd Sts.) | 6 to 33rd St. | 212-779-4550
Union Sq | 860 Broadway (17th St.) | 4/5/6/L/N/Q/R/W to 14th St./Union Sq. | 212-358-0692
W 90s | 2475 Broadway (92nd St.) | 1/2/3 to 96th St. | 212-877-1270
Howard Bch | 157-20 Cross Bay Blvd. (157th Ave.) | Queens | A to Howard Beach/JFK Airport | 718-845-3331
877-738-6742 | www.petco.com

"Yes, it's a big box", but the "Home Depot of pet supplies" offers "everything you need for Fido and Fluffy" and feathered and finny friends, including "valuable services" like vaccines; though the products are more "mainstream" than "fancy" and the service "nonexistent", the "reasonable" prices are enhanced by a "great frequent buyers' program."

Peter Elliot

25 | **20** | **20** | **E**

E 70s | 997 Lexington Ave. (72nd St.) | 6 to 68th St. | 212-570-2301
E 80s | 1067 Madison Ave. (81st St.) | 6 to 77th St. | 212-570-5747
E 80s | 1070 Madison Ave. (81st St.) | 6 to 77th St. | 212-570-2300
E 80s | 1071 Madison Ave. (81st St.) | 6 to 77th St. | 212-570-1551

Visitors to this series of "superbly edited small boutiques" leave the Upper East Side environs looking as if they're "setting up the country house" in "high-quality" "perfectly tailored" apparel; each one curates its own niche of "something a little different" among the men's, women's and boy's wear (1067 Madison Avenue acts as an outlet), and while "quirky" service "makes you laugh or cry depending on your mood", most find it worthwhile "to avoid the madness of larger stores."

▣ Peter Fox Shoes

28 | **25** | **25** | **E**

SoHo | 105 Thompson St. (bet. Prince & Spring Sts.) | C/E to Spring St. | 212-431-7426 | www.peterfox.com

"So original and unique!" – "when you find the right style, the combination rocks" rave Fox-y ladies who find "there are no better shoes for a night of dancing" or "special occasions" than the "well-made" numbers, some "evocative of Renaissance" or Victorian footwear, sold at this designer's quaint SoHo salon; the nuptials-bound find the Italian silk satin pumps and boots "especially beautiful for weddings", while actors galore walk the Broadway boards in these "lovely" offerings.

Peters Necessities for Pets

▽ **24** | **18** | **24** | **M**

E 70s | 236 E. 75th St. (bet. 2nd & 3rd Aves.) | 6 to 77th St. | 212-988-0769

Devotees who "love the delivery service rarely see the store", but those who frequent this "wonderful" East 70s pet emporium hail the "hard-to-find" "specialty" foods and "interesting merchandise"; the "helpful" owner and staff also earn plaudits.

Petit Bateau

27 | **24** | **20** | **E**

E 80s | 1094 Madison Ave. (82nd St.) | 4/5/6 to 86th St. | 212-988-8884 | www.petit-bateau.com

For some of the "best" French "T-shirts in town" "guaranteed to make you ooh and ahh at the sight of your little cherub", sail over to this "accommodating" Madison Avenue shop, which has the market cornered on "non-fussy", "comfortable" cotton duds; you "can't beat" basics like "excellent quality" pajamas and underwear – "there's a reason classics are classic"; P.S. the "cuddly" children's tees are also prized by "pre-teens", teens and petite moms.

Petland Discounts ⬤

| 18 | 12 | 15 | M |

W 40s | 734 Ninth Ave. (50th St.) | C/E to 50th St. | 212-459-9562 | www.petlanddiscounts.com
Additional locations throughout the NY area

"Convenient" locations, "competitive prices" and a "broad array" of pet products for a "variety of species" make this chain a "weekly" stop for urbanites; though service ranges from "informed" to "clueless" and the stock can be "disorganized", the "good value" for "basics" keeps bargain-hounds happy.

NEW Petrou 🅂Ⓜ

| – | – | – | VE |

E 60s | 850 Madison Ave. (bet. 69th & 70th Sts.) | 6 to 68th St. | 212-249-7111

A Euro-chic eveningwear extravaganza unfolds amid the elegant environs of upper Madison Avenue at this marble-columned boutique dedicated to the designs of Nicolas Petrou, aka Dennis Basso's creative director; his premiere collection boasts high-waisted cocktail dresses and taffeta gowns, embroidered jackets and carefully tailored coats, all handcrafted with luxurious laces, feathers and (of course) furs.

Ⓩ Pet Stop

| 26 | 21 | 25 | M |

W 80s | 564 Columbus Ave. (bet. 87th & 88th Sts.) | B/C to 86th St. | 212-580-2400 | www.petstopnyc.com

"You feel more like a friend than a customer" at this "unmatched" Upper West Side "institution" offering the "best selection" of "premium" pet products in an "enjoyable atmosphere"; the staff is "knowledgeable", the delivery service is "excellent" and on weekends you can adopt "purrfectly" "adorable" kitties.

NEW Petticoat Lane

| – | – | – | E |

TriBeCa | 149 Reade St. (bet. Greenwich & Hudson Sts.) | 1/2/3 to Chambers St. | 212-571-5115 | www.bagshop.com

This TriBeCa newcomer (the first NYC outpost of a Westchester-based chainlet) charms customers with a "nice combination" of lingerie (from Cosabella, DKNY, Hanro, La Perla and others) and handbags (from Botkier, Rafe, Lauren Merkin and Longchamp); a small selection of belts and jewelry as well as an "always helpful" staff keep accessory obsessives returning for "little things you don't see anywhere else."

Phat Farm

| 16 | 18 | 14 | E |

SoHo | 129 Prince St. (bet. W. B'way & Wooster St.) | N/R/W to Prince St. | 212-533-7428 | www.phatfarmstore.com

"Still going strong" assert citified agrarians who flock to "Russell Simmons' urbanwear staple" in SoHo for "clothes that are the height of cool", reflecting the music entrepreneur's sartorial blend of "hip-hop" culture and Ivy League Lacoste-like look; to the rear: wife Kimora Lee Simmons' sexy, "very wearable" Baby Phat women's collection and cat's meow kids' offerings; still, a phew phind the "help inattentive" and "prices beyond the means of its target audience."

Phi

- | - | - | VE

SoHo | 71 Greene St. (bet. Broome & Spring Sts.) | N/R/W to Prince St. | 212-966-0076 | www.phicollection.com

Slink into this loftlike SoHo shop with its soaring ceilings, mammoth pillars and standing vases filled with mulberry leaves to soak in designer Andreas Melbostad's sexy, minimalist womenswear from this edgy label backed by Susan Dell, wife of techie billionaire Michael; the clothes flatter a femme-fatale's curves with a bod-conscious cut in luxurious wools and luxe leathers, while the stratospheric prices seem in keeping with the company's provenance.

Philosophy di Alberta Ferretti

▽ 25 | 24 | 26 | VE

SoHo | 452 W. Broadway (bet. Houston & Prince Sts.) | C/E to Spring St. | 212-460-5500 | www.philosophy.it

Fashionistas don't have to know Plato to appreciate the cool sensibility of Alberta Ferretti's secondary line at this modern outpost in SoHo, which has a waterfall as a backdrop; the crowd-pleasing collection features polished suits, pretty cutwork sheaths, fluttery day-to-evening dresses and edgy inventory of accessories.

☑ Piaget ☒

28 | 28 | 27 | VE

E 50s | 730 Fifth Ave. (bet. 56th & 57th Sts.) | N/R/W to 5th Ave./ 59th St. | 212-246-5555 | www.piaget.com

"Very high-quality" Swiss dress watches that merge fine jewelry with haute horology – imagine your own fingerprint rendered in diamonds on the face – and signature gold-bracelet Polo timepieces are the focus at this East 50s store whose parent company dates back to 1874; the well-heeled warn: don't let the prices (up to $2 mil) tick you off.

Pieces of Brooklyn Ⓜ

▽ 21 | 22 | 20 | E

Prospect Hts | 671 Vanderbilt Ave. (Park Pl.) | Brooklyn | 2/3 to Grand Army Plaza | 718-857-7211 | www.piecesofbklyn.com

Pieces of Harlem Ⓜ

Harlem | 228 W. 135th St. (bet. Adam Clayton Powell & Frederick Douglass Blvds.) | 2/3 to 135th St. | 212-234-1725 | www.piecesofharlem.com

It's fitting that these "hip" boutiques in Prospect Heights and Harlem are owned by a husband-and-wife team with the last name of Daring, because that's a word that sums up the men's and women's jeans, T-shirts, European designer threads and "one-of-a-kind" accessories; the "great selection" is "eclectic" enough that you won't see your purchases "all over the place", plus the staff is "helpful", ensuring your pieces add up to a "style all your own."

Pier 1 Imports ◗

15 | 18 | 15 | I

E 80s | 1550 Third Ave. (87th St.) | 4/5/6 to 86th St. | 212-987-1746
Flatiron | 71 Fifth Ave. (15th St.) | 4/5/6/L/N/Q/R/W to 14th St./ Union Sq. | 212-206-1911
800-245-4595 | www.pier1.com

"Lots of wicker" and "assorted odds and ends" like "candles and glassware galore", Christmas ornaments, baskets, pillows and picture frames make home furnishings "accessorizing cheap and simple" for those "starting out" or just looking for "staples" at these Flatiron and Upper East Side chain links; but detractors dismiss them as "cookie-cutter" "tchotchkes places" whose quality is questionable.

	QUALITY	DISPLAY	SERVICE	COST

☑ Pierre Deux

	26	25	18	E

E 50s | 625 Madison Ave. (bet. 58th & 59th Sts.) | 4/5/6/F/N/R/W
to 59th St./Lexington Ave. | 212-521-8012 | www.pierredeux.com
East Side "class act" that makes customers feel as though they've
"stepped into the French countryside", where it is "a pleasure to stroll
through and find a treasure" among the "beautiful" antique and reproduction furniture, Provençal print fabrics, dishes, lamps and pewter.

Pilar Rossi ⚅

	–	–	–	VE

E 60s | 784 Madison Ave. (bet. 66th & 67th Sts.) | 6 to 68th St. |
212-288-2469 | www.pilarrossi.com
Dramatic and elegant, "Ms. Rossi's clothes are styled with real women's
curves in mind" assert admirers of the Brazilian eveningwear and
bridal designer who find a trip to her Madison Avenue store one of the
"most pleasurable shopping experiences you can have"; the glamorous
get-ups include day-into-night suits, gowns in rich brocade or silk satin
and sophisticated, entrance-worthy aisle-wear for that special day.

Pink Pussycat ●

	19	19	19	M

G Vill | 167 W. Fourth St. (bet. 6th & 7th Aves.) | A/B/C/D/E/F/V to
W. 4th St. | 212-243-0077
Park Slope | 355 Fifth Ave. (bet. 4th & 5th Sts.) | Brooklyn | F/M/R to
4th Ave./9th St. | 718-369-0088
www.pinkpussycat.com
The "grandaddy of all erotica" shops is this thirtysomething Greenwich
Village "icon" (with a Park Slope spin-off) where "horny" "out-of-
towners" and "giggling" "bachelorette" partiers peruse Rabbit Habit
vibrators, sex toys and S&M items; but the catty counter the "dingy"
digs and "low inventory" make this feline "a kitten of its former self."

Pink Slip ●

	▽ 23	19	23	M

E 40s | Grand Central | 42nd St. (Vanderbilt Ave.) | 4/5/6/7/S to 42nd St./
Grand Central | 212-949-9037 | 866-816-7465 | www.thepinkslip.com
Commuters "in a hurry" find something "mildly romantic" about buying lingerie in this Grand Central Station "little find" filled with a
"quickly rotating inventory" of "beautiful" camisole sets, panties,
bustiers, hosiery and sleepwear from designers like Arianne, Flirt and
On Gossamer; "great" for "quick gifts" (the staff makes men feel welcome) or "last-minute personal items", its only drawback is that all
"co-workers may see you" ducking in as they run for their trains.

Pintchik

	20	12	18	M

Park Slope | 478 Bergen St. (Flatbush Ave.) | Brooklyn | 2/3 to Bergen St. |
718-783-3333
Park Slope "shows its (paint) colors" at this pioneer hardware store
where "you can find just about anything" including a "large assortment of flooring" and lighting; sure, "you may not be able to see" everything, but the "informed staff" "can probably find it", so pintch
some free cappuccino and popcorn while you're waiting.

Pippin ●

	–	–	–	M

LES | 72 Orchard St. (bet. Broome & Grand Sts.) | F to East Broadway |
212-505-5159 | www.pippinvintagejewelry.com
Practically everything decorative is for sale at this long, narrow LES
vintage/costume jewelry shop run by husband-and-wife owners who

got their start at the 26th Street Flea Market; the display cases are filled with one-of-a-kind pieces like Bakelite bracelets and cameos dating from the late 1800s through 1970 at equally anachronistic prices.

Pir Cosmetics

-	-	-	E

NoLita | 14 Prince St. (Elizabeth St.) | 6 to Spring St. | 212-219-1290 | www.pircosmetics.com

If you're bored with beauty basics, check out this "brilliant" cosmetics boutique in NoLita specializing in "hard-to-find" luxury brands like Hamadi's shea butter hair mask and Kevyn Aucoin's "incredible makeup line"; the staff will "plop you down in a chair" and show you products that will "suit your skin tone, lifestyle and personal idiosyncrasies."

P.J. Huntsman & Co. 🖂

-	-	-	E

W 40s | 36 W. 44th St. (bet. 5th & 6th Aves.) | 7/B/D/F/V to 42nd St./ Bryant Park | 212-302-2463 | 800-968-3418

Don't let the name or the window display fool you: while this "small shop" does stock an assortment of hunting accessories – including shell bags, gun cases and sporting clays – its sights are clearly set on quality leisurewear for the urban jungle; the imported array of men's (and some women's) jackets, separates and waterproof boots are equally suited to a walk in adjacent Bryant Park as in the North Woods.

Planet Kids ◑

18	13	13	M

E 80s | 247 E. 86th St. (bet. 2nd & 3rd Aves.) | 4/5/6 to 86th St. | 212-426-2040
W 100s | 2688 Broadway (103rd St.) | 1 to 103rd St. | 212-864-8705 www.planetkidsny.com

"Good in a pinch", this "fun-to-browse" East Side–West Side pair of Uptown kids' supply stores fills the "need-it-now shopping" bill, squeezing a "surprisingly good selection" of "inexpensive", "cute" clothing, gear, furniture and toys into a "cramped", "limited space"; still, skeptics who wonder "what planet" the "disinterested staff" is on warn "it's every man for himself" here.

Plaza Too

21	21	21	E

W 70s | 2231 Broadway (bet. 79th & 80th Sts.) | 1 to 79th St. | 212-362-6871 | www.plazatoo.com

"Gives the UWS a little oomph" agree accessories addicts who kick up their heels over the "nicely edited shoe, bag", belt, scarf and jewelry selection that's "hip and beautiful without being pretentious" at this Westchester-based "favorite"; the "warm, friendly service is enough to keep you coming back" and so's the mix of brands like Aquatalia, Alexis Bittar, Arturo Chiang and Kate Spade suitable for "consumers of all budgets."

Pleasure Chest ◑

22	20	20	M

W Vill | 156 Seventh Ave. S. (bet. Charles & Perry Sts.) | 1 to Christopher St./ Sheridan Sq. | 212-242-2158 | 800-316-9222 | www.thepleasurechest.com

"Gay and straight" supporters of this sex shop say it peddles a "plethora of play things at palatable prices"; its "goodies to please other body parts besides your chest" range from "fantastic" to "shlock", arrayed in a "cheesy" but "not skeevy" space sporting a "window display that's one of the biggest attractions in the Village" – just "stay away during *Sex and the City* tours!"

Pleats Please

	-	-	-	E

SoHo | 128 Wooster St. (Prince St.) | N/R/W to Prince St. | 212-226-3600 | www.pleatsplease.com

This glass-encased shop at a busy hub in SoHo pleases patrons with "accommodating" salespeople wearing "Issey Miyake's less-expensive" line of "crazy cuts" in super-pleated polyester that is "made to travel", so "you're always chic"; however, those unimpressed by the pressed garb growl "at this point, we've all seen it."

Poggenpohl U.S. Inc.

	-	-	-	VE

E 50s | A&D Bldg. | 150 E. 58th St. (bet. Lexington & 3rd Aves.) | 4/5/6/F/N/R/W to 59th St./Lexington Ave. | 212-355-3666 🖾
Union Sq | 270 Park Ave. S. (19th St.) | 4/5/6/L/N/Q/R/W to 14th St./Union Sq. | 212-228-3334
www.poggenpohl-usa.com

Founded in 1892, this luxury bath and kitchen manufacturer in Union Square and the East 50s is up to the minute with "modern", German-made products, such as high-tech aluminum, stainless-steel, wood and glass cabinetry and appliances; aesthetes applaud the "superior design", but caution it may be "too expensive for any but the super-rich", who "also have maids to keep all that stainless spotless."

Ⓩ Point, The ●

	▽ 25	26	23	M

G Vill | 37A Bedford St. (Carmine St.) | 1 to Houston St. | 212-929-0800 | 877-607-6468 | www.thepointnyc.com

Crafters can "have a cappuccino and peruse" the skeins "in baskets on the walls" at this "beautiful" Greenwich Village store with a "delightful cafe"; it's a "comfortable place to gather with a knitting circle", thanks to a "supportive staff" and "good" prices, though some sticklers point out the selection in this venue is "a little thin."

Poleci

	22	22	23	E

Meatpacking | 414 W. 14th St. (bet. 9th Ave. & Washington St.) | A/C/E/L to 14th St./8th Ave. | 212-229-3701 | www.poleci.com

Leave it to two LA sisters to breathe a little 'ahh' into the Meatpacking District with a striking, 3,000-sq.-ft. shrine filled with the ladies' char-acteristic "cutting-edge" "camisoles, dresses and coats"; label-lovers also laud the policy (that's how the name is pronounced) of being "ex-tremely helpful"; skeptics say these "snippy bits of wrinkled fabric" "don't justify their prices" – but "if you catch a sale, [all's] affordable."

Poltrona Frau

	-	-	-	VE

SoHo | 145 Wooster St. (bet. Houston & Prince Sts.) | N/R/W to Prince St. | 212-777-7592 | www.frauusa.com

"You have to be the Donald, not the apprentice" to afford the "great" leather furniture featured in this minimalist SoHo showroom for the high-end Italian company that also outfits interiors for Ferrari, Maserati and Mercedes; there are over 90 shades to choose from for sofas, chairs, beds and even tables.

🆕 Pomellato 🖾

	-	-	-	VE

E 60s | 741 Madison Ave. (bet. 64th & 65th Sts.) | 6 to 68th St. | 212-879-2118 | 800-254-6020 | www.pomellato.com

Milan comes to Madison Avenue with the opening of this attractive Italian fine-jewelry store showcasing its own namesake brand; signature styles include clean, colorful square-cut rings and earrings with hand-faceted semiprecious stones in smoky quartz, amethyst and blue topaz, but there's also a more ornate line of carved cameo serpent designs.

Pomme Ⓜ
–	–	–	E

Dumbo | 81 Washington St. (York St.) | Brooklyn | F to York St. | 718-855-0623 | www.pommenyc.com

Urbane parents who prefer to dress their small fries like wee individuals turn to this Dumbo darling, a sprawling loft that doubles as a gallery/ workshop space; forget overexposure – stylesetters cherry pick limited quantities of exclusive, globally sourced items for sizes 0–4 from labels like Flora & Henri and Wooliweiss along with jewelry from Aurelie Bidermann, wicker cradles from Nume and felt dolls from MiniLabo.

⚡ Pompanoosuc Mills
25	21	24	E

TriBeCa | 124 Hudson St. (Ericsson Pl.) | 1 to Franklin St. | 212-226-5960 | www.pompy.com

Loyalists "love the simplicity" of this "handcrafted" traditional American furniture for the bedroom, office, living and dining room that's built-to-order in Vermont; the staff at the TriBeCa showroom "is helpful and patient, without being pushy", and proponents pronounce "prices amazing" given the "silky finishes" and "superb workmanship."

Pookie & Sebastian ◗
17	20	19	M

E 70s | 1488 Second Ave. (bet. 77th & 78th Sts.) | 6 to 77th St. | 212-861-0550
Murray Hill | 541 Third Ave. (36th St.) | 6 to 33rd St. | 212-951-7110
W 70s | 322 Columbus Ave. (75th St.) | B/C to 72nd St. | 212-580-5844
www.pookieandsebastian.com

This "fashion-forward" outfit "is constantly hopping", "overrun with Pookie Girls" jonesing for "stylish" jeans and the "latest knockoffs of designer pieces" including "flirty" jackets, "sparkly" party dresses and "high-style" extras with "a lot of charm"; "rabid shoppers" don't mind waiting for the "claustrophobic dressing rooms", because the "sales help is helpful and honest" – and "you can't leave without snagging a great find at a reasonable price."

Poppet ◗
(fka Psyche's Tears)
–	–	–	E

E Vill | 350 E. Ninth St. (bet. 1st & 2nd Aves.) | 6 to Astor Pl. | 212-924-3190 | www.poppetnyc.com

There's no shortage of vintage-clothing stores in the East Village, but "somebody finally got it right" with this recently revamped poppet whose clientele ranges from NYU students to Seventh Avenue stylists; the former find moderate, midcentury blouses and dresses, while the latter love the luminous labels from the '60s–'80s (think Ozzie Clark, Zandra Rhodes and Holly Harp); the tiny, red-walled space also holds a huge shoe collection that includes a plethora of platforms; everything's cleaned, pressed and ready to wear out the door.

Poppy
▽ 23	24	21	E

NoLita | 281 Mott St. (bet. Houston & Prince Sts.) | B/D/F/V to B'way/ Lafayette St. | 212-219-8934

"Stylish" women's "clothes are always in bloom" at this NoLita "shopper's paradise", which is "refreshingly spacious compared to other neighborhood boutiques", with racks and tables full of "sensual" "fashions" and "chic workplace-worthy attire" that "invite touching"; "go here whenever you need to reward" yourself – what better incentive than "very cute stuff" from hard-to-find lines, jeans from J Brand and jewelry from Moss Mills and Page Sargisson.

NEW Porsche Design

26 | 26 | 22 | VE

E 50s | 624 Madison Ave. (bet. 58th & 59th Sts.) | N/R/W to 5th Ave./59th St. | 212-308-1786 | www.porsche-design.com

"Your dollars speed out of your wallet faster than a 911 Turbo" at this "hi-tech" newcomer with a "gallery" feel featuring "handsome", "worth-the-money" accessories that fit the sports car driver's lifestyle; "just love all things Porsche" exclaim enthusiasts who get into manly gear like sunglasses, luggage, golf products, gloves and other "cool stuff" sold by a staff that "couldn't be nicer."

Porthault 🖾

▽ 29 | 28 | 23 | VE

E 60s | 18 E. 69th St. (Madison Ave.) | 6 to 68th St. | 212-688-1660

"Those who want the very best" get it at this grande dame of "extremely luxurious" French linens housed in a "lovely" Upper East Side converted townhouse; it's filled with signature printed sheets, table linens, scallop-edged bath towels, home fragrances and gifts, making it a resource for "great wedding presents"; prices are a nightmare though, so "take a loan before you go."

NEW Posey Baker 🅼

- | - | - | M

Park Slope | 167 Fifth Ave. (bet. Berkeley & Lincoln Pls.) | Brooklyn | M/R to Union St. | 718-623-2000

Southerner Karin McNair's home-furnishings store on Park Slope's ever-growing Fifth Avenue offers a mix of clean, colorful vintage furniture (like Swedish pieces from the '30s and '40s) along with contemporary pillows, candles and paintings from local artists; the name harkens back to McNair's grandmother, who would approve of the welcoming atmosphere and very non-New York City price tags.

Pottery Barn ●

20 | 22 | 18 | M

E 50s | 127 E. 59th St. (Lexington Ave.) | 4/5/6/F/N/R/W to 59th St./Lexington Ave. | 917-369-0050

SoHo | 600 Broadway (Houston St.) | B/D/F/V to B'way/Lafayette St. | 212-219-2420

W 60s | 1965 Broadway (67th St.) | 1 to 66th St./Lincoln Ctr. | 212-579-8477

888-779-5176 | www.potterybarn.com

"You can always find something you need here and it will last forever" declare devotees of this "easy-to-shop-in" chain with "quality" furniture and accessories like tableware, pillows and photo frames that are "great for house presents", even if "it's for your own"; chances are "all your friends have the exact same items in their apartments", but the "affordably priced" staples and "color-coordinated" offerings "prove that a tight budget does not preclude living well."

NEW Pottery Barn Bed & Bath ●

- | - | - | M

Chelsea | 100-104 Seventh Ave. (bet. 16th & 17th Sts.) | 1/2/3 to 14th St. | 646-336-7160 | www.potterybarn.com

The Williams-Sonoma–owned catalog comes to life at this new Chelsea outpost offering just what the name says – bed and bath furniture, fixtures and accessories; duvet covers, sheets, pillows, throws, mirrors, lamps, wall cabinets, robes, shower curtains and faucets are displayed vignette-style in the mostly white, Thomas O'Brien-designed space.

NEW Pottery Barn Kids

| - | - | - | M |

E 60s | 1311 Second Ave. (69th St.) | 6 to 68th St. | 212-879-4746 | www.potterybarn.com

Tots won't mind getting sent to their rooms if they're decked out with cool furniture and knickknacks from this new East 60s offshoot of the popular home chain; from French Rose to Train Junction, there's a kid-friendly decor theme to suit any style, plus a team of design experts on hand to help pull the look together; don't forget to check out the vast selection of toys including retro play kitchens, tea sets and xylophones.

Prada

| 26 | 26 | 21 | VE |

E 50s | 45 E. 57th St. (bet. Madison & Park Aves.) | 4/5/6/F/N/R/W to 59th St./Lexington Ave. | 212-308-2332
E 50s | 724 Fifth Ave. (bet. 56th & 57th Sts.) | N/R/W to 5th Ave./ 59th St. | 212-664-0010
E 70s | 841 Madison Ave. (70th St.) | 6 to 68th St. | 212-327-4200 🛇
SoHo | 575 Broadway (Prince St.) | N/R/W to Prince St. | 212-334-8888
www.prada.com

"Alluring", "artful" and "A+" are some of the adjectives awarded these showcases for Miuccia Prada's "impossibly chic and polished" Italian mens- and womenswear, "sexy shoes" and "adorable accessories"; it's "the first place" to take "fashion-forward" *touristas,* especially the Rem Koolhaas–designed SoHo flagship, which feels "more like a gallery than a store"; the savvy head to "the less-touristy Madison Avenue branch" where the service is "shockingly good" as opposed to "semi-friendly" elsewhere; wherever you go, though, get ready for prices that "make your wallet bleed"; N.B. 57th Street sells shoes and bags only.

🛇 Pratesi 🛇

| 29 | 24 | 24 | VE |

E 60s | 829 Madison Ave. (69th St.) | 6 to 68th St. | 212-288-2315 | www.pratesi.com

"Upper-class" East Side boutique that showcases the family-owned, 1893 Italian firm's sheets, which "are among the best on earth"; their table linens, towels and baby layettes also offer "luxury in every sense of the word"; of course, such "exquisite" merchandise is "*really* expensive", but patricians pronounce it "worth every penny."

Prato Fine Men's Wear Outlets

| ▽ 13 | 18 | 16 | I |

Financial Dist | 122 Nassau St., 1st fl. (Ann St.) | 2/3/4/5/A/C/J/M/Z to Fulton St./B'way/Nassau | 212-349-4150
Garment Dist | 28 W. 34th St. (bet. B'way & 5th Ave.) | B/D/F/N/Q/R/V/W to 34th St./Herald Sq. | 212-629-4730 ◗
Garment Dist | 492 Seventh Ave. (bet. 36th & 37th Sts.) | 1/2/3/A/C/E to 34th St./Penn Station | 212-564-9683 ◗
Dyker Hts | 8508 Fifth Ave. (85th St.) | Brooklyn | R to 86th St. | 718-491-1234
Astoria | 30-48 Steinway St. (bet. 30th & 31st Aves.) | Queens | G/R/V to Steinway St. | 718-274-2990 ◗
888-467-7286 | www.pratooutlets.com

The "low cost" and "good selection" of formal and business attire attract thrifty men to these discount warehouses scattered around NYC, Queens and Brooklyn; the "quality varies" and style advice doesn't extend beyond the basics, but what more "do you want for the price"?

	QUALITY	DISPLAY	SERVICE	COST

premium goods
– – – E

Park Slope | 347 Fifth Ave. (bet. 4th & 5th Sts.) | Brooklyn | F/M/R to 4th Ave./9th St. | 718-369-7477 | www.premiumgoods.net

It may be pocket-sized, but this Park Slope sneaker specialist packs plenty of punch thanks to its premium collection of footwear culled from major players like Nike, Puma and Vans, and a smattering of off-beat T-shirts; the distinctive trainers and tees aren't the only goods for sale – owner Clarence Nathan also mounts a rotating display of artwork from local talent.

Prince & Princess 🎌
– – – VE

E 70s | 41 E. 78th St. (Madison Ave.) | 6 to 77th St. | 212-879-8989 | www.princeandprincess.com

Just off Madison Avenue, this easy-to-overlook Upper East Side treasure trumpets high-end special-occasion finery that'll have your kids feeling like heirs to the throne; the crown jewels include luxe Italian-made silk party frocks for the little ladies and dapper silk suits, vests and bow ties for the lads; baby shoes and accessories supply the final flourishes.

Prince Charles III
– – – E

SoHo | 98 Thompson St. (Spring St.) | C/E to Spring St. | 212-334-9102 | www.princecharlesIII.com

You don't have to be royalty to stop by this SoHo boutique to stock up on European and American men's styles that aren't overly trendy; the inventory of small labels rotates seasonally, but what has remained constant during the past decade is the unique selection of belts, socks, ties and shirts – especially in larger sizes – and the reliable eye of owner Gina Karin.

Princeton Ski Shop ➊
21 17 17 M

Flatiron | 21 E. 22nd St. (bet. B'way & Park Ave.) | N/R/W to 23rd St. | 212-228-4400 | www.princetonski.com

Alpine enthusiasts whoosh over to this "old favorite" in the Flatiron District for a "reasonable selection" of "trendy, fashionable equipment" and clothing from "quality" names like Analog, Burton and Rossignol that are bound to make you one of the "best-dressed snow sport fans"; if a few find service "helpful" only "when you get them to focus" and the goods "pricey", most suggest waiting for the "terrific end-of-season sales", adding "if you're a serious skier, why shop anywhere else?"

Project 234 ➊
– – – M

NoLita | 234 Mulberry St. (bet. Prince & Spring Sts.) | 6 to Spring St. | 212-334-6431 | www.project234nyc.com

Owner Kim Phan fills her tiny NoLita gem with an artful mix of offbeat designers including Arrogant Cat, Buddhist Punk and Lundgren and Windinge – relatively-unheard-of labels that appeal to women who like to express their iconoclastic tendencies with strong doses of color; shoppers with a yen for retro-fitted fashions vie for vintage pieces that also project distinctive style.

Psny
– – – E

SoHo | 69 W. Houston St. (bet. W. B'way & Wooster St.) | B/D/F/V to B'way/Lafayette St. | 212-253-0630 | www.pslingnewyork.com

Done up with a cool chandelier and an orange ottoman, this sleek SoHo shop features the Japanese company's popular baby slings, designed to hold infants weighing up to 39 pounds; these fashionable, functional little linen or cotton helpers come in over 200 colorful, stylish prints and solids, and to go-with: sling-rings designed by Me & Ro, organic cotton onesies, and for mom, stretch silk maternity and nursing tops.

Pucci

26 | 25 | 24 | VE

E 50s | 701 Fifth Ave. (bet. 54th & 55th Sts.) | E/V to 5th Ave./53rd St. | 212-230-1135
E 60s | 24 E. 64th St. (bet. 5th & Madison Aves.) | 6 to 68th St. | 212-752-4777 🗷
www.emiliopucci.com

Revisit the "psychedelics of your youth" at either the East 60s boutique or the Fifth Avenue flagship where the legendary Italian designer's "swimming-in-color", "fun" fabrics are "back from the graveyard of fashion" in a big way; the "always distinctive" clothes and accessories are "sooo cute and easy-to-wear", you might well get a patented "Pucci high after purchasing one of the signature prints"; N.B. British designer Matthew Williamson has taken over from Christian Lacroix.

Puma

23 | 23 | 17 | M

Meatpacking | 421 W. 14th St. (bet. 9th & 10th Aves.) | A/C/E/L to 14th St./8th Ave. | 212-206-0109
SoHo | 521 Broadway (bet. Broome & Spring Sts.) | 6 to Spring St. | 212-334-7861 ●
NEW **Union Sq** | 33 Union Sq. W. (bet. 16th St. & Union Sq. W.) | 4/5/6/L/N/Q/R/W to 14th St./Union Sq. | 212-206-7761 ●
www.puma.com

"Pick up a pair" of "snazzy" "retro" "Euro-chic" "sneaks" in a "dazzling spectrum of colors" and "happening" athletic apparel at the two-floor SoHo showcase and you'll "stand out from the rest" and "be hip all over again"; also worth "checking out": the all-black, "super-trendy" Meatpacking District style-incubator and the new Union Square branch, a self-styled 'ship container' setting in which all the fixtures are mounted on walls, suspended from the ceiling or fastened to the floor.

Purdy Girl ●

18 | 21 | 20 | M

G Vill | 220 Thompson St. (bet. Bleecker & W. 3rd Sts.) | A/B/C/D/E/F/V to W. 4th St. | 212-529-8385
G Vill | 540 LaGuardia Pl. (bet. Bleecker & W. 3rd Sts.) | 6 to Bleecker St. | 646-654-6751
W 80s | 464 Columbus Ave. (bet. 82nd & 83rd Sts.) | B/C to 81st St. | 212-787-1980
www.purdygirlnyc.com

The "name says it all" confirm femme fans who "feel like a true Purdy girl" dressed in the house label's "darling" "workwear with flair", "super-affordable" "funky tees" and "cool, bohemian stuff" from Nanette Lepore and Trina Turk; it's not only a "charming" trio, "it's magic, because it makes money fly out of my wallet, the moment I walk in" – and the "no-pressure" staff makes me "walk out smiling."

☑ Purl

28 | 25 | 22 | E

SoHo | 137 Sullivan St. (bet. Houston & Prince Sts.) | C/E to Spring St. | 212-420-8796 | www.purlsoho.com

With a "surprisingly large selection" emphasizing natural fibers, this "little jewel" of a yarn shop in SoHo attracts local celebs plus "the hippest of the hip" who want to "sit and knit"; "charming old-world" storefront digs and a "knowledgeable staff" make for a "collegial" vibe, but claustrophobes charge the "tiny store" can "get uncomfortably crowded" – and all those "gorgeous imported" skeins are "expensive" (you may need enthusiast "Julia Roberts' wallet" to "afford them").

NEW Purple Reign Ⓜ | – | – | – | M |

Harlem | 171 Lenox Ave. (bet. 118th & 119th Sts.) | 2/3 to 116th St. | 212-222-7221 | www.purplereignshoes.com

When Junior's due for a new pair of shoes, shoppers in-the-know skip the long lines at the city's usual suspects and head straight to this Harlem haven where kids are given the royal treatment by the shop's "first-rate" staff; both moms and heirs to the throne will swoon over the splurge-worthy selection of stylish boots, sneakers and Mary Janes from European collections Aster, Geox, Oilily and Primigi.

Pylones ❶ | – | – | – | I |

E 60s | 842 Lexington Ave. (64th St.) | F to Lexington Ave./63rd St. | 212-317-9822
SoHo | 69 Spring St. (bet. Crosby & Lafayette Sts.) | 6 to Spring St. | 212-431-3244
NEW W Vill | 61 Grove St. (bet. Bleecker St. & 7th Ave. S.) | 1 to Christopher St./Sheridan Sq. | 212-727-2655
www.pylones-usa.com

For an inexpensive gift fix, hit this chainlet from France and scoop up brightly hued, whimsically designed knickknacks that look like they've been pulled from the pages of a children's book; the colorful mashup of household objects includes melamine plates and kitchen gadgets, stationery, desk accessories, toys and key chains, and a small pet section means you can pick up presents for pooches too.

Quiksilver Boardriders Club ❶ | 21 | 19 | 18 | M |

SoHo | 519 Broadway (Spring St.) | N/R/W to Prince St. | 212-226-1193
W 40s | 3 Times Sq. (42nd St. & 7th Ave.) | 1/2/3/7/N/Q/R/S/W to 42nd St./Times Sq. | 212-840-8111
800-576-4004 | www.quiksilver.com

Natch, it's "teenage boy heaven", but this "groovy" duo stocked with "unique" hang-ten "styles for surfers and non-surfers alike" has "something for everyone"; "it's an adventure just to walk into" the Times Square tourist-magnet that emphasizes apparel over boards ("if all else fails you can always play video games"); the sprawling SoHo "favorite" carries the whole nine yards, from skis and skiwear to beach-dude duds.

Quintessentials Ⓢ | 23 | 20 | 19 | E |

W 80s | 532 Amsterdam Ave. (bet. 85th & 86th Sts.) | 1 to 86th St. | 212-877-1919 | www.qkb.com

A "great place to go when you are renovating", this Upper West Side "kitchen- and bath-design store" offers a "terrific selection" of "top-of-the-line merchandise and appliances" along with "the best and most beautiful" high-end custom cabinetry, hardware, plumbing and fixtures; the "helpful" and "friendly staff" also "understands apartment spaces."

Rachel Ashwell's Shabby Chic | ▽ 23 | 27 | 22 | VE |

SoHo | 83 Wooster St. (bet. Broome & Spring Sts.) | N/R/W to Prince St. | 212-274-9842 | www.shabbychic.com

Slipcover queen Rachel Ashwell combined her "California-cool" lifestyle and English upbringing to create a fashionable flea-market look consisting of comfy, oversized furniture and faded floral fabrics, all on display at her SoHo shop; while some are tired of the "overpriced" pieces, others find them "perfect for the beach house."

Rachel Riley

	QUALITY	DISPLAY	SERVICE	COST
	-	-	-	E

E 90s | 1286 Madison Ave. (bet. 91st & 92nd Sts.) | 4/5/6 to 86th St. | 212-534-7477 | www.rachelriley.com

The private-school set and their fashionable mums embrace this romantic shop on Upper Madison Avenue, the brainchild of former model Rachel Riley, a Brit who designs her lovingly detailed fashions in the Loire Valley castle she lives in; the crystal chandeliers, velvet curtains and wood-carved vitrines create a genteel backdrop for retro classics that echo decades gone by, from tartan duffle coats to argyle sweaters, while astrakhan handbags add unexpected oomph.

RadioShack ⬤

	16	13	15	M

E 40s | 50 E. 42nd St. (bet. Madison & Park Aves.) | 4/5/6/7/S to 42nd St./ Grand Central | 212-953-6050 | 800-843-7422 | www.radioshack.com
Additional locations throughout the NY area

"Do-it-yourselfers" are devoted to this "solid" "corner drugstore for electronics" that's "a-clutter" with "techie basics", including "the odd cable or connector", "any battery you want" and "those electronics parts you need quickly"; the less-impressed, though, find it "fine for little things" "but not for big-ticket items", as the choices are "limited" and the staff's not always "as knowledgeable as advertised."

Rafe

	▽ 26	26	22	E

NoHo | 1 Bleecker St. (Bowery) | 6 to Bleecker St. | 212-780-9739 | 800-486-9544 | www.rafe.com

Expect a "great shopping experience" at this "gorgeous boutique on the Bowery" with a blue backdrop, "easy"-to-access displays filled with Ramon Felix [Rafe] Totengco's "trendy" accessories and a staff that's "ultrahip yet super-friendly"; sure, this designer made his name with "covetable", hot-ticket handbags for women, many boasting bohemian yet tasteful touches, but nowadays he also traffics in "fun" shoes, plus carryalls for guys, many at "not-too-horrible prices."

Ralph Lauren

	26	26	22	VE

E 70s | 867 Madison Ave. (72nd St.) | 6 to 68th St. | 212-606-2100
E 70s | 888 Madison Ave. (72nd St.) | 6 to 68th St. | 212-434-8000
SoHo | 379 W. Broadway (bet. Broome & Spring Sts.) | C/E to Spring St. | 212-625-1660
W Vill | 380 Bleecker St. (bet. Charles & Perry Sts.) | 1 to Christopher St./ Sheridan Sq. | 212-645-5513 ⬤
W Vill | 381 Bleecker St. (bet. Charles & Perry Sts.) | 1 to Christopher St./ Sheridan Sq. | 646-638-0684 ⬤
888-475-7674 | www.polo.com

"Feel like a million" ('cuz that's what you could spend) shopping these "preppy meccas" from the "king of American style", whose name's a by-word for "top-drawer basics", "tasteful, tailored" suits and gowns "evocative of another era"; the label "has several price ranges", but "whatever you end up with, the quality is usually spot-on" and the staff "is happy to help you put it all together"; if cynics sniff Ralph always produces the "same old standards", it's still "hard not to be seduced by the all-encompassing lifestyle"; P.S. the 867 Madison

	QUALITY	DISPLAY	SERVICE	COST

Avenue "mansion", with its "English-estate" "elegance", houses home furnishings that some say are even "better than the clothes."

Ralph Lauren Boys & Girls
| | 26 | 26 | 23 | E |

E 70s | 878 Madison Ave. (bet. 71st & 72nd Sts.) | 6 to 68th St. | 212-606-3370 | www.polo.com

"Stick with the classics" crow fans of the Prince of Prep's UES retail venture, which strives to make wardrobing for the shopaphobic boy or girl in your life as "painless" as possible; beef up on basics here, everything from khakis, cords and cable knit sweaters to rugbys, oxfords and barn coats, as well as "perfect attire for that special occasion", including "blazers for that party he just got invited to."

NEW Ralph Lauren Eyewear
| | – | – | – | E |

E 60s | 811 Madison Ave. (68th St.) | 6 to 68th St. | 212-988-4620 | www.polo.com

For sophisticated, super-stylish specs join the upmarket set at the latest addition to Ralph World on Madison Avenue; there's lots to covet at this corner shop, from classic eyeglasses that exude the essence of RL's understated chic to wide-framed wrap and square-framed sunglasses just right for seeking refuge from the paparazzi; N.B. opticians are on hand to fill existing prescriptions but no exams are given.

Ralph Lauren Layette & Toddler
| | 26 | 27 | 23 | VE |

E 70s | 872 Madison Ave. (71st St.) | 6 to 68th St. | 212-434-8099 | www.polo.com

The "first stop" for the town-and-country crowd after the stork strikes, this "absolutely darling" baby shop – just across from the designer's Madison Avenue flagship – lavishes little ones with "mini-versions" of "fabulous" "RL classics", including cashmere sweaters, madras plaid pants and those ubiquitous polo shirts; sure, it's pricey, but this "solid" "quality" "stuff" "will last."

Ray Beauty Supply ⊠
| | 24 | 9 | 19 | I |

W 40s | 721 Eighth Ave. (bet. 45th & 46th Sts.) | A/C/E to 42nd St./Port Authority | 212-757-0175 | 800-253-0993 | www.raybeauty.com

"One of the best, but certainly not best-looking, shops" for "all things hair" is this Hell's Kitchen retailer selling "gigantic bottles of name-brand conditioners", shampoos, dyes, dryers, curling irons and ceramic straighteners at "moderate prices"; "it's not for the weak" (the staff "looks like bikers" and the place is a "dungeon"), but it is nevertheless a "great resource" for "salon items" that's a "professional beauty secret."

Razor
| | – | – | – | E |

Park Slope | 329 Fifth Ave. (bet. 3rd & 4th Aves.) | Brooklyn | M/R to Union St. | 718-832-0717 ☽

NEW Park Slope | 463 Fourth St. (bet. 7th & 8th Aves.) | Brooklyn | F to 7th Ave. | 718-499-5314
www.razornyc.com

Park Slope hipsters don't have to spread themselves thin shopping for menswear now that this Fifth Avenue standby has opened a new offshoot nearby; fashion-minded dudes discover real "gems" among the funky professional-wear including shirts, ties and jewelry, plus an especially extensive selection of "high-end jeans" from premium labels like Antik, Buffalo by David Bitton, Chip & Pepper, 1921 and Yanuk.

| | QUALITY | DISPLAY | SERVICE | COST |

RCS Experience
17 | 15 | 14 | E

E 50s | 575 Madison Ave. (56th St.) | E/V to 5th Ave./53rd St. |
212-949-6935 | www.rcsnet.com

There's "a lot to choose from" at this East 50s electronics outlet, including a "good range of hard-to-find-items"; "high-quality computer" connoisseurs are keen on the fact that they "don't sell any crappy lines", leading most to say they "enjoy shopping here", but some wish they could switch off the "aggressive" staff.

Rebecca & Drew
– | – | – | E

Meatpacking | 342 W. 13th St. (Hudson St.) | A/C/E/L to 14th St./8th Ave. |
212-647-8904 | www.rebeccaanddrew.com

Women who prefer their shirts crisply tailored yet cutting-edge rejoice at the bounty of button-downs offered at this modest Meatpacking District shop owned by fashion-savvy friends Drew Paluba and alice + olivia co-founder Rebecca Winn; choose a solid, striped or plaid cotton number "based on your bra size", kitted out with ruffles or grosgrain ribbons and a variety of collars – it's "almost as good as buying custom-made."

Rebecca Taylor
23 | 23 | 20 | E

NoLita | 260 Mott St. (bet. Houston & Prince Sts.) | B/D/F/V to B'way/
Lafayette St. | 212-966-0406 | www.rebeccataylor.com

"Cute girlie" clothes "that even a 30-year-old can get away with" hold sway at this New Zealand designer's NoLita nugget, frequented by celebs like Chelsea Clinton and Sarah Michelle Gellar; "helpful" staffers find you "ultrafeminine" pieces that run the gamut from "fantastic pants" to "tailored suits" to "that adorable top you've been looking for."

Rebel Rebel ●
– | – | – | M

W Vill | 319 Bleecker St. (bet. Christopher & Grove Sts.) | 1 to Christopher St./
Sheridan Sq. | 212-989-0770

"The best excuse for not downloading music", this "excellent" indie in the West Village "specializes in imports", with an "extra focus on Euro pop and dance" CDs, and is jammed to the gills with "classic" and "off-beat" offerings ("the selection is especially great for Anglophiles", who also love the plethora of Brit mags); in fact, the only complaint is that owner David Shebiro "needs a larger store."

Redberi ● Ⓜ
– | – | – | E

Prospect Hts | 331 Flatbush Ave. (Park Pl.) | Brooklyn | B/Q to 7th Ave. |
718-622-1964 | www.redberi.com

"Another reason to stay in Brooklyn" brag boosters who bank on owner Carlene Brown's fine-tuned sense of color and style, plucking "quirky, individual", limited-edition and handcrafted clothing, jewelry and beauty products at this beri-cool boutique; the petite Prospect Heights digs offer finds from local designers and European and Asian indies like Arrogant Cat and Seneda.

Red Flower
– | – | – | M

NoLita | 13 Prince St. (bet. Bowery & Elizabeth St.) | J/M/Z to Bowery |
212-966-5301 | www.redflower.com

Fans of this flower say it's "worth the trip" to NoLita for "wonderful smelling" "unique candles" like the Moroccan Rose scented ones, along with botanically based bath and body products made out of ingredients like cherry blossoms and blood oranges; you can top off the soothing experience by taking home one of their equally evocative teas.

Reebok Concept Store ◐

| | 20 | 21 | 16 | M |

W 60s | 160 Columbus Ave. (bet. 67th & 68th Sts.) | 1 to 66th St./Lincoln Ctr. | 212-595-1480 | www.reebok.com

"True athletes" step on up to this "great-looking" 3,200-sq.-ft. West 60s outpost for a "good selection" of "cool brand merchandise" including men's and women's "trendy", top-"quality work-out clothing", sneakers and backpacks, plus NFL and NBA jerseys; but while they sell some of "the most comfortable shoes" around (including retro classics) and the "sales events" "can't be beat", gripers grumble that the "helpless help" can be easily "overwhelmed."

Reem Acra 🅂 Ⓜ

| ▽ | 29 | 29 | 28 | VE |

E 60s | 14 E. 60th St. (bet. 5th & Madison Aves.) | 4/5/6/F/N/R/W to 59th St./Lexington Ave. | 212-308-8760 | www.reemacra.com

Fiancées in search of a "sinfully beautiful gown at equally sinful prices" find the "most exquisite" big-day creations at this UES salon; when you see the "magnificent embroidery" "up close" "you understand why every bride would die to have" a beaded dress or a crystal tiara (fashioned by the designer's brother, Max); the "impeccable service" is "guaranteed to make you feel like royalty", so the end result is "worth every penny."

Refinery Ⓜ

| - | - | - | M |

Cobble Hill | 254 Smith St. (bet. Degraw & Douglass Sts.) | Brooklyn | F/G to Bergen St. | 718-643-7861 | www.brooklynrefinery.com

"Handmade in Brooklyn, what more could you want?" quip Cobble Hill cultists who covet owner-designer Suzanne Bagdade's "great bags made from vintage" ties and "very hip, durable" fabrics (no leather), all revealing her knack for "beautiful design and craftsmanship"; the spare, sleek space also boasts clogs and all-important 718 T-shirts for those big on announcing their borough pride.

Reinstein/Ross

| ▽ | 28 | 26 | 21 | VE |

E 70s | 29 E. 73rd St. (bet. 5th & Madison Aves.) | 6 to 68th St. | 212-772-1901 🅂

SoHo | 122 Prince St. (bet. Greene & Wooster Sts.) | N/R/W to Prince St. | 212-226-4513

www.reinsteinross.com

Upper East Side and SoHo jewelry shops showcasing "carefully handmade", "excellent quality" Egyptian- and Etruscan-inspired designs, from stacks of signature gemstone-set bands and rings in different shades of gold or platinum to multicolored sapphire cuffs and necklaces; just be sure to "save your pennies" in order to shop here.

Reiss

| 20 | 23 | 21 | E |

SoHo | 387 W. Broadway (bet. Broome & Spring Sts.) | C/E to Spring St. | 212-925-5707 ◐

NEW **W 60s** | 199 Columbus Ave. (69th St.) | 1 to 66th St./Lincoln Ctr. | 212-874-0245 Ⓜ

NEW **W Vill** | 311 Bleecker St. (bet. Barrow & Grove Sts.) | 1 to Christopher St./Sheridan Sq. | 212-488-2411 Ⓜ

www.reiss.co.uk

"Love the presentation" at this British import, which now has three "trendy megastores" around town, each boasting a sparkling chandelier, exposed-brick walls and "fun to shop" racks filled with "interesting" Reiss' "pieces that are simple yet different" for birds (and at the Downtown destinations, blokes too); if a few squawk it's "too expensive", flush twenty- and thirtysomethings taken with the "amazing styling" of the sexy cuts "stop in every time we're in the 'hood."

Reminiscence ●
19 | 19 | 17 | M

Flatiron | 50 W. 23rd St. (bet. 5th & 6th Aves.) | F/V to 23rd St. | 212-243-2292 | www.reminiscence.com

"Old, bold, flashy and trashy": "there's always something fun to be found" at this Flatiron "silly emporium", whose mirrored, beaded-curtained digs abound with vintage and "vintage-inspired items" ranging from "cutesy memorabilia" and "cool toys" to new Hawaiian shirts; while "it's changed since its heyday" – it's "mostly gag gifts and tchotchkes now" – "prices are manageable, if not cheap", and "if you don't find that '60s frock, you can always buy a glob of fake vomit."

Replay
▽ 23 | 21 | 19 | E

SoHo | 109 Prince St. (Greene St.) | N/R/W to Prince St. | 212-673-6300 | www.replay.it

While it's "usually quiet and often overlooked", this multifloor denim destination actually stocks a "huge choice" of what may be the "best jeans in SoHo" with a "friendly staff" to "help you navigate between dozens of styles"; "you have to know and love" this "cool" Italian label "to pay the price", but loyalists stand fast, advising "bring a lot of money" or "wait for the annual sale."

Restoration Hardware ●
21 | 23 | 19 | M

Flatiron | 935 Broadway (22nd St.) | N/R/W to 23rd St. | 212-260-9479 | 800-762-1005 | www.restorationhardware.com

"Much more than just hardware" is found at this Flatiron home-furnishings store with "dependable", "well-designed", "quality furniture", lighting, bathroom fixtures, towels, bedding, cleaning products, "cool gadgets" and retro toys; it's a "little limited on styles", but "prices are fair" and the staff is "knowledgeable and helpful."

Resurrection
- | - | - | VE

NoLita | 217 Mott St. (bet. Prince & Spring Sts.) | N/R/W to Prince St. | 212-625-1374 | www.resurrectionvintage.com

There's "sort of an arty take on vintage" mens- and womenswear at this NoLita hideaway, known among nostalgists as being "the best for Pucci, Courrèges" and other "coveted designers" from the Swinging '60s, '70s and '80s; with its "interesting mix of merch" in "remarkable" shape, "eye-catching window displays" and mod, blood-red interior, the scene is strictly "hipster central", so "don't even think about shopping here if you're not cool" or not flush (it "has gotten rather pricey").

Ricky's ●
19 | 15 | 14 | M

E 40s | 509 Fifth Ave. (bet. 42nd & 43rd Sts.) | 7 to 5th Ave. | 212-949-7230 | www.rickys-nyc.com
Additional locations throughout the NY area

These "freaky variety stores" exist because "you never know when you'll need a zebra-print boa, magenta wig, German deodorant or scented candle", along with Halloween costumes and "all the beauty products mentioned in magazines" from makeup and "top-quality hair" goop to "every lotion and potion you can think of"; then too there are those "naughty" back rooms with sex toys "without the Times Square smuttiness"; the "help is unhelpful", but that doesn't keep devotees from surrendering to "one-stop acid-trip shopping."

Rico

-	-	-	E

Boerum Hill | 384 Atlantic Ave. (bet. Bond & Hoyt Sts.) | Brooklyn | A/C/G to Hoyt/Schermerhorn Sts. | 718-797-2077 | www.shoprico.com

Amid the amorphous sea of antiques stores lining Boerum Hill's Atlantic Avenue stands this contemporary home-design hub, offering three floors of easygoing Mitchell Gold + Bob Williams sofas, minimalist Dellarobbia rugs, sculptural Emeco chairs and owner Rico Espinet's own atmospheric lighting.

☑ Rita's Needlepoint ☒

26	21	23	E

E 70s | 150 E. 79th St., 2nd fl. (bet. Lexington & 3rd Aves.) | 6 to 77th St. | 212-737-8613 | www.ritasneedlepoint.com

Needleworkers note that this Upper East Sider's "mind-boggling" selection of "beautiful hand-painted canvases" is almost certain to "contain what you're looking for" (if not, "helpful" staffers will "create your design" for you) and appreciate the "courteous" service that includes "free lessons for beginners who buy" there; though a few fret it could be more "cheerful" most agree these folks "get the point."

RK Bridal

19	11	15	M

Garment Dist | 318 W. 39th St. (bet. 8th & 9th Aves.) | A/C/E to 42nd St./Port Authority | 212-947-1155 | 800-929-9512 | www.rkbridal.com

When you want your "dream to be a princess on your wedding day to come true and you don't have much money", head to this "one-stop" Garment District "warehouse"; "it ain't fancy" and you need "patience" to sift through the "sea of white dresses" but the payoff is "bingo!" – "bridal and bridesmaids dresses galore" at a "large variety of price points" sold by an "accommodating staff"; P.S. "weekends are a zoo."

Roberta Freymann ☒

-	-	-	M

E 70s | 153 E. 70th St., 2nd fl. (Lexington Ave.) | 6 to 68th St. | 212-585-3767 | www.roberta-freymann.com

"A favorite for fashion editors", this Upper East Sider in the second floor of a brownstone gives you "a lot of look for the price" with its kurta tunics, Pakistani quilts, chic bohemian clothing and accessories imported from far-flung lands, including Argentina, India and Thailand; Freymann fans praise her sharp eye, confiding you'll find items "you can't get anywhere else", and "if you could", you'd "pay a lot more."

NEW Roberta Roller Rabbit ☒

-	-	-	M

E 70s | 1019 Lexington Ave. (73rd St.) | 6 to 77th St. | 212-772-7200 | www.roberta-freymann.com

Boho-chic clothing boutique owner Roberta Freymann brings her ethnically oriented eye to this new Indian-inspired home-furnishings' emporium in the East 70s; there are reasonably priced hand-painted armoires, chests and daybeds along with her signature hand-blocked fabrics, some of which turn up in childrenswear, and one of which inspired the offbeat name for the store.

☑ Robert Clergerie ⬛

28 | – | 22 | VE

E 60s | 19 E. 62nd St. (bet. 5th & Madison Aves.) | N/R/W to 5th Ave./ 59th St. | 212-207-8600 | www.robertclergerie.com

Whether it's "chunky" wedge sandals in wild colors, "always beautiful" "classic" heels or "great" lug-soled motorcycle-style boots, the French designer's "*très* expensive" footwear at his new East 60s boutique keeps "getting better", prompting patrons to "come back" "year after year"; the "last-forever" kicks are "comfortable" and "stylin'" – no wonder guys and gals swear you "can take them anywhere."

Robert Lee Morris Gallery

25 | 25 | 21 | E

SoHo | 400 W. Broadway (bet. Broome & Spring Sts.) | C/E to Spring St. | 212-431-9405 | 800-829-8444 | www.robertleemorris.com

"His jewelry is like artwork" "with a touch of nature", the tribal or the industrial influencing the pieces say fans of this pioneering SoHo designer and his gallerylike West Broadway haven that's headquarters for "handmade", sculptural silver cuffs and knuckle rings or more recent 18-karat gold orbital mobile necklaces.

Robert Marc

27 | 25 | 25 | VE

E 40s | 400 Madison Ave. (bet. 47th & 48th Sts.) | E/V to 5th Ave./ 53rd St. | 212-319-2900

E 50s | 551 Madison Ave. (bet. 55th & 56th Sts.) | N/R/W to 5th Ave./ 59th St. | 212-319-2000

E 60s | 782 Madison Ave. (bet. 66th & 67th Sts.) | 6 to 68th St. | 212-737-6000

E 70s | 1046 Madison Ave. (bet. 78th & 79th Sts.) | 6 to 77th St. | 212-988-9600

E 90s | 1300 Madison Ave. (bet. 92nd & 93rd Sts.) | 6 to 96th St. | 212-722-1600

SoHo | 436 W. Broadway (Prince St.) | N/R/W to Prince St. | 212-343-8300 ◗

W 60s | 190 Columbus Ave. (bet. 68th & 69th Sts.) | 1 to 66th St./ Lincoln Ctr. | 212-799-4600

W Vill | 386 Bleecker St. (Perry St.) | 1 to Christopher St./Sheridan Sq. | 212-242-6668 ◗

www.robertmarc.com

"If you have to wear glasses, you might as well have fun" shopping at this "outstanding" ocular octet of "well-designed" shops; the "fabulous selection of unusual frames" speaks to the "celebrity in all of us" with lots of "color options" in star-favored lines such as Freudenhaus and Lunor; sure, the wares are "costly", but the "quality is superb" and what's more, the "talented", "exacting" staff knows "just what looks best" on you – they even "try to find" specs that "fit your personality."

Roberto Cavalli

27 | 27 | 23 | VE

E 60s | 711 Madison Ave. (63rd St.) | 4/5/6/F/N/R/W to 59th St./ Lexington Ave. | 212-755-7722 | www.robertocavalli.it

Get ready to frock 'n' roll at this sleek, "absolutely fabulous" Madison Avenue bi-level boutique where the Italian designer lets it rip (sometimes literally) in his-and-hers skintight, "funky, sexy stuff", from ornate leather jackets to wrap dresses in wild animal prints; true, "friends might think you're crazy when you come back with $500 jeans with paint on them, but put them on and they'll understand" "the dent you just made in your budget."

Roberto Vascon
— | — | — | E

W 70s | 140 W. 72nd St. (bet. B'way & Columbus Ave.) | 1/2/3 to 72nd St. | 212-787-9050 | www.robertovascon.com

For a "unique" bag you "don't see all over town", head to this minimalist West 70s shop where cobbler Roberto creates "to your specifications", helping you choose the leather, handles and style to come up with an "absolutely beautiful handmade purse"; loyalists insist that these accessories are "addictive" enough to warrant a "closet full", but they better save space for the line of custom-made shoes.

Robert Talbott 🛇
28 | 25 | 23 | VE

E 60s | 680 Madison Ave. (bet. 61st & 62nd Sts.) | N/R/W to 5th Ave./59th St. | 212-751-1200 | 800-747-8778 | www.roberttalbott.com

It's not even close to a tie when it comes to the "finest neckwear in Manhattan" declare devotees of this East 60s haberdasher who also laud the "phenomenal" assortment of formalwear, including "the best tuxedo shirts you can get married in"; throw in more "colorful" dress and casual shirts and a smaller women's collection combined with "personalized" service and it's an obvious "first stop" on a Madison Avenue shopping spree.

☑ Roche Bobois
27 | 25 | 22 | VE

Murray Hill | 200 Madison Ave. (35th St.) | 6 to 33rd St. | 212-889-0700 | www.rochebobois.com

This Murray Hill store is a "modern" mainstay for "top-of-the-line French furniture" to "make a home more beautiful"; "great" pieces like luxe leather sofas and headboards of amazing "quality" and design "can break the bank", but connoisseurs who aren't hide-bound calmly counter that "perfection has a price."

Rochester Big & Tall ●
26 | 24 | 24 | E

W 50s | 1301 Sixth Ave. (52nd St.) | B/D/F/V to 47-50th Sts./Rockefeller Ctr. | 212-247-7500 | 800-282-8200 | www.rochesterclothing.com

"Find all the standard brands from Burberry to Ralph Lauren" at this Midtown chain link "for the man of height and girth", where "shopping is a pleasure" thanks to the "huge inventory" and "discreet, attentive" staff that "goes to great lengths" to help "chubby hubbies" find the right fit; "more-to-love guys" know to expect "big prices" here, but the "superior" selection and the "best tailoring" ease the sticker shock.

Rockit Scientist Records ●
— | — | — | M

E Vill | 33 St. Marks Pl. (bet. 2nd & 3rd Aves.) | 6 to Astor Pl. | 212-242-0066

Here's the prog-nosis: if "hard-to-find" progressive, psychedelic, garage, soul and '60s classics rock your world, this "hidden treasure" in the East Village will send you into orbit with one of the "best" selections of new and used CDs and vinyl; admirers are also over the moon about the "extremely knowledgeable staff", maintaining they make it a "great place to hang and talk about music."

Rocks in Your Head ●
— | — | — | M

Williamsburg | 133 Roebling St. (bet. N. 4th & 5th Sts.) | Brooklyn | G/L to Metropolitan Ave./Lorimer St. | 718-384-0049 | www.rocksinyourhead.com

After 28 years, the former "SoHo classic" music store where both Woody and Gwyneth shot footage, has moved to a bigger Williamsburg space; rockheads rejoice: they still have "tons of hard-to-find CDs" and LPs including "live recordings" and "interesting" indie discoveries.

NEW Rogan
25 | 21 | 21 | E

TriBeCa | 91 Franklin St. (bet. B'way & Church St.) | 1 to Franklin St. | 646-827-7554 | www.rogannyc.com

"Everything feels cool" at this lofty TriBeCa space with artfully rough edges (like exposed brick and metal pipes) where celebs and fashionistas pick up ultrahip dark denim that's deemed "exceptional, even for the price", as well as stylishly rumpled cashmere and silk separates from their A Ltil Btr line; furniture from recycled materials, rare books and handmade jewelry add to the all-around effortlessly chic aesthetic.

Romp M
- | - | - | E

Park Slope | 145 Fifth Ave. (bet. Lincoln & St. Johns Pls.) | Brooklyn | 2/3 to Bergen St. | 718-230-4373 | www.rompbklyn.com

Not your standard-issue toy shop, this Park Slope playhouse trumpets an unusual, sophisticated medley of merchandise, such as music boxes, make-and-shoot pinhole cameras, wood drums and other curiosities, from far-flung places like Thailand, Poland and The Netherlands; modern moms also romp over for the contemporary crib linens and furniture from local designers.

Room & Board
24 | 27 | 21 | M

SoHo | 105 Wooster St. (bet. Prince & Spring Sts.) | 1 to Houston St. | 212-334-4343 | 800-486-6554 | www.roomandboard.com

Minneapolis-based "minimalist" "modern furnishings" company that offers "excellent quality" "beautiful things" at "reasonable prices" in their four-floor SoHo store; there's a "great choice" of "smooth, clean-lined" sofas, side chairs, tables and beds, and service is "most helpful", leading enthusiasts to exclaim "thank you for coming to New York!"

Rosen & Chadick Textiles ⑤
- | - | - | E

Garment Dist | 561 Seventh Ave., 2nd fl. (bet. 39th & 40th Sts.) | 1/2/3/7/N/Q/R/S/W to 42nd St./Times Sq. | 212-869-0142 | 800-225-3838

After more than 25 years on West 40th Street, in mid-2005 this family-owned Garment District veteran moved around the corner to sunny, airy new digs; its clientele of professional designers, Broadway costumers and hobbyists has followed for the sake of its "beautiful fabrics" (e.g. custom-made linens, wools, cashmere, silks and men's suiting) and "helpful" staff.

Rothman's
23 | 19 | 22 | E

Union Sq | 200 Park Ave. S. (17th St.) | 4/5/6/L/N/Q/R/W to 14th St./Union Sq. | 212-777-7400 | www.rothmansny.com

Though perhaps "best-suited (pun intended) for those seeking traditional styles", this "Union Square institution" stocks a "wide variety of casual and business dress" for "grown-up guys" ready to "go that one step above the chains"; though it's no longer strictly a discounter, "you can find deals on top names" during sales, abetted by the "well-mannered staff"; N.B. the Display score may not reflect a recent renovation.

	QUALITY	DISPLAY	SERVICE	COST

Rubin Chapelle
| | - | - | - | VE |

Meatpacking | 410 W. 14th St. (bet. 9th Ave. & Washington St.) | A/C/E/L to 14th St./8th Ave. | 212-647-8636 | www.rubinchapelle.com

Enter the brave new world of Austrian Sonya Rubin and American Kip Chapelle at their modernistic brick-walled, art-filled store in the Meatpacking District; the pair is fearless in their pursuit of a crisp minimalism in all they design for men and women, be it a svelte gown, a knit sweater or a trim suit; accessories such as buttery leather jackets, vintage bags and customized fur-lined boots round out the look.

☑ Rubin Museum of Art Ⓜ
| | 26 | 23 | 24 | E |

Chelsea | 150 W. 17th St. (bet. 6th & 7th Aves.) | 1 to 18th St. | 212-620-5000 | www.rmanyc.org

"A beautiful little jewel" of a shop in a "charming" museum devoted to the arts of the Himalayas, this "find" offers "sumptuously designed books", lovely imported jewelry, clothing and other "unique" gift items (including "lovable stuffed yaks"); admittedly, some of the prices may be as "high" as Mt. Everest itself, but the "quality's terrific" and the staff "friendly", making it "worth a trip" to Barneys' former home in Chelsea.

Ruehl ❶
| | 21 | 23 | 17 | E |

W Vill | 370 Bleecker St. (bet. Charles & Perry Sts.) | 1 to Christopher St./Sheridan Sq. | 212-924-8506 | www.ruehl.com

What an "interesting retail concept: part club, part store, part cool" quip customers of Bleecker Street's "hip", "higher-end" accessories-only Abercrombie & Fitch spin-off who laud the "great feel" and "good display" of leather handbags, men's bags, gloves and belts; still, an unruly few scoff it's so "dark" you may need a "flashlight if you want to see what you are buying" and Ruehl out the "smug" staff.

Rue St. Denis ❶
| | - | - | - | E |

E Vill | 170 Ave. B (bet. 10th & 11th Sts.) | L to 1st Ave. | 212-260-3388 | www.vintagenyc.com

"Stocked with unique, unworn clothing from past eras", this East Village vintage shop is one of the few to focus on the menfolk – offering them everything from '60s slim-cut Cardin suits to narrow '80s ties – though femmes will find plenty to amuse them among the ruffled skirts and open-toe pumps; aside from the bell-bottoms and European biker gear, the clothes "eschew kitsch for subtle style"; and if some rue the "overpriced" goods, others kvell at the "cool collection."

Rugby
| | 22 | 23 | 18 | E |

G Vill | 99 University Pl. (12th St.) | 4/5/6/L/N/Q/R/W to 14th St./Union Sq. | 212-677-1895 | www.rugby.com

"Pick up one of Ralph Lauren's greatest hits, reworked and sized-down for the college crowd" at this "amazing concept" store in Greenwich Village; the "affordable" (compared to Ralph's other lines) clothes offer "preppy choices with a downtown edge" – i.e. "skull-and-crossbones on [corduroys], an interesting combination" – arranged in "terrific visual displays"; staff hotties and free concerts keep "the place packed with style-crazed young adults", and while some snap the shop and styles are too "small", if you want "a fun alternative to Polo", you might become "a big Rugby fan."

Rug Company, The

| | | | VE |

SoHo | 88 Wooster St. (bet. Broome & Spring Sts.) | C/E to Spring St. | 212-274-0444 | www.therugcompany.info

Sure, there are traditional woven classics like Berbers at this British import in SoHo, but it's the contemporary designs by boldface names in interiors and fashion like Nina Campbell, Cath Kidston and Paul Smith that generate the buzz with patterns that range from pale stalks of bamboo to bold stripes.

Ruzzetti & Gow 🖼

| | | | E |

E 70s | 22 E. 72nd St., 3rd fl. (bet. 5th & Madison Aves.) | 6 to 68th St. | 212-327-4281 | www.ruzzettiandgow.com

Tucked away on the third floor of an Upper East Side brownstone is "a lovely place to shop" for a gleaming assortment of silver-coated seashells, vegetables and fruits, which make for tony tabletop ornaments; the natural theme carries over into coral and rock crystal jewelry and semiprecious stone bowls and boxes.

Sabon

| 25 | 25 | 23 | E |

NEW Chelsea | 78 Seventh Ave. (15th St.) | 1/2/3 to 14th St. | 646-486-1809 🖼 M
NEW E 60s | 782 Lexington Ave. (bet. 60th & 61st Sts.) | 4/5/6/F/N/R/W to 59th St./Lexington Ave. | 212-308-5901 🖼 M
G Vill | 434 Sixth Ave. (10th St.) | A/B/C/D/E/F/V to W. 4th St. | 212-473-4346 ●
SoHo | 93 Spring St. (B'way) | N/R/W to Prince St. | 212-925-0742 ●
NEW W 50s | 1371 Sixth Ave. (bet. 55th & 56th Sts.) | F to 57th St. | 212-974-7352 🖼 M
W 70s | 2052 Broadway (70th St.) | 1/2/3 to 72nd St. | 212-362-0200 ●
866-697-2266 | www.sabonnyc.com

This Israeli bath and body chain with branches around town features a handmade, natural product line that includes jewel-colored and studded soaps that are sold by the pound, "fabulous body scrubs" with Dead Sea salts and shea butter lotions and creams with "original scents" like ginger/orange that are "luscious."

Sacco ●

| 22 | 19 | 20 | E |

Chelsea | 94 Seventh Ave. (bet. 15th & 16th Sts.) | 1 to 18th St. | 212-675-5180
E 50s | 118 E. 59th St. (bet. Lexington & Park Aves.) | 4/5/6/F/N/R/W to 59th St./Lexington Ave. | 212-207-3151
Flatiron | 14 E. 17th St. (bet. B'way & 5th Ave.) | 4/5/6/L/N/Q/R/W to 14th St./Union Sq. | 212-243-2070
NEW Flatiron | 6 E. 23rd St. (bet. B'way & Madison Ave.) | N/R/W to 23rd St. | 212-777-3414
SoHo | 111 Thompson St. (bet. Prince & Spring Sts.) | N/R/W to Prince St. | 212-925-8010
W 70s | 324 Columbus Ave. (75th St.) | 1/2/3/B/C to 72nd St. | 212-799-5229
www.saccoshoes.com

Finding "fashion and function in footwear" may seem like a highfalutin demand, but it's a thoroughly "realistic" requirement for women who "live, work and play in NYC" and this "stylish" "standby" rises to the challenge, turning out "edgy" "soft-leather" shoes that are also "unbelievably comfortable"; the "quality will outlast the trend", and surprise, the "staff goes out of its way to find what you need."

Safavieh Carpets

▽ 26 | 19 | 21 | E

E 50s | 238 E. 59th St. (bet. 2nd & 3rd Aves.) | 4/5/6/F/N/R/W to 59th St./Lexington Ave. | 212-888-0626
Murray Hill | 153 Madison Ave. (32nd St.) | 6 to 33rd St. | 212-683-8399

Safavieh Home Furnishings

Flatiron | 902 Broadway (bet. 20th & 21st Sts.) | N/R/W to 23rd St. | 212-477-1234
866-422-9070 | www.safaviehhome.com

You're covered because there's such a "great selection" of "tempting rugs" including "very fine quality" "antique Orientals" as well as reproductions, traditional, tribal and contemporary collections at these three Manhattan manufacturers and importers with "decent" prices; N.B. the Broadway store also carries furniture.

NEW Saja

- | - | - | E

NoLita | 250 Elizabeth St. (bet. Houston & Prince Sts.) | B/D/F/V to B'way/Lafayette St. | 212-226-7570 | www.sajainc.com

When the occasion calls for full-on femininity, sweep into designer Yoo Lee's boudoirlike NoLita enclave, a sliver of elegance with a bright white floor and exposed-brick wall; get your fix of "gorgeous" retro-modern dresses and girlie-girl separates inspired by the 1920s and '30s done up with tasteful details like French seaming, lace, beading and hand embroidery, all dispensed by a "sweet" staff.

☑ Saks Fifth Avenue

27 | 24 | 21 | VE

E 40s | 611 Fifth Ave. (50th St.) | B/D/F/V to 47-50th Sts./Rockefeller Ctr. | 212-753-4000 | 877-551-7257 | www.saks.com

An "essential stop on any shopping spree", this Midtown mainstay "sets the standard" for "elegant" emporia because it's "not as pompous" as some, but "hasn't lost its sophistication", either; you'll see tourists, "trendy teens and socialites, side by side" savoring the "selection of mid- and upper-end fashion" for her and him, accessories and jewelry sections "reminiscent of a museum" and "lots to play with" in cosmetics; and though the staff could "lower the pushiness factor a bit", "they'll check the computer for an item in your size and ship it to you."

Salvation Army ⊠

11 | 6 | 8 | I

W 40s | 536 W. 46th St. (bet. 10th & 11th Aves.) | A/C/E to 42nd St./Port Authority | 212-757-2311 | www.salvationarmy.org
Additional locations throughout the NY area

The "depressing atmosphere makes you feel like a poor relation" and much of the merch has that "thrift-shop whiff", but if you "take a deep breath and search for everything as fast as you can", this historic charity's chain offers "definitely the best deal in town" on anything from "aging appliances" to clothes to books; converts confide the flagship "46th Street location has the most stuff" – just think of the "dusty, dingy and dark" digs as "perfect for Halloween shopping."

☑ Salvatore Ferragamo

28 | 26 | 24 | VE

E 50s | 655 Fifth Ave. (bet. 52nd & 53rd Sts.) | E/V to 5th Ave./53rd St. | 212-759-3822 | 800-628-8916 | www.salvatoreferragamo.com

"Everything" at this "high-end" two-story Fifth Avenue "flagship of a European icon" "screams elegance" assert Sal-ivaters who "absolutely adore" the "exquisite", "classic, always appropriate" men's and women's footwear that's "worth every penny", all proffered by a "top-notch" staff; but there's also "nothing more "*bellissimo*" than the selection of "perfect scarves", "amazing ties" and "great leather accessories."

NEW Salviati — | — | — | VE

SoHo | 422 W. Broadway (bet. Prince & Spring Sts.) | C/E to Spring St. | 212-625-8390 | www.salviati.com

This Venetian glass blower dating back to 1859 has just debuted its first U.S. outpost, an über-modern, orange-tiled SoHo shop done by prestigious Milanese interior designer Paola Navone; there's boldly colored barware, limited-edition vases by emerging European names and exuberant Murano-glass jewelry, all with equally eye-popping prices.

Sam & Seb — | — | — | E

Williamsburg | 208 Bedford Ave. (bet. N. 5th & 6th Sts.) | Brooklyn | L to Bedford Ave. | 718-486-8300 | www.samandseb.com

"The place where hipsters shop" for their progeny, this feisty Williamsburg boutique's stock in trade is "awesomely edgy togs for tots" – in other words, "not the usual pink and blue" fare, and yeah, "they have other colors besides black"; take home some of the rockin' Ramones and AC/DC onesies, Wonder Woman T-shirts and way-cute camouflage cargo pants, and your tyke'll be "too cool for school."

NEW Samantha Thavasa  — | — | — | E

E 70s | 965 Madison Ave. (bet. 75th & 76th Sts.) | 6 to 77th St. | 212-535-3920

Groupies who go for the glitzy, girlie, star- or heart-patterned handbags of this Japanese label, rejoice: the company's opened its first stateside location in the East 70s; the all-white, rhinestone-studded store features purses in vibrant colors and various styles, with the lines designed by socialites or celebs – Tinsley Mortimer, Nicky Hilton, Beyoncé Knowles – well-represented; there are a few wallets as well.

Sam Flax 24 | 20 | 17 | E

E 50s | 900 Third Ave. (bet. 54th & 55th Sts.) | E/V to Lexington Ave./53rd St. | 212-813-6666

Flatiron | 12 W. 20th St. (bet. 5th & 6th Aves.) | F/V to 23rd St. | 212-620-3000 800-628-9512 | www.samflaxny.com

"Colorful" Herman Miller desks and chairs "to spice up a dull office" along with "inspirational" art supplies and a "hodgepodge of interesting" gift items are "attractively presented" at this East 50s and Flatiron duo; "don't ever submit a portfolio without checking here first" and remember it's the "last word in chic paper goods" too; there's some hue and cry about "hot and cold" service and "high" prices; nevertheless, most consider it "reliably trendy."

NEW Samsonite Black Label 24 | 21 | 19 | E

E 60s | 838 Madison Ave. (bet. 69th & 70th Sts.) | 6 to 68th St. | 212-861-2064 | www.samsoniteblacklabel.com

"Enthusiasm reigns" at this compact, mod Madison Avenue newcomer, the first U.S. location for the boldface maker's worldwide spin-off brand – and no wonder: who knew "Samsonite could be so hip"?; the "very comprehensive", colorful selection, including the Vintage Collection, super-light X' Lite line and futuristic Scope Collection, "makes you want to take a trip", while the latest luxury endeavor, a grouping from Alexander McQueen, ensures that you'll "travel in style."

	QUALITY	DISPLAY	SERVICE	COST

Samuel's Hats ⊠
	-	-	-	E

Financial Dist | 74 Nassau St. (John St.) | 2/3/4/5/A/C/J/M/Z to
Fulton St./B'way/Nassau | 212-513-7322 | www.samuelshats.com
"Hats off to the huge selection" at the Financial District's handmade
headpiece heaven where "expensive to moderate" –priced ladies' lids
from designers like Louise Green, Makins and Philip Treacy are available in limited quantities; whether you're looking for sleek cloches or
dressy pillboxes "you will definitely find it here" – or you can have it
custom-made; there's also a small crop of men's toppers from
Borsalino and Kangol.

S&W
	18	10	10	M

NEW **Chelsea** | 287 Seventh Ave. (26th St.) | 1 to 23rd St.⊠Ⓜ
Borough Pk | 4217 13th Ave. (43rd St.) | Brooklyn | D/M to
Fort Hamilton Pkwy.
Williamsburg | 160 Wallabout St. (Bedford Ave.) | Brooklyn | J/M/Z to
Marcy Ave.
718-431-2800 | www.swnewyork.com
"If you don't see what you want, just ask for it – it's there" declare disciples of this discount trio specializing in "conservative" – some say
"dowdy" – womenswear; however, the "heavy sales pressure" and
"noise levels can overwhelm shoppers", and opponents opine "they
used to have better selections."

Sanrio ●
	21	23	17	M

(aka Hello Kitty Store)
W 40s | 233 W. 42nd St. (bet. 7th & 8th Aves.) | 1/2/3/7/N/Q/R/S/W
to 42nd St./Times Sq. | 212-840-6011
Elmhurst | Queens Ctr. | 90-15 Queens Blvd. (bet. 57th & 59th Aves.) |
Queens | G/R/V to Woodhaven Blvd. | 718-760-4886
www.sanrio.com
Japan's famous feline fashionista "Hello Kitty reigns supreme" at
this slice of girl "heaven" in Times Square and the Queens Center mall;
gals of "all ages" "spend hours" purring over and pawing through
the "incredible variety of items" including "so cute" pencil cases,
purses, lip gloss, stationery and even toaster ovens featuring HK and
pals My Melody, Badtz Maru and Chococat – all the "characters we
love so much."

Sansha
	-	-	-	M

W 50s | 888 Eighth Ave. (bet. 52nd & 53rd Sts.) | C/E to 50th St. |
212-246-6212 | www.sansha.com
"This is the place to go if you do any kind of dancing" confide movers
and shakers who lead the way to this West 50s performer's haven for
"great" handcrafted, split-sole ballet slippers as well as ballroom,
character, jazz, tap and pointe shoes at "very good prices"; leotards
and tights plus performance-ready flamenco skirts and tutus set the
stage for encore visits.

⊠ Santa Maria Novella
	28	25	23	VE

NoLita | 285 Lafayette St. (bet. Jersey & Prince Sts.) | B/D/F/V to B'way/
Lafayette St. | 212-925-0001 | www.santamarianovellausa.com
With a gilded exterior and an imposing interior filled with an extensive
array of expensive Italian toiletries, this NoLita boutique is the place for
"absolute luxury", including heady scents such as tuber rose and over-

the-top offerings like Virgin's Milk toner for skin; the Florence-based company's legend says it was founded by 17th-century monks, which may be why converts call it a "heavenly" place for "divine products."

NEW Satellite

— | — | — | E

SoHo | 412 W. Broadway (bet. Prince & Spring Sts.) | C/E to Spring St. | 212-372-0016 | www.satelliteparis.com

Morocco meets Marie Antoinette and sometimes Queen Victoria at this French costume jewelry import newly arrived in SoHo; Sandrine Dulon's dramatic designs may incorporate semiprecious stones, elaborate beading, enamel, crystals and feathers in everything from chandelier earrings to multistrand bib necklaces, and all offer a big bang for the buck.

Satya ☻

21 | 22 | 22 | M

W Vill | 330 Bleecker St. (Christopher St.) | 1 to Christopher St./ Sheridan Sq. | 212-243-7313 | www.satyajewelry.com

When two jewelry veterans combined their interest in things Eastern, the result was Satya (meaning 'truth'), a "cool" West Village boutique with a Buddha in the window; "Indian-inspired pieces" in silver, 18-karat gold vermeil (particularly woven-metal cuffs and the thinnest bangles) and gemstones (chosen for their healing properties) appeal to celebs like Susan Sarandon and Bette Midler, but "reasonable prices" mean it's on the money for almost everyone; N.B. they've expanded into the space next door to sell scarves and soaps.

Scandinavian Ski and Sport Shop

22 | 16 | 17 | E

E 50s | 16 E. 55th St. (bet. 5th & Madison Aves.) | E/V to 5th Ave./ 53rd St. | 212-757-8524 | www.skishop.com

Snow bunnies "who want to look fabulous on the slopes" slalom over to this winter-wear mainstay in the East 50s to check out the "terrific inventory"; the shelves aren't limited to threads from "high-end" labels like Lange and Nils – the latest skis, sleds and equipment are also stocked; still, some consider the steep prices a "Scandinavian scandal", scoffing it's not "the only game in town" anymore.

Scaredy Kat ☻Ⓜ

▽ 24 | 23 | 25 | M

Park Slope | 229 Fifth Ave. (bet. Carroll & President Sts.) | Brooklyn | M/R to Union St. | 718-623-1839 | www.scaredykatstore.com

For the "best selection of hip, contemporary greeting cards" in Park Slope and "cool weird stuff" ranging from Frida Kahlo plastic totes to whimsical nightlights that make "fun gifts", skip over to this butter-cup-colored shop with a tongue-in-cheek "American mom-and-pop vibe" that hints at the owners' "sense of humor"; patrons purr there's "something for every occasion" here, including announcements and notes custom-made from your photos.

Schneider's ☒

▽ 25 | 16 | 19 | M

Chelsea | 41 W. 25th St. (bet. B'way & 6th Ave.) | F/V to 23rd St. | 212-228-3540 | www.schneidersbaby.com

Ok, it's "cluttered" but this "gem" of a baby general store – a New York "institution" for over 55 years, which relocated from Alphabet City to Chelsea "digs" a few years ago – stocks a "good selection of strollers, car seats, cribs and other basic supplies"; throw in an "incredibly helpful staff" and you've got a shop "definitely worth schlepping to."

	QUALITY	DISPLAY	SERVICE	COST

Scholastic Store, The

	24	24	21	M

SoHo | 557 Broadway (bet. Prince & Spring Sts.) | N/R/W to Prince St. |
212-343-6166 | 877-286-0137 | www.thescholasticstore.com

"Clifford and Harry Potter reside side by side" with Captain
Underpants at this "excellent, educational", always-"mobbed" SoHo
"wonderland" for little "learning minds"; the loftlike layout is stocked
solid with "engaging" toys, games, books, videos and CD-ROMs, plus
teachers can also nab "nice deals" on curriculum materials; stop in for
the "wonderful, interactive" character visits and story hour – it's a
"great way to instill [interest in] reading."

Schoolhouse Electric Co. 🖂

	–	–	–	E

TriBeCa | 27 Vestry St. (Hudson St.) | 1 to Franklin St. | 212-226-6113 |
www.schoolhouseelectric.com

Period-lighting lovers brighten at the sight of this TriBeCa showroom
selling classic 1900–1950s fixtures and hand-blown glass shades,
some out of production since the Depression; vintage molds are used to
create ceiling-mounted designs, hanging pendants and wall sconces.

School Products Co., Inc. 🖂

	25	16	22	M

Garment Dist | 1201 Broadway, 3rd fl. (bet. 28th & 29th Sts.) | N/R/W
to 23rd St. | 212-679-3516 | 800-847-4127 | www.schoolproducts.com

"Definitely old-school" (founded in 1947), Berta Karapetyan's "huge",
"no-atmosphere" fiber outlet near FIT is a "must-visit" for the savvy
crafter; knitters "racking up" "large quantities" make a beeline for
"high-quality", "bargain"-priced coned yarns left over from fashion
houses, pronouncing this "Garment Center classic" a "mecca for cashmere", silk and other luxury covetables; still, a handful feel it's a "hit-
or-miss" proposition – it just "depends on how lucky you are."

🛛 Schweitzer Linen

	27	16	21	E

E 70s | 1053 Lexington Ave. (bet. 74th & 75th Sts.) | 6 to 77th St. |
212-570-0236 🖂
E 80s | 1132 Madison Ave. (bet. 84th & 85th Sts.) | 4/5/6 to 86th St. |
212-249-8361 🖂
W 80s | 457 Columbus Ave. (bet. 81st & 82nd Sts.) | B/C to 81st St. |
212-799-9642
800-554-6367 | www.schweitzerlinen.com

Family-owned Uptown trio of "reasonably priced for the quality" linen
stores with a "great selection" of "beautiful", "upscale", European-
styled sheets that will help you "sleep better for having shopped
here", along with scallop-edged, Egyptian cotton towels with a
Porthault look for less; "small, cramped" quarters make it "hard to
browse" and service can vary, but that doesn't keep the "discerning"
from hunting for "great buys" here.

Scoop Kids ◉

	23	23	18	E

Meatpacking | 875 Washington St. (bet. 13th & 14th Sts.) | A/C/E/L to
14th St./8th Ave. | 212-691-1926 | 877-726-6777 | www.scoopnyc.com

"Kids can be hip too", especially after a stop at this Meatpacking
District mecca for all things child-size yet "trendy" that's "just like"
Scoop for grown-ups – what an "awesome idea"; "you know what's 'in'"
the moment you walk through the door: denim from Earnest Sewn, 7 for
All Mankind and Joe's Jeans, novelty tops from Tory Burch and comfy
basics from Juicy Couture – it's all "sooo kool but sooo expensive!"

Scoop Men's

23 | 23 | 18 | E

E 70s | 1277 Third Ave. (bet. 73rd & 74th Sts.) | 6 to 77th St. | 212-535-5577
Meatpacking | 873 Washington St. (bet. 13th & 14th Sts.) | A/C/E/L to 14th St./8th Ave. | 212-929-1244
www.scoopnyc.com

Anything from Scoop's sidekick for guys will "become the prized possessions of your wardrobe" insist insiders who snatch up the "latest styles" at these "easy-to-navigate" boutiques in the East 70s and "trendy Meatpacking District"; the "inventory is updated regularly, so stop in before your Thursday night date" for "great stuff" from Paul Smith and John Varvatos, store-commissioned lines from J.Crew and Theory, plus an "excellent selection of jeans" and T-shirts; still, some dish that service is "good – if you look like you're willing to spend major dollars."

Scoop NYC

23 | 22 | 16 | E

E 70s | 1273-1277 Third Ave. (bet. 73rd & 74th Sts.) | 6 to 77th St. | 212-535-5577
Meatpacking | 861 Washington St. (bet. 13th & 14th Sts.) | A/C/E/L to 14th St./8th Ave. | 212-691-1905
SoHo | 532 Broadway (bet. Prince & Spring Sts.) | N/R/W to Prince St. | 212-925-2886
877-726-6777 | www.scoopnyc.com

Bring "plenty of cash" to shop at this "effortlessly cool" outfit – it's the "ultimate closet" confide fashionistas who "scoop up" the "hottest jeans", "au courant" "fun stuff" from "fabulous" labels like alice + olivia, Marc Jacobs and Theory and "accessories to make them look even better"; some claim the "candid" staff is "helpful", but detractors declare their "laser-beam stares" can "send you running"; N.B. a 'mega store' is slated to open in early spring 2007 at 473-5 Broadway carrying men's, women's and kids' wear (plus a new fragrance line), while plans are afoot to turn 532 Broadway into an outlet.

Scott Jordan Furniture

▽ 27 | 26 | 29 | E

SoHo | 137 Varick St. (Spring St.) | C/E to Spring St. | 212-620-4682 | www.scottjordan.com

A "knowledgeable and low-pressure staff" presides over this SoHo showroom featuring "beautifully made", "clean-lined", "handcrafted" Mission-style furniture in American black-cherry wood; but while there is no quibble about the "high-quality" of the pieces, some aesthetes assert they are short on "style."

Scuba Network

- | - | - | M

Chelsea | 655 Sixth Ave. (bet. 20th & 21st Sts.) | F/V to 23rd St. | 212-243-2988
E 50s | 669 Lexington Ave. (bet. 55th & 56th Sts.) | 4/5/6/F/N/R/W to 59th St./Lexington Ave. | 212-750-9160
800-688-3483 | www.scubanetwork.com

Never mind the 30-ft. octopus stationed outside the Sixth Avenue location – Cousteau wannabes gladly hand themselves over to the "friendliest staff around" at this East 50s–Chelsea outfit because the "helpful" experts take the undersea world seriously; this "great diver's resource", in business for over 20 years, has expanded from the scuba basics to include snorkels, fins, swimsuits and kayaks, with prices leagues below others; P.S. "get your certification" here too.

☑ Scully & Scully

29 | 27 | 24 | VE

E 50s | 504 Park Ave. (59th St.) | 4/5/6/F/N/R/W to 59th St./
Lexington Ave. | 212-755-2590 | 800-223-3717 | www.scullyandscully.com
"Shop here" at this East 50s "classic" "Muffy/Buffy" home-furnishings
store if you have any "Republican friends who live on Park Avenue"; of
course, "lovely old-guard items" including Herend china animal figurines, sterling silver pheasants, faux sable throws and reproduction
antique furniture come at a premium price.

Seaman Schepps ☒

▽ 27 | 27 | 27 | VE

E 50s | 485 Park Ave. (58th St.) | 4/5/6/F/N/R/W to 59th St./
Lexington Ave. | 212-753-9520 | www.seamanschepps.com
"Wonderful, whimsical" turban-shell earrings wrapped with gold wire,
then crowned with colored stones are still the celebrated jeweler's signature, and the salon-style Park Avenue store he opened in 1934 to
feature his own designs, mixing precious gems with lesser materials
such as coral or wood, remains headquarters for the "creative, exuberant" "nonpareil" pieces that were (and are) coveted by the best-
dressed-list ladies; N.B. each pricey piece is numbered.

Sean ◑

▽ 24 | 24 | 26 | M

SoHo | 132 Thompson St. (bet. Houston & Prince Sts.) | C/E to Spring St. |
212-598-5980
W 70s | 224 Columbus Ave. (bet. 70th & 71st Sts.) | 1/2/3/B/C to
72nd St. | 212-769-1489
www.seanstore.com
This SoHo and West 70s pair can make almost any man "look like an
architect, or at least European" with breezy and basic French cuts
from labels such as Emile Lafaurie; the "reliably tasteful, hip" knits,
linens and shirts on the shelves come at what many consider a "good
price"; N.B. look for Sam, the seven-year-old chocolate Lab featured in
their ads, in person at the SoHo branch.

Sean John

18 | 22 | 18 | E

E 40s | 475 Fifth Ave. (41st St.) | 4/5/6/7/S to 42nd St./Grand Central |
212-220-2633 | www.seanjohn.com
The pseudonym-loving hip-hop entrepreneur parlays his fame and his
name into the fashion game with this marble-and-mahogany mecca
across from the NY Public Library; the too-cool-for-school menswear –
from jeans to suits to leather or suede sneakers – is "stylish and affordable" say aficionados aching for a bit of his inimitable lifestyle; but
skeptics sigh "why Diddy is doing this, I'll never know"; N.B. if bling is
your thing, ladies, check out the Sean by Sean Combs line.

☑ Seaport Yarn ⇄

28 | 15 | 23 | M

Seaport | 135 William St., 5th fl. (bet. Fulton & John Sts.) |
2/3/4/5/A/C/J/M/Z to Fulton St./B'way/Nassau | 212-220-5230 |
800-347-2662 | www.seaportyarn.com
A "den for knitaholics" stashed in a "hard-to-find" fifth-floor space
near the South Street Seaport, this 3,700-sq.-ft. office suite has "every
nook" and cubicle "crammed" full of "awesome yarns" and a
"tremendous selection of books, kits and supplies"; some shoppers
say it's "difficult to find things" in the "disorganized" environs, but
"knowledgeable", "no-attitude" staffers will "helpfully lead you to
the right room."

| | QUALITY | DISPLAY | SERVICE | COST |

Searle ◐

24 | 22 | 18 | E

E 60s | 1051 Third Ave. (62nd St.) | 4/5/6/F/N/R/W to 59th St./
Lexington Ave. | 212-838-5990
NEW **E 60s** | 1142 Third Ave. (67th St.) | 6 to 68th St. | 212-988-8361
E 60s | 635 Madison Ave. (60th St.) | 4/5/6/F/N/R/W to 59th St./
Lexington Ave. | 212-750-5153
E 60s | 805 Madison Ave. (68th St.) | 6 to 68th St. | 212-628-6665
E 70s | 1035 Madison Ave. (79th St.) | 6 to 77th St. | 212-717-4022
E 70s | 1296 Third Ave. (bet. 74th & 75th Sts.) | 6 to 77th St. | 212-717-5200
E 80s | 1124 Madison Ave. (84th St.) | 4/5/6 to 86th St. | 212-988-7318
Flatiron | 156 Fifth Ave. (bet. 20th & 21st Sts.) | N/R/W to 23rd St. |
212-924-4330
www.searlenyc.com

"All the sass without the 'tude" praise pros of this "high-caliber" "NY
staple for style", renowned for its "fabulous shearlings" and "lovely"
jackets; forget its "dowdy" past – this outfit has "an eye for modern",
"chic" looks, from its private label women's clothing "you'll reach for
again and again" to its "unique" designer selection; but "pick a branch
and stick with it", as "salespeople vary" from "excellent" to "pushy."

Sears ◐

17 | 13 | 13 | M

Bronx | 400 E. Fordham Rd. (bet. Park & Webster Aves.) | B/D to
Fordham Rd. | 718-817-7300
Flatbush | 2307 Beverley Rd. (E. 22nd St.) | Brooklyn | 2 to Beverley Rd. |
718-826-5800
Kings Plaza | Kings Plaza Shopping Ctr. | 5200 Kings Plaza (Flatbush Ave. &
Ave. U) | Brooklyn | 718-677-2100
Flushing | 137-61 Northern Blvd. (bet. Main St. & Parsons Blvd.) |
Queens | 7 to Main St. | 718-460-7000
Rego Pk | 96-05 Queens Blvd. (Junction Blvd.) | Queens | G/R/V to
63rd Dr./Rego Park | 718-830-5900
Staten Island | Staten Island Mall | 283 Platinum Ave. (Richmond Ave.) |
718-370-6200
www.sears.com

The "old standby" that served great-gramps seems "nearly unchanged"
after more than 110 years; "you cannot beat their home department"
("they back everything they sell, and now have a price-match guarantee") for washers, dryers, fridges or "anything to do with manual labor in
general"; but critics counsel "buy tools and appliances here, period" –
as most of the other merch is "boring" (though the "Lands' End clothing
is a plus"), plus many stores have "dowdy" digs, "service with a snarl"
and check-out "lines longer than the Great Wall of China."

Second Chance Designer Resale, A

▽ 21 | 15 | 15 | E

E 70s | 1109 Lexington Ave., 2nd fl. (bet. 77th & 78th Sts.) | 6 to 77th St. |
212-744-6041 | www.asecondchanceresale.com

Ladies "can find some lovely things" at this designer consignment
store; but getting "a good deal" can be "hit-or-miss", and the "packed-
to-the-gills" premises is "most unorganized", so some say this resale
shop's "not worth the bother, with so many others" on the UES.

NEW SEE Eyewear

- | - | - | M

W Vill | 312 Bleecker St. (bet. Barrow & Grove Sts.) | 1 to Christopher
St./Sheridan Sq. | 212-989-7060 | www.seeeyewear.com

Ciao, high-ticket logo-splashed eyewear, hello, über-stylish, no-name
specs – thanks to the arrival of this farsighted Michigan-based chain link

on the West Village's fashion row, the hipoisie can focus on finding chic frames with an upmarket look at, gulp, affordable prices; designed by a covey of creative talents from Europe's top frame houses, the tightly edited collection ranges from aviators to wraparounds to rhinestone-speckled celebutante shades, all displayed on easy-access shelving.

Seigo
▽ 28 26 27 E

E 80s | 1242 Madison Ave. (bet. 89th & 90th Sts.) | 4/5/6 to 86th St. | 212-534-6275

E 90s | 1248 Madison Ave. (90th St.) | 4/5/6 to 86th St. | 212-987-0191

Their "limited-edition ties" and bow ties "make the man" maintain mavens of this Madison Avenue mainstay who more likely than knot find a "superb selection" of "very beautiful, handmade" Asian silk neckwear in "inviting patterns" "so unique they could be framed when not worn"; for "one-of-a-kind handbags" and "interesting fashion jewelry" loop back to its accessories offshoot a few doors down.

Seize sur Vingt
25 23 20 E

NoLita | 243 Elizabeth St. (bet. Houston & Prince Sts.) | N/R/W to Prince St. | 212-343-0476 | www.16sur20.com

"You'll feel like you're at a fancy tailor in London" at this NoLita shop, which provides "gorgeous bespoke shirts" that are custom-made in Egyptian cottons "for the "hipster set", along with "spectacular" men's and women's suits, handmade Italian shoes, seven fold ties, cuff links and leather driving gloves; still, a handful huff that the staff is "standoffish, leaving inexperienced customers confused" – "maybe if you're anorexic and rich they'll look at you."

Selia Yang 🅼
▽ 26 23 18 E

E Vill | 324-328 E. Ninth St. (bet. 1st & 2nd Aves.) | L to 1st Ave. | 212-254-9073

NEW **TriBeCa** | 71 Franklin St. (bet. B'way & Church St.) | 1 to Franklin St. | 212-941-9073

www.seliayang.com

This "off-the-beaten" wedding path East Villager is the "ultimate for the downtown hipster bride with downtown hipster money" to burn as well as her entourage; the "gorgeous", "elegant" silk gowns "made for your special day" by the salon's owner are "unique", reflecting her "great fashion sense"; but while some praise the "one-on-one" attention, others "expected a more service-friendly" environment; N.B. the 324 East Ninth Street shop also sells cocktail dresses and daywear, while the new TriBeCa showroom focuses on bridalwear.

Selima Optique
27 24 22 E

E 70s | 899 Madison Ave. (bet. 72nd & 73rd Sts.) | 6 to 77th St. | 212-988-6690

E Vill | 84 E. Seventh St. (bet. 1st & 2nd Aves.) | F/V to Lower East Side/ 2nd Ave. | 212-677-8487 ◗

SoHo | 59 Wooster St. (Broome St.) | C/E to Spring St. | 212-343-9490 ◗

W Vill | 357 Bleecker St. (bet. Charles & W. 10th Sts.) | 1 to Christopher St./ Sheridan Sq. | 212-352-1640 ◗

www.selimaoptique.com

"Brilliant" designer Selima Salaun offers "colorful, funky and individual" spectacles and shades at her growing eyewear empire where the "stars go to get focused" in a "party atmosphere"; the staff "really cares" (though some surveyors squint at "ditzy service"), and "if your pocketbook is up to the challenge" you'll emerge sporting the "most unusual glasses in town"; P.S. "after a frame fitting", stop into the cafe at the Bleecker Street branch.

☑ Sephora ◑　　　　　　　　25 │ 24 │ 19 │ M

E 40s | 597 Fifth Ave. (bet. 48th & 49th Sts.) | B/D/F/V to 47-50th Sts./ Rockefeller Ctr. | 212-980-6534 | 877-737-4672 | www.sephora.com
Additional locations throughout the NY area

This "addictive" "candy shop for beauty junkies" offers over 100 brands (there's "something for every zit, wrinkle, stretch mark and split end"), and each has "try-before-you-buy" testers, making the chain "a great place to play" with products that range from the "reasonable" to the "pricey"; the walls are lined with men's and women's fragrances, along with tooth whiteners and brighteners – hey, they don't call it "the mother ship" of makeup for nothing.

Sergio Rossi　　　　　　　　　26 │ – │ 21 │ VE

E 50s | 694 Fifth Ave. (bet. 54th & 55th Sts.) | E/V to 5th Ave./53rd St. | 212-956-3303 | www.sergiorossi.com

For "hugely stylish" footwear of the "utmost quality", hit this spacious Midtown "winner" with a "sweet" staff; scoop up "godlike boots", the "best stilettos" and "sexy" sandals that "make women's legs attractive", plus edgy wingtips, luxe lizard loafers and the like for men, all designed by Edmundo Castillo and team; fetishists pay a bundle for "naughty shoes that never leave the apartment – the bedroom for that matter!" while on-the-towners "always find something for special occasions."

Seven New York　　　　　　▽ 26 │ 22 │ 19 │ E

SoHo | 110 Mercer St. (bet. Prince & Spring Sts.) | N/R/W to Prince St. | 646-654-0156 | www.sevennewyork.com

Fashion cultists recognize the esoteric lineup at this ultramodernist SoHo provocateur where international indie designers like Raf Simons from Belgium, Germany's Bernhard Willhelm, celebrity favorite Jeremy Scott and Antwerp's Christian Wijnants are procured for hipsters of both sexes along with jeans from on-trend labels like Acne and Cheap Monday; just note that these vanguard looks demand an adventurous spirit, a skinny bod and a fat wallet.

17 at 17 Thrift Shop 🅈　　　　18 │ 15 │ 14 │ M

Flatiron | 17 W. 17th St. (5th Ave.) | 4/5/6/L/N/Q/R/W to 14th St./ Union Sq. | 212-727-7516

"Like most thrifts, it can be hit-or-miss" at this store whose proceeds benefit the UJA-Federation of NY and Gilda's Club; "when it's hot, it's hot" with "bargains on piles of goodies", including womenswear in a "spectrum of styles" and "high-end" costume jewelry, but "when it's not", it suffers from a "not-very-helpful staff", "dowdy" wares and prices that seem "expensive" compared to "others on Thrift Shop Row" in the Flatiron District.

☑ S. Feldman Housewares　　　25 │ 17 │ 24 │ M

E 90s | 1304 Madison Ave. (92nd St.) | 6 to 96th St. | 212-289-3961 | 800-359-8558 | www.wares2u.com

"They sold your toaster to your mom before you were born" joke jesters about this eclectic, "old-fashioned" Upper East Sider dating back to 1929 that's still going strong for housewares like cooking equipment, "unique" tabletop accessories from Alessi, Mrs. Meyer's cleaning products and Miele vacuums; "friendly and helpful" service and "free delivery" make it a particular "must at Christmastime" for many.

Shanghai Tang
23 | 24 | 21 | E

E 60s | 714 Madison Ave. (bet. 63rd & 64th Sts.) | N/R/W to 5th Ave./59th St. | 212-888-0111 | 888-252-8264 | www.shanghaitang.com

"Each floor is a new adventure" at this Madison Avenue Chinese-themed (and -based) emporium; some beckon with the "brilliant colors" of the "fusion clothing" that tailors "wildly exotic" patterns and "traditional" Asian styles to Western sensibilities, others offer an "interesting mix" of accessories for home, bath and person; though they're "top-of-the-line for this kind" of thing, some grumble the goods are "impractical" and "overpriced" – unless you "consider you're saving the airfare" to Hong Kong (or a subway ride to Chinatown).

Sharper Image
21 | 22 | 19 | E

E 70s | 900 Madison Ave. (bet. 72nd & 73rd Sts.) | 6 to 68th St. | 212-794-4974

SoHo | 98 Greene St. (bet. Prince & Spring Sts.) | N/R/W to Prince St. | 917-237-0221

Seaport | South Street Seaport | 89 South St., Pier 17 (Fulton St.) | 2/3/4/5/A/C/J/M/Z to Fulton St./B'way/Nassau | 212-693-0477 ◖

W 40s | Rockefeller Ctr. | 50 Rockefeller Ctr. (bet. 5th & 6th Aves.) | B/D/F/V to 47-50th Sts./Rockefeller Ctr. | 646-557-0861 ◖

W 50s | 10 W. 57th St. (bet. 5th & 6th Aves.) | F to 57th St. | 212-265-2550 ◖

800-344-4444 | www.sharperimage.com

"Not your basic electronics stores", these "gadget marts" are "fun-to-explore" just to "get a buzz" "fiddling" with the "latest" "wonderful whatchamacallits", and you might just leave with "nifty" "novelties" "you never thought you'd buy" but suddenly "can't live without" (like that robotic floor vac); still, some cynics slam the "space-age prices" and claim the "cutting-edge products" are mostly "smoke and mirrors."

Sherle Wagner International ▣⊄
– | – | – | VE

E 50s | 60 E. 57th St. (Park Ave.) | 4/5/6/F/N/R/W to 59th St./Lexington Ave. | 212-758-3300 | www.sherlewagner.com

Considered by some to be the "Rolls-Royce of bathroom" plumbing accessories, this plummy Park Avenue purveyor, established in 1945, provides opulent hand-painted or gold-trimmed basins, fixtures, taps, tiles, lighting and linens; the "total collection can be a bit much", but most people could probably only afford a crystal soap dish or two anyway since prices are shattering and they don't take credit cards.

Shin Choi ◖▣
– | – | – | E

SoHo | 119 Mercer St. (bet. Prince & Spring Sts.) | N/R/W to Prince St. | 212-625-9202 | www.shinchoi.com

For a full-on SoHo shopping experience, spacious loft space, cool vibe and all, duck into this Mercer Street standby and peruse Korean-born designer Choi's lustrous lineup; the womenswear is "understated, but flattering", ranging from special-occasion suits and sumptuous cashmeres to sexy jeans – even visitors who cry "they're out of my price range" commend the "well-styled outfits."

	QUALITY	DISPLAY	SERVICE	COST

Shirt Store, The ⊠

| | 22 | 18 | 22 | E |

E 40s | 51 E. 44th St. (Vanderbilt Ave.) | 4/5/6/7/S to 42nd St./Grand Central | 212-557-8040 | 800-289-2744 | www.shirtstore.com

With shirt boxes stacked to the ceiling, the name really says it all as businessmen flock to this low-key "one-stop" for all their torso-covering needs at its "convenient location near Grand Central"; it's easy to nab the right fit from the 70 different ready-made sizes of "quality" button-downs, ranging from 14 x 32 to 18 1/2 x 37, or opt for a "custom" job; P.S. "they can make you feel important by having your initials sewn on" whatever you buy.

Shoe Box ◑

| | 23 | 19 | 17 | E |

E 70s | 1349 Third Ave. (77th St.) | 6 to 77th St. | 212-535-9615
Murray Hill | 537 Third Ave. (36th St.) | 6 to 33rd St. | 212-937-5750
800-320-7463 | www.theshoeboxonline.com

"Followed them from Long Island" to the East 70s and Murray Hill too reveal loyalists who hail this outfit as a big-city "favorite"; "my heart races every time I" eye the "excellent selection" of "better quality" "designer" footwear from the likes of Marc Jacobs, Sigerson Morrison and Vaneli – "this is one busy shoe store"; if a few fume "service is pushy", Box boosters believe they're "always friendly" and turn the other heel because the "fun" "merchandise keeps coming."

Shoe Mine Ⓜ

| | – | – | – | E |

Park Slope | 463 Seventh Ave. (bet. 16th St. & Windsor Pl.) | Brooklyn | F to 7th Ave. | 718-369-2624 | www.shoemine.com

There's lotsa gold in them there hills, er, the South Slope, for shoe buffs who fall for the "large selection" of way-funky footwear from hot-ticket labels like Frye, Kors by Michael Kors and La Canadienne, all showcased in a mad-cool, silver-ceilinged setting; kicks-cultists chill on the leather ottomans and contemplate the many splendors of hand-painted clogs from Holland and Switzerland and fab finds from Chie Mihara and Repetto, then stake their claim on unusual accessories and apparel.

Shoe New York, The

| | ▽ 24 | 23 | 21 | E |

NoLita | 262 Mott St. (bet. Houston & Prince Sts.) | 6 to Spring St. | 212-226-7366 | www.theshoeny.com

After creating a sensation with his women's footwear at his shop The Shoe, located in Chongdamdong, the avant-garde enclave of Seoul, Korean star Jae-min Lee brought his vision to the Manhattan market, opening this "chic" NoLita "hot spot"; the edgy emporium features his brightly colored, "fashion-forward" styles, plus bags, belts and clothing from other lines; N.B. you can also order versions with customized heels.

Shoofly

| | ▽ 26 | 21 | 19 | E |

TriBeCa | 42 Hudson St. (bet. Duane & Thomas Sts.) | 1/2/3 to Chambers St. | 212-406-3270 | www.shooflynyc.com

A favorite stomping ground of mini-stylehounds-in-training, this "fabulous" TriBeCa tot shop has laced up a loyal following by stocking "funky" footwear from Europe's premier labels, among them Buckle My Shoe and Aster; the accessorizing action doesn't end with the shoes: there's also an "interesting" array of "great tights" and hair tchotchkes.

	QUALITY	DISPLAY	SERVICE	COST

Shooz ◑
Chelsea | 128 Seventh Ave. (bet. 17th & 18th Sts.) | 1 to 18th St. | 212-727-7446

| | 19 | 18 | 20 | M |

"Gotta get my Shooz" gush groupies of this Chelsea standby, which stocks "sassy shoes for everyone" from laid-back labels, including Naot, Dansko and Robert Zur, along with what may be the "best collection of Wellies this side of the pond"; the "helpful", "knowledgeable staff" is sure to send you out the door stylishly shod and with "comfortable feet" to boot.

Shop
LES | 105 Stanton St. (Ludlow St.) | F/V to Lower East Side/2nd Ave. | 212-375-0304

| | ▽ 20 | 23 | 21 | E |

It may feel like you're visiting your "über-trendy, Lower East Side–dwelling older sister's closet", with a "few surprises thrown in" like Siwy jeans, tops from 3.1 Philip Lim and "handmade items by independent designers" like Sass & Bide at this girlie boutique; the "fun stuff" also includes "groovy jewelry", lingerie and bags, plus a "no-attitude staff."

Shu Uemura Beauty Boutique ◑
SoHo | 121 Greene St. (bet. Houston & Prince Sts.) | N/R/W to Prince St. | 212-979-5500 | 888-540-8181 | www.shuuemura.com

| | 27 | 26 | 22 | E |

This soaring, serene SoHo showroom for the Japanese cosmetics company features "gorgeous brushes and fantastic makeup", but the most iconic item is the legendary eyelash curler; as for the "helpful" staff, admirers enthuse "these people love what they're doing."

NEW Shvitz ◑
SoHo | 128 Thompson St. (bet. Houston & Prince Sts.) | C/E to Spring St. | 212-982-9465 | www.shvitznyc.com

| | - | - | - | E |

Female fashionistas who like their loungewear on the luxury side visit this small, sweet-as-icing SoHo boutique, whose pink/silver/white decor is like a little girl's dream boudoir (there's even a pink Mac) – all the better to offset the bright togs by the likes of Juicy, Joystick and PRIMP that fill the cool and cute requirement to a tee, tank or sweatsuit; buyers can also browse novelties like portable purse caddies or order up crystallized monograms (on the store-brand clothes).

NEW Sicis ▣
SoHo | 470 Broome St. (Greene St.) | 6 to Spring St. | 212-965-4100 | www.sicis.com

| | ▽ 25 | 25 | 21 | E |

"Great place and space" enthuse admirers of this new 13,000-sq.-ft. SoHo showcase for a long-standing manufacturer of Italian mosaics; "imaginative", "impeccably designed and executed" tiles in glass, marble and metal are displayed in a striking two-story landmark building with futuristic decor.

Sid's
Downtown | 345 Jay St. (Willoughby St.) | Brooklyn | A/C/F to Jay St./Borough Hall | 718-875-2259

| | ▽ 21 | 16 | 20 | M |

Skip the "hassle" of the big guns and head to this "classic local" in Downtown Brooklyn – it's the "kind of hardware store you could spend all day in", staffed with people hardwired to "help you find the stuff you need"; no wonder DIYers are hooked – they cut wood in the lumberyard, and stock "every kind of nail, light bulb" and garden tool imaginable.

| | QUALITY | DISPLAY | SERVICE | COST |

Sigerson Morrison
`25` `23` `19` `E`

NoLita | 28 Prince St. (Mott St.) | 6 to Spring St. | 212-219-3893 | www.sigersonmorrison.com

Urban "chic" rules at designers Kari Sigerson and Miranda Morrison's minimalist mecca proffering "perfect shoes for the NoLita girl, in every color of the rainbow"; cultists covet the "understated cool" aesthetic, stocking up on "kitten heels", "amazing flats", "pointy-toed" boots and other "unique, edgy" finds; sure, it's "pricey" (read: "not for the budget-minded"), but if you're serious about your SMs, snap up "the pair you want before it goes on sale", otherwise it "will be long gone."

Sigerson Morrison Bags
▽ `24` `23` `19` `E`

NoLita | 242 Mott St. (bet. Houston & Prince Sts.) | 6 to Spring St. | 212-941-5404 | www.sigersonmorrison.com

Stocked with "wonderful", "classy" bags that "might be the most sought after on the planet", this colorful NoLita spot also carries wallets, totes and accessories that are "luxurious without being ostentatious" and go nicely with the design duo's shoes, sold at their separate sister shop around the corner; but even fans who flip over the "fine detailing" still pooh-pooh the "high prices."

NEW Signoria ⊠
`25` `23` `22` `E`

E 60s | 764 Madison Ave. (bet. 65th & 66th Sts.) | 6 to 68th St. | 212-639-1121 | www.signoria.com

This long-standing, family-owned firm from Florence has opened a new Madison Avenue outpost featuring "very fancy" linens for both the bed and table that some wags wager are "too nice to use"; other "good quality items" include soaps, body creams and candles.

NEW Sigrid Olsen ●
`23` `21` `22` `E`

SoHo | 411 W. Broadway (bet. Prince & Spring Sts.) | C/E to Spring St. | 917-237-0140 | www.sigridolsen.com

"Lighten up your all-black wardrobe" at this bleached-wood SoHo emporium, which houses "classics for the corporate woman" – plus "sporty" apparel for "her weekend life" – in hues "much brighter than NYC wears"; detractors declare there's "no wow factor" in the "matchy-uppy" garb ("like Garanimals for women"), but the surprisingly hip handbags "have plenty of style", and "after a day of snotty salesgirls" elsewhere, it's nice to be welcomed with a glass of juice or champagne.

⊠ Simon Pearce
`27` `25` `23` `E`

E 50s | 500 Park Ave. (59th St.) | 4/5/6/F/N/R/W to 59th St./ Lexington Ave. | 212-421-8801 | www.simonpearce.com

"Solid", "simple and functional" glass like barware, bowls, lamps, cake plates and candlesticks make for good gifts say supporters of this Park Avenue purveyor that also offers "unique" inscribed pottery and engraved items; respondents remark on the "uncompromising quality" (even "the seconds are worth checking out"), and are thankful for "prices that don't make you fearful of using" the pieces.

⊠ Simon's Hardware & Bath ⊠
`26` `21` `19` `E`

Gramercy | 421 Third Ave. (bet. 29th & 30th Sts.) | 6 to 28th St. | 212-532-9220 | 888-274-6667 | www.simonshardwareandbath.com

There are "no hammers" at this Gramercy stalwart, just a "superb selection" of "gorgeous bathroom fixtures", shower systems, tiles, door and cabinet hardware for "every knob and handle in your apartment", all "artistically displayed"; if a handful huff that "service is sometimes a challenge" and pout about "stratospheric prices", those who've been Simon-ized declare "if you're doing home improvement, stop here" – "they have the best of everything", so "it's priced accordingly."

Sir Ⓜ

| | - | - | - | E |

Boerum Hill | 360 Atlantic Ave. (bet. Bond & Hoyt Sts.) | Brooklyn | A/C/G to Hoyt/Schermerhorn Sts. | 718-643-6877 | www.sirbrooklyn.com

It's "worth the trip" to Boerum Hill to check out this "hip, but not self-consciously so" two-room shop where "promising designer" Joanna Baum, a R.I.S.D. grad, peddles her vintage-y jackets, filmy cut-on-the-bias dresses and "wonderfully tactile" washed-silk blouses to style-istas and gamine stars like Brooklynite Michelle Williams; complete the look with the silver, glass bead and semiprecious stone jewelry from the Shee line by co-owner Nicole Rowars, along with cool-girl bags and shoes.

Sisley ●

| | 20 | 20 | 18 | M |

Flatiron | 133 Fifth Ave. (20th St.) | N/R/W to 23rd St. | 212-420-5700
G Vill | 753 Broadway (8th St.) | 6 to Astor Pl. | 212-979-2537
W 50s | The Shops at Columbus Circle, Time Warner Ctr. | 10 Columbus Circle, 2nd fl. (bet. 58th & 60th Sts.) | 1/A/B/C/D to 59th St./Columbus Circle | 212-823-9567
www.sisley.com

You "feel like you're sipping Campari and soda in Capri" upon donning the "sexy Euro styles" at this trio, Benetton's slightly "naughty cousin", a "one-stop shop" for guys and gals seeking "work gear that turns into night gear"; "if you're looking for sophisticated" staples "at fair prices" that are "a nice diversion from what everyone else is wearing", you may find them at these "simple settings" manned by an "attentive" crew.

Skechers ●

| | 19 | 18 | 15 | M |

Garment Dist | 140 W. 34th St. (bet. 6th & 7th Aves.) | B/D/F/N/Q/R/V/W to 34th St./Herald Sq. | 646-473-0490
W 40s | 3 Times Sq. (42nd St., bet. B'way & 6th Ave.) | 1/2/3/7/N/Q/R/S/W to 42nd St./Times Sq. | 212-869-9550
Astoria | 31-01 Steinway St. (31st Ave.) | Queens | G/R/V to 46th St. | 718-204-0040
Elmhurst | Queens Pl. | 88-01 Queens Blvd. (bet. 55th & 56th Aves.) | Queens | G/R/V to Grand Ave./Newtown | 718-699-2773
800-678-5019 | www.skechers.com

"The go-to spot for funky" footwear, this "friendly" chainster has got your back when it comes to filling the "what's-in-style-at-reasonable-prices" niche agree "tweens, teens" and twentysomethings; but while fans find the "walking-on-clouds" soles make for "happy feet", cynics cool their heels elsewhere, lamenting this outfit with "earsplitting music" and "strange" offerings is "long past having any hip factor."

Sleep ●

| | ▽ 22 | 20 | 19 | E |

Williamsburg | 110 N. Sixth St. (bet. Berry St. & Wythe Ave.) | Brooklyn | L to Bedford Ave. | 718-384-3211

Everything to give you sweet dreams is the draw at this welcome addition to the Williamsburg scene; the split-level, spiral staircase space has a boudoir feel, with luxe lingerie and sleepwear from the likes of Elle Macpherson and Princess Tam-Tam cohabiting with "unique" bedding; "it's an excellent place to spend any cash weighing your pocket down."

	QUALITY	DISPLAY	SERVICE	COST

Slope Sports

Park Slope | 70 Seventh Ave. (bet. Berkeley & Lincoln Pls.) | Brooklyn | B/Q to 7th Ave. | 718-230-4686 | www.slopesports.com

| - | - | - | M |

Though the name might imply skiing, this small shop for runners, cyclists, walkers and outdoor enthusiasts takes its name from its Park Slope environs; it may be "off the beaten path" for Gothamites, but fans feel it's "worth" the train ride to purchase performance apparel from labels like Hind, Pearl Izomi and Sugoi and sneakers from major players like Asics, Brooks and New Balance.

Smiley's 🗷🍃

| 16 | 14 | 18 | I |

Woodhaven | 92-06 Jamaica Ave. (bet. 92nd St. & Woodhaven Blvd.) | Queens | J/Z to Woodhaven Blvd. | 718-849-9873 | www.smileysyarns.com

Bargainistas salute this Queens stitchers stop, renowned since 1935 for its "cheap, and I mean *cheap,* prices" on a wide array of "mid- to low-end" "synthetics and blends"; "special sales" often make it "worth the trip" to Woodhaven ("check online" first), though fiber snobs sniff "you get what you pay for" at this "acrylic nightmare"; P.S. "you can make out like a bandit" at the annual 'Yarn Riots' held at area hotels.

Smith & Hawken ●

| 24 | 25 | 20 | E |

SoHo | 394 W. Broadway (bet. Broome & Spring Sts.) | C/E to Spring St. | 212-925-1190 | 800-776-3336 | www.smithandhawken.com

Root around "for gifts for your favorite gardener" at this "perfect" SoHo shop offering plants, pots, bulbs, books and "last-a-longtime tools"; fans of the brand also "love the teak furniture" and "big selection of Christmas ornaments and garlands", all sold by a "helpful staff"; city dwellers sigh the experience "makes you want to move to the suburbs and have a yard."

☑ Smythson of Bond Street 🗷

| 28 | 27 | 24 | VE |

W 50s | 4 W. 57th St. (5th Ave.) | F to 57th St. | 212-265-4573 | 866-769-8476 | www.smythson.com

For "bespoke stationery to say 'I've made it'", "luxurious" leather accessories like agendas, albums, passport covers, jewelry boxes and organizers with "unique color options" and gold and silver stamping, along with "luxurious" bags, briefcases and wallets, Anglophiles head to this "English import" on West 57th Street; needless to say, the holder of four royal warrants exclusively purveys products that go for a king's ransom.

NEW SOHO Ⓜ

| ▽ 20 | 18 | 16 | E |

NoLita | 228 Mott St. (bet. Prince & Spring Sts.) | 6 to Spring St. | 212-219-3734 | www.sohoenamel.com

At this small, new husband-and-wife-owned NoLita jewelry shop, the ancient Etruscan art of enameling is given an elegant contemporary edge when a "unique" collection of handmade bangles, earrings and necklaces is textured to look like marble, snakeskin, leopard spots or tiger stripes, then dusted with gold and dressed up with diamonds.

Sol Moscot

| 21 | 14 | 20 | M |

Flatiron | 69 W. 14th St. (6th Ave.) | F/L/V to 14th St./6th Ave. | 212-647-1550

LES | 118 Orchard St. (Delancey St.) | F/J/M/Z to Delancey/Essex Sts. | 212-477-3796

(continued)

Sol Moscot

Forest Hills | 107-20 Continental Ave. (bet. Austin St. & Queens Blvd.) |
Queens | E/F/G/R/V to Forest Hills/71st Ave. | 718-544-2200
www.solmoscotopticians.com

Even if it's "been around since the Flood", ok, 1920, this Lower East Side
optician and its Flatiron and Forest Hills progeny Noah from "stylish",
offering big names in frames from Fendi to Prada at "bargain" prices;
the staff's "ready, willing and able to help", and though some solilo-
quize you "have to know what you're looking for", its mascots maintain it's the epitome of "what an eyewear store should be."

Solstice

E 40s | 500 Fifth Ave. (42nd St.) | 7 to 5th Ave. | 212-730-2500
Garment Dist | 27 W. 34th St. (bet. 5th & 6th Aves.) | N/R/W to 28th St. |
212-563-7877 ◑
NEW   **SoHo** | 107 Spring St. (Mercer St.) | 6 to Spring St. | 212-219-3940 |
866-246-9043 ◑
W 50s | The Shops at Columbus Circle, Time Warner Ctr. | 10 Columbus
Circle, 3rd fl. (bet. 58th & 60th Sts.) | 1/A/B/C/D to 59th St./
Columbus Circle | 212-823-9590 ◑
www.solsticestores.com

With over 1,000 styles to choose from, you're guaranteed a "great selection" of sunglasses at this "pleasant" chain specializing in classic
and cutting-edge designers; the "friendly" staff can help you find a fit,
both facially and "fashion"-wise, in a "welcoming" atmosphere.

Some Odd Rubies ◑

LES | 151 Ludlow St. (bet. Rivington & Stanton Sts.) | F/V to Lower East Side/
2nd Ave. | 212-353-1736 | www.someoddrubies.com

In "tiny" Lower East Side digs, this "seriously cool store" owned by actress Summer Phoenix and her "nice" friends, Odessa Whitmire and
Ruby Canner, sparkles with a carefully "edited" selection of retro shoes
and jewelry; the "great goods" also spotlight reworked vintage must-
haves, some of which "look way more expensive than they are", plus
some new pieces from local designers.

Something Else

23 | 21 | 20 | E

Bensonhurst | 2051 86th St. (bet. Bay 25th & Bay 26th Sts.) |
Brooklyn | D/M to 20th Ave. | 718-372-1900
Boerum Hill | 144 Smith St. (Bergen St.) | Brooklyn | F/G to Bergen St. |
718-643-3204 ◑
Park Slope | 208 Fifth Ave. (Union St.) | Brooklyn | 2/3 to Bergen St. |
718-230-4063 ◑

"Bensonhurst babes [and dudes] know how to work it with style" and so
do Boerum Hill and Park Slope trendseekers hot for premium denim from
Joe's Jeans, AG Adriano Goldschmied and Citizens for Humanity and
"great" pieces from labels like Ben Sherman, The North Face and Triple
Five Soul; add in "cool" Adidas and Puma "sneaks" and Frye boots and
you've got a shopping experience that's, like, wow, something else.

Sonia Rykiel ⊠

26 | 24 | 22 | VE

E 70s | 849 Madison Ave. (bet. 70th & 71st Sts.) | 6 to 68th St. |
212-396-3060 | www.soniarykiel.com

Style-savvy surveyors know "why French women are thin" – it's so they
can slip into the "inventive" knits from this venerable Parisienne, whose

women's collection of cashmere coats and silken sweaters is instantly wearable; while some find the attitude in the East 70s boutique "a little intimidating", most "love every item", "including the fragrances."

Sons + Daughters

-	-	-	E

E Vill | 35 Ave. A (bet. 2nd & 3rd Sts.) | F/V to Lower East Side/2nd Ave. | 212-253-7797 | www.sonsanddaughtersinc.com

Wander off the beaten path to this refreshing East Village emporium, where you can easily whittle away hours exploring the eclectic selection of organic and fair-trade clothing, toys and other wares originating from far corners of the globe; it's also a great place to get "nifty gifts you don't see in other stores", like space-age ant farms, vintage dollhouses and made-to-order Moroccan slippers.

◪ Sony Style

26	26	18	E

E 50s | Sony Plaza | 550 Madison Ave. (bet. 55th & 56th Sts.) | E/V to 5th Ave./53rd St. | 212-833-8800 | www.sonystyle.com

"This is what an electronics store should look like" testify techheads taken with this "beautiful flagship store" in the East 50s, "a marvelous showcase" for all the "latest versions" of Sony's "coolest" equipment (about which the salespeople "know all the ins and outs"); though it's "entertaining" to "play with the new and fun products", deal-finders feel it's "strictly for browsing", saying you can "buy it cheaper elsewhere."

NEW Sophia Eugene ●

-	-	-	M

W Vill | 37 Cornelia St. (Bleecker St.) | A/B/C/D/E/F/V to W. 4th St. | 212-488-2124 | www.sophiaeugene.com

West Villagers applaud couturier Christopher Crawford's new teensy atelier with its ornate dressing room fashioned by a Broadway set designer; the in-store drama begins with his eclectic print separates, kittenish sweaters and retro jackets, and continues with a few fancy frocks from his Christopher Deane collection; tucked in a corner, but not to be upstaged, is vintage costume jewelry that's fit to be tried.

Soula ▣

-	-	-	M

Boerum Hill | 185 Smith St. (bet. Warren & Wyckoff Sts.) | Brooklyn | F/G to Bergen St. | 718-834-8423

"Cozy", top-of-the-Boerum-Hill-heap hangout that "sparkles" with a "fabulous display" of men's and women's "shoes and bags you just have to have"; "while the merchandise is as hip as it gets" – think labels like Camper, Gola and Puma – the exposed-brick walls and blond woodshelves create an "ambiance that's welcoming", with a "lovely staff" to boot; P.S. "comfort" is key – in other words, you won't find stilettos here.

◪ Sound by Singer

27	22	21	VE

Union Sq | 18 E. 16th St. (bet. 5th Ave. & Union Sq. W.) | 4/5/6/L/N/Q/R/W to 14th St./Union Sq. | 212-924-8600 | www.soundbysinger.com

The "audiophile's heaven" on earth, this "terrific place" in Union Square boasts 10 showrooms decked out in such "interesting lines" as Arcam, Burmester and Zanden and staffed by "people [who] really care about sound"; "those who can afford it" report that the "high-end products and service" blow away the competition "by a large margin", while the rest of us can always "go in and drool."

	QUALITY	DISPLAY	SERVICE	COST

Sound City ⊠

W 40s | 58 W. 45th St. (bet. 5th & 6th Aves.) | B/D/F/V to 47-50th Sts./
Rockefeller Ctr. | 212-575-0210 | www.soundcityny.com

| - | - | - | M |

There's no denying that this Midtown electronics emporium in the West 40s has the goods, whether you want to heat things up with the newest speakers or cool down with a remote-controlled air conditioner; true, it may be topsy-turvy and garishly lit, but there's a reason it's known for "great bargains."

Space Kiddets ⊠

Flatiron | 26 E. 22nd St. (bet. B'way & Park Ave.) | N/R/W to 23rd St. |
212-420-9878 | www.spacekiddets.com

| 26 | 18 | 22 | E |

For the "coolest kids' clothes this side of hip" from labels that fashionistas-in-training "want so badly", take off for this Flatiron emporium, home to one of the "most original collections" under the sun including "extra-special" rocker tees and toy robots; sure, it's "jam-packed" – but you can retreat to the expanded second floor, "service is beyond expectation", "sales are excellent" and your offspring may be the most "imaginatively" dressed "tyke on the block."

NEW Space Mercer

SoHo | 115 Mercer St. (Prince St.) | N/R/W to Prince St. | 212-730-2266

| - | - | - | E |

Housing smart, hip labels known to worldly shoppers (the Japanese line Green, Rick Owens knits, Lutz & Patmos sweaters), this large, brick-lined loft space in SoHo features 'look stations' of fully styled, accessorized mannequins enacting scenes of NYC life; complimentary cups of espresso and cosmetics, including an exclusive line from makeup artist Christine Chin, are also on tap.

Space107 ⊠ Ⓜ

W Vill | 107 Horatio St. (bet. Washington & West Sts.) | A/C/E/L to
14th St./8th Ave. | 212-206-7599 | www.space107.com

| - | - | - | E |

Redesigned furniture originals from the 1920s–1970s are displayed in vignettes throughout the gallerylike setting of this West Village space, giving it the air of an impeccable designerati's digs; owner Amir Dinkha starts with pieces from big names like Karl Springer, Paul Evans and Milo Baughman and then polishes, refinishes or reupholsters them with unique and poshly priced results.

Spence-Chapin Thrift Shops

E 80s | 1473 Third Ave. (bet. 83rd & 84th Sts.) | 4/5/6 to 86th St. |
212-737-8448
E 90s | 1850 Second Ave. (bet. 95th & 96th Sts.) | 6 to 96th St. | 212-426-7643
www.spence-chapin.org

| 16 | 14 | 12 | M |

From silk scarves to furniture to mens- and womenswear "finds", "classy castoffs can be yours" at this "cluttery" charity-store pair on the Upper East Side – and often "for very little, especially when they have sales"; pity that the "staff is sometimes more busy socializing with each other than focusing on clients."

Spoiled Brats ◗

W 40s | 340 W. 49th St. (bet. 8th & 9th Aves.) | C/E to 50th St. |
212-459-1615 | www.spoiledbratsnyc.com

| ▽ 24 | 19 | 25 | M |

Spoiled Hell's Kitchen Homo sapiens are hip to this "very service-oriented" pet store where the "great staff" "gets you whatever you want"; the "broad assortment" of "high-end, human-grade" food and "quirky" accessories may be a tad "pricey" for some, but the "shopping experience is enhanced by fragrant candles and soaps" that satisfy its "upscale" clientele; P.S. it also offers "good" kitty adoption assistance.

Sports Authority ●

	QUALITY	DISPLAY	SERVICE	COST
	17	14	11	M

E 50s | 845 Third Ave. (51st St.) | 6 to 51st St. | 212-355-9725
Flatiron | 636 Sixth Ave. (19th St.) | 1 to 18th St. | 212-929-8971
NEW **Forest Hills** | 73-25 Woodhaven Blvd. (74th Ave.) | Queens | G/R/V to 67th Ave. | 718-896-3826
Woodside | 51-30 Northern Blvd. (Newtown Rd.) | Queens | G/R/V to Northern Blvd. | 718-205-4075
888-801-9164 | www.thesportsauthority.com

"Big-box pickings mean" you'll find a "wide variety of sporting goods" from jerseys and athletic shoes to rackets and bats agree advocates of this athletic outfit; opponents opine that it "tries to be too many things" but instead "falls short" and leans toward the "middle-of-the-road"; even when "the products are there, the service isn't" always – "finding help is like going on a safari" through the "messy racks."

Spring Ⓜ

			E
–	–	–	E

Dumbo | 126A Front St. (Jay St.) | Brooklyn | F to York St. | 718-222-1054 | www.spring3d.net

Part gallery, part spare showcase, this curated Dumbo loftspace traffics in "quirky, interesting" tchotchkes like piggy banks and rubberband vases as well as one-of-a-kind accessories, jewelry, light fixtures, paintings and tabletop items from emerging artists and designers; never mind that the "practicality factor" is sometimes minimal – each piece is high-concept, plus the owners' "hearts are in the right place."

☑ Spring Flowers ⑤

	QUALITY	DISPLAY	SERVICE	COST
	28	21	17	VE

E 50s | 538 Madison Ave. (bet. 54th & 55th Sts.) | E/V to 5th Ave./53rd St. | 212-207-4606
E 60s | 1050 Third Ave. (62nd St.) | 6 to 68th St. | 212-758-2669
E 70s | 907 Madison Ave. (bet. 72nd & 73rd Sts.) | 6 to 68th St. | 212-717-8182
www.springflowerschildren.com

For your little "Cinderella's ball gown, a more perfect closet could not be found" believe boosters who throw bouquets to this Upper East Side childrenswear outfit, including a new double-decker shop in the East 70s, which sets the standard for special-occasion outfits with its "beautiful" "heirloom quality" party frocks and made-to-order flower-girl dresses and tot-sized tuxedos; still, a few thorny types tut "prices are not realistic" and service is "snobby."

Staples ●

	QUALITY	DISPLAY	SERVICE	COST
	19	16	13	M

W 80s | 2248 Broadway (bet. 80th & 81st Sts.) | 1 to 79th St. | 212-712-9617 | 800-378-2753 | www.staples.com
Additional locations throughout the NY area

A "reliable workhorse" "for anything office-related", this "no-frills" "super-chain" "wins over" one-stop shoppers with its "breadth of merchandise" – from computers and printers to humble "paper clips and ballpoint pens purchased *en masse*" – as well as its "superb no-hassle returns policy"; still, those who say the "inattentive" staffers "seem like they were born yesterday" suggest you "stick with the online" option.

| | QUALITY | DISPLAY | SERVICE | COST |

Stefano Ricci 🖾
▽ 27 | 25 | 25 | VE

E 50s | 407 Park Ave. (bet. 54th & 55th Sts.) | E/V to 5th Ave./53rd St. |
212-371-3901 | www.stefanoricci.com

"Feel like you've walked into a Stradivarius violin, lined with fragrant silks", glossy walnut woods and crocodile-upholstered furniture, when you enter this elite, "extravagant" East 50s men's store rooted in the Florentine tailoring tradition; the quality suiting, fine ties and glitzy accessories appeal to the "hip aristocrat", "mogul, sheik or pasha in every man"; you can bet "big bucks are required", but few there are who don't "find everything in this shop exactly to their liking."

Steinlauf & Stoller 🖾
– | – | – | M

Garment Dist | 239 W. 39th St. (bet. 7th & 8th Aves.) |
1/2/3/7/N/Q/R/S/W to 42nd St./Times Sq. | 212-869-0321 |
877-869-0321 | www.steinlaufandstoller.com

"You'll want to enroll in FIT after a trip" to this Garment District notions mecca that seamsters seek out for its 1,000-plus tailoring aids including fastenings, pads, trims, threads and pieces of workroom equipment – but no fabric; the 60-year-old venue's old-fashioned vibe makes it feel like you're "stepping back in time", but you can also shop 21st-century-style via the Web site.

Stella Dallas ◐
– | – | – | M

G Vill | 218 Thompson St. (bet. Bleecker & W. 3rd Sts.) | A/B/C/D/E/F/V to W. 4th St. | 212-674-0447

NEW **Williamsburg** | 285 N. Sixth St. (Havemeyer St.) | Brooklyn | G/L to Metropolitan Ave./Lorimer St. | 718-486-9482

"Long may she reign" cheer converts of this "quirky" queen of the vintage Village shops, which since 1970 has "specialized in women's apparel from the '40s and '50s" ("great for the domestic diva looking for a glam housedress and apron to match"); "reasonable prices keep 'em coming back" to explore the ever-changing stock that ranges from cowboy boots to pretty petticoats (hanging from the ceiling), and now there's also a new l'il filly to discover in Williamsburg.

Stella McCartney
26 | 25 | 20 | VE

Meatpacking | 429 W. 14th St. (bet. 9th & 10th Aves.) | A/C/E/L to 14th St./8th Ave. | 212-255-1556 | www.stellamccartney.com

If you're "reed thin", you'll fit right in at this "gorgeous", "fashionably trendy Meatpacking District" boutique, which offers pure "luxe for 'it' girls" who hog the arty dressing rooms trying on the eponymous designer's "clean-lined" trousers, Savile Row-styled jackets and little sack dresses that "are the reason you ask for a raise"; while it's an "elevating experience" to visit, critics castigate the "slowest and strangest salespeople around."

🖾 Stereo Exchange ◐
26 | 20 | 21 | VE

NoHo | 627 Broadway (bet. Bleecker & Houston Sts.) | B/D/F/V to B'way/Lafayette St. | 212-505-1111 | www.stereoexchange.com

Techheads "looking for first-rate equipment", from speakers and turntables to "the best home-theater" components, say this NoHo electronics extravaganza is "forever ahead of its time", adding that "nobody can argue with the expertise" of the "smart, low-pressure salespeople"; even though the "prices are as high as the quality" of products offered, regulars recommend you at least "go to learn" and "converse with the jet set of the stereo world."

☑ Steuben ⑤ | 29 | 28 | 25 | VE |

E 60s | 667 Madison Ave. (61st St.) | N/R/W to 5th Ave./59th St. | 212-752-1441 | 800-783-8236 | www.steuben.com

"When you want to be remembered", buy a gift from this "museum-like" East 60s store boasting "exquisitely crafted" "glass master-pieces" that include vases, bowls, barware, animals and apples; admirers of the century-old source for "the best American crystal" croon about "class all the way" and cite "charming service", but caution that the pieces are "breakable and so is your bank account"; N.B. you can also purchase limited-edition works from select artists including noted sculptor Michele Oka Doner.

Steve Madden ● | 16 | 17 | 15 | M |

E 80s | 150 E. 86th St. (bet. Lexington & 3rd Aves.) | 4/5/6 to 86th St. | 212-426-0538

Garment Dist | 41 W. 34th St. (bet. 5th & 6th Aves.) | B/D/F/N/Q/R/V/W to 34th St./Herald Sq. | 212-736-3283

SoHo | 540 Broadway (bet. Prince & Spring Sts.) | N/R/W to Prince St. | 212-343-1800

NEW Bensonhurst | 1402 Kings Hwy. (E. 14th St.) | Brooklyn | B/Q to Kings Highway | 718-645-0567

Kings Plaza | Kings Plaza Shopping Ctr. | 5380 Kings Plaza (Flatbush Ave. & Ave. U) | Brooklyn | 718-677-3985

NEW Bayside | 211-49 26th Ave. (bet. 2nd & 3rd Sts.) | Queens | 7 to Main St. | 718-224-4880

Staten Island | Staten Island Mall | 2655 Richmond Ave. (bet. Platinum Ave. & Richmond Hill Rd.) | 718-494-6459

800-747-6233 | www.stevemadden.com

This "crazy, fast-paced" "teenybopper"-targeted chain "has its finger on the pulse of what hip young thangs want for traipsing around the city", be it "funky" platforms", boots with "tons of style", "cork-wedge" clogs or moccasin-inspired loafers and the like for dudes; some styles may be "a little on the trashy side", but loads are "good to party in", and hey, they're so "reasonable" you "don't have worry if you'll ever wear them again!"

Steven ● | 18 | 19 | 17 | M |

SoHo | 529 Broadway (bet. Prince & Spring Sts.) | N/R/W to Prince St. | 212-431-6021 | www.stevemadden.com

The "large selection" of "funky", "good quality" shoes at this SoHo shop walks the "Steve Madden for grown-ups" line, and much like its better-known, teen-oriented sibling, it's "always über-crowded"; detractors quibble that it "tries too hard to be higher class", but instead falls short, turning out "sometimes uncomfortable" "middle-of-the-road" offerings that are neither "lowbrow" or "go-for-it" splurges.

Steven Alan | 24 | 23 | 19 | E |

TriBeCa | 103 Franklin St. (bet. Church St. & W. B'way) | 1 to Canal St. | 212-343-0692

W 80s | 465 Amsterdam Ave. (82nd St.) | 1 to 79th St. | 212-595-8451

Steven Alan annex

NoLita | 229 Elizabeth St. (bet. Houston & Prince Sts.) | 6 to Spring St. | 212-226-7482

(continued)

Steven Alan annex

NEW **W Vill** | 69 Eighth Ave. (W. 13th St.) | A/C/E/L to 14th St./8th Ave. | 212-242-2677 ●
www.stevenalan.com

The "go-to" "urban general store" "for hot brands", TriBeCa's "fashion landmark" and its West 80s offshoot represent the "21st-century cool" of "brilliant auteur" Steven Alan, who hand-picks "hip" his-and-hers collectibles from "emerging, offbeat, but accessible designers"; the Earnest Sewn jeans, Claudie Pierlot pieces, F-Troupe boots, "excellent jewelry" and McBride face creams "fit in" with the "laid-back yet chic" look and that "uniqueness" extends to the NoLita and West Village annex shops, home to the house-label's "great button-down shirts."

Z Stickley, Audi & Co.

28 | 24 | 24 | E

Flatiron | 160 Fifth Ave., 4th fl. (bet. 20th & 21st Sts.) | N/R/W to 23rd St. | 212-337-0700 | www.stickley.com

While the emphasis at this three-story Flatiron showroom is on "beautiful", "dark Mission-style" furniture made of "solid cherry or oak" and built "to last for the next 100 years", the Audi family also sells a "broad selection" of other lines like Craftsman Leather and designer rugs; the "heirloom quality comes at prices to match", but some "good bargains" can be had at their sales.

Z Stitches East 🖫

26 | 22 | 17 | E

E 50s | Park Avenue Plaza | 55 E. 52nd St. (bet. Madison & Park Aves.) | 6 to 51st St. | 212-421-0112

Unexpectedly located "in an office building lobby", this "fancy" Eastside store is "worth finding"; its floor-to-ceiling cubbyholes contain an "excellent selection" of yarns (from basic to novelty), and the spacious room also stocks patterns, tools and needlepoint equipment; it's "pricey", though – "as warranted by its location" – and some surveyors sigh the "knowledgeable" staffers "could use a sense of humor."

Z St. John

28 | 27 | 24 | VE

E 50s | 665 Fifth Ave. (bet. 52nd & 53rd Sts.) | E/V to 5th Ave./53rd St. | 212-755-5252 | www.stjohnknits.com

"A pleasure to shop in", this spacious Fifth Avenue flagship for a 45-year-old label still sets the gold standard for "investment" clothes, with "classically timeless" knits whose "flattering", "easy fit" is "forgiving" even "when the pounds sneak up on you"; once seen as "going after the over-50 cruise crowd", the "styles have gotten younger" – and the signing of Angelina Jolie as the label's face in advertising campaigns should ramp up the "glitz" quotient.

St. Marks Sounds ●⌿

19 | 15 | 17 | I

E Vill | 20 St. Marks Pl., 2nd fl. (bet. 2nd & 3rd Aves.) | 6 to Astor Pl. | 212-677-3444

Since 1979, this "classic used CD emporium" in the East Village has been attracting alt-finders with "obscure titles at great prices"; even if a handful sound off that its "heyday is past", more maintain this second-story "scavenger hunt's" "deep catalog" and "caring" staff make it a "must" – especially since they're now stocking vinyl again.

	QUALITY	DISPLAY	SERVICE	COST

Straight from the Crate ●

| | 13 | 9 | 13 | I |

E 60s | 1114 First Ave. (61st St.) | 4/5/6/F/N/R/W to 59th St./
Lexington Ave. | 212-838-8486
E 80s | 1251 Lexington Ave. (bet. 84th & 85th Sts.) | 4/5/6 to 86th St. |
212-717-4227
Flatiron | 50 W. 23rd St. (bet. 5th & 6th Aves.) | N/R/W to 23rd St. |
212-243-1844
NEW Gramercy | 140 E. 14th St. (bet. Irving Pl. & 3rd Ave.) |
4/5/6/L/N/Q/R/W to 14th St./Union Sq. | 212-358-8575
Murray Hill | 261 Madison Ave. (38th St.) | 4/5/6/7/S to 42nd St./
Grand Central | 212-867-4050
Murray Hill | 464 Park Ave. S. (bet. 31st & 32nd Sts.) | 6 to 33rd St. |
212-725-5383
W 70s | 161 W. 72nd St. (B'way) | 1/2/3 to 72nd St. |
212-579-6494
NEW W 90s | 103 W. 96th St. (bet. Amsterdam & Columbus Aves.) |
1/2/3 to 96th St. | 212-865-4754
www.straightfromthecrate.com

This string of "super-cramped" and "super-cheap" shops offers a
"good assortment" of "contemporary furnishings" – dressers, bookcases and shelving – that will "solve your storage or limited space is-
sues"; but the worldly warn shop here only if "dorm-room style" is
what you aspire to.

Strawberry ●

| | 11 | 12 | 10 | I |

E 40s | 129 E. 42nd St. (Lexington Ave.) | 4/5/6/7/S to 42nd St./
Grand Central | 212-986-7030 | www.strawberrystores.com
Additional locations throughout the NY area

Calling "the young and on-the-go" to this budget chain where shoppers "rummage through" the racks in "cramped quarters" searching
for "disposable" "trendy items for that weekend night out"; yes, you
get what you pay for here, including "inexperienced clerks" and a
"mess of clothes thrown on the floor", not to mention "one-time-
wear" quality levels, but to most this doesn't matter much when you
factor in the "cheapie prices."

Strider Records ⊠

| | - | - | - | M |

G Vill | 22 Jones St. (bet. Bleecker & W. 4th Sts.) | A/B/C/D/E/F/V to
W. 4th St. | 212-675-3040

Platters matter at this "vintage" Greenwich Villager vaunted for its
strictly vinyl vault of jazz, popular music, soul, R&B and rock 'n' roll;
you'll find everything from Louis Armstrong 78s to Chuck Berry 45s to
British Invasion and new wave LPs, and the staff will record your re-
quests for rare "collectors' items."

☑ String ⊠

| | 27 | 24 | 24 | E |

E 70s | 1015 Madison Ave. (bet. 78th & 79th Sts.) | 6 to 77th St. |
212-288-9276 | www.stringyarns.com

"The Bergdorf's of knitting stores", this Upper East Side "jewel"
specializes in the "highest-quality materials" (including what may well
be New York's "best selection of cashmere and other luxury yarns");
it's not surprising that "prices are much higher than elsewhere", but "if
cost is not a concern" buy your yarn here and as a bonus the "attentive" staff will "design and write you a custom pattern" for "anything
you want to make."

	QUALITY	DISPLAY	SERVICE	COST

NEW Stuart & Wright ● Ⓜ — — — E

Ft Greene | 85 Lafayette Ave. (bet. S. Elliott Pl. & S. Portland Ave.) |
Brooklyn | C to Lafayette Ave. | 718-797-0011

Don't be fooled by the vintage French Garment Cleaners sign outside –
it's merely a vestige of this Fort Greene newcomer's past life – just
duck inside and say *oui* to the urban-chic casualwear housed in its welcoming white-and-reclaimed-blond-wood space; the fashion-sleuth
owners, both Steven Alan alums, zero in on the right stuff: labels like
Engineered Garments and Mason's for guys, Lyell, Nina Stone and
Loeffler Randall shoes for her and A.P.C. for both.

Stuart Weitzman ● 27 24 23 E

E 50s | 625 Madison Ave. (bet. 58th & 59th Sts.) | N/R/W to 5th Ave./
59th St. | 212-750-2555
W 50s | The Shops at Columbus Circle, Time Warner Ctr. | 10 Columbus
Circle, ground fl. (bet. 58th & 60th Sts.) | 1/A/B/C/D to 59th St./
Columbus Circle | 212-823-9560
www.stuartweitzman.com

"Stewie is the best" confirm "well-heeled New Yorkers" who "feel like
Cinderella" in the namesake designer's "feminine, ultimately wearable" footwear that "lasts forever"; "playful" window displays and a
"great selection" of "expensive but sooo comfortable" "shoes for every reason and season" (and "cute bags too") make it "worth the trip
to his" Madison Avenue and Time Warner Center locales; here's the
kicker: the "impeccable" staff "bends over backwards" to "find you
just the right" style.

Stubbs & Wootton Ⓢ ▽ 26 27 23 E

E 70s | 1034 Lexington Ave. (74th St.) | 6 to 77th St. | 212-249-5200 |
877-478-8227 | www.stubbsandwootton.com

"If you want your feet noticed, step out" in "the most comfortable city
shoes around" order Wasps who Wootton go anywhere but this East
70s corner shop to purchase "unusual, comfy" European-made
slippers, loafers, heels, mules, slides, espadrilles and now boots too
in tapestry, needlepoint, brocade, merino wool or leather, all
tendered with "old-fashioned service"; they're all "showstoppers",
and the "clever designs" "ensure you'll have one for every mood";
N.B. monogramming available.

Studio Museum in Harlem Gift Shop Ⓜ — — — M

Harlem | 144 W. 125th St. (bet. Lenox & 7th Aves.) | 2/3 to 125th St. |
212-864-4500 | www.studiomuseum.org

An "extension of the museum" dedicated to African and African-
American art, this "small" shop features "good exhibition-related"
books and catalogs; it also offers a "varied selection" of "fun T-shirts",
"holiday gifts", jewelry and textiles as well as "cultural items" celebrating the history of Harlem.

Stussy NY ▽ 20 20 19 E

SoHo | 140 Wooster St. (bet. Houston & Prince Sts.) | N/R/W to
Prince St. | 212-995-8787 | www.stussy.com

What started as a small line of T-shirts by a California surfer is now a
young "classic" at age 27, representing West Coast style on the cob-
blestone streets of SoHo; established status notwithstanding, it's still
"home to graffiti writers, skaters" and other subculturists in need of

what students of steez consider the "coolest-in-town" tees, shoes, sunglasses and hoodies.

Suarez Ⓢ

27 | 23 | 24 | E

E 50s | 450 Park Ave. (57th St.) | 4/5/6/F/N/R/W to 59th St./ Lexington Ave. | 212-753-3758

It's "impossible to walk out without" buying one of the "unique" purses or "excellent" designer "knockoffs" at this Park Avenue family-owned "sleeper of the handbag world" where the "quality workmanship" extends to the nice "variety" of Italian leather accessories and shoes; though antisocial shoppers snap the "pushy" staff "doesn't leave you alone", others enjoy the "personal" "friendly" service.

Sude ◑

24 | 22 | 26 | E

Gramercy | 240 Third Ave. (20th St.) | 6 to 23rd St. | 212-420-1422
W 90s | 2470 Broadway (91st St.) | 1/2/3 to 96th St. | 212-721-5721

The Hell's Kitchen original may be no more but the styles are still "hotter than you know what" at Southern gal Sude Dellinger's "perfect little" Uptown-Downtown boutiques; there's "just enough great stuff to choose from" confirm customers who find "casual" to dressy garb from Ella Moss, Joe's Jeans, Splendid and the owner's own funky collection (along with a new selection of baby clothes), plus the "prices aren't bad" either.

Sugar ◑

▽ 22 | 21 | 23 | M

E Vill | 110 E. Seventh St. (bet. Ave. A & 1st Ave.) | 6 to Astor Pl. | 212-420-6499 | www.sugarshopping.com

Every girl likes a little sugar in her life and the savvy get a fashionable dose of it at this "funky East Village boutique"; indulge in the sweet satisfaction of finding "exciting", smart stuff for work, play or evening, "including Hudson jeans", feminine frocks, well-cut cords and "original" jackets; the "knowledgable" "staff is ready when you are", but do visit early and often, since "they don't overstock on items" – and what there is, "goes fast."

NEW Suite New York Ⓢ

- | - | - | VE

E 50s | 625 Madison Ave. (58th St.) | N/R/W to 5th Ave./59th St. | 212-421-3300 | www.suiteny.com

While this expensive Upper East Side contemporary furniture and lighting showroom may be a newcomer to the market, the owners – Kris Fuchs and Maria Isabel Sepulveda, formerly of the iconic store Troy – decidedly are not; they have harvested haute home furnishings from the boldest names in European and American design (think Wegner, Jacobsen and Lissoni) in a Chris Kraig–designed loftlike space to bring a little downtown edge to clients' uptown digs.

Super Runners Shop

26 | 20 | 25 | M

E 40s | Grand Central, main concourse | 42nd St. (Vanderbilt Ave.) | 4/5/6/7/S to 42nd St./Grand Central | 646-487-1120 ◑
E 70s | 1246 Third Ave. (72nd St.) | 6 to 68th St. | 212-249-2133
E 80s | 1337 Lexington Ave. (89th St.) | 4/5/6 to 86th St. | 212-369-6010
W 70s | 360 Amsterdam Ave. (77th St.) | 1 to 79th St. | 212-787-7665
www.superrunnersshop.com

"Quality, service, fit – that's what it's all about" at this "one-stop" "legend" that equips "hard-core" marathoners and "weekend warriors" with the "correct pair of sneaks" and apparel from labels like Asics, Saucony and Nike; the "trained staff" of "accomplished runners" "examines your stride as you walk" – and may even let you "test drive a pair around the block"; it's "not cheap", but loyalists go the distance, declaring "I won't buy athletic shoes anywhere else."

Supreme

| – | – | – | E |

SoHo | 274 Lafayette St. (bet. Houston & Prince Sts.) | B/D/F/V to B'way/Lafayette St. | 212-966-7799

Expect the wheel deal at SoHo's minimalist, white-and-chrome "skateboarders' oasis" where "hipsters" of all stripes congregate to work on their boards, watch action-packed video clips and peruse the artist-rendered equipment and wicked apparel; get in the game, or just look the part, with ramp-ready sweaters, hoodies, tees, sneakers and such from the house label plus brands like Girl Chocolate, Anti-Hero and City Stars.

Sur La Table ●

| 26 | 23 | 20 | E |

SoHo | 75 Spring St. (bet. Crosby & Lafayette Sts.) | 6 to Spring St. | 212-966-3375 | www.surlatable.com

Founded in Seattle's Pike Place Market in 1972, it took this kitchenware chain well over 30 years to make it to New York, but now local culinary connoisseurs call its 5,000-sq.-ft. SoHo space a "welcome addition" to the Apple; the "great selection" of "attractively displayed" barware, bakeware, "quality pots and pans", appliances, utensils, "neat gadgets" and tabletop accessories appeal to "everyone from the master chef to the take-out queen."

Surprise! Surprise!

| 15 | 10 | 13 | I |

E Vill | 91 Third Ave. (12th St.) | L to 3rd Ave. | 212-777-0990 | www.surprisesurprise.com

This East Village stalwart offers "affordable furniture for temporary living", plus a "jumble" of "cheap" housewares ranging "from window blinds to hampers and everything in between" that "seems geared to the yearly influx of NYU students and their dorm rooms"; but cynics say the only surprise is the "dumpy" setting and "nothing-special" merch.

Suzanne Couture Millinery Ⓢ

| ▽ 27 | 24 | 26 | VE |

E 60s | 27 E. 61st St. (bet. Madison & Park Aves.) | 4/5/6/F/N/R/W to 59th St./Lexington Ave. | 212-593-3232 | www.suzannemillinery.com

While the bridal veils and "handcrafted couture hats" festooned with feathers, mesh or jewels and "styled for you by elegant Suzanne" are "priced for a queen – hey, think she buys her hats here" too? – the cap-crazed consider these *chapeaux* some of the "most chic, creative designs" around; "for a special occasion", head to the old-world-style East 60s brownstone and "treat yourself to the best there is."

Swallow

| – | – | – | E |

Carroll Gdns | 361 Smith St. (2nd St.) | Brooklyn | F/G to Carroll St. | 718-222-8201 | www.swallowglass.com

Over 100 artists are represented at this eclectic Smith Street gallery selling a variety of handcrafted glass, ceramics, furniture and jewelry; some locals call it the "best place in Brooklyn to pick up a last-minute wedding gift", and the expertly edited offerings mean there is something for serious spendthrifts and wallet-watchers as well.

Swarovski

	25	25	22	E

E 40s | Rockefeller Ctr. | 30 Rockefeller Ctr. (bet. 49th & 50th Sts.) | B/D/F/V to 47-50th Sts./Rockefeller Ctr. | 212-332-4300

E 50s | 625 Madison Ave. (bet. 58th & 59th Sts.) | N/R/W to 5th Ave./ 59th St. | 212-308-1710

NEW E 50s | 731 Lexington Ave. (bet. 58th & 59th Sts.) | 4/5/6/F/N/R/W to 59th St./Lexington Ave. | 212-308-9560 ◗

NEW Staten Island | Staten Island Mall | 2655 Richmond Ave. (bet. Platinum Ave. & Richmond Hill Rd.) | 718-477-0469 ◗ 888-207-9873 | www.swarovski.com

"All that glitters is not gold" – in this quartet's case it's faceted Austrian crystal that "can really put a sparkle in your eye and on your lapel, finger or wrist"; there are other gleaming items like "small glass figurines" and tabletop accessories, but most maintain the bijoux are the best bling "for those who can't afford Harry Winston."

Swatch ◗

	20	22	18	M

E 40s | Grand Central | 42nd St. (Vanderbilt Ave.) | 4/5/6/7/S to 42nd St./ Grand Central | 212-297-9192

NoHo | 640 Broadway (Bleecker St.) | 6 to Bleecker St. | 212-777-1002

SoHo | 438 W. Broadway (Prince St.) | N/R/W to Prince St. | 646-613-0160

W 40s | 1528 Broadway (45th St.) | 1/2/3/7/N/Q/R/S/W to 42nd St./ Times Sq. | 212-764-5541

W 70s | 100 W. 72nd St. (Columbus Ave.) | 1/2/3 to 72nd St. | 212-595-9640

Elmhurst | Queens Ctr. | 90-15 Queens Blvd. (bet. 57th & 59th Aves.) | Queens | G/R/V to Grand Ave./Newtown | 718-760-7083 888-631-6037 | www.swatch.com

There's a "funky" and "fun" "Willy Wonka" quality to these watches that "come in a dizzying variety of styles and colors" and "tickle almost everyone's fancy" since they are "cheap" but "work well"; proponents also point out that "you don't have to worry about being mugged wearing one because these babies have no street value."

SwimBikeRun ◗

	–	–	–	E

W 50s | 203 W. 58th St. (7th Ave.) | N/Q/R/W to 57th St. | 212-399-3999 | www.sbrmultisports.com

This Midtown sports trifecta is staffed with "friendly" experts "that actually do triathlons" and "go above and beyond" attest admirers who "go in to just look and end up buying half the store"; fans "love" the "cool layout" and the "great" apparel and gear for, what else, swimming, biking and running; you need to be an Iron Man to handle the "expensive" prices, but hey, "you get what you pay for."

Swiss Army

	23	20	21	M

SoHo | 136 Prince St. (bet. W. B'way & Wooster St.) | N/R/W to Prince St. | 212-965-5714 | www.swissarmy.com

"Funny how we love the simple things in life like our Swiss Army watches" declare legions of fans who fall for the "efficient", "reasonably priced" "quality" timepieces at this spacious, modern SoHo haunt; but this "been-around" forever brand is "much more than" just chronographs, "top-notch" multitools and, of course, knives – you'll also find a "plethora" of "great-looking" luggage and men's and women's apparel from companion line Victorinox.

	QUALITY	DISPLAY	SERVICE	COST

Syms ●

	18	11	12	I

E 50s | 400 Park Ave. (54th St.) | 6 to 51st St. | 212-317-8200
Financial Dist | 42 Trinity Pl. (Rector St.) | R/W to Rector St. | 212-797-1199
www.syms.com

Whether Midtown or Downtown, "locals go" to this discount "delight" – "an old favorite" for clothes for the whole family, though some say you "do much better on men's than women's"; the apparel's all "organized by size", which "makes it a pleasure" (despite the "drab layout") "to pick through the plethora of racks"; however, some stock is "shop-worn" or "unmarked irregulars", so "inspect items closely for flaws."

Taffin ⊠ Ⓜ

	–	–	–	VE

By appointment only | inquiries: 212-421-6222

Born into an aristocratic and artistic family (his uncle is French fashion icon Hubert de Givenchy), James Taffin de Givenchy has been producing an "exquisite and exclusive" fine jewelry collection for over 10 years; his voluptuous, often playful and definitely inspired designs are based around colorful gemstones including favorite mandarin garnets, fire opals, red spinels and peridots.

Tah-Poozie ●

	▽ 18	20	17	M

G Vill | 50 Greenwich Ave. (bet. Charles & Perry Sts.) | 1 to Christopher St./ Sheridan Sq. | 212-647-0668

"Indulge your inner quirk" at this Greenwich Villager serving up "the best gags for cheap in NYC"; "get your rubber duckies and fridge magnets" along with "kitschy doodads for your home or office"; "anyone who has children, nieces or nephews should shop here" for "goofy gifts" that'll "leave 'em asking 'where did you get that?'"

☑ Takashimaya

	28	28	23	VE

E 50s | 693 Fifth Ave. (bet. 54th & 55th Sts.) | E/V to 5th Ave./53rd St. | 212-350-0100 | 800-753-2038

"Exquisite things in an exquisite setting" summarizes the scene at the "beautiful if austere" Midtown outpost of a Japanese chain; the mostly "modern" "high-end home goods and clothing" chosen "with an obvious Asian eye" are admittedly "an acquired taste" ("fine to browse, not much to buy" foes feel); but "beauty addicts stock up" on cosmetics brands "not usually found in the U.S.", and "vase fetishists" fawn over the "breathtaking floral" department; besides, the "laid-back help" and "Zen surroundings will automatically lower your blood pressure – until you see the prices"; P.S. there's also tea "in their lovely cafe."

☑ Talbots

	22	21	21	M

E 50s | 525 Madison Ave. (bet. 53rd & 54th Sts.) | E/V to 5th Ave./ 53rd St. | 212-838-8811
E 50s | 527 Madison Ave. (bet. 53rd & 54th Sts.) | E/V to 5th Ave./ 53rd St. | 212-371-5030
E 70s | 1251-1255 Third Ave. (72nd St.) | 6 to 68th St. | 212-988-8585 ●
Seaport | South Street Seaport | 189-191 Front St. (bet. Fulton & John Sts.) | 2/3/4/5/A/C/J/M/Z to Fulton St./B'way/Nassau | 212-425-0166
W 80s | 2289-2291 Broadway (bet. 82nd & 83rd Sts.) | 1 to 79th St. | 212-875-8753 ●
800-825-2687 | www.talbots.com

"If you're looking for preppy, look no further" than this "all-time favorite" chain proffering "excellent-quality" women's "classics" like "beautifully cut slacks" and "wrinkle-resistant shirts"; it's "not for the young and hip" and it may "have a reputation for matronly styling", but admirers say that only means its "lasts-for-years" clothing "never goes out of style", and they also laud the "affordable" prices; N.B. the 527 Madison branch houses the men's collection.

Talbots Kids and Babies

	24	23	22	E

E 50s | 527 Madison Ave. (54th St.) | E/V to 5th Ave./53rd St. | 212-758-4152
E 70s | 1523 Second Ave. (79th St.) | 6 to 77th St. | 212-570-1630
800-992-9010 | www.talbots.com

"Your little ones will look like they come from money" in the "preppy" apparel on parade at these East 50s and 70s "classic" "counterparts" to the adult chain; whether you're looking for "wonderful quality" "everyday stuff" or "party clothes", "they get it right" maintain parents who "don't want their children to have that J.Lo look at seven."

☑ T. Anthony Ltd. Ⓑ

	28	26	25	VE

E 50s | 445 Park Ave. (56th St.) | 4/5/6/F/N/R/W to 59th St./ Lexington Ave. | 212-750-9797 | www.tanthony.com

The "classic signature luggage that Gwyneth Paltrow made chic" and Donald Trump totes has actually "been around forever" and for good reason: the "beautiful coordinated sets", "elegant" duffel and wheeled styles and "gorgeous" garment bags at this "oh-so-proper" Park Avenue standby "always make you stand out when traveling"; expect "leather in all its glory" and "classy" canvas pieces, all offering "quality second to none", plus a staff that "treats you like you are royalty."

☑ Target ●

	17	17	13	I

Bronx | 40 W. 225th St. (I-87) | 1 to 225th St. | 718-733-7199
Downtown | Atlantic Terminal | 139 Flatbush Ave. (bet. Atlantic & 4th Aves.) | Brooklyn | 2/3/4/5/B/D/M/N/Q/R to Atlantic Ave. | 718-290-1109
Starrett City | Gateway Ctr. | 519 Gateway Dr. (bet. Fountain & Vandalia Aves.) | Brooklyn | A/C to Euclid Ave. | 718-235-6032
College Pt | 135-05 20th Ave. (Whitestone Expwy.) | Queens | 7 to Main St. | 718-661-4346
Elmhurst | Queens Pl. | 88-01 Queens Blvd. (bet. 55th & 56th Aves.) | Queens | G/R/V to Grand Ave./Newtown | 718-760-5656
800-440-0680 | www.target.com

Believers bellow this "neatly organized" outer-borough behemoth is the "best of the bargain mega-stores" for its "literally soup-to-nuts" variety; wheel down the "wide aisles" and "buy your outfit or outfit your home" with "lines created by designers" – like Proenza Schouler's fashions and the 500-piece housewares collection from Aero's Thomas O'Brien; if critics carp "you get tired traveling the immense space to find help", converts counter "what it [lacks] in service is balanced by its selections and prices", leaving only one question: "when will the bull's-eye land in Manhattan?"

NEW Tarina Tarantino

	▽ 22	24	20	E

SoHo | 117 Greene St. (Prince St.) | C/E to Spring St. | 212-226-6953 | www.tarinatarantino.com

You'll think pink at this rosy new SoHo outpost named for a California-based costume jewelry designer, who combines Swarovski crystal and Lucite in everything from eye-poppingly girlie multibead bracelets to oversized bib necklaces and drop earrings; for the even-more flamboyant, there are Barbie pendants and other pieces featuring Hello Kitty cartoon characters and storybook favorite *Alice in Wonderland*.

Taryn Rose
25 | - | 22 | VE

E 60s | 681 Madison Ave. (bet. 61st & 62nd Sts.) | N/R/W to 5th Ave./59th St. | 212-753-3939 | www.tarynrose.com

"Oh, to have a closet full of these shoes!" sigh admirers who swear that once you fall for the "like butter" men's and women's offerings, this "serene" shop, which recently moved to new Madison Avenue digs, "can be addictive"; trained as an orthopedic surgeon, the namesake designer creates "elegant" footwear that's "cute and good for your feet at the same time"; needless to say, such "extreme comfort" comes at an "extreme cost."

Tarzian True Value
21 | 14 | 21 | M

Park Slope | 193 Seventh Ave. (bet. 2nd & 3rd Sts.) | Brooklyn | F to 7th Ave. | 718-788-4120

"Got a brownstone? they've got what you need" at this "great" family-owned hardware store that's "provided for Park Slope throughout its renovation boom" – and eons before that, offering "a good selection of electronic and lighting" items, paint, plumbing supplies and garden tools "in a relatively small space"; natch, loyalists latch onto the "nice neighborhood vibe" and marvel that the "very helpful staff" "knows where everything is."

Tarzian West
21 | 17 | 20 | E

Park Slope | 194 Seventh Ave. (2nd St.) | Brooklyn | F to 7th Ave. | 718-788-4213

"It's a bit crowded" and the towering piles of product make you "feel as though things are about to fall on you", but Park Slopers salute this family-owned kitchen and bath store that "will satisfy most immediate needs", whether it's bakeware, cookware, cutlery or gadgets; locals like the fact that it "eliminates the need to trek into the city."

NEW té casan
- | - | - | E

SoHo | 382 W. Broadway (bet. Broome & Spring Sts.) | C/E to Spring St. | 212-584-8000 | www.tecasan.com

From the moment you whoosh up the spiral staircase of SoHo's champagne-colored 7,500-sq.-ft. showcase owned by a Spanish iconoclast, it's clear you're not in been-there-done-that footwear territory anymore; groupings of unique, limited-edition shoes from a rotating coterie of international designers, whose names may be unfamiliar but whose credentials, ranging from Alexander McQueen to Versace, speak volumes, are arranged like *objets d'art* and you can even try those wild wedges on in your own dressing room; after your Cinderella moment, dash downstairs for a spot of tea at the on-site T Salon.

Ted Baker
25 | 22 | 22 | E

SoHo | 107 Grand St. (Mercer St.) | 6/J/M/N/Q/R/W/Z to Canal St. | 212-343-8989 | www.tedbaker.co.uk

This dual-entrance SoHo boutique (one leads to womenswear, the other to men's) surprises with its "cute designs to spice up your wardrobe", like "great shirts" that come with complementary cuff links, floaty dresses and crease-resistant suits, including the famed Party

Animal Teflon-treated tuxedo; each dressing room has a fantasy mural, so you can envision wearing these "European-style clothes" on the Swiss Alps or at an English tea.

Ted Muehling 🅂🅼   ▽ 29 | 29 | 26 | E

SoHo | 27 Howard St. (bet. B'way & Lafayette St.) | 6/J/M/N/Q/R/W/Z to Canal St. | 212-431-3825 | www.tedmuehling.com

"No boyfriend or husband can go wrong buying" "beautiful", "timeless" jewelry from this SoHo designer whose striking "handcrafted" pieces – like pinecone or pussy willow earrings – are inspired by nature and "organic" forms; the "serene" shop also features his "incredible" porcelain and glass *objets* as well as gems by Gabriella Kiss.

🆉 Tekserve   26 | 16 | 23 | M

Chelsea | 119 W. 23rd St. (bet. 6th & 7th Aves.) | F/V to 23rd St. | 212-929-3645 | www.tekserve.com

Experience "Apple nirvana" at this "one-of-a-kind" Chelsea store whose renown rests with its reputation as the "quintessential" "computer rehab" "spot of choice for most Manhattan Mac owners"; "bring a book", though, and "expect to take a number" as "waits can be interminable"; P.S. the "quirky setting" includes a new glass-enclosed pro audio and video room featuring the original doors from the Las Vegas Sands Hotel.

Temperley 🅂   - | - | - | VE

SoHo | 453 Broome St., 2nd fl. (Mercer St.) | N/R/W to Prince St. | 212-219-2929 | www.temperleylondon.com

Visitors "love everything" about this light-filled, columned, second-story SoHo loft where British designer Alice Temperley houses her lavishly bedecked dresses and drapey feminine separates with a fin-de-siècle flair and attention to embroidered and beaded detail – all of which may account for their appeal to romantic icons like Gwyneth Paltrow and Kate Winslet; add in a new line of pillows, throws and bedspreads and "shopping here is amazing"; N.B. the store is slated to start carrying accessories again in 2007.

🆉 Tender Buttons 🅂⇗   28 | 26 | 21 | E

E 60s | 143 E. 62nd St. (bet. Lexington & 3rd Aves.) | 4/5/6/F/N/R/W to 59th St./Lexington Ave. | 212-758-7004

"Virtually a museum of buttons", this genteel, garden-level Upper East Sider "abounds" with "imported, antique" and "unusual" toggles and studs that make it "heaven to put the personal finishing touch on a jacket or sweater"; while it's "terribly hard to choose" among the "treasures" ("if you can't find what you're looking for here, it doesn't exist"), it's certainly "easy to see" the "splendid collection" in the uncluttered setting.

Tent and Trails   25 | 9 | 21 | M

Financial Dist | 21 Park Pl. (bet. B'way & Church St.) | A/C to Chambers St. | 212-227-1760 | 800-237-1760 | www.tenttrails.com

"Undeniably" one of the "best camping retailers" around, this "folksy" "grandpappy of sporting goods" is a "unique" Financial District "experience" for "outdoor groupies"; whether you're hiking to Central Park or pitching a tent in Kilimanjaro, you'll discover a bonanza of backpacking "treasure" – as long as you rely on the "knowledgeable staff", because the "crowded" quarters feel like a crazy "Tibetan bazaar."

Ten Thousand Things

`-` | `-` | `-` | VE

Meatpacking | 423 W. 14th St. (bet. 9th & 10th Aves.) | A/C/E/L to 14th St./8th Ave. | 212-352-1333

Way west on 14th Street, designers Ron Anderson and David Rees produce "simple, delicate" and "pricey" jewelry like signature cluster earrings and necklaces using gems ranging from keshi pearls to raw ruby skipping stones; N.B. there are also pieces from five other designers.

TG-170 ◗

▽ 20 | 17 | 18 | E

LES | 170 Ludlow St. (bet. Houston & Stanton Sts.) | F/V to Lower East Side/ 2nd Ave. | 212-995-8660 | www.tg170.com

The trek Downtown to this spacious, chandeliered Lower East Side style pioneer is well worth the mileage for the "hip and eclectic selection" of "one-of-a-kind" women's threads from labels like Corey Lynn Calter, Rebecca Taylor and less well-known designers; the "crisp aesthetic" of the clothes, jewelry and what may be the "largest assortment of messenger bags you'll ever see" "make this a neighborhood favorite."

Theory

23 | 22 | 21 | E

NEW **Meatpacking** | 38 Gansevoort St. (bet. Greenwich & Hudson Sts.) | A/C/E/L to 14th St./8th Ave. | 212-524-6790

NEW **SoHo** | 151 Spring St. (bet. W. B'way & Wooster St.) | 6 to Spring St. | 212-226-3691

W 70s | 230 Columbus Ave. (bet. 70th & 71st Sts.) | 1/2/3 to 72nd St. | 212-362-3676

www.theory.com

"Hip, but classic" "work attire" is not just theory but reality at this retail trio filled with an "always changing, always tempting" array of "no-fail outfits" in basic twill, gabardine and crepe; in particular, patrons praise "the perfectly fitting pants", provided you're a tall, "thin girl"; but "even if the trousers are cut for stick insects", the "staff tries to be honest", so "you won't regret buying the next day"; N.B. the new Meatpacking District behemoth also carries menswear.

37=1 Atelier Ⓜ

`-` | `-` | `-` | E

SoHo | 37 Crosby St. (bet. Broome & Grand Sts.) | N/R/W to Prince St. | 212-226-0067 | www.jeanyu.com

Discriminating stylesetters, celebs and the well-endowed who can pay "an arm and a leg" for wispy silk chiffon lingerie, filmy see-through dresses and glamorous satin halter gowns rely on designer Jean Yu for those champagne-worthy occasions; devotees can buy the willowy wearable art off the rack in the slinky SoHo space or "make an appointment" to have the meticulously crafted creations made to measure.

Thomas Pink

26 | 24 | 22 | E

E 50s | 520 Madison Ave. (53rd St.) | E/V to 5th Ave./53rd St. | 212-838-1928

W 40s | 1155 Sixth Ave. (44th St.) | 1/2/3/7/N/Q/R/S/W to 42nd St./ Times Sq. | 212-840-9663

W 50s | The Shops at Columbus Circle, Time Warner Ctr. | 10 Columbus Circle, ground fl. (bet. 58th & 60th Sts.) | 1/A/B/C/D to 59th St./ Columbus Circle | 212-823-9650 ◗

888-336-1192 | www.thomaspink.co.uk

Channeling the Jermyn Street school of shirtmaking, this British trio is a "mecca for Anglophiles" who want to "impress the boss" with "the finest off-the-rack shirt you can buy"; pink is just one of many "bright and lovely colors" available in a "vast selection of stripes, solids" and "unrivaled patterns" and displayed in "classy windows"; however, panners proclaim "they should blush [bright red] at their prices" and that often the "staff is less than helpful."

Thomasville ◗

23 | 21 | 19 | E

Bayside | 217-04 Northern Blvd. (217th St.) | Queens | 7 to Main St. | 718-224-2715 | www.thomasville.com

For more than a century, this North Carolina native with a Bayside showroom has crafted traditional living room, dining room and bedroom furniture in styles that range from French country to Shaker to Mission and more, including the popular Bogart and Hemingway collections; the "quality makes them well-worth the high price."

Thom Browne ⊠

- | - | - | VE

TriBeCa | 100 Hudson St. (Franklin St.) | 1/9 Franklin St. | 212-633-1197

Addressing a growing fan base, the menswear designer inspired by the bureaucratic look of the late '50s–early '60s – super-slim suits, short jackets and cropped trousers (Brad Pitt's been photographed wearing a pair) – recently moved to this sprawling TriBeCa space done up with a retro-office feel; acolytes call the distinctive custom-tailored togs "near perfect in every way" – plus there are also ready-to-wear ties, shirts and Corgi cashmeres for walk-ins (though not required, appointments are recommended).

Thos. Moser Cabinetmakers

▽ 29 | 29 | 25 | VE

E 60s | 699 Madison Ave., 2nd fl. (bet. 62nd & 63rd Sts.) | F to Lexington Ave./ 63rd St. | 212-753-7005 | 800-708-9016 | www.thomasmoser.com

The covetous confess it's "hard to keep your hands off the exquisite furniture in this Madison Avenue shop" where signed and dated Shaker, Scandinavian and Asian-influenced pieces "primarily in American black-cherry" are displayed; "prices are expensive, but justifiable" as the "workmanship is worth every cent."

3r Living ⊠

- | - | - | M

Park Slope | 276 Fifth Ave. (bet. 1st St. & Garfield Pl.) | Brooklyn | M/R to Union St. | 718-832-0951 | www.3rliving.com

Husband-and-wife-team Samantha Delman-Caserta and Mark Caserta make sure that all products in this "inventive, funky" Park Slope lifestyle store reflect the 3r's: reuse, recycle, reduce; the collection includes future-friendly offerings for body, baby, home and even pets, and the goods – from bike-chain bracelets to shotgun-shell vases – prove that the green lifestyle doesn't have to be "just for hippies."

NEW Tibi

- | - | - | E

SoHo | 120 Wooster St. (bet. Prince & Spring Sts.) | N/R/W to Prince St. | 212-226-5852 | www.tibi.com

"Embrace your girlieness" at this SoHo must-stop where the power of prettiness is captured by American designer Amy Smilovic's "feminine frocks", puffy-sleeved jackets and "cute" knit vests; "you can't beat it" if you're looking for "great quality", and you're welcome to lounge awhile in the loftlike space's mod sofas, taking in the eye-popping green, black and yellow color scheme that dominates the floral murals, zany couches and catchy prints.

	QUALITY	DISPLAY	SERVICE	COST

☑ Tiffany & Co.   28 | 27 | 24 | VE

E 50s | 727 Fifth Ave. (57th St.) | N/R/W to 5th Ave./59th St. | 212-755-8000 | 800-843-3269 | www.tiffany.com

"Any child, adult or ancient would love something" from Fifth Avenue's "American icon", whether it's "classic" silver, diamond or gold jewelry – including signature Elsa Peretti and Paloma Picasso pieces, plus a new Frank Gehry line – sterling, china and crystal for "memorable" wedding presents or the "best baby gifts"; despite "hordes of tourists" and mixed comments on service ("tops" vs "unless you're dressed to impress get ready to answer your own questions"), "who doesn't covet the little blue box?" N.B. the main-floor recently received a face-lift, plus plans are underway to open a Wall Street branch in 2007.

Timberland   23 | 19 | 17 | M

E 60s | 709 Madison Ave. (63rd St.) | F to Lexington Ave./63rd St. | 212-754-0436 | 800-445-5545 | www.timberland.com

"Top-shelf" footwear that "mixes style and rugged functionality" remains the foundation of this multilevel "showcase" in the East 60s; but Timber-fans holler "there's more" here – like outerwear, shirts, pants and accessories for the "mountain man set, or those playing it"; still, critics complain the "staff is not the most helpful" and put their foot down about "street shoes that [only] look like hiking boots."

Tiny Doll House ⊠   – | – | – | E

E 70s | 314 E. 78th St. (bet. 1st & 2nd Aves.) | 6 to 77th St. | 212-744-3719 | www.tinydollhousenyc.com

"I could spend an entire day" here – you "go inside and become six years old again" sigh house-hunters mesmerized by this "not-to-be-missed" East 70s destination for decadent dream homes, along with all of the little incidentals of life in miniature – everything from, say, pint-sized Persian rugs, lobster dinners and stiletto shoes to Starbucks coffee cups, radiators and Le Corbusier chairs.

Tiny Living ●   – | – | – | M

E Vill | 125 E. Seventh St. (bet. Ave. A & 1st Ave.) | L to 1st Ave. | 212-228-2748 | www.tinyliving.com

This affordable East Village shop lives up to its name by specializing in small-scaled, flexible furniture and accessories for the kind of cramped living room, kitchen, bath and office spaces that are so typical of Manhattan apartments; not only are there slim sofas, collapsible tables, chairs and even vases, many of the pieces are multipurpose and/or do double duty as storage as well.

Tip Top Kids   26 | 18 | 21 | E

W 70s | 149 W. 72nd St. (bet. B'way & Columbus Ave.) | 1 to 79th St. | 212-874-1003 | 800-925-5464 | www.tiptopshoes.com

"When your kid's sneakers are suddenly too small", stride over to this "old-fashioned", "conveniently located" West 70s shoe shop steps away from the grown-ups' standby, where the expert fitters "actually know how to measure feet" – a "rarity" nowadays; gravitate toward the "good selection" of "excellent quality" footwear "favorites" from mainstream labels like Timberland and Merrell or take the leap with budding brands like Blundstone, Keen and Umi.

Tip Top Shoes

25 | 18 | 22 | M

W 70s | 155 W. 72nd St. (bet. Amsterdam & Columbus Aves.) | 1/2/3 to 72nd St. | 212-787-4960 | 800-925-5464 | www.tiptopshoes.com

"Tip-top style and selection" assert admirers who stock their closets with an "excellent range" of "solid, comfortable" footwear from "international makers" galore from this "quintessential neighborhood store" that sets the "gold standard for shoe shopping on the Upper West Side"; the "window display calls me in whenever I walk by", while the "very accommodating staff" tends to my "weary feet", "fitting them correctly"; still, a handful huff the help is "grumpy" and caution it's "busy, busy, busy" on weekends.

✓ T.J. Maxx ●

16 | 10 | 8 | I

Flatiron | 620 Sixth Ave. (bet. 18th & 19th Sts.) | 1 to 18th St. | 212-229-0875
NEW College Pt | 136-05 20th Ave. (Parsons Blvd.) | Queens | 7 to Main St. | 718-353-2727
Staten Island | 1509 Forest Ave. (bet. Crystal & Decker Aves.) | 718-876-1995
Staten Island | 2530 Hylan Blvd. (New Dorp Ln.) | 718-980-4150
800-285-6299 | www.tjmaxx.com

"Savvy shoppers will be willing to overlook" the "time-consuming check-out lines" in order to "get an entire wardrobe for the price of one luxury item" at this "land of bargains" that also offers housewares, jewelry, luggage and other "great things mixed in with junk"; "spilling out onto the floor", the "picked-over" merch is "poorly organized" and often "not that clean, but hey, when you find a $15 Tahari shirt that retailed for $100, what's a little dirt?"

TLA Video ●

▽ 26 | 18 | 21 | M

G Vill | 52 W. Eighth St. (bet. 5th & 6th Aves.) | A/B/C/D/E/F/V to W. 4th St. | 212-228-8282 | www.tlavideo.com

"Blockbusting the competition" with its "amazing selection" of "great gay and lesbian", "international", art-house, indie and even mainstream films, this Village video/DVD store and rental repository is a "welcome" alternative; originally founded by the celebrated (and now defunct) Theatre of the Living Arts in Philadelphia, it boasts a "good" staff that's actually "seen the movies" and can help you "find anything you need."

Todd Hase

- | - | - | VE

SoHo | 261 Spring St. (bet. Hudson & Varick Sts.) | C/E to Spring St. | 212-871-9075 | www.toddhase.com

Known for his updates of classic furniture, designer Todd Hase's SoHo store features chaises, chairs, settees and sofas made with old-world techniques and upholstered in soft, neutral tones of mohair and silk that recall French design of the '30s and '40s; leather lamps add another quietly luxurious accent.

Todd Oldham for La-Z-Boy

19 | 21 | 19 | M

SoHo | 73 Wooster St. (bet. Broome & Spring Sts.) | C/E to Spring St. | 212-226-4908 | www.la-z-boy.com

Fashion designer Todd Oldham hits the home-furnishings market with this Wooster Street store, the first in a national chain for the Michigan-based manufacturer; he's taken a fresh look at gramps' favorite recliner, along with producing a line of sofas and sectionals available in a choice of 300 colorful fabrics, plus side tables and accessories, but whether his take is "hip" or hokey (a "limited style inspired by the *I Dream of Jeannie* era") will have to be your call.

⚡ Tod's
29 | 25 | 21 | VE

E 60s | 650 Madison Ave. (bet. 59th & 60th Sts.) | N/R/W to 5th Ave./59th St. | 212-644-5945 | www.todsonline.com

"Whether or not you" get behind the wheel, "your wardrobe must include a pair" of the "cute" signature "driving mocs" with "pebbled soles" that'll "spoil you for anything else" attest touters who feed their fetish for "clean-cut" shoes and "gorgeous bags" at this Madison Avenue flagship; if a few feel flustered by the "haughty" staff, even they admit the payoff is some of the "most comfortable" footwear "on the face of the earth" fashioned from "fabulous soft leather" ("like butter!"); N.B. the Display score may not reflect a dramatic renovation that tripled the store size.

⚡ Toga Bikes
26 | 19 | 24 | E

W 60s | 110 West End Ave. (64th St.) | 1 to 66th St./Lincoln Ctr. | 212-799-9625 | www.togabikes.com

A pedal pusher since 1971, this West 60s standby is not only the "sister to Gotham Bikes Downtown", but "an excellent place" for "enthusiasts and neophytes alike" to buy wheels; the "no-bull" staff "loves what it sells", including Cannondale road bikes and specialized all-terrain rides, and it also "tinkers with every new piece of equipment you add"; all bicycles have guaranteed lifetime service, which might explain the crowds (hint: "don't go on weekends").

Tokio 7 ◗
▽ 26 | 14 | 11 | M

E Vill | 64 E. Seventh St. (bet. 1st & 2nd Aves.) | 6 to Astor Pl. | 212-353-8443

It's a "good, solid resale shop" pronounce patrons of this long, low-ceilinged East Villager "chock-full" of male and female "basic, midrange" "designerwear that's definitely wearable", plus some "quirky" "higher-end goodies" at "fair prices" – and sometimes even "cheap" ones, "if you think wearing someone else's Marc Jacobs top from last year is worth 50 percent off the original cost."

Tokyo Joe ◗
22 | 15 | 15 | M

E Vill | 334 E. 11th St. (bet. 1st & 2nd Aves.) | L to 1st Ave. | 212-473-0724

This East Village "walk-in closet of a store" "looks dingy from the outside, but on the inside it's filled with wonderful" designer retreads for both genders, much of it "looking practically new"; the quarters can be close, "but the finds are worth the heat", especially those "at prices so low you'll have to put on your glasses to double-check that you aren't seeing things."

Tommy Hilfiger
20 | 20 | 18 | E

SoHo | 372 W. Broadway (Broome St.) | C/E to Spring St. | 917-237-0983 | www.tommy.com

Designer Tommy Hilfiger "has really stepped it up" at this "sleek" SoHo shop, delivering three floors of "classic, clean and preppy" his-and-hers "hip" wardrobe essentials infused with "European style" that are just right for "work or going out for a fine dinner"; but while it's "nice that it's all under one roof", critics cavil that the collection can "run hot and cold, depending on the season."

Top DJ Gear/Satellite Records ●◻ — — — | M

NoLita | 259 Bowery (bet. Houston & Prince Sts.) | F/V to Lower East Side/
2nd Ave. | 212-995-1744 | 888-998-6735 | www.topdjgear.com

Mixmasters of the universe make tracks to this NoLita nerve center
known for up-to-the-minute selections of progressive, trance, jungle,
techno, drum & bass and hip-hop; 20 vinyl and nine state-of-the-art
CD listening stations make it super easy to find that hot groove, and
the record store's recent mash-up with a major DJ equipment supplier
should send both pros and amateurs into lift-off.

Tory Burch 21 | 25 | 19 | E

NoLita | 257 Elizabeth St. (bet. Houston & Prince Sts.) | B/D/F/V to
B'way/Lafayette St. | 212-334-3000 | www.toryburch.com

"Tory hits the mark" maintain mavens of this "hot, hip boutique" – a
NoLita "must-stop" for the "must-haves" – that "feels like a glam '70s
living room"; it's "all presentation" protest pessimists who "don't
understand the buzz" about this socialite/designer's colorful wares,
but "well-maintained fortysomethings" find her "completely original
yet ultimately wearable" Me Decade–inspired pieces "perfect work-
day" attire and applaud the "special" wardrobe standouts that even
"take you into night."

Tourneau 27 | 24 | 21 | VE

E 50s | 500 Madison Ave. (52nd St.) | E/V to 5th Ave./53rd St. |
212-758-6098
Garment Dist | 200 W. 34th St. (7th Ave.) | 1/2/3/A/C/E to 34th St./
Penn Station | 212-563-6880
W 50s | The Shops at Columbus Circle, Time Warner Ctr. | 10 Columbus
Circle, ground fl. (bet. 58th & 60th Sts.) | 1/A/B/C/D to 59th St./
Columbus Circle | 212-823-9425 ●

Tourneau TimeMachine

E 50s | 12 E. 57th St. (Madison Ave.) | N/R/W to 5th Ave./59th St. |
212-758-7300
www.tourneau.com

"If you can't find it here you don't want it" assert admirers of this tony
ticker chain with perhaps "the most complete selection" of the "top
time pieces" in town (the TimeMachine outpost bills itself as the
world's largest watch store); while opinions on service range from
"spotty" and "snobby" ("if they think you can't afford it, they're not
interested") to "knowledgeable", the staff is "willing to negotiate
prices"; so "do your research" and note that there are "terrific pre-
owned deals" and they also "take trade-ins."

Town Shop 25 | 14 | 25 | M

W 80s | 2273 Broadway (bet. 81st & 82nd Sts.) | 1 to 79th St. |
212-787-2762 | www.townshop.com

It "might not be the most glamorous store", but this "all-pink",
"family-run" Upper West Side "institution" is the "last of the real lingerie shops" offering an "impressive array" of brand names and em-
ploying "no-nonsense" "expert" corsetieres who "size you up in a
second" with "fitting savvy that's beyond compare" ("yes, you were
probably wearing the wrong bra"); sure, the staff's approach is
"hands-on", but they'll "hook you up" with undergarments that provide the "support you've always wanted."

NEW Toy Space

23	21	24	E

Park Slope | 426 Seventh Ave. (bet. 14th & 15th Sts.) | Brooklyn | F to 7th Ave. | 718-369-9096 | www.toyspaceny.com

Travel "back in time" at this Park Slope funhouse where the "neat" and nostalgic selection of "classic, hard-to-find toys" from decades gone by will "remind you of your childhood"; from "gyroscopes, baby grand pianos" and Radio Flyer wagons to science kits and build-your-own-sports-car sets, this is *the* place" to go when you're "searching for something special" – "if you can't find it here, you can't find it anymore."

Toys "R" Us ●

20	20	14	M

W 40s | 1514 Broadway (44th St.) | 1/2/3/7/N/Q/R/S/W to 42nd St./Times Sq. | 646-366-8800 | 800-869-7787 | www.toysrus.com
Additional locations throughout the NY area

"Don't miss this show on Broadway" rave fans of Times Square's towering "toy universe" flagship offering a "carnival"-like "experience" complete with a "fantastic" Ferris wheel, an "unbelievable" animatronic T. rex, "awesome" Barbie playhouse, NYC landmarks done up in Legos and a Candyland sweet shop; though Scrooges dub it the "*Romper Room* of the suburbs" and grimace over "throngs" of "overstimulated" kids and "numbingly long lines", enthusiasts counter the "consolation is the hug you get from your child."

Tracy Feith

▽ 22	28	22	VE

NoLita | 209 Mulberry St. (bet. Kenmare & Spring Sts.) | 6 to Spring St. | 212-334-3097

You "gotta love it" – a "surfer dude designing fab ladies' gear" grin groupies who haunt this NoLita shop filled with "dresses made to fit you like a glove" in "colorful patterns" and "awesome fabrics" for those who "like to stand out at parties"; however, you may be hanging 10 on your own as the staff sometimes sends out a "don't-be-intrusive" vibe.

NEW Tracy Reese

25	25	23	E

Meatpacking | 641 Hudson St. (bet. Gansevoort & Horatio Sts.) | A/C/E/L to 14th St./8th Ave. | 212-807-0505 | www.tracyreese.com

"The ambiance alone will wow you" at this "airy" new va-va-voom boutique in the "über-hip Meatpacking District", showcasing the rapidly rising American designer known for her "adorable, grown-up yet girlie pieces for uptown and downtown types alike"; whether doing "womanly" work garb or a "kicky" party dress, "Reese has a great eye", imbuing garments with a vintage-modern mix of silk, satin and velvet, as well as ribbons and lace; the result is "a little pricey – but oh-so-pretty."

Training Camp ●

–	–	–	M

Garment Dist | 1412 Broadway (bet. 39th & 40th Sts.) | 7/B/D/F/V to 42nd St./Bryant Park | 212-398-3930

W 40s | 1079 Sixth Ave. (41st St.) | 7/B/D/F/V to 42nd St./Bryant Park | 212-921-4430

W 40s | 25 W. 45th St. (bet. 5th & 6th Aves.) | 7/B/D/F/V to 42nd St./Bryant Park | 212-840-7842

Canarsie | 1498 Rockaway Pkwy. (Flatlands Ave.) | Brooklyn | L to Canarsie/Rockaway Pkwy. | 718-876-6383

Staten Island | 1351 Forest Ave. (bet. Jewett & Veltman Aves.) | 718-273-9689

(continued)

(continued)

Training Camp

Staten Island | Staten Island Mall | 2655 Richmond Ave. (bet. Platinum Ave. & Richmond Hill Rd.) | 718-370-2893
Staten Island | 530 Bay St. (bet. Prospect & Sands Sts.) | 718-876-6383
www.trainingcampstores.com

"Every sneaker junkie in-the-know heads" to this military-themed "staple" with a "relaxed atmosphere" for the "hottest" kicks from Avirex, Phat Farm and Royal Elastics along with Nike Air Jordan and Bo Jackson Air Trainer finds; "whether you're looking for comfort or just want style, they have everything for everyone", and what's more, "when they have stuff on sale, it's really a sale."

Transit ●

| | 17 | 17 | 14 | M |

NoHo | 665 Broadway (bet. Bleecker & Bond Sts.) | 6 to Bleecker St. | 212-358-8726

"Grab your Metrocard" and "pass through" the "old-school turnstiles" at this multifloor NoHo standby, "one of the better places to go for midpriced", "casual, trendy" "urban streetwear" for the "hip-hop crowd" from labels like G-Unit, Sean Jean and Rocawear; don't forget to "check out the sneaker" wall filled with "cool" kicks including "hard-to-find" classics – the "transit train" vibe makes "you feel like you just stepped onto a subway platform."

Trash and Vaudeville ●

| | 16 | 18 | 14 | M |

E Vill | 4 St. Marks Pl. (bet. 2nd & 3rd Aves.) | 6 to Astor Pl. | 212-982-3590

"Hey, ho, let's go" to this "legendary" "CBGBs of clothing", housing "a treasure trove" of "awesome rock" paraphernalia and "great club wear", including, what else, "Ramones tees", bondage collars, rubber pants "with zippers and rings", "naughty mesh things" and the "occasional beautiful corset"; "hats off" to this "museum to punk" for being "one of the last remnants of the East Village as it used to be", and for providing a "unique experience", especially for "tourists."

NEW Treehouse Ⓜ

| | – | – | – | M |

Williamsburg | 430 Graham Ave. (bet. Frost & Withers Sts.) | Brooklyn | L to Graham Ave. | 718-482-8733 | www.treehousebrooklyn.com

Reawaken your childhood sense of wonder (not to mention memories of camp crocheting classes) at this former speakeasy, now a cozy shop filled with nooks and a knitted tree; the inventory is a mix of vintage clothes, quirky mens- and womenswear (from lines like Feral Childe, Bobbi and Papi's Mami) and tweet treasures in totes and home furnishings – most of them unique items from local designers; craft classes and knitting circles also keep this Williamsburg corner crowded.

Treillage Ⓢ

| | – | – | – | VE |

E 70s | 418 E. 75th St. (bet. 1st & York Aves.) | 6 to 77th St. | 212-535-2288 | www.treillageonline.com

For more than a decade, "decorators have flocked" to this Upper East Side, garden-inspired furnishings shop owned by interior designer Bunny Williams and antiques dealer John Rosselli; "unique" items, such as cast-stone bird baths from the 1920s and vintage French melon pots make for pretty pictures, but unless you are an "upscale client", these "beautiful" pieces may prove über-"expensive."

Tribeca Girls

- | - | - | E

TriBeCa | 171 Duane St. (bet. Greenwich & Hudson Sts.) | 1/2/3 to Chambers St. | 212-925-0049 | www.tribecagirls.com

"Top fashions for the littlest fashionista in your house", ranging from novelty T-shirts to colorful hoodies and kicky minis, fill the racks of this spacious TriBeCa yearling that caters to girls sizes 2T–14; the on-trend looks from prized labels like Diesel, Junk Food and Paul Frank are "sure-to-please" stylin' girls and their footstep-following younger sisters.

NEW Trico Field

- | - | - | E

SoHo | 65 W. Houston St. (Wooster St.) | B/D/F/V to B'way/Lafayette St. | 212-358-8484

The Japanese invasion of SoHo presses on with the arrival of this inviting new Houston Street shop, a thoughtfully merchandised, rectangular-shaped childrenswear find owned by Fith, an Asian powerhouse company; shoppers have a field day choosing sophisticated styles for fashionable kids, particularly boys, from wooden shelves and a chunky table, creating outfits with durable essentials like jean jackets, cargo pants, striped boatnecks and rugged button-down shirts, most made from natural fabrications.

NEW Trina Turk

- | - | - | E

Meatpacking | 67 Gansevoort St. (bet. Greenwich & Washington Sts.) | A/C/E/L to 14th St./8th Ave. | 212-206-7383 | www.trinaturk.com

Like an oasis in the desert, West Coast designer Trina Turk's new Meatpacking District boutique rejuvenates fashionistas thirsting for form-fitting sweaters and flattering frocks in Palm Springs shades and mod patterns; reminiscent of Big Sur, the '70s-styled white space boasts splashes of color and was designed by Jonathan Adler, whose ceramics the store carries, along with a small collection of menswear.

Triple Five Soul

21 | 20 | 18 | E

SoHo | 290 Lafayette St. (bet. Houston & Prince Sts.) | B/D/F/V to B'way/Lafayette St. | 212-431-2404

Williamsburg | 145 Bedford Ave. (N. 9th St.) | Brooklyn | L to Bedford Ave. | 718-599-5971 ●

www.triple5soul.com

"Love it!" say the "trendy young" things who flock to this SoHo-Williamsburg duo to scoop up "surprisingly innovative" hoodies, velour sweatpants, boyfriend jeans and satin parkas that "ooze coolness"; if you dig the "New York grunge-casual skateboarder" look, these "excellent cutting-edge" his-and-hers threads with an "unbelievable fit" are the "epitome of hipster" "urban" "fashion", plus there's plenty of music and art in store to keep your Triple Five Soul enlightened.

Z Trixie and Peanut ● M

27 | 28 | 24 | VE

Flatiron | 23 E. 20th St. (bet. B'way & Park Ave.) | 4/5/6/L/N/Q/R/W to 14th St./Union Sq. | 212-358-0881 | www.trixieandpeanut.com

A "beautiful" barks-and-mortar incarnation of an "amazing" online retail-er, this "upscale boutique" for animal companions has become a Flatiron "favorite" for "fabulous" apparel, carriers and "doggy jewelry" that "make your pet stand out in a crowd"; the staff supplies "great service", and "as long as you're not afraid of spending more money on your pooch than yourself", it's "as good as it gets."

Troy ⑤

	QUALITY	DISPLAY	SERVICE	COST
	-	-	-	VE

Gramercy | 99 Madison Ave. (bet. 29th & 30th Sts.) | 6 to 28th St. |
212-941-4777 | 888-941-4777 | www.troysoho.com

"I'd rather live without furnishings than live without Troy" proclaim
proponents of this airy, iconic and expensive store newly relocated
from SoHo to Gramercy Park digs; it now showcases an even larger
collection of "cool" contemporary beds, coffee tables, chairs and
couches from American and European designers like Fritz Hansen,
Living Davani and Porro, along with the namesake owner's home-
accessories collection that combines exotic wood with sterling silver
in items like bowls and napkin rings.

NEW True Religion

	-	-	-	VE

SoHo | 132 Prince St. (Wooster St.) | N/R/W to Prince St. | 212-966-6011 |
www.truereligionbrandjeans.com

A mainstay in the pages of *US Weekly*, this beloved-by-celebs denim
brand from LA has come to the chic streets of SoHo via its first NYC
boutique – a rough-hewn and woody space that complements the vintage feel of the artfully worn-in duds (which include T-shirts, flannels
and hoodies); the pricy premium jeans are the real stars here, with the
selection of mostly low-rise fits adorned with their signature curve-
hugging back pockets and distinctive horseshoe stitching.

NEW Trunkt ⑤

	▽ 23	23	22	M

TriBeCa | 393 Greenwich St. (bet. Beach & N. Moore Sts.) | 1 to
Franklin St. | 212-625-2997 | www.trunkt.com

This "interesting" and expansive new TriBeCa exposed-brick-and-
beam loft space is a showcase for indie design ranging from stationery,
spa products and home goods to women's accessories like handbags
and "trendy" costume jewelry; when it comes to the bijoux, wags wager: "you won't be leaving them to anyone in your will", but they'll
"make you smile now when you wear them."

TSE ⑤

	26	23	22	VE

Chelsea | 450 W. 15th St. (bet. 9th & 10th Aves.) | A/C/E/L to 14th St. &
8th Ave. | 212-472-7790 | www.tsecashmere.com

Oh, Tse can you see how "stylish" the stock is, a "sorbet assortment"
of colors and "contemporary" silhouettes that ensures these luxurious
knits are "not your grandma's cashmere"; admittedly "the prices are
thick for such thin ply", but the "pleasant" staff makes you believe "if
you could own one of these sweaters for every day of winter, your life
would be complete"; N.B. it's currently operating out of its by-
appointment-only showroom while searching for new digs.

Tsubi ◑

	-	-	-	E

NoLita | 219C Mulberry St. (bet. Prince & Spring Sts.) | 6 to Spring St. |
212-334-4690 | www.tsubi.com

Pick up a pair of Australia's premium, "soft against the body" Lean
Bean jeans (worn by Lindsay Lohan), pretty pastel tees and retro sunglasses beloved by Orlando Bloom, Ashley Olsen and Paddy Bloom of
the Scissors Sisters at this raw, glass-fronted Down Under export on a
relentlessly hip stretch of NoLita; slide into one of the retro chairs and
watch the skinny gals slip into the "expensive" denim that just may be
"worth the money."

Tucker Robbins 🛇

| | - | - | - | VE |

E 50s | 139 E. 57th St., 4th fl. (bet. Lexington & 3rd Aves.) | 4/5/6/F/N/R/W to 59th St./Lexington Ave. | 212-355-3383 Ⓜ

LIC | 33-02 Skillman Ave. (33rd St.) | Queens | 7 to 33rd St. | 718-764-0222
www.tuckerrobbins.com

Named after their eponymous and unusual owner – a former monk turned designer – these East 50s and Long Island City spaces showcase "interesting" furniture from around the world, which is made primarily from recycled wood and inspired by traditional Asian and African forms, leading loyalists to say it looks like "like no one else's."

Tuesday's Child

| | ▽ 26 | 16 | 19 | E |

Flatbush | 1904 Ave. M (E. 19th St.) | Brooklyn | Q to Ave. M | 718-375-1790 🛇 Ⓜ

Midwood | 2771 Nostrand Ave. (bet. Ave. N & Kings Hwy.) | Brooklyn | Q to Kings Hwy. | 718-252-8874 | 888-244-5388
www.tuesdayschild.com

It's "been around forever", but this Midwood mecca hasn't lost its edge when it comes to whipping the wardrobes of city kids into ship-shape; with a brand roster that reads like a who's who of "designer names" (Sonia Rykiel, Armani Junior and Burberry to name a few), "it's the right place to find high-priced" togs with "some regular European clothes mixed in"; if you don't have a fat wallet, check out the Avenue M outlet.

Ⓩ TUMI

| | 28 | 23 | 23 | VE |

E 40s | Grand Central | 42nd St. (Vanderbilt Ave.) | 4/5/6/7/S to 42nd St./Grand Central | 212-973-0015 ◐

E 50s | 520 Madison Ave. (54th St.) | E/V to 5th Ave./53rd St. | 212-813-0545

SoHo | 102 Prince St. (bet. Greene & Mercer Sts.) | N/R/W to Prince St. | 646-613-9101

W 40s | Rockefeller Ctr. | 53 W. 49th St. (bet. 5th & 6th Aves.) | B/D/F/V to 47-50th Sts./Rockefeller Ctr. | 212-245-7460

W 50s | The Shops at Columbus Circle, Time Warner Ctr. | 10 Columbus Circle, ground fl. (bet. 58th & 60th Sts.) | 1/A/B/C/D to 59th St./Columbus Circle | 212-823-9390 ◐

800-322-8864 | www.tumi.com

"Luggage for road warriors" sums up this "classy, unobtrusive" outfit renowned for its "extremely well-designed", "nothing short of fabulous" finds in "catchy au courant colors" and "gorgeous patterns"; "for those who appreciate workmanship and durability", these pieces "can take a beating", "survive the flight" and possibly even "last the rest of your life and beyond"; in short, "it's the only suitcase" to own and well "worth the investment."

Tupli 🛇 Ⓜ

| | - | - | - | VE |

E 60s | 780 Madison Ave., 2nd fl. (bet. 66th & 67th Sts.) | 6 to 68th St. | 212-472 2576 | www.tupli.com

There are unique, exquisite European-style custom-made shoes for every woman at this by-appointment-only Madison Avenue atelier where partners Kathy Myczkowski and Tamara Chubinidze strive to create a knockout pair just for you – as long as you don't mind shelling out lots of green; the staff researches your personal style, a mold is made of your foot for the best fit and, *voilà*: weeks later, your sole mate arrives.

⚡ Turnbull & Asser 🅢

	QUALITY	DISPLAY	SERVICE	COST
	28	27	25	VE

E 50s | 42 E. 57th St. (bet. Madison & Park Aves.) | 4/5/6/F/N/R/W to 59th St./Lexington Ave. | 212-752-5700 | 877-887-6285 | www.turnbullandasser.com

"Dapper only begins to describe" the "superb English offerings" at this multi-department "bespoke club" housed in a five-story townhouse on East 57th Street; since 1885, this "serious", "professional" haberdasher has "maintained the integrity" of its "classic, clean" dress shirts, suits and cashmere sweaters that run the gamut from banker to "dandy", and from lord to lady; service is highly "courteous", but beware – the bill for even a couple of the "great ties" may be "more expensive than the best dinner you ever had."

Two Jakes Ⓜ

	QUALITY	DISPLAY	SERVICE	COST
	∇ 21	14	20	M

Williamsburg | 320 Wythe Ave. (bet. Grand & S. 1st Sts.) | Brooklyn | L to Bedford Ave. | 718-782-7780 | www.twojakes.com

Within the 10,000-sq.-ft. industrial garagelike setting of this home- and office-furnishings store along the Williamsburg waterfront, there are "great vintage finds in wonderful condition" from Bisley to bludot, Offi to Emeco and Herman Miller to Knoll, along with new offerings like the owners' own J-line sofas and club chairs.

202

	QUALITY	DISPLAY	SERVICE	COST
	23	24	19	E

Chelsea | Chelsea Mkt. | 75 Ninth Ave. (bet. 15th & 16th Sts.) | 1 to 18th St. | 646-638-0115

We "love" that her "sweet" 202 Cafe is "right in the middle of it all – very innovative and truly the future of retail" predict prognosticators who praise Nicole Farhi's Chelsea Market "one-stop" concept shop where a "great variety" of the British-based designer's clothing for men and women, "beautiful furniture", home accessories and "unique gifts" comingle; "anything you buy would get compliments" confide brunchers and browsers who frequent this pretty, if admittedly "pricey" place.

NEW UGG Australia ◗

	QUALITY	DISPLAY	SERVICE	COST
	-	-	-	E

SoHo | 79 Mercer St. (bet. Broome & Spring Sts.) | 6 to Spring St. | 212-226-0602 | www.uggaustralia.com

Just when you thought the sheepskin trend had reached its expiration date, the California-based brand founded by a Down Under surfer stakes its claim on SoHo, unveiling footwear, accessories and outwear for the entire family in its new woodsy-colored digs; get your fill of fuzzy-wuzzy styles with the classic boot, lined flip-flops, slippers, even handbags, then dip into the smart selection of espadrilles, sandals and tote bags.

Umkarna Ⓜ

	QUALITY	DISPLAY	SERVICE	COST
	-	-	-	E

Park Slope | 69 Fifth Ave. (bet. St. Marks Pl. & Warren St.) | Brooklyn | D/M/N/R to Pacific St. | 718-398-5888 | www.umkarna.com

With an emphasis on antique and contemporary handicrafts created by women, owner Luisa Giugliano culls an expertly edited collection of exotic housewares, clothing and accessories largely from India and central and east Asia for her exotic Park Slope shop that's named after her Kashmiri husband's grandmother; the treasures range from Tibetan armoires to textiles from Uzbekistan.

	QUALITY	DISPLAY	SERVICE	COST

NEW **Uniqlo**   – | – | – | I

SoHo | 546 Broadway (bet. Prince & Spring Sts.) | N/R/W to Prince St. | 212-966-5374 | www.uniqlo.com

"Never do laundry again – just give the dirty stuff away and buy more" maintain mavens of this massive manufacturer from Japan, whose new multifloor SoHo flagship features a dizzying array of "cheap" casual cashmeres, cottons and cords "in a glow of colors"; yes, the "service could be nicer", and the garments "aren't the highest quality", but given that the line for the men's fitting room is as long as at the women's, clearly everyone enjoys the "disposable clothing at its finest."

Unis   – | – | – | E

NoLita | 226 Elizabeth St. (bet. Houston & Prince Sts.) | N/R/W to Prince St. | 212-431-5533 | www.unisnewyork.com

This tiny but tempting NoLita shop draws the generation of guys and gals who like their sportswear cut with nonchalant chic – and know designer-owner Eunice Lee delivers just that in blousy shirts, cargo-style trousers, military-inspired coats and teensy-strap dresses with a vintage feel.

Unisa   20 | 21 | 18 | M

E 60s | 701 Madison Ave. (bet. 62nd & 63rd Sts.) | 4/5/6/F/N/R/W to 59th St./Lexington Ave. | 212-753-7474 | www.unisa.com

For those seeking "a good quality shoe" in "a conservative-chic style" that's "not too flashy", this East 60s chainlet link serves up "fun designs at palatable prices"; not only are there "lots of flats and little heels", you may uncover the "best knockoffs in town", from "metallic slides" to "comfortable" mules, mocs and boots.

United Colors of Benetton   20 | 20 | 17 | M
(aka Benetton)

E 40s | 601 Fifth Ave. (bet. 48th & 49th Sts.) | E/V to 5th Ave./53rd St. | 212-317-2501 ◑

G Vill | 749 Broadway (bet. Astor Pl. & 8th St.) | N/R/W to 8th St. | 212-533-0230 ◑

Seaport | South Street Seaport | 10 Fulton St. (bet. Front & South Sts.) | 2/3/4/5/A/C/J/M/Z to Fulton St./B'way/Nassau | 212-509-3999 ◑

W 50s | The Shops at Columbus Circle, Time Warner Ctr. | 10 Columbus Circle, 2nd fl. (bet. 58th & 60th Sts.) | 1/A/B/C/D to 59th St./Columbus Circle | 212-245-5117 ◑

Bay Ridge | 409 86th St. (bet. 4th & 5th Aves.) | Brooklyn | R to 86th St. | 718-748-1555

Borough Pk | 4610 13th Ave. (bet. 46th & 47th Sts.) | Brooklyn | D/M to Fort Hamilton Pkwy. | 718-853-3420

Astoria | 31-17 Steinway St. (bet. B'way & 31st Ave.) | Queens | G/R/V to Steinway St. | 718-721-3333

Forest Hills | 71-27 Austin St. (71st Rd.) | Queens | E/F/G/R/V to Forest Hills/71st Ave. | 718-544-7117 ◑
www.benetton.com

Those nostalgic for their last "trip to Italy" head to this "'80s outpost" for "bright, happy" men's and women's apparel whose "clean looks" seem somewhat "original by American standards" and sport prices "any new professional can afford"; still, foes complain of "uninspiring" designs and a "bad return policy" – each store is independently owned, so you must take merchandise back to the location where you bought it.

	QUALITY	DISPLAY	SERVICE	COST

United Colors of Benetton Kids ◑
(aka UCB Kids)

21 | 22 | 18 | M

W 50s | The Shops at Columbus Circle, Time Warner Ctr. | 10 Columbus Circle, 2nd fl. (bet. 58th & 60th Sts.) | 1/A/B/C/D to 59th St./ Columbus Circle | 212-823-9569 | www.benetton.com

Proponents of "cute", "reasonably priced" children's clothes that "you won't see all of your friends' kids in" are united in their support of this Italian-style stallion's tot-oriented offshoot, with a "fabulous" Time Warner Center location next to sibling Sisley; snap up sassy school togs, winter jackets, activewear and accessories, available in a rainbow of "great colors" and patterns.

Urban Angler ⊠

- | - | - | E

Chelsea | 206 Fifth Ave., 3rd fl. (bet. 25th & 26th Sts.) | N/R/W to 23rd St. | 212-689-6400 | 800-255-5488 | www.urbanangler.com

Chelsea's fly-fishing mecca draws greenhorns and old salts alike with its "blue-ribbon quality" selection that "makes you proud" to be an angler; it's "nice to have a complete gear shop" in the "canyons of Manhattan" where you can pick up Sage rods, Abel reels, waders and a healthy dose of advice about local waters from "professionals"; P.S. sign up for casting lessons in nearby Madison Square Park with "appropriately named" owner Jon Fisher.

❷ Urban Archaeology ⊠

25 | 24 | 19 | VE

E 50s | 239 E. 58th St. (bet. 2nd & 3rd Aves.) | 4/5/6/F/N/R/W to 59th St./Lexington Ave. | 212-371-4646
TriBeCa | 143 Franklin St. (bet. Hudson & Varick Sts.) | 1 to Franklin St. | 212-431-4646
www.urbanarchaeology.com

For a "unique" collection of rescued and replica plunder, renovators recommend these TriBeCa and East 50s salvage shrines; "unusual handmade tiles", lighting, plumbing, pediments and statuary make them "fun places to scout", so the only dig is that sky-high prices mean that most can only "look, but not buy."

Urban Outfitters ◑

17 | 19 | 13 | M

Chelsea | 526 Sixth Ave. (14th St.) | F/L/V to 14th St./6th Ave. | 646-638-1646
E 50s | 999 Third Ave. (bet. 59th & 60th Sts.) | 4/5/6/F/N/R/W to 59th St./Lexington Ave. | 212-308-1518
E Vill | 162 Second Ave. (bet. 10th & 11th Sts.) | 6 to Astor Pl. | 212-375-1277
G Vill | 374 Sixth Ave. (Waverly Pl.) | A/B/C/D/E/F/V to W. 4th St. | 212-677-9350
G Vill | 628 Broadway (bet. Bleecker & Houston Sts.) | B/D/F/V to B'way/Lafayette St. | 212-475-0009
W 70s | 2081 Broadway (72nd St.) | 1/2/3 to 72nd St. | 212-579-3912
Rego Pk | Queens Ctr. | 90-15 Queens Blvd. (bet. 57th & 59th Aves.) | Queens | G/R/V to Woodhaven Blvd. | 718-699-7511
800-282-2200 | www.urbn.com

"Bohemian clothes" and "the funkiest" apartment kitsch bring budding hipsters who want to "look like an Olsen twin" to this "fun" chain; the feel's "overpriced Salvation Army" and service is mostly "subpar", but that doesn't keep the novelty books, "mass-produced vintage tees", "trenderrific" shoes and such from flying off the shelves.

	QUALITY	DISPLAY	SERVICE	COST

Utrecht
24 | 17 | 18 | M

Chelsea | 237 W. 23rd St. (bet. 7th & 8th Aves.) | 1 to 23rd St. | 212-675-8699 ●
E Vill | 111 Fourth Ave. (bet. 11th & 12th Sts.) | 4/5/6/L/N/Q/R/W to 14th St./Union Sq. | 212-777-5353
800-223-9132 | www.utrecht.com

"*Viva* Utrecht!" – a "favorite of art students", this "reliable, important standby" in the East Village stocks "quality products at reasonable prices" including its own "top-notch brand" of paints and brushes, plus "tools and materials galore"; the landscape may be a bit "cluttered" (don't expect "fancy displays"), but the staff's "knowledgeable" and the selection's "grand" at this 50-year-old "neighborhood resource"; N.B. artists across town can cruise the newer Chelsea branch.

☑ Valentino 🗷
28 | 27 | 25 | VE

E 60s | 747 Madison Ave. (bet. 64th & 65th Sts.) | 6 to 68th St. | 212-772-6969 | www.valentino.com

After four decades of designing "gorgeous grown-up clothes" for women and men, this Italian designer continues to please his "haute" clientele at this "spacious", limestone-floored Madison Avenue shop with "elegant styling" on "luscious" tailored jet-set suits and red-carpet-worthy gowns favored by Julia Roberts and Ashley Judd; if you're "serious about something fabulous", this is your go-to spot, but "have lots of $$$ to spend."

NEW Valley
- | - | - | E

LES | 48 Orchard St. (bet. Grand & Hester Sts.) | B/D to Grand St. | 212-274-8984 | www.valleynyc.com

A little bit of California makes its way to this large LES store, where West Coast sisters Nina and Julia Werman bring together a smart mix of LA-based lines like Mike + Chris, Sweet Tater and Borne displayed alongside clog boots and moccasins; the spirit of the San Fernando Valley lives in the woody environment that includes a lounge area and a spa for manicures and Brazilian wax treatments – so shoppers can look slick as they slip into the hip clothes.

☑ Van Cleef & Arpels 🗷
29 | 28 | 28 | VE

E 50s | 744 Fifth Ave. (57th St.) | N/R/W to 5th Ave./59th St. | 212-644-9500 | www.vancleef.com

"Exquisite" "drool jewelry" for "people made of money" sums up this estimable French firm, right next to Bergdorf's, whose celebrated clientele has ranged from The Duchess of Windsor (who suggested the zipper necklace that continues today) to Catherine Zeta-Jones; "truly classical beauties" here include the signature Alhambra quatrefoil (clover) necklace and "gorgeous", invisibly set floral gemstone pieces updated from their '20s and '30s origins; while a few sniff "snooty", most fans praise the "accommodating service"; N.B. a recent centennial face-lift that adds an art deco chandelier and fireplace to the stunning space may outdate the above Display score.

Vanessa Noel 🗷
- | - | - | VE

E 60s | 158 E. 64th St. (Lexington Ave.) | 6 to 68th St. | 212-906-0054
Celebs like Gwyneth Paltrow and Katie Couric take on the town in "trendy, but not way out" handmade-in-Italy pumps, sandals and

slingbacks from this designer's couture line, while mere mortals fall for the more affordable collection and brides scoop up "particularly good wedding shoes" at this East 60s townhouse; as you slip into "sexy" styles at the store, take note: your seat may match your feet, as Noel oftentimes uses the same fabrics for both.

Varda ▽ 27 | 21 | 21 | E
E 60s | 786 Madison Ave. (67th St.) | 6 to 68th St. | 212-472-7552
SoHo | 147 Spring St. (bet. W. B'way & Wooster St.) | C/E to Spring St. | 212-941-4990
W 70s | 2080 Broadway (71st St.) | 1/2/3 to 72nd St. | 212-873-6910 ◗
www.vardashoes.com

"These shoes are a treat" for the feet confirm fans who cool their heels at this his-and-hers trio-about-town, a veritable "savior" stocked with "comfortable and long-lasting" footwear that "never goes out of style"; for the ladies, "perfect boots", pointy pumps, ankle-strap sandals, and for the guys, luxe loafers, wing tips and hand-stitched moccasins, all "flattering", and, of course, "well-made" in Italy.

Variazioni 17 | 18 | 15 | E
Flatiron | 156 Fifth Ave. (20th St.) | N/R/W to 23rd St. | 212-627-4444 ◗
W 80s | 2389 Broadway (bet. 87th & 88th Sts.) | 1 to 86th St. | 212-595-1760 ◗
W 80s | 2395 Broadway (88th St.) | 1 to 86th St. | 212-595-8800

Variazioni is the spice of life at this trio of women's boutiques, boasting a "quirky mix" of "NYC hip" finds, including "perfect" denim, plus cashmere and shearling galore; "trendy, yet timeless" "pretty things" "abound", in fact, "you just may find a gem" assert admirers who also single out the "end-of-season blow-out sales" and confide that while the staff seems "pushy", they "know what they're talking about."

VeKa Bridal Couture – | – | – | E
NoLita | 284 Mulberry St. (bet. Houston & Prince Sts.) | 6 to Bleecker St. | 212-925-9044 | www.vekacc.com

"Modern" bridalwear that flies in the face of convention is the mainstay of this NoLita nuptials nook that showcases "excellent dresses by a select" handful of designers in a spare space done up with antique chandeliers; while these fanciful, neo-couture designs court romance, contemporary simplicity, from architectural lines to accents like waist-clinching obis, is also key to the sexy, edgy "impressive" ensembles.

Venture 22 | 16 | 16 | M
E 80s | 1156 Madison Ave. (bet. 85th & 86th Sts.) | 4/5/6 to 86th St. | 212-288-7235 | 888-388-2727

Upper East Siders venture that this long-standing stationer is a "handy" and "practical" "all-rounder" with everything from "Crane's to stickers for the kids", writing instruments, invitations, art supplies and leather goods from the likes of Longchamp; but they also call the service "unhelpful" and the store "a bit unkempt."

Vera Wang Bridal Salon ⊠ 27 | 25 | 22 | VE
E 70s | 991 Madison Ave. (77th St.) | 6 to 77th St. | 212-628-3400 | www.verawang.com

"Dreamy", with a "royal feel", Vera Wang's Madison Avenue salon (appointments preferred) is a matrimonial "must" if your "budget is on the large side"; the "dresses are divine" (you won't "look like a high school homecoming float"), the "lighting flattering" and the "dressing rooms larger than most NYC bedrooms", plus the staff has "a keen sense of what flatters every figure", "guiding you through the world of lace and silhouettes"; even budget-minded to-bes sigh if you "try on the wonderful designs then buy" elsewhere, "you'll always have that day of splendor."

Vera Wang Maids on Madison 🌀
27 | 24 | 23 | E

E 70s | 980 Madison Ave., 3rd fl. (bet. 76th & 77th Sts.) | 6 to 77th St. | 212-628-9898 | www.verawang.com

"If you're going to be in a wedding", "make an appointment" at this "super-luxurious", "top-notch" Madison Avenue salon where the designer "strikes again", this time with a "wide array of colors and shapes to suit" everyone in your party; "despite Vera's reputation for being expensive", many of these "beautiful, classic dresses" "look so un-bridesmaidy they could be worn again", and what's more, the "impeccable service makes you feel like the only girl in the store!"

Vercesi Hardware
23 | 14 | 25 | I

Gramercy | 152 E. 23rd St. (bet. Lexington & 3rd Aves.) | 6 to 23rd St. | 212-475-1883 | www.vercesihardware.com

"Last of the great old-fashioned hardware stores" insist hammer-wielders about this "comprehensive", "independent" Gramercy "treasure" "crammed with good stuff" "where they greet you by name" and "practically come home to assist with a repair"; that "personal touch" means the staff "will find the exact nail you asked for, then explain why you need a bolt instead."

Verdura 🌀
▽ 28 | 28 | 27 | VE

E 50s | 745 Fifth Ave. (bet. 57th & 58th Sts.) | N/R/W to 5th Ave./59th St. | 212-758-3388 | www.verdura.com

Between the rich Fifth Avenue penthouse feel, the "witty and creative jewelry" and the service – "they treat every customer like royalty" – it feels as if "Fulco Verdura were still around", whipping up deliciously colorful, Byzantine-inspired Maltese-cross cuffs and pieces like the wrapped-heart brooch and diamond bow-tied peridot ear clips that exude "elegance"; wistful worshipers sigh "oh, to win the Lottery."

Veronique
26 | 23 | 21 | E

E 90s | 1321 Madison Ave. (93rd St.) | 6 to 96th St. | 212-831-7800 | 888-265-5848 | www.veroniquematernity.com

An oasis for pregnant women who "want to sport the latest" fashions, this Upper East Sider stocks a "great selection" of designer items like Chaiken cords, Diane von Furstenberg wrap dresses and Chip & Pepper jeans "so chic" you'd "hardly know they're maternity clothes"; though the prices are "high", it's the "best of the bunch."

Versace
26 | 28 | 25 | VE

E 50s | 647 Fifth Ave. (bet. 51st & 52nd Sts.) | E/V to 5th Ave./53rd St. | 212-317-0224 | www.versace.com

Exhibitionist fashionistas who are "tall, thin and have a big bank account" are in "heaven, heaven, heaven" browsing in the multistoried Fifth Avenue flagship where the selection of "sexy" silhouettes in colorful silks and prints is "pretty outrageous"; while "intimidating at first glance", "the salespeople are always happy to help" ("they treated my son like he was a Trump").

Verve ●

QUALITY	DISPLAY	SERVICE	COST
24	19	22	M

W 70s | 282 Columbus Ave. (bet. 73rd & 74th Sts.) | 1/2/3 to 72nd St. | 212-580-7150
W Vill | 338 Bleecker St. (bet. Christopher & W. 10th Sts.) | 1 to Christopher St./Sheridan Sq. | 212-675-6693
W Vill | 353 Bleecker St. (bet. Charles & W. 10th Sts.) | 1 to Christopher St./Sheridan Sq. | 212-691-6516

"Up-to-the-minute NYC girls" strut into these "continually restocked" "treasure troves" "overflowing" with "great goodies" and "always wind up leaving with some fabulous find"; "the 'V' in 'Verve' is for variety", as in "funky jewelry" and "luscious, unusual" accessories from "local and European designers" "you haven't heard about yet, but will" at a "refreshing range" of prices; P.S. the shoes at 338 Bleecker "are to die for."

Vespa Ⓜ

–	–	–	E

SoHo | 13 Crosby St. (bet. Grand & Howard Sts.) | 6/J/M/N/Q/R/W/Z to Canal St. | 212-226-4410 | www.vespasoho.com

"The coolest" of cool, Piaggio USA showcases its mod motor scooters in a rainbow of "snazzy" colors and styles at this sleek, Euro-chic transportation boutique on the edge of SoHo; kick your "hip" quotient into high gear with a classic LX or a limited-edition PX 150, replete with customized details, and if you really want to look *bellissimo* in transit, add an eye-catching helmet made by Italian craftsmen.

Via Bus Stop

–	–	–	VE

SoHo | 172 Mercer St. (Houston St.) | B/D/F/V to B'way/Lafayette St. | 212-343-8810

"You won't be needing a Metrocard to enter this block-long Japanese import, but a year's worth of bus fare might be helpful to afford the "beautiful things" in this cavernous SoHo shop; the "jaw-dropping lineup" includes a nicely edited mix of Alexander McQueen, Easton Pearson, Trosman and Viktor & Rolf, making it a "must for any fashionista", especially those who make it into the upper VIP lounge area.

Victoria's Secret ●

18	21	18	M

Garment Dist | 1328 Broadway (34th St.) | B/D/F/N/Q/R/V/W to 34th St./Herald Sq. | 212-356-8380 | 800-888-1500 | www.victoriassecret.com
Additional locations throughout the NY area

Yes, the "Starbucks of lingerie" is "definitely for the masses", but for "Victoria's addicts", this "must-visit" chain is like "dipping your hand into a cookie jar" and emerging with "whipped cream and a cherry on top"; scout the "perfectly ordered" displays for "slinky sleepwear", a "tantalizing array of undergarments" or "something racy for that special night" and "leave feeling sexy from just being inside"; but while some tout the "tag-team" staff that even makes men feel "comfortable", others insist that service is "over-solicitous."

Vilebrequin

27	25	22	E

E 80s | 1070 Madison Ave. (81st St.) | 6 to 77th St. | 212-650-0353
SoHo | 436 W. Broadway (Prince St.) | C/E to Spring St. | 212-431-0673
888-458-0051 | www.vilebrequin.com

Sentimentalists say there's "nothing cuter than seeing a father and son in matching" bathing trunks from this "adorable, French" swim-

| | QUALITY | DISPLAY | SERVICE | COST |

wear pair in SoHo and the East 80s; "if you have it to spend, it doesn't get any better" – the "colors are bright, the quality amazing" and ze "unique" look is very "St. Tropez meets East Hampton" with "tons of tropical prints that aren't cheesy or loud" to choose from.

Village Tannery ⬤
| | 21 | 15 | 19 | M |

NoHo | 7 Great Jones St. (Lafayette St.) | 6 to Bleecker St. | 212-979-0013
W Vill | 173 Bleecker St. (bet. MacDougal & Sullivan Sts.) | A/B/C/D/E/F/V to W. 4th St. | 212-673-5444
www.villagetannery.com

"If you need anything leather" to carry your essentials, canter over to this NoHo–West Village duo that's "been around forever"; the "low-key vibe suits the down-to-earth" feel of the "distinctive", "well-priced" artisan-made totes, backpacks, duffels, briefcases and handbags scattered about; P.S. "they can make any design you have in mind", plus you can catch a glimpse of the workshop at the Great Jones store.

V.I.M. ⊠ M
| | 14 | 11 | 11 | I |

Harlem | 2239 Third Ave. (bet. 121st & 122nd Sts.) | 4/5/6 to 125th St. | 212-369-5033
Additional locations throughout the NY area

"Breeze in and breeze out" of this sneaker- and jean-centric chain, which makes sure its V.I.M. (Very Important Merchandise) includes "a good, basic collection of everyday wear, with a bit of jazz added in" from "trendy" brands like Fubu and Puma, all at "cheap prices"; "leave pretentiousness at the door", and scout out the basement for "cool" kicks.

Vintage Collections ⊠
| | ▽ 20 | 19 | 17 | E |

E 70s | 147 E. 72nd St. (bet. Lexington & 3rd Aves.) | 6 to 77th St. | 212-717-7702 | www.vintagecollectionsnyc.com
Looking like the sunny front parlor of an UES brownstone (which it probably once was), with Oriental rug, bay window and parquet floors, this young boutique offers "authentic vintage finds" from the '50s –'80s, in labels old (Mr. Blackwell, Norman Norell), relatively new (Christian Lacroix, Dolce & Gabbana) and forever young (Chanel, Pucci); yes, the mostly dressy womenswear is pretty (and some pout "pretentiously") "pricey", but "you could discover treasures" – if not among the clothes, then in the Vuitton luggage, jewelry or "funky" accessories.

Vintage Thrift Shop ⬤
| | 22 | 21 | 22 | M |

Gramercy | 286 Third Ave. (bet. 22nd & 23rd Sts.) | 6 to 23rd St. | 212-871-0777
"Loaded with nostalgic items", this "cozy" thrift store near Gramercy Park is "great for the prop designer" (many shop here) "and those who long for another era"; they'll find it represented by the "mostly high-end merchandise", including "art deco armchairs", "shabby-chic" clothing, "good glassware", books and jewelry; usually the wares are "well presented", but it can be "messy", so maybe, some say, it's better if you "don't go (more for me)"; N.B. closed Saturdays.

Vinylmania ⬤◒⊠
| | – | – | – | M |

G Vill | 60 Carmine St. (bet. Bedford St. & 7th Ave. S.) | 1 to Houston St. | 212-924-7223
This haven for house lovers has vended vinyl in the Village to pro and aspiring DJs for nearly 30 years; it's still considered a reliable source

for the latest progressive dance tracks including R&B, hip-hop, trance, garage and acid jazz as well as classic club mixes and accessories in a space that is stuffed to the rafters; sure, it can be "ear-splittingly loud", but that doesn't deter raving maniacs.

⚡ Virgin Megastore ◑

23 | 21 | 15 | M

Union Sq | 52 E. 14th St. (B'way) | 4/5/6/L/N/Q/R/W to 14th St./ Union Sq. | 212-598-4666

W 40s | 1540 Broadway, level 2 (bet. 45th & 46th Sts.) | 1/2/3/7/N/Q/R/S/W to 42nd St./Times Sq. | 212-921-1020 www.virgin.com

Megastore virgins beware: the recently refurbed "multifloor" Times Square "mother ship" can be "a little dizzying", what with "really 21st-century" listening stations, a story-high video screen and "hordes" of tourists checking out the "impressive" offerings from CDs to DVDs to clothing; the Union Square outpost is "more civilized" with a "fabulous" selection of imports, and even if they're "not the cheapest", you're "almost guaranteed" to get satisfaction at these "temples of sound."

Vitra

- | - | - | VE

Meatpacking | 29 Ninth Ave. (bet. 13th & 14th Sts.) | A/C/E/L to 14th St./ 8th Ave. | 212-463-5750 | www.vitra.com

"A leader in modern furnishings" for the home and office, this "cool" Swiss-owned company with a Meatpacking District showroom has a "museumlike quality" that's "fitting, considering many of the pieces displayed *are* in a museum" and priced accordingly; two "dramatic" levels display designs from different eras and re-editions of '30s and '40s classics like George Nelson clocks and Jean Prouvé chairs.

Vivienne Tam

▽ 24 | 24 | 22 | E

SoHo | 99 Greene St. (bet. Prince & Spring Sts.) | N/R/W to Prince St. | 212-966-2398 | www.viviennetam.com

There's a "very cool vibe" emanating from the namesake designer's womenswear with "signature Asian flair" at this SoHo shop; though it's "a little on the dark side", "it's still nice to look through the merchandise", marveling at the "intricate" designs and "lush fabrics", especially the trademark printed velvets and stretch mesh tops; N.B. the boutique is slated to move to 40 Mercer Street in late spring 2007.

Vogel ⑤

- | - | - | VE

SoHo | 19 Howard St. (bet. B'way & Lafayette St.) | 6/J/M/N/Q/R/W/Z to Canal St. | 212-925-2460 | www.vogelboots.com

"Makes you want to go horseback riding" exclaims a certain stratum of society that gallops over to this SoHo "classic" that's been cherished for its handiwork since 1879 and chosen repeatedly to outfit the U.S. Olympic equestrian team; from the outside it may seem "fuddy-duddy"-ish, but inside it's a "high-end" stomping ground where sporting folk order custom-made, über-expensive English riding boots, jodhpur-style (short) booties and alligator belts.

NEW Von Dutch ⑤ Ⓜ

- | - | - | M

SoHo | 109 Spring St. (bet. Greene & Mercer Sts.) | 6 to Spring St. | 212-965-8794 | www.vondutch.com

Catering to California-casual car culturists (both real and wannabe), this LA-born brand has just opened a pit stop in SoHo, where guys and gals can fill up on tees, trucker hats, bomber sunglasses and other samples of highway chic; the dimly lit environs also contain a logo-crazed line of tops and jeans sold only at this outpost.

Walter Steiger 🖾

28 | 27 | 25 | VE

E 50s | 417 Park Ave. (55th St.) | E/V to Lexington Ave./53rd St. | 212-826-7171 | www.walter-steiger.com

"When you want the very best" his-and-hers footwear at Steigering prices, stride over to this designer's "luxurious" Park Avenue boutique and treat yourself to "beautiful, so well-made" shoes fashioned from "incredibly soft leather that tenderly hug your foot"; "love every minute of shopping here" sigh sybarites who extol the "excellent service" and can't help but fall for the "terrific styles", exotic skins and interesting details; N.B. check out the recently added line of women's handbags.

Warren Edwards 🖾

28 | 27 | 26 | VE

E 60s | 107 E. 60th St. (Park Ave.) | 4/5/6/F/N/R/W to 59th St./Lexington Ave. | 212-223-4374 | www.warrenedwards.com

The "true couture fan can create the exact shoes" of his or her "dreams" following a "personal consultation with Warren" himself or "salespeople that know their stuff" at this East 60s stomping ground where you can also gobble up "gorgeous", "terrific-looking" hand-made footwear from the bi-annual collections; sure, "prices are off the charts, but so are the designs and quality", and you get to shop alongside two fox terriers who scamper about, completing the Wasp tableau.

☑ Waterworks

28 | 28 | 21 | VE

E 50s | 225 E. 57th St. (bet. 2nd & 3rd Aves.) | 4/5/6/F/N/R/W to 59th St./Lexington Ave. | 212-371-9266 🖾
NEW **Flatiron** | 7 E. 20th St. (Park Ave. S.) | N/R/W to 23rd St. | 212-254-6025
SoHo | 469 Broome St. (Greene St.) | C/E to Spring St. | 212-966-0605
www.waterworks.com

"Elegant bath fittings for apartments and lofts alike" can be found at these "exquisite" SoHo and East 50s stores whose "marvelous presentation" of "excellent quality", "gorgeous bathroom tiles, sinks", faucets, fixtures and furnishings is "first class"; of course, the "self-important staff" and "stratospheric" prices "will bring the Waterworks to your eyes", even if you are buying "for that seven-figure fixer-upper"; N.B. there's now a new branch in the Flatiron District.

Watts on Smith 🅼

- | - | - | E

Carroll Gdns | 248 Smith St. (bet. Degraw & Douglass Sts.) | Brooklyn | F/G to Carroll St. | 718-596-2359 | www.wattsonsmith.com

Channeling the "relaxed style" of Carroll Gardens, this site is an unassuming but charming stop for all types of men's urban-wear; light-hearted, emergent designers like Trovata, Sacque Suit, Oliver Spencer and Modern Amusement are all packed into one modern room alongside established lines like Wrangler and Vans.

Wedding Library ●🖾🅼

25 | 21 | 21 | E

E 70s | 43 E. 78th St. (bet. Madison & Park Aves.) | 6 to 77th St. | 212-327-0100 | www.theweddinglibrary.com

"An oasis for stressed-out brides" and "anything wedding"-related (except the gown) is "all packed into one beautiful brownstone" in the

East 70s; multitaskers maintain it's "great for everything from planning your city" nuptials "to buying trinkets" and "cute accessories" for the wedding party, plus there's a "good selection of bridesmaid's dresses"; the icing on the cake: the staff is "nothing but lovely."

Wedding Things

`20` `22` `19` `E`

E 60s | 1039 Third Ave. (bet. 61st & 62nd Sts.) | 4/5/6/F/N/R/W to 59th St./Lexington Ave. | 212-308-4680 | www.weddingthings.com
It's "fun to browse" at this "cute little" white-and-periwinkle East 60s wedding wunderkind, a Vancouver offshoot that sells nuptials essentials (but no gowns), along with "adorable baby items"; choose from cards and invitations from Crane's and Vera Wang, plus big-day basics like cake knives, photo albums and ring pillows; still, a handful huff it's "overpriced", lamenting there's "not much in this itty-bitty store."

☒ Wempe ☒

`29` `27` `26` `VE`

E 50s | 700 Fifth Ave. (55th St.) | E/V to 5th Ave./53rd St. | 212-397-9000 | 800-513-1131 | www.wempe.com
This recently expanded, European-style emporium in Midtown gets high marks as "a museum" for an aristocratic array of some of "the best watches anywhere", "from the merely expensive to collectibles priced in the stratosphere"; touters tick off other pluses like "tip-top service" and "the best repair department in New York."

Wendy Mink

`-` `-` `-` `E`

G Vill | 10 Morton St. (bet. Bleecker St. & 7th Ave. S.) | 1 to Christopher St./Sheridan Sq. | 212-367-9137 | www.wendyminkjewelry.com
East meets West at the designer-owner's Greenwich Village namesake, a "wonderful example of a neighborhood store" with a stone's-throw-away studio where a team of 10 Tibetan women craft fine gold, silver and semiprecious stone jewelry; the collection includes chandelier earrings from gold filigree to quartz fountain styles, long tassel necklaces and vermeil chain-link ones, plus delicate charms representing faith, hope and charity.

NEW! WeSC ●

`-` `-` `-` `E`

SoHo | 282 Lafayette St. (bet. Houston & Prince Sts.) | B/D/F/V to B'way/Lafayette St. | 212-925-9372 | www.wesc.com
Even if you don't quite get the meaning of the insiderish acronym that stands for We Are the Superlative Conspiracy, you're sure to grasp the style inherent in the skateboarder- and snowboard-inspired attire for guys and gals at this huge Lafayette Street newcomer from the globally expanding Swedish company; the airy, wood-paneled setting is just as sleek as the hoodies, vests, cardigans and premium denim all displayed on leather tabletops.

West Elm

`17` `23` `18` `M`

Chelsea | 112 W. 18th St. (bet. 6th & 7th Aves.) | 1 to 18th St. | 212-929-4464 ●
Dumbo | 75 Front St. (Main St.) | Brooklyn | F to York St. | 718-875-7757 866-937-8356 | www.westelm.com
A "simple" but "sophisticated" "urban vibe" permeates these Williams Sonoma–owned stores in Chelsea and Dumbo with "appealingly displayed", "affordable" furniture and "trendy" accessories like lamps and pillows in offbeat colors that are geared to "young New

| | QUALITY | DISPLAY | SERVICE | COST |

York professionals"; but a rising chorus of skeptics suggests "you get what you pay for", warning "what looks glam in the catalog" is actually "hit-or-miss" in real life in the "quality" department.

West Side Kids
24 | 20 | 20 | M

W 80s | 498 Amsterdam Ave. (84th St.) | 1 to 86th St. | 212-496-7282
Shoppers in search of "a special something for a special little person" swing by this "wonderful" West 80s "mom-and-pop" "independent" shop, always well stocked with a "fantastic" selection of toys "for all ages" from top brands like Lego and Playmobil; procrastinators in need of a present pronto can count on the "excellent" staff to conjure up the "perfect" gift and "wrap it too" in "10 minutes" flat.

Wet Seal ●
10 | 13 | 11 | I

Garment Dist | Manhattan Mall | 901 Sixth Ave. (bet. 32nd & 33rd Sts.) | B/D/F/N/Q/R/V/W to 34th St./Herald Sq. | 212-216-0622 | www.wetseal.com
The "racks and racks of inexpensive, trendy clothes" – going-out tops, flirty skirts and such, plus funky accessories – at this cheapie chain draw "teenyboppers" in droves to this Midtown mall address; the of-the-moment offerings are perhaps "not the best quality", but then most buyers are "only going to throw them out" after a few wearings anyway.

What Comes Around Goes Around ●
▽ 26 | 22 | 18 | E

SoHo | 351 W. Broadway (bet. Broome & Grand Sts.) | A/C/E to Canal St. | 212-343-9303 | www.nyvintage.com
. . . "And you hope it comes to you" declare devotees of this SoHo shop that sells a century's worth (1880–1980) of used and recon-structed clothing for men, women and children; after 13 years, it's "still great for cowboy stuff" including boots and fringed shirts, plus vintage Levis from the legendary denim bar, but a few feel it's "not as good" in the newer women's designer salon and deem prices "ridiculous" – unless "you have the disposable income to buy used rock T-shirts at 12 times the original" cost.

Z Whiskers ●
27 | 18 | 25 | M

E Vill | 235 E. Ninth St. (bet. 2nd & 3rd Aves.) | 6 to Astor Pl. | 212-979-2532 | 800-944-7537 | www.1800whiskers.com
It's "worth the trip to the East Village" to shop at the "Whole Foods for four-legged kids", where the staff "advocates holistic pet care"; you'll also find "lots of toys, treats and homeopathic remedies" "packed in a small space", and if the "preachy nature of the place" gives paws to some, more maintain "they know their stuff" – and the "price is right."

NEW White House Black Market ●
– | – | – | M

Flatiron | 136 Fifth Ave. (19th St.) | 4/5/6/L/N/Q/R/W to 14th St./ Union Sq. | 212-741-8685 | www.whiteandblack.com
Yes, it's taken years for this retail chain to land in NYC, but now fans of the classic womenswear that is true to its name (ahem, everything is in black and white) have 3,000-plus sq.-ft of easy and elegant tops, suits, eveningwear and jeans (ok, there's some indigo too) to choose from; within the well-appointed Flatiron District interior, a pseudo-Victorian ambiance reigns: crystal chandelier, a cozy fireplace, silk-curtained dressing rooms and a few antique seats for male companions to wait patiently on.

	QUALITY	DISPLAY	SERVICE	COST

White on White 🆉
Murray Hill | New York Design Center Bldg. | 200 Lexington Ave. (32nd St.) | 6 to 33rd St. | 212-213-0393 | www.whiteonwhiteny.com

| – | – | – | VE |

"Everything is so feminine" at this "inviting" home-furnishings shop now in Murray Hill; it's a showcase for classic Swedish style like reproduction and antique Gustavian pieces, embroidered textiles, china, bedding and baby items mostly – as the name states – in various shades of white; all is serene and "pristine" "until you look at the prices."

Whitney Museum Store Ⓜ
E 70s | 945 Madison Ave. (75th St.) | 6 to 77th St. | 212-570-3614 | www.whitney.org

| 21 | 17 | 16 | M |

Whether you browse the "great book selection" on the ground floor or the restaurant-adjacent shop below, the offerings are of "good quality" at this "venerable" UES American art museum; fans find "creative gifts" including housewares and toys for "every taste", but the blasé "yawn", bemoaning the "limited" merchandise and "crowded" conditions.

William Barthman
Financial Dist | 176 Broadway (bet. John St. & Maiden Ln.) | 2/3/4/5/A/C/J/M/Z to Fulton St./B'way/Nassau | 212-732-0890 🆉
Gravesend | 1118 Kings Hwy. (Coney Island Ave.) | Brooklyn | N to Kings Hwy. | 718-375-1818
800-727-9725 | www.williambarthman.com

| ▽ 26 | 23 | 24 | E |

Since 1884, this traditional Financial District and Gravesend gift establishment has offered a "beautiful selection" of the "best" brands; baubles from Bulgari and David Yurman, Lalique crystal, Lladró porcelains, watches and Montblanc pens; admirers also applaud "exceptional" service "that goes the extra mile", including "excellent repairs."

🆉 Williams-Sonoma
Chelsea | 110 Seventh Ave. (bet. 16th & 17th Sts.) | 1 to 18th St. | 212-633-2203 ●
E 50s | 121 E. 59th St. (Lexington Ave.) | 4/5/6/F/N/R/W to 59th St./Lexington Ave. | 917-369-1131 ●
E 80s | 1175 Madison Ave. (86th St.) | 4/5/6 to 86th St. | 212-289-6832
W 50s | The Shops at Columbus Circle, Time Warner Ctr. | 10 Columbus Circle, ground fl. (bet. 58th & 60th Sts.) | 1/A/B/C/D to 59th St./Columbus Circle | 212-823-9750 ●
800-541-2233 | www.williams-sonoma.com

| 26 | 26 | 22 | E |

With "foodie eye candy" everywhere, this "classic cook's paradise" and national chain "has it all", "from blenders to bread makers", copper and stainless-steel pots and pans, linens and accessories, gourmet oils, infusions and "I-didn't-know-I-needed-that gadgets"; "pristine" layouts and a "friendly" staff also make it "great" for "housewarming and wedding gifts" – just note that "the products somehow find their way into your basket while your money finds its way out of your wallet."

William-Wayne & Co.
E 60s | 846-850 Lexington Ave. (bet. 64th & 65th Sts.) | 6 to 68th St. | 212-737-8934 🆉
G Vill | 40 University Pl. (9th St.) | N/R/W to 8th St. | 212-533-4711
800-318-3435 | www.william-wayne.com

| ▽ 26 | 22 | 22 | M |

"If you need something" "lovely" "for your home" or for a gift, "you'll find it here" at these Greenwich Village and Upper East Side shops stocked with tasteful tableware, mirrors, linens and other accessories "chosen with a discerning eye"; devotees declare the "selection" "great", although Wasp-weary wags lament the "Muffy/Buffy"-style merch, particularly the proliferation of the signature "monkey-themed products."

Willoughby's

20	15	16	M

Garment Dist | 298 Fifth Ave. (31st St.) | N/R/W to 28th St. | 212-564-1600 | 800-378-1898 | www.willoughbys.com

More than a century old (though only three years in its current location), this "great camera store" in the Garment District is still a "standard for photographers", offering some of the "best discounts in the city", especially if you "aren't afraid to bargain"; the inventory is "spread out and well presented", but some savvy sorts say "be careful" of certain "slick salesmen looking for a quick sale."

Wink ●

21	21	21	E

SoHo | 155 Spring St. (bet. W. B'way & Wooster St.) | C/E to Spring St. | 212-334-3646

W 60s | 188 Columbus Ave. (bet. 68th & 69th Sts.) | 1 to 66th St./Lincoln Ctr. | 212-877-7727
www.winknyc.com

"Always on-trend", this "cute" West 60s–SoHo twosome stocks so many "of-the-moment accessories" "you cannot walk in without buying something", be it "cool, trendy" earrings from Kipepeo, skimmers from Seychelles, slouch boots from Fornarina, handbags from Moni Moni or "unique finds" like ILI's leather mittens; in the wink of an eye, the "friendly staff" including the owner, former model Ilse Werther, can help you "pull together" a "gorgeous" look.

Wolford

28	22	22	VE

E 50s | 619 Madison Ave. (bet. 58th & 59th Sts.) | 4/5/6/F/N/R/W to 59th St./Lexington Ave. | 212-688-4850 ⑤

E 70s | 996 Madison Ave. (bet. 77th & 78th Sts.) | 6 to 77th St. | 212-327-1000 ⑤

SoHo | 122 Greene St. (Prince St.) | N/R/W to Prince St. | 212-343-0808
800-965-3673 | www.wolford.com

"Legends are made" of stockings this "superb" sigh "happy girlfriends" and smitten socialites who take a "second mortgage" to buy the "latest styles" of this Austrian company's "unique", "superb quality" "leg coverings", "sexy" bodysuits and underthings, at this Uptown-Downtown trio; the luxe hosiery "costs a pretty penny" but it's "worth the price" – "at least" my gams "think so" – plus it "lasts and lasts!"; N.B. check out the new limited-edition designer lines from Zac Posen and Kenzo.

Wonk

–	–	–	E

Dumbo | 68 Jay St. (bet. Front & Water Sts.) | Brooklyn | F to York St. | 718-596-8026

NEW **Williamsburg** | 160A N. Fourth St. (bet. Bedford & Driggs Aves.) | Brooklyn | L to Bedford Ave. | 718-218-7750 ●
www.wonknyc.com

Contemporary furniture in wood or lacquer finishes – from dining tables to seating, shelving, desks, cabinets and dressers – is the focus at this Brooklyn duo in Dumbo and Williamsburg; space-starved surveyors like the fact that the emphasis is on pieces with storage possibilities, like the popular Mod Quad coffee table with concealed cubbies.

Wool Gathering

▽ **24** | **21** | **20** | **E**

E 80s | 318 E. 84th St. (bet. 1st & 2nd Aves.) | 4/5/6 to 86th St. | 212-734-4747 | www.thewoolgathering.com

If you "yearn for wonderful yarns" but "aren't sure what you want or need" drop in for a consultation at this "quiet", "hospitable" shop "tucked away" in a vintage East 80s building, where the "very friendly" owner will provide "lots of help with a project"; given the "great selection" of materials plus the option of custom ordering, it's "terrific for experts" too; N.B. there are also lessons for kids.

Woolworks Needlepoint 🖼🔁

24 | **19** | **19** | **E**

E 70s | 1045 Lexington Ave., 2nd fl. (bet. 74th & 75th Sts.) | 6 to 77th St. | 212-861-8700

"Everything you need" for "serious" "projects" can be found at this "teensy", long-standing second-floor needlepoint nook on the Upper East Side, a "wonderful" and "convenient" one-stop shop for "fine yarns", needles and patterns that also offers private tutorials and finishing services; while the store stocks a variety of floral, animal and geometric designs, the staff is also happy to customize an original motif or translate a pre-made drawing into a needlepoint canvas.

World of Disney ●

22 | **25** | **20** | **E**

E 50s | 711 Fifth Ave. (55th St.) | E/V to 5th Ave./53rd St. | 212-702-0702 | www.worldofdisney.com

"Great for a Disney fix when neither California nor Florida is in your immediate" travel plans, this "multifloored" funland brings all of the "magic" of Walt's "theme park" to Fifth Avenue, with its "eye-candy presentation" of character "stuff" and "special" attractions like meet-and-greets with "perky" Mickey and friends, a Mr. Potato Head station and Cinderella-hosted princess-themed parties; everything's "ridiculously overpriced" but when it comes to "bringing a smile to even a curmudgeon's face" "ya gotta love" the "mouse house."

World of Golf, The

24 | **18** | **20** | **E**

E 40s | 147 E. 47th St. (bet. Lexington & 3rd Aves.) | 6 to 51st St. | 212-755-9398

NEW **Financial Dist** | 74 Broad St. (bet. Beaver & Stone Sts.) | 4/5 to Bowling Green | 212-385-1246 🖼
800-499-7491 | www.theworldofgolf.com

A "golf fanatic's" hole-in-one "heaven" housing a "great range" of the latest putters and irons for the links (Callaway, Cobra, MacGregor) as well as "nice" clothes for the clubhouse confirm fans of this East 40s flagship and its new Financial District offshoot; lower your handicap at either location with staff pros that analyze your swing – "they know their stuff" and "almost always have what you need."

☒ Yarn Co., The 🖼Ⓜ

26 | **18** | **14** | **E**

W 80s | 2274 Broadway, 2nd fl. (bet. 81st & 82nd Sts.) | 1 to 79th St. | 212-787-7878 | 888-927-6261 | www.theyarnco.com

"It's hip to knit" at this "bustling" second-floor West 80s "hideaway" run by a pair of best friends known for their trendy *Yarn Girls* pattern books; fans love to "stitch and schmooze" amid an "inspiring" range of "high-end" materials, but foes frown at "cramped" conditions, "top-dollar" pricing and a "snooty", "cliquish" attitude toward newcomers ("you want to stab someone with a needle"); P.S. it "turns into a mosh pit on Saturdays."

Yarn Connection, The ⑤

22	15	22	M

Murray Hill | 218 Madison Ave. (bet. 36th & 37th Sts.) | 6 to 33rd St. | 212-684-5099 | www.theyarnconnection.com

Take "a quick walk from Grand Central" to this Murray Hill "knitters' haven" showcasing a "diverse" selection of "top-brand yarns" at "not-bad" prices (with "excellent" deals in the "great sale section"); staffers are "knowledgeable" and "patient" to boot, but needleworkers note "if you've got claustrophobia, go elsewhere" – the "tiny" shop feels "cluttered" even with its high ceilings and large front window.

Yarn Tree, The ❶

-	-	-	M

Williamsburg | 347 Bedford Ave. (3rd St.) | Brooklyn | J/M/Z to Marcy Ave. | 718-384-8030 | www.theyarntree.com

Would-be artists and artisans eager not only to knit and crochet but also to felt, dye, spin and weave wend their way to this "warm" natural-fiber yarn boutique near the Williamsburg Bridge, where shop owner and "true fiber expert" Linda LaBelle teaches classes (limited to six people) that are "thorough" and "well worth the money"; N.B. late hours (till 10 PM Monday–Thursday) allow for after-work visits.

Yellow Door

-	-	-	E

NoLita | 4 Prince St. (bet. Bowery & Elizabeth St.) | N/R/W to Prince St. | 212-274-0020 Ⓜ

Midwood | 1308 Ave. M (bet. 13th & 14th Sts.) | Brooklyn | Q to Ave. M | 718-998-7382

www.theyellowdoor.com

These "go-to" "giftware oases" in NoLita and Midwood offer an eclectic mix of "expensive and inexpensive" jewelry, from cubic zirconia studs to select gems from La Nouvelle Bague, Penny Preville and SeidenGang, along with home furnishings from a surefire lineup of resources like Baccarat.

Yellow Rat Bastard ❶

16	17	13	M

SoHo | 478 Broadway (bet. Broome & Grand Sts.) | 6/J/M/N/Q/R/W/Z to Canal St. | 212-334-2150

NEW **Elmhurst** | Queens Ctr. | 90-15 Queens Blvd. (bet. 57th & 59th Aves.) | Queens | G/R/V to Grand Ave./Newtown | 718-393-2030

877-935-5728 | www.yellowratbastard.com

"If you're looking for trend and funk, you'll find it at the Bastard", SoHo's "common stomping ground" for "urban guerrillas", "punk" skaters, "hip-hoppers" and "suburban" tweens and teens alike; "you know what you're getting" at this "underground staple": "witty T-shirts" and "cool" threads from Ecko, Penguin and Vans, all piled high inside a "graffiti"-strewn, warehouselike space with music pumping "so loud you have to shout over it"; N.B. there's a younger brother Rat in Elmhurst.

Yigal Azrouel

-	-	-	VE

Meatpacking | 408 W. 14th St. (bet. 9th Ave. & Washington St.) | A/C/E/L to 14th St./8th Ave. | 212-929-7525 | www.yigal-azrouel.com

"Don't let the secret out" that within the "loungey atmosphere" of this Meatpacking District shop, with its crystal chandelier and brick walls, are some of the "best [evening] dresses in the city" – an assortment of "ultrasexy and feminine showstoppers", favored by the likes of Natalie Portman and Cynthia Nixon; whether you prefer a sleek suit or a slinky gown, the "fit is amazing."

NEW Ylli ●

– | – | – | E

Williamsburg | 482 Driggs Ave. (N. 10th St.) | Brooklyn | L to Bedford Ave. | 718-302-3555 | www.yllibklyn.com

In a Williamsburg loft that's more SoHo than boho, with gleaming wood floors, exposed beams and space between the racks, this show-case for rising designers maintains a youthful aesthetic pumped up with denim aplenty (labels like Sass & Bide and The Proportion of Blu) and Brooklyn-inspired tees by Barking Irons; men find sharp plaid shirts and jackets, while women choose from a wider selection ranging from neck-tied silk dresses to hot hoodies.

Yohji Yamamoto

27 | 27 | 24 | VE

SoHo | 103 Grand St. (Mercer St.) | C/E to Spring St. | 212-966-9066 | www.yohjiyamamoto.co.jp

"What the thinking artist/architect wears" can be found at this artwork-filled SoHo standby featuring the collections of Japanese designer Yohji Yamamoto, aka "a god" to "discerning" types for his "impeccable tailor-ing of genius fabrics"; the clothes can be "costume-y" ("admirable and unwearable" some say), "but the more sober" architectural pieces be-come "wardrobe staples" if you're "unself-conscious – and have a fat wallet", plus you'll find "great sneakers" from the Y-3 line, an Adidas collaboration; N.B. plans are underway to open a shop on Gansevoort Street in spring 2007.

NEW Yoko Devereaux Ⓜ

– | – | – | E

Williamsburg | 338 Broadway (bet. Keap & Rodney Sts.) | Brooklyn | J/M/Z to Marcy Ave. | 718-302-1450 | www.yokod.com

You'll never meet Yoko at this Williamsburg haunt – it's a made-up name, after all – but if you're an urbane guy or even a "tailored hip-ster", sooner or later you'll become familiar with this "alterna-chic menswear" line, the brainchild of founder-designer Andy Salzer; hunt down this stark sub-rosa shop with an off-kilter boys' club feel, then stake your claim on cool wardrobe essentials like fleece cardigans, houndstooth pants and one-button blazers, plus collaborative limited-editions from names like In God We Trust.

Yoya

▽ 27 | 28 | 19 | VE

W Vill | 636 Hudson St. (bet. Horatio & Jane Sts.) | A/C/E/L to 14th St./8th Ave. | 646-336-6844

Yoya Mart

W Vill | 15 Gansevoort St. (Hudson St.) | A/C/E/L to 14th St./8th Ave. | 212-242-5511

www.yoyashop.com

"Virtual museums for children's clothing", this dynamic duo, located just blocks apart on the West Village/Meatpacking District border, has shoppers spellbound over its "stunningly original" selection of "chichi" fashions "almost too pretty to touch"; the huge Hudson Street shop is "*the* place to find great, new lines" like Lucy Sykes and imps & elfs, plus you'll find the latest gotta-have-it gadgets and Montessori toys at its sibling nearby.

Yves Delorme 🗷
28 | 27 | 23 | E

E 70s | 985 Madison Ave. (bet. 76th & 77th Sts.) | 6 to 77th St. |
212-439-5701 | www.yvesdelorme.com

Luxe-linen lovers run for covers in this stateside venture from the venerable Paris-based company nestled next to the Carlyle Hotel; white cabinets and a marble floor set the stage for "beautiful" goods, including Egyptian cotton sheets in rich colors or "feminine" florals reminiscent of the French countryside and jacquard-woven tablecloths, as well as caned Louis XVI headboards, mahogany sleighbeds and silk pillows.

Yves Saint Laurent Rive Gauche
26 | 26 | 24 | VE

E 50s | 3 E. 57th St. (bet. 5th & Madison Aves.) | N/R/W to 5th Ave./
59th St. | 212-980-2970
E 70s | 855 Madison Ave. (bet. 70th & 71st Sts.) | 6 to 68th St. |
212-988-3821 🗷
www.ysl.com

"There's nothing gauche" about this venerable French label, whose "elegant", "impeccably tailored" men's and women's clothes in "gorgeous fabrics" are "well worth the price if it fits your budget"; whether in the East 50s or the East 70s, the "friendlier-than-you'd-think" staff "takes care of you as if you're a celebrity", making sure you find the Mombasa bag, waist-cinching suit or platform shoes "that you want more than one should want an article of clothing."

Ⓩ Zabar's ⬤
26 | 17 | 17 | M

W 80s | 2245 Broadway (80th St.) | 1 to 79th St. | 212-787-2000 |
800-697-6301 | www.zabars.com

"If you can get past the foodies downstairs" at this "legendary" gourmet store and "mainstay of the Upper West Side", you'll be privy to "the best-known secret in New York", which is that "the best selection" of "the cheapest cookware, gadgets", appliances and utensils is found on its mezzanine; it can be "crowded", "cramped" and "chaotic" and "if your feelings get hurt easily don't ask for help", but beaming bargain-hunters shrug that just "adds to the NYC charm" of the experience.

Zachary's Smile ◖
▽ 24 | 24 | 19 | M

G Vill | 9 Greenwich Ave. (6th Ave.) | 1 to Christopher St./Sheridan Sq. |
212-924-0604
NoHo | 317 Lafayette St. (bet. Bleecker & Houston Sts.) | 6 to Bleecker St. |
212-965-8248
www.zacharyssmile.com

Surveyors smile upon this colorful Villager and its newer NoHo sibling, which offer "oodles of cool vintage" garments for both he and she; spanning the 1940s–'80s, the diverse stock includes famed labels (peruse the Puccis to the rear), "affordable dresses", "fresh" "original pieces" made from old fabrics and "great lingerie and shoes", including cowboy boots; small wonder actresses Sarah Jessica Parker and Gretchen Mol have been spotted among the racks.

Zales Jewelers ⬤
12 | 14 | 15 | M

Garment Dist | 142 W. 34th St. (bet. B'way & 7th Ave.) | 1/2/3/A/C/E to
34th St./Penn Station | 646-473-0727 | 800-311-5393 | www.zales.com
Additional locations throughout the NY area

With more than 2,300 outposts, "the fast food of jewelry" carries "a lot of inexpensive" pieces from cubic zirconia to the real (diamond) thing, but most surveyors sniff at the chain's "tawdry" quality, "tacky" styles and "pushy salespeople" "who act like your favorite long-lost cousin."

Zara ⬤ | 18 | 19 | 15 | M |

E 50s | 689 Fifth Ave. (54th St.) | E/V to 5th Ave./53rd St. | 212-371-2555
E 50s | 750 Lexington Ave. (59th St.) | 4/5/6/F/N/R/W to 59th St./Lexington Ave. | 212-754-1120
Flatiron | 101 Fifth Ave. (bet. 17th & 18th Sts.) | 4/5/6/L/N/Q/R/W to 14th St./Union Sq. | 212-741-0555
Garment Dist | 39 W. 34th St. (bet. B'way & 5th Ave.) | B/D/F/N/Q/R/V/W to 34th St./Herald Sq. | 212-868-6551
SoHo | 580 Broadway (bet. Houston & Prince Sts.) | N/R/W to Prince St. | 212-343-1725
www.zara.com

Everyone's "favorite" "chain from Spain", this men's and women's standby offers "reasonable", "right-on-trend" styles for "young professionals on a budget"; the organization by color "saves a lot of time" when browsing collections that most consider "well made for the price" and "terrific for the long-legged' gal, if "not a woman with hips."

Zarin Fabrics and Home Furnishings | 23 | 13 | 16 | M |

LES | 318 Grand St. (bet. Allen & Orchard Sts.) | F/J/M/Z to Delancey/Essex Sts. | 212-925-6112 | www.harryzarin.com

Decorators, designers and DIYers are wild about Harry because this 71-year-old discount "fabric emporium" on the Lower East Side "almost always has what you need" (including "wondrous" wares from "many different fashion houses") at "great prices"; browsers do best "when not looking for something specific" amid the vast environs and "huge selection", while those who get "overwhelmed" readily rely on "knowledgeable" staffers; N.B. it now sells its own line of furniture.

Z'Baby Company | 24 | 21 | 19 | E |

E 70s | 996 Lexington Ave. (72nd St.) | 6 to 68th St. | 212-472-2229
W 70s | 100 W. 72nd St. (Columbus Ave.) | 1/2/3/B/C to 72nd St. | 212-579-2229 ⬤
www.zbabycompany.com

"For superb baby presents" and "cute, cute, cute" "creative" European clothes for the "special" babies, tots and tweens "in your life", head over to these "trendy" East 70s–West 70s twins, "well laid-out" and solidly stocked with a "sophisticated" selection of wardrobe wows that are definitely "not the norm"; it's "a little on the pricey side" but there's always the "legendary sales" when bargain-hunters "clean up."

Z Chemists ⬤ | 25 | 20 | 20 | E |

W 50s | 40 W. 57th St. (bet. 5th & 6th Aves.) | F to 57th St. | 212-956-6000 | www.zchemists.com

Zitomer ⬤

E 70s | 969 Madison Ave. (bet. 75th & 76th Sts.) | 6 to 77th St. | 212-737-5560 | 888-219-2888 | www.zitomer.com

"Crowded and chaotic", this expensive Upper East Side über-drugstore (with a Midtown Z Chemists offshoot) "has a little bit of everything for everyone" from "the crème de la crème" of beauty products to perfumes and candles; in addition, there's Zittles for children's clothing and toys and a pet boutique called Z-Spot with an "almost scarily complete" collection of pampered puppy paraphernalia that includes pearl necklaces.

	QUALITY	DISPLAY	SERVICE	COST
	-	-	-	E

Zero/Maria Cornejo

NoLita | 225 Mott St. (bet. Prince & Spring Sts.) | 6 to Spring St. |
212-925-3849 ●
NEW **W Vill** | 807 Greenwich St. (Jane St.) | A/C/E/L to 14th St./8th Ave. |
212-620-0460 ⑤ Ⓜ
www.mariacornejo.com

Offering "a wonderful reprieve" from the often-frazzling "SoHo shopping experience" is this grottolike NoLita store/studio nearby and its lovely new West Village sibling showcasing the sensual styles of Chilean designer Maria Cornejo; her "simple, elegant looks" – bubble-hemmed dresses, cowl-neck tops, dramatic coats and draped Venus gowns – "push the design envelope without ripping it to shreds", a reason why loyal clients are said to include Sofia Coppola, Cindy Sherman and Marisa Tomei.

	-	-	-	E

NEW Zoë ●

Dumbo | 70 Washington St. (bet. Front & York Sts.) | Brooklyn | F to York St. | 718-237-4002 | www.shopzoeonline.com

This 3,400-sq.-ft. mucho-modern sleek sibling of the same-named Princeton, NJ, mother ship strides into Dumbo with derring-do, winning over fashionistas with its cultivated mix of high-end collections and contemporary essentials; shoppers make the rounds, perusing show-stopping pieces from Mayle, Matthew Williamson and Stella McCartney on circular wheeled racks, then moving on to covetables from James Perse, Jovovich Hawk and Marc by Marc Jacobs, plus 19 brands of denim, bags from Miu Miu and shoes from Hogan and Pedro Garcia.

	▽ 29	26	28	E

Zoomies

W Vill | 434 Hudson St. (bet. Leroy & Morton Sts.) | 1 to Houston St. |
212-462-4480 | www.zoomiesnyc.com

"Extremely pampered pets and owners" zoom in on this Village boutique offering "high style for Buster" in the form of apparel, bedding and accessories, some designed by the former fashion exec co-owner; "dogs love" the "fresh-baked", "gourmet" cookies and treats made by a French chef, and even if it's a *peu* "expensive", it's a "bonus that the staff truly aims to please."

INDEXES

LOCATION MAPS

Locations

Includes store names and merchandise type, where necessary. ⨂ indicates highest ratings, popularity and importance.

Manhattan

CHELSEA

(24th to 30th Sts., west of 5th; 14th to 24th Sts., west of 6th)

Alexandros | *Furs*

Angel St. Thrift Shop

Arcadia | *Cosmetics/Toiletries*

⨂ Balenciaga | *Designer*

Barking Zoo | *Pet Supplies*

Barneys CO-OP | *Men's & Women's Clothing*

Birnbaum & Bullock | *Bridal*

BoConcept | *Home*

Bowery Kitchen Supplies | *Major Appliances*

Brooklyn Industries | *Men's & Women's Clothing*

Burlington Coat | *Discount*

⨂ buybuy BABY

Camouflage | *Men's Clothing*

⨂ Carlyle Convertibles | *Home*

⨂ City Quilter | *Fabrics/Notions*

Comme des Garçons | *Designer*

Container Store | *Home*

Dave's Army Navy | *Men's Clothing*

DaVinci Art Supply

Door Store | *Home*

Ellen Christine | *Accessories*

Family Jewels | *Vintage*

Find Outlet | *Discount*

Fisch for the Hip | *Consignment*

Gerry's | *Men's & Women's Clothing*

Giraudon | *Shoes*

Habu Textiles

Here Comes Bridesmaid

Housing Works Thrift

Jazz Record Center

Jensen-Lewis | *Home*

Karim Rashid Shop | *Home*

Kleinfeld | *Bridal*

Knoll | *Home*

Kremer Pigments | *Art Supplies*

La Cafetière | *Home*

LaCrasia Gloves

Lightforms | *Lighting*

⨂ Loehmann's | *Discount*

Lucky Wang | *Children's*

Malin + Goetz | *Cosmetics/Toiletries*

Myoptics | *Eyewear*

New Mus./Contemp. Art

New York Golf

Noose | *Sex Shop*

Olde Good Things | *Home*

Parke & Ronen | *Men's Clothing*

NEW Pottery Barn Bed/Bath

⨂ Rubin Museum

Sabon | *Cosmetics/Toiletries*

Sacco | *Shoes*

S&W | *Discount*

Schneider's | *Children's*

Scuba Network | *Sporting Goods*

Shooz | *Shoes*

⨂ Tekserve | *Computers*

TSE | *Designer*

202 | *Designer*

Urban Angler | *Sporting Goods*

Urban Outfitters | *Men's & Women's Clothing*

Utrecht | *Art Supplies*

West Elm | *Home*

⨂ Williams-Sonoma | *Home*

CHINATOWN

(Canal to Pearl Sts., west of Bway)

Canal Hi-Fi | *Electronics*

⨂ Pearl Paint | *Art Supplies*

EAST 40S

Airline Stationery

⨂ Allen Edmonds | *Shoes*

American Girl Place | *Toys*

⨂ Ann Taylor Loft | *Women's Clothing*

Aveda | *Cosmetics/Toiletries*

Barami | *Women's Clothing*

Bloom | *Jewelry*

Botticelli | *Shoes*

⨂ Bridge Kitchenware

Z Brooks Brothers | *Men's & Women's Clothing*

Z Build-A-Bear | *Toys*

Caché | *Women's Clothing*

Caswell-Massey | *Cosmetics/ Toiletries*

Cellini | *Jewelry*

Charles Tyrwhitt | *Men's Clothing*

Children's Gen. Store | *Toys*

Clarks England | *Shoes*

Crabtree & Evelyn | *Cosmetics/ Toiletries*

Crouch & Fitzgerald | *Luggage*

DeNatale Jewelers

Denimaxx | *Men's & Women's Clothing*

Douglas Cosmetics

Erwin Pearl | *Jewelry*

Fila | *Activewear*

For Eyes | *Eyewear*

Fossil | *Watches*

Grand Central Racquet

Innovation Luggage

J.Crew | *Men's & Women's Clothing*

Johnston & Murphy | *Shoes*

Z Joon | *Stationery*

Jos. A. Bank | *Men's Clothing*

Joseph Edwards | *Watches*

J. Press | *Men's Clothing*

NEW K&G Fashion | *Discount*

Kavanagh's | *Consignment/Vintage*

Kenneth Cole NY | *Designer*

La Brea | *Gifts/Novelties*

Lacoste | *Men's & Women's Clothing*

Laila Rowe | *Accessories*

Links of London | *Jewelry*

Men's Wearhse. | *Men's Clothing*

Z Michael C. Fina | *Fine China/ Crystal*

Missha | *Cosmetics/Toiletries*

New York Look | *Women's Clothing*

New York Public Library

New York Transit Mus.

Nintendo World | *Toys*

Origins | *Cosmetics/Toiletries*

Orvis | *Activewear*

Paul Stuart | *Men's Clothing*

Pink Slip | *Hosiery/Lingerie*

RadioShack | *Electronics*

Ricky's | *Cosmetics/Toiletries*

Robert Marc | *Eyewear*

Sean John | *Designer*

Z Sephora | *Cosmetics/Toiletries*

Shirt Store | *Men's Clothing*

Solstice | *Eyewear*

Strawberry | *Women's Clothing*

Super Runners Shop

Swarovski | *Jewelry*

Swatch | *Watches*

Z TUMI | *Luggage*

UnitedColors/Benetton | *Men's & Women's Clothing*

World of Golf

EAST 50S

Abercrombie & Fitch | *Tween/Teen*

Agatha Paris | *Jewelry*

Alain Mikli | *Eyewear*

Z A La Vieille Russie | *Jewelry*

Alexandros | *Furs*

Z Allen Edmonds | *Shoes*

Amsale | *Bridal*

Anne Fontaine | *Designer*

Z Ann Sacks | *Tile*

Z Apple Store | *Electronics*

Z Artistic Tile

A. Testoni | *Shoes*

Aveda | *Cosmetics/Toiletries*

A/X Armani Exchange | *Men's & Women's Clothing*

Z Baccarat | *Home*

Bally | *Handbags*

Z Banana Republic | *Men's & Women's Clothing*

Z B&B Italia | *Home*

Barami | *Women's Clothing*

Bebe | *Women's Clothing*

Z Belgian Shoes

Z Bergdorf Goodman | *Dept. Store*

Z Bergdorf Men's | *Dept. Store*

Z Bernardaud | *Home*

Blanc de Chine | *Designer*

Z Bloomingdale's | *Dept. Store*

Bochic | *Jewelry*

Z Bottega Veneta | *Designer*

Botticelli | *Shoes*

Bric's | *Luggage*

- ☒ Brioni | *Designer*
- British Amer. Hse. | *Men's Clothing*
- ☒ Brooks Brothers | *Men's & Women's Clothing*
- ☒ Buccellati | *Home/Jewelry*
- Bulgari | *Jewelry*
- Burberry | *Designer*
- Camera Land
- ☒ Cartier | *Jewelry*
- Cassina USA | *Home*
- Cellini | *Jewelry*
- ☒ Chanel | *Designer*
- City Sports | *Sneakers*
- ☒ Coach | *Handbags*
- Cole Haan | *Shoes*
- Conran Shop | *Home*
- Container Store | *Home*
- Crabtree & Evelyn | *Cosmetics/ Toiletries*
- ☒ Crate & Barrel | *Home*
- Dana Buchman | *Designer*
- Davis & Warshow | *Bathroom Fixtures*
- DeBeers | *Jewelry*
- ☒ Dempsey & Carroll | *Stationery*
- Destination Maternity
- Dior Homme | *Designer*
- ☒ Dior New York | *Designer*
- Domenico Vacca | *Designer*
- Door Store | *Home*
- Dunhill | *Accessories*
- Eileen Fisher | *Women's Clothing*
- Einstein-Moomjy | *Home*
- Emporio Armani | *Designer*
- Enzo Angiolini | *Shoes*
- Eres | *Hosiery/Lingerie*
- ☒ Ermenegildo Zegna | *Designer*
- Escada | *Designer*
- Façonnable | *Men's & Women's Clothing*
- FAO Schwarz | *Toys*
- Fendi | *Designer*
- Florsheim Shoe
- ☒ Fogal/Switzerland | *Hosiery/ Lingerie*
- Fortunoff | *Home/Jewelry*
- Fratelli Rossetti | *Shoes*
- Furla | *Handbags*
- Furry Paws | *Pet Supplies*
- Gant | *Men's Clothing*
- Geox | *Shoes*
- NEW Golfsmith
- Gruen Optika | *Eyewear*
- Gucci | *Designer*
- Gym Source | *Sporting Goods*
- Hammacher Schlemmer | *Electronics*
- ☒ H&M | *Men's & Women's Clothing*
- ☒ Harry Winston | *Jewelry*
- Hastings Tile
- ☒ Henri Bendel | *Dept. Store*
- H. Herzfeld | *Men's Clothing*
- Hickey Freeman | *Men's Clothing*
- H.L. Purdy | *Eyewear*
- NEW Honora | *Jewelry*
- ☒ H. Stern | *Jewelry*
- H2O Plus | *Cosmetics/Toiletries*
- Hugo Boss | *Designer*
- Ideal Tile
- Il Makiage | *Cosmetics/Toiletries*
- Innovative Audio | *Electronics*
- Jacob & Co. | *Jewelry*
- James Robinson | *Jewelry/Home*
- Jay Kos | *Men's Clothing*
- Jil Sander | *Designer*
- Jimmy Choo | *Shoes*
- Johnston & Murphy | *Shoes*
- ☒ Joon | *Stationery*
- Jubilee | *Shoes*
- Kenneth Cole NY | *Designer*
- Kiton | *Designer*
- Kreiss Collection | *Home*
- Lacoste | *Men's & Women's Clothing*
- Lederer de Paris | *Handbags*
- Levi's Store | *Jeans*
- Linda Dresner | *Women's Clothing*
- Links of London | *Jewelry*
- Louis Vuitton | *Designer*
- Lowell/Edwards | *Electronics*
- ☒ MacKenzie-Childs | *Home*
- Mark Ingram Bridal
- Mason's Tennis Mart
- ☒ Maurice Villency | *Home*
- Mexx | *Men's & Women's Clothing*
- ☒ Mikimoto | *Jewelry*
- Molton Brown | *Cosmetics/Toiletries*

Montblanc | *Stationery*

🆕 MoonSoup | *Children's*

🆕 Mulberry | *Handbags*

NBA Store | *Activewear*

New Balance | *Sneakers*

Niketown NY | *Activewear/Sneakers*

Nine West | *Shoes*

🆕 Nokia | *Electronics*

☑ Oxxford Clothes | *Men's Clothing*

☑ Piaget | *Watches*

☑ Pierre Deux | *Home*

Poggenpohl U.S. | *Home*

🆕 Porsche Design | *Accessories*

Pottery Barn | *Home*

Prada | *Designer*

Pucci | *Designer*

RCS Experience | *Electronics*

Robert Marc | *Eyewear*

Sacco | *Shoes*

Safavieh | *Home*

☑ Saks Fifth Ave. | *Dept. Store*

☑ Salvatore Ferragamo | *Designer*

Sam Flax | *Art Supplies*

Scandinavian Sport

Scuba Network | *Sporting Goods*

☑ Scully & Scully | *Home*

Seaman Schepps | *Jewelry*

Sergio Rossi | *Shoes*

Sherle Wagner Int'l | *Bathroom Fixtures*

☑ Simon Pearce | *Home*

☑ Sony Style | *Electronics*

Sports Authority

☑ Spring Flowers | *Children's*

Stefano Ricci | *Designer*

☑ Stitches East | *Knitting/ Needlepoint*

☑ St. John | *Designer*

Stuart Weitzman | *Shoes*

Suarez | *Handbags*

🆕 Suite New York | *Home*

Swarovski | *Jewelry*

Syms | *Discount*

☑ Takashimaya | *Clothing/Home*

☑ Talbots | *Men's & Women's Clothing*

Talbots Kids/Babies

☑ T. Anthony | *Luggage*

Thomas Pink | *Men's Clothing*

☑ Tiffany & Co. | *Jewelry*

Tourneau | *Watches*

Tucker Robbins | *Home*

☑ TUMI | *Luggage*

☑ Turnbull & Asser | *Men's Clothing*

☑ Urban Archaeology | *Home*

Urban Outfitters | *Men's & Women's Clothing*

☑ Van Cleef & Arpels | *Jewelry*

Verdura | *Jewelry*

Versace | *Designer*

Walter Steiger | *Shoes*

☑ Waterworks | *Bathroom Fixtures*

☑ Wempe | *Watches*

☑ Williams-Sonoma | *Home*

Wolford | *Hosiery/Lingerie*

World of Disney | *Toys*

Yves Saint Laurent | *Designer*

Zara | *Men's & Women's Clothing*

EAST 60S

Aaron Basha | *Jewelry*

☑ Akris | *Designer*

Alessandro Dell'Acqua | *Designer*

American Kennels | *Pet Supplies*

Anne Fontaine | *Designer*

🆕 Anne Klein | *Designer*

☑ Ann Taylor | *Women's Clothing*

Anya Hindmarch | *Handbags*

Arche | *Shoes*

Arden B. | *Women's Clothing*

Aveda | *Cosmetics/Toiletries*

Bare Escentuals | *Cosmetics/ Toiletries*

☑ Barneys New York | *Dept. Store*

BCBG Max Azria | *Designer*

Bebe | *Women's Clothing*

☑ Bed Bath & Beyond | *Home*

Bellini | *Children's Furniture*

Betsey Johnson | *Designer*

Billy Martin's Western | *Men's & Women's Clothing*

☑ Bonpoint | *Children's*

Borrelli Boutique | *Men's Clothing*

Breguet | *Watches*

Bulgari | *Jewelry*

Calvin Klein | *Designer*

Calypso | *Women's Clothing*
Camilla Bergeron | *Jewelry*
⚡ Canine Styles | *Pet Supplies*
Canyon Beachwear | *Swimwear*
Capezio | *Activewear*
⚡ Carlyle Convertibles | *Home*
Caron Paris | *Cosmetics/Toiletries*
⚡ Cartier | *Jewelry*
⚡ Celine | *Designer*
⚡ Cesare Paciotti | *Shoes*
⚡ Chanel | *Accessories*
Chanel Jewelry
⚡ Chopard | *Jewelry/Watches*
⚡ Christofle | *Home*
Chrome Hearts | *Jewelry*
Chuckies | *Shoes*
Church's Shoes
Club Monaco | *Men's & Women's Clothing*
Cohen Optical
Cole Haan | *Shoes*
Damiani | *Jewelry*
Daum | *Home*
⚡ Davide Cenci | *Men's Clothing*
David Webb | *Jewelry*
David Yurman | *Jewelry*
de Grisogono | *Jewelry*
Dennis Basso | *Furs*
Design Within Reach | *Home*
Diesel | *Jeans*
DKNY | *Designer*
Dolce & Gabbana | *Designer*
Domain | *Home*
Domenico Vacca | *Designer*
Donna Karan | *Designer*
Dooney & Bourke | *Handbags*
Dylan's Candy Bar | *Gifts/Novelties*
E. Braun & Co. | *Bed/Bath*
Elgot | *Cabinetry*
Emanuel Ungaro | *Designer*
Equinox Energy Wear | *Activewear*
Erwin Pearl | *Jewelry*
Ethan Allen | *Home*
Etro | *Designer*
Floris of London | *Cosmetics/Toiletries*
⚡ Fred Leighton | *Jewelry*
⚡ Frette | *Bed/Bath*

Furla | *Handbags*
Gallery/Wearable Art | *Bridal*
Galo | *Shoes*
⚡ Georg Jensen | *Home/Jewelry*
⚡ Ghurka | *Luggage*
⚡ Giorgio Armani | *Designer*
⚡ Giuseppe Zanotti | *Shoes*
Givenchy | *Designer*
⚡ Graff | *Jewelry*
Gruen Optika | *Eyewear*
Gucci | *Designer*
Gymboree | *Children's*
⚡ Hermès | *Designer*
Innovation Luggage
Issey Miyake | *Designer*
Jacadi | *Children's*
Janovic Plaza | *Hardware*
Jeri Cohen Jewelry
Jimmy Choo | *Shoes*
⚡ J. Mendel | *Furs*
J.M. Weston | *Shoes*
⚡ John Lobb | *Shoes*
⚡ Joon | *Stationery*
Joseph | *Designer*
⚡ Judith Leiber | *Accessories*
Judith Ripka | *Jewelry*
Kraft | *Bathroom Fixtures*
Krizia | *Designer*
La Boutique Resale | *Vintage*
La Brea | *Gifts/Novelties*
Lalaounis | *Jewelry*
⚡ Lalique | *Home*
Lana Marks | *Handbags*
⚡ La Perla | *Hosiery/Lingerie*
Lara Hélène | *Bridal*
Le Chien Pet Salon
Lee Anderson | *Designer*
Léron | *Bed/Bath*
Le Sabon & Baby Too | *Cosmetics/Toiletries*
Lexington Luggage
Lingerie on Lex
Lockes Diamonds | *Jewelry*
Longchamp | *Handbags*
⚡ Loro Piana | *Men's & Women's Clothing*
Luca Luca | *Designer*
Lucky Brand Jeans

MaxMara | *Designer*
Miriam Rigler | *Bridal*
Miu Miu | *Designer*
Molton Brown | *Cosmetics/Toiletries*
Morgane Le Fay | *Designer*
Morgenthal Frederics | *Eyewear*
Ⓩ Mrs. John L. Strong | *Stationery*
Munder-Skiles | *Garden*
Myla | *Sex Shop*
Natalie & Friends | *Children's*
New York Doll | *Toys*
Nicholas Perricone | *Cosmetics/ Toiletries*
Nicole Farhi | *Designer*
Nicole Miller | *Designer*
Oilily | *Children's/Women's Clothing*
Oliver Peoples | *Eyewear*
Oriental Lamp Shade | *Lighting*
Ⓩ Oscar de la Renta | *Designer*
Paul & Shark | *Men's Clothing*
NEW Petrou | *Designer*
Pilar Rossi | *Bridal*
NEW Pomellato | *Jewelry*
Porthault | *Bed/Bath*
NEW Pottery Barn Kids | *Home*
Ⓩ Pratesi | *Bed/Bath*
Pucci | *Designer*
Pylones | *Gifts/Novelties*
NEW Ralph Lauren Eyewear
Reem Acra | *Bridal*
Ⓩ Robert Clergerie | *Shoes*
Robert Marc | *Eyewear*
Roberto Cavalli | *Designer*
Robert Talbott | *Men's Clothing*
Sabon | *Cosmetics/Toiletries*
NEW Samsonite Black Label | *Luggage*
Searle | *Women's Clothing*
Shanghai Tang | *Designer*
NEW Signoria | *Bed/Bath*
Ⓩ Spring Flowers | *Children's*
Ⓩ Steuben | *Home*
Straight from Crate | *Home*
Suzanne Couture | *Accessories*
Taryn Rose | *Shoes*
Ⓩ Tender Buttons
Thos. Moser Cabinets
Timberland | *Shoes*

Ⓩ Tod's | *Shoes*
Tupli | *Shoes*
Unisa | *Shoes*
Ⓩ Valentino | *Designer*
Vanessa Noel | *Shoes*
Varda | *Shoes*
Warren Edwards | *Shoes*
Wedding Things | *Bridal*
William-Wayne | *Home*

EAST 70S

ABH Design | *Home*
Adrien Linford | *Home*
Alain Mikli | *Eyewear*
Anik | *Women's Clothing*
Arche | *Shoes*
AsiaStore/Asia Society
Ⓩ Asprey | *Clothing/Home*
Ⓩ Bang & Olufsen | *Electronics*
Bardith | *Fine China/Crystal*
Beneath | *Hosiery/Lingerie*
Berkley Girl | *Tween/Teen*
Berluti | *Shoes*
Betsey Bunky Nini | *Women's Clothing*
Big Drop | *Men's & Women's Clothing*
Bond No. 9 | *Cosmetics/Toiletries*
Bonne Nuit | *Hosiery/Lingerie*
Bra Smyth | *Hosiery/Lingerie*
By Boe | *Jewelry*
Calling All Pets
Calypso | *Women's Clothing*
Cantaloup/Luxe | *Women's Clothing*
Ⓩ Carolina Herrera | *Designer*
Chambers Outlet | *Bed/Bath*
Chico's | *Women's Clothing*
Chloé | *Designer*
Ⓩ Christian Louboutin | *Shoes*
CK Bradley | *Women's Clothing*
Claudia Ciuti | *Shoes*
Clea Colet | *Bridal*
Clyde's | *Cosmetics/Toiletries*
delfino | *Handbags*
Eileen Fisher | *Women's Clothing*
Elizabeth Locke | *Jewelry*
Emmelle | *Women's Clothing*
Eric | *Shoes*
Essentials | *Cosmetics/Toiletries*

Etcetera | *Gifts/Novelties*

flora and henri | *Children's*

F.M. Allen | *Home/Clothing*

Forréal | *Women's Clothing*

45rpm/R | *Jeans*

Fragments | *Jewelry*

Frank Stella | *Men's Clothing*

French Sole | *Shoes*

Fresh | *Cosmetics/Toiletries*

Frick Collection

Galo | *Shoes*

Gianfranco Ferré | *Designer*

Giggle | *Children's*

🖸 Gracious Home

Greenstones | *Children's*

Gymboree | *Children's*

NEW Heidi Klein | *Swimwear*

Hom Boms | *Toys*

Homer | *Home*

Housing Works Thrift

🖸 Il Papiro | *Stationery*

Ina | *Consignment*

Intermix | *Women's Clothing*

Jacadi | *Children's*

Jackie Rogers | *Designer*

Jaime Mascaró | *Shoes*

Jane | *Women's Clothing*

Jane Wilson-Marquis | *Bridal*

Jay Kos | *Men's Clothing*

Jennifer Miller Jewelry

J. McLaughlin | *Men's & Women's Clothing*

Jo Malone | *Cosmetics/Toiletries*

Jubilee | *Shoes*

NEW Juicy Couture | *Designer*

🖸 Kate's Paperie | *Stationery*

Knits Incredible

Knitting 321

La Boutique Resale

Larry & Jeff Bicycle

L' Avenue des Reves | *Maternity*

Leonard Opticians

Lexington Gardens

Liz Lange Maternity

Luca Luca | *Designer*

Malia Mills Swimwear

Mariko | *Jewelry*

Marimekko | *Home*

🖸 Mary Arnold Toys

Mecox Gardens

Michael Ashton | *Jewelry*

Michael Kors | *Designer*

Michael's/Consignment

Michal Negrin | *Jewelry*

Mish | *Jewelry*

Missoni | *Designer*

Morgenthal Frederics | *Eyewear*

Naturino | *Children's*

Penhaligon's | *Cosmetics/Toiletries*

Peter Elliot | *Men's Clothing*

Peters Necessities/Pets

Pookie & Sebastian | *Women's Clothing*

Prada | *Designer*

Prince & Princess | *Children's*

Ralph Lauren | *Designer*

Ralph Lauren Boys/Girls

Ralph Lauren Layette

Reinstein/Ross | *Jewelry*

🖸 Rita's Needlepoint

Roberta Freymann | *Women's Clothing*

NEW Roberta Roller Rabbit | *Home*

Robert Marc | *Eyewear*

Ruzzetti & Gow | *Home*

NEW Samantha Thavasa | *Handbags*

🖸 Schweitzer Linen

Scoop Men's | *Men's Clothing*

Scoop NYC | *Women's Clothing*

Searle | *Women's Clothing*

Second Chance | *Consignment*

Selima Optique | *Eyewear*

Sharper Image | *Electronics*

Shoe Box

Sonia Rykiel | *Designer*

🖸 Spring Flowers | *Children's*

🖸 String | *Knitting*

Stubbs & Wootton | *Shoes*

Super Runners Shop

Taffin | *Jewelry*

🖸 Talbots | *Men's & Women's Clothing*

Talbots Kids/Babies

Tiny Doll House | *Toys*

Treillage | *Home*

Vera Wang Bridal
Vera Wang Maids | *Bridal*
Vintage Collections
Wedding Library
Whitney Museum
Wolford | *Hosiery/Lingerie*
Woolworks Needlepoint
Yves Delorme | *Bed/Bath*
Yves Saint Laurent | *Designer*
Z'Baby Company
Z Chemists/Zitomer | *Cosmetics/
Toiletries*

EAST 80S

Agnès B. | *Designer*
Anik | *Women's Clothing*
Artbag | *Handbags*
Bambini | *Children's*
☑ Barbour/Peter Elliot | *Men's &
Women's Clothing*
☑ Best Buy | *Electronics*
Betsey Johnson | *Designer*
Bis Designer Resale | *Consignment*
Blacker & Kooby | *Stationery*
Bombay Company | *Home*
Calling All Pets
☑ Canine Styles
Cardeology | *Stationery*
Catimini | *Children's*
Cécile et Jeanne | *Jewelry*
Chuckies | *Shoes*
Circuit City | *Electronics*
Clarins | *Cosmetics/Toiletries*
Cosmophonic Sound | *Electronics*
Council Thrift Shop
Designer Resale
Didi's Children's | *Toys*
E.A.T. Gifts | *Toys*
Emmelle | *Women's Clothing*
Encore | *Consignment*
Eric | *Shoes*
G.C. William | *Tween/Teen*
Gentlemen's Resale
Great Feet | *Children's*
Greenstones | *Children's*
Gruen Optika | *Eyewear*
Guggenheim Museum
Gymboree | *Children's*
H.L. Purdy | *Eyewear*

Housing Works Thrift
Hyde Park Stationers
Infinity | *Tween/Teen*
Jaded | *Jewelry*
NEW J.J. Marco | *Jewelry*
Jonathan Adler | *Home*
Kidville Boutique | *Children's*
Kieselstein-Cord | *Accessories*
La Brea | *Gifts/Novelties*
Larry & Jeff Bicycle
L'Artisan Parfumeur | *Cosmetics/
Toiletries*
Laytner's Linen
LeSportsac | *Handbags*
Lester's | *Children's*
Little Eric | *Children's*
Livi's Lingerie
☑ Lyric Hi-Fi | *Electronics*
NEW Madura | *Home*
Magic Windows | *Children's*
Marie-Chantal | *Designer*
Marsha D.D. | *Children's*
Mem. Sloan-Kettering | *Thrift*
Metro Bicycles
☑ Met. Museum of Art
Montmartre | *Women's Clothing*
Nancy & Co. | *Women's Clothing*
Naturino | *Children's*
Nellie M. Boutique | *Women's
Clothing*
☑ Neue Galerie NY
New York Pipe Dreams | *Sporting
Goods*
Occhiali | *Eyewear*
Olive & Bette's | *Women's Clothing*
Petco | *Pet Supplies*
Peter Elliot | *Men's Clothing*
Petit Bateau | *Children's*
Pier 1 Imports | *Home*
Planet Kids | *Baby Gear*
☑ Schweitzer Linen
Searle | *Women's Clothing*
Seigo | *Accessories*
Spence-Chapin Thrift
Steve Madden | *Shoes*
Straight from Crate | *Home*
Super Runners Shop
Venture | *Stationery*

Vilebrequin | *Swimwear*

Ⓩ Williams-Sonoma | *Home*

Wool Gathering | *Knitting/ Needlepoint*

EAST 90S & 100S

(90th to 110th Sts.)

Adrien Linford | *Home*

Ann Crabtree | *Women's Clothing*

Annie Needlepoint

Blue Tree | *Toys*

Ⓩ Bonpoint | *Children's*

Capezio | *Activewear*

Children's Gen. Store | *Toys*

Cooper-Hewitt | *Museum Shops*

El Museo Del Barrio | *Museum Shops*

Furry Paws | *Pet Supplies*

Intimacy | *Hosiery/Lingerie*

Jacadi | *Children's*

Jewish Museum

J. McLaughlin | *Men's & Women's Clothing*

NEW Mish Mish | *Children's*

Museum/City of NY

New York Replacement | *Bathroom Fixtures*

Rachel Riley | *Children's*

Robert Marc | *Eyewear*

Seigo | *Accessories*

Ⓩ S.Feldman Houseware

Spence-Chapin Thrift

Veronique | *Maternity*

EAST VILLAGE

(14th to Houston Sts., east of Bway)

Academy Records

a. cheng | *Designer*

Alpana Bawa | *Designer*

Alphabets | *Gifts/Novelties*

Amarcord Vintage

Andy's Chee-Pees | *Thrift*

Angela's Vintage

Anna | *Women's Clothing*

Archangel Antiques | *Vintage*

Arche | *Shoes*

Azaleas | *Hosiery/Lingerie*

Barbara Feinman | *Accessories*

Barbara Shaum | *Shoes*

Blue | *Women's Clothing*

Body Shop | *Cosmetics/Toiletries*

Centricity | *Vintage*

CoCo & Delilah | *Women's Clothing*

Crembebè | *Children's*

Crunch | *Activewear*

Dave's Quality Meat | *Sneakers*

Dinosaur Hill | *Toys*

D/L Cerney | *Men's & Women's Clothing*

Ⓩ Downtown Yarns

Eileen Fisher | *Women's Clothing*

Etherea | *Records*

Fabulous Fanny's | *Eyewear*

Finyl Vinyl | *Records*

NEW Gabay's Home

Gabay's Outlet | *Discount*

GapBody | *Hosiery/Lingerie*

Girly NYC | *Hosiery/Lingerie*

Gringer & Sons | *Appliances*

Jammyland | *CDs/Records*

John Derian | *Home*

Ⓩ Kiehl's | *Cosmetics/Toiletries*

Knit New York

LaoLao Handmade | *Home*

NEW Little Stinkers | *Children's*

Love Saves The Day | *Vintage*

Mavi | *Jeans*

Metro Bicycles

Min-K | *Women's Clothing*

Kim's Mediapolis | *CDs/DVDs/ Records/Videos*

Myoptics | *Eyewear*

New York Central Art

99X | *Men's Clothing*

Norman's Sound/Vision | *CDs/ DVDs/Records/Videos*

NYC Velo | *Sporting Goods*

Odin | *Men's Clothing*

NEW Paulina Quintana | *Children's*

Poppet | *Vintage*

Rockit Sci. Records

Rue St. Denis | *Vintage*

Selia Yang | *Bridal*

Selima Optique | *Eyewear*

Sons + Daughters | *Children's*

St. Marks Sounds | *CDs/Records*

Sugar | *Women's Clothing*

Surprise! Surprise! | *Home*

Tiny Living | *Home*

Tokio 7 | *Consignment*

Tokyo Joe | *Consignment*

Trash and Vaudeville | *Men's & Women's Clothing*

Urban Outfitters | *Men's & Women's Clothing*

Utrecht | *Art Supplies*

Z Whiskers | *Pet Supplies*

FINANCIAL DISTRICT

(South of Murray St.)

Boomerang Toys

Z Century 21 | *Discount*

Compact Impact | *Electronics*

DeNatale Jewelers

Z DSW | *Shoes*

Erwin Pearl | *Jewelry*

Hickey Freeman | *Men's Clothing*

Z J&R Music/Computer | *Electronics*

Kenjo | *Watches*

Montmartre | *Women's Clothing*

New York & Co. | *Women's Clothing*

Prato Fine Men's Wear

Samuel's Hats

Syms | *Discount*

Tent and Trails | *Sporting Goods*

William Barthman | *Jewelry*

World of Golf

FLATIRON DISTRICT

(14th to 24th Sts., 6th Ave. to Park Ave. S., excluding Union Sq.)

Z ABC Carpet & Home

Z ABC Carpets/Rugs

Abracadabra | *Toys*

Academy Records

Z Adorama Camera

A.I. Friedman | *Art Supplies*

Alkit | *Cameras/Video*

Z Ann Sacks | *Tile*

Z Anthropologie | *Women's Clothing/Home*

Apartment 48 | *Home*

Arden B. | *Women's Clothing*

Z Artistic Tile

Aveda | *Cosmetics/Toiletries*

A/X Armani Exchange | *Men's & Women's Clothing*

Banana Republic Men

Z Bang & Olufsen | *Electronics*

BCBG Max Azria | *Designer*

Beads of Paradise | *Jewelry*

Bebe | *Women's Clothing*

Beckenstein Fabrics

Z Bed Bath & Beyond

Z Best Buy | *Electronics*

Blackman | *Bathroom Fixtures*

Bombay Company | *Home*

Bridal Garden

Z Charles P. Rogers | *Bed/Bath*

Classic Sofa

Club Monaco | *Men's & Women's Clothing*

David Z. | *Shoes*

Design Within Reach | *Home*

Domain | *Home*

Eileen Fisher | *Women's Clothing*

Eisenberg Eisenberg | *Men's Clothing*

Essentials | *Cosmetics/Toiletries*

Z Filene's Basement | *Discount*

Fishs Eddy | *Home*

Fresh | *Cosmetics/Toiletries*

Z Home Depot

Innovation Luggage

Intermix | *Women's Clothing*

J.Crew | *Men's & Women's Clothing*

Jennifer Convertibles | *Home*

Jo Malone | *Cosmetics/Toiletries*

NEW Juicy Couture | *Designer*

Just Bulbs | *Lighting*

Kenneth Cole NY | *Designer*

Z Kidding Around | *Toys*

Z Krup's Kitchen/Bath

LF Stores | *Women's Clothing*

Z Ligne Roset | *Home*

Lucky Brand Jeans

M.A.C. Cosmetics

Manhattan Ctr. | *Major Appliances*

Metro Bicycles

My Glass Slipper | *Bridal*

Nemo Tile

Origins | *Cosmetics/Toiletries*

Otto Tootsi Plohound | *Shoes*
Paper Presentation | *Stationery*
Paul Smith | *Designer*
Pier 1 Imports | *Home*
Princeton Ski Shop
Reminiscence | *Vintage*
Restoration Hardware | *Home*
Sacco | *Shoes*
Safavieh | *Home*
Sam Flax | *Art Supplies*
Searle | *Women's Clothing*
17 at 17 Thrift
Sisley | *Men's & Women's Clothing*
Sol Moscot | *Eyewear*
Space Kiddets | *Children's*
Sports Authority
☑ Stickley, Audi & Co. | *Home*
Straight from Crate | *Home*
☑ T.J. Maxx | *Discount*
☑ Trixie and Peanut | *Pet Supplies*
Variazioni | *Women's Clothing*
☑ Waterworks | *Bathroom Fixtures*
NEW White Hse. Black Mkt. |
   Women's Clothing
Zara | *Men's & Women's Clothing*

GARMENT DISTRICT

(30th to 40th Sts., west of 5th)
Aerosoles | *Shoes*
Aldo | *Shoes*
Alixandre Furs
Am. Eagle Outfitters | *Tween/Teen*
BabyGap
☑ B&H Photo-Video
☑ B&J Fabrics
Barami | *Women's Clothing*
Blades Board & Skate
Bloom & Krup | *Appliances*
Brookstone | *Electronics*
Capitol Fishing | *Sporting Goods*
Charlotte Russe | *Tween/Teen*
Cheap Jack's | *Thrift/Vintage*
Children's Place
Claire's Accessories
CompUSA | *Electronics*
☑ Daffy's | *Discount*
Dr. Jay's | *Activewear*
Enzo Angiolini | *Shoes*
Express | *Women's Clothing*

Florsheim Shoe
Foot Locker | *Sneakers*
Forever 21 | *Women's Clothing*
42nd St. Photo
☑ Gap | *Men's & Women's Clothing*
GapKids
Gerry Cosby | *Sporting Goods*
Hyman Hendler | *Fabrics/Notions*
J.J. Hat Center
KB Toys
Kmart | *Clothing/Home*
LaDuca Shoes
Lady Foot Locker | *Sneakers*
Lush | *Cosmetics/Toiletries*
☑ Macy's | *Dept. Store*
M&J Trimming | *Fabrics/Notions*
Modell's Sport
Mood | *Fabrics/Notions*
New York Golf
Olden Camera/Lens
Old Navy | *Men's & Women's*
   Clothing
Payless Shoe
Perfumania | *Cosmetics/Toiletries*
Prato Fine Men's Wear
RK Bridal
Rosen & Chadick | *Fabrics/Notions*
School Products | *Knitting*
Skechers | *Shoes*
Solstice | *Eyewear*
Steinlauf & Stoller | *Fabrics/Notions*
Steve Madden | *Shoes*
Tourneau | *Watches*
Training Camp | *Sneakers*
Victoria's Secret | *Hosiery/Lingerie*
Wet Seal | *Tween/Teen*
Willoughby's | *Cameras/Video*
Zales Jewelers
Zara | *Men's & Women's Clothing*

GRAMERCY PARK

(24th to 30th Sts., east of 5th; 14th
to 24th Sts., east of Park)
Casual Male XL | *Men's Clothing*
City Opera Thrift
Door Store | *Home*
Furry Paws | *Pet Supplies*
Housing Works Thrift
Jam Paper | *Stationery*

Manhattan Saddlery | *Sporting Goods*

Museum of Sex

Paparazzi | *Gifts/Novelties*

Park Ave. Audio | *Electronics*

P.C. Richard & Son | *Major Appliances*

☑ Pearl Paint | *Art Supplies*

☑ Simon's Hardware

Straight from Crate | *Home*

Sude | *Women's Clothing*

Troy | *Home*

Vercesi Hardware

Vintage Thrift Shop

GREENWICH VILLAGE

(Houston to 14th Sts., west of Bway, east of 7th Ave. S., excluding NoHo)

☑ Aedes De Venustas | *Cosmetics/ Toiletries*

Albertine | *Women's Clothing*

Alphabets | *Gifts/Novelties*

Arthur's Invitations | *Stationery*

Bag House | *Luggage*

Bleecker Bob's | *Records*

Bleecker St. Records

☑ Broadway Panhandler | *Cookware*

Canal Jean

☑ Canine Styles | *Pet Supplies*

C.O. Bigelow | *Cosmetics/Toiletries*

David Z. | *Shoes*

Disc-O-Rama | *CDs*

environment337 | *Home*

Eskandar | *Designer*

Estella | *Children's*

Fat Beats | *CDs/Records*

Forever 21 | *Women's Clothing*

Furry Paws | *Pet Supplies*

Generation Records

☑ Geppetto's Toy Box

Girl Props | *Accessories*

Gotta Knit

House of Oldies | *Records*

Ibiza Kidz | *Children's*

Ibiza NY | *Women's Clothing*

Joyce Leslie | *Women's Clothing*

Jubilee | *Shoes*

☑ Kate's Paperie | *Stationery*

kid o. | *Toys*

Kmart | *Clothing/Home*

Kuhlman | *Men's & Women's Clothing*

Laina Jane | *Hosiery/Lingerie*

La Petite Coquette | *Hosiery/ Lingerie*

Lucien Pellat-Finet | *Designer*

Lucky Wang | *Children's*

Ludivine | *Women's Clothing*

Make Up For Ever

Olde Good Things | *Home*

Pink Pussycat | *Sex Shop*

☑ Point | *Knitting/Needlepoint*

Purdy Girl | *Women's Clothing*

Rugby | *Men's & Women's Clothing*

Sabon | *Cosmetics/Toiletries*

Sisley | *Men's & Women's Clothing*

Stella Dallas | *Vintage*

Strider Records

Tah-Poozie | *Gifts/Novelties*

TLA Video

UnitedColors/Benetton | *Men's & Women's Clothing*

Urban Outfitters | *Men's & Women's Clothing*

Vinylmania | *CDs/Records*

Wendy Mink | *Jewelry*

William-Wayne | *Home*

Zachary's Smile | *Vintage*

HARLEM/EAST HARLEM

(110th to 157th Sts., excluding Columbia U. area)

B. Oyama Homme | *Men's Clothing*

Carol's Daughter | *Cosmetics/ Toiletries*

Champs | *Sporting Goods*

Davis & Warshow | *Bathroom Fixtures*

Demolition Depot | *Home*

M.A.C. Cosmetics

NEW N | *Men's & Women's Clothing*

New York Public Library | *Museum Shop*

Pieces | *Men's & Women's Clothing*

NEW Purple Reign | *Children's*

Studio Museum/Harlem

V.I.M. | *Jeans*

LITTLE ITALY

(Canal to Kenmare Sts., Bowery to Lafayette St.)

Built by Wendy | *Designer*
No. 6 | *Vintage*

LOWER EAST SIDE

(Houston to Canal Sts., east of Bowery)

Adriennes | *Bridal*
Alife | *Sneakers*
Altman Luggage
A.W. Kaufman | *Hosiery/Lingerie*
Z Babeland | *Sex Shop*
NEW Bblessing | *Men's Clothing*
Bike Works NYC | *Sporting Goods*
NEW Blibetroy | *Handbags*
Bowery Lighting
DeMask | *Sex Shop*
Dolce Vita | *Shoes/Women's Clothing*
Doyle and Doyle | *Jewelry*
NEW Dulcinée | *Vintage*
Edith and Daha | *Women's Clothing*
Foley + Corinna | *Women's Clothing*
NEW Freemans Sporting | *Men's Clothing*
Frock | *Vintage*
NEW Hairy Mary's | *Vintage*
Z Harris Levy | *Bed/Bath*
Itsasickness | *Activewear*
Joe's Fabrics
Jutta Neumann | *Shoes*
NEW Kaight | *Women's Clothing*
Lighting By Gregory
Lower E. S. Tenement | *Museum Shop*
Marmalade | *Vintage*
Mary Adams The Dress | *Bridal*
miks | *Women's Clothing*
Nakedeye | *Eyewear*
O'Lampia Studio | *Lighting*
Orchard Corset Center
Peggy Pardon | *Vintage*
Pippin | *Jewelry*
Shop | *Women's Clothing*
Sol Moscot | *Eyewear*
Some Odd Rubies | *Vintage*
TG-170 | *Women's Clothing*

NEW Valley | *Women's Clothing*
Zarin Fabrics

MEATPACKING DISTRICT

(Gansevoort to 15th Sts., west of 9th Ave.)

Z Alexander McQueen | *Designer*
Artsee | *Eyewear*
auto | *Home*
B8 | *Men's Clothing*
Bodum | *Home*
Boucher | *Jewelry*
Buckler | *Men's Clothing*
Carlos Miele | *Designer*
Catriona Mackechnie | *Hosiery/Lingerie*
Charles Nolan | *Designer*
DDC Lab | *Jeans*
Dernier Cri | *Women's Clothing*
Design Within Reach | *Home*
Destination | *Accessories*
Diane von Furstenberg | *Designer*
Earnest Cut & Sew | *Jeans*
NEW Ed Hardy | *Men's & Women's Clothing*
Elizabeth Charles | *Women's Clothing*
NEW Esthete | *Men's & Women's Clothing*
Girlshop | *Women's Clothing*
Henry Beguelin | *Designer*
Jean Shop
Jeffrey | *Men's & Women's Clothing*
Z La Perla | *Hosiery/Lingerie*
Lucy Barnes | *Designer*
Poleci | *Designer*
Puma | *Activewear/Sneakers*
Rebecca & Drew | *Designer*
Rubin Chapelle | *Designer*
Scoop Kids | *Children's*
Scoop Men's | *Men's Clothing*
Scoop NYC | *Women's Clothing*
Stella McCartney | *Designer*
Ten Thousand Things | *Jewelry*
Theory | *Men's & Women's Clothing*
NEW Tracy Reese | *Designer*
NEW Trina Turk | *Designer*
Vitra | *Home*
Yigal Azrouel | *Designer*

MURRAY HILL

(30th to 40th Sts., east of 5th)

BoConcept | *Home*
NEW Bridal Reflect.
City Sports | *Sneakers*
DataVision | *Electronics*
David Z. | *Shoes*
ddc domus design | *Home*
Eneslow | *Shoes*
Etcetera | *Gifts/Novelties*
Ethan Allen | *Home*
Furry Paws | *Pet Supplies*
Z Lord & Taylor | *Dept. Store*
McGuire | *Home*
NEW Morgan Library | *Museum Shops*
On Stage Dance
Petco | *Pet Supplies*
Pookie & Sebastian | *Women's Clothing*
Z Roche Bobois | *Home*
Safavieh | *Home*
Shoe Box
Straight from Crate | *Home*
White on White | *Home*
Yarn Connection | *Knitting*

NOHO

(Houston to 4th Sts., Bowery to Bway)

Adidas | *Activewear/Sneakers*
American Apparel | *Men's & Women's Clothing*
Andy's Chee-Pees | *Thrift*
Atrium | *Men's & Women's Clothing*
Z Best Buy | *Electronics*
Blades Board & Skate
Z Blick Art Materials
Bond No. 9 | *Cosmetics/Toiletries*
Bond 07 by Selima | *Women's Clothing*
NEW Caravan | *Men's & Women's Clothing*
Classic Kicks | *Sneakers*
Z Crate & Barrel | *Home*
Daryl K | *Designer*
David Z. | *Shoes*
Edge nyNoHo | *Men's & Women's Clothing*
Eye Candy | *Jewelry*

French Connection | *Men's & Women's Clothing*
Ghost | *Designer*
In Living Stereo | *Electronics*
KD Dance & Sport | *Activewear*
Nat'l Wholesale Liquid | *Discount*
Necessary Clothing | *Tween/Teen*
Nom de Guerre | *Men's Clothing*
Nort/Recon | *Sneakers*
Z Other Music
Patricia Field | *Men's & Women's Clothing*
Rafe | *Handbags*
Z Stereo Exchange | *Electronics*
Swatch | *Watches*
Transit | *Men's & Women's Clothing*
Village Tannery | *Leather Goods*
Zachary's Smile | *Vintage*

NOLITA

(Houston to Kenmare Sts., Bowery to Lafayette St.)

Blue Bag | *Handbags*
Cadeau | *Maternity*
NEW Calvin Tran | *Designer*
Calypso | *Women's Clothing*
Calypso Bijoux | *Jewelry*
Calypso Home
Cath Kidston | *Home*
Chip & Pepper | *Jeans*
Christopher Totman | *Designer*
Coclico | *Shoes*
C. Ronson | *Women's Clothing*
Crumpler Bags
Dinosaur Designs | *Jewelry*
Dö Kham | *Accessories*
Duncan Quinn | *Designer*
NEW EMc2 | *Women's Clothing*
Erica Tanov | *Women's Clothing*
Femmegems | *Jewelry*
Find Outlet | *Discount*
Fresh | *Cosmetics/Toiletries*
Good, Bad & Ugly | *Women's Clothing*
Groupe | *Men's Clothing*
Helen Ficalora | *Jewelry*
Henry Lehr | *Jeans*
Highway | *Handbags*
Hollywould | *Shoes*
I Heart | *Women's Clothing*

Ina | *Consignment*
Jack Gomme | *Handbags*
Jamin Puech | *Handbags*
John Fluevog Shoes
Just Shades | *Lighting*
NEW Kipepeo | *Accessories*
NEW Laces | *Sneakers*
NEW Le Labo | *Cosmetics/Toiletries*
Lilith | *Designer*
Lilliput | *Children's*
NEW Linda Derector | *Eyewear*
NEW Lord Willy's | *Men's Clothing*
NEW Lulu Castagnette | *Women's Clothing*
Lyell | *Designer*
Malia Mills Swimwear
Market NYC | *Women's Clothing*
Matta | *Women's Clothing*
Mayle | *Designer*
Me & Ro | *Jewelry*
Min-K | *Women's Clothing*
Mixona | *Hosiery/Lingerie*
Nancy Koltes Home | *Bed/Bath*
Odin | *Men's Clothing*
Only Hearts | *Hosiery/Lingerie*
Otto Tootsi Plohound | *Shoes*
NEW Parasuco | *Jeans*
Paul Frank | *Tween/Teen*
Pearldaddy | *Jewelry*
Pir Cosmetics
Poppy | *Women's Clothing*
Project 234 | *Women's Clothing*
Rebecca Taylor | *Designer*
Red Flower | *Cosmetics/Toiletries*
Resurrection | *Vintage*
NEW Saja | *Designer*
Z Santa Maria Novella | *Cosmetics/Toiletries*
Seize sur Vingt | *Men's & Women's Clothing*
Shoe New York
Sigerson Morrison | *Shoes*
Sigerson Morrison Bags
NEW SOHO | *Jewelry*
Steven Alan | *Men's & Women's Clothing*
Top DJ Gear
Tory Burch | *Designer*

Tracy Feith | *Designer*
Tsubi | *Jeans*
Unis | *Designer*
VeKa Bridal Couture | *Bridal*
Yellow Door | *Jewelry*
Zero/Maria Cornejo | *Designer*

SOHO

(Canal to Houston Sts., west of Lafayette St.)
Active Wearhouse
Add Accessories
Adidas | *Activewear/Sneakers*
Z Aero | *Home*
AG Adriano Goldschmied | *Jeans*
Agatha Ruiz de la Prada | *Designer*
Agent Provocateur | *Hosiery/Lingerie*
Agnès B. | *Designer*
NEW Alessi | *Home*
Alexis Bittar | *Jewelry*
Amarcord Vintage
Am. Eagle Outfitters | *Tween/Teen*
Anna Sui | *Designer*
Anne Fontaine | *Designer*
Z Anthropologie | *Women's Clothing/Home*
Anya Hindmarch | *Handbags*
A.P.C. | *Designer*
Z Apple Store | *Electronics*
Arden B. | *Women's Clothing*
Armani Casa | *Home*
Artemide | *Lighting*
Atelier NY | *Men's Clothing*
Aveda | *Cosmetics/Toiletries*
A/X Armani Exchange | *Men's & Women's Clothing*
Z Babeland | *Sex Shop*
Banana Republic Men
Z B&B Italia | *Home*
Barbara Bui | *Designer*
Barneys CO-OP | *Men's & Women's Clothing*
Bathing Ape | *Sneakers*
BCBG Max Azria | *Designer*
BDDW | *Home*
Beau Brummel | *Men's Clothing*
NEW Ben Sherman | *Men's & Women's Clothing*

Betsey Johnson | *Designer*

Bicycle Habitat | *Sporting Goods*

Big Drop | *Men's & Women's Clothing*

Bisazza | *Tile*

🅩 Bloomingdale's | *Dept. Store*

NEW Blue in Green | *Men's Clothing*

BoConcept | *Home*

Boffi SoHo | *Major Appliances*

Brooklyn Industries | *Men's & Women's Clothing*

Burberry | *Designer*

Burton Store | *Sporting Goods*

By Boe | *Jewelry*

Calvin Klein Underwear

Calypso | *Women's Clothing*

Calypso Enfant/Kids

Camper | *Shoes*

Cappellini | *Home*

Catherine Malandrino | *Designer*

Catherine Memmi | *Home*

Cécile et Jeanne | *Jewelry*

Ceramica | *Home*

🅩 Chanel | *Designer*

Chelsea Girl | *Vintage*

Christopher Fischer | *Designer*

Clarins | *Cosmetics/Toiletries*

Clio | *Home*

Cloak | *Designer*

Club Monaco | *Men's & Women's Clothing*

Costume National | *Designer*

NEW Crew Cuts | *Children's*

Custo Barcelona | *Men's Clothing*

D & G | *Designer*

Dane 115 | *Accessories*

David Lee Holland | *Jewelry*

David Z. | *Shoes*

NEW DC Shoes

🅩 Dean & Deluca | *Cookware*

Design Within Reach | *Home*

Desiron | *Home*

Diesel | *Jeans*

Diesel Denim Gallery | *Jeans*

Diesel Kids

DKNY | *Designer*

Doggystyle | *Pet Supplies*

Domenico Vacca | *Designer*

Dosa | *Designer*

Dunderdon Workshop | *Men's Clothing*

Dusica Dusica | *Shoes*

Eileen Fisher | *Women's Clothing*

Elie Tahari | *Designer*

Emporio Armani | *Designer*

EMS | *Sporting Goods*

Eres | *Hosiery/Lingerie*

Esprit | *Men's & Women's Clothing*

FACE Stockholm | *Cosmetics/Toiletries*

Facial Index | *Eyewear*

Federico de Vera | *Home/Jewelry*

Flou | *Bed/Bath*

Flying A | *Men's & Women's Clothing*

Fort St. Studio | *Home*

45rpm/R | *Jeans*

Fragments | *Jewelry*

French Connection | *Men's & Women's Clothing*

Garrard | *Jewelry*

George Smith | *Home*

🅩 Georg Jensen | *Home/Jewelry*

Giggle | *Children's*

Girl Props | *Accessories*

Global Table | *Home*

G-Star Raw | *Jeans*

Guess | *Jeans*

NEW Hastens | *Bed/Bath*

Hat Shop

Helen Wang | *Designer*

Hogan | *Shoes*

Hugo Boss | *Designer*

Hunting World | *Luggage*

NEW IC Zinco | *Men's & Women's Clothing*

IF | *Men's & Women's Clothing*

Il Bisonte | *Handbags*

Ina | *Consignment*

Ingo Maurer Light | *Lighting*

Institut NYC | *Women's Clothing*

Intermix | *Women's Clothing*

IS: Ind. Stationery | *Stationery*

Jack Spade | *Luggage*

Jaime Mascaró | *Shoes*

J.Crew | *Men's & Women's Clothing*

Jill Platner | *Jewelry*

Jill Stuart | *Designer*

J. Lindeberg | *Men's Clothing*

Joan Michlin Gallery | *Jewelry*

Joël Name Optique | *Eyewear*

John Varvatos | *Designer*

Jonathan Adler | *Home*

Joseph | *Designer*

Julian & Sara | *Children's*

Kartell | *Home*

NEW Kate's At Home

Kate Spade | *Accessories*

Z Kate's Paperie | *Stationery*

Kenneth Cole NY | *Designer*

Key | *Women's Clothing*

Kid Robot | *Toys*

NEW Kiki De Montparnasse | *Hosiery/Lingerie*

Kirna Zabête | *Women's Clothing*

Kuhlman | *Men's & Women's Clothing*

Lacoste | *Men's & Women's Clothing*

Lady Foot Locker | *Sneakers*

Z La Perla | *Hosiery/Lingerie*

L'Artisan Parfumeur | *Cosmetics/Toiletries*

Les Petits Chapelais | *Children's*

LeSportsac | *Handbags*

Levi's Store | *Jeans*

LF Stores | *Women's Clothing*

Z Ligne Roset | *Home*

Lilliput | *Children's*

Links of London | *Jewelry*

L'Occitane | *Cosmetics/Toiletries*

Longchamp | *Handbags*

Louis Vuitton | *Designer*

Lounge | *Men's & Women's Clothing*

Lucky Brand Jeans

NEW Lucky Kid | *Children's*

M.A.C. Cosmetics

Marc Jacobs | *Designer*

Marni | *Designer*

Marston & Langinger | *Home*

Mastic Spa | *Cosmetics/Toiletries*

NEW Max Azria | *Designer*

MaxMara | *Designer*

Max Studio | *Designer*

NEW Meg Cohen Design | *Accessories*

Metropolitan Lumber

Mexx | *Men's & Women's Clothing*

Michele Varian | *Home*

Missha | *Cosmetics/Toiletries*

Miss Sixty | *Women's Clothing*

Miu Miu | *Designer*

NEW M Missoni | *Designer*

Modernica | *Home*

Molton Brown | *Cosmetics/Toiletries*

Z MoMA Store

Z Montblanc | *Stationery*

Morgane Le Fay | *Designer*

Morgenthal Frederics | *Eyewear*

Z Moss | *Home*

Movado | *Watches*

Myoptics | *Eyewear*

M Z Wallace | *Handbags*

Nanette Lepore | *Designer*

NEW Napapijri | *Activewear*

Natuzzi | *Home*

NEW Nave | *Women's Clothing*

Necessary Clothing | *Tween/Teen*

New York Look | *Women's Clothing*

Nicole Miller | *Designer*

North Face | *Activewear*

Oakley | *Eyewear*

NEW Ochre | *Home*

Oilily | *Children's/Women's Clothing*

Olive & Bette's | *Women's Clothing*

Oliver Peoples | *Eyewear*

Opening Ceremony | *Men's & Women's Clothing*

Origins | *Cosmetics/Toiletries*

NEW Oska | *Men's & Women's Clothing*

Patagonia | *Activewear*

Patina | *Vintage*

Paul Smith | *Designer*

Pearl River Mart | *Home*

Z Peter Fox Shoes

Phat Farm | *Men's & Women's Clothing*

Phi | *Designer*

Philosophy/A.Ferretti | *Designer*

Pleats Please | *Designer*

Poltrona Frau | *Home*

Pottery Barn | *Home*

Prada | *Designer*

Prince Charles III | *Men's Clothing*
Psny | *Children's*
Puma | *Activewear/Sneakers*
🆕 Purl | *Knitting/Needlepoint*
Pylones | *Gifts/Novelties*
Quiksilver | *Activewear/Swimwear*
Rachel Ashwell's | *Home*
Ralph Lauren | *Designer*
Reinstein/Ross | *Jewelry*
Reiss | *Women's Clothing*
Replay | *Jeans*
Robert Lee Morris | *Jewelry*
Robert Marc | *Eyewear*
Room & Board | *Home*
Rug Company | *Home*
Sabon | *Cosmetics/Toiletries*
Sacco | *Shoes*
🆕 Salviati | *Fine China/Crystal*
🆕 Satellite | *Jewelry*
Scholastic Store | *Toys*
Scoop NYC | *Women's Clothing*
Scott Jordan | *Home*
Sean | *Men's Clothing*
Selima Optique | *Eyewear*
Seven NY | *Women's Clothing*
Sharper Image | *Electronics*
Shin Choi | *Designer*
Shu Uemura | *Cosmetics/Toiletries*
🆕 Shvitz | *Women's Clothing*
🆕 Sicis | *Bathroom Fixtures/Tiles*
🆕 Sigrid Olsen | *Women's Clothing*
Smith & Hawken | *Garden*
Solstice | *Eyewear*
🆕 Space Mercer | *Women's Clothing*
Steve Madden | *Shoes*
Steven | *Shoes*
Stussy NY | *Men's Clothing*
Supreme | *Activewear*
Sur La Table | *Cookware*
Swatch | *Watches*
Swiss Army | *Accessories*
🆕 Tarina Tarantino | *Jewelry*
🆕 té casan | *Shoes*
Ted Baker | *Designer*
Ted Muehling | *Jewelry*
Temperley | *Designer*

Theory | *Men's & Women's Clothing*
37=1 Atelier | *Hosiery/Lingerie*
🆕 Tibi | *Designer*
Todd Hase | *Home*
Todd Oldham/La-Z-Boy | *Home*
Tommy Hilfiger | *Designer*
🆕 Trico Field | *Children's*
Triple Five Soul | *Men's & Women's Clothing*
🆕 True Religion | *Jeans*
Ⓩ TUMI | *Luggage*
🆕 UGG Australia | *Shoes*
🆕 Uniqlo | *Men's & Women's Clothing*
Varda | *Shoes*
Vespa | *Sporting Goods*
Via Bus Stop | *Women's Clothing*
Vilebrequin | *Swimwear*
Vivienne Tam | *Designer*
Vogel | *Shoes*
🆕 Von Dutch | *Men's & Women's Clothing*
Ⓩ Waterworks | *Bathroom Fixtures*
🆕 WeSC | *Men's & Women's Clothing*
What Comes Around | *Vintage*
Wink | *Accessories*
Wolford | *Hosiery/Lingerie*
Yellow Rat Bastard | *Tween/Teen*
Yohji Yamamoto | *Designer*
Zara | *Men's & Women's Clothing*

SOUTH STREET SEAPORT

Abercrombie & Fitch | *Tween/Teen*
Brookstone | *Electronics*
Express Men | *Men's Clothing*
Guess | *Jeans*
J.Crew | *Men's & Women's Clothing*
🆕 Leontine | *Women's Clothing*
Ⓩ Met. Museum of Art
Ⓩ Seaport Yarn
Sharper Image | *Electronics*
Ⓩ Talbots | *Men's & Women's Clothing*
UnitedColors/Benetton | *Men's & Women's Clothing*

TRIBECA

(Canal to Murray Sts., west of Bway)

Anbar | *Shoes*

A Uno/Walk | *Shoes/Women's Clothing*

Babylicious | *Children's*

Baker Tribeca | *Home*

Blue Bench | *Children's Furniture*

Boomerang Toys

🔲 Brooks Brothers | *Men's & Women's Clothing*

Bu and the Duck | *Children's*

Butter and Eggs | *Home*

Calypso | *Women's Clothing*

Capucine | *Maternity*

Design Within Reach | *Home*

Disrespectacles | *Eyewear*

Donzella | *Home*

Dudley's Paw | *Pet Supplies*

Dune | *Home*

🔲 Fountain Pen | *Stationery*

Gotham Bikes

Issey Miyake | *Designer*

Koh's Kids | *Children's*

NEW LuLuLemon | *Activewear*

Metro Bicycles | *Sporting Goods*

Mika Inatome | *Bridal*

NEW Moulin Bleu | *Home*

Myoptics | *Eyewear*

NEW Nili Lotan | *Designer*

Number (N)ine | *Designer*

P&S Fabrics

NEW Petticoat Lane | *Hosiery/Lingerie*

🔲 Pompanoosuc Mills | *Home*

NEW Rogan | *Jeans*

Schoolhouse Electric | *Lighting*

Selia Yang | *Bridal*

Shoofly | *Children's*

Steven Alan | *Men's & Women's Clothing*

Thom Browne | *Designer*

Tribeca Girls | *Children's*

NEW Trunkt | *Jewelry*

🔲 Urban Archaeology | *Home*

UNION SQUARE

(14th to 17th Sts., 5th Ave. to Union Sq. E.)

Agnès B. | *Designer*

Am. Eagle Outfitters | *Tween/Teen*

Babies "R" Us

Circuit City | *Electronics*

🔲 Country Floors | *Tiles*

David Z. | *Shoes*

Diesel | *Jeans*

Disc-O-Rama | *CDs*

🔲 DSW | *Shoes*

Esprit | *Men's & Women's Clothing*

🔲 Filene's Basement | *Discount*

JackRabbit Sports | *Activewear*

Levi's Store | *Jeans*

🔲 Paragon | *Sporting Goods*

Petco | *Pet Supplies*

Poggenpohl U.S. | *Home*

Puma | *Activewear/Sneakers*

Rothman's | *Men's Clothing*

🔲 Sound by Singer | *Electronics*

🔲 Virgin Megastore | *CDs/DVDs/Videos*

WASHINGTON HTS./INWOOD

(North of W. 157th St.)

🔲 Met. Museum of Art

WEST 40S

NEW Adrienne Vittadini | *Women's Clothing*

Alcone | *Cosmetics/Toiletries*

NEW alice + olivia | *Women's Clothing*

🔲 Arthur Brown & Bro. | *Stationery*

🔲 Best Buy | *Electronics*

🔲 Billabong | *Activewear/Swimwear*

Bra*Tenders | *Hosiery/Lingerie*

Champs | *Sporting Goods*

Colony Music

🔲 Crane & Co. | *Stationery*

Delphinium | *Home*

Dykes Lumber

NEW Giorgio Fedon 19 | *Accessories/Handbags*

Gothic Cabinet Craft | *Home*

🔲 Harvey Electronics

🔲 International Photo

Metro Bicycles

Metropolitan Lumber

☑ Met. Museum of Art

Movado | *Watches*

New Balance | *Sneakers*

New York Fabric

New York Look | *Women's Clothing*

Original Penguin | *Men's Clothing*

Pan Aqua Diving | *Sporting Goods*

Papyrus | *Stationery*

Paron Fabrics

Petland Discounts

P.J. Huntsman | *Men's Clothing*

Quiksilver | *Activewear/Swimwear*

Ray Beauty Supply | *Cosmetics/ Toiletries*

Salvation Army | *Thrift*

Sanrio | *Toys*

Sharper Image | *Electronics*

Skechers | *Shoes*

Sound City | *Electronics*

Spoiled Brats | *Pet Supplies*

Swatch | *Watches*

Thomas Pink | *Men's Clothing*

Toys "R" Us | *Toys*

Training Camp | *Sneakers*

☑ TUMI | *Luggage*

☑ Virgin Megastore | *CDs/DVDs/ Videos*

WEST 50S

Aaron Faber | *Jewelry/Watches*

American Folk Art

☑ Anthropologie | *Women's Clothing/Home*

Arche | *Shoes*

Ascot Chang | *Men's Clothing*

Aveda | *Cosmetics/Toiletries*

A/X Armani Exchange | *Men's & Women's Clothing*

Bebe | *Women's Clothing*

Beverly Feldman | *Shoes*

Blair Delmonico | *Jewelry/Women's Clothing*

Blockbuster Video

Bolton's | *Discount*

☑ Bose | *Electronics*

BOSS Hugo Boss | *Designer*

Brookstone | *Electronics*

Caché | *Women's Clothing*

Calvin Klein Underwear

Capezio | *Activewear*

Charles Tyrwhitt | *Men's Clothing*

Club Monaco | *Men's & Women's Clothing*

Cole Haan | *Shoes*

CompUSA | *Electronics*

Crabtree & Evelyn | *Cosmetics/ Toiletries*

delfino | *Handbags*

Eileen Fisher | *Women's Clothing*

Erwin Pearl | *Jewelry*

Esprit | *Men's & Women's Clothing*

Eve's Garden | *Sex Shop*

FACE Stockholm | *Cosmetics/ Toiletries*

Frank Stella | *Men's Clothing*

French Connection | *Men's & Women's Clothing*

f.y.e. | *CDs/DVDs/Videos*

NEW Guy Laroche | *Designer*

Innovation Luggage

J.Crew | *Men's & Women's Clothing*

J.W. Cooper | *Accessories*

☑ Kate's Paperie | *Stationery*

Kenjo | *Watches*

Kuhlman | *Men's & Women's Clothing*

Lee's Art Shop

Lee's Studio | *Home*

Leonard Opticians | *Eyewear*

☑ Manolo Blahnik | *Shoes*

Maternity Works

☑ MoMA Store

Montmartre | *Women's Clothing*

Morgenthal Frederics | *Eyewear*

☑ Museum Arts/Design

New York Running | *Sneakers*

OMO Norma Kamali | *Designer*

Rochester Big/Tall | *Men's Clothing*

Sabon | *Cosmetics/Toiletries*

Sansha | *Activewear*

Sharper Image | *Electronics*

Sisley | *Men's & Women's Clothing*

☑ Smythson of Bond St. | *Stationery*

Solstice | *Eyewear*

Stuart Weitzman | *Shoes*

SwimBikeRun | *Sporting Goods*
Thomas Pink | *Men's Clothing*
Tourneau | *Watches*
☒ TUMI | *Luggage*
UnitedColors/Benetton | *Men's & Women's Clothing*
United Colors/Kids | *Children's*
☒ Williams-Sonoma | *Cookware*
Z Chemists/Zitomer | *Cosmetics/ Toiletries*

WEST 60S

Agatha Paris | *Jewelry*
American Folk Art
BCBG Max Azria | *Designer*
☒ Bed Bath & Beyond
Danskin | *Activewear*
Domain | *Home*
Ethan Allen | *Home*
Furry Paws | *Pet Supplies*
☒ Gracious Home
Gruen Optika | *Eyewear*
Gymboree | *Children's*
Innovation Luggage
Intermix | *Women's Clothing*
Jacadi | *Children's*
Kangol Columbus Ave. | *Accessories*
☒ Kiehl's | *Cosmetics/Toiletries*
NEW Lancôme | *Cosmetics/ Toiletries*
NEW LuLuLemon | *Activewear*
M.A.C. Cosmetics
Met. Opera Shop | *Gifts/Novelties*
New York Look | *Women's Clothing*
Pottery Barn | *Home*
Reebok Concept Store | *Activewear*
Reiss | *Men's & Women's Clothing*
Robert Marc | *Eyewear*
☒ Toga Bikes
Wink | *Accessories*

WEST 70S

Am. Museum/Nat.Hist.
☒ Bang & Olufsen | *Electronics*
Barneys CO-OP | *Men's & Women's Clothing*
Beacon Paint/Hardware
Beau Brummel | *Men's Clothing*

Berkley Girl | *Tween/Teen*
Betsey Johnson | *Designer*
Blades Board & Skate
Bloch | *Activewear*
Boyd's of Madison | *Cosmetics/ Toiletries*
Bra Smyth | *Hosiery/Lingerie*
Brief Encounters | *Hosiery/Lingerie*
Cardeology | *Stationery*
Clarins | *Cosmetics/Toiletries*
Design Within Reach | *Home*
Eileen Fisher | *Women's Clothing*
FACE Stockholm | *Cosmetics/ Toiletries*
☒ Filene's Basement | *Discount*
G.C. William | *Tween/Teen*
Granny-Made | *Children's*
Housing Works Thrift
Jewish Museum
Jubilee | *Shoes*
Kenneth Cole NY | *Designer*
La Boutique Resale | *Vintage*
La Brea | *Gifts/Novelties*
Lord of the Fleas | *Tween/Teen*
Lucky Brand Jeans
Lush | *Cosmetics/Toiletries*
Malia Mills Swimwear
Montmartre | *Women's Clothing*
North Face | *Activewear*
Olive & Bette's | *Women's Clothing*
Only Hearts | *Hosiery/Lingerie*
Oriental Lamp Shade | *Lighting*
Paterson Silks | *Fabrics/Notions*
Plaza Too | *Accessories*
Pookie & Sebastian | *Women's Clothing*
Roberto Vascon | *Handbags*
Sabon | *Cosmetics/Toiletries*
Sacco | *Shoes*
Sean | *Men's Clothing*
Straight from Crate | *Home*
Super Runners Shop
Swatch | *Watches*
Theory | *Men's & Women's Clothing*
Tip Top Kids
Tip Top Shoes

Urban Outfitters | *Men's & Women's Clothing*

Varda | *Shoes*

Verve | *Handbags/Shoes*

Z'Baby Company | *Children's*

WEST 80S

Allan & Suzi | *Consignment/Vintage*

🄩 Avventura | *Fine China/Crystal*

Bicycle Renaissance | *Sporting Goods*

Böc | *Women's Clothing*

Cardeology | *Stationery*

Circuit City | *Electronics*

Club Monaco | *Men's & Women's Clothing*

NEW C.P.W. | *Children's*

Door Store | *Home*

Essentials | *Cosmetics/Toiletries*

Eye Man | *Eyewear*

Frank Stella | *Men's Clothing*

Greenstones | *Children's*

Gruen Optika | *Eyewear*

Gymboree | *Children's*

Harry's Shoes

NEW Harry's Shoes/Kids

Kidville Boutique

Laina Jane | *Hosiery/Lingerie*

Laytner's Linen

Lightforms | *Lighting*

Maxilla & Mandible | *Toys*

Medici | *Shoes*

Morris Brothers | *Children's*

Origins | *Cosmetics/Toiletries*

Patagonia | *Activewear*

Penny Whistle | *Toys*

🄩 Pet Stop

Purdy Girl | *Women's Clothing*

Quintessentials | *Major Appliances*

🄩 Schweitzer Linen

Staples | *Electronics*

Steven Alan | *Men's & Women's Clothing*

🄩 Talbots | *Men's & Women's Clothing*

Town Shop | *Hosiery/Lingerie*

Variazioni | *Women's Clothing*

West Side Kids | *Toys*

🄩 Yarn Co. | *Knitting*

🄩 Zabar's | *Cookware*

WEST 90S

Albee Baby Carriage

La Brea | *Gifts/Novelties*

Liberty House | *Children's*

Metro Bicycles

Petco | *Pet Supplies*

Straight from Crate | *Home*

Sude | *Women's Clothing*

WEST 100S

(See also Harlem/East Harlem)

Kim's Mediapolis | *CDs/DVDs/ Records/Videos*

Liberty House | *Children's*

🄩 Marshalls | *Discount*

Planet Kids | *Baby Gear*

WEST VILLAGE

(Houston to 14th Sts., west of 7th Ave. S., excluding Meatpacking District)

Annelore | *Designer*

🄩 Bathroom | *Cosmetics/Toiletries*

Beasty Feast | *Pet Supplies*

Belly Dance Maternity

blush | *Women's Clothing*

Bond No. 9 | *Cosmetics/Toiletries*

🄩 Bonpoint | *Children's*

Brooklyn Industries | *Men's & Women's Clothing*

NEW Brunello Cucinelli | *Designer*

Butik | *Women's Clothing*

Calypso | *Women's Clothing*

Castor & Pollux | *Women's Clothing*

Catherine Malandrino | *Designer*

Cherry | *Vintage*

🄩 Christian Louboutin | *Shoes*

City Cricket | *Children's*

Crumpler Bags

Cynthia Rowley | *Designer*

Darling | *Women's Clothing*

Disrespectacles | *Eyewear*

Flight 001 | *Luggage*

Fresh | *Cosmetics/Toiletries*

Geminola | *Women's Clothing*

Gerry's | *Men's & Women's Clothing*

NEW Greenwich Letterpress | *Stationery*

Hable Construction | *Home*

Housing Works Thrift

Intermix | *Women's Clothing*

Irma | *Women's Clothing*

James Perse | *Men's & Women's Clothing*

NEW Juicy Couture | *Designer*

Kaas GlassWorks | *Home*

Kids Rx | *Cosmetics/Toiletries*

Kim's Mediapolis | *CDs/DVDs/ Records/Videos*

Ⅾ Leather Man | *Sex Shop*

Le Fanion | *Home*

Lulu Guinness | *Handbags*

L'Uomo | *Men's Clothing*

Maison Martin Margiela | *Designer*

Marc and Max | *Hosiery/Lingerie*

Marc/Marc Jacobs | *Designer*

Marc Jacobs Access.

Mick Margo | *Women's Clothing*

NEW Mulberry | *Handbags*

Mxyplyzyk | *Home*

Olatz | *Bed/Bath*

Olive & Bette's | *Women's Clothing*

NEW Oliver Spencer | *Men's Clothing*

Otte | *Women's Clothing*

Peanutbutter & Jane | *Children's*

P.E. Guerin | *Hardware*

Pleasure Chest | *Sex Shop*

Pylones | *Gifts/Novelties*

Ralph Lauren | *Designer*

Rebel Rebel | *CDs/Records*

Reiss | *Women's Clothing*

Robert Marc | *Eyewear*

Ruehl | *Accessories*

Satya | *Jewelry*

NEW SEE Eyewear

Selima Optique | *Eyewear*

NEW Sophia Eugene | *Designer*

Space107 | *Home*

Steven Alan | *Men's & Women's Clothing*

Verve | *Handbags/Shoes*

Village Tannery | *Leather Goods*

Yoya/Yoya Mart | *Children's*

Zero/Maria Cornejo | *Designer*

Zoomies | *Pet Supplies*

Bronx

ABC Carpet/Whse. Outlet | *Home*

Athlete's Foot | *Sneakers*

Casual Male XL | *Men's Clothing*

Davis & Warshow | *Bathroom Fixtures*

Dykes Lumber

Kmart | *Clothing/Home*

Ⅾ Loehmann's | *Discount*

Ⅾ Marshalls | *Discount*

Nat'l Wholesale Liquid | *Discount*

Sears | *Dept. Store*

Ⅾ Target | *Dept. Store*

Brooklyn

BAY RIDGE

Ⅾ Century 21 | *Discount*

Joyce Leslie | *Women's Clothing*

KB Toys

Ⅾ Michael C. Fina | *Fine China/ Crystal*

UnitedColors/Benetton | *Men's & Women's Clothing*

BENSONHURST

Babies "R" Us

Ⅾ Best Buy | *Electronics*

Ⅾ Marshalls | *Discount*

Mylo Dweck Maternity

Nat'l Wholesale Liquid | *Discount*

Something Else | *Men's & Women's Clothing*

Steve Madden | *Shoes*

BOERUM HILL

Brooklyn Industries | *Men's & Women's Clothing*

Flight 001 | *Luggage*

GRDN Bklyn | *Garden*

NEW Hollander & Lexer | *Men's Clothing*

Knit-A-Way | *Knitting/Needlepoint*

Michelle NY | *Bridal/Women's Clothing*

Rico | *Home*

Sir | *Designer*

Something Else | *Men's & Women's Clothing*

Soula | *Shoes*

BOROUGH PARK

Jacadi | *Children's*

Mimi Maternity

Nat'l Wholesale Liquid | *Discount*

S&W | *Discount*

UnitedColors/Benetton | *Men's & Women's Clothing*

BROOKLYN HEIGHTS

NEW Abitare | *Home*

Design Within Reach | *Home*

Heights Kids | *Children's*

Housing Works Thrift

M.A.C. Cosmetics

New York Transit Mus.

CANARSIE

Casual Male XL | *Men's Clothing*

Training Camp | *Sneakers*

CARROLL GARDENS

Area | *Children's*

Brooklyn Gen. Store | *Knitting/ Needlepoint*

Debbie Fisher | *Jewelry*

environment337 | *Home*

NEW Hasker | *Home*

Living Fifth/Seventh/Smith | *Home/Women's Clothing*

Oculus 20/20 | *Eyewear*

NEW Olá Baby | *Children's Furniture*

Swallow | *Home*

Watts on Smith | *Men's Clothing*

CLINTON HILL

Circuit City | *Electronics*

COBBLE HILL

A Brooklyn Table | *Home*

Bird | *Women's Clothing*

Dear Fieldbinder | *Women's Clothing*

Diane T | *Women's Clothing*

Green Onion | *Children's*

LF Stores | *Women's Clothing*

Refinery | *Handbags*

CONEY ISLAND

Z Loehmann's | *Discount*

DITMAS PARK

NEW Belle & Maxie | *Children's*

DOWNTOWN

Acorn | *Toys*

Burlington Coat | *Discount*

Butter | *Women's Clothing*

Carol's Daughter | *Cosmetics/ Toiletries*

NEW Consignment

Door Store | *Home*

Z DSW | *Shoes*

Forever 21 | *Women's Clothing*

Goodwill | *Thrift*

Layla | *Home*

Maleeka | *Home/Women's Clothing*

Z Marshalls | *Discount*

Sid's | *Hardware*

Z Target | *Dept. Store*

DUMBO

Blueberi | *Women's Clothing*

BoConcept | *Home*

halcyon the shop | *CDs/DVDs/ Records/Videos*

Half Pint | *Baby Gear*

NEW Loopy Mango | *Women's Clothing*

Pomme | *Children's*

Spring | *Accessories*

West Elm | *Home*

Wonk | *Home*

NEW Zoë | *Women's Clothing*

DYKER HEIGHTS

Casual Male XL | *Men's Clothing*

Prato Fine Men's Wear

EAST NEW YORK

Athlete's Foot | *Sneakers*

FLATBUSH

Canal Jean

Sears | *Dept. Store*

Tuesday's Child | *Children's*

FORT GREENE

Addy & Ferro | *Men's & Women's Clothing*

Carol's Daughter | *Cosmetics/ Toiletries*

Cloth | *Women's Clothing*

Hot Toddie | *Children's*

NEW Stuart & Wright | *Men's & Women's Clothing*

GOWANUS

Lowe's | *Hardware*

GRAVESEND

Lester's | *Children's*

William Barthman | *Jewelry*

KINGS PLAZA/MARINE PARK

Am. Eagle Outfitters | *Tween/Teen*

Express Men | *Men's Clothing*

Forever 21 | *Women's Clothing*

Guess | *Jeans*

Joyce Leslie | *Women's Clothing*

Lady Foot Locker | *Sneakers*

Limited Too | *Tween/Teen*

Sears | *Dept. Store*

Steve Madden | *Shoes*

MIDWOOD

Diva | *Tween/Teen*

Drimmers | *Major Appliances*

Katz in the Cradle | *Children's Furniture*

Tuesday's Child | *Children's*

Yellow Door | *Jewelry*

MILL BASIN

Casual Male XL | *Men's Clothing*

Joyce Leslie | *Women's Clothing*

PARK SLOPE

Area | *Children's*

Baby Bird | *Children's*

Beacon's Closet | *Consignment/ Thrift/Vintage*

Bird | *Women's Clothing*

Brooklyn Industries | *Men's & Women's Clothing*

Clay Pot | *Jewelry*

Cog & Pearl | *Accessories*

Diana Kane | *Women's Clothing/ Lingerie*

Dykes Lumber | *Hardware*

Eidolon | *Women's Clothing*

4PlayBK | *Tween/Teen*

Goldy + Mac | *Women's Clothing*

JackRabbit Sports | *Activewear*

Lion in the Sun | *Stationery*

Living Fifth/Seventh/Smith | *Home/Women's Clothing*

Loom | *Accessories/Women's Clothing*

Luilei | *Cosmetics/Toiletries*

Matter | *Home*

Nest | *Home*

Oak | *Men's & Women's Clothing*

Orange Blossom | *Children's*

Pink Pussycat | *Sex Shop*

Pintchik | *Hardware*

NEW Posey Baker | *Home*

premium goods | *Sneakers*

Razor | *Men's Clothing*

Romp | *Toys*

Scaredy Kat | *Gifts/Novelties*

Shoe Mine | *Men's & Women's Shoes*

Slope Sports | *Sporting Goods*

Something Else | *Men's & Women's Clothing*

Tarzian True Value | *Hardware*

Tarzian West | *Home*

3r Living | *Home*

NEW Toy Space | *Toys*

Umkarna | *Women's Clothing*

PROSPECT HEIGHTS

Brooklyn Museum

Hooti Couture | *Vintage*

Pieces | *Men's & Women's Clothing*

Redberi | *Women's Clothing*

RED HOOK

Brooklyn Collective | *Women's Clothing*

STARRETT CITY

Babies "R" Us

Z Bed Bath & Beyond | *Home*

Circuit City | *Electronics*

- ▣ Marshalls | *Discount*
- ▣ Target | *Dept. Store*

SUNSET PARK

- ▣ Costco Wholesale | *Discount*
- Lady Foot Locker | *Sneakers*

WILLIAMSBURG

- Academy Records
- Amarcord Vintage
- Beacon's Closet | *Consignment/ Thrift/Vintage*
- Brooklyn Industries | *Men's & Women's Clothing*
- Built by Wendy | *Designer*
- Catbird | *Clothing: Women's*
- CB I Hate Perfume | *Cosmetics/ Toiletries*
- Flying Squirrel | *Children's*
- NEW Fresh Kills | *Home*
- Future Perfect | *Home*
- NEW Jumelle | *Women's Clothing*
- NEW Lisa Levine Jewelry
- NEW Love Brigade | *Women's Clothing*
- Michael Anchin Glass | *Home*
- Mini Mini Market | *Accessories*
- Natan Borlam's | *Children's*
- Noisette | *Women's Clothing*
- Oak | *Men's & Women's Clothing*
- Oculus 20/20 | *Eyewear*
- Otte | *Women's Clothing*
- Rocks in Your Head | *CDs/DVDs*
- Sam & Seb | *Children's*
- S&W | *Discount*
- Sleep | *Bed/Bath*
- Stella Dallas | *Consignment/Thrift/ Vintage*
- NEW Treehouse | *Men's & Women's Clothing*
- Triple Five Soul | *Men's & Women's Clothing*
- Two Jakes | *Home*
- Wonk | *Home*
- Yarn Tree | *Knitting/Needlepoint*
- NEW Ylli | *Men's & Women's Clothing*
- NEW Yoko Devereaux | *Designer*

Queens

ASTORIA

- Loveday31 | *Consignment/Thrift/ Vintage*
- Metropolitan Lumber
- NEW Mimi's Closet | *Women's Clothing*
- Prato Fine Men's Wear
- Skechers | *Shoes*
- UnitedColors/Benetton | *Men's & Women's Clothing*

BAYSIDE

- Am. Eagle Outfitters | *Tween/Teen*
- Bombay Company | *Home*
- Chico's | *Women's Clothing*
- Hazel's Shoes
- Steve Madden | *Shoes*
- Thomasville | *Home*

COLLEGE POINT

- Babies "R" Us
- Circuit City | *Electronics*
- ▣ Target | *Dept. Store*
- ▣ T.J. Maxx | *Discount*

CORONA

- Metropolitan Lumber

ELMHURST

- Am. Eagle Outfitters | *Tween/Teen*
- A/X Armani Exchange | *Men's & Women's Clothing*
- Bare Escentuals | *Cosmetics/ Toiletries*
- Bebe | *Women's Clothing*
- ▣ Bed Bath & Beyond | *Home*
- ▣ Best Buy | *Electronics*
- Champs | *Sporting Goods*
- Clarks England | *Shoes*
- Club Monaco | *Men's & Women's Clothing*
- ▣ DSW | *Shoes*
- Forever 21 | *Women's Clothing*
- Fossil | *Watches*
- Geox | *Shoes*
- Lady Foot Locker | *Sneakers*
- Limited Too | *Tween/Teen*
- Lush | *Cosmetics/Toiletries*

Sanrio | *Toys*

Skechers | *Shoes*

Swatch | *Watches*

☒ Target | *Dept. Store*

Yellow Rat Bastard | *Tween/Teen*

FLORAL PARK

Paterson Silks | *Fabrics/Notions*

FLUSHING

Athlete's Foot | *Sneakers*

Blackman | *Bathroom Fixtures*

☒ Filene's Basement | *Discount*

Grand Central Racquet

Joyce Leslie | *Women's Clothing*

KB Toys

Nat'l Wholesale Liquid | *Discount*

Sears | *Dept. Store*

FOREST HILLS

Ethan Allen | *Home*

Jubilee | *Shoes*

Sol Moscot | *Eyewear*

Sports Authority

UnitedColors/Benetton | *Men's & Women's Clothing*

GLENDALE

Bombay Company | *Home*

Gymboree | *Children's*

HOWARD BEACH

Petco | *Pet Supplies*

JACKSON HEIGHTS

KB Toys

JAMAICA

Athlete's Foot | *Sneakers*

Metropolitan Lumber

Nemo Tile

LITTLE NECK

Eneslow | *Shoes*

LONG ISLAND CITY

☒ Best Buy | *Electronics*

☒ Costco Wholesale | *Discount*

David's Bridal

Dykes Lumber | *Hardware*

☒ Marshalls | *Discount*

Nat'l Wholesale Liquid | *Discount*

Tucker Robbins | *Home*

MASPETH

Davis & Warshow | *Bathroom Fixtures*

MIDDLE VILLAGE

Kmart | *Clothing/Home*

QUEENS VILLAGE

Blackman | *Bathroom Fixtures*

REGO PARK

☒ Bed Bath & Beyond | *Home*

Circuit City | *Electronics*

CompUSA | *Electronics*

☒ Marshalls | *Discount*

Sears | *Dept. Store*

Urban Outfitters | *Men's & Women's Clothing*

RIDGEWOOD

Joyce Leslie | *Women's Clothing*

KB Toys

WOODHAVEN

Missha | *Cosmetics/Toiletries*

Smiley's | *Knitting/Needlepoint*

WOODSIDE

Sports Authority

Staten Island

Am. Eagle Outfitters | *Tween/Teen*

☒ Apple Store | *Electronics*

Bath & Body Works | *Cosmetics/Toiletries*

BCBG Max Azria | *Designer*

Bebe | *Women's Clothing*

☒ Bed Bath & Beyond | *Home*

☒ Best Buy | *Electronics*

Bombay Company | *Home*

Brookstone | *Electronics*

☒ Build-A-Bear | *Toys*

Burlington Coat | *Discount*

Caché | *Women's Clothing*

Casual Male XL | *Men's Clothing*

Champs | *Sporting Goods*

Charlotte Russe | *Tween/Teen*

Circuit City | *Electronics*

☒ Costco Wholesale | *Discount*

Crabtree & Evelyn | *Cosmetics/Toiletries*

Esprit | *Men's & Women's Clothing*
Ethan Allen | *Home*
Forever 21 | *Women's Clothing*
Guess | *Jeans*
Gymboree | *Children's*
Joyce Leslie | *Women's Clothing*
KB Toys
Kmart | *Clothing/Home*
Lady Foot Locker | *Sneakers*
Limited Too | *Tween/Teen*

Lowe's | *Hardware*
Z Marshalls | *Discount*
Mimi Maternity
Nat'l Wholesale Liquid | *Discount*
Sears | *Dept. Store*
Steve Madden | *Shoes*
Swarovski | *Jewelry*
Z T.J. Maxx | *Discount*
Training Camp | *Sneakers*

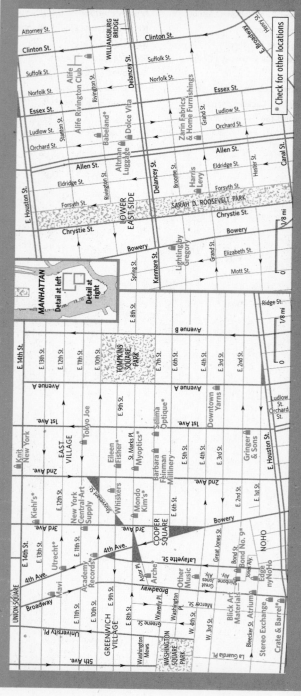

MAPS

1/8 mi
0

East River

Staten Island Ferry Terminal

FDR Dr.

BROOKLYN BRIDGE

Dover St.
Peck Slip
South Street Seaport
Sharper Image*
United Colors of Benetton*
Front St.
Water St.
Pearl St.
J. Crew*
Guess*
Fulton St.
Talbots*
Brookstone*
Metropolitan Museum of Art Store*
South St.
Gouverneur Ln.
Old Slip
South St.
Pearl St.
Water St.
Front St.
Pine St.
Hanover Sq.
William St.
Stone St.
Broad St.
Moore St.

Frankfort St.
Gold St.
Spruce St.
Beekman St.
Ann St.
Cliff St.
Ryders Aly.
Seaport Yarn*
Dutch St.
Pratt St.
Gold St.
Cedar St.
Malden La.
William St.
Wall St.
Exchange Pl.
Nassau St.
New St.
Beaver St.
FINANCIAL DISTRICT
Bridge St.
Stone St.
State St.
BOWLING GREEN
Whitehall St.

CITY HALL PARK
Park Row
J&R Music & Computer World
Fulton St.
Broadway
Dey St.
DeNatale Jewelers*
World Of Golf*
Hickey Freeman*
Dutch St.
Kenjo*

Tent & Trails*
Park Pl.
W. Broadway
Barclay St.
Vesey St.
Church St.
Century 21*
Cortlandt St.
Liberty St.
Cedar St.
Thames St.
Albany St.
Carlisle St.
Broadway
Trinity Pl.
Greenwich St.
Rector St.
Washington St.
Little West St.
Brooklyn Battery Tunnel Entrance
Battery Pl.
BATTERY PARK

West St.
Liberty St.
Brooks Brothers*
Erwin Pearl*
Montmartre*
World Financial Center
DSW*
North End Ave.
Vesey St.
BATTERY PARK CITY
South End Ave.
Albany St.
Rector Pl.
W. Thames St.
3rd Pl.
2nd Pl.
1st Pl.

ESPLANADE
Hudson River

* Check for other locations

MANHATTAN
Detail at left
Detail at right

SOHO
Howard St.
Centre St.
Lafayette St.
Canal St.
Greene St.
Mercer St.
Wooster St.
W. Broadway
Lispenard St.
Walker St.
White St.
Cortlandt Aly.
Franklin St.
Benson St.
Catherine La.
Worth St.
Broadway
Elk St.
City Hall

TRIBECA
Rogan
Leonard St.
Thomas St.
Anbar
Duane St.
Chambers St.
Warren St.
Church St.
Bu & the Duck
Steven Alan*
Worth St.
Calypso*
Reade St.
W. Broadway
Murray St.
Fountain Pen Hospital

Ave. of the Americas
St. Johns La.
Beach St.
Ericsson Pl.
Franklin St.
Hudson St.
Staple St.
DUANE PARK
Design Within Reach*
Urban Archaeology*
Varick St.
Canal St.
Vestry St.
Laight St.
Holland Tunnel Approach
Pompanoosuc Mills*
Issey Miyake*
Collester St.
Beach St.
Jay St.
Harrison St.
Duane St.
Myoptics*
WASHINGTON MARKET PARK
Greenwich St.
Warren St.

Watts St.
Desbrosses St.
Hudson St.
Greenwich St.
Washington St.
Hubert St.
N. Moore St.
West St.
Chambers St.
North End Ave.
Hudson River

1/8 mi
0

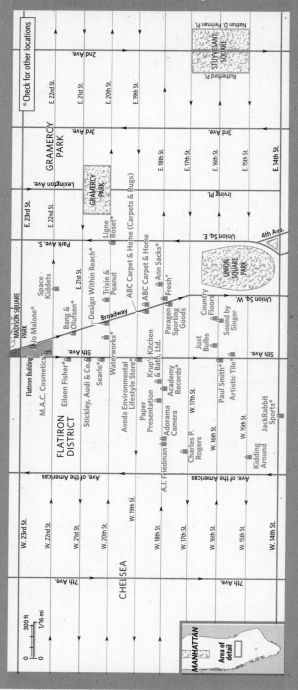

FLATIRON · UNION SQUARE

*Check for other locations

MADISON SQUARE PARK

GRAMERCY PARK

GRAMERCY PARK

UNION SQUARE PARK

FLATIRON DISTRICT

CHELSEA

Flatiron Building

M.A.C. Cosmetics*

Jo Malone*

Space Kiddets

Bang & Olufsen*

Design Within Reach*

Trixie & Peanut

Ligne Roset*

ABC Carpet & Home (Carpets & Rugs)

ABC Carpet & Home

Ann Sacks*

Fresh*

Eileen Fisher*

Waterworks*

Searle*

Broadway

Krup's Kitchen & Bath, Ltd.

Paragon Sporting Goods

Country Floors

Just Bulbs

Sound by Singer

Stickley, Audi & Co.*

Aveda Environmental Lifestyle Store*

Academy Records*

Paul Smith*

Artistic Tile*

Paper Presentation

Adorama Camera

A.I. Friedman

Charles P. Rogers

Kidding Around

JackRabbit Sports*

E. 23rd St.
E. 22nd St.
E. 22nd St.
E. 21st St.
E. 20th St.
E. 19th St.
E. 18th St.
E. 17th St.
E. 16th St.
E. 15th St.
E. 14th St.

2nd Ave.
3rd Ave.
Lexington Ave.
Irving Pl.
Park Ave. S.
Union Sq. E.
Union Sq. W.
4th Ave.
5th Ave.
Ave. of the Americas
7th Ave.

Nathan D. Perlman Pl.
Rutherford Pl.

STUYVESANT SQUARE

W. 23rd St.
W. 22nd St.
W. 21st St.
W. 20th St.
W. 19th St.
W. 18th St.
W. 17th St.
W. 16th St.
W. 15th St.
W. 14th St.

0   300 ft
0   1/16 mi

MANHATTAN

Area of detail

CENTRAL PARK

The Pond

Doris C. Freedman Plaza

5th Ave.

Madison Ave.

Park Ave.

* Check for other locations

E. 60th St.

Scully & Scully

A La Vieille Russie

E. 59th St.

Central Park S.

Baccarat

Bernardaud

Grand Army Plaza

W. 58th St.

Bergdorf Goodman

E. 58th St.

Bergdorf Goodman Men's

Van Cleef & Arpels

Chanel*

Dior New York

Brioni

W. 57th St.

Smythson of Bond St.

Piaget

E. 57th St.

Turnbull & Asser

Anthony Ltd

Mikimoto

Buccellati

W. 56th St.

Harry Winston

Oxxford Clothes

E. 56th St.

Allen Edmonds*

W. 55th St.

Wempe

E. 55th St.

Belgian Shoes

Manolo Blahnik

Bottega Veneta

Spring Flowers*

W. 54th St.

E. 54th St.

5th Ave.

St. John

E. 53rd St.

W. 53rd St.

Ermenegildo Zegna

Park Ave.

Brioni

Salvatore Ferragamo

Cartier*

W. 52nd St.

E. 52nd St.

H. Stern

W. 51st St.

E. 51st St.

St. Patrick's Cathedral

W. 50th St.

E. 50th St.

Rockefeller Center

5th Ave.

E. 49th St.

W. 49th St.

W. 48th St.

E. 48th St.

MANHATTAN

Area of detail

W. 47th St.

E. 47th St.

W. 46th St.

Madison Ave.

E. 46th St.

W. 45th St.

E. 45th St.

Bridge Kitchenware

Met Life Building

W. 44th St.

Allen Edmonds*

Vanderbilt Ave.

W. 43rd St.

Grand Central Terminal

W. 42nd St.

E. 42nd St.

BRYANT PARK

New York Public Library

0   1/8 mi

Park Ave.

MAPS

Chrystie St.

Stanton St.

Rivington St.

Bowery

Delancey St.

Bowery

Elizabeth St.

Grand St.

Prince St.

Elizabeth St.

Seize sur
Vingt

Ina*

Spring St.

Mott St.

Broome St.

NOLITA

Sigerson
Morrison

Find
Outlet*

Hollywould

Malia Mills
Swimwear*

LITTLE
ITALY

Mulberry St.

Ina*

Lilith

Crumpler
Bags*

Kenmare St.

Mott St.

Mulberry St.

Centre Market
Pl.

Calypso Kids
& Home

Cleveland
Pl.

Enfant

Calypso
& Bebe

Aero

Centre St.

Lafayette St.

Jersey St.

Prince St.

Crosby St.

Lafayette St.

Calypso's

Nanette
Lepore

W. Houston St.

Broadway

Bloomingdale's
SoHo*

Puma*

Crosby St.

Grand St.

**See SoHo detail map
on facing page below**

Mercer St.

Kiki De Montparnasse

Nicole Miller*

Diesel Denim
Gallery

Catherine
Malandrino*

Broadway

Broome St.

Kate
Spade

Babeland*

Ted-Baker

Greene St.

Jack
Spade

Alexis
Bittar

Yohji
Yamamoto

SOHO

Wooster St.

Spring St.

Eileen Fisher*

Morgane
Le Fay*

Selima
Optique*

Waterworks*

Greene St.

W. Broadway

Prince St.

Thompson St.

W. Broadway

Smith &
Hawken

Ralph Lauren*

Broome St.

Oliver
Peoples*

Wooster St.

Grand St.

Sullivan St.

MacDougal St.

Ave. of the Americas

Varick St.

Broome St.

Dominick St.

Watts St.

Varick St.

Spring St.

Holland Tunnel

Holland Tunnel
Entrance

W. Houston St.

King St.

Charlton St.

Vandam St.

Hudson St.

Canal St.

Hudson St.

300 ft

1/16 mi

0

0

* Check for other locations

MANHATTAN

Area of
detail

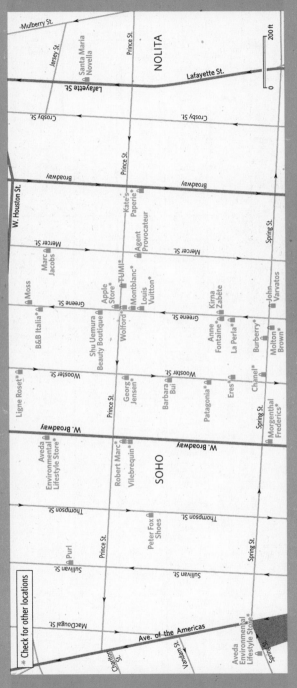

SoHo · NoLita

Mulberry St.

Jersey St.

Santa Maria Novella

Prince St.

NOLITA

Lafayette St.

Lafayette St.

0   200 ft

Crosby St.

Crosby St.

Prince St.

W. Houston St.

Broadway

Broadway

Spring St.

Kate's Paperie*

Mercer St.

Agent Provocateur

Mercer St.

Marc Jacobs

TUMI*

Moss

Apple Store*

Montblanc*

Louis Vuitton*

Greene St.

B&B Italia*

Greene St.

Kirna Zabête

John Varvatos

Shu Uemura Beauty Boutique

Wolford*

Anne Fontaine*

La Perla*

Burberry*

Ligne Roset*

Wooster St.

Georg Jensen*

Barbara Bui

Patagonia*

Eres*

Chanel*

Molton Brown*

Wooster St.

Prince St.

Spring St.

W. Broadway

W. Broadway

Morgenthal Frederics*

Aveda Environmental Lifestyle Store*

Robert Marc*

Vilebrequin*

SOHO

Thompson St.

Thompson St.

Peter Fox Shoes

Prince St.

Spring St.

Purl

Sullivan St.

Sullivan St.

* Check for other locations

MacDougal St.

Ave. of the Americas

Charlton St.

Vandam St.

Aveda Environmental Lifestyle Store*

Spring St.

Spring St.

MAPS

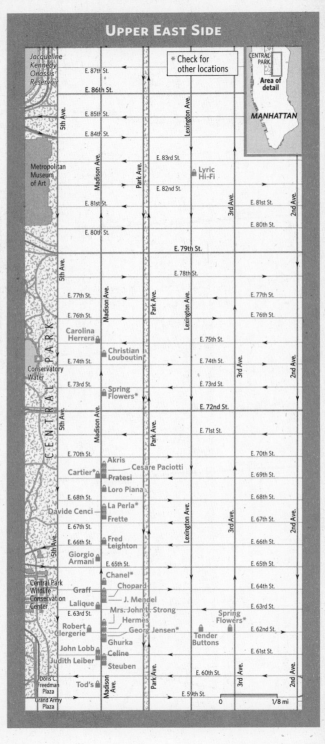

UPPER EAST SIDE

* Check for other locations

CENTRAL PARK

Area of detail

MANHATTAN

Jacqueline Kennedy Onassis Reservoir

E. 87th St.
E. 86th St.
E. 85th St.
E. 84th St.
E. 83rd St.
E. 82nd St.
E. 81st St.
E. 80th St.
E. 79th St.
E. 78th St.
E. 77th St.
E. 76th St.
E. 75th St.
E. 74th St.
E. 73rd St.
E. 72nd St.
E. 71st St.
E. 70th St.
E. 69th St.
E. 68th St.
E. 67th St.
E. 66th St.
E. 65th St.
E. 64th St.
E. 63rd St.
E. 62nd St.
E. 61st St.
E. 60th St.
E. 59th St.

5th Ave.
Madison Ave.
Park Ave.
Lexington Ave.
3rd Ave.
2nd Ave.

Metropolitan Museum of Art

Lyric Hi-Fi

Carolina Herrera

Christian Louboutin*

Spring Flowers*

Conservatory Water

CENTRAL PARK

Akris
Cartier*
Cesare Paciotti
Pratesi
Loro Piana
La Perla*
Davide Cenci
Frette
Fred Leighton
Giorgio Armani
Chanel*
Chopard
Graff
J. Mendel
Lalique
Mrs. John L. Strong
Hermes
Spring Flowers*
Robert Clergerie
Georg Jensen*
Tender Buttons
Ghurka
John Lobb
Celine
Judith Leiber
Steuben

Central Park Wildlife Conservation Center

Doris C. Freedman Plaza

Tod's

Grand Army Plaza

0   1/8 mi

374

subscribe to zagat.com

Albee Baby
Carriage Co.

W. 88th St.

Pet
Stop

CENTRAL
PARK

Area of
detail

MANHATTAN

Gruen
Optika*

W. 87th St.

W. 86th St.

West End Ave.

Broadway

Amsterdam Ave.

W. 85th St.

Columbus Ave.

W. 84th St.

W. 83rd St.

Harry's
Shoes

Avventura

W. 82nd St.

Central Park West

Schweitzer Linen*

Town
Shop

Yarn Co.

Greenstones*

W. 81st St.

Zabar's

Broadway

Patagonia*

W. 80th St.

Oriental Lamp
Shade Co.*

W. 79th St.

American
Museum
of
Natural
History

W. 78th St.

Super Runners
Shop*

Columbus Ave.

W. 77th St.

Bra
Smyth*

Jewish
Museum
Stores*

Amsterdam Ave.

Eileen Fisher*

W. 76th St.

Broadway

Bang &
Olufsen*

W. 75th St.

West End Ave.

W. 74th St.

North
Face*

VERDI
SQ.

W. 73rd St.

Tip Top
Kids

Columbus Ave.

CENTRAL

W. 73rd St.

Tip Top Shoes

W. 72nd St.

Strawberry
Fields

W. 72nd St.

Clarins*

W. 71st St.

W. 71st St.

Sabon*

Malia Mills
Swimwear*

W. 70th St.

Lancôme

Broadway

W. 69th St.

Gruen Optika*

Robert
Marc*

W. 68th St.

PARK

Gracious Home*

W. 67th St.

West End Ave.

Kiehl's*

M.A.C. Cosmetics*

Central Park West

Adventure
Playground

W. 66th St.

W. 66th St.

Alice Tully Hall/
Juilliard School

Tavern
on the
Green

W. 65th St.

W. 65th St.

Toga Bikes

Mitzi E. Newhouse/
Vivian Beaumont
Theaters

Avery
Fischer
Hall

Broadway

W. 64th St.

Amsterdam Ave.

Metropolitan
Opera House

Lincoln
Center

W. 63rd St.

W. 63rd St.

DAMROSCH
PARK

New York
State
Theater

Columbus Ave.

W. 62nd St.

W. 61st St.

W. 61st St.

W. 60th St.

Jacadi*

0   1/8 mi

Time Warner
Center

Columbus
Circle

MAPS

WEST VILLAGE · MEATPACKING DISTRICT

UNION SQUARE

E. 13th St.
E. 12th St.
4th Ave.
Broadway
Lafayette St.
Great Jones St.
Bond St.
Jones Aly.
E. Houston St.
Astor Pl.
NOHO
Great Jones Aly.
Shinbone Aly.
Broadway
La Petite Coquette
Broadway Panhandler
E. 11th St.
E. 10th St.
University Pl.
5th Ave.
Mercer St.
Waverly Pl.
Washington Pl.
W. 4th St.
W. 3rd St.
Bleecker St.
GREENWICH VILLAGE
Greene St.
Mercer St.
Washington Pl.
Generation Records
E. 9th St.
Greene St.
Washington Mews
E. 8th St.
Washington Sq. N.
La Guardia Pl.
Kate's Paperie*
W. 14th St.
W. 13th St.
W. 11th St.
W. 10th St.
W. 9th St.
Washington Sq. S.
Thompson St.
Sullivan St.
MacDougal St.
W. Houston St.
Sabon*
C.O. Bigelow Chemists
Geppetto's Toy Box
MacDougal Aly.
WASHINGTON SQUARE PARK
Minetta Ln.
Ave. of the Americas
Ave. of the Americas
Aedes De Venustas*
Greenwich Letterpress
Gay St.
Cornelia St.
Jones St.
Bleecker St.
Carmine St.
Downing St.
W. 12th St.
Canine Styles*
Waverly Pl.
W. 4th St.
Leroy St.
1/8 mi
0
Greenwich Ave.
7th Ave.
SHERIDAN SQUARE
Christopher St.
Perry St.
Charles St.
W. 10th St.
Grove St.
Barrow St.
Commerce St.
Bedford St.
7th Ave. S.
Morton St.

* Check for other locations

7th Ave.
W. 12th St.
W. 13th St.
Greenwich Ave.
Bank St.
Perry St.
7th Ave. S.
Waverly Pl.
Grove St.
Christopher St.
WEST VILLAGE
W. 11th St.
W. 4th St.
Marc by Marc Jacobs
Marc by Marc Jacobs Accessories
The Bathroom
James Perse
Selima Optique*
W. 10th St.
Leather Man
Ralph Lauren*
Bleecker St.
Christopher St.
W. 14th St.
8th Ave.
Jane St.
W. 4th St.
W. 12th St.
James Perse
Bond No. 9*
Lulu Guinness
Bonpoint*
Fresh*
Robert Marc*
Ralph Lauren*
W. 11th St.
Charles St.
Hudson St.
Horatio St.
Greenwich Ave.
Design Within Reach*
Alexander McQueen
Tracy Reese
9th Ave.
Christian Louboutin
Greenwich St.
W. 13th St.
W. 12th St.
Jane St.
Bethune St.
Bank St.
Washington St.
MEATPACKING DISTRICT
Little W. 12th St.
Gansevoort St.
Horatio St.
Jane St.
W. 12th St.
West St.
Bodum
Bloomfield St.
Jeffrey New York
Stella McCartney
La Perla*
10th Ave.
West St.
Hudson River
1/8 mi
0

MANHATTAN
Left detail
Right detail

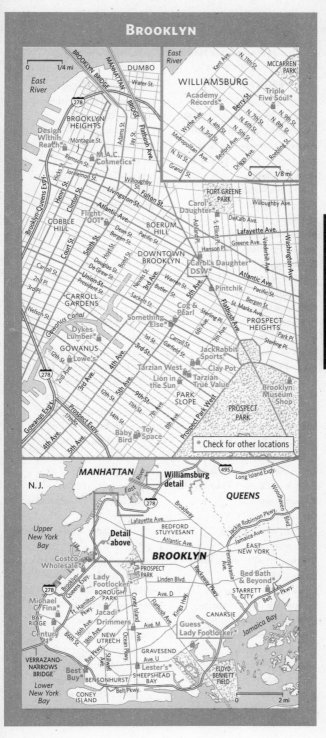

BROOKLYN

DUMBO

Water St.

East River

WILLIAMSBURG

N. 11th St.

Kent Ave.
N. 10th St.
MCCARREN PARK

Academy Records*
Berry St.
N. 9th St.
N. 8th St.
Triple Five Soul*

Wythe Ave.
N. 7th St.

N. 6th St.
N. 5th St.

Metropolitan Ave.
N. 4th St.
N. 3rd St.
Bedford Ave.

N. 1st St.
Driggs Ave.
Roebling St.

Grand St.

0   1/8 mi

0   1/4 mi

East River

BROOKLYN BRIDGE

MANHATTAN BRIDGE

278

BROOKLYN HEIGHTS

Adams St.

Tillary St.

Flatbush Ave.

Design Within Reach*

Montague St.

Remsen St.
Joralemon St.

M.A.C. Cosmetics*

Hicks St.

Henry St.

Clinton St.

Court St.

Willoughby St.

Fulton St.

Livingston St.

Atlantic Ave.

Flight 001*

COBBLE HILL

Smith St.

Dean St.
Bergen St.

Pacific St.

BOERUM HILL

FORT GREENE PARK

Willoughby Ave.

Carol's Daughter*

S. Elliott Pl.

DeKalb Ave.

Lafayette Ave.

Greene Ave.

Vanderbilt Ave.

Washington Ave.

Ashland Pl.

Hanson Pl.

DOWNTOWN BROOKLYN

Hoyt St.

Bond St.

Nevins St.

Douglass St.

De Graw St.

Union St.

President St.

CARROLL GARDENS

Carroll St.

2nd St.
3rd Pl.

Nelson St.

Warren St.

Carol's Daughter*

DSW*

Atlantic Ave.

Pacific St.

Bergen St.

St. Marks Ave.

Pintchik

3rd Ave.

4th Ave.

5th Ave.

Butler St.

Sackett St.

Cog & Pearl

Something Else*

1st St.

Carroll St.

3rd St.

Garfield St.

Sterling Pl.

6th St.

7th St.

PROSPECT HEIGHTS

Park Pl.

Sterling Pl.

JackRabbit Sports*

Clay Pot

Gowanus Canal

Dykes Lumber*

GOWANUS

Lowe's*

12th St.

3rd Ave.

2nd Ave.

278

Tarzian West*

Lion in the Sun

Tarzian True Value

PARK SLOPE

Brooklyn Museum Shop

PROSPECT PARK

5th Ave.

9th St.

11th St.

12th St.

14th St.

7th Ave.

Prospect Park West

Prospect Expy.

Gowanus Expy.

17th St.

4th Ave.

5th Ave.

Baby Bird

Toy Space

* Check for other locations

MANHATTAN

N.J.

East River

Williamsburg detail

495

Long Island Expy.

QUEENS

Broadway

278

Lafayette Ave.

Upper New York Bay

Detail above

BEDFORD STUYVESANT

Atlantic Ave.

Jackie Robinson Pkwy.

Jamaica Ave.

Woodhaven Blvd.

EAST NEW YORK

Costco Wholesale*

PROSPECT PARK

Linden Blvd.

BROOKLYN

Rockaway Ave.

Pennsylvania Ave.

Bed Bath & Beyond*

Belt Pkwy.

STARRETT CITY

278

Lady Footlocker

Ft. Hamilton Pkwy.

BOROUGH PARK

Jacadi

Drimmers

Ave. D

Kings Hwy.

Flatbush Ave.

CANARSIE

Jamaica Bay

Michael C. Fina*

BAY RIDGE

10th Ave.

18th Ave.

NEW UTRECH

Ave. M

Ocean Pkwy.

Guess*
Lady Footlocker

Century 21*

VERRAZANO-NARROWS BRIDGE

86th St.

Bay Pkwy.

Stillwell Ave.

GRAVESEND

Ave. U

Lester's*

SHEEPSHEAD BAY

FLOYD BENNETT FIELD

Best Buy*

BENSONHURST

Belt Pkwy.

Lower New York Bay

CONEY ISLAND

0   2 mi

MAPS

Merchandise

Includes store names and locations. ☑ indicates highest ratings, popularity and importance.

ACCESSORIES

Add Accessories | **SoHo**
🆕 Adrienne Vittadini | **W 40s**
Alessandro Dell'Acqua | **E 60s**
Amarcord Vintage | **multi. loc.**
Am. Eagle Outfitters | **multi. loc.**
Anna Sui | **SoHo**
🆕 Anne Klein | **E 60s**
Ascot Chang | **W 50s**
☑ Asprey | **E 70s**
A Uno/Walk | **TriBeCa**
Barbara Feinman | **E Vill**
Barneys CO-OP | **multi. loc.**
☑ Barneys New York | **E 60s**
🆕 Ben Sherman | **SoHo**
☑ Bergdorf Goodman | **E 50s**
☑ Bergdorf Men's | **E 50s**
Bird | **multi. loc.**
Blair Delmonico | **W 50s**
Bloom | **E 40s**
☑ Bloomingdale's | **multi. loc.**
Blueberi | **Dumbo**
🆕 Blue in Green | **SoHo**
Böc | **W 80s**
Bond 07 by Selima | **NoHo**
☑ Bottega Veneta | **E 50s**
B. Oyama Homme | **Harlem**
🆕 Bridal Reflect. | **Murray Hill**
Burberry | **multi. loc.**
Cantaloup/Luxe | **E 70s**
Catbird | **Williamsburg**
☑ Chanel | **multi. loc.**
Charles Tyrwhitt | **multi. loc.**
Cherry | **W Vill**
Chloé | **E 70s**
Christopher Fischer | **SoHo**
CK Bradley | **E 70s**
Claire's Accessories | **multi. loc.**
☑ Coach | **multi. loc.**
Cog & Pearl | **Park Slope**
🆕 Consignment | **Downtown**
D & G | **SoHo**
Dane 115 | **SoHo**
Daryl K | **NoHo**

Dear Fieldbinder | **Cobble Hill**
Destination | **Meatpacking**
Diane T | **Cobble Hill**
Dior Homme | **E 50s**
☑ Dior New York | **E 50s**
Dö Kham | **NoLita**
Dolce & Gabbana | **E 60s**
Dunhill | **E 50s**
Edith and Daha | **LES**
Eidolon | **Park Slope**
Ellen Christine | **Chelsea**
Etcetera | **multi. loc.**
Eye Candy | **NoHo**
Fabulous Fanny's | **E Vill**
Fendi | **E 50s**
Flying A | **SoHo**
4PlayBK | **Park Slope**
Geminola | **W Vill**
☑ Giorgio Armani | **E 60s**
🆕 Giorgio Fedon 19 | **W 40s**
Girl Props | **multi. loc.**
Good, Bad & Ugly | **NoLita**
Groupe | **NoLita**
Gucci | **multi. loc.**
🆕 Guy Laroche | **W 50s**
🆕 Hairy Mary's | **LES**
Hat Shop | **SoHo**
☑ Henri Bendel | **E 50s**
Henry Beguelin | **Meatpacking**
☑ Hermès | **E 60s**
🆕 Hollander & Lexer | **Boerum Hill**
Hooti Couture | **Prospect Hts**
Ibiza NY | **G Vill**
Institut NYC | **SoHo**
Intermix | **multi. loc.**
Jack Spade | **SoHo**
Jane | **E 70s**
J.Crew | **multi. loc.**
Jeffrey | **Meatpacking**
J.J. Hat Center | **Garment Dist**
☑ Judith Leiber | **E 60s**
🆕 Juicy Couture | **multi. loc.**
Jutta Neumann | **LES**

J.W. Cooper | **W 50s**
Kangol Columbus Ave. | **W 60s**
Kate Spade | **SoHo**
Kavanagh's | **E 40s**
Kieselstein-Cord | **E 80s**
NEW Kipepeo | **NoLita**
Kirna Zabête | **SoHo**
Lacoste | **multi. loc.**
LaCrasia Gloves | **Chelsea**
Laila Rowe | **multi. loc.**
Loom | **Park Slope**
NEW Loopy Mango | **Dumbo**
Z Lord & Taylor | **Murray Hill**
Z Loro Piana | **E 60s**
Louis Vuitton | **multi. loc.**
Loveday31 | **Astoria**
Ludivine | **G Vill**
Lulu Guinness | **W Vill**
Z Macy's | **multi. loc.**
Maleeka | **Downtown**
Marc Jacobs Access. | **W Vill**
Market NYC | **NoLita**
Marsha D.D. | **E 80s**
Z Marshalls | **Rego Pk**
NEW Max Azria | **SoHo**
NEW Meg Cohen Design | **SoHo**
Mexx | **multi. loc.**
Mick Margo | **W Vill**
Mini Mini Market | **Williamsburg**
Miriam Rigler | **E 60s**
Missoni | **E 70s**
Miss Sixty | **SoHo**
NEW Mulberry | **multi. loc.**
NEW N | **Harlem**
New York & Co. | **multi. loc.**
Nicole Miller | **SoHo**
NEW Nili Lotan | **TriBeCa**
Number (N)ine | **TriBeCa**
Odin | **multi. loc.**
Olive & Bette's | **multi. loc.**
Patina | **SoHo**
Patricia Field | **NoHo**
Paul Frank | **NoLita**
Paul Smith | **multi. loc.**
Pearl River Mart | **SoHo**
Plaza Too | **W 70s**
Poppy | **NoLita**
NEW Porsche Design | **E 50s**

Prince Charles III | **SoHo**
Pucci | **multi. loc.**
Ralph Lauren | **multi. loc.**
Rebecca Taylor | **NoLita**
Redberi | **Prospect Hts**
Resurrection | **NoLita**
Robert Talbott | **E 60s**
Ruehl | **W Vill**
Ruzzetti & Gow | **E 70s**
Sacco | **multi. loc.**
Z Saks Fifth Ave. | **E 50s**
Z Salvatore Ferragamo | **E 50s**
Samuel's Hats | **Financial Dist**
Searle | **multi. loc.**
Seigo | **multi. loc.**
Shop | **LES**
Some Odd Rubies | **LES**
Spring | **Dumbo**
Stella Dallas | **Williamsburg**
Steve Madden | **multi. loc.**
Steven Alan | **multi. loc.**
NEW Stuart & Wright | **Ft Greene**
Suzanne Couture | **E 60s**
Swiss Army | **SoHo**
Z Takashimaya | **E 50s**
TG-170 | **LES**
Thomas Pink | **multi. loc.**
Thom Browne | **TriBeCa**
Tory Burch | **NoLita**
NEW Tracy Reese | **Meatpacking**
NEW Trina Turk | **Meatpacking**
Triple Five Soul | **multi. loc.**
NEW Trunkt | **TriBeCa**
Z Turnbull & Asser | **E 50s**
NEW Uniqlo | **SoHo**
Urban Outfitters | **multi. loc.**
NEW Valley | **LES**
Versace | **E 50s**
Verve | **multi. loc.**
Warren Edwards | **E 60s**
Watts on Smith | **Carroll Gdns**
Wink | **multi. loc.**
Zachary's Smile | **G Vill**

ACTIVEWEAR
Active Wearhouse | **SoHo**
Adidas | **multi. loc.**
Athlete's Foot | **Flushing**
Z Billabong | **W 40s**

Bloch | **W 70s**

Capezio | **multi. loc.**

Champs | **multi. loc.**

City Sports | **multi. loc.**

Crunch | **multi. loc.**

Danskin | **W 60s**

Dave's Quality Meat | **E Vill**

NEW DC Shoes | **SoHo**

Dr. Jay's | **multi. loc.**

Equinox Energy Wear | **multi. loc.**

Fila | **E 40s**

NEW Golfsmith | **E 50s**

Itsasickness | **LES**

JackRabbit Sports | **multi. loc.**

KD Dance & Sport | **NoHo**

Lady Foot Locker | **multi. loc.**

NEW LuLuLemon | **multi. loc.**

NEW Napapijri | **SoHo**

NBA Store | **E 50s**

New Balance | **multi. loc.**

New York Running | **W 50s**

Niketown NY | **E 50s**

North Face | **multi. loc.**

NYC Velo | **E Vill**

On Stage Dance | **Murray Hill**

Orvis | **E 40s**

☑ Paragon | **Union Sq**

Patagonia | **multi. loc.**

P.J. Huntsman | **W 40s**

Princeton Ski Shop | **Flatiron**

Puma | **multi. loc.**

Quiksilver | **multi. loc.**

Reebok Concept Store | **W 60s**

Sansha | **W 50s**

Slope Sports | **Park Slope**

Sports Authority | **multi. loc.**

Super Runners Shop | **multi. loc.**

Supreme | **SoHo**

SwimBikeRun | **W 50s**

☑ Target | **multi. loc.**

Temperley | **SoHo**

ART SUPPLIES

A.I. Friedman | **Flatiron**

☑ Blick Art Materials | **NoHo**

DaVinci Art Supply | **Chelsea**

Kremer Pigments | **Chelsea**

Lee's Art Shop | **W 50s**

New York Central Art | **E Vill**

☑ Pearl Paint | **multi. loc.**

Sam Flax | **multi. loc.**

Utrecht | **multi. loc.**

BABY GEAR

Albee Baby Carriage | **W 90s**

Babies "R" Us | **multi. loc.**

☑ Bloomingdale's | **E 50s**

☑ buybuy BABY | **Chelsea**

Giggle | **multi. loc.**

Half Pint | **Dumbo**

Heights Kids | **Brooklyn Hts**

Kidville Boutique | **multi. loc.**

Kmart | **multi. loc.**

☑ Macy's | **multi. loc.**

NEW MoonSoup | **E 50s**

Planet Kids | **multi. loc.**

Psny | **SoHo**

Schneider's | **Chelsea**

Sears | **multi. loc.**

☑ Target | **multi. loc.**

BATHROOM FIXTURES/ TILES

☑ Ann Sacks | **multi. loc.**

☑ Artistic Tile | **multi. loc.**

☑ Bed Bath & Beyond | **multi. loc.**

Bisazza | **SoHo**

Blackman | **multi. loc.**

Boffi SoHo | **SoHo**

☑ Country Floors | **Union Sq**

Davis & Warshow | **multi. loc.**

☑ Gracious Home | **multi. loc.**

Hastings Tile | **E 50s**

☑ Home Depot | **multi. loc.**

Ideal Tile | **E 50s**

Kraft | **E 60s**

☑ Krup's Kitchen/Bath | **Flatiron**

Lowe's | **multi. loc.**

Manhattan Ctr. | **Flatiron**

Nemo Tile | **multi. loc.**

New York Replacement | **E 90s**

NEW Pottery Barn Bed/Bath | **Chelsea**

Quintessentials | **W 80s**

Restoration Hardware | **Flatiron**

Sears | **multi. loc.**

Sherle Wagner Int'l | **E 50s**

NEW Sicis | **SoHo**

Sid's | **Downtown**
☑ Simon's Hardware | **Gramercy**
☑ Urban Archaeology | **multi. loc.**
☑ Waterworks | **multi. loc.**

BED/BATH

☑ ABC Carpet & Home | **Flatiron**
ABC Carpet/Whse. Outlet | **Bronx**
NEW Abitare | **Brooklyn Hts**
Apartment 48 | **Flatiron**
Armani Casa | **SoHo**
auto | **Meatpacking**
Baker Tribeca | **TriBeCa**
☑ Bed Bath & Beyond | **multi. loc.**
☑ Bergdorf Goodman | **E 50s**
☑ Bloomingdale's | **E 50s**
Calvin Klein | **E 60s**
Calypso Home | **NoLita**
Chambers Outlet | **E 70s**
☑ Charles P. Rogers | **Flatiron**
Conran Shop | **E 50s**
☑ Crate & Barrel | **multi. loc.**
Dö Kham | **NoLita**
E. Braun & Co. | **E 60s**
environment337 | **multi. loc.**
Ethan Allen | **multi. loc.**
☑ Filene's Basement | **multi. loc.**
Flou | **SoHo**
☑ Frette | **E 60s**
☑ Gracious Home | **multi. loc.**
☑ Harris Levy | **LES**
NEW Hastens | **SoHo**
John Derian | **E Vill**
NEW Kate's At Home | **SoHo**
Kmart | **multi. loc.**
Kreiss Collection | **E 50s**
La Cafetière | **Chelsea**
Layla | **Downtown**
Laytner's Linen | **multi. loc.**
Léron | **E 60s**
☑ Macy's | **multi. loc.**
NEW Madura | **E 80s**
☑ Marshalls | **multi. loc.**
☑ Maurice Villency | **E 50s**
Michele Varian | **SoHo**
Nancy Koltes Home | **NoLita**
Olatz | **W Vill**
Pearl River Mart | **SoHo**
Pier 1 Imports | **multi. loc.**

Porthault | **E 60s**
Pottery Barn | **multi. loc.**
☑ Pratesi | **E 60s**
Rachel Ashwell's | **SoHo**
Restoration Hardware | **Flatiron**
☑ Schweitzer Linen | **multi. loc.**
Sears | **multi. loc.**
NEW Signoria | **E 60s**
Sleep | **Williamsburg**
☑ Takashimaya | **E 50s**
☑ Target | **multi. loc.**
Tarzian West | **Park Slope**
Temperley | **SoHo**
Thomasville | **Bayside**
☑ Waterworks | **multi. loc.**
West Elm | **multi. loc.**
Yves Delorme | **E 70s**

BRIDAL

Adriennes | **LES**
Amsale | **E 50s**
☑ Bergdorf Goodman | **E 50s**
Birnbaum & Bullock | **Chelsea**
Blue | **E Vill**
Bridal Garden | **Flatiron**
NEW Bridal Reflect. | **Murray Hill**
☑ Carolina Herrera | **E 70s**
Clea Colet | **E 70s**
David's Bridal | **LIC**
Gallery/Wearable Art | **E 60s**
Hazel's Shoes | **Bayside**
Here Comes Bridesmaid | **Chelsea**
Jane Wilson-Marquis | **E 70s**
Kleinfeld | **Chelsea**
Lara Hélène | **E 60s**
☑ Macy's | **multi. loc.**
Mark Ingram Bridal | **E 50s**
Mary Adams The Dress | **LES**
Michael's/Consignment | **E 70s**
Michelle NY | **Boerum Hill**
Mika Inatome | **TriBeCa**
Miriam Rigler | **E 60s**
My Glass Slipper | **Flatiron**
☑ Peter Fox Shoes | **SoHo**
Pilar Rossi | **E 60s**
Reem Acra | **E 60s**
RK Bridal | **Garment Dist**
☑ Saks Fifth Ave. | **E 50s**
Selia Yang | **multi. loc.**

Stuart Weitzman | **multi. loc.**
Suzanne Couture | **E 60s**
VeKa Bridal Couture | **NoLita**
Vera Wang Bridal | **E 70s**
Vera Wang Maids | **E 70s**
Wedding Library | **E 70s**
Wedding Things | **E 60s**

CABINETRY

Boffi SoHo | **SoHo**
Elgot | **E 60s**
🔲 Home Depot | **multi. loc.**
🔲 Krup's Kitchen/Bath | **Flatiron**
Lowe's | **multi. loc.**
Manhattan Ctr. | **Flatiron**
Poggenpohl U.S. | **multi. loc.**
Quintessentials | **W 80s**

CAMERAS/VIDEO EQUIPMENT

🔲 Adorama Camera | **Flatiron**
Alkit | **Flatiron**
🔲 B&H Photo-Video | **Garment Dist**
🔲 Best Buy | **multi. loc.**
🔲 Bloomingdale's | **E 50s**
Camera Land | **E 50s**
Circuit City | **multi. loc.**
42nd St. Photo | **Garment Dist**
🔲 J&R Music/Computer | **Financial Dist**
Olden Camera/Lens | **Garment Dist**
Sears | **multi. loc.**
🔲 Sony Style | **E 50s**
🔲 Target | **multi. loc.**
Willoughby's | **Garment Dist**

CDS/VIDEOS/RECORDS/DVDS

Academy Records | **multi. loc.**
🔲 Best Buy | **multi. loc.**
Bleecker Bob's | **G Vill**
Bleecker St. Records | **G Vill**
Blockbuster Video | **multi. loc.**
Colony Music | **W 40s**
Disc-O-Rama | **multi. loc.**
Etherea | **E Vill**
Fat Beats | **G Vill**
Finyl Vinyl | **E Vill**
f.y.e. | **W 50s**
Generation Records | **G Vill**

halcyon the shop | **Dumbo**
House of Oldies | **G Vill**
Jammyland | **E Vill**
🔲 J&R Music/Computer | **Financial Dist**
Jazz Record Center | **Chelsea**
Kim's Mediapolis | **multi. loc.**
Met. Opera Shop | **W 60s**
Norman's Sound/Vision | **E Vill**
🔲 Other Music | **NoHo**
Rebel Rebel | **W Vill**
Rockit Sci. Records | **E Vill**
Rocks in Your Head | **Williamsburg**
St. Marks Sounds | **E Vill**
Strider Records | **G Vill**
TLA Video | **G Vill**
Top DJ Gear | **NoLita**
Vinylmania | **G Vill**
🔲 Virgin Megastore | **multi. loc.**

CHILDREN'S BEDDING/LAYETTE

Babies "R" Us | **multi. loc.**
Baby Bird | **Park Slope**
Bambini | **E 80s**
Bellini | **E 60s**
Burlington Coat | **multi. loc.**
🔲 buybuy BABY | **Chelsea**
Erica Tanov | **NoLita**
Heights Kids | **Brooklyn Hts**
Jacadi | **multi. loc.**
🔲 Lord & Taylor | **Murray Hill**
🔲 Macy's | **multi. loc.**
NEW Olá Baby | **Carroll Gdns**
NEW Pottery Barn Kids | **E 60s**
Ralph Lauren Layette | **E 70s**
🔲 Saks Fifth Ave. | **E 50s**

CLOTHING: CHILDREN'S

Agatha Ruiz de la Prada | **SoHo**
Area | **multi. loc.**
Babies "R" Us | **multi. loc.**
BabyGap | **multi. loc.**
Babylicious | **TriBeCa**
Bambini | **E 80s**
🔲 Barneys New York | **E 60s**
NEW Belle & Maxie | **Ditmas Pk**
🔲 Bergdorf Goodman | **E 50s**
🔲 Bloomingdale's | **E 50s**

Bonne Nuit | **E 70s**

🆉 Bonpoint | **multi. loc.**

Bu and the Duck | **TriBeCa**

Burlington Coat | **multi. loc.**

🆉 buybuy BABY | **Chelsea**

Calypso Enfant/Kids | **SoHo**

Capucine | **TriBeCa**

Catimini | **E 80s**

🆉 Century 21 | **multi. loc.**

Children's Place | **multi. loc.**

City Cricket | **W Vill**

NEW C.P.W. | **W 80s**

Crembebè | **E Vill**

NEW Crew Cuts | **SoHo**

🆉 Daffy's | **multi. loc.**

Didi's Children's | **E 80s**

Diesel Kids | **SoHo**

Diva | **Midwood**

Erica Tanov | **NoLita**

Estella | **G Vill**

🆉 Filene's Basement | **multi. loc.**

flora and henri | **E 70s**

Flying Squirrel | **Williamsburg**

GapKids | **multi. loc.**

Giggle | **multi. loc.**

Granny-Made | **W 70s**

Green Onion | **Cobble Hill**

Greenstones | **multi. loc.**

Gymboree | **multi. loc.**

Heights Kids | **Brooklyn Hts**

NEW Juicy Couture | **W Vill**

Julian & Sara | **SoHo**

Kid Robot | **SoHo**

Kidville Boutique | **multi. loc.**

Kmart | **multi. loc.**

Koh's Kids | **TriBeCa**

Lacoste | **multi. loc.**

Le Sabon & Baby Too | **E 60s**

Les Petits Chapelais | **SoHo**

Lester's | **multi. loc.**

Liberty House | **W 100s**

Lilliput | **multi. loc.**

NEW Little Stinkers | **E Vill**

🆉 Lord & Taylor | **Murray Hill**

NEW Lucky Kid | **SoHo**

Lucky Wang | **multi. loc.**

NEW Lulu Castagnette | **NoLita**

🆉 Macy's | **multi. loc.**

Magic Windows | **E 80s**

Marie-Chantal | **E 80s**

🆉 Marshalls | **multi. loc.**

NEW Mish Mish | **E 90s**

NEW MoonSoup | **E 50s**

Morris Brothers | **W 80s**

Natalie & Friends | **E 60s**

Natan Borlam's | **Williamsburg**

Naturino | **multi. loc.**

North Face | **multi. loc.**

Oilily | **multi. loc.**

Old Navy | **multi. loc.**

NEW Paulina Quintana | **E Vill**

Peanutbutter & Jane | **W Vill**

Pearl River Mart | **SoHo**

Peter Elliot | **E 70s**

Pomme | **Dumbo**

Prince & Princess | **E 70s**

Rachel Riley | **E 90s**

Ralph Lauren Boys/Girls | **E 70s**

Ralph Lauren Layette | **E 70s**

NEW Roberta Roller Rabbit | **E 70s**

🆉 Saks Fifth Ave. | **E 50s**

Sam & Seb | **Williamsburg**

Scoop Kids | **Meatpacking**

Sears | **multi. loc.**

Shoofly | **TriBeCa**

Sons + Daughters | **E Vill**

Space Kiddets | **Flatiron**

🆉 Spring Flowers | **multi. loc.**

Talbots Kids/Babies | **multi. loc.**

🆉 Target | **multi. loc.**

Tribeca Girls | **TriBeCa**

NEW Trico Field | **SoHo**

Tuesday's Child | **Midwood**

Umkarna | **Park Slope**

NEW Uniqlo | **SoHo**

United Colors/Kids | **W 50s**

World of Disney | **E 50s**

Yoya/Yoya Mart | **W Vill**

CLOTHING: DESIGNER

a. cheng | **E Vill**

Agatha Ruiz de la Prada | **SoHo**

Agnès B. | **multi. loc.**

🆉 Akris | **E 60s**

Alessandro Dell'Acqua | **E 60s**

🆉 Alexander McQueen | **Meatpacking**

Alpana Bawa | **E Vill**

Anna Sui | **SoHo**

Anne Fontaine | **multi. loc.**

NEW Anne Klein | **E 60s**

Annelore | **W Vill**

Z Asprey | **E 70s**

Z Balenciaga | **Chelsea**

Barbara Bui | **SoHo**

BCBG Max Azria | **multi. loc.**

Betsey Johnson | **multi. loc.**

Blanc de Chine | **E 50s**

BOSS Hugo Boss | **W 50s**

Z Bottega Veneta | **E 50s**

Z Brioni | **E 50s**

NEW Brunello Cucinelli | **W Vill**

Built by Wendy | **multi. loc.**

Burberry | **multi. loc.**

Calvin Klein | **E 60s**

NEW Calvin Tran | **NoLita**

Carlos Miele | **Meatpacking**

Z Carolina Herrera | **E 70s**

Catherine Malandrino | **multi. loc.**

Z Celine | **E 60s**

Z Chanel | **multi. loc.**

Charles Nolan | **Meatpacking**

Chloé | **E 70s**

Christopher Fischer | **SoHo**

Christopher Totman | **NoLita**

Cloak | **SoHo**

Comme des Garçons | **Chelsea**

Costume National | **SoHo**

C. Ronson | **NoLita**

Cynthia Rowley | **W Vill**

Dana Buchman | **E 50s**

D & G | **SoHo**

Daryl K | **NoHo**

Diane von Furstenberg |
   Meatpacking

Dior Homme | **E 50s**

Z Dior New York | **E 50s**

DKNY | **multi. loc.**

Dolce & Gabbana | **E 60s**

Domenico Vacca | **multi. loc.**

Donna Karan | **E 60s**

Dosa | **SoHo**

Duncan Quinn | **NoLita**

Elie Tahari | **SoHo**

Emanuel Ungaro | **E 60s**

Emporio Armani | **multi. loc.**

Z Ermenegildo Zegna | **E 50s**

Escada | **E 50s**

Eskandar | **G Vill**

Etro | **E 60s**

Fendi | **E 50s**

Ghost | **NoHo**

Gianfranco Ferré | **E 70s**

Z Giorgio Armani | **E 60s**

Givenchy | **E 60s**

Gucci | **multi. loc.**

NEW Guy Laroche | **W 50s**

Helen Wang | **SoHo**

Henry Beguelin | **Meatpacking**

Z Hermès | **E 60s**

Hugo Boss | **multi. loc.**

Issey Miyake | **multi. loc.**

Jackie Rogers | **E 70s**

Jill Stuart | **SoHo**

Jil Sander | **E 50s**

John Varvatos | **SoHo**

Joseph | **multi. loc.**

NEW Juicy Couture | **multi. loc.**

Kenneth Cole NY | **multi. loc.**

Kiton | **E 50s**

Krizia | **E 60s**

Lee Anderson | **E 60s**

Lilith | **NoLita**

Louis Vuitton | **multi. loc.**

Luca Luca | **multi. loc.**

Lucien Pellat-Finet | **G Vill**

Lucy Barnes | **Meatpacking**

Lyell | **NoLita**

Maison Martin Margiela | **W Vill**

Marc/Marc Jacobs | **W Vill**

Marc Jacobs | **SoHo**

Marie-Chantal | **E 80s**

Marni | **SoHo**

NEW Max Azria | **SoHo**

MaxMara | **multi. loc.**

Max Studio | **SoHo**

Mayle | **NoLita**

Michael Kors | **E 70s**

Missoni | **E 70s**

Miu Miu | **multi. loc.**

NEW M Missoni | **SoHo**

Morgane Le Fay | **multi. loc.**

Nanette Lepore | **SoHo**

Nicole Farhi | **E 60s**
Nicole Miller | **multi. loc.**
NEW Nili Lotan | **TriBeCa**
Number (N)ine | **TriBeCa**
OMO Norma Kamali | **W 50s**
⊿ Oscar de la Renta | **E 60s**
NEW Paulina Quintana | **E Vill**
Paul Smith | **multi. loc.**
NEW Petrou | **E 60s**
Phi | **SoHo**
Philosophy/A.Ferretti | **SoHo**
Pleats Please | **SoHo**
Poleci | **Meatpacking**
Prada | **multi. loc.**
Pucci | **multi. loc.**
Rachel Riley | **E 90s**
Ralph Lauren | **multi. loc.**
Ralph Lauren Boys/Girls | **E 70s**
Ralph Lauren Layette | **E 70s**
Rebecca & Drew | **Meatpacking**
Rebecca Taylor | **NoLita**
Roberto Cavalli | **E 60s**
Rubin Chapelle | **Meatpacking**
NEW Saja | **NoLita**
Sean John | **E 40s**
Shanghai Tang | **E 60s**
Shin Choi | **SoHo**
Sir | **Boerum Hill**
Sonia Rykiel | **E 70s**
NEW Sophia Eugene | **W Vill**
Stefano Ricci | **E 50s**
Stella McCartney | **Meatpacking**
⊿ St. John | **E 50s**
Ted Baker | **SoHo**
Temperley | **SoHo**
Theory | **multi. loc.**
Thom Browne | **TriBeCa**
NEW Tibi | **SoHo**
Tommy Hilfiger | **SoHo**
Tory Burch | **NoLita**
Tracy Feith | **NoLita**
NEW Tracy Reese | **Meatpacking**
NEW Trina Turk | **Meatpacking**
TSE | **Chelsea**
202 | **Chelsea**
Unis | **NoLita**
⊿ Valentino | **E 60s**
Versace | **E 50s**

Vivienne Tam | **SoHo**
Yigal Azrouel | **Meatpacking**
Yohji Yamamoto | **SoHo**
NEW Yoko Devereaux |
    Williamsburg
Yves Saint Laurent | **multi. loc.**
Zero/Maria Cornejo | **multi. loc.**

CLOTHING: MEN'S

Abercrombie & Fitch | **multi. loc.**
Addy & Ferro | **Ft Greene**
Alessandro Dell'Acqua | **E 60s**
Alife | **LES**
Allan & Suzi | **W 80s**
Alpana Bawa | **E Vill**
American Apparel | **multi. loc.**
Am. Eagle Outfitters | **multi. loc.**
Andy's Chee-Pees | **multi. loc.**
Anna Sui | **SoHo**
A.P.C. | **SoHo**
Ascot Chang | **W 50s**
⊿ Asprey | **E 70s**
Atelier NY | **SoHo**
Atrium | **NoHo**
A/X Armani Exchange | **multi. loc.**
B8 | **Meatpacking**
⊿ Banana Republic | **multi. loc.**
Banana Republic Men | **multi. loc.**
⊿ Barbour/Peter Elliot | **E 80s**
Barneys CO-OP | **multi. loc.**
⊿ Barneys New York | **E 60s**
Bathing Ape | **SoHo**
NEW Bblessing | **LES**
Beau Brummel | **multi. loc.**
NEW Ben Sherman | **SoHo**
⊿ Bergdorf Men's | **E 50s**
Big Drop | **E 70s**
Billy Martin's Western | **E 60s**
Blanc de Chine | **E 50s**
⊿ Bloomingdale's | **multi. loc.**
NEW Blue in Green | **SoHo**
Borrelli Boutique | **E 60s**
BOSS Hugo Boss | **W 50s**
B. Oyama Homme | **Harlem**
⊿ Brioni | **E 50s**
British Amer. Hse. | **E 50s**
Brooklyn Industries | **multi. loc.**
⊿ Brooks Brothers | **multi. loc.**
NEW Brunello Cucinelli | **W Vill**

MERCHANDISE

Buckler | **Meatpacking**
Burberry | **multi. loc.**
Burlington Coat | **multi. loc.**
Calvin Klein | **E 60s**
Camouflage | **Chelsea**
🆕 Caravan | **NoHo**
Casual Male XL | **multi. loc.**
Ⓩ Century 21 | **multi. loc.**
Charles Tyrwhitt | **multi. loc.**
Christopher Fischer | **SoHo**
Cloak | **SoHo**
Club Monaco | **multi. loc.**
Comme des Garçons | **Chelsea**
Costume National | **SoHo**
Custo Barcelona | **SoHo**
Ⓩ Daffy's | **multi. loc.**
D & G | **SoHo**
Dave's Army Navy | **Chelsea**
Dave's Quality Meat | **E Vill**
Ⓩ Davide Cenci | **E 60s**
Denimaxx | **E 40s**
Dior Homme | **E 50s**
DKNY | **multi. loc.**
Dolce & Gabbana | **E 60s**
Domenico Vacca | **multi. loc.**
Donna Karan | **E 60s**
Dr. Jay's | **multi. loc.**
Duncan Quinn | **NoLita**
Dunderdon Workshop | **SoHo**
Edge nyNoHo | **NoHo**
🆕 Ed Hardy | **Meatpacking**
Eisenberg Eisenberg | **Flatiron**
Emporio Armani | **multi. loc.**
Ⓩ Ermenegildo Zegna | **E 50s**
Eskandar | **G Vill**
Esprit | **multi. loc.**
🆕 Esthete | **Meatpacking**
Etro | **E 60s**
Express Men | **multi. loc.**
Façonnable | **E 50s**
Ⓩ Filene's Basement | **multi. loc.**
Flying A | **SoHo**
F.M. Allen | **E 70s**
Frank Stella | **multi. loc.**
🆕 Freemans Sporting | **LES**
French Connection | **multi. loc.**
Gabay's Outlet | **E Vill**
Gant | **E 50s**

Ⓩ Gap | **multi. loc.**
Gerry's | **multi. loc.**
Gianfranco Ferré | **E 70s**
Ⓩ Giorgio Armani | **E 60s**
Givenchy | **E 60s**
Groupe | **NoLita**
Gucci | **multi. loc.**
🆕 Guy Laroche | **W 50s**
Ⓩ H&M | **multi. loc.**
Henry Beguelin | **Meatpacking**
Ⓩ Hermès | **E 60s**
H. Herzfeld | **E 50s**
Hickey Freeman | **multi. loc.**
🆕 Hollander & Lexer | **Boerum Hill**
Hugo Boss | **multi. loc.**
🆕 IC Zinco | **SoHo**
IF | **SoHo**
Issey Miyake | **multi. loc.**
Itsasickness | **LES**
James Perse | **W Vill**
Jay Kos | **multi. loc.**
J.Crew | **multi. loc.**
Jeffrey | **Meatpacking**
Jil Sander | **E 50s**
J. Lindeberg | **SoHo**
J. McLaughlin | **E 90s**
John Varvatos | **SoHo**
Jos. A. Bank | **E 40s**
Joseph | **SoHo**
J. Press | **E 40s**
🆕 Juicy Couture | **W Vill**
🆕 K&G Fashion | **E 40s**
Kenneth Cole NY | **multi. loc.**
Kiton | **E 50s**
Kmart | **multi. loc.**
Krizia | **E 60s**
Kuhlman | **multi. loc.**
Lacoste | **multi. loc.**
Ⓩ Loehmann's | **multi. loc.**
Ⓩ Lord & Taylor | **Murray Hill**
🆕 Lord Willy's | **NoLita**
Ⓩ Loro Piana | **E 60s**
Louis Vuitton | **multi. loc.**
Lounge | **SoHo**
Lucien Pellat-Finet | **G Vill**
L'Uomo | **W Vill**
Ⓩ Macy's | **multi. loc.**

Maison Martin Margiela | **W Vill**
Marc/Marc Jacobs | **W Vill**
Marc Jacobs | **SoHo**
Marni | **SoHo**
🔲 Marshalls | **multi. loc.**
Men's Wearhse. | **multi. loc.**
Mexx | **multi. loc.**
Michael Kors | **E 70s**
🔳 NEW N | **Harlem**
🔳 NEW Napapijri | **SoHo**
Nicole Farhi | **E 60s**
99X | **E Vill**
Nom de Guerre | **NoHo**
North Face | **multi. loc.**
Number (N)ine | **TriBeCa**
Oak | **multi. loc.**
Odin | **multi. loc.**
Old Navy | **multi. loc.**
🔳 NEW Oliver Spencer | **W Vill**
Opening Ceremony | **SoHo**
Original Penguin | **W 40s**
🔳 NEW Oska | **SoHo**
🔲 Oxxford Clothes | **E 50s**
Parke & Ronen | **Chelsea**
Paul & Shark | **E 60s**
Paul Smith | **multi. loc.**
Paul Stuart | **E 40s**
Peter Elliot | **multi. loc.**
Phat Farm | **SoHo**
Pieces | **multi. loc.**
P.J. Huntsman | **W 40s**
Prada | **multi. loc.**
Prato Fine Men's Wear | **multi. loc.**
Prince Charles III | **SoHo**
Ralph Lauren | **multi. loc.**
Razor | **Park Slope**
Reiss | **multi. loc.**
Reminiscence | **Flatiron**
Roberto Cavalli | **E 60s**
Robert Talbott | **E 60s**
Rochester Big/Tall | **W 50s**
Rothman's | **Union Sq**
Rubin Chapelle | **Meatpacking**
Rugby | **G Vill**
🔲 Saks Fifth Ave. | **E 50s**
🔲 Salvatore Ferragamo | **E 50s**
Scoop Men's | **multi. loc.**
Sean | **multi. loc.**

Sean John | **E 40s**
Sears | **multi. loc.**
Seize sur Vingt | **NoLita**
Shanghai Tang | **E 60s**
Shirt Store | **E 40s**
Sisley | **multi. loc.**
Something Else | **multi. loc.**
Stefano Ricci | **E 50s**
Steven Alan | **multi. loc.**
🔳 NEW Stuart & Wright | **Ft Greene**
Stussy NY | **SoHo**
🔲 Takashimaya | **E 50s**
🔲 Talbots | **E 50s**
🔲 Target | **multi. loc.**
Ted Baker | **SoHo**
Thomas Pink | **multi. loc.**
Thom Browne | **TriBeCa**
Timberland | **E 60s**
🔲 T.J. Maxx | **multi. loc.**
Tokio 7 | **E Vill**
Tommy Hilfiger | **SoHo**
Transit | **NoHo**
Trash and Vaudeville | **E Vill**
🔳 NEW Treehouse | **Williamsburg**
🔳 NEW Trina Turk | **Meatpacking**
Triple Five Soul | **multi. loc.**
🔲 Turnbull & Asser | **E 50s**
202 | **Chelsea**
🔳 NEW Uniqlo | **SoHo**
Unis | **NoLita**
Urban Outfitters | **multi. loc.**
🔲 Valentino | **E 60s**
Versace | **E 50s**
Vilebrequin | **multi. loc.**
🔳 NEW Von Dutch | **SoHo**
Watts on Smith | **Carroll Gdns**
🔳 NEW WeSC | **SoHo**
🔳 NEW Ylli | **Williamsburg**
Yohji Yamamoto | **SoHo**
🔳 NEW Yoko Devereaux |
    Williamsburg
Yves Saint Laurent | **multi. loc.**
Zara | **multi. loc.**

CLOTHING: MEN'S/ WOMEN'S

(Stores carrying both)
Addy & Ferro | **Ft Greene**
American Apparel | **multi. loc.**

A.P.C. | **SoHo**

A/X Armani Exchange | **multi. loc.**

☑ Banana Republic | **multi. loc.**

☑ Barbour/Peter Elliot | **E 80s**

Barneys CO-OP | **multi. loc.**

☑ Barneys New York | **E 60s**

NEW Ben Sherman | **SoHo**

Big Drop | **multi. loc.**

Billy Martin's Western | **E 60s**

☑ Bloomingdale's | **multi. loc.**

Brooklyn Industries | **multi. loc.**

☑ Brooks Brothers | **multi. loc.**

NEW Caravan | **NoHo**

Club Monaco | **multi. loc.**

Denimaxx | **E 40s**

Dö Kham | **NoLita**

Dr. Jay's | **multi. loc.**

Edge nyNoHo | **NoHo**

NEW Ed Hardy | **Meatpacking**

Esprit | **multi. loc.**

NEW Esthete | **Meatpacking**

Façonnable | **E 50s**

Flying A | **SoHo**

French Connection | **multi. loc.**

☑ Gap | **multi. loc.**

Gerry's | **multi. loc.**

☑ H&M | **multi. loc.**

NEW IC Zinco | **SoHo**

IF | **SoHo**

James Perse | **W Vill**

J.Crew | **multi. loc.**

Jeffrey | **Meatpacking**

J. McLaughlin | **E 90s**

Kmart | **multi. loc.**

Kuhlman | **multi. loc.**

Lacoste | **multi. loc.**

☑ Lord & Taylor | **Murray Hill**

☑ Loro Piana | **E 60s**

Lounge | **SoHo**

☑ Macy's | **multi. loc.**

Mexx | **multi. loc.**

NEW N | **Harlem**

Oak | **multi. loc.**

Old Navy | **multi. loc.**

Opening Ceremony | **SoHo**

NEW Oska | **SoHo**

Phat Farm | **SoHo**

Pieces | **multi. loc.**

Reiss | **multi. loc.**

Rugby | **G Vill**

☑ Saks Fifth Ave. | **E 50s**

Seize sur Vingt | **NoLita**

Sisley | **multi. loc.**

Something Else | **multi. loc.**

Steven Alan | **multi. loc.**

NEW Stuart & Wright | **Ft Greene**

☑ Talbots | **multi. loc.**

☑ Target | **multi. loc.**

Transit | **NoHo**

Trash and Vaudeville | **E Vill**

NEW Treehouse | **Williamsburg**

Triple Five Soul | **multi. loc.**

NEW Uniqlo | **SoHo**

UnitedColors/Benetton | **multi. loc.**

Urban Outfitters | **multi. loc.**

NEW Von Dutch | **SoHo**

NEW WeSC | **SoHo**

NEW Ylli | **Williamsburg**

Zara | **multi. loc.**

CLOTHING: TWEEN/ TEEN

Abercrombie & Fitch | **multi. loc.**

Adidas | **multi. loc.**

Am. Eagle Outfitters | **multi. loc.**

☑ Anthropologie | **multi. loc.**

Arden B. | **multi. loc.**

Bebe | **multi. loc.**

Berkley Girl | **multi. loc.**

Betsey Johnson | **multi. loc.**

☑ Billabong | **W 40s**

☑ Bloomingdale's | **multi. loc.**

☑ Century 21 | **multi. loc.**

Charlotte Russe | **multi. loc.**

Diva | **Midwood**

Dr. Jay's | **multi. loc.**

Express | **multi. loc.**

Forever 21 | **multi. loc.**

4PlayBK | **Park Slope**

French Connection | **multi. loc.**

G.C. William | **multi. loc.**

☑ H&M | **multi. loc.**

Infinity | **E 80s**

J.Crew | **multi. loc.**

Joyce Leslie | **multi. loc.**

Kmart | **multi. loc.**

Lester's | **multi. loc.**

Limited Too | multi. loc.
Ⓩ Loehmann's | multi. loc.
Lord of the Fleas | W 70s
Ⓩ Macy's | multi. loc.
Magic Windows | E 80s
Marsha D.D. | E 80s
NEW Mish Mish | E 90s
Morris Brothers | W 80s
Natalie & Friends | E 60s
Old Navy | multi. loc.
Patagonia | multi. loc.
Paul Frank | NoLita
Petit Bateau | E 80s
Phat Farm | SoHo
Planet Kids | multi. loc.
Puma | multi. loc.
Quiksilver | multi. loc.
Rugby | G Vill
Ⓩ Saks Fifth Ave. | E 50s
Strawberry | multi. loc.
Tribeca Girls | TriBeCa
Triple Five Soul | multi. loc.
Tuesday's Child | Midwood
Urban Outfitters | multi. loc.
V.I.M. | multi. loc.
Wet Seal | Garment Dist
Yellow Rat Bastard | multi. loc.

CLOTHING: WOMEN'S

Abercrombie & Fitch | multi. loc.
ABH Design | E 70s
a. cheng | E Vill
Addy & Ferro | Ft Greene
NEW Adrienne Vittadini | W 40s
Agatha Ruiz de la Prada | SoHo
Agnès B. | multi. loc.
Ⓩ Akris | E 60s
Albertine | G Vill
Alessandro Dell'Acqua | E 60s
Ⓩ Alexander McQueen |
   Meatpacking
NEW alice + olivia | W 40s
Allan & Suzi | W 80s
Alpana Bawa | E Vill
American Apparel | multi. loc.
Am. Eagle Outfitters | multi. loc.
Anik | multi. loc.
Anna | E Vill
Anna Sui | SoHo

Ann Crabtree | E 90s
Anne Fontaine | multi. loc.
Annelore | W Vill
Ⓩ Ann Taylor | multi. loc.
Ⓩ Ann Taylor Loft | multi. loc.
Ⓩ Anthropologie | multi. loc.
A.P.C. | SoHo
Arden B. | multi. loc.
Ⓩ Asprey | E 70s
Atrium | NoHo
A Uno/Walk | TriBeCa
A/X Armani Exchange | multi. loc.
Ⓩ Balenciaga | Chelsea
Ⓩ Banana Republic | multi. loc.
Barami | multi. loc.
Barbara Bui | SoHo
Ⓩ Barbour/Peter Elliot | E 80s
Barneys CO-OP | multi. loc.
Ⓩ Barneys New York | E 60s
Bathing Ape | SoHo
BCBG Max Azria | multi. loc.
Bebe | multi. loc.
Beneath | E 70s
Ⓩ Bergdorf Goodman | E 50s
Betsey Bunky Nini | E 70s
Betsey Johnson | multi. loc.
Big Drop | multi. loc.
Billy Martin's Western | E 60s
Bird | multi. loc.
Blair Delmonico | W 50s
Blanc de Chine | E 50s
Ⓩ Bloomingdale's | multi. loc.
Blue | E Vill
Blueberi | Dumbo
blush | W Vill
Böc | W 80s
Bond 07 by Selima | NoHo
BOSS Hugo Boss | W 50s
Brooklyn Collective | Red Hook
Brooklyn Industries | multi. loc.
Ⓩ Brooks Brothers | multi. loc.
NEW Brunello Cucinelli | W Vill
Built by Wendy | Little Italy
Burberry | multi. loc.
Burlington Coat | multi. loc.
Butik | W Vill
Butter | Downtown

Caché | multi. loc.
Calvin Klein | E 60s
NEW Calvin Tran | NoLita
Calypso | multi. loc.
Cantaloup/Luxe | E 70s
NEW Caravan | NoHo
Carlos Miele | Meatpacking
Z Carolina Herrera | E 70s
Castor & Pollux | W Vill
Catbird | Williamsburg
Catherine Malandrino | multi. loc.
Z Celine | E 60s
Z Century 21 | multi. loc.
Z Chanel | multi. loc.
Charles Nolan | Meatpacking
Charles Tyrwhitt | multi. loc.
Chico's | multi. loc.
Chloé | E 70s
Christopher Fischer | SoHo
Christopher Totman | NoLita
CK Bradley | E 70s
Cloth | Ft Greene
Club Monaco | multi. loc.
CoCo & Delilah | E Vill
Comme des Garçons | Chelsea
Costume National | SoHo
NEW C.P.W. | W 80s
C. Ronson | NoLita
Custo Barcelona | SoHo
Cynthia Rowley | W Vill
Z Daffy's | multi. loc.
Dana Buchman | E 50s
D & G | SoHo
Darling | W Vill
Daryl K | NoHo
Dave's Quality Meat | E Vill
Dear Fieldbinder | Cobble Hill
Denimaxx | E 40s
Dernier Cri | Meatpacking
Designer Resale | E 80s
Destination | Meatpacking
Diana Kane | Park Slope
Diane T | Cobble Hill
Diane von Furstenberg |
    Meatpacking
Z Dior New York | E 50s
DKNY | multi. loc.
D/L Cerney | E Vill

Dolce & Gabbana | E 60s
Dolce Vita | LES
Domenico Vacca | multi. loc.
Donna Karan | E 60s
Dosa | SoHo
Edge nyNoHo | NoHo
NEW Ed Hardy | Meatpacking
Eidolon | Park Slope
Eileen Fisher | multi. loc.
Elie Tahari | SoHo
Elizabeth Charles | Meatpacking
Emanuel Ungaro | E 60s
NEW EMc2 | NoLita
Emmelle | multi. loc.
Emporio Armani | multi. loc.
Erica Tanov | NoLita
Z Ermenegildo Zegna | E 50s
Escada | E 50s
Eskandar | G Vill
Esprit | multi. loc.
NEW Esthete | Meatpacking
Etro | E 60s
Express | multi. loc.
Façonnable | E 50s
Fendi | E 50s
Z Filene's Basement | multi. loc.
Find Outlet | multi. loc.
Flying A | SoHo
F.M. Allen | E 70s
Foley + Corinna | LES
Forever 21 | multi. loc.
Forréal | E 70s
4PlayBK | Park Slope
French Connection | multi. loc.
Gabay's Outlet | E Vill
Gallery/Wearable Art | E 60s
Z Gap | multi. loc.
G.C. William | multi. loc.
Geminola | W Vill
Gerry's | multi. loc.
Ghost | NoHo
Gianfranco Ferré | E 70s
Z Giorgio Armani | E 60s
Girlshop | Meatpacking
Girly NYC | E Vill
Givenchy | E 60s
Goldy + Mac | Park Slope
Good, Bad & Ugly | NoLita

Gucci | **multi. loc.**
NEW Guy Laroche | **W 50s**
NEW Hairy Mary's | **LES**
Ⓩ H&M | **multi. loc.**
Helen Wang | **SoHo**
Ⓩ Henri Bendel | **E 50s**
Henry Beguelin | **Meatpacking**
Ⓩ Hermès | **E 60s**
Hugo Boss | **multi. loc.**
Ibiza NY | **G Vill**
NEW IC Zinco | **SoHo**
IF | **SoHo**
I Heart | **NoLita**
Institut NYC | **SoHo**
Intermix | **multi. loc.**
Irma | **W Vill**
Issey Miyake | **multi. loc.**
Itsasickness | **LES**
Jackie Rogers | **E 70s**
James Perse | **W Vill**
Jane | **E 70s**
J.Crew | **multi. loc.**
Jeffrey | **Meatpacking**
Jill Stuart | **SoHo**
Jil Sander | **E 50s**
J. McLaughlin | **multi. loc.**
Joseph | **multi. loc.**
Joyce Leslie | **multi. loc.**
NEW Juicy Couture | **multi. loc.**
NEW Jumelle | **Williamsburg**
NEW Kaight | **LES**
NEW K&G Fashion | **E 40s**
Kenneth Cole NY | **multi. loc.**
Key | **SoHo**
Kirna Zabête | **SoHo**
Kiton | **E 50s**
Kmart | **multi. loc.**
Krizia | **E 60s**
Kuhlman | **multi. loc.**
Lacoste | **multi. loc.**
Lee Anderson | **E 60s**
NEW Leontine | **Seaport**
LF Stores | **multi. loc.**
Lilith | **NoLita**
Linda Dresner | **E 50s**
Living Fifth/Seventh/Smith | **multi. loc.**
Ⓩ Loehmann's | **multi. loc.**

Loom | **Park Slope**
NEW Loopy Mango | **Dumbo**
Ⓩ Lord & Taylor | **Murray Hill**
Lord of the Fleas | **W 70s**
Ⓩ Loro Piana | **E 60s**
Louis Vuitton | **multi. loc.**
Lounge | **SoHo**
NEW Love Brigade | **Williamsburg**
Luca Luca | **multi. loc.**
Lucien Pellat-Finet | **G Vill**
Lucy Barnes | **Meatpacking**
Ludivine | **G Vill**
NEW Lulu Castagnette | **NoLita**
Lyell | **NoLita**
Ⓩ Macy's | **multi. loc.**
Maison Martin Margiela | **W Vill**
Maleeka | **Downtown**
Marc/Marc Jacobs | **W Vill**
Marc Jacobs | **SoHo**
Marimekko | **E 70s**
Market NYC | **NoLita**
Marni | **SoHo**
Ⓩ Marshalls | **multi. loc.**
Matta | **NoLita**
NEW Max Azria | **SoHo**
MaxMara | **multi. loc.**
Max Studio | **SoHo**
Mayle | **NoLita**
Mexx | **multi. loc.**
Michael Kors | **E 70s**
Michelle NY | **Boerum Hill**
Mick Margo | **W Vill**
miks | **LES**
NEW Mimi's Closet | **Astoria**
Min-K | **multi. loc.**
Missoni | **E 70s**
Miss Sixty | **SoHo**
Miu Miu | **multi. loc.**
NEW M Missoni | **SoHo**
Montmartre | **multi. loc.**
Morgane Le Fay | **multi. loc.**
NEW N | **Harlem**
Nancy & Co. | **E 80s**
Nanette Lepore | **SoHo**
NEW Napapijri | **SoHo**
NEW Nave | **SoHo**
Necessary Clothing | **multi. loc.**
Nellie M. Boutique | **E 80s**

New York & Co. | **multi. loc.**
New York Look | **multi. loc.**
Nicole Farhi | **E 60s**
Nicole Miller | **multi. loc.**
NEW Nili Lotan | **TriBeCa**
Noisette | **Williamsburg**
North Face | **multi. loc.**
Number (N)ine | **TriBeCa**
Oak | **multi. loc.**
Oilily | **multi. loc.**
Old Navy | **multi. loc.**
Olive & Bette's | **multi. loc.**
OMO Norma Kamali | **W 50s**
Opening Ceremony | **SoHo**
Z Oscar de la Renta | **E 60s**
NEW Oska | **SoHo**
Otte | **multi. loc.**
Patricia Field | **NoHo**
Paul Smith | **SoHo**
Paul Stuart | **E 40s**
Pearl River Mart | **SoHo**
Peter Elliot | **E 80s**
NEW Petrou | **E 60s**
Phat Farm | **SoHo**
Phi | **SoHo**
Philosophy/A.Ferretti | **SoHo**
Pieces | **multi. loc.**
Pleats Please | **SoHo**
Poleci | **Meatpacking**
Pookie & Sebastian | **multi. loc.**
Poppy | **NoLita**
Prada | **multi. loc.**
Project 234 | **NoLita**
Pucci | **multi. loc.**
Puma | **multi. loc.**
Purdy Girl | **multi. loc.**
Ralph Lauren | **multi. loc.**
Rebecca & Drew | **Meatpacking**
Rebecca Taylor | **NoLita**
Redberi | **Prospect Hts**
Reiss | **multi. loc.**
Roberta Freymann | **E 70s**
Roberto Cavalli | **E 60s**
Rubin Chapelle | **Meatpacking**
Rue St. Denis | **E Vill**
Rugby | **G Vill**
NEW Saja | **NoLita**
Z Saks Fifth Ave. | **E 50s**

Z Salvatore Ferragamo | **E 50s**
S&W | **multi. loc.**
Scoop NYC | **multi. loc.**
Searle | **multi. loc.**
Sears | **multi. loc.**
Seize sur Vingt | **NoLita**
Seven NY | **SoHo**
Shanghai Tang | **E 60s**
Shin Choi | **SoHo**
Shop | **LES**
NEW Shvitz | **SoHo**
NEW Sigrid Olsen | **SoHo**
Sir | **Boerum Hill**
Sisley | **multi. loc.**
Something Else | **multi. loc.**
Sonia Rykiel | **E 70s**
NEW Sophia Eugene | **W Vill**
NEW Space Mercer | **SoHo**
Stella McCartney | **Meatpacking**
Steven Alan | **multi. loc.**
Z St. John | **E 50s**
Strawberry | **multi. loc.**
NEW Stuart & Wright | **Ft Greene**
Sude | **multi. loc.**
Sugar | **E Vill**
Z Takashimaya | **E 50s**
Z Talbots | **multi. loc.**
Z Target | **multi. loc.**
Ted Baker | **SoHo**
Temperley | **SoHo**
TG-170 | **LES**
Theory | **multi. loc.**
37=1 Atelier | **SoHo**
Thomas Pink | **multi. loc.**
NEW Tibi | **SoHo**
Z T.J. Maxx | **multi. loc.**
Tommy Hilfiger | **SoHo**
Tory Burch | **NoLita**
Tracy Feith | **NoLita**
NEW Tracy Reese | **Meatpacking**
Trash and Vaudeville | **E Vill**
NEW Treehouse | **Williamsburg**
NEW Trina Turk | **Meatpacking**
Triple Five Soul | **multi. loc.**
TSE | **Chelsea**
Z Turnbull & Asser | **E 50s**
202 | **Chelsea**
Umkarna | **Park Slope**

NEW Uniqlo | **SoHo**

Unis | **NoLita**

UnitedColors/Benetton | **multi. loc.**

Urban Outfitters | **multi. loc.**

Z Valentino | **E 60s**

NEW Valley | **LES**

Variazioni | **multi. loc.**

Versace | **E 50s**

Via Bus Stop | **SoHo**

Vivienne Tam | **SoHo**

NEW Von Dutch | **SoHo**

NEW WeSC | **SoHo**

NEW White Hse. Black Mkt. |
   Flatiron

Yigal Azrouel | **Meatpacking**

NEW Ylli | **Williamsburg**

Yohji Yamamoto | **SoHo**

Yves Saint Laurent | **multi. loc.**

Zara | **multi. loc.**

Zero/Maria Cornejo | **multi. loc.**

NEW Zoë | **Dumbo**

CONSIGNMENT/ THRIFT/VINTAGE

Allan & Suzi | **W 80s**

Amarcord Vintage | **multi. loc.**

Andy's Chee-Pees | **multi. loc.**

Angela's Vintage | **E Vill**

Angel St. Thrift Shop | **Chelsea**

Archangel Antiques | **E Vill**

Beacon's Closet | **multi. loc.**

Bis Designer Resale | **E 80s**

Centricity | **E Vill**

Cheap Jack's | **Garment Dist**

Chelsea Girl | **SoHo**

Cherry | **W Vill**

City Opera Thrift | **Gramercy**

NEW Consignment | **Downtown**

Council Thrift Shop | **E 80s**

Designer Resale | **E 80s**

NEW Dulcinée | **LES**

Edith and Daha | **LES**

Ellen Christine | **Chelsea**

Encore | **E 80s**

Eye Candy | **NoHo**

Family Jewels | **Chelsea**

Fisch for the Hip | **Chelsea**

Foley + Corinna | **LES**

Frock | **LES**

Geminola | **W Vill**

Gentlemen's Resale | **E 80s**

Goodwill | **multi. loc.**

NEW Hairy Mary's | **LES**

Hooti Couture | **Prospect Hts**

Housing Works Thrift | **multi. loc.**

Ina | **multi. loc.**

Kavanagh's | **E 40s**

La Boutique Resale | **multi. loc.**

NEW Loopy Mango | **Dumbo**

Loveday31 | **Astoria**

Love Saves The Day | **E Vill**

Marmalade | **LES**

Mem. Sloan-Kettering | **E 80s**

Michael's/Consignment | **E 70s**

No. 6 | **Little Italy**

Patina | **SoHo**

Peggy Pardon | **LES**

Poppet | **E Vill**

Project 234 | **NoLita**

Reminiscence | **Flatiron**

Resurrection | **NoLita**

Rue St. Denis | **E Vill**

Salvation Army | **multi. loc.**

Second Chance | **E 70s**

17 at 17 Thrift | **Flatiron**

Some Odd Rubies | **LES**

Spence-Chapin Thrift | **multi. loc.**

Stella Dallas | **multi. loc.**

Tokio 7 | **E Vill**

Tokyo Joe | **E Vill**

Vintage Collections | **E 70s**

Vintage Thrift Shop | **Gramercy**

What Comes Around | **SoHo**

Zachary's Smile | **multi. loc.**

COOKWARE

NEW Alessi | **SoHo**

Z Bed Bath & Beyond | **multi. loc.**

Z Bloomingdale's | **E 50s**

Bodum | **Meatpacking**

Bowery Kitchen Supplies | **Chelsea**

Z Bridge Kitchenware | **E 40s**

Z Broadway Panhandler | **G Vill**

Z Crate & Barrel | **multi. loc.**

Z Dean & Deluca | **SoHo**

NEW Gabay's Home | **E Vill**

Z Gracious Home | **multi. loc.**

Kmart | **multi. loc.**

☑ Macy's | **multi. loc.**

Pearl River Mart | **SoHo**

Sears | **multi. loc.**

☑ S.Feldman Houseware | **E 90s**

Sur La Table | **SoHo**

☑ Target | **multi. loc.**

Tarzian West | **Park Slope**

☑ Williams-Sonoma | **multi. loc.**

☑ Zabar's | **W 80s**

COSMETICS/TOILETRIES

☑ Aedes De Venustas | **G Vill**

Alcone | **W 40s**

Anna Sui | **SoHo**

Arcadia | **Chelsea**

Aveda | **multi. loc.**

Bare Escentuals | **multi. loc.**

Barneys CO-OP | **multi. loc.**

☑ Barneys New York | **E 60s**

Bath & Body Works | **multi. loc.**

☑ Bathroom | **W Vill**

☑ Bergdorf Goodman | **E 50s**

☑ Bergdorf Men's | **E 50s**

☑ Bloomingdale's | **multi. loc.**

Body Shop | **multi. loc.**

Bond No. 9 | **multi. loc.**

Boyd's of Madison | **W 70s**

Calvin Klein | **E 60s**

Carol's Daughter | **multi. loc.**

Caron Paris | **E 60s**

Caswell-Massey | **E 40s**

CB I Hate Perfume | **Williamsburg**

☑ Chanel | **multi. loc.**

Clarins | **multi. loc.**

Clyde's | **E 70s**

C.O. Bigelow | **G Vill**

Crabtree & Evelyn | **multi. loc.**

Diane von Furstenberg |
   Meatpacking

Donna Karan | **E 60s**

Douglas Cosmetics | **E 40s**

Essentials | **multi. loc.**

FACE Stockholm | **multi. loc.**

Floris of London | **E 60s**

Fresh | **multi. loc.**

☑ Henri Bendel | **E 50s**

H2O Plus | **E 50s**

Il Makiage | **E 50s**

Jeffrey | **Meatpacking**

Jo Malone | **multi. loc.**

Kids Rx | **W Vill**

☑ Kiehl's | **multi. loc.**

NEW Kiki De Montparnasse | **SoHo**

NEW Lancôme | **W 60s**

L'Artisan Parfumeur | **multi. loc.**

NEW Le Labo | **NoLita**

Le Sabon & Baby Too | **E 60s**

L'Occitane | **multi. loc.**

☑ Loehmann's | **multi. loc.**

☑ Lord & Taylor | **Murray Hill**

Luilei | **Park Slope**

Lulu Guinness | **W Vill**

Lush | **multi. loc.**

M.A.C. Cosmetics | **multi. loc.**

☑ Macy's | **multi. loc.**

Make Up For Ever | **G Vill**

Malin + Goetz | **Chelsea**

Mastic Spa | **SoHo**

Missha | **multi. loc.**

Molton Brown | **multi. loc.**

NEW N | **Harlem**

Nanette Lepore | **SoHo**

Nicholas Perricone | **E 60s**

NEW Oliver Spencer | **W Vill**

OMO Norma Kamali | **W 50s**

Origins | **multi. loc.**

Penhaligon's | **E 70s**

Perfumania | **Garment Dist**

Pir Cosmetics | **NoLita**

Prada | **multi. loc.**

Ray Beauty Supply | **W 40s**

Red Flower | **NoLita**

Ricky's | **multi. loc.**

Sabon | **multi. loc.**

☑ Saks Fifth Ave. | **E 50s**

☑ Santa Maria Novella | **NoLita**

☑ Sephora | **multi. loc.**

Shu Uemura | **SoHo**

Steven Alan | **multi. loc.**

☑ Takashimaya | **E 50s**

Z Chemists/Zitomer | **multi. loc.**

DEPARTMENT STORES

Barneys CO-OP | **multi. loc.**

☑ Barneys New York | **E 60s**

☑ Bed Bath & Beyond | **multi. loc.**

☑ Bergdorf Goodman | **E 50s**

☑ Bergdorf Men's | **E 50s**

☑ Bloomingdale's | **multi. loc.**
☑ Gracious Home | **multi. loc.**
☑ Henri Bendel | **E 50s**
Jeffrey | **Meatpacking**
☑ Lord & Taylor | **Murray Hill**
☑ Macy's | **multi. loc.**
☑ Saks Fifth Ave. | **E 50s**
Sears | **multi. loc.**
☑ Takashimaya | **E 50s**
☑ Target | **multi. loc.**

DISCOUNT STORES

Anbar | **TriBeCa**
☑ B&H Photo-Video | **Garment Dist**
Bolton's | **multi. loc.**
☑ Century 21 | **multi. loc.**
Chambers Outlet | **E 70s**
☑ Costco Wholesale | **multi. loc.**
☑ Daffy's | **multi. loc.**
☑ DSW | **multi. loc.**
☑ Filene's Basement | **multi. loc.**
Find Outlet | **multi. loc.**
NEW Gabay's Home | **E Vill**
Gabay's Outlet | **E Vill**
☑ J&R Music/Computer | **Financial Dist**
☑ Loehmann's | **multi. loc.**
☑ Marshalls | **multi. loc.**
Nat'l Wholesale Liquid | **multi. loc.**
Payless Shoe | **multi. loc.**
Petland Discounts | **multi. loc.**
Prato Fine Men's Wear | **multi. loc.**
S&W | **multi. loc.**
Syms | **multi. loc.**
☑ T.J. Maxx | **multi. loc.**

ELECTRONICS

☑ Apple Store | **multi. loc.**
☑ Bang & Olufsen | **multi. loc.**
☑ Best Buy | **multi. loc.**
☑ Bloomingdale's | **E 50s**
☑ Bose | **W 50s**
Brookstone | **multi. loc.**
Canal Hi-Fi | **Chinatown**
Circuit City | **multi. loc.**
Compact Impact | **Financial Dist**
CompUSA | **multi. loc.**
Cosmophonic Sound | **E 80s**
DataVision | **Murray Hill**

Hammacher Schlemmer | **E 50s**
☑ Harvey Electronics | **W 40s**
In Living Stereo | **NoHo**
Innovative Audio | **E 50s**
☑ J&R Music/Computer | **Financial Dist**
Lowell/Edwards | **E 50s**
☑ Lyric Hi-Fi | **E 80s**
NEW Nokia | **E 50s**
Park Ave. Audio | **Gramercy**
P.C. Richard & Son | **multi. loc.**
RadioShack | **multi. loc.**
RCS Experience | **E 50s**
Sears | **multi. loc.**
Sharper Image | **multi. loc.**
☑ Sony Style | **E 50s**
☑ Sound by Singer | **Union Sq**
Sound City | **W 40s**
Staples | **multi. loc.**
☑ Stereo Exchange | **NoHo**
☑ Target | **multi. loc.**
☑ Tekserve | **Chelsea**

EYEWEAR

Alain Mikli | **multi. loc.**
Artsee | **Meatpacking**
Cohen Optical | **multi. loc.**
Disrespectacles | **multi. loc.**
Eye Man | **W 80s**
Fabulous Fanny's | **E Vill**
Facial Index | **SoHo**
For Eyes | **E 40s**
Gruen Optika | **multi. loc.**
H.L. Purdy | **multi. loc.**
Joël Name Optique | **SoHo**
Leonard Opticians | **multi. loc.**
NEW Linda Derector | **NoLita**
Morgenthal Frederics | **multi. loc.**
Myoptics | **multi. loc.**
Nakedeye | **LES**
Oakley | **SoHo**
Occhiali | **E 80s**
Oculus 20/20 | **multi. loc.**
Oliver Peoples | **multi. loc.**
NEW Porsche Design | **E 50s**
NEW Ralph Lauren Eyewear | **E 60s**
Robert Marc | **multi. loc.**
NEW SEE Eyewear | **W Vill**
Selima Optique | **multi. loc.**

MERCHANDISE

Sol Moscot | **multi. loc.**

Solstice | **multi. loc.**

FABRICS/NOTIONS

☑ B&J Fabrics | **Garment Dist**

Beckenstein Fabrics | **Flatiron**

Brooklyn Gen. Store | **Carroll Gdns**

☑ City Quilter | **Chelsea**

Habu Textiles | **Chelsea**

Hyman Hendler | **Garment Dist**

Joe's Fabrics | **LES**

M&J Trimming | **Garment Dist**

Mood | **Garment Dist**

New York Fabric | **W 40s**

P&S Fabrics | **TriBeCa**

Paron Fabrics | **W 40s**

Paterson Silks | **multi. loc.**

Rosen & Chadick | **Garment Dist**

Steinlauf & Stoller | **Garment Dist**

☑ Tender Buttons | **E 60s**

Zarin Fabrics | **LES**

FINE CHINA/CRYSTAL

A Brooklyn Table | **Cobble Hill**

☑ Avventura | **W 80s**

☑ Baccarat | **E 50s**

Bardith | **E 70s**

☑ Barneys New York | **E 60s**

☑ Bergdorf Goodman | **E 50s**

☑ Bernardaud | **E 50s**

☑ Bloomingdale's | **E 50s**

☑ Cartier | **E 60s**

☑ Christofle | **E 60s**

Daum | **E 60s**

Fortunoff | **E 50s**

☑ Georg Jensen | **E 60s**

James Robinson | **E 50s**

☑ Lalique | **E 60s**

☑ Macy's | **multi. loc.**

☑ Michael C. Fina | **multi. loc.**

☑ Moss | **SoHo**

☑ Saks Fifth Ave. | **E 50s**

NEW Salviati | **SoHo**

☑ Simon Pearce | **E 50s**

☑ Steuben | **E 60s**

Swarovski | **multi. loc.**

☑ Takashimaya | **E 50s**

☑ Tiffany & Co. | **E 50s**

Vera Wang Bridal | **E 70s**

FURNITURE/HOME FURNISHINGS

BABIES'/CHILDREN'S

☑ ABC Carpet & Home | **Flatiron**

Albee Baby Carriage | **W 90s**

Bellini | **E 60s**

Blue Bench | **TriBeCa**

Burlington Coat | **multi. loc.**

☑ buybuy BABY | **Chelsea**

Calypso Enfant/Kids | **SoHo**

Capucine | **TriBeCa**

Ethan Allen | **multi. loc.**

Giggle | **multi. loc.**

☑ Gracious Home | **multi. loc.**

Katz in the Cradle | **Midwood**

kid o. | **G Vill**

NEW Olá Baby | **Carroll Gdns**

Pomme | **Dumbo**

☑ Pompanoosuc Mills | **TriBeCa**

NEW Pottery Barn Kids | **E 60s**

Room & Board | **SoHo**

Schneider's | **Chelsea**

Straight from Crate | **multi. loc.**

White on White | **Murray Hill**

GENERAL

☑ ABC Carpet & Home | **Flatiron**

☑ ABC Carpets/Rugs | **Flatiron**

ABC Carpet/Whse. Outlet | **Bronx**

ABH Design | **E 70s**

NEW Abitare | **Brooklyn Hts**

A Brooklyn Table | **Cobble Hill**

Adrien Linford | **multi. loc.**

☑ Aero | **SoHo**

NEW Alessi | **SoHo**

American Folk Art | **multi. loc.**

☑ Anthropologie | **multi. loc.**

Apartment 48 | **Flatiron**

Arcadia | **Chelsea**

Armani Casa | **SoHo**

AsiaStore/Asia Society | **E 70s**

auto | **Meatpacking**

Baker Tribeca | **TriBeCa**

☑ B&B Italia | **multi. loc.**

☑ Barneys New York | **E 60s**

BDDW | **SoHo**

☑ Bed Bath & Beyond | **multi. loc.**

☑ Bergdorf Goodman | **E 50s**

☑ Bloomingdale's | **E 50s**

BoConcept | **multi. loc.**
Bodum | **Meatpacking**
Bombay Company | **multi. loc.**
Butter and Eggs | **TriBeCa**
Calvin Klein | **E 60s**
Calypso Home | **NoLita**
Cappellini | **SoHo**
◪ Carlyle Convertibles | **multi. loc.**
Cassina USA | **E 50s**
Catherine Memmi | **SoHo**
Cath Kidston | **NoLita**
Ceramica | **SoHo**
◪ Charles P. Rogers | **Flatiron**
Classic Sofa | **Flatiron**
Clio | **SoHo**
Cog & Pearl | **Park Slope**
Conran Shop | **E 50s**
Container Store | **multi. loc.**
Cooper-Hewitt | **E 90s**
◪ Crate & Barrel | **multi. loc.**
ddc domus design | **Murray Hill**
Delphinium | **W 40s**
Demolition Depot | **Harlem**
Design Within Reach | **multi. loc.**
Desiron | **SoHo**
Dinosaur Designs | **NoLita**
Domain | **multi. loc.**
Donna Karan | **E 60s**
Donzella | **TriBeCa**
Door Store | **multi. loc.**
Dune | **TriBeCa**
Einstein-Moomjy | **E 50s**
environment337 | **multi. loc.**
Etcetera | **multi. loc.**
Ethan Allen | **multi. loc.**
Federico de Vera | **SoHo**
Fishs Eddy | **Flatiron**
Flou | **SoHo**
F.M. Allen | **E 70s**
Fort St. Studio | **SoHo**
Fortunoff | **E 50s**
NEW Fresh Kills | **Williamsburg**
Future Perfect | **Williamsburg**
NEW Gabay's Home | **E Vill**
George Smith | **SoHo**
◪ Georg Jensen | **SoHo**
Global Table | **SoHo**
Goodwill | **multi. loc.**

Gothic Cabinet Craft | **multi. loc.**
◪ Gracious Home | **multi. loc.**
Hable Construction | **W Vill**
Hammacher Schlemmer | **E 50s**
NEW Hasker | **Carroll Gdns**
Henry Beguelin | **Meatpacking**
◪ Home Depot | **multi. loc.**
Homer | **E 70s**
Housing Works Thrift | **multi. loc.**
Jennifer Convertibles | **multi. loc.**
Jensen-Lewis | **Chelsea**
John Derian | **E Vill**
Jonathan Adler | **multi. loc.**
Kaas GlassWorks | **W Vill**
Karim Rashid Shop | **Chelsea**
Kartell | **SoHo**
NEW Kate's At Home | **SoHo**
Kmart | **multi. loc.**
Knoll | **Chelsea**
Kraft | **E 60s**
Kreiss Collection | **E 50s**
La Cafetière | **Chelsea**
LaoLao Handmade | **E Vill**
Laytner's Linen | **multi. loc.**
Lee's Studio | **W 50s**
Le Fanion | **W Vill**
◪ Ligne Roset | **multi. loc.**
Living Fifth/Seventh/Smith | **multi. loc.**
Lower E. S. Tenement | **LES**
◪ MacKenzie-Childs | **E 50s**
◪ Macy's | **multi. loc.**
NEW Madura | **E 80s**
Marimekko | **E 70s**
◪ Marshalls | **multi. loc.**
Marston & Langinger | **SoHo**
Matter | **Park Slope**
◪ Maurice Villency | **E 50s**
McGuire | **Murray Hill**
Mecox Gardens | **E 70s**
NEW Meg Cohen Design | **SoHo**
Mem. Sloan-Kettering | **E 80s**
◪ Met. Museum of Art | **multi. loc.**
Michael Anchin Glass | **Williamsburg**
Michele Varian | **SoHo**
Modernica | **SoHo**
◪ MoMA Store | **multi. loc.**

Moss | **SoHo**
NEW Moulin Bleu | **TriBeCa**
Mxyplyzyk | **W Vill**
NEW N | **Harlem**
Natuzzi | **SoHo**
Nest | **Park Slope**
Neue Galerie NY | **E 80s**
Nicole Farhi | **E 60s**
NEW Ochre | **SoHo**
Olde Good Things | **multi. loc.**
Pearl River Mart | **SoHo**
P.E. Guerin | **W Vill**
Pier 1 Imports | **multi. loc.**
Pierre Deux | **E 50s**
Poltrona Frau | **SoHo**
Pompanoosuc Mills | **TriBeCa**
NEW Posey Baker | **Park Slope**
Pottery Barn | **multi. loc.**
Rachel Ashwell's | **SoHo**
Restoration Hardware | **Flatiron**
Rico | **Boerum Hill**
NEW Roberta Roller Rabbit | **E 70s**
Roche Bobois | **Murray Hill**
Room & Board | **SoHo**
Rug Company | **SoHo**
Ruzzetti & Gow | **E 70s**
Safavieh | **multi. loc.**
Saks Fifth Ave. | **E 50s**
Salvation Army | **multi. loc.**
NEW Salviati | **SoHo**
Scott Jordan | **SoHo**
Scully & Scully | **E 50s**
Sears | **Flushing**
17 at 17 Thrift | **Flatiron**
S.Feldman Houseware | **E 90s**
Shanghai Tang | **E 60s**
Space107 | **W Vill**
Spence-Chapin Thrift | **multi. loc.**
Stickley, Audi & Co. | **Flatiron**
Straight from Crate | **multi. loc.**
NEW Suite New York | **E 50s**
Surprise! Surprise! | **E Vill**
Swallow | **Carroll Gdns**
Takashimaya | **E 50s**
Tarzian West | **Park Slope**
Thomasville | **Bayside**
Thos. Moser Cabinets | **E 60s**
3r Living | **Park Slope**

Tiny Living | **E Vill**
Todd Hase | **SoHo**
Todd Oldham/La-Z-Boy | **SoHo**
Troy | **Gramercy**
Tucker Robbins | **multi. loc.**
Two Jakes | **Williamsburg**
202 | **Chelsea**
Umkarna | **Park Slope**
Vintage Thrift Shop | **Gramercy**
Vitra | **Meatpacking**
West Elm | **multi. loc.**
White on White | **Murray Hill**
William-Wayne | **multi. loc.**
Wonk | **multi. loc.**
Yellow Door | **multi. loc.**

FURS

Alexandros | **multi. loc.**
Alixandre Furs | **Garment Dist**
Bergdorf Goodman | **E 50s**
Bloomingdale's | **E 50s**
Dennis Basso | **E 60s**
Fendi | **E 50s**
J. Mendel | **E 60s**
Saks Fifth Ave. | **E 50s**

GARDEN

Bed Bath & Beyond | **multi. loc.**
Gracious Home | **multi. loc.**
GRDN Bklyn | **Boerum Hill**
Home Depot | **multi. loc.**
Kmart | **multi. loc.**
Lexington Gardens | **E 70s**
Lowe's | **multi. loc.**
Mecox Gardens | **E 70s**
Munder-Skiles | **E 60s**
Sears | **multi. loc.**
Smith & Hawken | **SoHo**
Takashimaya | **E 50s**
Target | **multi. loc.**
Treillage | **E 70s**

GIFTS/NOVELTIES

Abracadabra | **Flatiron**
Alphabets | **multi. loc.**
American Folk Art | **multi. loc.**
Am. Museum/Nat.Hist. | **W 70s**
Arcadia | **Chelsea**
AsiaStore/Asia Society | **E 70s**
Brooklyn Museum | **Prospect Hts**

Cooper-Hewitt | **E 90s**
Delphinium | **W 40s**
Dylan's Candy Bar | **E 60s**
E.A.T. Gifts | **E 80s**
El Museo Del Barrio | **E 100s**
environment337 | **multi. loc.**
Etcetera | **multi. loc.**
Frick Collection | **E 70s**
Guggenheim Museum | **E 80s**
☒ International Photo | **W 40s**
Jewish Museum | **multi. loc.**
Karim Rashid Shop | **Chelsea**
La Brea | **multi. loc.**
Loom | **Park Slope**
Lower E. S. Tenement | **LES**
☒ Met. Museum of Art | **multi. loc.**
Met. Opera Shop | **W 60s**
☒ MoMA Store | **multi. loc.**
NEW Morgan Library | **Murray Hill**
☒ Museum Arts/Design | **W 50s**
Museum/City of NY | **E 100s**
Nest | **Park Slope**
☒ Neue Galerie NY | **E 80s**
New Mus./Contemp. Art | **Chelsea**
New York Public Library | **multi. loc.**
New York Transit Mus. | **multi. loc.**
Paparazzi | **Gramercy**
Papyrus | **multi. loc.**
Pylones | **multi. loc.**
☒ Rubin Museum | **Chelsea**
Sanrio | **multi. loc.**
Scaredy Kat | **Park Slope**
Studio Museum/Harlem | **Harlem**
Tah-Poozie | **G Vill**
Whitney Museum | **E 70s**
World of Disney | **E 50s**

HANDBAGS

Add Accessories | **SoHo**
NEW Adrienne Vittadini | **W 40s**
Alessandro Dell'Acqua | **E 60s**
NEW alice + olivia | **W 40s**
NEW Anne Klein | **E 60s**
Anya Hindmarch | **multi. loc.**
Artbag | **E 80s**
☒ Balenciaga | **Chelsea**
Bally | **E 50s**
Barneys CO-OP | **multi. loc.**
☒ Barneys New York | **E 60s**

☒ Bergdorf Goodman | **E 50s**
NEW Blibetroy | **LES**
☒ Bloomingdale's | **multi. loc.**
Blue Bag | **NoLita**
Böc | **W 80s**
☒ Bottega Veneta | **E 50s**
Botticelli | **multi. loc.**
Catbird | **Williamsburg**
☒ Celine | **E 60s**
☒ Chanel | **multi. loc.**
Chelsea Girl | **SoHo**
Chloé | **E 70s**
☒ Christian Louboutin | **multi. loc.**
☒ Coach | **multi. loc.**
Cole Haan | **multi. loc.**
Crouch & Fitzgerald | **E 40s**
D & G | **SoHo**
Dane 115 | **SoHo**
delfino | **multi. loc.**
Destination | **Meatpacking**
☒ Dior New York | **E 50s**
DKNY | **multi. loc.**
Dolce & Gabbana | **E 60s**
Dooney & Bourke | **E 60s**
Fendi | **E 50s**
Fisch for the Hip | **Chelsea**
Fratelli Rossetti | **E 50s**
Furla | **multi. loc.**
Gabay's Outlet | **E Vill**
☒ Ghurka | **E 60s**
Gianfranco Ferré | **E 70s**
NEW Giorgio Fedon 19 | **W 40s**
Gucci | **multi. loc.**
NEW Guy Laroche | **W 50s**
☒ Henri Bendel | **E 50s**
Henry Beguelin | **Meatpacking**
☒ Hermès | **E 60s**
Highway | **NoLita**
Hogan | **SoHo**
Il Bisonte | **SoHo**
Jack Gomme | **NoLita**
Jaime Mascaró | **multi. loc.**
Jamin Puech | **NoLita**
Jeffrey | **Meatpacking**
☒ Judith Leiber | **E 60s**
Kate Spade | **SoHo**
NEW Kipepeo | **NoLita**
Lana Marks | **E 60s**

Lederer de Paris | **E 50s**
LeSportsac | **multi. loc.**
Longchamp | **multi. loc.**
Ⓩ Lord & Taylor | **Murray Hill**
Louis Vuitton | **multi. loc.**
NEW Love Brigade | **Williamsburg**
Lulu Guinness | **W Vill**
Ⓩ Macy's | **multi. loc.**
Marc Jacobs Access. | **W Vill**
NEW Max Azria | **SoHo**
Miu Miu | **multi. loc.**
NEW Mulberry | **multi. loc.**
M Z Wallace | **SoHo**
NEW N | **Harlem**
NEW Nave | **SoHo**
Nine West | **multi. loc.**
Olive & Bette's | **multi. loc.**
NEW Petticoat Lane | **TriBeCa**
Prada | **multi. loc.**
Pucci | **multi. loc.**
Rafe | **NoHo**
Refinery | **Cobble Hill**
Ⓩ Robert Clergerie | **E 60s**
Roberto Vascon | **W 70s**
Ⓩ Saks Fifth Ave. | **E 50s**
Ⓩ Salvatore Ferragamo | **E 50s**
NEW Samantha Thavasa | **E 70s**
Seigo | **E 80s**
Sergio Rossi | **E 50s**
Sigerson Morrison Bags | **NoLita**
Steve Madden | **multi. loc.**
Steven | **SoHo**
Stuart Weitzman | **W 50s**
Suarez | **E 50s**
Ⓩ T. Anthony | **E 50s**
Taryn Rose | **E 60s**
Ⓩ Tod's | **E 60s**
NEW Trina Turk | **Meatpacking**
Triple Five Soul | **multi. loc.**
NEW Valley | **LES**
Versace | **E 50s**
Verve | **multi. loc.**
Village Tannery | **multi. loc.**
Walter Steiger | **E 50s**
Wink | **multi. loc.**
Yves Saint Laurent | **multi. loc.**

HARDWARE

Beacon Paint/Hardware | **W 70s**

Dykes Lumber | **multi. loc.**
Ⓩ Gracious Home | **multi. loc.**
Ⓩ Home Depot | **multi. loc.**
Janovic Plaza | **multi. loc.**
Kmart | **multi. loc.**
Lowe's | **multi. loc.**
Metropolitan Lumber | **multi. loc.**
P.E. Guerin | **W Vill**
Pintchik | **Park Slope**
Sears | **multi. loc.**
Sid's | **Downtown**
Ⓩ Simon's Hardware | **Gramercy**
Ⓩ Target | **multi. loc.**
Tarzian True Value | **Park Slope**
Vercesi Hardware | **Gramercy**

HOSIERY/LINGERIE

ABH Design | **E 70s**
Agent Provocateur | **SoHo**
A.W. Kaufman | **LES**
Azaleas | **E Vill**
Ⓩ Barneys New York | **E 60s**
Beneath | **E 70s**
Ⓩ Bergdorf Goodman | **E 50s**
Ⓩ Bloomingdale's | **E 50s**
Blueberi | **Dumbo**
Bond 07 by Selima | **NoHo**
Bonne Nuit | **E 70s**
Bra Smyth | **multi. loc.**
Bra*Tenders | **W 40s**
Brief Encounters | **W 70s**
Burlington Coat | **multi. loc.**
Calvin Klein Underwear | **multi. loc.**
Catriona Mackechnie |
   Meatpacking
Ⓩ Century 21 | **multi. loc.**
Ⓩ Daffy's | **multi. loc.**
Diana Kane | **Park Slope**
Eres | **multi. loc.**
Ⓩ Filene's Basement | **multi. loc.**
Ⓩ Fogal/Switzerland | **E 50s**
GapBody | **E Vill**
Girly NYC | **E Vill**
Ⓩ H&M | **multi. loc.**
Ⓩ Henri Bendel | **E 50s**
Intimacy | **E 90s**
NEW Kiki De Montparnasse | **SoHo**
Laina Jane | **multi. loc.**
Ⓩ La Perla | **multi. loc.**

La Petite Coquette | **G Vill**

Lingerie on Lex | **E 60s**

Livi's Lingerie | **E 80s**

🛒 Loehmann's | **multi. loc.**

🛒 Lord & Taylor | **Murray Hill**

🛒 Macy's | **multi. loc.**

Marc and Max | **W Vill**

🛒 Marshalls | **multi. loc.**

Mixona | **NoLita**

Myla | **E 60s**

Only Hearts | **multi. loc.**

Orchard Corset Center | **LES**

NEW Petticoat Lane | **TriBeCa**

Pink Slip | **E 40s**

Redberi | **Prospect Hts**

🛒 Saks Fifth Ave. | **E 50s**

Sleep | **Williamsburg**

Syms | **multi. loc.**

🛒 Takashimaya | **E 50s**

🛒 Target | **multi. loc.**

37=1 Atelier | **SoHo**

🛒 T.J. Maxx | **multi. loc.**

Town Shop | **W 80s**

Victoria's Secret | **multi. loc.**

Wolford | **multi. loc.**

JEANS

Abercrombie & Fitch | **multi. loc.**

AG Adriano Goldschmied | **SoHo**

Am. Eagle Outfitters | **Garment Dist**

Atrium | **NoHo**

Barneys CO-OP | **multi. loc.**

🛒 Bergdorf Goodman | **E 50s**

Bird | **Park Slope**

🛒 Bloomingdale's | **E 50s**

NEW Blue in Green | **SoHo**

Canal Jean | **multi. loc.**

Cantaloup/Luxe | **E 70s**

Catbird | **Williamsburg**

Chip & Pepper | **NoLita**

DDC Lab | **Meatpacking**

Diane T | **Cobble Hill**

Diesel | **multi. loc.**

Diesel Denim Gallery | **SoHo**

Dr. Jay's | **multi. loc.**

Dunderdon Workshop | **SoHo**

Earnest Cut & Sew | **Meatpacking**

Forréal | **E 70s**

45rpm/R | **multi. loc.**

G-Star Raw | **SoHo**

Guess | **multi. loc.**

🛒 Henri Bendel | **E 50s**

Henry Lehr | **NoLita**

Jean Shop | **Meatpacking**

Levi's Store | **multi. loc.**

Lounge | **SoHo**

Lucky Brand Jeans | **multi. loc.**

NEW Lucky Kid | **SoHo**

🛒 Macy's | **multi. loc.**

Mavi | **E Vill**

Miss Sixty | **SoHo**

NEW N | **Harlem**

Oak | **Williamsburg**

Old Navy | **multi. loc.**

NEW Parasuco | **NoLita**

Pieces | **Harlem**

Pookie & Sebastian | **multi. loc.**

Razor | **Park Slope**

Replay | **SoHo**

NEW Rogan | **TriBeCa**

Rugby | **G Vill**

🛒 Saks Fifth Ave. | **E 50s**

Scoop Men's | **Meatpacking**

Scoop NYC | **multi. loc.**

Sean John | **E 40s**

NEW Stuart & Wright | **Ft Greene**

Transit | **NoHo**

Triple Five Soul | **multi. loc.**

NEW True Religion | **SoHo**

Tsubi | **NoLita**

V.I.M. | **multi. loc.**

What Comes Around | **SoHo**

JEWELRY

COSTUME/ SEMIPRECIOUS

Add Accessories | **SoHo**

Agatha Paris | **multi. loc.**

Alexis Bittar | **SoHo**

Arcadia | **Chelsea**

Beads of Paradise | **Flatiron**

Blair Delmonico | **W 50s**

🛒 Bloomingdale's | **E 50s**

Boucher | **Meatpacking**

By Boe | **multi. loc.**

Calypso Bijoux | **NoLita**

Claire's Accessories | **multi. loc.**

Cog & Pearl | **Park Slope**
Cooper-Hewitt | **E 90s**
Debbie Fisher | **Carroll Gdns**
Dinosaur Designs | **NoLita**
Dö Kham | **NoLita**
Erwin Pearl | **multi. loc.**
Femmegems | **NoLita**
⊠ Henri Bendel | **E 50s**
Jaded | **E 80s**
Jennifer Miller Jewelry | **E 70s**
NEW Kipepeo | **NoLita**
Laila Rowe | **multi. loc.**
⊠ Lord & Taylor | **Murray Hill**
⊠ Macy's | **multi. loc.**
Mariko | **E 70s**
Marni | **SoHo**
⊠ Met. Museum of Art | **multi. loc.**
Michal Negrin | **E 70s**
Pearldaddy | **NoLita**
⊠ Saks Fifth Ave. | **E 50s**
NEW Satellite | **SoHo**
NEW SOHO | **NoLita**
Swarovski | **multi. loc.**
NEW Tarina Tarantino | **SoHo**
NEW Trunkt | **TriBeCa**
Yellow Door | **multi. loc.**

FINE
Aaron Basha | **E 60s**
Aaron Faber | **W 50s**
⊠ ABC Carpet & Home | **Flatiron**
⊠ Asprey | **E 70s**
⊠ Barneys New York | **E 60s**
⊠ Bergdorf Goodman | **E 50s**
Blair Delmonico | **W 50s**
Bloom | **E 40s**
⊠ Bloomingdale's | **E 50s**
Bochic | **E 50s**
Breguet | **E 60s**
⊠ Buccellati | **E 50s**
Bulgari | **multi. loc.**
Camilla Bergeron | **E 60s**
⊠ Cartier | **multi. loc.**
Castor & Pollux | **W Vill**
Cécile et Jeanne | **multi. loc.**
Cellini | **multi. loc.**
Chanel Jewelry | **E 60s**
⊠ Chopard | **E 60s**
Chrome Hearts | **E 60s**

Clay Pot | **Park Slope**
Damiani | **E 60s**
David Lee Holland | **SoHo**
David Webb | **E 60s**
David Yurman | **E 60s**
DeBeers | **E 50s**
de Grisogono | **E 60s**
DeNatale Jewelers | **multi. loc.**
Diana Kane | **Park Slope**
Doyle and Doyle | **LES**
Elizabeth Locke | **E 70s**
Federico de Vera | **SoHo**
Fortunoff | **E 50s**
Fragments | **multi. loc.**
Garrard | **SoHo**
⊠ Georg Jensen | **multi. loc.**
⊠ Graff | **E 60s**
⊠ Harry Winston | **E 50s**
Helen Ficalora | **NoLita**
NEW Honora | **E 50s**
⊠ H. Stern | **E 50s**
Jacob & Co. | **E 50s**
Jeffrey | **Meatpacking**
Jennifer Miller Jewelry | **E 70s**
Jeri Cohen Jewelry | **E 60s**
Jill Platner | **SoHo**
NEW J.J. Marco | **E 80s**
Joan Michlin Gallery | **SoHo**
Judith Ripka | **E 60s**
Kieselstein-Cord | **E 80s**
Lalaounis | **E 60s**
⊠ Lalique | **E 60s**
Links of London | **multi. loc.**
NEW Lisa Levine Jewelry |
    Williamsburg
Lockes Diamonds | **E 60s**
⊠ Lord & Taylor | **Murray Hill**
⊠ Macy's | **multi. loc.**
Marc and Max | **W Vill**
Me & Ro | **NoLita**
⊠ Met. Museum of Art | **multi. loc.**
⊠ Michael C. Fina | **multi. loc.**
⊠ Mikimoto | **E 50s**
Mish | **E 70s**
⊠ MoMA Store | **multi. loc.**
⊠ Piaget | **E 50s**
NEW Pomellato | **E 60s**
Reinstein/Ross | **multi. loc.**

Robert Lee Morris | **SoHo**

☑ Saks Fifth Ave. | **E 50s**

Satya | **W Vill**

Seaman Schepps | **E 50s**

Swallow | **Carroll Gdns**

Taffin | **E 70s**

☑ Takashimaya | **E 50s**

Ted Muehling | **SoHo**

Ten Thousand Things |
   Meatpacking

☑ Tiffany & Co. | **E 50s**

☑ Van Cleef & Arpels | **E 50s**

Verdura | **E 50s**

Wendy Mink | **G Vill**

William Barthman | **multi. loc.**

Yellow Door | **multi. loc.**

Zales Jewelers | **multi. loc.**

VINTAGE

Aaron Faber | **W 50s**

☑ ABC Carpet & Home | **Flatiron**

☑ A La Vieille Russie | **E 50s**

Allan & Suzi | **W 80s**

Angela's Vintage | **E Vill**

Archangel Antiques | **E Vill**

☑ Barneys New York | **E 60s**

Camilla Bergeron | **E 60s**

Doyle and Doyle | **LES**

Eye Candy | **NoHo**

☑ Fred Leighton | **E 60s**

James Robinson | **E 50s**

Michael Ashton | **E 70s**

Pippin | **LES**

☑ Saks Fifth Ave. | **E 50s**

Some Odd Rubies | **LES**

KNITTING/ NEEDLEPOINT

Annie Needlepoint | **E 90s**

Brooklyn Gen. Store | **Carroll Gdns**

☑ Downtown Yarns | **E Vill**

Gotta Knit | **G Vill**

Knit-A-Way | **Boerum Hill**

Knit New York | **E Vill**

Knits Incredible | **E 70s**

Knitting 321 | **E 70s**

☑ Point | **G Vill**

☑ Purl | **SoHo**

☑ Rita's Needlepoint | **E 70s**

School Products | **Garment Dist**

☑ Seaport Yarn | **Seaport**

Smiley's | **Woodhaven**

☑ Stitches East | **E 50s**

☑ String | **E 70s**

Wool Gathering | **E 80s**

Woolworks Needlepoint | **E 70s**

☑ Yarn Co. | **W 80s**

Yarn Connection | **Murray Hill**

Yarn Tree | **Williamsburg**

LIGHTING

☑ ABC Carpet & Home | **Flatiron**

Artemide | **SoHo**

Bowery Lighting | **LES**

Calypso Home | **NoLita**

environment337 | **multi. loc.**

☑ Gracious Home | **multi. loc.**

☑ Home Depot | **multi. loc.**

Ingo Maurer Light | **SoHo**

Just Bulbs | **Flatiron**

Just Shades | **NoLita**

Lee's Studio | **W 50s**

Lightforms | **multi. loc.**

Lighting By Gregory | **LES**

Living Fifth/Seventh/Smith | **Park
   Slope**

Lowe's | **multi. loc.**

Michael Anchin Glass |
   Williamsburg

O'Lampia Studio | **LES**

Oriental Lamp Shade | **multi. loc.**

Restoration Hardware | **Flatiron**

Rico | **Boerum Hill**

Schoolhouse Electric | **TriBeCa**

🆕 Suite New York | **E 50s**

West Elm | **Dumbo**

LUGGAGE

Altman Luggage | **LES**

Bag House | **G Vill**

☑ Bloomingdale's | **E 50s**

Bric's | **E 50s**

☑ Chanel | **E 60s**

Crouch & Fitzgerald | **E 40s**

Crumpler Bags | **multi. loc.**

EMS | **SoHo**

Fendi | **E 50s**

Flight 001 | **multi. loc.**

F.M. Allen | **E 70s**
🗷 Ghurka | **E 60s**
NEW Giorgio Fedon 19 | **W 40s**
Gucci | **multi. loc.**
Hunting World | **SoHo**
Innovation Luggage | **multi. loc.**
Jack Spade | **SoHo**
Kmart | **multi. loc.**
LeSportsac | **E 80s**
Lexington Luggage | **E 60s**
Longchamp | **multi. loc.**
Louis Vuitton | **multi. loc.**
🗷 Macy's | **multi. loc.**
NEW Mulberry | **multi. loc.**
M Z Wallace | **SoHo**
Patagonia | **multi. loc.**
NEW Porsche Design | **E 50s**
Rafe | **NoHo**
🗷 Saks Fifth Ave. | **E 50s**
NEW Samsonite Black Label | **E 60s**
Swiss Army | **SoHo**
🗷 T. Anthony | **E 50s**
🗷 Target | **multi. loc.**
🗷 TUMI | **multi. loc.**
Village Tannery | **multi. loc.**

MAJOR APPLIANCES

🗷 Best Buy | **multi. loc.**
Bloom & Krup | **Garment Dist**
Boffi SoHo | **SoHo**
Bowery Kitchen Supplies | **Chelsea**
Drimmers | **Midwood**
Elgot | **E 60s**
🗷 Gracious Home | **multi. loc.**
Gringer & Sons | **E Vill**
🗷 Home Depot | **multi. loc.**
Kmart | **multi. loc.**
🗷 Krup's Kitchen/Bath | **Flatiron**
Lowe's | **multi. loc.**
Manhattan Ctr. | **Flatiron**
P.C. Richard & Son | **multi. loc.**
Poggenpohl U.S. | **multi. loc.**
Quintessentials | **W 80s**
Sears | **multi. loc.**

MATERNITY

🗷 Barneys New York | **E 60s**
Belly Dance Maternity | **W Vill**
🗷 Bloomingdale's | **E 50s**

Cadeau | **NoLita**
Capucine | **TriBeCa**
Destination Maternity | **E 50s**
🗷 H&M | **multi. loc.**
Kmart | **multi. loc.**
L' Avenue des Reves | **E 70s**
Liz Lange Maternity | **E 70s**
🗷 Macy's | **multi. loc.**
Maternity Works | **W 50s**
Mimi Maternity | **multi. loc.**
Mylo Dweck Maternity |
   Bensonhurst
Old Navy | **multi. loc.**
🗷 Target | **multi. loc.**
Veronique | **E 90s**

MUSEUM SHOPS

American Folk Art | **multi. loc.**
Am. Museum/Nat.Hist. | **W 70s**
AsiaStore/Asia Society | **E 70s**
Brooklyn Museum | **Prospect Hts**
Cooper-Hewitt | **E 90s**
El Museo Del Barrio | **E 100s**
Frick Collection | **E 70s**
Guggenheim Museum | **E 80s**
🗷 International Photo | **W 40s**
Jewish Museum | **multi. loc.**
Lower E. S. Tenement | **LES**
🗷 Met. Museum of Art | **multi. loc.**
🗷 MoMA Store | **multi. loc.**
NEW Morgan Library | **Murray Hill**
🗷 Museum Arts/Design | **W 50s**
Museum of Sex | **Gramercy**
Museum/City of NY | **E 100s**
🗷 Neue Galerie NY | **E 80s**
New Mus./Contemp. Art | **Chelsea**
New York Public Library | **multi. loc.**
New York Transit Mus. | **multi. loc.**
🗷 Rubin Museum | **Chelsea**
Studio Museum/Harlem | **Harlem**
Whitney Museum | **E 70s**

PET SUPPLIES

American Kennels | **E 60s**
Barking Zoo | **Chelsea**
Beasty Feast | **W Vill**
Calling All Pets | **multi. loc.**
🗷 Canine Styles | **multi. loc.**
Doggystyle | **SoHo**

Dudley's Paw | **TriBeCa**
Furry Paws | **multi. loc.**
Le Chien Pet Salon | **E 60s**
Petco | **multi. loc.**
Peters Necessities/Pets | **E 70s**
Petland Discounts | **multi. loc.**
🔲 Pet Stop | **W 80s**
Spoiled Brats | **W 40s**
🔲 Trixie and Peanut | **Flatiron**
🔲 Whiskers | **E Vill**
Zoomies | **W Vill**

SEX SHOPS

🔲 Babeland | **multi. loc.**
DeMask | **LES**
Eve's Garden | **W 50s**
🔲 Leather Man | **W Vill**
Museum of Sex | **Gramercy**
Myla | **E 60s**
Noose | **Chelsea**
Pink Pussycat | **multi. loc.**
Pleasure Chest | **W Vill**

SHOES: CHILDREN

Area | **multi. loc.**
NEW Belle & Maxie | **Ditmas Pk**
🔲 Bloomingdale's | **multi. loc.**
🔲 Bonpoint | **multi. loc.**
Burlington Coat | **multi. loc.**
🔲 Century 21 | **multi. loc.**
NEW Crew Cuts | **SoHo**
Eneslow | **Little Neck**
flora and henri | **E 70s**
Geox | **multi. loc.**
Great Feet | **E 80s**
NEW Harry's Shoes/Kids | **W 80s**
Ibiza Kidz | **G Vill**
Kmart | **multi. loc.**
Lester's | **multi. loc.**
Little Eric | **E 80s**
NEW Little Stinkers | **E Vill**
🔲 Lord & Taylor | **Murray Hill**
🔲 Macy's | **multi. loc.**
Naturino | **multi. loc.**
Oilily | **multi. loc.**
NEW Purple Reign | **Harlem**
Rachel Riley | **E 90s**
🔲 Saks Fifth Ave. | **E 50s**
Sears | **multi. loc.**

Shoofly | **TriBeCa**
Skechers | **multi. loc.**
🔲 Target | **multi. loc.**
Tip Top Kids | **W 70s**

SHOES: MEN'S/ WOMEN'S

Aerosoles | **multi. loc.**
Aldo | **multi. loc.**
🔲 Allen Edmonds | **multi. loc.**
Anbar | **TriBeCa**
Arche | **multi. loc.**
A. Testoni | **E 50s**
A Uno/Walk | **TriBeCa**
Barbara Shaum | **E Vill**
Barneys CO-OP | **multi. loc.**
🔲 Barneys New York | **E 60s**
🔲 Belgian Shoes | **E 50s**
🔲 Bergdorf Goodman | **E 50s**
🔲 Bergdorf Men's | **E 50s**
Berluti | **E 70s**
Beverly Feldman | **W 50s**
🔲 Bloomingdale's | **multi. loc.**
Botticelli | **multi. loc.**
Butter | **Downtown**
Camper | **SoHo**
🔲 Century 21 | **multi. loc.**
🔲 Cesare Paciotti | **E 60s**
🔲 Christian Louboutin | **multi. loc.**
Chuckies | **multi. loc.**
Church's Shoes | **E 60s**
Clarks England | **multi. loc.**
Claudia Ciuti | **E 70s**
Coclico | **NoLita**
Cole Haan | **multi. loc.**
🔲 Daffy's | **multi. loc.**
David Z. | **multi. loc.**
NEW DC Shoes | **SoHo**
Dolce Vita | **LES**
🔲 DSW | **multi. loc.**
Dusica Dusica | **SoHo**
Eneslow | **multi. loc.**
Enzo Angiolini | **multi. loc.**
Eric | **multi. loc.**
🔲 Filene's Basement | **multi. loc.**
Florsheim Shoe | **multi. loc.**
Fratelli Rossetti | **E 50s**
French Sole | **E 70s**
Galo | **multi. loc.**

Geox | **multi. loc.**

Giraudon | **Chelsea**

Z Giuseppe Zanotti | **E 60s**

Harry's Shoes | **W 80s**

Hazel's Shoes | **Bayside**

Hollywould | **NoLita**

Jaime Mascaró | **multi. loc.**

J.Crew | **multi. loc.**

Jimmy Choo | **multi. loc.**

J.M. Weston | **E 60s**

John Fluevog Shoes | **NoLita**

Z John Lobb | **E 60s**

Johnston & Murphy | **multi. loc.**

Jubilee | **multi. loc.**

Jutta Neumann | **LES**

Kenneth Cole NY | **multi. loc.**

Kmart | **multi. loc.**

LaDuca Shoes | **Garment Dist**

Z Loehmann's | **multi. loc.**

Z Lord & Taylor | **Murray Hill**

Z Macy's | **multi. loc.**

Manhattan Saddlery | **Gramercy**

Z Manolo Blahnik | **W 50s**

Medici | **W 80s**

My Glass Slipper | **Flatiron**

Nine West | **multi. loc.**

Otto Tootsi Plohound | **multi. loc.**

Payless Shoe | **multi. loc.**

Z Peter Fox Shoes | **SoHo**

Prada | **multi. loc.**

Z Robert Clergerie | **E 60s**

Sacco | **multi. loc.**

Z Saks Fifth Ave. | **E 50s**

Z Salvatore Ferragamo | **E 50s**

Sergio Rossi | **E 50s**

Shoe Box | **multi. loc.**

Shoe Mine | **Park Slope**

Shoe New York | **NoLita**

Shooz | **Chelsea**

Sigerson Morrison | **NoLita**

Skechers | **multi. loc.**

Soula | **Boerum Hill**

Steve Madden | **multi. loc.**

Steven | **SoHo**

Stuart Weitzman | **multi. loc.**

Stubbs & Wootton | **E 70s**

Syms | **multi. loc.**

Z Target | **multi. loc.**

Taryn Rose | **E 60s**

NEW té casan | **SoHo**

Timberland | **E 60s**

Tip Top Shoes | **W 70s**

Z Tod's | **E 60s**

Tupli | **E 60s**

NEW UGG Australia | **SoHo**

Unisa | **E 60s**

Vanessa Noel | **E 60s**

Varda | **multi. loc.**

Verve | **W Vill**

Vogel | **SoHo**

Walter Steiger | **E 50s**

Warren Edwards | **E 60s**

SHOES: TWEEN/TEEN

Aldo | **multi. loc.**

Z Bloomingdale's | **multi. loc.**

Z Century 21 | **multi. loc.**

David Z. | **multi. loc.**

NEW DC Shoes | **SoHo**

Dr. Jay's | **multi. loc.**

NEW Harry's Shoes/Kids | **W 80s**

Kmart | **multi. loc.**

Lester's | **multi. loc.**

Limited Too | **multi. loc.**

Z Macy's | **multi. loc.**

Patagonia | **multi. loc.**

Z Saks Fifth Ave. | **E 50s**

Skechers | **multi. loc.**

Steve Madden | **multi. loc.**

Timberland | **E 60s**

NEW UGG Australia | **SoHo**

SILVER

A Brooklyn Table | **Cobble Hill**

Z A La Vieille Russie | **E 50s**

Z Asprey | **E 70s**

Z Barneys New York | **E 60s**

Z Bergdorf Goodman | **E 50s**

Z Bloomingdale's | **E 50s**

Z Buccellati | **E 50s**

Z Cartier | **multi. loc.**

Z Christofle | **E 60s**

Fortunoff | **E 50s**

Z Georg Jensen | **multi. loc.**

James Robinson | **E 50s**

Z Michael C. Fina | **multi. loc.**

Z Moss | **SoHo**

Ruzzetti & Gow | **E 70s**
☑ Saks Fifth Ave. | **E 50s**
☑ Scully & Scully | **E 50s**
☑ Tiffany & Co. | **E 50s**

SNEAKERS

Active Wearhouse | **SoHo**
Adidas | **multi. loc.**
Alife | **LES**
Athlete's Foot | **multi. loc.**
Bathing Ape | **SoHo**
Blades Board & Skate | **multi. loc.**
Champs | **multi. loc.**
City Sports | **multi. loc.**
Classic Kicks | **NoHo**
Dave's Quality Meat | **E Vill**
David Z. | **multi. loc.**
NEW DC Shoes | **SoHo**
Dr. Jay's | **multi. loc.**
☑ DSW | **multi. loc.**
EMS | **SoHo**
Fila | **E 40s**
Foot Locker | **multi. loc.**
Geox | **multi. loc.**
Grand Central Racquet | **E 40s**
Harry's Shoes | **W 80s**
NEW Harry's Shoes/Kids | **W 80s**
JackRabbit Sports | **Union Sq**
Karim Rashid Shop | **Chelsea**
Kmart | **multi. loc.**
NEW Laces | **NoLita**
Lacoste | **multi. loc.**
Lady Foot Locker | **multi. loc.**
Lester's | **multi. loc.**
☑ Lord & Taylor | **Murray Hill**
☑ Macy's | **multi. loc.**
Mason's Tennis Mart | **E 50s**
Modell's Sport | **multi. loc.**
NBA Store | **E 50s**
New Balance | **multi. loc.**
New York Running | **W 50s**
Niketown NY | **E 50s**
99X | **E Vill**
Nom de Guerre | **NoHo**
Nort/Recon | **NoHo**
Number (N)ine | **TriBeCa**
☑ Paragon | **Union Sq**
Payless Shoe | **multi. loc.**
premium goods | **Park Slope**

Puma | **multi. loc.**
Reebok Concept Store | **W 60s**
Shooz | **Chelsea**
Slope Sports | **Park Slope**
Sports Authority | **multi. loc.**
Steve Madden | **multi. loc.**
Super Runners Shop | **multi. loc.**
SwimBikeRun | **W 50s**
☑ Target | **multi. loc.**
Timberland | **E 60s**
Tip Top Shoes | **W 70s**
Training Camp | **multi. loc.**
Transit | **NoHo**
V.I.M. | **multi. loc.**

SPORTING GOODS

Bicycle Habitat | **SoHo**
Bicycle Renaissance | **W 80s**
Bike Works NYC | **LES**
Blades Board & Skate | **multi. loc.**
Burton Store | **SoHo**
Capitol Fishing | **Garment Dist**
Champs | **multi. loc.**
City Sports | **E 50s**
EMS | **SoHo**
Gerry Cosby | **Garment Dist**
NEW Golfsmith | **E 50s**
Gotham Bikes | **TriBeCa**
Grand Central Racquet | **multi. loc.**
Gym Source | **E 50s**
JackRabbit Sports | **multi. loc.**
Kmart | **multi. loc.**
Larry & Jeff Bicycle | **multi. loc.**
Manhattan Saddlery | **Gramercy**
Mason's Tennis Mart | **E 50s**
Metro Bicycles | **multi. loc.**
Modell's Sport | **multi. loc.**
New York Golf | **multi. loc.**
New York Pipe Dreams | **E 80s**
NYC Velo | **E Vill**
Orvis | **E 40s**
Pan Aqua Diving | **W 40s**
☑ Paragon | **Union Sq**
Princeton Ski Shop | **Flatiron**
Scandinavian Sport | **E 50s**
Scuba Network | **multi. loc.**
Sears | **Flushing**
Slope Sports | **Park Slope**
Sports Authority | **multi. loc.**

Supreme | **SoHo**

SwimBikeRun | **W 50s**

🛒 Target | **multi. loc.**

Tent and Trails | **Financial Dist**

🛒 Toga Bikes | **W 60s**

Urban Angler | **Chelsea**

Vespa | **SoHo**

World of Golf | **multi. loc.**

STATIONERY

Airline Stationery | **E 40s**

🛒 Arthur Brown & Bro. | **W 40s**

Arthur's Invitations | **G Vill**

Blacker & Kooby | **E 80s**

Cardeology | **multi. loc.**

🛒 Crane & Co. | **W 40s**

🛒 Dempsey & Carroll | **E 50s**

🛒 Fountain Pen | **TriBeCa**

NEW Greenwich Letterpress | **W Vill**

Hyde Park Stationers | **E 80s**

🛒 Il Papiro | **E 70s**

IS: Ind. Stationery | **SoHo**

Jam Paper | **Gramercy**

🛒 Joon | **multi. loc.**

🛒 Kate's Paperie | **multi. loc.**

Lion in the Sun | **Park Slope**

🛒 Montblanc | **multi. loc.**

🛒 Mrs. John L. Strong | **E 60s**

Paper Presentation | **Flatiron**

Papyrus | **multi. loc.**

🛒 Smythson of Bond St. | **W 50s**

Venture | **E 80s**

SWIMWEAR

Azaleas | **E Vill**

🛒 Billabong | **W 40s**

🛒 Bloomingdale's | **multi. loc.**

Calypso | **multi. loc.**

Canyon Beachwear | **E 60s**

Catriona Mackechnie | **Meatpacking**

🛒 Daffy's | **multi. loc.**

Eres | **multi. loc.**

NEW Heidi Klein | **E 70s**

J.Crew | **multi. loc.**

🛒 Lord & Taylor | **Murray Hill**

🛒 Macy's | **multi. loc.**

Malia Mills Swimwear | **multi. loc.**

Quiksilver | **multi. loc.**

🛒 Saks Fifth Ave. | **E 50s**

SwimBikeRun | **W 50s**

🛒 Target | **multi. loc.**

Vilebrequin | **multi. loc.**

TOYS

Abracadabra | **Flatiron**

Acorn | **Downtown**

American Girl Place | **E 40s**

Area | **multi. loc.**

Blue Tree | **E 90s**

Boomerang Toys | **multi. loc.**

🛒 Build-A-Bear | **multi. loc.**

Children's Gen. Store | **multi. loc.**

Didi's Children's | **E 80s**

Dinosaur Hill | **E Vill**

E.A.T. Gifts | **E 80s**

FAO Schwarz | **E 50s**

🛒 Geppetto's Toy Box | **G Vill**

Heights Kids | **Brooklyn Hts**

Hom Boms | **E 70s**

Hot Toddie | **Ft Greene**

Ibiza Kidz | **G Vill**

KB Toys | **multi. loc.**

🛒 Kidding Around | **Flatiron**

kid o. | **G Vill**

Kid Robot | **SoHo**

Kidville Boutique | **multi. loc.**

Kmart | **multi. loc.**

Lee's Art Shop | **W 50s**

🛒 Macy's | **multi. loc.**

🛒 Mary Arnold Toys | **E 70s**

Maxilla & Mandible | **W 80s**

NEW MoonSoup | **E 50s**

New York Doll | **E 60s**

Nintendo World | **E 40s**

Penny Whistle | **W 80s**

Pomme | **Dumbo**

Romp | **Park Slope**

Sanrio | **multi. loc.**

Scholastic Store | **SoHo**

Sears | **multi. loc.**

🛒 Target | **multi. loc.**

Tiny Doll House | **E 70s**

NEW Toy Space | **Park Slope**

Toys "R" Us | **multi. loc.**

West Side Kids | **W 80s**

World of Disney | **E 50s**
Z Chemists/Zitomer | **E 70s**

WATCHES

Aaron Faber | **W 50s**
Z Asprey | **E 70s**
Z Barneys New York | **E 60s**
Blair Delmonico | **W 50s**
Z Bloomingdale's | **E 50s**
Breguet | **E 60s**
Z Buccellati | **E 50s**
Bulgari | **multi. loc.**
Z Cartier | **multi. loc.**
Cellini | **multi. loc.**
Chanel Jewelry | **E 60s**
Z Chopard | **E 60s**
Chrome Hearts | **E 60s**
Damiani | **E 60s**
David Webb | **E 60s**
David Yurman | **E 60s**
Dunhill | **E 50s**
Fortunoff | **E 50s**
Fossil | **multi. loc.**
Z Fred Leighton | **E 60s**
Z Georg Jensen | **SoHo**

Gucci | **multi. loc.**
Z Harry Winston | **E 50s**
Z H. Stern | **E 50s**
Jacob & Co. | **E 50s**
Joan Michlin Gallery | **SoHo**
Joseph Edwards | **E 40s**
Kenjo | **multi. loc.**
Z Lord & Taylor | **Murray Hill**
Z Macy's | **multi. loc.**
Michael Ashton | **E 70s**
Z MoMA Store | **multi. loc.**
Movado | **multi. loc.**
Z Piaget | **E 50s**
Z Saks Fifth Ave. | **E 50s**
Swatch | **multi. loc.**
Swiss Army | **SoHo**
Taffin | **E 70s**
Z Tiffany & Co. | **E 50s**
Tourneau | **multi. loc.**
Z Van Cleef & Arpels | **E 50s**
Z Wempe | **E 50s**
William Barthman | **multi. loc.**
Zales Jewelers | **multi. loc.**

Special Features

Listings cover the best in each category and include store names and locations. ☒ indicates highest ratings, popularity and importance.

ADDITIONS

(Properties added since the last edition of the book)

Abitare | **Brooklyn Hts**

A Brooklyn Table | **Cobble Hill**

Adrienne Vittadini | **W 40s**

Alessi | **SoHo**

alice + olivia | **W 40s**

Anne Klein | **E 60s**

Arcadia | **Chelsea**

Area | **multi. loc.**

Bblessing | **LES**

Belle & Maxie | **Ditmas Pk**

Ben Sherman | **SoHo**

Blibetroy | **LES**

Blue in Green | **SoHo**

Bra*Tenders | **W 40s**

Bridal Reflect. | **Murray Hill**

Brooklyn Collective | **Red Hook**

Brunello Cucinelli | **W Vill**

Calvin Tran | **NoLita**

Caravan | **NoHo**

Caron Paris | **E 60s**

Catbird | **Williamsburg**

Centricity | **E Vill**

Consignment | **Downtown**

C.P.W. | **W 80s**

Crew Cuts | **SoHo**

Crumpler Bags | **multi. loc.**

DC Shoes | **SoHo**

de Grisogono | **E 60s**

DeNatale Jewelers | **multi. loc.**

Dolce Vita | **LES**

Dulcinée | **LES**

Ed Hardy | **Meatpacking**

EMc2 | **NoLita**

Essentials | **multi. loc.**

Esthete | **Meatpacking**

45rpm/R | **multi. loc.**

Freemans Sporting | **LES**

Fresh Kills | **Williamsburg**

Gabay's Home | **E Vill**

GapBody | **E Vill**

Giorgio Fedon 19 | **W 40s**

Golfsmith | **E 50s**

Greenwich Letterpress | **W Vill**

Groupe | **NoLita**

Guy Laroche | **W 50s**

Hairy Mary's | **LES**

Harry's Shoes/Kids | **W 80s**

Hasker | **Carroll Gdns**

Hastens | **SoHo**

Heidi Klein | **E 70s**

Hollander & Lexer | **Boerum Hill**

Honora | **E 50s**

IC Zinco | **SoHo**

Institut NYC | **SoHo**

Irma | **W Vill**

Itsasickness | **LES**

JackRabbit Sports | **multi. loc.**

Jaime Mascaró | **E 70s**

Jennifer Miller Jewelry | **E 70s**

J.J. Marco | **E 80s**

Juicy Couture | **multi. loc.**

Jumelle | **Williamsburg**

Kaight | **LES**

K&G Fashion | **E 40s**

Kate's At Home | **SoHo**

Kids Rx | **W Vill**

Kidville Boutique | **W 80s**

Kiki De Montparnasse | **SoHo**

Kipepeo | **NoLita**

Laces | **NoLita**

Lancôme | **W 60s**

Lara Hélène | **E 60s**

Le Labo | **NoLita**

Leontine | **Seaport**

Le Sabon & Baby Too | **E 60s**

LF Stores | **multi. loc.**

Limited Too | **multi. loc.**

Linda Derector | **NoLita**

Lion in the Sun | **Park Slope**

Lisa Levine Jewelry | **Williamsburg**

Little Stinkers | **E Vill**

Loopy Mango | **Dumbo**

Lord Willy's | **NoLita**

Love Brigade | **Williamsburg**

Loveday31 | **Astoria**

Lulu Castagnette | **NoLita**

LuLuLemon | **multi. loc.**

Madura | **E 80s**

Marc and Max | **W Vill**

Max Azria | **SoHo**
Meg Cohen Design | **SoHo**
miks | **LES**
Mimi's Closet | **Astoria**
Miriam Rigler | **E 60s**
Mish Mish | **E 90s**
M Missoni | **SoHo**
MoonSoup | **E 50s**
Morgan Library | **Murray Hill**
Moulin Bleu | **TriBeCa**
Mulberry | **multi. loc.**
N | **Harlem**
Napapijri | **SoHo**
Nave | **SoHo**
Nili Lotan | **TriBeCa**
Nokia | **E 50s**
Number (N)ine | **TriBeCa**
Ochre | **SoHo**
Olá Baby | **Carroll Gdns**
Oliver Spencer | **W Vill**
Oska | **SoHo**
Parasuco | **NoLita**
Paulina Quintana | **E Vill**
Petrou | **E 60s**
Petticoat Lane | **TriBeCa**
Pomellato | **E 60s**
Porsche Design | **E 50s**
Posey Baker | **Park Slope**
Pottery Barn Bed/Bath | **Chelsea**
Pottery Barn Kids | **E 60s**
Purple Reign | **Harlem**
Pylones | **multi. loc.**
Quintessentials | **W 80s**
Ralph Lauren Eyewear | **E 60s**
Roberta Roller Rabbit | **E 70s**
Rogan | **TriBeCa**
Saja | **NoLita**
Salviati | **SoHo**
Samantha Thavasa | **E 70s**
Samsonite Black Label | **E 60s**
Satellite | **SoHo**
SEE Eyewear | **W Vill**
Shooz | **Chelsea**
Shvitz | **SoHo**
Sicis | **SoHo**
Signoria | **E 60s**
Sigrid Olsen | **SoHo**
SOHO | **NoLita**
Sophia Eugene | **W Vill**
Space Mercer | **SoHo**

Space107 | **W Vill**
Spring | **Dumbo**
Stuart & Wright | **Ft Greene**
Suite New York | **E 50s**
Tarina Tarantino | **SoHo**
té casan | **SoHo**
Tibi | **SoHo**
Tiny Living | **E Vill**
Toy Space | **Park Slope**
Tracy Reese | **Meatpacking**
Treehouse | **Williamsburg**
Trico Field | **SoHo**
Trina Turk | **Meatpacking**
True Religion | **SoHo**
Trunkt | **TriBeCa**
UGG Australia | **SoHo**
Uniqlo | **SoHo**
Valley | **LES**
Village Tannery | **multi. loc.**
Vintage Collections | **E 70s**
Von Dutch | **SoHo**
WeSC | **SoHo**
White Hse. Black Mkt. | **Flatiron**
Wonk | **multi. loc.**
Woolworks Needlepoint | **E 70s**
Ylli | **Williamsburg**
Yoko Devereaux | **Williamsburg**
Zoë | **Dumbo**

AVANT-GARDE

Agent Provocateur | **SoHo**
Alain Mikli | **E 70s**
🖬 Alexander McQueen |
    Meatpacking
auto | **Meatpacking**
🖬 Balenciaga | **Chelsea**
🖬 Barneys New York | **E 60s**
Bathing Ape | **SoHo**
NEW Bblessing | **LES**
Bond 07 by Selima | **NoHo**
Butter | **Downtown**
CB I Hate Perfume | **Williamsburg**
Chrome Hearts | **E 60s**
Cloak | **SoHo**
Comme des Garçons | **Chelsea**
Compact Impact | **Financial Dist**
Costume National | **SoHo**
Dernier Cri | **Meatpacking**
Design Within Reach | **multi. loc.**
Destination | **Meatpacking**

Dolce & Gabbana | **E 60s**
Edge nyNoHo | **NoHo**
45rpm/R | **E 70s**
Fragments | **SoHo**
Future Perfect | **Williamsburg**
Garrard | **SoHo**
Good, Bad & Ugly | **NoLita**
IF | **SoHo**
Ingo Maurer Light | **SoHo**
Issey Miyake | **multi. loc.**
Jean Shop | **Meatpacking**
Jeffrey | **Meatpacking**
John Fluevog Shoes | **NoLita**
Kirna Zabête | **SoHo**
Lilith | **NoLita**
Market NYC | **NoLita**
Matter | **Park Slope**
☑ MoMA Store | **multi. loc.**
☑ Moss | **SoHo**
Opening Ceremony | **SoHo**
☑ Other Music | **NoHo**
Patricia Field | **NoHo**
Pleats Please | **SoHo**
Prada | **multi. loc.**
Roberto Cavalli | **E 60s**
Seven NY | **SoHo**
Spring | **Dumbo**
☑ Takashimaya | **E 50s**
37=1 Atelier | **SoHo**
Tupli | **E 60s**
Via Bus Stop | **SoHo**
Vitra | **Meatpacking**
Yohji Yamamoto | **SoHo**
Zero/Maria Cornejo | **NoLita**

CELEBRITY CLIENTELE
Aaron Basha | **E 60s**
☑ ABC Carpet & Home | **Flatiron**
☑ Aedes De Venustas | **G Vill**
Alain Mikli | **E 70s**
Alessandro Dell'Acqua | **E 60s**
☑ Alexander McQueen |
   Meatpacking
Alexis Bittar | **SoHo**
Annelore | **W Vill**
☑ Balenciaga | **Chelsea**
☑ Barneys New York | **E 60s**
BDDW | **SoHo**
☑ Bergdorf Goodman | **E 50s**

☑ Bergdorf Men's | **E 50s**
Berluti | **E 70s**
Beverly Feldman | **W 50s**
Billy Martin's Western | **E 60s**
Blue Tree | **E 90s**
☑ Bottega Veneta | **E 50s**
Breguet | **E 60s**
Burberry | **multi. loc.**
Burton Store | **SoHo**
Butik | **W Vill**
Calvin Klein | **E 60s**
NEW Calvin Tran | **NoLita**
Calypso | **multi. loc.**
Camilla Bergeron | **E 60s**
NEW Caravan | **NoHo**
Carlos Miele | **Meatpacking**
☑ Carolina Herrera | **E 70s**
Catherine Malandrino | **SoHo**
CB I Hate Perfume | **Williamsburg**
☑ Chanel | **multi. loc.**
Chloé | **E 70s**
☑ Christian Louboutin | **E 70s**
Chrome Hearts | **E 60s**
Claudia Ciuti | **E 70s**
Damiani | **E 60s**
DDC Lab | **Meatpacking**
de Grisogono | **E 60s**
Dernier Cri | **Meatpacking**
Dior Homme | **E 50s**
☑ Dior New York | **E 50s**
Dolce & Gabbana | **E 60s**
Domenico Vacca | **multi. loc.**
Donna Karan | **E 60s**
Dylan's Candy Bar | **E 60s**
Earnest Cut & Sew | **Meatpacking**
NEW Ed Hardy | **Meatpacking**
Elizabeth Charles | **Meatpacking**
NEW EMc2 | **NoLita**
Fat Beats | **G Vill**
Fendi | **E 50s**
Fragments | **SoHo**
☑ Fred Leighton | **E 60s**
Fresh | **multi. loc.**
Garrard | **SoHo**
Geminola | **W Vill**
☑ Giorgio Armani | **E 60s**
Gucci | **multi. loc.**
NEW Guy Laroche | **W 50s**
NEW Hastens | **SoHo**
Helen Ficalora | **NoLita**

Henry Beguelin | **Meatpacking**
⛧ Hermès | **E 60s**
Hogan | **SoHo**
Hollywould | **NoLita**
Hugo Boss | **multi. loc.**
Issey Miyake | **multi. loc.**
Jacob & Co. | **E 50s**
Jeffrey | **Meatpacking**
Jennifer Miller Jewelry | **E 70s**
Jill Platner | **SoHo**
Jimmy Choo | **E 50s**
J.M. Weston | **E 60s**
Jonathan Adler | **SoHo**
Joseph | **multi. loc.**
NEW Juicy Couture | **multi. loc.**
Kangol Columbus Ave. | **W 60s**
Key | **SoHo**
NEW Kiki De Montparnasse | **SoHo**
NEW Kipepeo | **NoLita**
Kiton | **E 50s**
LaDuca Shoes | **Garment Dist**
Lana Marks | **E 60s**
La Petite Coquette | **G Vill**
Longchamp | **SoHo**
NEW Lord Willy's | **NoLita**
Louis Vuitton | **SoHo**
Lowell/Edwards | **E 50s**
Lulu Guinness | **W Vill**
Manhattan Saddlery | **Gramercy**
⛧ Manolo Blahnik | **W 50s**
Marc Jacobs Access. | **W Vill**
Marc Jacobs | **SoHo**
Marie-Chantal | **E 80s**
Marni | **SoHo**
NEW Max Azria | **SoHo**
Mayle | **NoLita**
Michael Kors | **E 70s**
Michele Varian | **SoHo**
Mish | **E 70s**
Miu Miu | **multi. loc.**
Mixona | **NoLita**
⛧ Moss | **SoHo**
NEW Mulberry | **multi. loc.**
Oliver Peoples | **multi. loc.**
NEW Oliver Spencer | **W Vill**
⛧ Oscar de la Renta | **E 60s**
NEW Petrou | **E 60s**
Poleci | **Meatpacking**
Prada | **multi. loc.**
Pucci | **E 60s**

⛧ Purl | **SoHo**
Rafe | **NoHo**
Ralph Lauren | **multi. loc.**
Ralph Lauren Boys/Girls | **E 70s**
NEW Ralph Lauren Eyewear | **E 60s**
Rebecca Taylor | **NoLita**
Reem Acra | **E 60s**
Robert Marc | **multi. loc.**
Roberto Cavalli | **E 60s**
Roberto Vascon | **W 70s**
NEW Rogan | **TriBeCa**
Rubin Chapelle | **Meatpacking**
NEW Samantha Thavasa | **E 70s**
⛧ Santa Maria Novella | **NoLita**
Satya | **W Vill**
Sean John | **E 40s**
Shin Choi | **SoHo**
Some Odd Rubies | **LES**
Stella McCartney | **Meatpacking**
Swarovski | **E 50s**
Taffin | **E 70s**
NEW Tarina Tarantino | **SoHo**
Temperley | **SoHo**
Todd Hase | **SoHo**
⛧ Tod's | **E 60s**
NEW Trina Turk | **Meatpacking**
NEW True Religion | **SoHo**
Tsubi | **NoLita**
Tupli | **E 60s**
⛧ Urban Archaeology | **multi. loc.**
⛧ Valentino | **E 60s**
Vanessa Noel | **E 60s**
Versace | **E 50s**
Vogel | **SoHo**
Yigal Azrouel | **Meatpacking**
Yohji Yamamoto | **SoHo**

COOL LOOS

⛧ ABC Carpet & Home | **Flatiron**
⛧ Apple Store | **SoHo**
⛧ Asprey | **E 70s**
⛧ Barneys New York | **E 60s**
⛧ Bergdorf Goodman | **E 50s**
Burton Store | **SoHo**
NEW Caravan | **NoHo**
Chanel Jewelry | **E 60s**
Charles Nolan | **Meatpacking**
Earnest Cut & Sew | **Meatpacking**
NEW Ed Hardy | **Meatpacking**
NEW Esthete | **Meatpacking**

SPECIAL FEATURES

Fendi | **E 50s**

Marimekko | **E 70s**

NEW N | **Harlem**

NEW Nili Lotan | **TriBeCa**

Patricia Field | **NoHo**

Phi | **SoHo**

Poleci | **Meatpacking**

Reiss | **SoHo**

Rugby | **G Vill**

NEW Sophia Eugene | **W Vill**

Z Takashimaya | **E 50s**

NEW Tracy Reese | **Meatpacking**

CUSTOM-MADE GOODS

Aaron Basha | **E 60s**

Aaron Faber | **W 50s**

Z ABC Carpets/Rugs | **Flatiron**

ABH Design | **E 70s**

NEW Abitare | **Brooklyn Hts**

Z Aero | **SoHo**

Airline Stationery | **E 40s**

NEW Alessi | **SoHo**

Alexandros | **multi. loc.**

Alexis Bittar | **SoHo**

Alixandre Furs | **Garment Dist**

Amsale | **E 50s**

Annelore | **W Vill**

Z Ann Sacks | **multi. loc.**

Anya Hindmarch | **multi. loc.**

Armani Casa | **SoHo**

Artbag | **E 80s**

Arthur's Invitations | **G Vill**

Z Artistic Tile | **multi. loc.**

Ascot Chang | **W 50s**

Z Asprey | **E 70s**

Atelier NY | **SoHo**

Baker Tribeca | **TriBeCa**

Barbara Feinman | **E Vill**

Barbara Shaum | **E Vill**

BDDW | **SoHo**

Beacon Paint/Hardware | **W 70s**

Beckenstein Fabrics | **Flatiron**

Z Bergdorf Goodman | **E 50s**

Z Bergdorf Men's | **E 50s**

Berluti | **E 70s**

Z Bernardaud | **E 50s**

Birnbaum & Bullock | **Chelsea**

Bisazza | **SoHo**

Blacker & Kooby | **E 80s**

Blackman | **multi. loc.**

Blue | **E Vill**

BoConcept | **multi. loc.**

Bond No. 9 | **multi. loc.**

Borrelli Boutique | **E 60s**

Z Bottega Veneta | **E 50s**

B. Oyama Homme | **Harlem**

Bra*Tenders | **W 40s**

Breguet | **E 60s**

Bric's | **E 50s**

NEW Bridal Reflect. | **Murray Hill**

Z Brioni | **E 50s**

Brooklyn Collective | **Red Hook**

Z Buccellati | **E 50s**

Buckler | **Meatpacking**

Z Build-A-Bear | **multi. loc.**

Butter and Eggs | **TriBeCa**

Calypso Bijoux | **NoLita**

Calypso Enfant/Kids | **SoHo**

Calypso Home | **NoLita**

Canal Hi-Fi | **Chinatown**

Cappellini | **SoHo**

Z Carlyle Convertibles | **multi. loc.**

Carol's Daughter | **multi. loc.**

Caron Paris | **E 60s**

Cassina USA | **E 50s**

CB I Hate Perfume | **Williamsburg**

Cécile et Jeanne | **multi. loc.**

Cellini | **multi. loc.**

Charles Nolan | **Meatpacking**

Z Charles P. Rogers | **Flatiron**

Chrome Hearts | **E 60s**

Z City Quilter | **Chelsea**

Classic Sofa | **Flatiron**

Clea Colet | **E 70s**

Cloak | **SoHo**

Cog & Pearl | **Park Slope**

Compact Impact | **Financial Dist**

Cosmophonic Sound | **E 80s**

Z Country Floors | **Union Sq**

Z Crane & Co. | **W 40s**

Crumpler Bags | **multi. loc.**

Damiani | **E 60s**

Daum | **E 60s**

Z Davide Cenci | **E 60s**

David Lee Holland | **SoHo**

ddc domus design | **Murray Hill**

Z Dempsey & Carroll | **E 50s**

DeNatale Jewelers | **multi. loc.**
Dennis Basso | **E 60s**
Desiron | **SoHo**
Dinosaur Designs | **NoLita**
Dö Kham | **NoLita**
Domain | **multi. loc.**
Domenico Vacca | **multi. loc.**
Dudley's Paw | **TriBeCa**
Duncan Quinn | **NoLita**
Dune | **TriBeCa**
Dykes Lumber | **multi. loc.**
Earnest Cut & Sew | **Meatpacking**
E. Braun & Co. | **E 60s**
Einstein-Moomjy | **E 50s**
Elgot | **E 60s**
Elizabeth Locke | **E 70s**
Ellen Christine | **Chelsea**
NEW EMc2 | **NoLita**
environment337 | **multi. loc.**
Z Ermenegildo Zegna | **E 50s**
Federico de Vera | **SoHo**
Flou | **SoHo**
Fort St. Studio | **SoHo**
45rpm/R | **multi. loc.**
Z Fred Leighton | **E 60s**
NEW Freemans Sporting | **LES**
NEW Fresh Kills | **Williamsburg**
Z Frette | **E 60s**
Future Perfect | **Williamsburg**
Gallery/Wearable Art | **E 60s**
Garrard | **SoHo**
George Smith | **SoHo**
Z Ghurka | **E 60s**
Granny-Made | **W 70s**
NEW Greenwich Letterpress | **W Vill**
NEW Guy Laroche | **W 50s**
Z Harris Levy | **LES**
Z Harry Winston | **E 50s**
NEW Hasker | **Carroll Gdns**
NEW Hastens | **SoHo**
Hat Shop | **SoHo**
Z Henri Bendel | **E 50s**
Henry Beguelin | **Meatpacking**
H. Herzfeld | **E 50s**
Hickey Freeman | **multi. loc.**
Highway | **NoLita**
Z Home Depot | **multi. loc.**

Hyde Park Stationers | **E 80s**
IF | **SoHo**
Il Makiage | **E 50s**
Z Il Papiro | **E 70s**
In Living Stereo | **NoHo**
Innovative Audio | **E 50s**
IS: Ind. Stationery | **SoHo**
Jacob & Co. | **E 50s**
Jaded | **E 80s**
Jane Wilson-Marquis | **E 70s**
Jay Kos | **multi. loc.**
Jean Shop | **Meatpacking**
Jennifer Miller Jewelry | **E 70s**
Jeri Cohen Jewelry | **E 60s**
J.J. Hat Center | **Garment Dist**
NEW J.J. Marco | **E 80s**
Z J. Mendel | **E 60s**
J.M. Weston | **E 60s**
Joan Michlin Gallery | **SoHo**
John Derian | **E Vill**
Z John Lobb | **E 60s**
Z Judith Leiber | **E 60s**
Just Shades | **NoLita**
Jutta Neumann | **LES**
J.W. Cooper | **W 50s**
Kaas GlassWorks | **W Vill**
Karim Rashid Shop | **Chelsea**
Z Kate's Paperie | **multi. loc.**
Katz in the Cradle | **Midwood**
Kenjo | **multi. loc.**
NEW Kiki De Montparnasse | **SoHo**
Kiton | **E 50s**
Knoll | **Chelsea**
Kraft | **E 60s**
Kreiss Collection | **E 50s**
Z Krup's Kitchen/Bath | **Flatiron**
La Cafetière | **Chelsea**
LaDuca Shoes | **Garment Dist**
Lalaounis | **E 60s**
Z Lalique | **E 60s**
Lana Marks | **E 60s**
LaoLao Handmade | **E Vill**
L' Avenue des Reves | **E 70s**
Z Leather Man | **W Vill**
Lee Anderson | **E 60s**
Lee's Art Shop | **W 50s**
Le Fanion | **W Vill**
Léron | **E 60s**

Lightforms | **multi. loc.**

Lighting By Gregory | **LES**

Lion in the Sun | **Park Slope**

Lockes Diamonds | **E 60s**

Longchamp | **multi. loc.**

NEW Lord Willy's | **NoLita**

NEW Love Brigade | **Williamsburg**

Lowe's | **multi. loc.**

Lucien Pellat-Finet | **G Vill**

Z Lyric Hi-Fi | **E 80s**

Magic Windows | **E 80s**

Manhattan Ctr. | **Flatiron**

Marimekko | **E 70s**

Mary Adams The Dress | **LES**

Z Maurice Villency | **E 50s**

McGuire | **Murray Hill**

Mecox Gardens | **E 70s**

Michael Anchin Glass |
   Williamsburg

Michele Varian | **SoHo**

Michelle NY | **Boerum Hill**

Mika Inatome | **TriBeCa**

Miriam Rigler | **E 60s**

Mish | **E 70s**

Z Montblanc | **E 50s**

NEW MoonSoup | **E 50s**

NEW Morgan Library | **Murray Hill**

Z Moss | **SoHo**

NEW Moulin Bleu | **TriBeCa**

Z Mrs. John L. Strong | **E 60s**

NEW Mulberry | **multi. loc.**

Munder-Skiles | **E 60s**

Mxyplyzyk | **W Vill**

Nemo Tile | **multi. loc.**

NEW Nokia | **E 50s**

NYC Velo | **E Vill**

Occhiali | **E 80s**

Oculus 20/20 | **multi. loc.**

O'Lampia Studio | **LES**

OMO Norma Kamali | **W 50s**

On Stage Dance | **Murray Hill**

Oriental Lamp Shade | **multi. loc.**

Z Oxxford Clothes | **E 50s**

Papyrus | **multi. loc.**

Park Ave. Audio | **Gramercy**

Parke & Ronen | **Chelsea**

Paterson Silks | **multi. loc.**

P.E. Guerin | **W Vill**

Z Pierre Deux | **E 50s**

Poggenpohl U.S. | **multi. loc.**

Poltrona Frau | **SoHo**

NEW Pomellato | **E 60s**

Pomme | **Dumbo**

Z Pompanoosuc Mills | **TriBeCa**

Porthault | **E 60s**

Z Pratesi | **E 60s**

Quintessentials | **W 80s**

Rachel Ashwell's | **SoHo**

Rafe | **NoHo**

Reem Acra | **E 60s**

Refinery | **Cobble Hill**

Reinstein/Ross | **multi. loc.**

NEW Roberta Roller Rabbit | **E 70s**

Robert Lee Morris | **SoHo**

Robert Marc | **multi. loc.**

Roberto Vascon | **W 70s**

Z Roche Bobois | **Murray Hill**

Romp | **Park Slope**

Rosen & Chadick | **Garment Dist**

Rubin Chapelle | **Meatpacking**

Rug Company | **SoHo**

Ruzzetti & Gow | **E 70s**

Safavieh | **multi. loc.**

NEW Salviati | **SoHo**

Samuel's Hats | **Financial Dist**

Z Santa Maria Novella | **NoLita**

Scandinavian Sport | **E 50s**

Schoolhouse Electric | **TriBeCa**

Z Schweitzer Linen | **multi. loc.**

Scott Jordan | **SoHo**

Seigo | **E 80s**

Seize sur Vingt | **NoLita**

Selia Yang | **multi. loc.**

Sherle Wagner Int'l | **E 50s**

Shirt Store | **E 40s**

Shoe Mine | **Park Slope**

NEW Shvitz | **SoHo**

Sid's | **Downtown**

NEW Signoria | **E 60s**

Sir | **Boerum Hill**

Sleep | **Williamsburg**

NEW SOHO | **NoLita**

Sound City | **W 40s**

Space Kiddets | **Flatiron**

Space107 | **W Vill**

Spring | **Dumbo**

Stefano Ricci | **E 50s**
🅩 Steuben | **E 60s**
🅩 Stickley, Audi & Co. | **Flatiron**
🅩 String | **E 70s**
Stubbs & Wootton | **E 70s**
Suzanne Couture | **E 60s**
Taffin | **E 70s**
Ted Muehling | **SoHo**
37=1 Atelier | **SoHo**
Thom Browne | **TriBeCa**
Thos. Moser Cabinets | **E 60s**
🅩 Tiffany & Co. | **E 50s**
Tiny Doll House | **E 70s**
Todd Hase | **SoHo**
Town Shop | **W 80s**
NEW Treehouse | **Williamsburg**
Treillage | **E 70s**
Troy | **Gramercy**
Tucker Robbins | **multi. loc.**
Tupli | **E 60s**
🅩 Turnbull & Asser | **E 50s**
Umkarna | **Park Slope**
🅩 Van Cleef & Arpels | **E 50s**
Vanessa Noel | **E 60s**
Venture | **E 80s**
Vera Wang Bridal | **E 70s**
Vera Wang Maids | **E 70s**
Village Tannery | **multi. loc.**
Vogel | **SoHo**
Walter Steiger | **E 50s**
Warren Edwards | **E 60s**
White on White | **Murray Hill**
Wonk | **multi. loc.**
World of Golf | **E 40s**
Yigal Azrouel | **Meatpacking**
Yoya/Yoya Mart | **W Vill**
Yves Delorme | **E 70s**
Zarin Fabrics | **LES**

FREQUENT-BUYER PROGRAMS

Alkit | **Flatiron**
🅩 Allen Edmonds | **E 40s**
Aveda | **multi. loc.**
🅩 Barneys New York | **E 60s**
BCBG Max Azria | **Flatiron**
🅩 Bergdorf Goodman | **E 50s**
🅩 Bergdorf Men's | **E 50s**
🅩 Bloomingdale's | **SoHo**

Carol's Daughter | **multi. loc.**
Casual Male XL | **multi. loc.**
Chico's | **multi. loc.**
Dana Buchman | **E 50s**
🅩 DSW | **multi. loc.**
NEW Ed Hardy | **Meatpacking**
Eileen Fisher | **multi. loc.**
Esprit | **W 50s**
GapBody | **E Vill**
Harry's Shoes | **W 80s**
NEW Harry's Shoes/Kids | **W 80s**
JackRabbit Sports | **multi. loc.**
🅩 Marshalls | **multi. loc.**
Montmartre | **multi. loc.**
Naturino | **multi. loc.**
Papyrus | **multi. loc.**
Petco | **multi. loc.**
Poggenpohl U.S. | **multi. loc.**
Prato Fine Men's Wear | **multi. loc.**
Sacco | **multi. loc.**
🅩 Saks Fifth Ave. | **E 50s**
Sharper Image | **multi. loc.**
Staples | **multi. loc.**
Syms | **multi. loc.**
🅩 T.J. Maxx | **multi. loc.**
Tourneau | **multi. loc.**
Toys "R" Us | **multi. loc.**
Utrecht | **E Vill**
Victoria's Secret | **multi. loc.**
NEW White Hse. Black Mkt. | **Flatiron**

HIP/HOT PLACES

a. cheng | **E Vill**
Adidas | **multi. loc.**
🅩 Aedes De Venustas | **G Vill**
AG Adriano Goldschmied | **SoHo**
Agent Provocateur | **SoHo**
Albertine | **G Vill**
Alessandro Dell'Acqua | **E 60s**
NEW Alessi | **SoHo**
🅩 Alexander McQueen | **Meatpacking**
Alexis Bittar | **SoHo**
NEW alice + olivia | **W 40s**
American Apparel | **multi. loc.**
Anna Sui | **SoHo**
🅩 Apple Store | **SoHo**
Artsee | **Meatpacking**

Baby Bird | **Park Slope**
◪ Balenciaga | **Chelsea**
Barneys CO-OP | **SoHo**
◪ Barneys New York | **E 60s**
◪ Bathroom | **W Vill**
BCBG Max Azria | **multi. loc.**
NEW Ben Sherman | **SoHo**
Big Drop | **SoHo**
Bird | **multi. loc.**
Blades Board & Skate | **multi. loc.**
Blueberi | **Dumbo**
Bond 07 by Selima | **NoHo**
◪ Bottega Veneta | **E 50s**
Burberry | **multi. loc.**
Burton Store | **SoHo**
Butter | **Downtown**
Calypso | **multi. loc.**
Calypso Enfant/Kids | **SoHo**
Calypso Home | **NoLita**
Camper | **SoHo**
◪ Canine Styles | **G Vill**
Cantaloup/Luxe | **E 70s**
NEW Caravan | **NoHo**
Carlos Miele | **Meatpacking**
Catherine Malandrino | **SoHo**
Cherry | **W Vill**
Chloé | **E 70s**
◪ Christian Louboutin | **E 70s**
Chrome Hearts | **E 60s**
Cloak | **SoHo**
Conran Shop | **E 50s**
Costume National | **SoHo**
Crembebè | **E Vill**
NEW Crew Cuts | **SoHo**
C. Ronson | **NoLita**
D & G | **SoHo**
Darling | **W Vill**
Daryl K | **NoHo**
Dernier Cri | **Meatpacking**
Diana Kane | **Park Slope**
Diane T | **Cobble Hill**
Diane von Furstenberg |
    Meatpacking
Diesel | **multi. loc.**
Diesel Denim Gallery | **SoHo**
Dior Homme | **E 50s**
◪ Dior New York | **E 50s**
Doggystyle | **SoHo**
Dolce & Gabbana | **E 60s**
Dylan's Candy Bar | **E 60s**

Earnest Cut & Sew | **Meatpacking**
Edge nyNoHo | **NoHo**
NEW Ed Hardy | **Meatpacking**
Erica Tanov | **NoLita**
Fat Beats | **G Vill**
Flight 001 | **W Vill**
Flying A | **SoHo**
Foley + Corinna | **LES**
NEW Fresh Kills | **Williamsburg**
Future Perfect | **Williamsburg**
G.C. William | **E 80s**
Giggle | **multi. loc.**
◪ Giuseppe Zanotti | **E 60s**
Good, Bad & Ugly | **NoLita**
Gucci | **multi. loc.**
◪ H&M | **multi. loc.**
NEW Hasker | **Carroll Gdns**
Henry Beguelin | **Meatpacking**
Henry Lehr | **NoLita**
I Heart | **NoLita**
Infinity | **E 80s**
Intermix | **multi. loc.**
Jack Spade | **SoHo**
Jacob & Co. | **E 50s**
James Perse | **W Vill**
Jean Shop | **Meatpacking**
Jeffrey | **Meatpacking**
Jill Stuart | **SoHo**
Jimmy Choo | **E 50s**
John Derian | **E Vill**
John Varvatos | **SoHo**
Jonathan Adler | **SoHo**
NEW Juicy Couture | **Flatiron**
Kate Spade | **SoHo**
Key | **SoHo**
◪ Kiehl's | **multi. loc.**
NEW Kiki De Montparnasse | **SoHo**
NEW Kipepeo | **NoLita**
Kirna Zabête | **SoHo**
Lacoste | **E 40s**
LeSportsac | **multi. loc.**
NEW Lisa Levine Jewelry |
    Williamsburg
NEW Loopy Mango | **Dumbo**
NEW Lord Willy's | **NoLita**
Lounge | **SoHo**
Ludivine | **G Vill**
Lulu Guinness | **W Vill**
Lyell | **NoLita**
Maison Martin Margiela | **W Vill**

Malin + Goetz | **Chelsea**

Ⓩ Manolo Blahnik | **W 50s**

Marc/Marc Jacobs | **W Vill**

Marc Jacobs Access. | **W Vill**

Marc Jacobs | **SoHo**

Marni | **SoHo**

Marsha D.D. | **E 80s**

Matter | **Park Slope**

Mayle | **NoLita**

Me & Ro | **NoLita**

NEW Mimi's Closet | **Astoria**

Min-K | **NoLita**

Missha | **multi. loc.**

Miss Sixty | **SoHo**

Miu Miu | **multi. loc.**

Ⓩ Moss | **SoHo**

NEW Mulberry | **multi. loc.**

NEW N | **Harlem**

Nanette Lepore | **SoHo**

99X | **E Vill**

Noisette | **Williamsburg**

No. 6 | **Little Italy**

Oakley | **SoHo**

Odin | **multi. loc.**

Olive & Bette's | **multi. loc.**

Opening Ceremony | **SoHo**

Ⓩ Other Music | **NoHo**

Paul Frank | **NoLita**

Paul Smith | **multi. loc.**

Phat Farm | **SoHo**

Pieces | **Prospect Hts**

Poleci | **Meatpacking**

Pookie & Sebastian | **multi. loc.**

Poppy | **NoLita**

Prada | **multi. loc.**

Pucci | **multi. loc.**

Puma | **multi. loc.**

Rafe | **NoHo**

Rebecca Taylor | **NoLita**

Redberi | **Prospect Hts**

Red Flower | **NoLita**

Resurrection | **NoLita**

Robert Marc | **multi. loc.**

Roberto Cavalli | **E 60s**

Ruehl | **W Vill**

Rugby | **G Vill**

NEW Saja | **NoLita**

Sam & Seb | **Williamsburg**

Ⓩ Santa Maria Novella | **NoLita**

NEW Satellite | **SoHo**

Satya | **W Vill**

Scoop Kids | **Meatpacking**

Scoop NYC | **multi. loc.**

Sean John | **E 40s**

Searle | **multi. loc.**

Seize sur Vingt | **NoLita**

Selima Optique | **multi. loc.**

Seven NY | **SoHo**

Shoe Box | **multi. loc.**

Shoe Mine | **Park Slope**

Sigerson Morrison | **NoLita**

Sigerson Morrison Bags | **NoLita**

Sleep | **Williamsburg**

Space Kiddets | **Flatiron**

NEW Space Mercer | **SoHo**

Stella McCartney | **Meatpacking**

Steven Alan | **multi. loc.**

NEW Stuart & Wright | **Ft Greene**

Swarovski | **multi. loc.**

NEW Tarina Tarantino | **SoHo**

NEW té casan | **SoHo**

Ted Baker | **SoHo**

Ⓩ Tekserve | **Chelsea**

TG-170 | **LES**

Theory | **multi. loc.**

Thom Browne | **TriBeCa**

Top DJ Gear | **NoLita**

Tory Burch | **NoLita**

Tracy Feith | **NoLita**

NEW Tracy Reese | **Meatpacking**

NEW Trina Turk | **Meatpacking**

Triple Five Soul | **SoHo**

Troy | **Gramercy**

Tsubi | **NoLita**

NEW Uniqlo | **SoHo**

Urban Outfitters | **multi. loc.**

Vespa | **SoHo**

Vitra | **Meatpacking**

Watts on Smith | **Carroll Gdns**

NEW WeSC | **SoHo**

Wink | **multi. loc.**

Yellow Rat Bastard | **multi. loc.**

NEW Ylli | **Williamsburg**

Zachary's Smile | **multi. loc.**

Zero/Maria Cornejo | **multi. loc.**

INSIDER SECRETS

NEW Abitare | **Brooklyn Hts**

Adriennes | **LES**

Alcone | **W 40s**

Alexandros | **multi. loc.**

SPECIAL FEATURES

Alife | **LES**

Alixandre Furs | **Garment Dist**

Alpana Bawa | **E Vill**

Amarcord Vintage | **multi. loc.**

Anbar | **TriBeCa**

Anna | **E Vill**

Annelore | **W Vill**

Barbara Shaum | **E Vill**

NEW Bblessing | **LES**

Beneath | **E 70s**

NEW Blibetroy | **LES**

Blue | **E Vill**

NEW Blue in Green | **SoHo**

Bowery Kitchen Supplies | **Chelsea**

B. Oyama Homme | **Harlem**

Bra*Tenders | **W 40s**

Built by Wendy | **Little Italy**

Butik | **W Vill**

By Boe | **E 70s**

Camilla Bergeron | **E 60s**

Capucine | **TriBeCa**

Catbird | **Williamsburg**

CB I Hate Perfume | **Williamsburg**

Classic Kicks | **NoHo**

Cloth | **Ft Greene**

NEW Consignment | **Downtown**

Dane 115 | **SoHo**

David Lee Holland | **SoHo**

Dear Fieldbinder | **Cobble Hill**

Diva | **Midwood**

D/L Cerney | **E Vill**

Dosa | **SoHo**

Doyle and Doyle | **LES**

Duncan Quinn | **NoLita**

Dunderdon Workshop | **SoHo**

Dusica Dusica | **SoHo**

Edith and Daha | **LES**

Elizabeth Charles | **Meatpacking**

Ellen Christine | **Chelsea**

environment337 | **multi. loc.**

Family Jewels | **Chelsea**

Finyl Vinyl | **E Vill**

Fort St. Studio | **SoHo**

45rpm/R | **multi. loc.**

NEW Fresh Kills | **Williamsburg**

Garrard | **SoHo**

Geminola | **W Vill**

Gentlemen's Resale | **E 80s**

Good, Bad & Ugly | **NoLita**

NEW Greenwich Letterpress | **W Vill**

halcyon the shop | **Dumbo**

NEW Heidi Klein | **E 70s**

NEW Hollander & Lexer | **Boerum Hill**

IF | **SoHo**

Itsasickness | **LES**

Jammyland | **E Vill**

Jane | **E 70s**

Jay Kos | **E 70s**

Jeri Cohen Jewelry | **E 60s**

Jill Platner | **SoHo**

NEW Jumelle | **Williamsburg**

Kavanagh's | **E 40s**

KD Dance & Sport | **NoHo**

Key | **SoHo**

Kiton | **E 50s**

Koh's Kids | **TriBeCa**

Kremer Pigments | **Chelsea**

NEW Laces | **NoLita**

L'Artisan Parfumeur | **multi. loc.**

Layla | **Downtown**

Lee Anderson | **E 60s**

NEW Le Labo | **NoLita**

NEW Leontine | **Seaport**

NEW Linda Derector | **NoLita**

NEW Love Brigade | **Williamsburg**

Lowell/Edwards | **E 50s**

Lucky Wang | **G Vill**

Luilei | **Park Slope**

Maleeka | **Downtown**

Mariko | **E 70s**

Market NYC | **NoLita**

Mary Adams The Dress | **LES**

Matta | **NoLita**

NEW Meg Cohen Design | **SoHo**

Mick Margo | **W Vill**

Mika Inatome | **TriBeCa**

Mini Mini Market | **Williamsburg**

Min-K | **E Vill**

NEW Moulin Bleu | **TriBeCa**

Myla | **E 60s**

Mylo Dweck Maternity | **Bensonhurst**

M Z Wallace | **SoHo**

NEW Nave | **SoHo**

New York Replacement | E 90s
Noisette | Williamsburg
Nom de Guerre | NoHo
Nort/Recon | NoHo
Number (N)ine | TriBeCa
NYC Velo | E Vill
Occhiali | E 80s
Otte | multi. loc.
Peggy Pardon | LES
P.E. Guerin | W Vill
Pippin | LES
Pomme | Dumbo
premium goods | Park Slope
Prince Charles III | SoHo
Project 234 | NoLita
Psny | SoHo
Razor | Park Slope
Rebecca & Drew | Meatpacking
Rico | Boerum Hill
Roberto Vascon | W 70s
Romp | Park Slope
Ruzzetti & Gow | E 70s
Schoolhouse Electric | TriBeCa
Sean | multi. loc.
Sir | Boerum Hill
Some Odd Rubies | LES
NEW Sophia Eugene | W Vill
Sugar | E Vill
Taffin | E 70s
Temperley | SoHo
Tiny Living | E Vill
NEW Trico Field | SoHo
Tupli | E 60s
Two Jakes | Williamsburg
Umkarna | Park Slope
Unis | NoLita
Urban Angler | Chelsea
Vintage Collections | E 70s
Vogel | SoHo
NEW Yoko Devereaux |
    Williamsburg
NEW Zoë | Dumbo

LEGENDARY

(Date company founded)
1730 | Floris of London | E 60s
1752 | Caswell-Massey | E 40s
1775 | Breguet | E 60s
1781 | Asprey | E 70s
1801 | Crane & Co. | W 40s
1816 | Baccarat | E 50s
1818 | Brooks Brothers | multi. loc.
1825 | Clarks England | E 40s
1826 | Lord & Taylor | Murray Hill
1830 | Christofle | E 60s
1831 | Takashimaya | E 50s
1837 | Hermès | E 60s
1837 | Tiffany & Co. | E 50s
1838 | C.O. Bigelow | G Vill
1847 | Cartier | multi. loc.
1848 | Hammacher Schlemmer | E
    50s
1851 | A La Vieille Russie | E 50s
1851 | Bally | E 50s
1851 | Kiehl's | multi. loc.
1852 | Hastens | SoHo
1853 | Levi's Store | multi. loc.
1854 | Louis Vuitton | multi. loc.
1855 | Charles P. Rogers | Flatiron
1856 | Burberry | multi. loc.
1856 | Orvis | E 40s
1857 | P.E. Guerin | W Vill
1858 | Macy's | multi. loc.
1860 | Chopard | E 60s
1860 | Frette | E 60s
1860 | Ligne Roset | multi. loc.
1862 | FAO Schwarz | E 50s
1863 | Bernardaud | E 50s
1870 | Met. Museum of Art | multi.
    loc.
1870 | Penhaligon's | E 70s
1872 | Bloomingdale's | multi. loc.
1873 | Church's Shoes | E 60s
1874 | Piaget | E 50s
1878 | Daum | E 60s
1878 | Dempsey & Carroll | E 50s
1878 | Salvation Army | multi. loc.
1878 | Wempe | E 50s
1879 | Vogel | SoHo
1881 | Movado | multi. loc.
1882 | Danskin | W 60s
1884 | William Barthman | multi.
    loc.
1885 | Turnbull & Asser | E 50s
1887 | Capezio | multi. loc.
1887 | Smythson of Bond St. | W
    50s
1888 | Town Shop | W 80s
1889 | Modell's Sport | multi. loc.

1890 | H. Herzfeld | **E 50s**
1891 | J.M. Weston | **E 60s**
1892 | Poggenpohl U.S. | **multi. loc.**
1893 | Dunhill | **E 50s**
1893 | Mikimoto | **E 50s**
1893 | Pratesi | **E 60s**
1893 | Sears | **multi. loc.**
1894 | Bulgari | **multi. loc.**
1894 | Harris Levy | **LES**
1895 | Berluti | **E 70s**
1895 | Swarovski | **multi. loc.**
1896 | Henri Bendel | **E 50s**
1897 | ABC Carpet & Home | **Flatiron**
1897 | ABC Carpets/Rugs | **Flatiron**
1897 | Swiss Army | **SoHo**
1898 | Eisenberg Eisenberg | **Flatiron**
1898 | Lederer de Paris | **E 50s**
1898 | Willoughby's | **Garment Dist**
1899 | Bergdorf Goodman | **E 50s**
1899 | Hickey Freeman | **multi. loc.**
1900 | Hyman Hendler | **Garment Dist**
1900 | New York Doll | **E 60s**
1900 | Stickley, Audi & Co. | **Flatiron**
1900 | Tourneau | **multi. loc.**
1902 | Goodwill | **multi. loc.**
1902 | J. Press | **E 40s**
1903 | Steuben | **E 60s**
1904 | Caron Paris | **E 60s**
1904 | Georg Jensen | **multi. loc.**
1904 | Seaman Schepps | **E 50s**
1905 | Jos. A. Bank | **E 40s**
1905 | Lalique | **E 60s**
1905 | Thomasville | **Bayside**
1906 | Aaron Basha | **E 60s**
1906 | Montblanc | **multi. loc.**
1906 | Van Cleef & Arpels | **E 50s**
1908 | DeNatale Jewelers | **multi. loc.**
1908 | Filene's Basement | **multi. loc.**
1908 | Paragon | **Union Sq**
1908 | Spence-Chapin Thrift | **multi. loc.**
1910 | Ermenegildo Zegna | **E 50s**
1910 | Léron | **E 60s**

1911 | Fila | **E 40s**
1911 | J.J. Hat Center | **Garment Dist**
1911 | New York Public Library | **E 40s**
1912 | James Robinson | **E 50s**
1912 | Manhattan Saddlery | **Gramercy**
1913 | Prada | **multi. loc.**
1914 | Chanel | **multi. loc.**
1914 | Salvatore Ferragamo | **E 50s**
1915 | Sol Moscot | **multi. loc.**
1916 | Oxxford Clothes | **E 50s**
1917 | Alixandre Furs | **Garment Dist**
1918 | Beckenstein Fabrics | **Flatiron**
1918 | Gringer & Sons | **E Vill**
1918 | Jaime Mascaró | **multi. loc.**
1918 | Paterson Silks | **Floral Pk**
1919 | Buccellati | **E 50s**
1919 | Giorgio Fedon 19 | **W 40s**
1919 | Greenstones | **W 80s**
1920 | Adidas | **multi. loc.**
1920 | Altman Luggage | **LES**
1920 | Harry Winston | **E 50s**
1920 | Oriental Lamp Shade | **multi. loc.**
1921 | Alessi | **SoHo**
1921 | Blackman | **multi. loc.**
1921 | Gucci | **multi. loc.**
1921 | Loehmann's | **multi. loc.**
1922 | Allen Edmonds | **multi. loc.**
1922 | Fortunoff | **E 50s**
1923 | Barneys New York | **E 60s**
1923 | Fogal/Switzerland | **E 50s**
1924 | Arthur Brown & Bro. | **W 40s**
1924 | A.W. Kaufman | **LES**
1924 | Damiani | **E 60s**
1924 | Loro Piana | **E 60s**
1924 | Saks Fifth Ave. | **E 50s**
1925 | Bang & Olufsen | **multi. loc.**
1925 | Capitol Fishing | **Garment Dist**
1925 | Davis & Warshow | **multi. loc.**
1925 | Fendi | **E 50s**
1926 | Davide Cenci | **E 60s**

1926 | Eneslow | **multi. loc.**
1927 | Cassina USA | **E 50s**
1927 | Furla | **multi. loc.**
1927 | Harvey Electronics | **W 40s**
1928 | Bloom & Krup | **Garment Dist**
1928 | Cole Haan | **multi. loc.**
1929 | A.I. Friedman | **Flatiron**
1929 | A. Testoni | **E 50s**
1929 | Mrs. John L. Strong | **E 60s**
1929 | S.Feldman Houseware | **E 90s**
1930 | Cappellini | **SoHo**
1930 | Princeton Ski Shop | **Flatiron**
1930 | Signoria | **E 60s**
1930 | Whitney Museum | **E 70s**
1931 | Mary Arnold Toys | **E 70s**
1932 | Artbag | **E 80s**
1932 | Ethan Allen | **multi. loc.**
1932 | H.L. Purdy | **multi. loc.**
1932 | Maurice Villency | **E 50s**
1932 | Sid's | **Downtown**
1933 | Albee Baby Carriage | **W 90s**
1933 | Lacoste | **multi. loc.**
1933 | Pearl Paint | **multi. loc.**
1934 | Alkit | **Flatiron**
1934 | Boffi SoHo | **SoHo**
1934 | Scully & Scully | **E 50s**
1935 | Frick Collection | **E 70s**
1935 | Kraft | **E 60s**
1935 | Michael C. Fina | **multi. loc.**
1935 | Smiley's | **Woodhaven**
1936 | M&J Trimming | **Garment Dist**
1936 | Olden Camera/Lens | **Garment Dist**
1936 | Zarin Fabrics | **LES**
1937 | Gym Source | **E 50s**
1938 | Kangol Columbus Ave. | **W 60s**
1938 | Knoll | **Chelsea**
1938 | Paul Stuart | **E 40s**
1938 | Suarez | **E 50s**
1939 | Gerry Cosby | **Garment Dist**
1939 | Verdura | **E 50s**
1940 | Coach | **multi. loc.**
1940 | Gabay's Home | **E Vill**
1940 | Gabay's Outlet | **E Vill**
1940 | Tip Top Shoes | **W 70s**
1941 | Kleinfeld | **Chelsea**

1945 | Brioni | **E 50s**
1945 | Celine | **E 60s**
1945 | Elgot | **E 60s**
1945 | H. Stern | **E 50s**
1945 | Sherle Wagner Int'l | **E 50s**
1946 | Bridge Kitchenware | **E 40s**
1946 | Dior New York | **E 50s**
1946 | Fountain Pen | **TriBeCa**
1946 | Honora | **E 50s**
1946 | T. Anthony | **E 50s**
1947 | F.M. Allen | **E 70s**
1947 | H&M | **multi. loc.**
1947 | Jewish Museum | **E 90s**
1947 | Pucci | **multi. loc.**
1947 | Steinlauf & Stoller | **Garment Dist**
1947 | Talbots | **multi. loc.**
1948 | Colony Music | **W 40s**
1948 | David Webb | **E 60s**
1948 | Lester's | **multi. loc.**
1948 | Lexington Luggage | **E 60s**
1948 | Longchamp | **SoHo**
1948 | Mem. Sloan-Kettering | **E 80s**
1948 | Puma | **multi. loc.**
1948 | Scandinavian Sport | **E 50s**
1949 | Gant | **E 50s**
1949 | Miriam Rigler | **E 60s**
1949 | Pottery Barn | **multi. loc.**
1949 | Pottery Barn Bed/Bath | **Chelsea**
1949 | Wolford | **multi. loc.**
1950 | Adriennes | **LES**
1950 | Alcone | **W 40s**
1950 | Kreiss Collection | **E 50s**
1950 | Leonard Opticians | **multi. loc.**
1950 | Morris Brothers | **W 80s**
1950 | Ray Beauty Supply | **W 40s**
1950 | Robert Talbott | **E 60s**
1950 | Schneider's | **Chelsea**
1950 | Z Chemists/Zitomer | **E 70s**

ONLY IN NEW YORK

🄩 ABC Carpet & Home | **Flatiron**
Academy Records | **multi. loc.**
Alexandros | **multi. loc.**
Alixandre Furs | **Garment Dist**
🄩 B&H Photo-Video | **Garment Dist**
Capitol Fishing | **Garment Dist**
Colony Music | **W 40s**

Demolition Depot | **Harlem**
Dylan's Candy Bar | **E 60s**
Earnest Cut & Sew | **Meatpacking**
E.A.T. Gifts | **E 80s**
Edge nyNoHo | **NoHo**
🆕 EMc2 | **NoLita**
FAO Schwarz | **E 50s**
Hyman Hendler | **Garment Dist**
Jacob & Co. | **E 50s**
Jean Shop | **Meatpacking**
Love Saves The Day | **E Vill**
Lower E. S. Tenement | **LES**
Maxilla & Mandible | **W 80s**
Met. Opera Shop | **W 60s**
🔲 MoMA Store | **multi. loc.**
🆕 Morgan Library | **Murray Hill**
Museum/City of NY | **E 100s**
🔲 Neue Galerie NY | **E 80s**
New York Public Library | **E 40s**
New York Transit Mus. | **E 40s**
Ray Beauty Supply | **W 40s**
Ricky's | **multi. loc.**
🔲 Tender Buttons | **E 60s**
🔲 Zabar's | **W 80s**

REGISTRY: BABY

Acorn | **Downtown**
Area | **multi. loc.**
Babies "R" Us | **multi. loc.**
Baby Bird | **Park Slope**
🔲 Bed Bath & Beyond | **Staten Is**
🔲 Bergdorf Goodman | **E 50s**
🔲 Bloomingdale's | **SoHo**
Blue Bench | **TriBeCa**
Burlington Coat | **multi. loc.**
🔲 buybuy BABY | **Chelsea**
Calypso Enfant/Kids | **SoHo**
City Cricket | **W Vill**
Crembebè | **E Vill**
Destination Maternity | **E 50s**
FAO Schwarz | **E 50s**
flora and henri | **E 70s**
🔲 Georg Jensen | **SoHo**
Giggle | **multi. loc.**
Green Onion | **Cobble Hill**
Half Pint | **Dumbo**
Ibiza Kidz | **G Vill**
Julian & Sara | **SoHo**
Katz in the Cradle | **Midwood**
🔲 Kidding Around | **Flatiron**
kid o. | **G Vill**

Kidville Boutique | **W 80s**
Le Sabon & Baby Too | **E 60s**
Les Petits Chapelais | **SoHo**
🆕 Little Stinkers | **E Vill**
Lucky Wang | **Chelsea**
🆕 Mish Mish | **E 90s**
🆕 MoonSoup | **E 50s**
Natalie & Friends | **E 60s**
🆕 Olá Baby | **Carroll Gdns**
Peanutbutter & Jane | **W Vill**
Planet Kids | **multi. loc.**
Pomme | **Dumbo**
🆕 Pottery Barn Kids | **E 60s**
Prince & Princess | **E 70s**
Ralph Lauren Layette | **E 70s**
Sam & Seb | **Williamsburg**
Schneider's | **Chelsea**
Sons + Daughters | **E Vill**
Space Kiddets | **Flatiron**
🔲 Target | **multi. loc.**
🔲 Tiffany & Co. | **E 50s**
Tiny Doll House | **E 70s**
Umkarna | **Park Slope**
Yoya/Yoya Mart | **W Vill**
Z'Baby Company | **multi. loc.**

REGISTRY: BRIDAL/GIFT

🔲 ABC Carpet & Home | **Flatiron**
🆕 Abitare | **Brooklyn Hts**
A Brooklyn Table | **Cobble Hill**
Adrien Linford | **multi. loc.**
🔲 Aero | **SoHo**
Agent Provocateur | **SoHo**
Area | **multi. loc.**
Armani Casa | **SoHo**
🔲 Asprey | **E 70s**
🔲 Avventura | **W 80s**
🔲 Baccarat | **E 50s**
Bardith | **E 70s**
🔲 Barneys New York | **E 60s**
🔲 Bed Bath & Beyond | **multi. loc.**
🔲 Bergdorf Goodman | **E 50s**
🔲 Bloomingdale's | **multi. loc.**
Blue Tree | **E 90s**
Bonne Nuit | **E 70s**
Borrelli Boutique | **E 60s**
Boucher | **Meatpacking**
🔲 Bridge Kitchenware | **E 40s**
🔲 Broadway Panhandler | **G Vill**
🔲 Buccellati | **E 50s**
Calvin Klein | **E 60s**

Z Charles P. Rogers | **Flatiron**
Z Christofle | **E 60s**
Clio | **SoHo**
Conran Shop | **E 50s**
Z Crate & Barrel | **multi. loc.**
Daum | **E 60s**
E. Braun & Co. | **E 60s**
environment337 | **multi. loc.**
Ethan Allen | **multi. loc.**
Fishs Eddy | **Flatiron**
Fortunoff | **E 50s**
Z Frette | **E 60s**
Z Georg Jensen | **multi. loc.**
Girlshop | **Meatpacking**
Global Table | **SoHo**
Z Gracious Home | **multi. loc.**
Z Harris Levy | **LES**
Z Hermès | **E 60s**
NEW Honora | **E 50s**
Jensen-Lewis | **Chelsea**
John Derian | **E Vill**
NEW Jumelle | **Williamsburg**
NEW Kiki De Montparnasse | **SoHo**
La Cafetière | **Chelsea**
Laina Jane | **multi. loc.**
Z Lalique | **E 60s**
Z La Perla | **multi. loc.**
L' Avenue des Reves | **E 70s**
Laytner's Linen | **multi. loc.**
Léron | **E 60s**
Longchamp | **multi. loc.**
Z MacKenzie-Childs | **E 50s**
Z Macy's | **multi. loc.**
NEW Meg Cohen Design | **SoHo**
Z Michael C. Fina | **multi. loc.**
NEW MoonSoup | **E 50s**
Z Moss | **SoHo**
Nancy Koltes Home | **NoLita**
Nicole Farhi | **E 60s**
Pier 1 Imports | **multi. loc.**
Z Pierre Deux | **E 50s**
Porthault | **E 60s**
Pottery Barn | **multi. loc.**
Z Pratesi | **E 60s**
Restoration Hardware | **Flatiron**
Z Saks Fifth Ave. | **E 50s**
NEW Satellite | **SoHo**
Z Scully & Scully | **E 50s**
Sherle Wagner Int'l | **E 50s**
Z Simon Pearce | **E 50s**

Sleep | **Williamsburg**
Z Steuben | **E 60s**
Z Takashimaya | **E 50s**
Z Target | **multi. loc.**
NEW Tarina Tarantino | **SoHo**
37=1 Atelier | **SoHo**
Z Tiffany & Co. | **E 50s**
NEW Trunkt | **TriBeCa**
Victoria's Secret | **multi. loc.**
Z Williams-Sonoma | **multi. loc.**
William-Wayne | **G Vill**
Yellow Door | **multi. loc.**
Z Zabar's | **W 80s**

STATUS GOODS

Z Aedes De Venustas | **G Vill**
Agent Provocateur | **SoHo**
Z Akris | **E 60s**
Z A La Vieille Russie | **E 50s**
Alessandro Dell'Acqua | **E 60s**
Z Alexander McQueen |
  Meatpacking
Z Allen Edmonds | **multi. loc.**
Z Ann Sacks | **multi. loc.**
Z Apple Store | **multi. loc.**
Armani Casa | **SoHo**
Z Asprey | **E 70s**
A. Testoni | **E 50s**
Z Baccarat | **E 50s**
Z Balenciaga | **Chelsea**
Z B&B Italia | **E 50s**
Z Bang & Olufsen | **multi. loc.**
Z Barbour/Peter Elliot | **E 80s**
Z Barneys New York | **E 60s**
Z Belgian Shoes | **E 50s**
Bellini | **E 60s**
Z Bergdorf Goodman | **E 50s**
Berluti | **E 70s**
Z Bernardaud | **E 50s**
Beverly Feldman | **W 50s**
Blue Tree | **E 90s**
Boffi SoHo | **SoHo**
Z Bonpoint | **multi. loc.**
Z Bose | **W 50s**
Z Bottega Veneta | **E 50s**
Breguet | **E 60s**
Bric's | **E 50s**
Z Brioni | **E 50s**
NEW Brunello Cucinelli | **W Vill**
Z Buccellati | **E 50s**
Bulgari | **multi. loc.**

Burberry | **multi. loc.**
Burton Store | **SoHo**
Calvin Klein | **E 60s**
Camilla Bergeron | **E 60s**
Cappellini | **SoHo**
Carlos Miele | **Meatpacking**
☑ Carolina Herrera | **E 70s**
Caron Paris | **E 60s**
☑ Cartier | **E 50s**
Cassina USA | **E 50s**
Catherine Memmi | **SoHo**
Catimini | **E 80s**
Catriona Mackechnie |
   Meatpacking
☑ Celine | **E 60s**
Cellini | **multi. loc.**
☑ Cesare Paciotti | **E 60s**
☑ Chanel | **multi. loc.**
Chloé | **E 70s**
☑ Chopard | **E 60s**
☑ Christian Louboutin | **E 70s**
☑ Christofle | **E 60s**
Claudia Ciuti | **E 70s**
Comme des Garçons | **Chelsea**
☑ Country Floors | **Union Sq**
Daum | **E 60s**
☑ Davide Cenci | **E 60s**
David Webb | **E 60s**
David Yurman | **E 60s**
☑ Dean & Deluca | **SoHo**
de Grisogono | **E 60s**
☑ Dempsey & Carroll | **E 50s**
Dennis Basso | **E 60s**
Design Within Reach | **multi. loc.**
Dior Homme | **E 50s**
☑ Dior New York | **E 50s**
Dolce & Gabbana | **E 60s**
Domenico Vacca | **multi. loc.**
Donna Karan | **E 60s**
Doyle and Doyle | **LES**
Dunhill | **E 50s**
Earnest Cut & Sew | **Meatpacking**
Elizabeth Locke | **E 70s**
Emanuel Ungaro | **E 60s**
☑ Ermenegildo Zegna | **E 50s**
Escada | **E 50s**
Etro | **E 60s**
FAO Schwarz | **E 50s**
Fendi | **E 50s**
Fisch for the Hip | **Chelsea**

F.M. Allen | **E 70s**
Fort St. Studio | **SoHo**
45rpm/R | **E 70s**
Fratelli Rossetti | **E 50s**
☑ Fred Leighton | **E 60s**
☑ Frette | **E 60s**
Garrard | **SoHo**
George Smith | **SoHo**
☑ Georg Jensen | **E 60s**
☑ Ghurka | **E 60s**
Gianfranco Ferré | **E 70s**
☑ Giorgio Armani | **E 60s**
☑ Giuseppe Zanotti | **E 60s**
Givenchy | **E 60s**
☑ Graff | **E 60s**
Gucci | **multi. loc.**
NEW Guy Laroche | **W 50s**
☑ Harry Winston | **E 50s**
NEW Hastens | **SoHo**
☑ Henri Bendel | **E 50s**
Henry Beguelin | **Meatpacking**
☑ Hermès | **E 60s**
Hickey Freeman | **multi. loc.**
Hogan | **SoHo**
Hugo Boss | **E 50s**
Ingo Maurer Light | **SoHo**
Issey Miyake | **multi. loc.**
Jacadi | **multi. loc.**
Jackie Rogers | **E 70s**
Jacob & Co. | **E 50s**
Jennifer Miller Jewelry | **E 70s**
Jil Sander | **E 50s**
Jimmy Choo | **E 50s**
☑ J. Mendel | **E 60s**
J.M. Weston | **E 60s**
☑ John Lobb | **E 60s**
Johnston & Murphy | **multi. loc.**
John Varvatos | **SoHo**
☑ Joon | **multi. loc.**
☑ Judith Leiber | **E 60s**
Judith Ripka | **E 60s**
Kavanagh's | **E 40s**
NEW Kiki De Montparnasse | **SoHo**
Kiton | **E 50s**
Krizia | **E 60s**
☑ Lalique | **E 60s**
Lana Marks | **E 60s**
L'Artisan Parfumeur | **multi. loc.**
Lederer de Paris | **E 50s**
Léron | **E 60s**

Lexington Gardens | **E 70s**
🆕 Linda Derector | **NoLita**
Linda Dresner | **E 50s**
Ⓩ Loro Piana | **E 60s**
Louis Vuitton | **multi. loc.**
Lowell/Edwards | **E 50s**
Lucien Pellat-Finet | **G Vill**
Ⓩ Lyric Hi-Fi | **E 80s**
Manhattan Saddlery | **Gramercy**
Ⓩ Manolo Blahnik | **W 50s**
Marc Jacobs | **SoHo**
Marie-Chantal | **E 80s**
Marni | **SoHo**
Marston & Langinger | **SoHo**
MaxMara | **multi. loc.**
Michael Ashton | **E 70s**
Michael Kors | **E 70s**
Mika Inatome | **TriBeCa**
Ⓩ Mikimoto | **E 50s**
Mish | **E 70s**
Missoni | **E 70s**
Miu Miu | **multi. loc.**
Morgenthal Frederics | **multi. loc.**
Ⓩ Moss | **SoHo**
Movado | **SoHo**
Ⓩ Mrs. John L. Strong | **E 60s**
🆕 Nokia | **E 50s**
Oakley | **SoHo**
🆕 Ochre | **SoHo**
Olatz | **W Vill**
Oliver Peoples | **multi. loc.**
Ⓩ Oscar de la Renta | **E 60s**
Ⓩ Oxxford Clothes | **E 50s**
Paul & Shark | **E 60s**
Paul Smith | **multi. loc.**
P.E. Guerin | **W Vill**
Phi | **SoHo**
Ⓩ Piaget | **E 50s**
Pilar Rossi | **E 60s**
Poltrona Frau | **SoHo**
🆕 Porsche Design | **E 50s**
Porthault | **E 60s**
Prada | **multi. loc.**
Ⓩ Pratesi | **E 60s**
Pucci | **multi. loc.**
Ralph Lauren | **multi. loc.**
Ralph Lauren Boys/Girls | **E 70s**
🆕 Ralph Lauren Eyewear | **E 60s**
Ralph Lauren Layette | **E 70s**
Reem Acra | **E 60s**

Resurrection | **NoLita**
Robert Marc | **multi. loc.**
Roberto Cavalli | **E 60s**
Robert Talbott | **E 60s**
Ⓩ Salvatore Ferragamo | **E 50s**
🆕 Samsonite Black Label | **E 60s**
Ⓩ Santa Maria Novella | **NoLita**
Seaman Schepps | **E 50s**
Sherle Wagner Int'l | **E 50s**
🆕 Sicis | **SoHo**
Sigerson Morrison | **NoLita**
Sigerson Morrison Bags | **NoLita**
Ⓩ Smythson of Bond St. | **W 50s**
🆕 SOHO | **NoLita**
Sonia Rykiel | **E 70s**
Ⓩ Sound by Singer | **Union Sq**
Stella McCartney | **Meatpacking**
Ⓩ Stereo Exchange | **NoHo**
Ⓩ Steuben | **E 60s**
Stubbs & Wootton | **E 70s**
Suarez | **E 50s**
🆕 Suite New York | **E 50s**
Taffin | **E 70s**
Ⓩ Takashimaya | **E 50s**
Ⓩ T. Anthony | **E 50s**
Ted Muehling | **SoHo**
Temperley | **SoHo**
Thomas Pink | **multi. loc.**
Thom Browne | **TriBeCa**
Thos. Moser Cabinets | **E 60s**
Ⓩ Tiffany & Co. | **E 50s**
Ⓩ Tod's | **E 60s**
TSE | **Chelsea**
Tupli | **E 60s**
Ⓩ Turnbull & Asser | **E 50s**
Ⓩ Valentino | **E 60s**
Ⓩ Van Cleef & Arpels | **E 50s**
Vanessa Noel | **E 60s**
Vera Wang Bridal | **E 70s**
Verdura | **E 50s**
Versace | **E 50s**
Vintage Collections | **E 70s**
Vitra | **Meatpacking**
Vogel | **SoHo**
Walter Steiger | **E 50s**
Ⓩ Waterworks | **multi. loc.**
Ⓩ Wempe | **E 50s**
Yigal Azrouel | **Meatpacking**
Yohji Yamamoto | **SoHo**
Yves Delorme | **E 70s**

SPECIAL FEATURES

Yves Saint Laurent | **E 70s**
NEW Zoë | **Dumbo**

TWEEN/TEEN APPEAL

Abracadabra | **Flatiron**
Adidas | **multi. loc.**
Alphabets | **multi. loc.**
American Apparel | **multi. loc.**
Am. Eagle Outfitters | **multi. loc.**
Z Apple Store | **multi. loc.**
Arden B. | **multi. loc.**
Atrium | **NoHo**
Beacon's Closet | **multi. loc.**
Bebe | **multi. loc.**
NEW Ben Sherman | **SoHo**
Berkley Girl | **multi. loc.**
Z Billabong | **W 40s**
Blades Board & Skate | **multi. loc.**
Body Shop | **multi. loc.**
Brooklyn Industries | **multi. loc.**
Burton Store | **SoHo**
Canal Jean | **multi. loc.**
Capezio | **multi. loc.**
NEW Caravan | **NoHo**
Cardeology | **multi. loc.**
Charlotte Russe | **Garment Dist**
Cheap Jack's | **Garment Dist**
Claire's Accessories | **multi. loc.**
CoCo & Delilah | **E Vill**
Compact Impact | **Financial Dist**
Crumpler Bags | **multi. loc.**
Dave's Army Navy | **Chelsea**
Dave's Quality Meat | **E Vill**
David Z. | **multi. loc.**
NEW DC Shoes | **SoHo**
Diesel Kids | **SoHo**
Diva | **Midwood**
Dylan's Candy Bar | **E 60s**
NEW Ed Hardy | **Meatpacking**
Essentials | **E 70s**
Flying A | **SoHo**
Forever 21 | **multi. loc.**
Fossil | **E 40s**
4PlayBK | **Park Slope**
G.C. William | **E 80s**
Girl Props | **multi. loc.**
Guess | **multi. loc.**
NEW Hairy Mary's | **LES**
Jubilee | **multi. loc.**
NEW Juicy Couture | **Flatiron**
Laila Rowe | **multi. loc.**

Levi's Store | **multi. loc.**
Limited Too | **multi. loc.**
Lord of the Fleas | **W 70s**
NEW Love Brigade | **Williamsburg**
NEW Lulu Castagnette | **NoLita**
M.A.C. Cosmetics | **multi. loc.**
Marmalade | **LES**
Marsha D.D. | **E 80s**
Maxilla & Mandible | **W 80s**
Metro Bicycles | **multi. loc.**
NEW Mimi's Closet | **Astoria**
Missha | **E 40s**
Necessary Clothing | **SoHo**
Niketown NY | **E 50s**
North Face | **multi. loc.**
Oakley | **SoHo**
Z Paragon | **Union Sq**
Paul Frank | **NoLita**
Pearl River Mart | **SoHo**
Plaza Too | **W 70s**
Puma | **multi. loc.**
Pylones | **multi. loc.**
Quiksilver | **multi. loc.**
Reminiscence | **Flatiron**
Ruehl | **W Vill**
Rugby | **G Vill**
Sanrio | **multi. loc.**
Scaredy Kat | **Park Slope**
Scoop Kids | **Meatpacking**
Sean John | **E 40s**
Z Sephora | **multi. loc.**
Something Else | **multi. loc.**
Z Sony Style | **E 50s**
Steve Madden | **multi. loc.**
Strawberry | **multi. loc.**
Supreme | **SoHo**
Tah-Poozie | **G Vill**
Tokio 7 | **E Vill**
Trash and Vaudeville | **E Vill**
NEW Treehouse | **Williamsburg**
Tribeca Girls | **TriBeCa**
Tuesday's Child | **Midwood**
NEW UGG Australia | **SoHo**
NEW Uniqlo | **SoHo**
Urban Outfitters | **multi. loc.**
Z Virgin Megastore | **multi. loc.**
NEW Von Dutch | **SoHo**
NEW WeSC | **SoHo**
Yellow Rat Bastard | **multi. loc.**

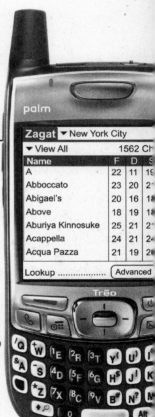